Constraints to Leisure

Constraints to Leisure

edited by Edgar L. Jackson

Venture Publishing, Inc.
State College, Pennsylvania

Copyright © 2005
Venture Publishing, Inc.
1999 Cato Avenue
State College, PA 16801
Phone (814) 234-4561
Fax   (814) 234-1651

Production Manager: Richard Yocum

Manuscript Editing: Valerie Fowler and Richard Yocum

Cover: Echelon Design

Library of Congress Catalogue Card Number: 2004116649
ISBN-10: 1-892132-54-0
ISBN-13: 978-1-892132-54-3

For

Linda

and

in memory of

Stewart P. Wheler

List of Contributors

Cheryl K. Baldwin

M. Deborah Bialeschki

Linda L. Caldwell

Garry Chick

Andrew Church

Duane W. Crawford

John L. Crompton

Erwei Dong

Myron F. Flyod

Paul Gilchrist

Geoffrey Godbey

Karla Henderson

Susan L. Hutchinson

Yoshi Iwasaki

Edgar L. Jackson

Douglas A. Kleiber

Angela Loucks-Atkinson

Roger C. Mannell

Francis McGuire

William Norman

R. P. Porter

Neil Ravenscroft

Cecilia Y. Rider

Diane M. Samdahl

Stuart J. Schleien

David Scott

Susan M. Shaw

Kimberly J. Shinew

Monika Stodolska

Charlsena F. Stone

M. A. Tarrant

Randy J. Virden

Michael G. Wade

Gordon J. Walker

Peter Witt

Jouyeon Yi-Kook

Table of Contents

Section 1:
Retrospect

Section 2:
Impacts of Constraints on
Diverse Populations

Section 3:
New Approaches to
the Study of Constraints

List of Tables and Figures

Chapter 15

Chapter 16

Chapter 18

Preface

In a recent best-selling mystery novel (*Private Eyes*, by Jonathan Kellerman), the main character, Alex Delaware, an investigator based in Los Angeles, consults a leading research psychologist at a top east coast university. During the course of their conversation they discuss a mutual acquaintance. "Until four years ago," says the psychologist, "X was still cranking the stuff out. Then all of a sudden, it stopped. No more experiments, just a couple of essays—very soft stuff. Resumè filler." "Essays on what?" Delaware asks. "Philosophical issues…" "Doesn't sound too controversial." "No. Maybe it's old age," the psychologist replies. "What is?" "Getting philosophical and abandoning real science. I've seen other guys go through it when they hit menopause. Gotta tell my students if *I* ever start doing it, take me out and shoot me."

Amusing though it may be, this passage neatly summarizes an attitude widely followed if not always enthusiastically embraced by academics of all stripes and disciplines in North America. It causes Deans to rub their hands in glee in anticipation of more publications, more funding, more equipment, and more buildings, and hangs like a black cloud over the deliberations of tenure and promotion committees. Perhaps, as Kellerman's character suggests, it is indeed "an age thing," but I now find myself decreasingly satisfied with molding yet more "academic bricks" (empirical research papers). My interests have shifted toward trying to see if all these bricks so many of us have been diligently producing over the years actually fit together into some sort of structure.

In this context, what I hope to achieve in this book is to provide the reader with a sense of what has been accomplished in leisure constraints research. My former colleague, Tim Burton, was fond of a quote that satirized Columbus's voyage to the New World: "When he set out, he didn't know where he was going; when he arrived, he didn't know where he was; and when he returned, he didn't know where he had been" (Burton, 1980, p. 380). Knowing where we have been, where we are, and where we are going in the future in leisure constraints research are, I strongly believe, crucial if the field is to fulfill its potential to add to the body of knowledge about leisure, and ultimately to help enhance the quality of people's lives.

My first involvement with "constraints to leisure" research occurred in the early 1980s when I was invited to contribute to writing a contract report based on survey data collected in Alberta, Canada. The data dealt with what were then called "barriers to recreation participation." At that time there was very little relevant research literature on which to draw for inspiration. As far as I could determine, only four research articles investigated factors limiting people's participation and enjoyment in leisure and recreation (Boothby, Tungatt & Townsend, 1981; Francken & van Raiij, 1981; Romsa & Hoffman, 1980; Witt & Goodale, 1981). The situation began to change quite rapidly—and radically—through the mid-1980s, however. For example, Michael Wade published his edited collection of essays, *Constraints on Leisure* (Wade, 1985), and there was a flurry of activity along several fronts: empirical research, some early modeling, and suggestions as to how barriers research could be applied to enhancing the delivery of leisure services.

Between about 1985 and 1995 a virtual explosion occurred in attention to constraints in North American leisure research, and to a lesser extent in other parts of the world. This was signified by numerous papers presented at conferences and articles published in the refereed journals, and perhaps best exemplified in 1991 by the unprecedented simultaneous publication of special editions of the two leading North American leisure research journals, the *Journal of Leisure Research* and *Leisure Sciences*, for which I was the guest editor. The fact that by then there was both a sufficiently large number of researchers interested in constraints and an equally critical mass of research waiting to be published to fill these two special editions almost goes without saying.

For about 10 years, beginning in the mid-1980s, I compiled and continually updated an informal bibliography of leisure constraints research publications, although deciding what was to be included and what should be omitted was often troublesome. I was frequently reminded of Tom Goodale's (1992) remarks during an invited talk at an NRPA Leisure Research Symposium:

> Virtually all studies of women and leisure are studies of constraints…Studies of the elderly, of those who have disabilities [and] of various races and ethnic groups are mainly studies of constraints….Constraints research, titles aside, encompasses a very large portion of psychological and social psychological research on leisure behavior.

As I later observed in a commentary article, it began to be difficult to resist an image of leisure constraints research as a sort of gigantic conceptual Pac-Man, swallowing up everything in leisure studies in its path (Jackson, 1997).

By about 1996 I could no longer ignore Goodale's comments or my own concerns. I abandoned the bibliography. So much research was being conducted and so many articles and papers were appearing that were at least tangentially related to understanding constraints—even if they did not explicitly acknowledge the terms and concepts—that the bibliography was beginning to be so all-encompassing as to be useless. Also, by the mid-1990s a process of assimilation had set in, by which I mean that many papers and articles appeared that touched rather than focused centrally on constraints as part of wider endeavors to understand leisure and leisure behavior. By then it had almost become routine to refer to constraints in studies concerned with other themes and issues.

In recent years I have come to believe strongly the two main distinct but reciprocally interconnected thrusts in research—theoretical development and the conduct of empirical studies (incidentally, it is these that seem to garner the most rewards from university tenure and promotion committees)—sometimes overshadow what I view as being a third and equally important scholarly endeavor. This third element consists of synthesis of what is frequently fragmented and fugitive knowledge, particularly given recent growth in the number of journals and the difficulty of keeping up with the current literature (Jackson, 2003). Indeed, keeping track of the literature and trying to make sense of how it all fits together was the primary reason behind why I began compiling the bibliography and then published an article that attempted to summarize what was known about leisure constraints by the end of the 1980s (Jackson, 1988).

As the field began to grow exponentially, and to put tentacles into many if not all areas of North American leisure research, I felt the need for synthesis even more strongly. I decided this could best be accomplished by inviting leading and established scholars, and some of the finer minds among younger and emerging scholars in our field, to contribute chapters to a book that would not only bring together what we already know about constraints to leisure, but also adopt a critical posture toward that knowledge, draw on concepts and theories elsewhere in leisure studies and the social sciences, and look ahead to prospects for the future.

The results were enormously gratifying. I began by identifying broadly defined topics that, arising out of two decades of activity in the field, I had good reason to believe were important to consolidating knowledge about constraints. I also selected authors based on my judgment as to who were the leading authorities in each area. I provided only the most skeletal of guidelines as to what each chapter might include. I asked each author, having summarized what is known about the selected topic or theme, to keep in mind two reciprocal questions: (1) To what extent has leisure constraints research contributed to our understanding of a given issue (e.g., constraints and gender, adolescence, race and ethnicity)? and (2) How can the existing literature in each of these areas be adapted to enhance our understanding of constraints?

I did not in any way anticipate the depth and breadth of scholarship, the innovative thinking, nor indeed, the enthusiasm with which the invited authors tackled their

mandates. As I read the chapters both in draft and final form, I became increasingly aware of hidden depths in the deceptively simple concept of "constraints to leisure" and numerous connections with topics, themes, concepts, and theories elsewhere in leisure studies and the social sciences we have only just begun to explore. The tiny amount of literature available some two decades or more ago has now been replaced by a very large body of knowledge, as well as the potential for future research and understanding that was, to put it bluntly, beyond the imaginations of the early, pioneer researchers in the field (and I include myself in this comment).

The goals of this book are threefold. Adapting the cartographic metaphor Tim Burton and I used at the end of the 1980s when we attempted a broad overview of leisure studies as a whole in our edited book, *Understanding Leisure: Mapping the Past, Charting the Future* (Jackson & Burton, 1989), the first objective is to lay out a series of "local maps," at a fine scale, of what we know about specific aspects of constraints to leisure after 25 years of attention. The second purpose is to integrate this knowledge by moving sufficiently far back from the detail to provide a sort of continental-scale view, perhaps a satellite image, of the constraints to leisure "topography." The third goal is to use these maps to chart journeys in the future.

Like the previous books I helped to edit, this book is the product of a collective effort, in which the most important participants, and those to be thanked first, are the 40 or so authors who willingly sacrificed their time to write their chapters with the sole reward of knowing they were unselfishly contributing to this effort to enhance the growth of the field. Thanks to all for agreeing to write the chapters, for responding rapidly (in most cases!) and with good humor to my reviews, and for your forbearance during unavoidable delays.

At Venture Publishing, Inc., I should like to thank the editors, Richard Yocum, Valerie Fowler, and Michele Barbin. Thanks to the Department of Earth and Atmospheric Sciences, University of Alberta, and Brian Jones, Department Chair. Finally, I am blessed with a wonderful family who have supported me through some difficult times. Thank you Linda, Patrick, Nicholas, and Katherine.

Ed Jackson
University of Alberta

References

Boothby, J., Tungatt, M. F., and Townsend, A. R. (1981). Ceasing participation in sports activity: Reported reasons and their implications. *Journal of Leisure Research, 13,* 1–14.

Burton, T. L. (1980). The maturation of leisure research. In T. L. Goodale and P. A. Witt (Eds.), *Recreation and leisure: Issues in an era of change* (pp. 373–385). State College, PA: Venture Publishing, Inc.

Francken, D. A. and van Raiij, M. F. (1981). Satisfaction with leisure time activities. *Journal of Leisure Research, 13,* 337–352.

Goodale, T. L. (1992). *Constraints research: Performing without a net next time.* Featured speaker, Psychological/Social Psychological Aspects of Leisure Behavior, Part I, NRPA Symposium on Leisure Research, Cincinnati, OH.

Jackson, E. L. (1988). Leisure constraints: A survey of past research. *Leisure Sciences, 10,* 203–215.

Jackson, E. L. (1997). In the eye of the beholder: A comment on Samdahl and Jekubovich, "A critique of leisure constraints: Comparative analyses and understandings." *Journal of Leisure Research, 29,* 458–468.

Jackson, E. L. (2003). Leisure research by Canadians and Americans: One community or two solitudes? *Journal of Leisure Research, 35,* 292–315.

Jackson, E. L. and Burton, T. L. (Eds.) (1989). *Understanding leisure and recreation: Mapping the past, charting the future.* State College, PA: Venture Publishing, Inc.

Romsa, G. and Hoffman, W. (1980). An application of non-participation data in recreation research: Testing the opportunity theory. *Journal of Leisure Research, 12,* 321–328.

Wade, M. G. (Ed.). (1985). *Constraints on leisure.* Springfield, IL: Charles C. Thomas.

Witt, P. A. and Goodale, T. L. (1981). The relationship between barriers to leisure enjoyment and family stages. *Leisure Sciences, 4,* 29–49.

Section 1

Retrospect

Chapter 1

Leisure Constraints Research: Overview of a Developing Theme in Leisure Studies

Edgar L. Jackson (University of Alberta)

Objectives and Evolution of Leisure Constraints Research

Origins and Early Assumptions

Leisure constraints research aims to "investigate factors that are assumed by researchers and/or perceived or experienced by individuals to limit the formation of leisure preferences and/or to inhibit or prohibit participation and enjoyment in leisure" (Jackson, 2000, p. 62). There are essentially three general justifications for leisure constraints research. First, to understand individuals' leisure choices and behavior requires investigation of all the factors, both positive (e.g., motivations, anticipated benefits) and negative (e.g., constraints) that influence those choices. Studies of constraints can also help to explain why observed relationships among values and attitudes, leisure preferences, and overt leisure behavior are frequently tenuous. Second, constraints research has assisted in generating new insights into aspects of leisure previously thought to be well-understood, such as leisure participation, motivations, satisfactions, and recreational conflict. Third, the field has become a sort of conceptual Esperanto, proving to be a useful device to enhance communication among scholars with diverse disciplinary training, topical interests, and methodological orientations.

Systematic research on leisure constraints has existed as a distinct subfield of investigation within leisure studies for a little over two decades, beginning with key papers published in the early 1980s (Boothby, Tungatt & Townsend, 1981; Francken & van Raiij, 1981; Romsa & Hoffman, 1980; Witt & Goodale, 1981). As Goodale and Witt (1989) pointed out, however, the origins of this field of interest can be traced back over a much longer time period—at least to the Outdoor Recreation Research Review Commission (ORRRC) studies of the early 1960s (Ferris, 1962; Mueller, Gurin & Wood, 1962), and even to the origins of the North American parks and recreation movement in the 19th century.

Most of the research conducted in the 1980s was empirical, being based on theory at only the deepest and most implicit level (Stockdale, 1989).[1] Consequently, researchers tended to make certain assumptions about constraints, and their impacts on people's leisure and recreation, not uncovered as limiting the development of the field until much later. Two important early assumptions included (1) constraints are immovable, static, obstacles to participation; and (2) the most significant, if perhaps not the only, effect of constraints on leisure is to block or limit participation. In other words, the absence or presence of constraints would explain why a person does or does not participate in an activity. To use subsequent language, structural constraints (those that intervene between preferences and participation) were thought to be the only significant type of constraint. As a corollary, the emphasis was on activities and participation as outcomes of constraints, which, like the constraints items, were the most easily quantifiable and measurable aspects of leisure to investigate.

The implicit model employed reflected the thinking summarized in **Figure 1a** (p. 4): a person is presumed to have a preference, desire, or demand for a leisure activity, but fulfillment of this preference may be compromised by the presence of a constraint—or "barrier" as the then conventional terminology had it. A slightly more sophisticated model is shown in **Figure 1b** (p. 4): participation results from the absence of constraints, but the outcome of encountering a constraint is nonparticipation. Little if any attention was paid to outcomes of constraints other than nonparticipation, nor were constraints acknowledged to affect preferences. Thus, a nonparticipant was assumed to be constrained in some way but a participant was not constrained.

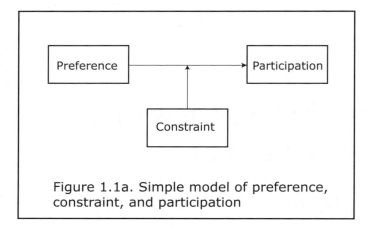

Figure 1.1a. Simple model of preference, constraint, and participation

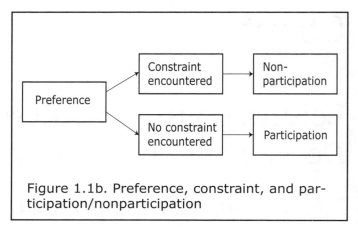

Figure 1.1b. Preference, constraint, and participation/nonparticipation

Another characteristic of the early stages of leisure constraints research was that a rather narrow range of methods was employed to collect data for the statistical analysis of relationships among leisure, constraints, and other variables thought to be important (e.g., socioeconomic and demographic factors, the most influential of which were found to be age, gender, and income). The dominant orientation was quantitative, usually consisting of a questionnaire survey in which lists of constraints or "barriers" thought to be important by researchers were rated by respondents in terms of their perceived effects on participation. Thus, from both a methodological and an empirical/conceptual standpoint, much of what was published about barriers to recreation participation in the early to mid 1980s was itself constrained.

Changes in the Late 1980s

The picture changed considerably in several distinct, but in hindsight interconnected, ways in the late 1980s and the 1990s. First, the field began to be characterized by more explicit and increasingly sophisticated theorizing, as researchers began to uncover previous false assumptions and explore new concepts. There were two facets to this development: innovative interpretation of new and more complex empirical research, and the emergence of a series of theoretical, model-based articles that challenged previous assumptions and attempted to set the stage for the more sophisticated empirical research to follow.

Second, the language changed. Jackson and Scott (1999) discussed this superficially trivial but in reality fundamental change in some detail:

In the early 1980s, the field of interest, had it been recognized as distinct, would have been referred to as "barriers to recreation participation." The conventional terminology is now "constraints to leisure," a change that represents

much more than a semantic difference: it is indicative of three fundamental shifts in focus and conceptualization. First, the more inclusive term "constraints" is now preferred to "barriers," because the latter fails to capture the entire range of explanations of constrained leisure behavior. Moreover…the word "barrier" tends to direct researchers' attention toward only one type of constraint, that which intervenes between preferences and participation. Now, however, a much more comprehensive and complex range of constraints is recognized.…Second, replacement of the word "recreation" with leisure simultaneously represents both broadening the focus of investigation and forging closer links than before with the mainstream of thinking in leisure studies. The third change, dropping the word "participation," is based on recognition that constraints influence far more than the choice to participate or not.…It is also consistent with the evolution of definitions of leisure, away from activity- and time-based conceptualizations and toward the meaning of leisure as experienced by the participant rather than as defined by the researcher. (modified from Jackson & Scott, 1999, p. 300; citations omitted)

The third way in which leisure constraints research changed in the late 1980s and early 1990s was the widened array of methods, in particular with the incorporation of qualitative methods and the declining domination of the questionnaire—as, of course, was also happening more widely in leisure studies and indeed in the social sciences as a whole. Fourth, vocal criticism began to be aired about constraints research and concepts, which generated a vigorous and healthy scholarly debate about the value and accuracy of the insights to be gained from research conducted using a constraints-based perspective (e.g., Samdahl & Jekubovich, 1997a, followed by replies from Henderson, 1997, and Jackson, 1997, and a rebuttal by Samdahl & Jekubovich, 1997b). This debate continues in specific themes addressed in this book (see McGuire & Norman's discussion of the beneficial role that constraints sometimes play) as well as in Samdahl's critical concluding chapter.

Theories and Models

Three specific developments occurred between 1987 and 1991 that challenged the somewhat naïve thinking of early constraints research and changed its course. First, stimulated in part by an integrative review (Jackson, 1988), there was an increase in new empirical research activity coupled with a growing awareness among leisure scholars of the pervasive importance of constraints, both in people's leisure lives and in diverse areas of leisure studies in which constraints had not previously been investigated. For example, and related to Crawford and Godbey's (1987) work on expanding the range of constraints, some initial attempts were made to go beyond the simple preferences/constraints/participation model and investigate what at that time were called "antecedent constraints"—limiting factors thought to shape the development of interests and preferences (e.g., Henderson, Stalnaker & Taylor, 1988; Jackson, 1990a, 1990b). On a different tack, some very innovative research was published that later proved to be the foundation for subsequent theoretical exploration of the concept of "leisure constraints negotiation." For example, Scott (1991), in a qualitative study of contract bridge, showed that people often take quite innovative steps to negotiate the constraints they face. (This was the first time the term "negotiation" appeared in the constraints literature.) Kay and Jackson (1991) demonstrated how many people manage to participate in their chosen leisure activities "despite constraint." Shaw, Bonen, and McCabe (1991), having identified the counterintuitive finding it is often the more constrained people who participate more frequently than the less constrained, questioned the assumption that "more constraints mean less leisure."

The third development—new theorizing and the construction of models—was intimately connected with the other two. Indeed, it would not likely have occurred had it not been for the stimulus of the articles by Scott, Kay and Jackson, and Shaw et al., among others. The result of this development was the publication of an increasingly sophisticated set of models of leisure and constraints. Several such models had been published earlier in the 1980s. Most notable among them was an application-oriented choice/flow model in which Godbey (1985) attempted to isolate a range of factors that affect participation. He concluded from a management perspec-

tive the most fruitful strategy for recreation providers to pursue is to provide information to nonparticipants about activities and opportunities, since lack of awareness appeared to be the most influential barrier to participation. A model conceptually similar, although displayed in an entirely different way, consisted of a decision matrix developed by Jackson and Searle (1985). The model was based on concepts derived from geographic research on human adaptation to natural hazards more than 20 years earlier (White, 1961). In this model, the presence or absence of constraints is viewed as defining leisure choices as open, inhibited, or blocked, with participation or nonparticipation once again being the assumed outcome. Although neither of these models was subsequently adopted as a framework for research, it does not, in hindsight, take a great deal of imagination to detect elements of constraints negotiation concepts and strategies in both of these models, even if they were not apparent to the authors at the time.

In retrospect, the single most important conceptual development in leisure constraints research in the 1980s was the publication in *Leisure Sciences* of a seminal paper, "Reconceptualizing Barriers to Family Leisure," by Crawford and Godbey (1987). Crawford and Godbey made two main contributions, which have been adopted as axiomatic by subsequent leisure constraints researchers. First, they argued constraints affected not only participation and nonparticipation, but also preferences. In other words, lack of desire for an activity or lack of awareness could also be subject to and therefore explained in part by constraints. Second, and in a sense a corollary of the first contribution, they broadened the range of constraints that could be recognized as affecting leisure behavior. Thus, constraints not only intervene between preferences and participation, as shown in Figure 1.1 (Crawford and Godbey referred to this type of constraint as "structural"), but also affect preferences in several significant ways, most notably through the operation of two other types of constraints, which Crawford and Godbey referred to as intrapersonal and interpersonal.

The next step in the modeling process occurred in the form of an hierarchical model in which Crawford, Jackson, and Godbey (1991) recast the thinking that had gone into the Crawford and Godbey paper in terms of a sequential hierarchy of constraints. They argued although most research attention had been paid to structural constraints, these were the most distal and therefore probably the least important in shaping leisure behavior, whereas intrapersonal and interpersonal constraints, being more proximal, were likely more important influences on leisure. The notion people might negotiate through these sequentially arranged constraints was only implicit in the hierarchical model, but became more explicit as the focus of attention in a subsequent article by Jackson, Crawford, and Godbey (1993).[2] The "negotiation thesis," as it came to be known, was based on the idea, derived from Kay and Jackson (1991) and Scott (1991) that, despite experiencing constraints, people do find ways to participate in and enjoy leisure, even if such participation and enjoyment may differ from what they would have been in the absence of constraints.

A flow-diagram model (**Figure 1.2**) summarized the negotiation thesis, and six specific propositions were presented:

1. Participation is dependent not on the absence of constraints (although this may be true for some people) but on negotiation through them. Such negotiation may modify rather than foreclose participation.

2. Variations in the reporting of constraints can be viewed not only as variations in the experience of constraints, but also as variations in success in negotiating them.

3. Absence of the desire to change current leisure behavior may be partly explained by prior successful negotiation of structural constraints.

4. Anticipation of one or more insurmountable interpersonal or structural constraints may suppress the desire for participation.

5. Anticipation consists of not simply the anticipation of the presence or intensity of a constraint, but also the anticipation of the ability to negoitate it.

6. Both the initiation and the outcome of the negotiation process depend on the relative strength of, and interactions between, constraints on participating in an activity and motivations for such participation.

In addition to the aforementioned propositions, Jackson et al. (1993, p. 8) proposed a three-category typology of people with respect to their responses to constraints:

(1) people who do not participate in their desired activity (reactive response); (2) people who, despite experiencing a constraint, do not reduce or otherwise change their participation at all (successful proactive response); and (3) people who participate but in an altered manner (partly successful proactive response).

This conceptual typology, based on speculation, has been empirically supported in a qualitative study of constraints negotiation among women with physical disabilities (Henderson, Bedini, Hecht & Shuler 1995), in which the three preceding groups were referred to, respectively, as "passive responders," "achievers," and "attempters." Regardless of the terminology, the importance of these typologies was they explicitly rejected one of the assumptions in early constraints research, namely constraints are insurmountable obstacles to participation.

Empirically Based Knowledge About Constraints

Research on Structural Constraints

Although the situation is changing, the bulk of published empirical research on constraints to leisure has focused on what Crawford and Godbey (1987) called structural constraints. Moreover, in the early stages of research much of the analysis was conducted on an item-by-item basis, consisting essentially of cross-sectional correlations between scores on constraints items and two other sets of variables: measures of participation and nonparticipation, and socioeconomic and demographic vari-

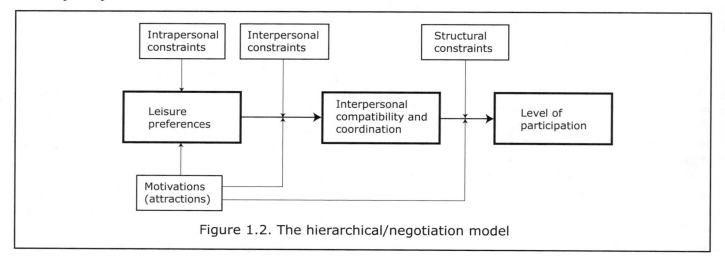

Figure 1.2. The hierarchical/negotiation model

ables. Following the lead of McGuire (1984), however, methods to reduce the complexity of item-by-item analysis were introduced into the field, such as factor analysis (Hawkins & Freeman, 1993), cluster analysis (Jackson, 1993; Norman, 1995), and multidimensional scaling (Hultsman, 1995). Results from the use of these methods allowed patterns describing the impact of constraints to emerge that would likely have been obscured at the finer level of analysis previously utilized, as well as to pinpoint more robust and generalizable relationships with associated variables. Key findings from the analysis of structural constraints (based on Jackson, 2000) are outlined next.

There is a stable and virtually universal range of categories of constraints to leisure, typically consisting of

1. costs of participating.

2. time and other commitments.

3. problems with facilities.

4. isolation (sometimes subdivided into social isolation and geographical isolation).

5. lack of skills and abilities.

With minor variations, these dimensions represent the kinds of empirical groupings commonly reported in quantitative (usually factor analysis-based) classifications of constraints items and scales.

No constraint or type of constraint is experienced with equal intensity by everyone, although time-related and cost-related constraints rank among the most widely and intensely experienced inhibitors of the achievement of leisure goals and a balanced lifestyle.

The experience of constraints varies among individuals and groups. No subgroup of the population, and probably no individual, is entirely free from constraints to leisure.

Relationships between categories of constraints and personal characteristics, such as age and income, also tend to be stable. The idealized composite graph shown in **Figure 1.3** is a good example both of the kinds of the analysis and the graphic presentation of quantitative data that typically emerge from questionnaire surveys, in which respondents are asked to rate the importance of varying numbers of constraints items (e.g., being too busy with their family, the costs of participating) in relation to aspects of constrained leisure. As the graph shows, when analyzed and presented at this highly aggregate and general level, some interesting and stable patterns emerge about apparent changes in constraints across the life cycle. Moreover, each category of constraint not coincidentally exhibits a distinct pattern of association with age. Thus, a lack of skills and abilities,

although consistently rated as least important among every age group when averaged across a survey sample, gradually increases in importance as the life cycle progresses. In contrast—both in terms of the relative importance of the constraint and the direction of the relationship—costs as a negative influence on participation decline with advancing age. Perhaps not surprisingly, because the category of constraints may be viewed as "external" to the individual, most studies have shown the amount and quality of facilities as a constraint to leisure do not vary with age. As far as the remaining two categories are concerned, isolation is typically characterized by a U-shaped relationship with age, meaning it is most important in the early stages of the life cycle, declines until early middle age, and increases once again in the later stages of life. In dramatic contrast, commitments and time constraints are usually characterized by a very strong inverted U-shaped relationship.

A similar picture emerges when variations in the reporting of constraints are analyzed by income. **Figure 1.4** (p. 8) demonstrates—as one would expect—the costs of participation decline with increasing income. However, time commitments increase, a trend that can be interpreted to suggest not only that increasing income is achieved at the cost of giving up free time, but also that individuals make conscious choices about tradeoffs between free time and disposable income (see Godbey, this volume).

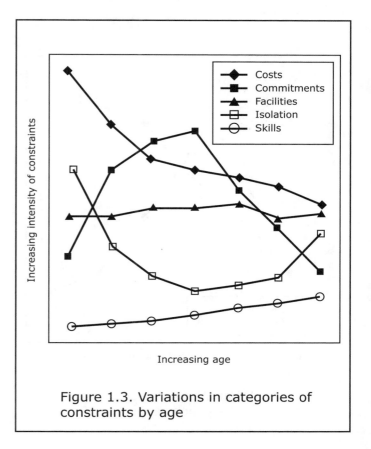

Figure 1.3. Variations in categories of constraints by age

Allowing for the limitations of drawing developmental-like inferences about individuals from cross-sectional aggregate data, what appears to emerge from the kinds of findings displayed in Figures 1.3 and 1.4 is there is not only *change* in the individual constraints and combinations of constraints that people experience as they move through the life cycle or through income categories, but also a process of *exchange*—of one combination of constraints for another.

Research on the Hierarchical Model and the Process of Leisure Constraints Negotiation

There has been less research on the other types of constraints besides structural. However, although there have been exceptions (e.g., Gilbert & Hudson, 2000; Hawkins, Peng, Hsieh & Eklund, 1999), the empirical evidence to date supports the validity of distinguishing among intrapersonal, interpersonal, and structural constraints, and these are arranged in a sequential hierarchy (e.g., Raymore, Godbey & Crawford, 1994; Raymore, Godbey, Crawford & von Eye, 1993). Research has also shown people adopt strategies to negotiate through the various levels to fulfill their leisure. For example Scott

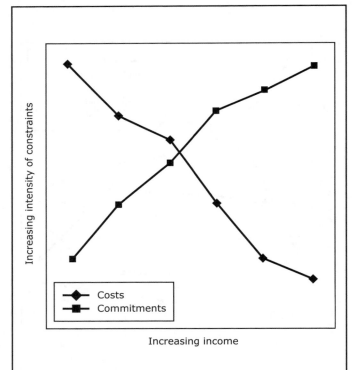

Figure 1.4. Variations in costs and time commitments by income

(1991), in his study of participants in contract bridge, identified three main options: acquisition of information about limited opportunities for play, altered scheduling of games to adjust to reduced group membership and individuals' time commitments, and skill development to permit participation in advanced play. Strategies to adjust to time and financial constraints on leisure in general identified by Kay and Jackson (1991) included reducing (but not entirely foregoing) participation, saving money to participate, trying to find the cheapest opportunity, making other (non-leisure-related) economies, reducing the amount of time spent on household tasks, and reducing work time. Similarly, Samdahl and Jekubovich (1997a) described how people change work schedules, alter their routines, and select activities that meet their leisure goals. At a more general level, Jackson and Rucks (1995) distinguished between cognitive and behavioral strategies, the latter being subdivided into modifications of leisure and nonleisure, and further categorized into modifying the use of time, acquiring skills, changing interpersonal relations, improving finances, physical therapy, and changing leisure aspirations.

One of the most innovative, and potentially fruitful, recent directions in this aspect of leisure constraints research has been conducted by Mannell and his colleagues (Hubbard & Mannell, 2001; Mannell & Loucks-Atkinson, this volume). Using structural equation modeling in empirical tests of alternative models of the leisure constraints negotiation process, these researchers greatly improved our understanding of how constraints operate in people's lives, and how they interact with other key variables, such as preferences and motivations. For example, Hubbard and Mannell (2001) tested four alternative constraint–negotiation models that specified different links between motivation, constraint, negotiation, and participation. They found the strongest support for the constraints/effects/mitigation model, which showed while there was no direct relationship between motivation and perceived constraint, motivation appeared to be strongly related to participation through its strong positive influence on efforts to negotiate constraints.

The Contributions of Qualitative Research

Although some would argue it is anachronistic to separate research conducted using quantitative and qualitative methods, the unique contributions of the latter to leisure constraints research are worthy of a brief but distinct discussion. In sharp contrast to the predominantly quantitative, usually survey-based research of the 1980s, there is now a growing body of qualitative constraints research. Although its proponents and practitioners have made many contributions, I view three as particularly significant and substantial.

To begin with, qualitative researchers have greatly extended the identification of the range of constraints that affect people's leisure, and, indeed, their lives as a whole. It is perhaps no coincidence this strand in leisure constraints research has been contributed mainly if not exclusively by women researchers, usually working within a feminist framework (see Henderson, 1991; Henderson, Bialeschki, Shaw & Freysinger, 1996; Shaw, 1994), and no doubt influenced by counterpart work from the UK, such as Deem (1986) and Wimbush and Talbot (1988). Thus, much of the work on constraints from a qualitative perspective was initially aimed at uncovering constraints thought to be particularly pertinent to women, but which had been overlooked in previous quantitative research based on constraints items and scales stemming from the assumptions of researchers.[3] Consequently, a substantial number of research articles appeared beginning in the early 1990s, contributed by researchers such as Susan Shaw, Karla Henderson, Deborah Bialeschki, and their associates and students. Their research examined constraints such as ethic of care (Henderson & Allen, 1991), lack of a sense of entitlement to leisure (Henderson & Bialeschki, 1991), fear (Whyte & Shaw, 1994), and body image (Frederick & Shaw, 1995), or focused on particular aspects or circumstances of women's lives, such as immigration, language difficulties and isolation (Rublee & Shaw, 1991), ethnicity and adolescence (Tirone & Shaw, 1997), maturation of children (Bialeschki & Michener, 1994), menopause (Parry & Shaw, 1999), and the death of a spouse (Patterson & Carpenter, 1994). It is worth noting, however, based on this new knowledge, there is an emerging recognition much of what has been learned about women, leisure, and constraints may apply equally well to men. Thus, we are now witnessing the appearance of pieces such as Shaw and Henderson's (2003) conference paper, *Leisure research about gender and men: The weaker link?* In addition, the chapter by these authors in this book adopts a gender-based perspective that encompasses both women and men.

A second important contribution from qualitative researchers has been to challenge and criticize conventional wisdom derived from the conclusions and inferences from survey research. This has occurred on several levels:

1. the relatively narrow and specific questioning of the hierarchical sequence in the experience of constraints proposed by Crawford et al. (1991), both from an empirical perspective (e.g., Gilbert & Hudson, 2000; Ravenscroft, 2004) and a theoretical perspective (Henderson & Bialeschki, 1993).

2. a somewhat broader critique of terminology and its hidden implications (e.g., Samdahl, Hutchinson & Jacobson, 1999, on "navigation" vs. "negotiation").

3. outright skepticism about the value of approaching leisure from a constraints-based perspective (Samdahl, this volume; Samdahl & Jekubovich, 1997a).

One need not agree with these challenges, especially the last, to acknowledge their value in generating debate and prompting other researchers to clarify and to sharpen their concepts.

The third contribution from qualitative research has been to provide a much clearer sense of context at both the micro scale (individual's lives) and macro scale (society) for understanding the experience and effects of constraints. Quantitative surveys provide cross-sectional, instantaneous data equivalent to a narrowly framed, slightly out-of-focus, black-and-white snapshot of a tiny slice of people's lives. As I comment elsewhere in this book (see the chapter on transitions and constraints), constraints-related surveys say

> very little if anything about the rest of people's lives, except indirectly and at an aggregate level by using statistical methods to correlate constraints with various socioeconomic and demographic variables. In short, much constraints research is bereft of context, whether this be at the personal, familial, or societal levels. It is almost as if we have said to our survey respondents, "Tell us about your leisure and constraints, but don't tell us about anything else important in your life."

There is also no question we have not achieved much understanding of the leisure of people whose very lives may consist almost entirely of constraint: the poor, many unemployed people, single parents, the elderly, some members of some minority groups, and so on. If such people have been included in our surveys (and one wonders here about response rates and how far we can generalize from, say, 40% questionnaire return rates if the other 60% may, because of personal circumstances, be precisely those who are most constrained), we have typically asked them what, for them, must be viewed as superficial and trivial questions met with puzzlement if not outright derision or anger.

Qualitative research has done much to redress these problems, weaving a far richer tapestry of how constraints fit into the context of people's lives and of how these in turn are shaped and affected by the broader social, political, economic, and environmental milieu within which we live. Although it typically begins with the individual—as does most quantitative research—the qualitative orientation is far better placed to examine the antecedents and context of constraints. Moreover, this overall trend does much toward helping to "close the gap" between the predominantly social psychological orientation of most North American leisure research and the more sociological approach typically adopted in Britain and western Europe, as presented by Coalter (1997, 1999; see also Beckers, 1995; Mommaas, 1997; Shaw, 1997) and discussed by Ravenscroft (this volume). As a result, North American leisure constraints research—and indirectly leisure studies—is able to incorporate, to adapt, and to be enriched by alternative perspectives, approaches, concepts, and theory from outside the continent, and thus to alleviate the detrimental intellectual and geographical isolation recently decried in the literature (Jackson, in press; Samdahl & Kelly, 1999; Valentine, Allison & Schneider, 1999).

In conclusion, it is worth emphasizing none of these significant contributions to leisure constraints research would have emerged in the absence of qualitative research and researchers. They should therefore be acknowledged as being equally as important as other developments, such as innovative quantitative research and the shift toward a deeper understanding of constraints via the modeling process.

Conclusions About the State of Research on Constraints to Leisure

Considerable progress has been made in the understanding of constraints to leisure over the last two to three decades. Atheoretical empirical research no longer dominates the field, nor are the empirical and theoretical "branches" as isolated from each other as they used to be. As exemplified by Hubbard and Mannell (2001), the most recent developments in leisure constraints research reflect an intimate intertwining of theoretical thinking and empirical analysis, with the field moving ahead as new findings stimulate new interpretations, which in turn power the next stage of research. "Leisure constraints research" is now well-established as a recognizable and distinct subfield within leisure studies, and thinking about constraints has also been assimilated into leisure research that is not overtly directed toward the specific goal of understanding leisure constraints. These developments, together with the innovative ideas contained in

this book, provide significant and exciting opportunities for future research. Scholars do not need to reinvent the conceptual wheel, but are in the enviable position of being able to capitalize on an existing body of knowledge and, with care, apply it to the kinds of phenomena and behaviors in which they are interested.

Reasons for and Outcomes of Leisure Constraints Research

This section briefly tackles three distinct but connected and somewhat broader issues related to leisure constraints research:

1. types of and themes in research and how they fit together.

2. the place of leisure constraints research within leisure studies and the social sciences.

3. the rationale for and outcomes of such research.

Types of Research

As far as the types of research are concerned, I believe the two dominant ways in which knowledge is advanced—the development of concepts and theory, and the conduct of empirical research—should be complemented by synthesis. By this I mean periodic efforts, such as this book, should stand back from the detail of individual research projects and hundreds of conference papers and journal articles to try and detect—or construct—the big picture. It is each of these strands together, plus interrelationships among them, that constitute a body of knowledge such as leisure constraints research (**Figure 1.5**). They also provide general directions individual researchers might wish to follow, or at least emphasize, in their future endeavors.

Thus, it should almost go without saying empirical research is enhanced by being based on explicit theory as a framework for asking questions, while the results are interpreted—and perhaps later reinterpreted—within the context of that theory and new and evolving theories. Conversely, theory does not exist in a vacuum, but needs to be tested, supported, or modified in the empirical realm. Without this combination of theoretical development and empirical investigation, leisure constraints research would still be at the stage it reached two or more decades ago—untested assumptions and guesses guiding atheoretical, empirical studies with little effort toward or concern for interpreting the findings, not only for understanding constraints and their impacts on people's lives, but even less as a contribution to enhancing our understanding of the phenomenon of leisure in general. Without theory, empirical research—in which statistical significance is frequently mistaken for substantive importance—merely produces information, and that information is often faulty or tainted; with theory, we stand a good chance of translating that information into knowledge. (For further discussion, see Crawford & Jackson, this volume.)

As argued previously, however, recent years have witnessed both growth and improvements in empirical research and theoretical development in leisure constraints research. Even more importantly, both in recent research and in the chapters of this book, leisure constraints research is now less engaged with the themes lying within the two relevant circles in Figure 1.5, but is concentrating to a much greater extent, and far more fruitfully, on the relationships, or reciprocal arrow, between them. Having said this, however, I also want to reiterate the need for and the value of synthesis—the integration of what we know (or at least what we think we know)—to avoid the pitfalls of fragmentation that characterize much of present-day research, based partly on the difficulty of keeping up with an exploding literature

that is often difficult to find, pressures to publish, and an academic culture that tends to value information over knowledge. With synthesis, however, we stand a good chance of ensuring that knowledge becomes more than the sum of its individual parts, but truly becomes a foundation for asking new questions while discouraging the trivial exercise of asking old ones over and over again.

To emphasize this point, I should like to quote from an article I published in 2003, in which I drew on my experience as a geographer housed in an earth sciences department about the need

> to "stand back" from time to time and reflect on what is going on in leisure studies, and what factors…account for the patterns. [This]…involves discerning what I call the "Big Picture." I have always been a "big picture" person: thus, even though I have been happy to spend a large portion of my academic career attempting to understand the minutiae of detailed quantitative data on topics such as constraints to leisure, and outdoor recreation and environmental attitudes, I have also always thought it necessary to try and develop a sense of context, an overview or overall framework of how things

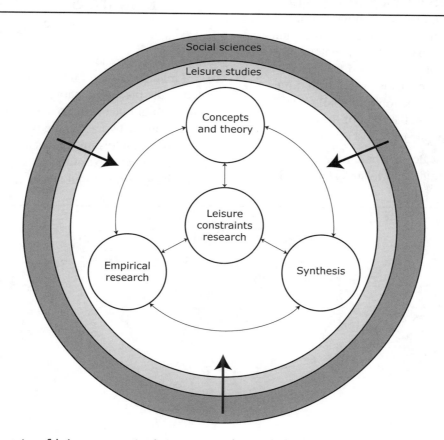

Figure 1.5. Elements of leisure constraints research, and the place of leisure constraints research within leisure studies and the social sciences

fit together....I also try to emphasize the "big picture" in my discipline-based course on human impacts on the environment. One of the points I make in this course is the desirability of forging linkages across disciplines, not only within the natural sciences but also between and among the natural sciences, the social sciences, the humanities, education, engineering, and so on. There is an enormous diversity across the earth, atmospheric, and biological sciences, and partly because of this there is a great danger of further fragmentation of knowledge in these areas. This has been particularly the case in the last five to ten years, during which science and scientific knowledge have advanced incredibly, but during which, also, researchers have become increasingly more specialized and consequently less able to communicate with others. In my environmental impacts course I refer to this as "Digging Disciplines Deeper," and I illustrate the point using a cartoon drawn by my son [**Figure 1.6**], which shows the production of more and more in-depth, specialized knowledge with very little connection to anything else, and the difficulty, the deeper we get, of peering across boundaries between these disciplinary "holes." I readily concede to having been one of the "hole-diggers" illustrated on the left and center of the cartoon for a good proportion of my academic career....However, I have also tried, from time to time, to "look over the top of the hole," as does the third figure on the right of the cartoon. (Jackson, 2003b, p. 345)

Even though the "scale" is smaller—leisure constraints research as a subfield of leisure studies—I

believe these remarks apply equally well to leisure constraints research, both in terms of specific themes within the subfield as well as its relationships with other issues in leisure studies, and I have been an advocate of such efforts for some considerable period of time. Thus, synthesis of what was known about leisure constraints was the purpose behind two previous pieces in which I have been involved: an essay published in the late 1980s (Jackson, 1988) and a more recent chapter written with David Scott (Jackson & Scott, 1999), published as part of a larger synthesis of knowledge about leisure as a whole (Jackson & Burton, 1999). But it is also important to recognize each of the individual chapters in this book is a work of synthesis, whether it be about constraints and gender, race, adolescents, migration, culture, methodology, or applications. It is my hope the book as a whole will be used as a synthesis of knowledge about leisure constraints as it exists halfway through the first decade of the 21st century. I have no doubt the picture will be quite different in 5, 10, or 20 years, but at least we have now charted the territory.

Leisure Constraints Research, Leisure Studies, and the Social Sciences

When I first sketched out the diagram shown in Figure 1.5, I intended to limit it to the central section, as elaborated in the preceding paragraphs. However, it occurred to me it might be useful to extend the diagram to encompass a word or two about the place of leisure constraints research within leisure studies as a whole (as well in the more general context of the social sciences), and to make some observations about actual and desirable directions

Figure 1.6. "Digging disciplines deeper"

in the flow of ideas. Thus, as shown in the diagram, leisure constraints research does not exist in an intellectual vacuum, but is part of and informed by the progress of constructing knowledge in leisure studies (although perhaps not to the extent some scholars would wish). This process of immediate fertilization is amply demonstrated by the chapters assembled here, and in many cases we also witness the incorporation and adaptation of concepts, theory, and methods from the broader social sciences to a much greater extent than in the past. Two specific examples spring to mind:

1. the use of the concept of "selective optimization with compensation" as a guiding principle in several chapters, most notably Caldwell and Baldwin on adolescents, McGuire and Norman on the elderly, and Kleiber, Wade, and Loucks-Atkinson on the concept of affordance.

2. the use of structural equation modeling by Mannell and his colleagues as a recently introduced technique to identify and disentangle complex relationships among many leisure-related variables defining and connected with leisure constraints.

Although not shown in the diagram, there are also actual and potential influences and flows of ideas in the opposite direction (i.e., from constraints research to knowledge about leisure). I noted earlier one detectable change in leisure studies by about the mid-1990s was the assimilation of constraints-related ideas, concepts, and questions into research on other themes and topics. This, then, is an example of four ways in which leisure constraints research has shaped the more general field of which it is a part:

1. quantitatively, in terms of the number of research studies and publications.

2. substantively, in terms of the kinds of questions that researchers ask and pursue.

3. conceptually, with respect to how the concept of "constraint" changes our understanding of leisure as perceived freedom.

4. theoretically, in terms of how the various models outlined here have enhanced understanding of the components of and processes that affect people's leisure decisions and enjoyment.

It would probably still be true to say, however, neither leisure constraints research nor leisure studies as a whole generated much impact on or interest within other social sciences. This is to be regretted, although perhaps expected in view of the intellectual isolation of the field as discussed by Samdahl and Kelly (1999), coupled with limitations imposed by the small number of active and productive leisure researchers in North America and the individual and institutional concentration of the production of knowledge about leisure as detected by Jackson (2000–2001, 2003a, in press).

Rationale and Outcomes

As far as the third theme of this section of the chapter is concerned, I should like to discuss briefly what I see as being simultaneously the rationale for and some of the benefits of research on constraints to leisure. This is not the place to defend leisure studies as a whole—that has been done adequately by many others before now (e.g., Cooper, 1999, who raises and then refutes three "objections" to the idea that leisure is worthy of scholarly investigation). However, it is worth suggesting what I want to argue, as summarized in **Figure 1.7** (p. 14), not only applies equally well to other themes and topics in leisure studies but also provides a perspective on the value of research that may sometimes be overlooked in these days of emphasizing the practical applications of what researchers do. In constructing Figure 1.7, and drawing on Driver (1999), I tried to suggest—in concert with the central portion of Figure 1.5—three interconnected components of the reasons why we study leisure constraints and what outcomes, or benefits, this endeavor brings. First is knowledge—the role of social scientific research in advancing the state of understanding of the phenomena that research was designed to investigate. As argued previously, this does not encompass solely empirical research, but also philosophical and theoretical/conceptual and synthesizing work, the purpose of which is to develop a deeper, more general understanding of the phenomena. Second is education, which refers to formal education gained in universities and colleges and includes undergraduate and graduate levels. Third is practice, which involves the translation of knowledge into new or improved policies and practices.

Clearly, as Driver (1999) acknowledged, each pair of outcomes is interconnected. First, the quality of education is obviously enhanced by incorporating the latest research-based knowledge, as well as an instructor's comprehensive understanding of the depth, accomplishments, limitations, and context of the field. Although it is not universally accepted, I would also argue—potentially, at least—the best researchers make the best teachers. At a minimum, instructors should have some hands-on experience of research in curriculum topics; otherwise, courses are in danger of degenerating into "teaching from the textbook." In the reverse direction, education can enhance research. This can occur by supporting innovative graduate students, encouraging enquiring young minds to challenge the status quo, and treating graduate students as research colleagues. It can also happen in the undergraduate classroom, in terms of the clarification and enhanced understanding of complex concepts that often ensue when attempting to explain the latter.

Second, turning to the reciprocal relationship between research and practice, the conventional wisdom seems to be practitioners ought to be more aware than they appear to be of ongoing developments in leisure research (Godbey, 1989; Jordan & Roland, 1999; Shaw, 2000). Given this awareness, they should then be better positioned to take advantage of new research that has the potential to improve the quality and efficiency of recreation resource allocation and leisure service delivery (see Scott, this volume). Conversely, the specific needs of practitioners may lead to new questions for researchers, which may in turn enhance theoretical knowledge of the phenomena under empirical investigation. Ideally, of course, we should perhaps strive for the level of cooperation between researchers and practitioners advocated by Driver and Bruns (1999) in their discussion of the benefits approach to leisure.

Finally, enhancing the quality of education should produce better-trained practitioners who can translate their knowledge into practice, and who are more aware of and able to use the results of research in their everyday and ongoing activities. Thus, the practical value of research does not lie solely in undertaking research to answer practitioners' immediate needs and questions—

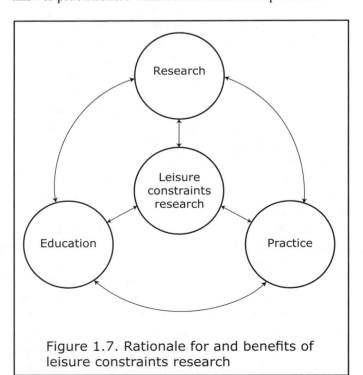

Figure 1.7. Rationale for and benefits of leisure constraints research

by appending paragraphs about applications to research articles, by orienting some or our journals to applied issues, or by organizing "Research Round Tables."[4] It lies, too, in ensuring our students are exposed to research and armed with knowledge and a critical keenness they can subsequently use to ask the right questions if and when they become practitioners.

Organizing Knowledge About Constraints: Structure of the Book

The editor of a collection such as this book inevitably faces the problem of how to structure it and how to organize the sequence of chapters. Themes are typically identified at the outset, but new ones replace them as chapters are drafted and unexpected connections emerge. Also, it is rare for a chapter to be concerned solely with the single theme related to a given subheading. Ultimately, however, the editor must make a decision, and for this book I opted for four main groupings of chapters, meanwhile urging the reader to remember that many alternatives could have been followed, and these are "open" rather than "closed" sections. Most of the chapters cut across several themes, and the reader is urged to keep in mind connections among chapters as well as the specific content of each chapter. The chapters can be read in any order and with alternative groupings should instructors and students decide to pursue connections and themes other than the ones reflected in my own choices.

To begin with, there is a section of eight chapters broadly linked under the heading of *Impacts of Constraints on Diverse Populations*. A typical journal article usually starts with a theoretical framework followed by empirical evidence, and it was tempting to follow this order when deciding which section to place first. However, I have chosen to start the book with chapters that summarize—and extend—our knowledge about the populations often thought to be the most affected by constraints to their leisure. These chapters also cover issues and frameworks that simultaneously help to draw together what we already know and which, following the careful guidance of the authors involved, point to innovative directions for future research. Thus, this section contains chapters on gender, race, ethnicity and immigration, adolescents, and the elderly. It also includes an integrative chapter on women and fear in the outdoors that brings together three key elements related to the experience of constraints: people, constraint, and place. This part of the book concludes with a pair of chapters that cut across much of what has already been said in the section. They focus on transitions and constraints over the lifespan, and then on a particular kind of transition—negative life events.

Armed with this knowledge, the reader should be able to move on to the more theoretical and abstract chapters in the next section, *New Approaches to the Study of Constraints*. This section begins with theory and concludes with method, while in between there is consideration of broad issues of culture, time, outdoor recreation, disciplinary foundations and interdisciplinary connections, new concepts (affordance), and an integrating framework (benefits and constraints). The penultimate section, *Constraints Research and Practice*, comprises three chapters that focus largely on applications. While the first of these chapters takes applications as its central theme, the reader is urged to recognize the other two chapters, on geographic information systems and therapeutic recreation, could easily have been placed elsewhere, as they contain material of a conceptual nature that sets the foundation for the applications they cover. Moreover, many of the chapters in the earlier sections of the book contain material that either explicitly or implicitly contributes to applying knowledge about constraints.

The book concludes with a section entitled *Critique* that consists of two chapters that in a sense "stand back" from everything that has preceded them. There has been an increasing recognition in recent years that there is effectively a "North American paradigm" in leisure research on this side of the Atlantic; this is equally true of leisure constraints research as it is of the broader field of which it is a part. Thus, the first of the two chapters in the *Critique* section reminds us that there are other approaches. Finally, to forestall the idea there is universal agreement about the value and contributions of leisure constraints research, the last chapter of the book adopts an intentionally critical posture toward the field.

References

Backman, S. J. and Crompton, J. L. (1989). Discriminating between continuers and discontinuers of two public leisure services. *Journal of Park and Recreation Administration, 7*, 56–71.

Backman, S. J. and Crompton, J. L. (1990). Differentiating between active and passive discontinuers of two leisure activities. *Journal of Leisure Research, 22*, 197–212.

Beckers, T. (1995). Back to basics: International communication in leisure research. *Leisure Sciences, 17*, 327–336.

Bella, L. (1989). Women and leisure: Beyond androcentrism. In E. L. Jackson and T. L. Burton (Eds.), *Understanding leisure and recreation: Mapping the past, charting the future* (pp. 150–180). State College, PA: Venture Publishing, Inc.

Bialeschki, M. D. and Henderson, K. A. (1988). Constraints to trail use. *Journal of Park and Recreation Administration, 6*, 20–28.

Bialeschki, M. D. and Michener, S. (1994). Re-entering leisure: Transition within the role of motherhood. *Journal of Leisure Research, 26*, 57–74.

Blazey, M. (1987). The differences between participants and non-participants in a senior travel program. *Journal of Travel Research, 26*, 7–12.

Boothby, J., Tungatt, M. F., and Townsend, A. R. (1981). Ceasing participation in sports activity: Reported reasons and their implications. *Journal of Leisure Research, 13*, 1–14.

Buchanan, T. and Allen, L. (1985). Barriers to recreation participation in later life cycle stages. *Therapeutic Recreation Journal, 19*, 39–50.

Coalter, F. (1997). Leisure sciences and leisure studies: Different concept, same crisis? *Leisure Sciences, 19*, 255–268.

Coalter, F. (1999). Leisure sciences and leisure studies: The challenge of meaning. In E. L. Jackson and T. L. Burton (Eds.), *Leisure studies: Prospects for the twenty-first century* (pp. 507–519). State College, PA: Venture Publishing, Inc.

Cooper, W. E. (1999). Some philosophical aspects of leisure theory. In E. L. Jackson and T. L. Burton (Eds.), *Leisure studies: Prospects for the twenty-first century* (pp. 3–15). State College, PA: Venture Publishing, Inc.

Crawford, D. W. and Godbey, G. (1987). Reconceptualizing barriers to family leisure. *Leisure Sciences, 9*, 119–127.

Crawford, D. W., Jackson, E. L., and Godbey, G. (1991). A hierarchical model of leisure constraints. *Leisure Sciences, 13*, 309–320.

Deem, R. (1986). *All work and no play? The sociology of women and leisure*. Milton Keynes, England: Open University Press.

Driver, B. L. (1999). Recognizing and celebrating progress in leisure studies. In E. L. Jackson and T. L. Burton (Eds.), *Leisure studies: Prospects for the twenty-first century* (pp. 523–534). State College, PA: Venture Publishing, Inc.

Driver, B. L. and Bruns, D. H. (1999). Concepts and uses of the benefits approach to leisure. In E. L. Jackson and T. L. Burton (Eds.), *Leisure studies: Prospects for the twenty-first century* (pp. 349–369). State College, PA: Venture Publishing, Inc.

Ferris, A. L. (1962). *National Recreation Survey, Outdoor Recreation Resources Review Commission* (Study Report No. 19). Washington, DC: U.S. Government Printing Office.

Francken, D. A. and Van Raiij, M. F. (1981). Satisfaction with leisure time activities. *Journal of Leisure Research, 13*, 337–352.

Frederick, C. J. and Shaw, S. M. (1995). Body image as a leisure constraint: Examining the experience of aerobic exercise classes for young adults. *Leisure Sciences, 17*, 57–89.

Gilbert, D. and Hudson, S. (2000). Tourism demand constraints: A skiing participation. *Annals of Tourism Research, 27*, 906–925.

Godbey, G. (1985). Non-participation in public leisure services: A model. *Journal of Park and Recreation Administration, 3*, 1–13.

Godbey, G. (1989). Implications of recreation and leisure research for professionals. In E. L. Jackson and T. L. Burton (Eds.), *Understanding leisure and recreation: Mapping the past, charting the future* (pp. 613–628). State College, PA: Venture Publishing, Inc.

Goodale, T. L. and Witt, P. A. (1989). Recreation non-participation and barriers to leisure. In E. L. Jackson and T. L. Burton (Eds.), *Understanding leisure and recreation: Mapping the past, charting the future* (pp. 421–449). State College, PA: Venture Publishing, Inc.

Harrington, M. A. (1991). Time after work: Constraints on the leisure of working women. *Loisir et Société, 14*(1), 115–132.

Hawkins, B. A. and Freeman, P. (1993). *Factor analysis of leisure constraints for aging adults with mental retardation*. Paper presented at the NRPA Symposium on Leisure Research, San Jose, CA.

Hawkins, B. A., Peng, J., Hsieh, C.-M., and Eklund, S. J. (1999). Leisure constraints: A replication and extension of construct development. *Leisure Sciences, 21*, 179–192.

Henderson, K. A. (1991). The contribution of feminism to an understanding of leisure constraints. *Journal of Leisure Research, 23*, 363–377.

Henderson, K. A. (1997). A critique of constraints theory: A response. *Journal of Leisure Research, 29*, 453–457.

Henderson, K. A. and Allen, K. (1991). The ethic of care: Leisure possibilities and constraints for women. *Loisir et Société, 14*(1), 97–113.

Henderson, K. A., Bedini, L. A., Hecht, L., and Schuler, R. (1995). Women with physical disabilities and the negotiation of leisure constraints. *Leisure Studies, 14*, 17–31.

Henderson, K. A. and Bialeschki, M. D. (1991). A sense of entitlement to leisure as constraint and empowerment for women. *Leisure Sciences, 13*, 51–65.

Henderson, K. A. and Bialeschki, M. D. (1993). Exploring an expanded model of women's leisure constraints. *Journal of Applied Recreation Research, 18*, 229–252.

Henderson, K. A., Bialeschki, M. D., Shaw, S. M., and Freysinger, V. J. (1996). *Both gains and gaps: Feminist perspectives on women's leisure*. State College, PA: Venture Publishing, Inc.

Henderson, K. A., Stalnaker, D., and Taylor, G. (1988). The relationship between barriers to recreation and gender-role personality traits for women. *Journal of Leisure Research, 20*, 69–80.

Howard, D. R. and Crompton, J. L. (1984). Who are the consumers of public park and recreation services? An analysis of the users and non-users of three municipal leisure service organizations. *Journal of Park and Recreation Administration, 2*, 33–48.

Hubbard, J. and Mannell, R. (2001). Testing competing models of the leisure constraint negotiation process in a corporate employee recreation setting. *Leisure Sciences, 23*, 145–163.

Hultsman, W. Z. (1995). Recognizing patterns of leisure constraints: An extension of the exploration of dimensionality. *Journal of Leisure Research, 27*, 228–244.

Jackson, E. L. (1983). Activity specific barriers to recreation participation. *Leisure Sciences, 6*, 47–60.

Jackson, E. L. (1988). Leisure constraints: A survey of past research. *Leisure Sciences, 10*, 203–215.

Jackson, E. L. (1990a). Variations in the desire to begin a leisure activity: Evidence of antecedent constraints? *Journal of Leisure Research, 22*, 55–70.

Jackson, E. L. (1990b). Trends in leisure preferences: Alternative constraints-related explanations. *Journal of Applied Recreation Research, 15*(3), 129–145.

Jackson, E. L. (1993). Recognizing patterns of leisure constraints: Results from alternative analyses. *Journal of Leisure Research*, *25*, 129–149.

Jackson, E. L. (1997). In the eye of the beholder: A comment on Samdahl and Jekubovich, "A critique of leisure constraints: Comparative analyses and understandings." *Journal of Leisure Research*, *29*, 458–468.

Jackson, E. L. (2000). Will research on leisure constraints still be relevant in the twenty-first century? *Journal of Leisure Research*, *32*, 62–68.

Jackson, E. L. (2000–2001). The North American leisure research community in the 1990s: An exploratory quantitative analysis of participation in the Leisure Research Symposium and the Canadian Congress on Leisure Research, *Leisure/Loisir*, *25*(1–2), 79–107.

Jackson, E. L. (2003a). Leisure research by Canadians and Americans: One community or two solitudes? *Journal of Leisure Research*, *35*, 292–315.

Jackson, E. L. (2003b). Digging disciplines deeper: Thoughts arising from commentaries by Shaw, Samdahl, Dawson, and Witt. *Journal of Leisure Research*, *35*, 335–347.

Jackson, E. L. (in press). Individual and institutional concentration of leisure research in North America. *Leisure Sciences*.

Jackson, E. L. and Burton, T. L. (Eds.). (1999). *Leisure studies: Prospects for the twenty-first century*. State College, PA: Venture Publishing, Inc.

Jackson, E. L., Crawford, D. W., and Godbey, G. (1993). Negotiation of leisure constraints. *Leisure Sciences*, *15*, 1–11.

Jackson, E. L. and Rucks, V. C. (1995). Negotiation of leisure constraints by junior-high and high-school students: An exploratory study. *Journal of Leisure Research*, *27*, 85–105.

Jackson, E. L. and Scott, D. (1999). Constraints to leisure. In E. L. Jackson and T. L. Burton (Eds.), *Leisure studies: Prospects for the twenty-first century* (pp. 299–321). State College, PA: Venture Publishing, Inc.

Jackson, E. L. and Searle, M. S. (1983). Recreation non-participation: Variables related to the desire for new recreational activities. *Recreation Research Review*, *10*(2), 5–12.

Jackson, E. L. and Searle, M. S. (1985). Recreation non-participation and barriers to participation: Concepts, and models. *Loisir et Société*, *8*, 693–707.

Jordan, D. J. and Roland, M. (1999). An examination of differences between academics and practitioners in frequency of reading research and attitudes toward research. *Journal of Leisure Research*, *31*, 166–170.

Kay, T. and Jackson, G. (1991). Leisure despite constraint: The impact of leisure constraints on leisure participation. *Journal of Leisure Research*, *23*, 301–313.

McGuire, F. A. (1984). A factor analytic study of leisure constraints in advanced adulthood. *Leisure Sciences*, *6*, 313–326.

McGuire, F. A., Dottavio, D., and O'Leary, J. T. (1986). Constraints to participation in outdoor recreation across the life span: A nationwide study of limitors and prohibitors. *The Gerontologist*, *26*, 538–544.

McGuire, F. A. and O'Leary, J. T. (1992). The implications of leisure constraint research for the delivery of leisure services. *Journal of Park and Recreation Administration*, *10*, 31–40.

McGuire, F. A., O'Leary, J. T., Yeh, C.-K., and Dottavio, F. D. (1989). Integrating ceasing participation with other aspects of leisure behavior: A replication and extension. *Journal of Leisure Research*, *21*, 316–326.

Mommaas, H. (1997). European leisure studies at the crossroads? A history of leisure research in Europe. *Leisure Sciences*, *19*, 241–255.

Mueller, E., Gurin, G., and Wood, M. (1962). Participation in outdoor recreation: Factors affecting demand among American adults. *Outdoor Recreation Resources Review Commission* (Study Report No. 20). Washington, DC: U.S. Government Printing Office.

Norman, W. (1995). *Perceived constraints: A new approach to segmenting the vacation travel market*. Paper presented at the NRPA Symposium on Leisure Research, San Antonio, TX.

Parry, D. C. and Shaw, S. M. (1999). The role of leisure in women's experiences of menopause and mid-life. *Leisure Sciences*, *21*, 197–212.

Patterson, I. and Carpenter, G. (1994). Participation in leisure activities after the death of a spouse. *Leisure Sciences*, *16*, 105–117.

Ravenscroft, N. (2004). Tales from the tracks: Discourses of constraint in the use of mixed cycle and walking routes. *International Review for the Sociology of Sport*, *39*(1), 27–44.

Raymore, L. A., Godbey, G. C., and Crawford, D. W. (1994). Self-esteem, gender, and socioeconomic status: Their relation to perceptions of constraint on leisure among adolescents. *Journal of Leisure Research 26*, 99–118.

Raymore, L. A., Godbey, G. C., Crawford, D. W., and von Eye, A. (1993). Nature and process of leisure constraints: An empirical test. *Leisure Sciences*, *15*, 99–113.

Romsa, G. and Hoffman, W. (1980). An application of non-participation data in recreation research: Testing the opportunity theory. *Journal of Leisure Research*, *12*, 321–328.

Rublee, C. B. and Shaw, S. M. (1991). Constraints on the leisure and community participation of immigrant women: Implications for social integration. *Loisir et Société*, *14*(1), 133–150.

Samdahl, D. M., Hutchinson, S. L., and Jacobson, S. (1999). *Navigating constraints? A critical commentary on negotiation in leisure studies.* Paper presented at the Ninth Canadian Congress on Leisure Research, Acadia University, Wolfville, Nova Scotia, Canada.

Samdahl, D. and Jekubovich, N. (1997a). A critique of leisure constraints: Comparative analyses and understandings. *Journal of Leisure Research*, *29*, 430–452.

Samdahl, D. and Jekubovich, N. (1997b). A rejoinder to Henderson's and Jackson's commentaries on "A critique of leisure constraints." *Journal of Leisure Research*, *29*, 469–471.

Samdahl, D. M. and Kelly, J. J. (1999). Speaking only to ourselves? Citation analysis of *Journal of Leisure Research* and *Leisure Sciences*. *Journal of Leisure Research*, *31*, 171–180.

Scott, D. (1991). The problematic nature of participation in contract bridge: A qualitative study of group-related constraints. *Leisure Sciences*, *13*, 321–336.

Searle, M. S. and Jackson, E. L. (1985a). Socioeconomic variations in perceived barriers to recreation participation among would-be participants. *Leisure Sciences*, *7*, 227–249.

Searle, M. S. and Jackson, E. L. (1985b). Recreation non-participation and barriers to participation: Considerations for the management of recreation delivery systems. *Journal of Park and Recreation Administration*, *3*, 23–36.

Shaw, S. M. (1994). Gender, leisure, and constraint: Towards a framework for the analysis of women's leisure. *Journal of Leisure Research*, *26*, 8–22.

Shaw, S. M. (1997). Cultural determination, diversity, and coalition in leisure research: A commentary on Coalter and Mommaas. *Leisure Sciences*, *19*, 277–279.

Shaw, S. M. (2000). If our research is relevant, why is nobody listening? *Journal of Leisure Research*, *32*, 147–151.

Shaw, S. M., Bonen, A., and McCabe, J. F. (1991). Do more constraints mean less leisure? Examining the relationship between constraints and participation. *Journal of Leisure Research*, *23*, 286–300.

Shaw, S. M. and Henderson, K. A. (2003). *Leisure research about gender and men: The weaker link?* Paper presented at the NRPA Symposium on Leisure Research, St. Louis, MO.

Stockdale, J. E. (1989). Concepts and measures of leisure participation and preference. In E. L. Jackson and T. L. Burton (Eds.), *Understanding leisure and recreation: Mapping the past, charting the future* (pp. 113–150). State College, PA: Venture Publishing, Inc.

Tirone, S. C. and Shaw, S. M. (1997). At the center of their lives: Indo Canadian women, their families and leisure. *Journal of Leisure Research*, *29*, 225–244.

Valentine, K., Allison, M. T., and Schneider, I. (1999). The one-way mirror of leisure research: A need for cross-national social scientific perspectives. *Leisure Sciences*, *21*, 241–246.

Virden, R. J. (1990). A comparison study of wilderness users and nonusers: Implications for managers and policy makers. *Journal of Park and Recreation Administration*, *8*, 13–24.

White, G. F. (1961). The choice of use in resource management. *Natural Resources Journal, 1*, 23–40.

Whyte, L. B. and Shaw, S. M. (1994). Women's leisure: An exploratory study of fear of violence as a leisure constraint. *Journal of Applied Recreation Research*, *19*, 5–21.

Wimbush, E. and Talbot, M. (1988). *Relative freedoms: Women and leisure.* Milton Keynes, England: Open University Press.

Witt, P. A. and Goodale, T. L. (1981). The relationship between barriers to leisure enjoyment and family stages. *Leisure Sciences*, *4*, 29–49.

Wright, B. A. and Goodale, T. L. (1991). Beyond non-participation: Validation of interest and frequency of participation categories in constraints research. *Journal of Leisure Research*, *23*, 314–331.

Endnotes

1. A representative but not exhaustive list of work conducted in the mid- to late-1980s includes the following: (1) *Empirical research:* Backman & Crompton, 1989, 1990; Bialeschki & Henderson, 1988; Blazey, 1987; Buchanan & Allen, 1985; Harrington, 1991; Henderson & Allen, 1991; Henderson & Bialeschki, 1991; Jackson, 1983; Jackson & Searle, 1983; McGuire, Dottavio & O'Leary, 1986; McGuire, O'Leary, Yeh & Dottavio, 1989; Rublee & Shaw, 1991; Searle & Jackson, 1985a; (2) *Early modeling:* Godbey, 1985; Jackson & Searle, 1985; Wright & Goodale, 1991; (3) *On applications:* Howard & Crompton, 1984; McGuire & O'Leary, 1992; Searle & Jackson, 1985b; Virden, 1990.

2. It should be acknowledged that this linear, quantitatively oriented model was not the only one to appear in the 1990s. For example, Henderson and Bialeschki (1993) developed a more holistic, interactive model suitable for use in qualitative research.

3. It would not be unreasonable to argue early leisure constraints research exhibited the characteristics of "androcentrism" as described by Bella (1989, p. 151), which she defined as "a pattern of thought that takes male experience as central, and studies and evaluates women's experiences by referring to those of men."

4. This comment should not be interpreted as disparaging these efforts to ensure research is grounded in the "real world." I simply want to suggest that there is more to it than that.

Section 2

Impacts of Constraints on Diverse Populations

Chapter 2

Gender Analysis and Leisure Constraints: An Uneasy Alliance

Susan M. Shaw (University of Waterloo) and Karla Henderson (North Carolina State University)

Over the past 20 years, research on gender and leisure has made rapid gains. Gender has been shown to have a substantial impact on leisure practices, opportunities, and experiences, affecting the quantity and quality of leisure. Although some questions remain about the degree of recognition and acceptance of this body of research (Deem, 1999), advances in scholarship are evident, particularly an understanding of the problems women face in terms of their access to quality leisure (Henderson, Bialeschki, Shaw & Freysinger, 1996). Early research tended to use an "add women and stir" approach (Henderson, 1991), quickly replaced by research on gender differences, and later by women-centered research focusing on women's experiences and ensuring women's voices were heard (Henderson, 1994a). In recent years, research on gender and leisure adopted a gender relations approach, in which the linkages are explored between women's disadvantaged position in terms of access to leisure and their lack of power in society in general (Aitchison, 2001). To date, most of this research has been concerned with the gendered nature of women's leisure, with relatively little attention to understanding men's leisure from a gendered perspective.

Over approximately the same time period, considerable progress has been made in understanding and documenting leisure constraints. Constraints research moved from a narrow focus on barriers to participation toward a broader conceptualization of constraints. In addition, typologies of leisure constraints have been developed, and the three categories of intrapersonal, interpersonal, and structural constraints, originally introduced by Crawford and Godbey (1987), have become widely accepted and adopted by researchers (Jackson & Scott, 1999). The relationship between these categories of constraints has been theorized, including the development of a hierarchical model (Crawford, Jackson & Godbey,

1991), and a set of propositional statements about how this model works (Jackson, Crawford & Godbey, 1993). The interrelationships between constraints and their impact on participation have been empirically tested (e.g., Raymore, Godbey, Crawford & von Eye, 1993). Further, based on evidence constraints are not necessarily impenetrable barriers, attention has also been directed toward the idea of negotiation, recognizing constraints can be negotiated around to a greater or lesser degree (Jackson & Rucks, 1993).

Despite the fact these two areas of research (i.e., gender research and constraints research) have grown and developed over approximately the same period of time, they have remained somewhat separate and independent of each other. This separation of the two bodies of literature is surprising in some ways, because gender research has focused on women's disadvantaged position with respect to leisure, and so can be seen to relate to the notion of constraints (Shaw, 1994). Also, a number of constraints researchers have recognized sociodemographics do play a role in the prevalence and extent of constraints (e.g., Jackson & Henderson, 1995; Scott & Munson, 1994; Searle & Jackson, 1985). The frequently disconnected nature of these subareas, however, leads to the suggestion the relationship between gender research and constraints research is an uneasy alliance rather than an integration or consolidation. Despite some commonality of interest, gender has not been a major focus of attention for constraints researchers, and gender scholars have not typically adopted or supported a constraints framework for their research. Conceptual and theoretical advances have developed independently, and for the most part, in different directions.

In this chapter, the uneasy alliance between gender scholarship and constraints scholarship will be explored and discussed. First, the contribution gender or feminist research has made in terms of understanding constraints will be identified, by examining the extent to which the insights from this research fit into a constraints framework. This will be done by focusing primarily on constraints on women's leisure, because of the lack of research on men's leisure. Second, the reasons why gender researchers seem to be uncomfortable with a constraints approach will be examined, with particular attention to the theoretical and conceptual differences between constraints research and gender research. In the final section of the chapter suggestions will be made, based on an integration of ideas related to both gender and constraints, about ways to expand our understanding and to combine the knowledge and insight gained from both areas of research.

Gender Research and the Constraints Framework

Research on Women's Leisure

Much of the research on women's leisure has been motivated by the assumption of a leisure gap between men and women, as well as a gap caused by conflict between leisure and the various responsibilities and demands women experience (Henderson et al., 1996). This idea of a leisure gap is based on documentation of the lack of leisure time women have compared to men (Firestone & Shelton, 1994; Shaw, 1985), as well as awareness of other factors that prevent women from accessing leisure (Deem, 1986). The growing body of research on women's leisure indicates women's position in society, their lack of access to valued resources, and societal expectations about women's lives, roles, and responsibilities reduce their freedom and constrain their options (Green, Hebron & Woodward, 1990; Henderson, 1994b; Shaw & de la Durantaye, 1992; Wimbush & Talbot, 1988).

Most of this research on women's leisure has not used a constraints framework. Rather than looking at specific types of constraints that reduce levels of participation in desired activities, the majority of feminist researchers have directed their attention toward the linkages between women's gendered lives and women's leisure. When a constraints framework has been adopted, however, the research has shown women do indeed face more constraints in their leisure than do men (Jackson & Henderson, 1995), and these constraints relate to culturally based gender role expectations. Moreover, although traditional constraints categories have not typically been employed by feminist researchers, the findings from empirical studies of women's leisure can be adapted

to correspond to these categories, thus providing some information and understanding about questions of structural, intrapersonal, and interpersonal constraints (Shaw, 1994). This adaptation suggests linkages do exist between feminist research and constraints research, but the linkages have been implicit rather than explicit, in part because of the separation of the two bodies of research.

Structural Constraints

Many of the constraints on women's leisure, as revealed through the feminist literature, can be conceptualized as structural constraints, or factors that intervene between a desire for leisure activities and levels of actual participation. Women's lack of financial resources, and the fact that they often lack financial independence, can be seen in this way. Labor market statistics continue to indicate the low earning power of women compared to men (Office of the President, 2001; Statistics Canada, 2000), and some women, particularly single mothers and older women living on their own, are often severely economically deprived. Moreover, women's economic dependency can lead to constraints on spending money on personal leisure, and is associated with other types of constraints as well, such as lack of transportation (Deem, 1986).

Lack of leisure opportunities and programs can also be seen as structural constraints on women's leisure. Sports and physical activities are an obvious example. Despite the fact that few sports activities remain exclusively male today, opportunities to participate, to join teams, or to be involved in sports leagues continue to be considerably limited for girls and women compared to boys and men (Messner & Sabo, 1990; Robinson & Godbey, 1993). For example, opportunities for soccer tend to be relatively equal for preteen girls and boys, but females have considerably fewer opportunities to continue to participate through adolescence and into adulthood compared to males. In addition, despite growth in women's and girls' hockey participation in Canada, females continue to face greater constraints than males in terms of the number of teams and competitive opportunities available (Theberge, 2000).

Although some of the research on women's leisure has provided insight into these structural constraints, considerably more attention has been paid by feminist researchers to the issue of women's lack of time for leisure. Time stress and lack of time for self are major constraints on women's leisure lives. For women, it is not only paid work, but unpaid work and household responsibilities that together leave little time for personal rest, relaxation, or the development of personal leisure activities (Green et al., 1990). Paid work, for example, has some advantages for women (e.g., economic independence and resources, more leisure choices, and more out of home leisure), but it comes at a cost in terms of time stress and reduced time for leisure (Henderson et al., 1996; Shaw, 1988). This dearth of time is largely because women continue to do the major share of household labor whether or not they are employed (Hochschild & Machung, 1990; Horna, 1989; Pittman, Teng, Kerpelman & Solheim, 1999; Shank, 1986). Recent research in the United Kingdom, for example, found even though many British couples believed domestic responsibility should be shared in a dual working household, women were still doing a disproportionate amount of the housework (Kay, 1998). This household labor, added to paid labor, leads to lack of leisure, and this conclusion is further reinforced by statistics that show employed mothers have the highest time stress of all sociodemographic groups (Statistics Canada, 2000).

Time spent in family-related work is more difficult to define, operationalize, and measure for research purposes compared to paid work and housework, but clearly family responsibilities impact women's opportunities for personal leisure as well. Indeed the significance of family responsibilities as a leisure constraint for women is evident from research on life transitions (see Crawford & Huston, 1993; and Jackson, this volume), which indicates the birth of the first child has a dramatic effect, especially on women's leisure. Other types of family-related responsibilities, such as caring for elderly relatives, are also disproportionately shouldered by women (Frederick & Fast, 1999).

Thompson (1999) suggested Australian women are highly likely to establish their leisure around their family responsibilities and tasks, while men are much less likely to place such restrictions on their leisure. Research on family leisure has also shown this form of activity can sometimes constrain rather than enable women's own leisure experiences. For example, several research studies have shown how women put considerable time and effort into ensuring family leisure is a positive experience for their children, husbands, and other family members at the expense of their own leisure interests and desires (Bella, 1992; Hunter & Whitson, 1992). Thus, family activities that appear to be leisure may not be experienced that way by women, but may be an extension of their unpaid work (Shaw, 1992b).

Intrapersonal Constraints

Apart from time and other structural constraints, researchers also examined a variety of factors that may

be viewed as representing intrapersonal constraints for women. Perhaps the issue that has received the most attention is the ethic of care. While caring behavior can facilitate social relationships (Dupuis & Smale, 2000; Henderson & Ainsworth, 2001), and self-care can have a positive effect on personal leisure (Bialeschki & Michener, 1994), the overriding consensus in the gender literature is women's caring behavior is a major constraining factor on women's leisure (Henderson et al., 1996). This constraint is particularly true for married women with children or women caring for aging relatives (e.g., Harrington, Dawson & Bolla, 1992; Rogers, 1997). Closely associated with the ethic of care is the lack of sense of entitlement to leisure evident among some women. As women internalize the ethic of care and direct attention to the well-being of others, they may not develop a sense of their own needs or feel they have a right to leisure for themselves (Bedini & Guinan, 1996; Henderson & Bialeschki, 1991). Clearly, the ethic of care and lack of sense of entitlement relate to women's family roles, and to the obligation to put the well-being of others first. Thus, distinguishing between structural constraints of lack of time from intrapersonal constraints related to caring behaviors and an internalized sense of responsibility to others is difficult.

Although a strongly developed ethic of care and a lack of sense of entitlement seem to be most pronounced among women with children, adolescent females appear to be more likely than males to report participation in activities to please others (Shaw, Caldwell & Kleiber, 1996). This perception may be indicative of an emerging ethic of care and a willingness even among young women to give up personal leisure for the sake of others. College-age women involved in dating relationships have also been found to constrain their own independent leisure to please their male partners (Herridge, Shaw & Mannell, 2003). These findings suggest the constraining effect of caring behavior is not restricted to women who are mothers. On a more positive note, some evidence suggests the constraining effect of the ethic of care may lessen as women age. For example, research by Bialeschki and Michener (1994) showed mothers often regained some sense of entitlement to their own leisure as their children grew up, became independent, and left home. The researchers described this process as a full cycle of leisure as women reclaimed time for themselves. Anderton, Fitzgerald, and Laidler (1995) reached similar conclusions in their study of older women, as did Parry and Shaw (1999) in their research with women in midlife. In both of these studies, the women interviewed seemed to have reached a stage in their lives when they were interested in, and had a sense of entitlement to, personal leisure.

Another intrapersonal constraint that emerges from analysis of the literature on women's leisure relates to women's self-attitudes, including lack of self-esteem. The decline of confidence and self-esteem in teenage girls, as well as an obsession with body image and appearance, have been documented by a number of researchers (e.g., Henderson & King, 1998; Shaw, 1992a). Concerns about appearance, skill level, and fear of being embarrassed by not fitting in or not looking right can constrain participation in different activities. For example, such concerns may affect participation in aerobics (Frederick & Shaw, 1995) or swimming (James, 2000). Young women may be particularly vulnerable to social pressures to conform to the correct or ideal body image. Nevertheless, concerns over appearance and body weight clearly seem to be more constraining for women of all ages compared to men (Lafrance, Zivian & Myers, 2000). Body image has been found to be a constraint to leisure among low-income overweight women (Dattilo, Dattilo & Samdahl, 1994). In general, women's and girls' concerns about appearance may make them reluctant to participate in any activities where they feel their bodies will be on display.

Embarrassment can also reduce the desire to participate in leisure when the desired activity is considered by others to be inappropriate. For example, Culp (1998) found gender roles, including both peer and family expectations about appropriate roles for females, constrained girls interested in outdoor recreation. Such activities may also affect the desire to participate in other activities normatively perceived to be male, such as ice hockey, football, rugby, boxing, or wrestling (Wiley, Shaw & Havitz, 2000). It is important to note here the perception of specific activities as appropriate or not is a culturally based determination. Thus, the nature and degree of this type of intrapersonal constraint will vary between cultural groups (e.g., Khan, 1997; Manrai & Manrai, 1995; Tirone & Pedlar, 2000; Tirone & Shaw, 1997).

An additional factor that could be considered an intrapersonal constraint on women's leisure is fear of violence (Bialeschki & Hicks, 1998; Carr, 2000). Research has consistently shown levels of fear of violence are higher among women than men (e.g., National Crime Prevention Council, 1999; Statistics Canada, 2000). These elevated levels of fear can clearly affect women's participation in leisure, and may be inhibitory factors reducing the desire to participate in activities that might be considered risky. For example, women are often reluctant to go out to leisure activities on their own after dark, or in areas where they feel unsafe, such as walking in the woods, hiking, or cycling on their own (Carr, 2000; Delamere, 1999).

Interpersonal Constraints

Very little research focuses on factors that could be considered interpersonal constraints on women's leisure. This scarcity may be because women tend to have a greater number of social relationships than men, and are thus less likely to lack leisure partners (Henderson & Ainsworth, 2000). Indeed, some research has indicated women have relatively easy access to social leisure, and women's friendships are an important context for leisure (Green, 1998). In this instance, then, gender may be an enabler rather than a constraint. In addition, the lack of attention to constraints of an interpersonal nature may be because one of the major problems women face is lack of time for self or time to be alone. Therefore, time for personal leisure may be a more common and salient concern for many women than lack of friends or partners for leisure activities.

There are indications, though, that other types of interpersonal constraints may negatively affect women's leisure. For example, social disapproval of activities considered to be inappropriate may be a type of interpersonal constraint through friends, family members, or others making their disapproval evident. Similarly, the social control of women's lives by husbands discouraging or making it difficult for wives to participate in desired leisure activities (e.g., Green & Hebron, 1988; Green, Hebron & Woodward, 1987) constrains some women's leisure. However, the extent to which social disapproval and social control influence women's leisure in our society remains essentially unknown, because virtually no research or discussion surrounds this type of constraint. It is also possible women face additional interpersonal constraints not yet fully recognized.

Constraints on Men's Leisure

The lack of research on men, leisure, and gender means relatively little is known about the gendered nature of men's leisure constraints. That is, although much of the research on leisure has been about men, this research has rarely used gender or masculinity as analytic concepts. It could be argued gender should be seen as an enabling factor for men rather than as a constraint. This is because of men's higher levels of participation and what appears to be a stronger sense of entitlement to leisure compared to women. On the other hand, some research in sport sociology and men's studies has pointed to a number of the problems men face because of their gender (e.g., Kimmel & Messner, 1998; Messner & Sabo, 1990). For example, men who do not fit the ideal image of masculinity or who are not competitive, tough, successful, or heterosexual may face a variety of problems in their lives, including their leisure lives. In addition, Kaufman's research (1994) discussed the ways men typically learn to suppress a range of emotions, needs, and possibilities (e.g., nurturing, empathy, and receptivity) inconsistent with dominant ideologies of masculinity. Thus they may reject leisure activities and possibilities they otherwise might enjoy because of the desire to appear masculine. Indeed, this line of research suggests intrapersonal or interpersonal constraints associated with societal views of appropriate male gender role behaviors may be particularly strong for men.

A related line of research with relevance for understanding leisure constraints is sports as an obligatory activity for males. Messner (1998), for example, showed how sports can be experienced as a compulsory leisure activity by some boys and men, in that they feel compelled to participate to reinforce a masculine image of themselves to the outside world. This research suggests leisure participation needs to be understood not only as factors that reduce or prevent participation (i.e., constraints from participation), but also as factors that cause some activities to become obligatory, and thus act as constraints into participation (Shaw, 1994). The same idea can also be applied to women's leisure. For example, some women may feel compelled to participate in family activities or other social activities because of a sense of responsibility, or feel compelled to participate in fitness activities to lose weight.

Overall, the research on gender and leisure illustrates the important contribution this area of research can make to an enhanced understanding of constraints. Exploring the literature of women's leisure from a constraints perspective clearly illustrates the powerful effect of structural constraints (especially lack of time) and intrapersonal constraints (especially the ethic of care, as well as self-attitudes and body attitudes) on women's opportunities for and participation in leisure. In addition, initial research on the gendered nature of men's leisure participation suggests the importance of expanding the research on gender and leisure to look at men and masculinities as well as women and femininities. An expansion of this area of research may provide additional insights into the diversity of leisure experiences among men (as well as among women), the role of gender as a leisure enabler, the gendered nature of some intrapersonal constraints, and the need to examine compulsory dimensions of leisure participation for both women and men.

The Theoretical Bases of Gender and Constraints Research

Despite the evidence of important linkages between research on gender and research on constraints, and despite the argument research on women's leisure has already made an important contribution to understanding constraints, there remains an uncomfortable fit between gender scholarship and constraints scholarship. We suggest this discomfort may be due not to the different areas of interest of the two groups of researchers, but rather to the use of different theoretical and explanatory systems. Given this suggestion, examination and comparison of the theoretical and conceptual bases of these two areas of research can help to explain the difficulties in integrating the two literatures.

Sociocultural Versus Social Psychological Approaches

A number of reasons exist for the uneasy alliance between gender and constraints researchers. Perhaps the most obvious is feminist research focuses on sociocultural explanations for gendered constraints, with particular attention to the total context of women's lives, including the intersections of work, home, family, and leisure. This concern with social context is particularly true of the more recent research that rejected simple comparisons of men's and women's leisure in favor of developing a gender relations approach (Aitchison, 2001). Further, this emphasis on gender relations leads to consideration of the relative positions of women and men in the broader society and the influence of societal values, ideologies, and structures in people's lives. The assumption is the lives of individual women are linked through common or shared experiences of being female in a culture in which power is differentiated by gender (Scraton, 1994), an assumption that could be applied to men as well. Thus, explanations for the difficulties women have in accessing leisure need to be examined within the broader cultural context of societal gender relations. This perspective, in many ways, reflects a British or European approach to leisure research, although it is evident in North American feminist research on leisure as well (see Coalter, 1999).

Constraints research, on the other hand, being more closely aligned with the North American social psychological approach to the study of leisure (Coalter, 1999), tended to focus on individual experiences or perceptions. Attention has been paid to distinguishing and documenting the types of constraints individuals face and the relationship between these constraints and leisure behavior. Moreover, the idea of negotiation strategies also focuses on individual decisions and behaviors. Thus, the social context within which such decisions are made may not be taken into account or may be given only scant attention. This lack of acknowledgment of how social structures constrain people can be criticized for leading to a blame the victim approach, directed at individuals who are not able, for a variety of reasons, to negotiate around constraints (Henderson, 1998).

Distinguishing Categories of Constraints

A second reason for the uneasy alliance may be researchers studying women's leisure found it difficult to distinguish among structural, intrapersonal, and interpersonal constraints (Henderson & Bialeschki, 1993). For example, lack of time due to family responsibilities and obligations could be seen as a structural constraint that intervenes between women's desire for leisure and their actual levels of participation. On the other hand, the same family responsibilities could be seen as an intrapersonal constraint as women learn to internalize an ethic of care and to develop an outlook that leads to caring for others and putting the needs of family members before their own personal needs. Moreover, lack of time could also be seen to arise as an interpersonal constraint, resulting from interactions with husbands/partners and with other family members who have particular expectations about women's roles within the family.

It is not only family responsibilities that fall simultaneously into all three constraints categories. The difficulty in distinguishing clearly among categories is also true for other constraints associated with societal gender roles, such as fear of violence or body image. Body image, because it represents an internalized conception of self, can be classified as an intrapersonal constraint that decreases desire to participate in activities such as swimming, gymnastics, or aerobics. Further, it can also be seen as either a structural constraint that deters desired participation because of embarrassment or self-consciousness (James, 2000), or as an interpersonal constraint related to the sense that other people are watching or judging one's appearance (James, 2000). Likewise, fear of violence based on fear of attack or assault by others may result from interpersonal relations between men and women, represent an intrapersonal internalized attitude, or be a structural constraint that reduces participation (Delamere, 1999; Whyte & Shaw, 1994).

In a study by Samdahl and Jekubovich (1997) the difficulties of adopting the traditional constraints categories for understanding leisure were further revealed. This study explored the constraints of a group of men and women, most of whom were employed. Initially, the researchers used the three concepts of structural, interpersonal, and intrapersonal to classify the constraints reported. They found the data could indeed be categorized according to these predetermined concepts. When they reanalyzed the data, however, using an interpretive approach of developing categories based on the words and meanings of the people in their study, a different view of constraints emerged. Specifically, other-oriented or interpersonal concerns of women as well as men were shown to be important. The people interviewed in this study were motivated to create space and time for their leisure, but the researchers felt the predetermined definition and categorization of constraints seemed to limit, rather than facilitate, explanations for leisure behavior.

Based on the second approach to analysis of their data, Samdahl and Jekubovich (1997) were also critical of the idea of negotiation, as it has been developed in the constraints literature. They felt the concept of negotiation required further consideration and development. Specifically, they suggested greater recognition needs to be directed toward the dynamic and ongoing nature of negotiation processes in everyday life. In addition, they suggested negotiation does not always imply conscious and deliberate attempts to find ways around constraints, but that negotiations may also occur unconsciously or subconsciously (see also Samdahl, this volume, and Crawford & Jackson, this volume).

Conceptualizing Constraints

The research by Samdahl and Jekubovich (1997) and others (e.g., Henderson & Bialeschki, 1993) indicated the traditional way of defining constraints may need further consideration. This traditional conceptualization may be too narrow and may not always lead to fruitful explanations of leisure behavior (Henderson & Bialeschki, 1993). In a study of constraints on women's leisure, for example, Harrington et al. (1992) used the concepts of subjective and objective constraints. This conceptualization was based on the idea constraints are both external to the individual (e.g., lack of time or lack of financial resources), and internalized as a set of experiences, attitudes or beliefs (e.g., individuals may feel time stressed or financially stressed). Harrington et al.'s approach allowed for examination of whether objective and subjective components of specific types of constraints had differential or similar effects on leisure behavior. Another way to conceptualize constraints might be to examine the effect of clusters of constraints on people's leisure lives, as suggested previously by Jackson (1993). For example, some people (especially employed mothers) may be predominantly affected by lack of time and time constraints, while others (e.g., caregivers) may be constrained primarily by caring behaviors and an internalized ethic of care. Yet others may experience constraints associated with disability or health-related problems.

Whatever approach is taken to the categorization of constraints, most feminist researchers argue the conceptualization needs to be grounded in people's lived experiences. In line with feminist thinking and feminist methodology (e.g., Harding, 1987), more research studies using interpretive methods are required to ensure the categorization and definition of constraints are consistent with the meaning of constraints in people's (men's and women's) lives. The same argument also applies to ensuring the ideas of negotiation and negotiation strategies are consonant with people's experiences and meanings.

Constraints to the Experience of Leisure

Another reason why some feminist scholars, as well as others, have criticized the constraints literature is it has tended to focus only on constraints on participation rather than constraints on the quality of leisure experiences. In other words, this body of research adopted an activity definition of leisure rather than an experiential definition (Samdahl & Jekubovich, 1997). This focus may have been because the initial impetus for this research was to explain patterns of participation and the use of resources and facilities (see Jackson & Scott, 1999). A number of studies of women's leisure, however, have indicated constraints on the *quality* of leisure experience are just as important in women's lives as constraints on activity participation. Frederick and Shaw (1995), for example, found constraints associated with appearance, body image, and self-consciousness in aerobics did not necessarily reduce levels of participation in this activity, but did reduce levels of enjoyment. Similarly, women may continue to participate in certain activities, such as outdoor activities, despite elevated levels of fear, but if they do so this fear is likely to reduce the quality of the leisure they experience (Whyte & Shaw, 1994). In addition, the constraints many women face related to time pressure, family obligations, and exhaustion constrain the quality of family leisure and make it difficult for them to enjoy family activities (Larson, Gillman & Richards, 1997),

but may not decrease participation because of a sense of responsibility or compulsion. The issue of constraints on experience has been recognized in the literature (e.g., see Jackson & Scott, 1999). To date, however, few researchers in the constraints field have given much consideration to the issue of experience, or the relationship between experience and obligation, either in terms of empirical research or in terms of theoretical development.

Theoretical Underpinnings

Overall, the conceptual and theoretical basis of the gender and leisure literature differs from many of the premises of the constraints literature. Constraints researchers tend to focus on individual behaviors and explanations, while gender researchers focus more on the social and cultural context. The more holistic approach of gender research, including research on masculinities as well as femininities, means constraints are seen as culturally based, and as such are seen to be related to social structures and structured power relations as well. Even the terminology causes some confusion here, because feminist researchers use the word "structures" to talk about systems of power or stratification (e.g., Shaw, Bonen & McCabe, 1991), whereas constraints researchers use the term "structural constraints" to mean factors that affect individual leisure participation levels. In addition, the relationships among the categories of structural, interpersonal, and intrapersonal constraints are not mutually exclusive. Considerable overlap exists in the meanings of these groupings.

Differences in terminology reflecting the different theoretical underpinnings are also evident with respect to ways of dealing with or overcoming constraints. Although some constraints researchers use the term "negotiation" to depict individual strategies to enable greater leisure participation, feminist researchers might be more likely to use the term "resistance." For feminists, resistance means not only finding ways to overcome constraints, but also challenging dominant ideologies or dominant power relations (Wearing, 1990). Resistance is also seen as a collective strategy (e.g., a group of girls demanding equal access to sports facilities), as well as an individual strategy used to increase personal power and freedom (Shaw, 2001).

Conclusions

Although some major differences appear in the way constraints are understood and theorized in the constraints literature compared to the gender literature, some commonality of interest also clearly exists. The extent to which interests overlap suggests it would be fruitful to move toward a greater integration of these two somewhat separate but important areas of research. The literature on gender and leisure could benefit from greater attention to the constraints field, while constraints research could also be advanced through insights developed by gender researchers.

A number of strategies can be suggested that would help to bring the somewhat separate literatures on gender and on constraints together, to reduce the uneasy alliance that currently exists, and to promote mutually interdependent and beneficial new insights. First, we need to explore both individual and societal levels of analysis, because both affect the existence of and the perception of constraints. With regard to the constraints literature, this approach requires moving beyond examining only individual experiences toward taking account of social context and placing more emphasis on the holistic aspects of people's lives. In conjunction with this, more studies using interpretive methodologies to develop an understanding of the social and cultural context of people's leisure lives are needed. For gender researchers, greater attention to advances in the constraints field are warranted. Participation in the ongoing debate on constraints might alleviate the isolation of gender research literature and lead to a better integration of ideas and theories.

Second, as indicated earlier, a need arises to use grounded methodologies to examine current constraints concepts and categories with particular attention to the meaningfulness of these concepts. Moreover, apart from assessing the relevance of current concepts, the question of whether constraints are always obvious and overt, or whether there might be hidden constraints, could also be addressed. For example, intrapersonal constraints, such as fear of violence, the ethic of care, or social disapproval of activities, may not always be consciously recognized by individuals, yet may affect their behaviors. Constraints associated with normative behaviors and societal roles, such as gender roles, may be particularly likely to go unrecognized because of the taken-for-granted nature of role expectations. In addition, negotiation strategies to increase levels of leisure participation may also be either conscious and intended, or subconscious and unintended. For example, applying for a new job or for a promotion could increase an individual's level of self-confidence, and that may, in turn, help to overcome certain intrapersonal constraints linked to body image or self-esteem. The idea of unintended outcomes is also consistent with recent research and theorizing about leisure and resistance (Shaw, 2001), where different types of resistance, both purposeful and unintended, have been recognized. A discussion of the similarities and differences between negotiation strategies and resistance could indeed facilitate a greater understanding and integration of ideas.

Another strategy that would lead to a better integration of the gender literature and the constraints literature would be to adopt a more comprehensive conceptualization of leisure itself. While most of the literature on the social psychology of leisure adopted a broad definition of leisure as experience, and as a combination of perceptual and experiential factors (e.g., see Mannell & Kleiber, 1997), continuing emphasis on leisure participation as the outcome of constraints and negotiations appears to be unwarranted. More research is needed on the ways enjoyment and the quality of leisure experiences are constrained. Such research could spawn a new way of thinking about constraints and would likely lead to the identification of new types and categories of constraints as well. A focus on experience would also lead to a better understanding of the compulsory nature of certain types of leisure activities and the ways in which men or women are sometimes constrained into participation. Moreover, this type of research may well lead to explorations of the ways in which participation itself might constrain experiences (Shaw, 1994). For example, activities with an obligatory or purposeful component may well diminish or compromise the quality of experience. Examples include boys' participation in sports to conform to dominant ideas of masculinity, girls' participation in fitness activities for weight loss, or mothers' participation in family activities out of a sense of duty.

A final strategy for integrating feminist and constraints research and for developing an expanded understanding of constraints would be to pay more attention to a range of demographic and social structural factors. First, the lack of research on the gendered nature of men's leisure needs to be addressed. This means not simply doing analysis that compares men's and women's leisure participation, enjoyment, or constraints, but examining in more detail the ways in which societal gender relations affect the leisure practices of men as well as women. Studies may confirm, as feminist researchers have indicated, men are advantaged in terms of leisure, and this may lead to research on the ways in which gender facilitates rather than constrains participation or enjoyment. At the same time, research on men will also show the ways in which narrow constructions of masculinity may disadvantage or constrain men, reducing their options. Further, such research will be able to determine which specific categories of men are particularly disadvantaged. Clearly this kind of research has the potential to greatly enhance our understanding of constraints as well as of gender. Examining gender and leisure for men might focus on men's emotions, including self-reflection, studying men in groups, placing men's experience in structural context, and focusing on power and identity to understand participation, enjoyment, and constraint.

We also need to move beyond gender to describe the multiple systems of inequality (McKay, Messner & Sabo, 2000) and the ways in which they influence and constrain leisure. Some initial research explored the constraints reported by different age groups (e.g., Hultsman, 1992; Mannell & Zuzanek, 1991) and by different racial and ethnic groups (e.g., Floyd, 1998; Stodolska & Jackson, 1998). Relatively little research, however, explicitly addressed the question of diversity. Research on a variety of social groups, including both men and women, and research involving people of different cultural backgrounds, would greatly enhance the constraints literature. Constraints researchers could apply their particular expertise to the question of diversity. At the same time, gender researchers could bring an awareness of the cultural construction of gender, and the need to take social construction into consideration in research with different population groups.

In sum, an important start has been made in the constraints research field. This research is both challenged and complemented by insights from the research on gender and leisure, particularly the research on women's leisure. We hope future research will seek to strengthen the alliance between these two areas of investigation. Bringing together information on individual behaviors, negotiation strategies, attitudes, and experiences, along with an understanding of the influence of social structures and sociocultural contexts, should lead to a stronger basis for understanding leisure constraints, an enhanced understanding of this important aspect of people's lives, and new and innovative directions for future research.

References

Aitchison, C. (2001). Gender and leisure research: The "codification of knowledge." *Leisure Sciences, 23*(1), 1–19.

Anderton, J., Fitzgerald, C., and Laidler, A. (1995). Leisure lost, leisure regained? Leisure in the lives of older women. *ANZALS Leisure Research Series, 2*, 2–25.

Bedini, L. A. and Guinan, D. M. (1996). The leisure of caregivers of older adults: Implications for CRTS's in non-traditional settings. *Therapeutic Recreation Journal, 30*, 274–288.

Bella, L. (1992). *The Christmas imperative.* Halifax, Nova Scotia, Canada: Fernwood Publishing.

Bialeschki, M. D. and Hicks, H. (1998). *"I refuse to live in fear": The influence of violence on women's outdoor recreation activities.* Paper presented at the Leisure Studies Association Conference, Leeds, England.

Bialeschki, M. D. and Michener, S. (1994). Re-entering leisure: Transition within the role of motherhood. *Journal of Leisure Research, 26*(1), 57–74.

Carr, N. (2000). An exploratory study of young women's use of leisure spaces and times: Constrained, negotiated, or unconstrained behavior? *World Leisure, 3*, 25–32.

Coalter, F. (1999). Leisure sciences and leisure studies: The challenge of meaning. In E. L. Jackson and T. L. Burton (Eds.), *Leisure studies: Prospects for the twenty-first century* (pp. 507–519). State College, PA: Venture Publishing, Inc.

Crawford, D. W. and Godbey, G. (1987). Reconceptualizing barriers to family leisure. *Leisure Sciences, 9*(2), 119–127.

Crawford, D. W. and Huston, T. L. (1993). The impact of the transition to parenthood on marital leisure. *Personality and Social Psychology Bulletin, 19*, 39–46.

Crawford, D. W., Jackson, E. L., and Godbey, G. (1991). A hierarchical model of leisure constraints. *Leisure Sciences, 13*(4), 309–320.

Culp, R. H. (1998). Adolescent girls and outdoor recreation: A case study examining constraints and effective programming. *Journal of Leisure Research, 30*(3), 356–379.

Dattilo, J., Dattilo, A., and Samdahl, D. M. (1994). Leisure orientations and self-esteem in women with low incomes who are overweight. *Journal of Leisure Research, 25*(1), 23–38.

Deem, R. (1986). *All work and no play? The sociology of women and leisure.* Milton Keynes, England: Open University Press.

Deem, R. (1999). How do we get out of the ghetto? Strategies for research on gender and leisure for the twenty-first century. *Leisure Studies, 18*(3), 161–177.

Delamere, F. (1999). *A critical examination of fear of violence as a form of social control and the impact of this fear on women's leisure experience.* Paper presented at the 9th Canadian Congress on Leisure Research, Acadia University, Wolfville, Nova Scotia, Canada.

Dupuis, S. L. and Smale, B. J. A. (2000). Bittersweet journeys: Meanings of leisure in the institution-based caregiving context. *Journal of Leisure Research, 32*(3), 303–340.

Firestone, J. and Shelton, B. A. (1994). A comparison of women's and men's leisure time: Subtle effects of the double day. *Leisure Sciences, 16*(1), 45–60.

Floyd, M. F. (1998). Getting beyond marginality and ethnicity: The challenge for race and ethnic studies in leisure research. *Journal of Leisure Research, 30*(1), 3–22.

Frederick, C. J. and Shaw, S. M. (1995). Body image as a leisure constraint: Examining the experience of aerobic exercises classes for young women. *Leisure Sciences, 17*(2), 57–73.

Frederick, J. A. and Fast, J. E. (1999, Autumn). Elder-care in Canada: Who does how much? *Canadian Social Trends*, 26–30.

Green, E. (1998). "Women doing friendship": An analysis of women's leisure as a site of identity construction, empowerment and resistance. *Leisure Studies, 17*(2), 171–185.

Green, E. and Hebron, S. (1988). Leisure and male partners. In E. Wimbush and M. Talbot (Eds.), *Relative freedoms: Women and leisure* (pp. 75–92). Milton Keynes, England: Open University Press.

Green, E., Hebron, S., and Woodward, D. (1987). Women, leisure and social control. In J. Hanmer and M. Maynard (Eds.), *Women, violence and social control.* London, England: Macmillan.

Green, E., Hebron, S., and Woodward, D. (1990). *Women's leisure, what leisure?* Basingstoke, England: Macmillan.

Harding, S. (Ed.). (1987). *Feminism and methodology.* Milton Keynes, England: Open University Press.

Harrington, M., Dawson, D., and Bolla, P. (1992). Objective and subjective constraints on women's enjoyment of leisure. *Loisir et Sociètè, 15*(1), 203–222.

Henderson, K. A. (1991). The contribution of feminism to an understanding of leisure constraints. *Journal of Leisure Research, 23*(4), 363–377.

Henderson, K. A. (1994a). Broadening an understanding of women, gender and leisure. *Journal of Leisure Research, 26*(1), 1–7.

Henderson, K. A. (1994b). Special issue on women, gender and leisure. *Journal of Leisure Research, 26*(1), 1–96.

Henderson, K. A. (1998). Enhancing physical activity. *Women in Sport and Physical Activity Journal, 7*(1), 13–26.

Henderson, K. A. and Ainsworth, B. E. (2000). Enablers and constraints to walking for African and American Indian women. *Research Quarterly for Exercise and Sport, 71*(4), 313–321.

Henderson, K. A. and Ainsworth, B. E. (2001). Researching leisure and physical activity with women of color: Issues and emerging questions. *Leisure Sciences, 23*(1), 21–34.

Henderson, K. A. and Bialeschki, M. D. (1991). A sense of entitlement to leisure as constraint and empowerment for women. *Leisure Sciences, 12*(1), 51–65.

Henderson, K. A. and Bialeschki, M. D. (1993). Exploring an expanded model of women's leisure constraints. *Journal of Applied Recreation Research, 18*(4), 229–252.

Henderson, K. A., Bialeschki, M. D., Shaw, S. M., and Freysinger, V. J. (1996). *Both gains and gaps: Feminist perspectives on women's leisure.* State College, PA: Venture Publishing, Inc.

Henderson, K. A. and King, K. (1998). Recreation programming for adolescent girls: Rationale and foundations. *Journal of Park and Recreation Administration, 16*(2), 1–14.

Herridge, K. L., Shaw, S. M., and Mannell, R. C. (2003). An exploration of women's leisure within heterosexual romantic relationships. *Journal of Leisure Research, 35*(3), 274–291.

Hochschild, A. and Machung, A. (1990). *The second shift.* New York, NY: Viking Press.

Horna, J. (1989). The leisure component of the parental role. *Journal of Leisure Research, 21*(3), 228–241.

Hultsman, W. Z. (1992). Constraints to activity participation in early adolescence. *Journal of Early Adolescence, 12*(3), 280–299.

Hunter, P. L. and Whitson, D. J. (1992). Women's leisure in a resource industry town: Problems and issues. *Loisir et Sociètè, 15*(1), 223–244.

Jackson, E. L. (1993). Recognizing patterns of leisure constraints: Results from alternative analyses. *Journal of Leisure Research, 25*(2), 129–149.

Jackson, E. L., Crawford, D. W., and Godbey, G. (1993). Negotiation of leisure constraints. *Leisure Sciences, 15*(1), 1–11.

Jackson, E. L. and Henderson, K. A. (1995). Gender-based analysis of leisure constraints. *Leisure Sciences, 17*(1), 31–51.

Jackson, E. L. and Rucks, V. C. (1993). Reasons for ceasing participation and barriers to participation: Further examination of constrained leisure as an internally homogeneous concept. *Leisure Sciences, 17*(1), 217–230.

Jackson, E. L. and Scott, D. (1999). Constraints to leisure. In E. L. Jackson and T. L. Burton (Eds.), *Leisure studies: Prospects for the twenty-first century* (pp. 299–321). State College, PA: Venture Publishing, Inc.

James, K. (2000). "You can feel them looking at you": The experiences of adolescent girls at swimming pools. *Journal of Leisure Research, 32*(2), 262–280.

Kaufman, M. (1994). Men, feminism, and men's contradictory experiences of power. In H. Brod and M. Kaufman (Eds.), *Theorizing masculinities* (pp. 142–163). Thousand Oaks, CA: Sage Publications.

Kay, T. (1998). Having it all or doing it all? The construction of women's lifestyles in time-crunched households. *Loisir et Sociètè, 21*(2), 435–454.

Khan, N. A. (1997). Leisure and recreation among women of selected hill-farming families in Bangladesh. *Journal of Leisure Research, 29*(1), 5–20.

Kimmel, M. S. and Messner, M. A. (Eds.). (1998). *Men's lives* (4th ed.). Boston, MA: Allyn & Bacon.

Lafrance, M. N., Zivian, M. T., and Myers, A. M. (2000). Women, weight and appearance satisfaction: An ageless pursuit of thinness. In B. McCauley (Ed.), *Women's bodies/women's lives* (pp. 277–302). Toronto, Ontario, Canada: Sumach Press.

Larson, R. W., Gillman, S. A., and Richards, M. H. (1997). Divergent experiences of family leisure: Fathers, mothers, and young adolescents. *Journal of Leisure Research, 29*(1), 78–97.

Mannell, R. and Zuzanek, J. (1991). The nature and variability of leisure constraints in daily life: The case of the physically active leisure of older adults. *Leisure Sciences, 13*(4), 337–351.

Mannell, R. C. and Kleiber, D. A. (1997). *A social psychology of leisure*. State College, PA: Venture Publishing, Inc.

Manrai, L. A. and Manrai, A. K. (1995). Effects of cultural context, gender, and acculturation on perceptions of work versus social/leisure time usage. *Journal of Business Research, 32*, 115–128.

McKay, J., Messner, M., and Sabo, D. (2000). *Masculinities, gender relations and sport*. Thousand Oaks, CA: Sage Publications.

Messner, M. A. (1998). Boyhood, organized sports, and the construction of masculinities. In M. S. Kimmel and M. A. Messner (Eds.), *Men's lives* (4th ed.; pp. 109–121). Boston, MA: Allyn & Bacon.

Messner, M. A. and Sabo, D. (Eds.). (1990). *Sport, men, and the gender order: Critical feminist perspectives*. Champaign, IL: Human Kinetics.

National Crime Prevention Council. (1999). *Preventing violence against women: Not just a women's issue*. Washington, DC: Author.

Office of the President. (2001, January). *Economic report of the President*. Washington, DC: U.S. Government Printing Office. Retrieved from http://www.gpoaccess.gov/eop/download.html

Parry, D. C. and Shaw, S. M. (1999). The role of leisure in women's experiences of menopause and mid-life. *Leisure Sciences, 21*(3), 197–212.

Pittman, J. F., Teng, W., Kerpelman, J. L., and Solheim, C. A. (1999). Satisfaction with performance of housework: The roles of time spent, quality assessment, and stress. *Journal of Family Issues, 20*(6), 746–770.

Raymore, L. A., Godbey, G., Crawford, D. W., and von Eye, A. (1993). Nature and process of leisure constraints: An empirical test. *Leisure Sciences, 15*(2), 99–113.

Robinson, J. P. and Godbey, G. (1993). Sport, fairness, and the gender gap. *Leisure Sciences, 15*(4), 291–307.

Rogers, N. B. (1997). Centrality of the caregiving role and integration of leisure in everyday life: A naturalistic study of older wife caregivers. *Therapeutic Recreation Journal, 31*(4), 230–243.

Samdahl, D. M. and Jekubovich, N. J. (1997). A critique of leisure constraints: Comparative analyses and understandings. *Journal of Leisure Research, 29*(4), 430–452.

Scott, D. and Munson, W. (1994). Perceived constraints to park usage among individuals with low incomes. *Journal of Park and Recreation Administration, 12*(1), 52–69.

Scraton, S. (1994). The changing world of women and leisure: Feminism, 'postfeminism' and leisure. *Leisure Studies, 13*(4), 249–261.

Searle, M. S. and Jackson, E. L. (1985). Socioeconomic variations in perceived barriers to recreation participation among would-be participants. *Leisure Sciences, 2*, 227–249.

Shank, J. (1986). An exploration of leisure in the lives of dual-career women. *Journal of Leisure Research, 18*(4), 300–319.

Shaw, S. M. (1985). Gender and leisure: Inequality in the distribution of leisure time. *Journal of Leisure Research, 17*(4), 266–282.

Shaw, S. M. (1988). Leisure in the contemporary family: The effect of female employment on the leisure of Canadian wives and husbands. *International Review of Modern Sociology, 18*(1), 1–15.

Shaw, S. M. (1992a). Body image among adolescent women: The role of sports and physically active leisure. *Journal of Applied Recreation Research, 16*(4), 349–357.

Shaw, S. M. (1992b). Dereifying family leisure: An examination of women's and men's everyday experiences and perceptions of family time. *Leisure Sciences, 14*(4), 271–286.

Shaw, S. M. (1994). Gender, leisure, and constraint: Towards a framework for the analysis of women's leisure. *Journal of Leisure Research, 26*(1), 8–22.

Shaw, S. M. (2001). Conceptualizing resistance: Women's leisure as political practice. *Journal of Leisure Research, 33*(2), 186–201.

Shaw, S. M., Bonen, A. and McCabe, J. F. (1991). Do more constraints mean less leisure? Examining the relationship between constraints and participation. *Journal of Leisure Research, 23*(4), 349–367.

Shaw, S. M., Caldwell, L. L., and Kleiber, D. A. (1996). Stress and social control in the daily activities of adolescents. *Journal of Leisure Research, 28*(4), 274–292.

Shaw, S. M. and de la Durantaye, C. V. (1992). Special issue on feminist perspectives on leisure. *Loisir et Sociètè, 15*(1).

Statistics Canada. (2000). *Women in Canada 2000: A gender-based statistical report*. Ottawa, Ontario, Canada: Canadian Ministry of Industry.

Stodolska, M. and Jackson, E. L. (1998). Discrimination in leisure and work experienced by a white minority group. *Journal of Leisure Research, 30*(1), 23–46.

Theberge, N. (2000). *Higher goals: Women's ice hockey and the politics of gender*. New York, NY: SUNY Press.

Thompson, S. M. (1999). *Mother's taxi: Sport and women's labor*. Albany, NY: State University of New York Press.

Tirone, S. and Pedlar, A. (2000). Understanding the leisure experiences of a minority ethnic group: South Asian teens and young adults in Canada. *Loisir et Sociètè 23*(1), 145–169.

Tirone, S. and Shaw, S. M. (1997). At the center of their lives: Indo Canadian women, their families and leisure. *Journal of Leisure Research, 29*(2), 225–244.

Wearing, B. M. (1990). Beyond the ideology of motherhood: Leisure as resistance. *Australian and New Zealand Journal of Sociology, 26*(1), 36–58.

Whyte, L. and Shaw, S. M. (1994). Women's leisure: An exploratory study of fear of violence as a leisure constraint. *Journal of Leisure Research, 19*(1), 5–21.

Wiley, C. G. E., Shaw, S. M., and Havitz, M. (2000). Men's and women's involvement in sports: An examination of the gendered aspects of leisure involvement. *Leisure Sciences, 22*(1), 19–31.

Wimbush, E. and Talbot, M. (1988). *Relative freedoms: Women and leisure*. Milton Keynes, England: Open University Press.

Chapter 3

Racial Inequality and Constraints to Leisure in the Post-Civil Rights Era: Toward an Alternative Framework

Kimberly J. Shinew (University of Illinois) and Myron F. Floyd (University of Florida)

The coauthors are listed in random order. We thank Ed Jackson for his helpful comments on the early drafts of this chapter. We also wish to acknowledge insights provided by Susan Shaw.

Over the past decade, an impressive amount of scholarship has been devoted to understanding constraints to leisure. Over the same period, the number of studies investigating racial and ethnic influences on leisure participation also increased significantly. While common issues and concerns have been addressed within these respective areas (Jackson & Scott, 1999), only a limited number of studies focused specifically on race and constraints. Race and constraints research has been conducted largely along separate tracks, despite overlapping theoretical concerns and foci of application. Leisure research on constraints sought to understand the "complex ways in which leisure is constrained" (Jackson & Scott, 1999), while a primary concern among researchers working in race and leisure has been to understand how racial prejudice, discrimination, and structural inequality constrain leisure among racial minorities. Future research and practice stand to benefit from bridging the gap between research on race and leisure constraints. As Stodolska (1998, p. 521) argued, "it is difficult to study the leisure of minorities effectively without understanding the constraints they face."

In this chapter we explore the consequences of racial inequality for constraints to leisure among African Americans and suggest avenues for further study of constraints to leisure among this subgroup of the population. First, we provide a broad overview of trends in inequality on selected indicators of social and economic well-being of African Americans. Second, we review the literature on race and leisure constraints. In this section we highlight themes and challenges presented by this limited body of research. Third, we introduce a general framework for understanding constraints to leisure and

constraints negotiation among African Americans. We proceed with a discussion of race and constraints that focuses exclusively on African Americans and not other racial and ethnic minority groups for three reasons. First, even though current population figures show the Hispanic population has become the largest minority group in the United States, the distinctive social, historical, and political circumstances of African Americans continue to warrant focused research attention (Loury, 2002). Further, as Glenn Loury (2002, p. 11) argued, status attainment of African Americans has been impeded primarily by forces "indigenous to the U.S. society" rather than by social, economic, and political circumstances found outside of the United States, such as countries of origin for many immigrant populations. Finally, the "severe and protracted" nature of racial discrimination against African Americans over time makes the case of African Americans unique. Loury admits the "severe and protracted" disadvantaged status of Native Americans is comparable, but is deserving of "its own treatment." We feel current accounts of constraints to leisure and the associated negotiation processes among African Americans are incomplete because much of the research on leisure constraints has yet to acknowledge theoretically or empirically that leisure constraints experienced by African Americans are shaped by historic and contemporary social and economic inequalities. In many ways social practices enacted toward Blacks in American society and their overall social status serve as a barometer of sorts for how society treats other minority groups. With this in mind, our discussion may shed light on ways to understand constraints and negotiation among other marginalized subpopulations defined by race or ethnicity.

Trends in Social Well-Being

Racial inequality is an enduring feature of the American social landscape. Passage of a series of civil rights laws and court decisions during the 1950s and 1960s dismantled the framework that legitimated and perpetuated institutional racial discrimination and inequality in the United States. Accompanying this change was a lessening of racial prejudice toward African Americans expressed by White Americans (Schuman, Steeh & Bobo, 1985) and greater integration of African Americans into the economy and other social institutions. Toward the end of the 20th century, because of the successes of the Civil Rights era, some scholars argued the social and economic well-being of African Americans had more to do with economic class position than with interracial conflict stemming from White Americans (Wilson, 1980). We believe it would be premature to downplay the importance of racial inequality. A number of scholars have argued race still matters and remains a significant factor in determining life chances of African Americans (e.g., Feagin, 1991; Massey & Denton, 1993; Willie, 1978). Data support both positions, however. The 2000 census revealed 51% of African American households reported incomes of $50,000 or higher. Yet racial inequalities persist on many broad socioeconomic indicators, such as education, labor market participation, affordable housing and neighborhoods, and health status (Blank, 2001). Despite the improvement in their social status, middle-class African Americans continue to face discrimination in a range of public social settings (Feagin, 1991; Feagin & Vera, 1995), including many leisure-type settings (Hibbler & Shinew, 2002; Phillip, 2000).

To provide an overview of the social and economic well-being of African American in the post-Civil Rights era, we examine trends in income, educational attainment, labor force participation, residential segregation, and interracial interaction. Specifically, we wish to highlight both gaps and gains with respect to well-being by comparing Whites and African Americans. Our purpose is to use these trends to highlight the socioeconomic contexts that condition leisure constraints and their negotiation among African Americans.

Income

We examine income first because it provides perspective on the overall economic status of African Americans (Farley & Allen, 1987). Two indicators of income are used: personal income and family income. Income depends to a large extent on education and labor force participation and serves as a broad parameter for assessing access to material resources that facilitate or constrain leisure participation.

An examination of trends in personal and family incomes since 1960 reveals both gaps and gains. Incomes for African American men and women increased over time relative to their racial counterparts. For African American men, their median income as a percentage of White male income increased steadily over four decades, from 55% in 1960 to 73% in 2000 (**Table 3.1**). Focusing on absolute differences, however, there was rising inequality in male incomes from 1960 to 1990, with a slight decrease in 2000. This is noteworthy, because it suggests while income for African American males increased relative to Whites, substantial differences in personal income and access to material resources remain.

Table 3.1. Racial differences in personal income from 1960 to 2000

	1960	1970	1980	1990	2000
MEN					
Median Income (All)	4,080	6,670	12,530	20,293	28,343
Black	2,260	4,157	8,009	12,868	21,659
White	4,080	7,011	13,328	21,170	29,696
Racial Gap	−1,820	−2,854	−5,319	−8,302	−8,037
Percent*	55%	59%	60%	61%	73%
WOMEN					
Median Income (All)	1,261	2,237	4,920	10,070	16,063
Black	837	2,063	4,580	8,328	16,084
White	1,352	2,266	4,947	10,317	16,216
Racial Gap	−515	−203	−367	−1,989	−132
Percent	62%	91%	93%	81%	99%

*African American income as a percentage of White income
Source: U.S. Bureau of the Census

Thus, while some progress is evident, the current situation remains disturbing. On the other hand, African American women closed the income gap more rapidly than did their male counterparts. Among women, the percentage of African American income as a percentage of White income rose from 62% to 99%. Absolute racial difference was at its lowest level in 2000, and its highest level in 1990. The trends observed here mirror those reported by Farley and Allen (1991).

Inequality in family income may be an even more important indicator, because family serves as a primary context for leisure participation. However, the prospect of narrowing the income gap between White and African American families appears less tractable (**Table 3.2**). While median income from all sources among African Americans has increased over time, the gap between White and African American families persists. There was only a small gain in relative terms from 1960 to 2000 (an 8% increase). The racial difference in absolute dollars grew to nearly $20,000, suggesting when it comes to family income, race remains a significant factor.

Education

The most impressive gains in status attainment among African Americans occurred in educational attainment. In 1970 nearly twice as many Whites completed high school or college than African Americans. By 2000 the difference between Whites and African Americans was less than 10% (see **Table 3.3**, p. 38). This pattern prevailed among both men and women. However, a more detailed analysis controlling for region, age group, and employment would probably show a different pattern of inequality. In addition, other indicators, such as quality and type of education, may also reveal different patterns of inequality. Overall, however, social policy interventions designed to reduce inequalities in educational systems have been relatively effective and probably account for some of these gains (Farley, 1984).

Employment

Data on employment are not as clear-cut as those on income and education due to different definitions of employment and unemployment used by demographers (Farley, 1984). Also, data for 1960–1970 for Blacks is not available. For our purposes employment refers to the labor force participation rate (i.e., labor force participation as a percentage of the noninstitutional population). Unemployment rate refers to the number of people unemployed as a percentage of the labor force. Employment is critical to generating income and sustaining socioeconomic mobility (Blank, 2001). Annual rates of employment and unemployment for 1970, 1980, 1990, and 2000 are shown in **Table 3.4** (p. 39).

Since 1970 racial differences in overall employment rates have remained consistent and small, yet employment by gender and race show a different pattern. For men, employment rates are declining relative to rates of employment for women. In addition, among men, Whites experience higher rates of employment than Blacks, and the "racial gap" has remained unchanged across the decades. Among women, Black rates of employment exceed those of Whites. This reflects the historical tendency for White women not to work outside of the home as compared to Black women (Blank, 2001), though White women's participation is increasing.

Unemployment figures for the four decades show African Americans experienced double-digit unemployment in three of four years reported (**Table 3.5**, p. 40). Black unemployment was consistently two to three times higher than rates of unemployment for Whites. Thus, while there has been some convergence in employment, based on unemployment figures, Blacks experience greater difficulty in finding and keeping a job (Farley, 1984). It is not our purpose to explain the gap in unemployment, but rather to simply highlight unemployment poses a hardship for individuals and families that influences the context of the experience of leisure constraints. Moreover, the data, however general and broad, indicate

Table 3.2. Racial differences in family income from 1960 to 2000

	1960	1970	1980	1990	2000
Median Income (All)	5,620	9,876	2,1530	35,353	50,732
Black	3,230	6,279	12,674	21,423	33,676
White	5,835	10,236	21,904	36,915	53,256
Racial Gap	−2,605	−3,957	−9,230	−15,492	−19,580
Percent*	55%	61%	58%	58%	63%

*African American income as a percentage of White income
Source: U.S. Bureau of the Census

Table 3.3. Percent of population 25 years and older who have completed high school or college by race, 1970 to 2000

	1970	1980	1990	2000
% Completed 4 Years of High School or More				
Total Population	55.2	68.6	77.6	84.1
Total White Population	57.4	70.5	79.1	84.9
Total Black Population	33.7	51.2	66.2	79.7
Racial Gap	−23.7	−19.3	−12.9	−5.2
MALES				
Blacks	32.4	51.1	65.8	78.7
Whites	57.2	71.0	79.1	84.8
Racial Gap	−24.8	−19.9	−13.3	−6.1
FEMALES				
Blacks	34.8	51.3	66.5	78.3
Whites	57.6	70.1	79.0	85.0
Racial Gap	−22.8	−18.8	−12.5	−6.7

Source: U.S. Bureau of the Census

men (Black men in particular) may be subject to greater constraint associated with employment compared to women. This is consistent with a litany of reports on chronic low unemployment among Black males.

Segregation

Patterns of residential segregation are of concern for two primary reasons. First, residential segregation sets the context and tone for intergroup interaction (Massey & Denton, 1993). Generally, both interpersonal and institutional discrimination vary according to the extent of residential segregation (Farley & Allen, 1991; Fossett & Seibert, 1997; Massey & Denton, 1993). The extent of residential segregation has also been theorized as a precursor to convergence of leisure lifestyles among Whites and African Americans (Floyd & Shinew, 1999). Second, residential segregation negatively impacts the quality of community services. Because of continued discrimination in housing and mortgage lending, potential tax revenues and concomitant services tend to migrate to affluent suburbs (Massey & Denton, 1993). The movement of tax revenue and services concentrates poverty and undermines improvement in public services (Wilson, 1991). Two indicators of "White–Black" residential segregation include isolation and dissimilarity. *Isolation* represents the "degree of potential contact, or possibility of interaction, between minority and majority group members" (Massey & Denton, 1993, p. 287). *Dissimilarity* measures the percentage of a group's population that would have to move from one residential area to another to eliminate segregation. The dissimilarity index ranges from 0 (complete integration) to 100 (complete segrega-

tion). We examine these indicators for the largest metropolitan areas in the United States since 1980. Isolation measures the "extent to which Blacks live only among other blacks" and gauges "the potential for interracial contact within neighbourhoods" (Massey & Denton, 1993, p. 65). Like the dissimilarity index, it ranges from 0 to 100, where 100 indicates all Blacks live in all-Black neighborhoods.

While residential segregation decreased since 1980, for African Americans the dissimilarity index remains fairly high (Massey & Denton, 1993). As indicated in **Table 3.6** (p. 41), in 1980 at least 73% of Blacks would have to had changed residences to achieve an even distribution or integration in a city, compared to at least 64% in 2000. According to the Massey and Denton (1993), values under 30 are considered low, values from 30 to 60 are considered as moderate, and values 60 or above are high. Isolation measures also indicate relatively high occurrence of low interracial contact between Blacks and Whites in neighborhood settings. While isolation appears to be increasing for Latinos, isolation among African Americans continues to be higher than the other groups. Thus, according to these criteria, comparisons with other racial and ethnic minority groups show that African Americans were, and still are, the most residentially segregated subpopulation group.

As these data indicate, even though other minority groups experience residential segregation, its extent does not rival that experienced by African Americans. Blacks tend to be more segregated from Whites and more segregated than Latinos and Asian Americans. The legacy of sanctioned, systematic, and institutional racial discrimination targeting African Americans in housing, real

Table 3.4. Labor force participation rate by race and gender, 1970 to 2000 (civilian employment for persons 20 years and older)

	1970	1980	1990	2000
Total White Population	60.2	64.1	66.9	67.4
Total Black Population	59.9	61.0	64.0	65.8
Racial Gap	0.3	3.1	2.9	1.6
MALES				
Black	78.5	75.1	75.0	72.6
White	82.8	79.8	78.5	77.0
Racial Gap	4.3	4.7	3.5	4.4
FEMALES				
Black	51.2	55.6	60.6	65.6
White	42.2	50.6	57.6	60.2
Racial Gap	+9	+5	+3	+5.4

Source: U.S. Department of Labor, Bureau of Statistics

estate, and the labor market helps to explain these trends. This continuing pattern well into the 1990s and 2000 suggests attention must be given to how residential segregation impacts leisure, and leisure constraints, among African Americans.

Interracial Interaction

Many believe, after decades of struggle, race relations have not significantly improved (Jones, 1997). Regrettably, recent events such as racially related deaths and anti-affirmative action proposals have augmented an increasingly visible division between African Americans and Whites (Kohatsu et al., 2000). Despite these intergroup tensions, many Whites remain oblivious to racial issues and continue to endorse the idea that America is a country of equal opportunity for all racial groups (Robinson & Ginter, 1999; Sears, 1998). Furthermore, based on a long history of bigotry, prejudice, and discrimination, many African Americans believe Whites are insensitive to racial problems (National Conference of Christians and Jews, 1994). More specifically, these two groups differ substantially in their perceptions of the prevalence and impact of discrimination in society: African Americans, in general, perceive racial discrimination to be more insidious and damaging than do Whites. Dovidio, Gaertner, Kawakami, and Hodson (2002) reported in a recent public poll (Gallup, 2001) nearly half of African Americans (47%) indicated they were treated unfairly in their own community in at least one of five common situations (e.g., shopping, at work) during the previous month. Sigelman and Welch (1993) found in their examination of interracial contact and levels of hostility that 26% of African Americans, compared to only 5% of Whites, estimated most White Americans share the racial

attitudes of the Ku Klux Klan. More generally, Whites see White racism as the providence of "only a tiny portion of the public," while African Americans perceive it as "rampant." "Simply stated, Blacks are much more likely than Whites to perceive Black–White relations as problematic....By contrast, Whites are much more likely to perceive Black–White relations as smooth and congenial" (Sigelman & Welch, 1993, p. 792). Given the magnitude and persistence of these different views, it is not surprising current race relations between African Americans and Whites in the United States could be characterized by racial distance and racial distrust. Sigelman, Bledsoe, Welch, and Combs (1996) described the situation as "hostile and unequal."

Summary of Trends

While racial differences in major indicators of social well-being have decreased in the post-Civil Rights era, inequalities between Whites and African Americans persist. While our review of these indicators was presented in broad strokes, we can point to several trends and issues with relevance to constraints to leisure that warrant focused analysis. In particular, inequality in personal and family income, employment and unemployment, gender differences in labor force participation, persistent and high levels of residential segregation, and tension surrounding interracial interaction appear to be factors that shape the context for how African Americans experience and negotiate constraints to leisure. Racial disparities on these and other socioeconomic indicators, and the generally lower access to social power and prestige among African Americans, are often acknowledged but are not reflected in conceptual development and empirical analyses of leisure constraints and race (see Phillip,

Table 3.5. Unemployment rate by race and gender, 1970–2000 (civilian employment for persons 20 years and older)

	1970	1980	1990	2000
Total White Population	4.5	6.3	4.8	3.5
Total Black Population	10.4	14.3	11.4	7.6
Racial Gap	5.9	8.0	6.6	4.1
MALES				
Black	7.0	12.4	10.4	7.0
White	3.2	5.3	4.3	2.8
Racial Gap	3.8	7.1	6.1	4.2
FEMALES				
Black	9.0	11.9	9.7	6.3
White	4.4	5.6	4.1	3.1
Racial Gap	4.6	6.3	5.6	3.2

Source: U.S. Department of Labor, Bureau of Statistics

1995). We wish to bring attention to these trends to argue that contexts of inequality must be included in any examination of African Americans' constraints given the continued inequities that exist in society. The next section examines the leisure studies literature on racial inequality and constraints. In this section we highlight themes and challenges presented by this limited body of research to identify critical areas for theoretical development and empirical studies.

Racial Inequality and Leisure Constraints

Some researchers suggested examining the constraints of subgroups of the population might help us to better understand the leisure habits of the general population (e.g., Jackson & Henderson, 1995; Jackson & Scott, 1999). Similarly, it could be proposed that understanding the relationship between race and leisure constraints is important not only for furthering our knowledge of leisure, but also for gaining greater insight into broader societal issues surrounding race. Clearly, issues surrounding race and leisure constraints warrant further research attention.

Stodolska (1998) commented that most of the existing research focused on the constraints of the general population, with less attention given to special populations, such as people with disabilities, ethnic and racial minorities, or immigrants. Although increasingly more research is being conducted with these populations, we still do not fully understand the complex nature and multifaceted impact of constraints associated with racial stratification (Henderson & Ainsworth, 2001). It has been established, however, that race and its relationship

to constraints is a worthwhile, although complicated, construct to study (Floyd, 1998; Philipp, 2000).

Summary of the Relevant Literature

Both Washburne (1978) and Woodard (1988) made significant early contributions to this line of research and laid the foundation for future studies on the relationship between race and leisure constraints. Washburne (1978), in one of the first studies that examined race and its connection to leisure and recreation, presented two possible explanations to describe African Americans' limited participation in wildland recreation. His two frameworks, the marginality and ethnicity perspectives, then became the basis for understanding racial differences in leisure behavior. The marginality perspective suggests African Americans do not participate in certain leisure activities due to socioeconomic discrimination that can result in a lifestyle constrained by "unmet basic needs, poor transportation, and limited opportunities due to their urban 'ghetto' residence" (p. 177). The alternative explanation, ethnicity, contends the leisure choices of African Americans are based on their subcultural style and leisure is a reflection of one's unique culture. Washburne stated cultural explanations for African Americans' distinct leisure patterns are connected to their values, social organization, and normative elements. For example, African Americans may value the natural environment differently than their White counterparts because nature and open space may hold more negative connotations for African Americans (e.g., White domination of land ownership). Further, while such values may serve as the genesis of distinct leisure activities and patterns, social organizations may be responsible for preserving them. For example, among African Americans normative structures may influence leisure choices and discourage the adoption of White mainstream lifestyles. Moreover, due to historical discrimination, African American communities attempt to protect their members from additional discrimination by discouraging contact with mainstream society and encouraging adherence to normative codes. "Thus, there may be powerful forces within the community that discourage participation in 'white' activities" (p. 178).

Woodard (1988) focused his study on a single group, African Americans, and examined the extent to which social class and intragroup regionality affected leisure participation. Although his study did not address constraints directly, his findings did add to this body of research, because the study examined the impact of four discrimination-related factors on the leisure choices of African Americans. More specifically, he examined

- "fear of race prejudice" (feeling safe from racial prejudice when recreating within one's own neighborhood).

- "discrimination" (experiencing some form of racial discrimination the preceding year).

- "coracialism" (interacting socially with other African Americans).

- "criticism" (receiving peer or family criticism for interracial social interaction) and their influence on leisure participation.

His findings indicated many of these factors affected African Americans' participation in the three categories of leisure activities studied ("metropolitan activities," "informal domestic activities," and "night life activities"),

suggesting the importance of discrimination as a constraint to leisure participation.

Most of the studies that followed these seminal papers used marginality, ethnicity, and/or discrimination to explain their findings. For example, Edwards (1981) explored relationships among race, residence, and leisure style and employed the marginality and ethnicity perspectives to explain her findings. In relation to constraints, she found few racial differences in the factors that inhibited recreational participation, with the exception that African American men perceived greater time constraints and White women felt more constrained because "suitable programs" were not offered. She concluded in terms of inequitable distribution of recreational services (marginality), African Americans were no more likely than their White counterparts to identify program constraints resulting from differential allocation of resources: "Transportation, inadequate information, or the lack of interesting programs do not appear to be problems for the black sample" (p. 108). However, the ethnicity perspective was supported by her findings as an explanation of racial differences in leisure *preferences*. She concluded subcultural variations in leisure choices were evident, in that Whites favored skill classes and organized outdoor activities, while African Americans preferred physical conditioning and dance instruction.

West's (1989) study of Detroit residents found African American residents participated more than Whites in Detroit city parks, but visited the surrounding regional parks less. West's paper explored possible explanations for these findings and concluded, in contrast to Edwards's findings, that marginality, particularly as it

Table 3.6. Residential segregation indexes for African Americans, Hispanics, and Asians, 1980 to 2000

AFRICAN AMERICANS

Segregation Index	Year			Percent Change
	1980	1990	2000	
Dissimilarity	.727	.678	.640	-12.0
Isolation	.655	.614	.591	-9.8

LATINOS

	Year			Percent Change
	1980	1990	2000	
Dissimilarity	.502	.500	.509	1.3
Isolation	.454	.508	.552	21.6

ASIAN AND PACIFIC ISLANDERS

	Year			Percent Change
	1980	1990	2000	
Dissimilarity	.405	.412	.411	1.5
Isolation	.233	.264	.306	31.3

Source: U.S. Bureau of the Census

relates to transportation, played more of a role than ethnicity factors in these park use patterns. However, West stated "neither factor explains a large percentage of this difference" (p. 24), and concluded interracial relations among different racial groups affected respondents' park use, in that African Americans felt more "unwelcome/ uneasy" because of interracial factors. West postulated it is likely their responses with respect to interracial factors were "only the tip of a larger iceberg" in that more respondents might have been affected by these types of factors but were hesitant to discuss them with a stranger over the phone. He concluded "these results indicate that interracial relations may be a contributing factor in inhibiting use of region parks by inner-city minorities in Detroit" (p. 22).

Johnson, Bowker, English, and Worthen (1998) empirically examined marginality and ethnicity factors in relation to wildland visitation patterns among rural African Americans and Whites. They found African Americans were more than three times as likely as Whites to report they were unaware of nearby wildland areas (marginality). The ethnicity factors (no interest, discomfort in wildland settings, family and friends not liking wildland areas, not having anyone to go with) were not significantly different between the two groups. Johnson and colleagues (1998) concluded an alternative explanation for nonvisitation not addressed in their study was racial antagonism or discrimination in recreation settings. One of the authors of the study had several informal conversations with African Americans, and noted residents believed there were racially demarcated recreation areas in the study area because African Americans and Whites tended to use different sites in the Apalachicola National Forest.

> The small number of African Americans also commented they would not feel comfortable camping in the forest because they were concerned about being hassled by groups of (white) drunks or "rednecks." They felt there would be little or no security in isolated camping areas. (p. 116)

Gobster's (2002) study of a popular urban park in Chicago also found racial discrimination was a problem for some park users. In his study, park users were asked, "In your past use of the park were there any times or situations where you felt discriminated against because of your race or ethnic background?" Reports of racial discrimination were highest among African Americans (14%). Gobster concluded discrimination can lead to feelings of discomfort among users and lower their enjoyment of the leisure experience. He acknowledged that in more severe cases it can lead to feelings of anger and physical violence, which may ultimately lead to user displacement or even nonuse by some groups.

In another study, Johnson, Bowker, and Cordell (2001) explored whether groups historically marginalized in society—African Americans, women, and rural dwellers—perceived more constraints to outdoor recreation participation than did other groups. The findings for African Americans indicated that while race did not seem to be a significant factor in predicting whether individuals perceive constraints in a favorite outdoor activity, it did appear to be a factor among nonparticipants. More specifically, nonparticipating African Americans were more likely than Whites to feel safety concerns deterred their outdoor recreation opportunities. Thus, African Americans who did not participate in outdoor recreational activities had concerns about safety not shared by participating African Americans. The authors noted, therefore, this difference suggests constraints for Blacks may not be "uniform," and applied Wilson's (1978) diverging class structure argument as support. Likewise, constraints experienced by African Americans may also vary by sex. Henderson and Ainsworth (2001) conducted a study focused specifically on constraints to physical activity among women of color (African American and American Indian women). The women indicated finding time and space for physical activity was problematic, and concluded several specific constraints (e.g., job demands, physical tiredness, physical illnesses and ailments, expectations and needs of the family and others in the community) limited their participation. Further, many of the women believed opportunities for physical activity had not always existed for them due to historical, marginality, cultural, and daily living issues.

Phillip conducted two studies related to race and leisure constraints. His first study (Philipp, 1995) examined the relationship between race and two measures related to leisure constraints: appeal and comfort. His findings indicated African Americans and Whites rated the appeal of many activities differently, and African Americans felt significantly less comfortable in approximately half of the leisure activities examined. To explain his findings he applied the marginality, ethnicity, and prejudice/discrimination frameworks. He stated that many of the leisure activities that take place outside the home and local community are associated with lower appeal and comfort among African Americans, and this may be related to perceptions of present or historical patterns of discrimination. He concluded it is difficult to discount centuries of discrimination against African Americans when considering leisure constraints.

In a later study, Philipp (1999) examined the perceived "welcomeness" of several leisure pursuits by asking both racial groups how welcome they thought African Americans would feel in a variety of activities. Results indicated African Americans reportedly felt unwelcome in a number of leisure pursuits, whereas Whites reported they thought African Americans would feel welcome in these same activities, thus indicating failure to appreciate or to recognize these feelings among African Americans. However, Arnold and Shinew's (1998) study of urban park use found Whites, not African Americans, felt more constrained in their use of parks. They speculated this might be due, in part, to the different standards more privileged people in society, namely middle-class Whites, have for their parks. In summary, despite some mixed findings, these studies do offer insight into the leisure constraints African Americans face, and how they might differ from those experienced by Whites.

Lack of Viable Theoretical Frameworks

A number of issues regarding the relationship between race and constraints have not been examined in the literature reviewed previously. As noted by Floyd (1998) and Henderson and Ainsworth (2001), one of the critical issues facing the race and ethnic studies research is the paucity of viable theoretical frameworks to guide this line of research. Most of the studies on race and constraints have used one of three theories to guide their research: the marginality hypothesis, the ethnicity hypothesis, and perceived discrimination. Floyd (1998) presented some of the limitations of the marginality and ethnicity theories, and contended that discrimination as an explanatory concept needs further theoretical development. In particular, he noted "more work elaborating the types and range of discrimination and how they impact leisure choices and constraints should be pursued" (p. 7). Philipp (1995) maintained leisure constraint models fail to address the influence of race and argued:

> Race, as a category of measurement, should not be hidden in other measurement categories that appear to transcend race because the assumption then becomes racial differences are no longer of primary importance to leisure participation, preferences, and choices. In effect, such conceptual schemes render race secondary to more basic analytical categories. (p. 110)

Philipp stated he preferred a framework that links marginality, socialization, and discrimination "in a theoretically complex, and difficult to separate, manner" (p. 118) and called for models of constraints that reflect these multiple theories on race. These links among marginal-

ity, ethnicity, and discrimination, while evident in the literature (Floyd, 1998; Johnson et al., 2001; West, 1989), need to be explored further.

Others noted the lack of frameworks to guide this line of research. For example, Tsai and Coleman (1999) called for conceptual frameworks that incorporate the social and cultural perspectives of specific subgroups of the population to better understand their leisure attitudes, behaviors, and constraints. More specifically they found "racial and cultural constraints" experienced by Chinese immigrants included such factors as "language barriers, feeling uncomfortable for race-related reasons, and feeling uncomfortable because of different cultures, together with other previously acknowledged social constraints, such as feeling insecure, and lack of sense of belonging." (p. 255).

Jackson and Scott (1999) also supported this argument and suggested studies of subgroups of the population have provided in-depth information about the constraint negotiation processes for that particular group. Further, this relates to the concept of examining constraints within the appropriate and relevant contexts associated with that particular subgroup. For example, studies of the constraints women often face have highlighted ethic of care, lack of a sense of entitlement, body image, and violence (Henderson & Bialeschki, 1991; Henderson, Bialeschki, Shaw & Freysinger, 1996; Whyte & Shaw, 1994) as constraint issues that may impact women more often than men. Further, researchers raised questions about how multiple identities, such as gender, race, social class, and residence, interact and influence leisure preferences and constraints (Arnold & Shinew, 1998; Edwards, 1981; Johnson et al., 1998; Shinew, Floyd, McGuire & Noe, 1995; Virden & Walker, 1999; Woodard, 1988), thereby suggesting multiple factors should also be taken into account in a model reflecting constraints and race.

The negotiation processes associated with constraints should also be part of any discussion of conceptual models that address race and constraints. As suggested by Jackson and Scott (1999), in the past much of the constraints research focused on participation versus nonparticipation. More recently, however, "a variety of other criterion variables have been used against which to measure the impact of constraints" (p. 305). Jackson and Scott summarized these variables to include, among others, the inability to maintain participation at a desired level and inadequate enjoyment of current leisure participation. Gobster (2002) supported this view when he stated discrimination might lead to lower levels of enjoyment by some minority groups, but not necessarily nonparticipation, although that could also occur. Jackson and

Scott (1999) further contended although core constraints emerge regardless of the criterion variables chosen, the strength and importance of these variables differ enough to warrant attention, and thus encouraged researchers to consider selecting multiple variables when designing their studies.

If we apply these concepts to a framework that examines African Americans' leisure constraints, then we should take into consideration the importance of race, the multiple identities within the African American population (this is supported by Johnson et al.'s [2001] finding that constraints for Blacks may not be uniform), the need for broad criterion variables most salient to African Americans (e.g., lower levels of enjoyment, feeling unwelcome, fear of personal safety), and the application of multiple constraint variables.

It is important to reiterate our general overview of racial inequality. Several indicators of social well-being suggest African Americans experience and negotiate constraints under different sets of socioeconomic conditions. We have also argued this has been neglected in leisure research. Because African Americans hold a minority status, their relative lack of access to socioeconomic resources is usually assumed but not accounted for in conceptual development and empirical studies. In short, the relevance and viability of current constraints models to racial and ethnic minorities has been assumed more than demonstrated.

Resistance-Based Framework

In view of the limited theoretical understanding of and empirical research on how racial inequality impacts constraints to leisure and negotiation, we now introduce a general framework for filling these gaps in the literature. We believe our ideas will provide a useful perspective on issues currently incomplete and unaddressed in the literature. We also wish to point out while this chapter focuses on constraints among African Americans, it can also provide perspective on the study of constraints for other racial and ethnic minority populations who experience similar societal inequities. Our framework rests on two concepts: resistance and resourcefulness. We build on ideas from feminist studies (Shaw, 1994, 2001) and human development (Rapoport & Rapoport, 1975). We begin with a brief discussion of resistance, defining its meaning and its application to leisure. This discussion helps to explain how the resistance concept can further our understanding of racial inequality and leisure constraints. We then link resistance to resourcefulness, centering on introducing types of resources that facilitate

and support resistance activities. Our basic premise is African Americans continue to hold less social power and to have less access to socioeconomic resources, and these conditions shape how constraints are experienced. Further, we submit constraint negotiation under such conditions can be reconceptualized as resistance (Shaw, 1994, 2001).

Leisure as Resistance

The conceptualization of leisure as resistance is based on the notion that leisure choices and activities are linked to hegemonic power and power relations in the social world (Shaw, 2001). Leisure is seen as a space in which people, either individually or collectively, can challenge power distributions and the ways in which power is distributed within society. Leisure becomes one arena where power can be gained, reinforced, diminished, or lost. Shaw (2001) explored the notion of women's leisure as a form of resistance, but stated leisure could also be a context for resistance to racism. Regarding the experiences of African Americans and racism, resistance appears to be relevant because of the enduring nature of structural inequality and domination arrayed against Blacks. First, the history of Africans in America has been one extended discourse of resistance, from quiet acts of resistance by enslaved Africans and free Blacks, to the organized political activities of the Civil Rights Movement. Second, Omi and Winant (1994) noted:

> As the voluminous literature on black culture under slavery shows, black slaves developed cultures of resistance based on music, religion, African traditions, and family ties through which they sustained their own ideological project: the development of a "free" black identity and a collectivity dedicated to emancipation. (p. 80)

To fully appreciate African Americans' leisure as a site for resistance and thus political practice, the notion of resistance and how it applies to race and leisure must be explored.

Resistance can be approached from several theoretical standpoints, and thus it can take on different meanings (Shaw, 2001). From a *structuralist* position, resistance is conceptualized as "acts that challenge the structured power relations of class, race, disability, ethnicity, gender, sexual orientation, or other forms of societal stratifications" (p. 188). Resistance in this case focuses on disadvantaged groups or individuals seeking to challenge power structures and to gain individual or collective empowerment. However, a structuralist approach also recognizes leisure can be a site that reinforces or reproduces inequalities (Deem, 1988), and thus leisure is also seen as a setting for "cultural contestation between dominant and subordinate groups" (Clark & Critchener, cited in Shaw, 2001). In other words, hegemony may be perpetuated through leisure, because it can also be a site for the reproduction or legitimization of unequal access to power and resources. However, given that hegemony is continuous and never complete, resistance is also plausible and might be considered the "flip side" of reproduction. Resistance to racial power relations may be explored through African Americans' resistance to the confinement of society's restraining role expectations of them and through the promotion of counterhegemonic activities. Further, according to Shaw (2001), scholars who adopt a structualist perspective view the outcomes of resistance as both individual and collective. She posited, "individual empowerment, arising out of resistance to constraining material and ideological conditions, has the potential to empower others in similar situations, and to reduce systemic inequalities" (p. 189), thus leading to broader social change.

A *poststructuralist* or *postmodern* approach conceptualizes resistance as linked "to personal deployment of power, and the freedom to develop new identities and new freedoms not subject to someone else's control" (Shaw, 2001, p. 190). Thus, poststructuralist or postmodern leisure researchers focus more on personal empowerment and individual resistance. Power is seen as having multiple sources, which suggests there are also many possibilities for resistance. Diversity is emphasized in this approach, and thus it is not assumed African Americans share a "common world" or common repression. African Americans experience different oppression due to their social class, sexual orientation, age, and gender. This perspective focuses more on individual resistance as opposed to collective resistance, with the outcome being individual empowerment rather than broad social change.

A third approach used to conceptualize resistance is the *interactionist* perspective. Researchers who apply this perspective focus on the subjective experiences of leisure in different social and interactional contexts. This approach attempts to combine aspects of the structuralist and poststructuralist or postmodern perspectives and reflects both individual and collective outcomes of resistance. Leisure reflects resistance from the interactionist perspective when African Americans make choices that provide them with personal empowerment while simultaneously challenging traditional and constrictive views. For example, if an African American chooses activities nontraditional for his or her race, such as downhill skiing, that is considered an individual act of resistance that may also have broader implications in its ability to create social change.

Whether approached from a structuralist, poststructuralist/postmodernist, or interactionist perspective, the notion of resistance emerges when African Americans use their leisure or gain from their leisure a sense of empowerment. However, as suggested by Shaw (2001), resistance does not always take the form of a conscious deliberation or intent. For example, some acts may not be motivated by a desire to challenge hegemony, whereas other acts may clearly have that as their goal. Furthermore, resistance can be both individual and collective, and thus intentions may relate to one or both levels. These issues notwithstanding, leisure's link with resistance to hegemonic forces suggests its potential to play a pivotal role in the leisure lives of African Americans. Through leisure experiences African Americans may gain a sense of autonomy, personal control, and entitlement that may be lacking in other aspects of their lives.

With these different theoretical perspectives in mind, we posit resistance can take several forms. One type of resistance among African Americans could be what Washburne (1978) referred to as *pioneers*—those individuals or collectives who participate in leisure activities despite constraints and despite being an extreme minority. Such individuals resist conformity and sanctions associated with their particular group and break through the barriers that exclude their participation. This type of resistance could be viewed as intentional resistance, with the outcome being individual or collective empowerment. Another type of resistance can be seen through African Americans' participation in *parallel* or corresponding activities, yet doing so exclusively within their own race. For example, this could be in the form of exclusively Black ski clubs and scuba clubs for the more affluent, or in the form of street cultural activities for the less affluent. In this type of resistance, the focus is intentional resistance, with the goal being to create one's own sphere of influence and control. *Abstention* among African Americans who deliberately choose not to participate in certain leisure activities as a form of protest might also be a demonstration of resistance. African Americans who intentionally and freely choose not to participate in stereotypical White leisure pursuits suggests an individual form of resistance and self-determination. In other words, this type of resistance could be taken to indicate African Americans do not feel the need to conform, or rather they resist, participation in what might be considered White mainstream activities (e.g., nature-based activities), thereby consciously choosing pursuits more attractive to them and also reinforce their own unique subculture. This concept is similar to ethnic boundary maintenance, when a group finds ways to emphasize differences between themselves and out-group members (Gramann & Allison, 1999; Washburne & Wall, 1980).

Similarly, Washburne and Wall (1980) suggested leisure choices might be made to confirm traditions valued by the group, and "to avoid activities that may be interpreted by members as inconsistent with ethnic norms, values, or tradition" (p. 11). Further, they concluded some leisure activities may have "White" identities associated with them, and consequently be "across the boundary" for African Americans. It is difficult, however, to identify which leisure choices are intended to be resistance activities, in that clearly not all leisure choices are political—a problem acknowledged by Shaw (2001).

What Facilitates Resistance? The Role of Agency and Resources

Even though some definitional issues associated with different conceptualizations of resistance are unresolved, the general concept holds promise for understanding both the nature of constraints to leisure and constraints negotiation among African Americans. Shaw's (2001, p. 190) discussion concluded by suggesting "leisure can also be a context for resistance to racism" and other forms of oppression. We illustrated the forms resistance might take related to leisure styles among African Americans. The next logical step is to extend the discussion by elaborating on the meaning of agency and the role of resources. We recognize this discussion will require additional elaboration beyond the confines of this chapter.

The concept of resourcefulness put forward by Rapoport and Rapoport (1975) in *Leisure and the Family Life Cycle* provides a strategic starting point to bridge resistance to agency and resources. Rapoport and Rapoport defined resourcefulness by describing its characteristics as (1) "the capacity to develop interests which have meaning in themselves as well as expressing underlying preoccupation" and (2) "it entails the ability to carry through the interests to realization in activities" (p. 26). Further, they stated "resourcefulness means knowing and being able to make a meaningful life for oneself with the *realities* of one's existence as well as how to change these realities" (p. 26). While Rapoport and Rapoport (1975) focused attention on activities and tasks associated with developmental stages over the life course, we propose the concept opens up theoretical space to elaborate on the question of what facilitates leisure as resistance. Specifically, it permits an analysis of the different types of resources that enable individuals and groups to negotiate constraints to leisure related to racial inequality.

Resourcefulness, in the Rapoports' use of the term, is homologous to human agency. Both concepts describe a condition in which individual actors (or groups) respond to the demands of social structure, roles, and expectations. Resourcefulness and agency both speak to the capacity to exploit available resources and alternatives to effect change. Indeed, Sewell (1992, p. 19) viewed agency as the "capacity to reinterpret and mobilize an array of resources in terms of cultural schema other than those that initially constituted the array." Stated differently, agency arises from the ability of individuals and groups to recognize and exploit resources and transfer them to different contexts. Hays (1994) placed agency on a continuum ranging from structurally reproductive agency to structurally transformative agency. She described the former as individual or group action that leads to reproduction and further solidification of structural inequality. Findings from Outley's (2000) analysis of leisure socialization among African American youth provided an illustration of how this might be relevant. Outley observed youth, particularly boys, sanctioned their peers known to participate in middle-class activities such as golf or tennis. In their neighborhood and in their school, such activities were labeled as "White activities" and those who participated in such activities were "acting White." By rejecting middle-class activities, and favoring the activities of the neighborhood (e.g., basketball and football), they potentially perpetuate a perceived boundary between so-called "White activities" and those perceived to be appropriate for Black youth from the urban core. This can be linked back to abstention as a form of resistance described earlier.

Hays's (1994) latter point described the type of action that facilitates visible or radical change or the dismantling of social structures. Hays described this form of agency as revolutionary in effect. An example would be the breakdown of racial segregation and discrimination in public accommodations. According to Hays, both kinds of agency "can be understood as human social action involving choices among alternatives made available by the enabling features of social structure" (p. 64). We wish to bring attention to these enabling features or resources inherent in social structures. Resources come about from the enabling features of social structure. They have the potential to provide individuals or collective groups with power to resist and possibly transform constraints associated with social inequalities (Hays, 1994; Sewell, 1992).

Our central idea is there is value in conceptualizing and describing the kinds of resources needed to mount resistance activities in leisure. At this point we suggest four exploratory analytical categories for moving in this direction: material resources, relational resources, symbolic resources, and option resources. *Material resources* refer to socioeconomic and physical resources available to individuals or collective groups. Examples of material resources include time, money, education, requisite knowledge, equipment, and skills. *Relational (social) resources* come through social capital and social networks. These are resources to which an individual or group can be linked directly or indirectly through their social ties. Social resources include companions and access to voluntary organizations and institutions. *Symbolic resources* refer to intangible attributes related to racial or subcultural identity that support resistance activities. Ethnic pride can be a source of motivation for individual and collective group action. In the 1970s, for example, "Blackness" and Black identity were essential features of the Civil Rights and Black Power movements. *Option resources* refer to the availability of leisure choices and alternatives. This set of resources (options) could expand or contract depending on the level of possession of the other types. As such, the categories of resources are not mutually exclusive. Indeed, it might be possible to show variation in single or a combination of resource possession leads to dependence or increased salience of another type of resource. For example, for individuals lacking in material resources, relational and symbolic resources may become more important.

Obviously, more extensive theorizing and review of existing theoretical and empirical studies is needed to flesh these categories out in greater detail. While space does not permit us to do that here, a number of quick examples can be given. As an initial sketch, focusing on resources might help to identify linkages between resistance and agency in several key ways. First, by proposing different analytical categories of resources, we may be able to identify avenues for understanding whether and how differential possession of resources relates to different patterns of constraints negotiation among racial minorities. Second, we can begin to speculate on how resources are acquired, shared, and transferred. Third, we can speculate on how different types of resources interrelate. Addressing such issues should lead to more explicit statements about what enables and facilitates resistance activities. Fourth, such categories permit examination of intraracial variation. This would recognize the class heterogeneity within the African American population (Shinew et al., 1995, 1996). Fifth, the introduction of categories of resources to facilitate constraint resources expands on the conventional types of structural constraints. Such constraints, we argue, are more relevant to the socioeconomic context of African Americans and other marginalized subpopulations. Thus, a framework based on the concept of resistance, resources, and agency can serve as a heuristic model for future research on constraints among African Americans and other racial minorities.

Conclusions

The purpose of this chapter was to bring attention to conceptual needs in research on race and constraints to leisure. While common issues and concerns are addressed by constraints researchers and researchers of race and ethnic issues, little attention has been given to how to exploit commonalities between them to advance scholarship in both areas. Jackson and Scott (1999) stated the "explosion" of constraints research can be attributed to the extent it has informed theory and methods in diverse topical areas. Only recently have researchers begun to look for ways to bridge the gap between race and ethnicity and constraints to leisure.

In this chapter we argued advancing this cause could be based on three observations. First, while the social and economic well-being of African Americans has improved markedly since the 1960s, this subpopulation is still subject to significant racial inequality, even in the post-Civil Rights era. Among the general indicators we reviewed, evidence of inequality is manifested in racial differences in personal and family income, employment, job opportunities for African American men, persistence of high levels of racial segregation, and tension surrounding interracial social interaction. Current constraints research approaches do not appear to be sensitive to the socioeconomic contexts shaping the lives of many African Americans. Perhaps the greater emphasis on psychological and social psychological aspects of constraints/negotiation can account for the limited attention to structural inequalities. To the extent this is an accurate statement, the role of structural factors and how they link to intrapersonal and interpersonal constraints warrants greater research attention. Moreover, the persistence of racial inequality calls for greater understanding of how African Americans and other racial and ethnic subpopulations negotiate constraints to leisure.

Second, we reviewed the existing literature on race and constraints, focusing on studies of African Americans. Several factors were identified that suggest a more relevant theoretical framework is needed to guide future research. Specifically, we suggested appropriate and relevant contexts for African Americans have been neglected in constraints research. Moreover, we stated selecting criterion variables most salient to particular subgroups would provide greater in-depth information about the constraints negotiation process for diverse populations.

Third, we introduced a framework based on resistance to offer possibilities for reconceptualizing the study of race and leisure constraints/negotiation. By doing so, we make several contributions. We believe our main contribution is the attempt to extend the conceptual analysis of resistance to identifying and describing the role of agency and resources in facilitating resistance in leisure. This kind of approach seems to be a more relevant alternative theoretical perspective for understanding leisure participation and constraints among African Americans. Further, we extended Shaw's (2001) discussion of resistance and women's leisure and applied it to leisure as a context for resistance to racism. As stated by Shaw, a greater understanding of the various forms of leisure resistance will enhance our appreciation of leisure as a form of political practice. We also identified some possible paths of resistance, such as pioneers, parallel activities, and abstention, and suggested some analytical categories describing the kinds of resources needed to mount resistance activities in leisure.

Undoubtedly, limitations and challenges to what we have proposed exist. First, we have made broad sweeping characterizations regarding the socioeconomic status of the African American population. We acknowledge the heterogeneity of this group and recognize regional-related (Johnson et al., 1998; Woodard, 1988), gender-related (Henderson & Ainsworth, 2001), and participation-related factors (Johnson et al., 2001) exist within the African American population, and these variations would likely affect the application of the framework. Second, we have not taken into consideration the role of racial identity and the impact it may have on resistance, resources, and agency. Racial identity, and the issues associated with multiple racial identities, is a heavily researched feature of African Americans' psychological lives (Sellers, Rowley, Chavous, Shelton & Smith, 1997). Despite the prolific nature of this literature, relatively little consensus exists beyond the belief that racial identity does plays a role, yet it is unclear as to the exact nature of that role, in the lives of African Americans. Further, more individuals are expressing a connection to multiple racial identities, and this could impact the nature of the framework's variables. Thus, racial identity and its relationship to the key variables in the framework will need further exploration. Third, we stated resistance can be approached from several theoretical standpoints (Shaw, 2001) and outlined how these various approaches can impact whether leisure is a space where power can be gained, reinforced, or lost. We have not, however, connected these various resistance approaches to the continuum of agency described by Hays (1994), or to the four types of resources described earlier.

We nevertheless stress that we believe the ideas presented here open up new insights into constraints theory and its relevance to African Americans. Stodolska (2000) questioned whether race and ethnicity studies contribute to our understanding of leisure behavior. In our intro-

duction we noted that leisure constraints and race and ethnicity research are rarely linked. As we have stated, a resistance–resources framework appears to be useful for bridging these two bodies of research. The framework will need further conceptual elaboration and empirical evaluation, but we hope it will be useful in advancing understanding of constraints to leisure and racial inequality. Ultimately, however, we hope such understanding will provide insight into ways in which leisure can empower and improve the lives of individuals and bring about broader social change.

References

Arnold, M. L. and Shinew, K. J. (1998). The role of gender, race and income on park use constraints. *Journal of Park and Recreation Administration, 16,* 39–56.

Blank, R. M. (2001). An overview of trends in social and economic well-being, by race. In N. J. Smelser, W. J. Wilson, and F. Mitchell (Eds.), *America becoming: Racial trends and their consequences* (Vol. 1; pp. 21–39).

Clark, J. and Critchener, C. (1985). *The devil makes work: Leisure in capitalist Britain.* London, England: Mac-Millan Publishers.

Deem, R. (1988). Feminism and leisure studies: Opening up new directions. In E. Wimbush and M. Talbot (Eds.), *Relative freedoms: Women and leisure* (pp. 5–17). Milton Keynes, England: Open University Press.

Dovidio, J. F., Gaertner, S. L., Kawakami, K., and Hodson, G. (2002). Why can't we just get along? Interpersonal biases and interracial distrust. *Cultural Diversity and Ethnic Minority Psychology, 8,* 88–102.

Edwards, P. K. (1981). Race, residence and leisure style: Some policy implications. *Leisure Sciences, 4,* 95–112.

Farley, R. (1984). *Blacks and whites narrowing the gap?* Cambridge, MA: Harvard University Press.

Farley, R. and Allen, W. R. (1987). *The color line and the quality of life in America.* New York, NY: Oxford University Press.

Feagin, J. R. (1991). The continuing significance of race: Antiblack discrimination in public places. *American Sociological Review, 56,* 101–116.

Feagin, J. R. and Vera, H. (1995). *White racism.* New York, NY: Routledge.

Floyd, M. F. (1998). Getting beyond marginality and ethnicity: The challenge for race and ethnic studies in leisure research. *Journal of Leisure Research, 30,* 3–22.

Floyd, M. F. and Shinew, K. J. (1999). Convergence and divergences in leisure style among Whites and African-Americans: Towards an interracial contact hypothesis. *Journal of Leisure Research, 31,* 359–384.

Fossett, M. A. and Seibert, M. T. (1997). *Long time coming: Racial inequality in the nonmetropolitan south, 1940–1990.* Boulder, CO: Westview Press.

Gallup (2001). *Black–white relations in the United States: 2001 update.* Washington, DC: Gallup Organization.

Gobster, P. H. (2002) Managing urban parks for a racially and ethnically diverse clientele. *Leisure Sciences, 24,* 143–159.

Gramann, J. H. and Allison, M. T. (1999). Ethnicity, race, and leisure. In E. L. Jackson and T. L. Burton (Eds.), *Leisure Studies: Prospects for the twenty-first century* (pp. 283–291). State College, PA: Venture Publishing, Inc.

Hays, S. (1994). Structure and agency and the sticky problem of culture. *Sociological Theory, 12*(1), 57–72.

Henderson, K. A. and Ainsworth, B. E. (2001). Researching leisure and physical activity with women of color: Issues and emerging questions. *Leisure Sciences, 23,* 21–34.

Henderson, K. A. and Bialeschki, M. D. (1991). A sense of entitlement to leisure as constraint and empowerment for women. *Leisure Sciences, 13,* 51–65.

Henderson, K. A., Bialeschki, M. D., Shaw, S. M., and Freysinger, V. (1996). *Both gains and gaps: Feminist perspectives on women's leisure.* State College, PA: Venture Publishing, Inc.

Hibbler, D. K. and Shinew, K. J. (2002). Interracial couples' experience of leisure: A social construction of a racialized other. *Journal of Leisure Research, 34,* 135–156.

Jackson, E. L. and Henderson, K. A. (1995). Gender-based analysis of leisure constraints. *Leisure Sciences, 17,* 31–51.

Jackson, E. L. and Scott, D. (1999). Constraints to leisure. In E. L. Jackson and T. L. Burton (Eds.), *Leisure studies: Prospects for the twenty-first century* (pp. 299–321). State College, PA: Venture Publishing, Inc.

Johnson, C. Y., Bowker, J. M., and Cordell, H. K. (2001). Outdoor recreation constraints: An examination of race, gender, and rural dwelling. *Southern Rural Sociology, 17,* 111–133.

Johnson, C. Y., Bowker, J. M., English, D. B. K., and Worthen, D. (1998). Wildland recreation in the rural south: An examination of marginality and ethnicity theory. *Journal of Leisure Research, 30,* 101–120.

Jones, J. M. (1997). *Prejudice and racism* (2nd ed.). New York, NY: McGraw-Hill.

Kohatsu, E. L., Dulay, M., Lam, C., Concepcion, W., Perez, P., Lopez, C., and Euler, J. (2000). Using racial identity theory to explore racial mistrust and interracial contact among Asian Americans. *Journal of Counseling & Development, 78,* 334–342.

Loury, G. C. (2002). *The anatomy of racial inequality.* Cambridge, MA: Harvard University Press.

Massey, D. S. and Denton, N. A. (1993). *American apartheid: Segregation and the making of the underclass.* Cambridge, MA: Harvard University Press.

National Conference of Christians and Jews. (1994). *Taking America's pulse: The full report of the national conference survey on inter-group relations.* New York, NY: Author.

Omi, M. and Winant, H. (1994). *Racial formation in the United States: From the 1960's to the 1990's* (2nd ed.). New York, NY: Routledge.

Outley, C. W. (2000). *Kickin' it: An investigation of leisure behavior among inner city African American children*. Unpublished doctoral dissertation, Texas A&M University, College Station, TX.

Philipp, S. F. (1995). Race and leisure constraints. *Leisure Sciences*, *17*, 109–120.

Philipp, S. F. (1999). Are we welcome? African-American racial acceptance in leisure activities and the importance given to children's leisure. *Journal of Leisure Research*, *31*, 385–403.

Philipp, S. F. (2000). Race and the pursuit of happiness. *Journal of Leisure Research*, *32*, 121–124.

Rapoport, R. and Rapoport, R. N. (1975). *Leisure and the family life cycle*. London, England: Routledge & Kegan Paul.

Robinson, T. L. and Ginter, E. J. (1999). Introduction to the *Journal of Counseling & Development's* special issue on racism. *Journal of Counseling & Development*, *77*, 3.

Schuman, H., Steeh, C. and Bobo, L. (1985). *Racial attitudes in America: Trends and interpretations*. Cambridge, MA: Harvard University Press.

Sears, D. O. (1998). Racism and politics in the United States. In J. L. Eberhardt and S. T. Fiske (Eds.), *Confronting racism: The problem and the response* (pp. 76–100). Thousand Oaks, CA: Sage Publications.

Sellers, R. M., Rowley, S. A., Chavous, T., Shelton, J., and Smith, M. (1997). Multidimensional inventory of black identity: A preliminary investigation of reliability and construct validity. *Journal of Personality and Social Psychology, 73*, 805–815.

Sewell, W. H., Jr. (1992). A theory of structure: Duality, agency, and transformation. *American Journal of Sociology, 98*(1), 1–29.

Shaw, S. M. (1994). Gender, leisure and constraint: Towards a framework for the analysis of women's leisure. *Journal of Leisure Research, 26*, 8–22.

Shaw, S. M. (2001). Conceptualizing resistance: Women's leisure as political practice. *Journal of Leisure Research, 33*, 186–201.

Shinew, K. J., Floyd, M. F., McGuire, F. A., and Noe, F. P. (1995). Gender, race, and subjective social class and their association with leisure preferences. *Leisure Sciences, 17*, 75–89.

Shinew, K. J., Floyd, M. F., McGuire, F. A., and Noe, F. P. (1996). Class polarization and leisure activity preferences of African Americans: Intragroup comparisons. *Journal of Leisure Research, 28*, 219–232.

Sigelman, L., and Welch, S. (1993). The contact hypothesis revisited: Black–white interaction and positive racial attitudes. *Social Forces, 71*, 781–795.

Sigelman, L., Bledsoe, T., Welch, S., and Combs, W. (1996). Making contact? Black–white social interaction in an urban setting. *American Journal of Sociology, 101,* 1306–1332.

Stodolska, M. (1998). Assimilation and leisure constraints: Dynamics of constraint on leisure in immigrant populations. *Journal of Leisure Research, 3,* 521–551.

Stodolska, M. (2000). Looking beyond the invisible: Can research on leisure of ethnic and racial minorities contribute to leisure theory? *Journal of Leisure Research, 32,* 156–160.

Tsai, E. H. and Coleman, D. J. (1999). Leisure constraints of Chinese immigrants: An exploratory study. *Society and Leisure, 22,* 243–264.

U.S. Census Bureau (n.d.). Table 7-1. Descriptive statistics for residential segregation indexes for American Indians and Alaska Natives, Asians and Pacific Islanders, Blacks, and Hispanics: 1980, 1990, and 2000. Retrieved December 6, 2002, from http://landview.census.gov/hhes/www/housing/resseg/tab7-1.html

U.S. Census Bureau (n.d.). Table A-2. Percent of people 25 years old and over who have completed high school or college by race, Hispanic origin, and sex: Selected years 1940 to 2000. Retrieved December 5, 2002, from http://landview.census.gov/population/socdemo/education/tableA-2.txt

U.S. Census Bureau (n.d.). Table F -5. Race and Hispanic origin of householder—Families by median and mean income: 1947 to 2001. Retrieved December 5, 2002, from http://www.census.gov/hhes/income/histinc/f05.html

U.S. Census Bureau. (n. d.). Table P-2. Race and Hispanic origin of people by median income and sex: 1947 to 2001. Retrieved December 5, 2002, from http://www.census.gov/hhes/income/histinc/p02.html

U.S. Department of Labor, Bureau of Labor Statistics (n.d.). Employment status of the civilian population by race, sex, age, and Hispanic origin. Retrieved December 23, 2002, from http://data.bls.gov/news.release/empsit.t02.htm

U.S. Department of Labor, Bureau of Labor Statistics (n.d.). Labor force statistics from the current population survey. Retrieved January 27, 2003, from http://data.bls.gov/servlet/SurveyOutputServlet

Virden, R. J. and Walker, G. J. (1999). Ethnic/racial and gender variations among meanings given to, preferences for, the natural environment. *Leisure Sciences, 21*, 219–239.

Washburne, R. (1978). Black under-participation in wildland recreation: Alternative explanations. *Leisure Sciences, 1*, 175–189.

Washburne, R. and Wall, P. (1980). *Black–white ethnic differences in outdoor recreation.* (USDA Forest Service Research Paper INT-249). Ogden, UT: Intermountain Forest and Range Experiment Station.

West, P. C. (1989). Urban region parks and black minorities: Subculture, marginality, and interracial relations in park use in the Detroit metropolitan area. *Leisure Sciences, 11,* 11–28.

Whyte, L. B. and Shaw, S. M. (1994). Women's leisure: An exploratory study of fear of violence as a leisure constraint. *Journal of Applied Recreation Research, 19,* 5–21.

Willie, C. V. (1978). The inclining significance of race. *Society, 15,* 15.

Wilson, W. J. (1978). *The declining significance of race.* Chicago, IL: University of Chicago Press.

Wilson, W. J. (1980). *The declining significance of race* (2nd ed.). Chicago, IL: University of Chicago Press.

Wilson, W. J. (1991). Studying inner city dislocations: The challenge of public agenda research. *American Sociological Review, 56,* 1–14.

Woodard, M. D. (1988). Class, regionality, and leisure among urban Black Americans: The post-civil rights era. *Journal of Leisure Research, 20,* 87–105.

Chapter 4

Ethnicity, Immigration, and Constraints

Monika Stodolska (University of Illinois at Urbana–Champaign) and Jouyeon Yi-Kook (Seoul National University)

While both the United States and Canada are often described as "nations of immigrants," the leisure of immigrants only recently attracted significant interest in our field. Immigration is often perceived as a thing of the past, a phenomenon that used to define us as nations but has little relevance today. With a few exceptions, such as history lessons or genealogical research, the very term "immigrant" appears to carry negative connotations. One tends to forget that immigration is not only a part of our heritage, but also an important factor that continues to affect our culture and economic prosperity today. Its significance is likely to grow in the foreseeable future.

The goal of this chapter is to provide an overview of the theoretical constructs used in the study of constraints on the leisure of ethnic minorities and to survey the empirical research that focused on or otherwise tackled the effects of constraints on the leisure behavior of ethnic minorities and immigrants. First, to illustrate the significance of research on minority populations and to establish its context, we briefly review current demographic trends in the United States and Canada and describe the role minorities play in the economic and cultural lives of both countries. Second, we review current conceptualizations of the term "ethnicity" and discuss major problems in research on constraints on leisure among ethnic minorities and immigrants. Third, we discuss major theoretical constructs employed in the study of ethnicity, immigration, and leisure constraints among ethnic minority members. Lastly, we overview constraints experienced by ethnic minorities using the marginality/ethnicity/discrimination framework and discuss the specific constraints on leisure experienced by immigrant populations.

Ethnic Minorities in the United States and Canada

The 20th century witnessed a transformation of the United States and Canada from nations composed mostly of Whites to ones whose populations represent a wide range of racial and ethnic minorities. While at the beginning of the 20th century the American population was 87% White, 100 years later non-Hispanic Whites account for less than 75% of the nation's inhabitants, and their share in the total population of the United States is steadily decreasing. African Americans, the second largest minority group, account for 13% of the American population or 36 million people (McKinnon, 2003). Currently, Hispanic Americans (primarily Mexicans, Puerto Ricans, and Cubans) constitute the largest minority group in the United States, accounting for 13.7% percent of the population, or approximately 37.4 million people (Ramirez & de la Cruz, 2003). Asian Americans, the third minority group in terms of size, account for 4.4% of the total population or 12.5 million people (Reeves & Bennett, 2003). America's ethnic landscape also includes a rapidly growing south Asian population (with India and Pakistan being the largest source countries), an Arab population, a sizeable Jewish population, as well as other ethnic groups, including those of European origins such as Italians, Russians, and Poles. The most recent projections from the U.S. Census Bureau forecast a net addition of 820,000 immigrants annually until 2050 (Cheeseman Day, 1996). In 2050 the American population is expected to reach 409 million, including 52% non-Hispanic Whites, 25% Hispanics, 13% Blacks, and 10% Asian/Pacific Islanders (U.S. Census Bureau, 2003). If these projections do materialize, today's minority groups will constitute tomorrow's "average American citizens" and thus the culture of the mainstream, including its leisure patterns, is likely to be permanently redefined.

The growth of the ethnic minority population in the United States and Canada can be attributed to two major factors. First, immigration has accounted for more than one third of the growth of the minorities since 1980 (Martin & Midgley, 2003). The majority of immigrants (51%) come from Latin America and another 30% from Asia. Similarly, in Canada at the turn of the century, almost half of the population growth rate could be attributed to immigration (Statistics Canada, 2003). The second major reason for the rapid increase in the minority populations in the United States and Canada is higher fertility rates among minority women. Many of the minorities come from countries where large families are the norm. Moreover, many minority women, particularly those of Hispanic background, tend to have their first child at a younger age than their White counterparts, which contributes to a larger total family size (Pollard & O'Hare, 1999). As some argue, even if the United States accepted no more immigrants after 1995, the higher fertility rates among minorities, combined with their younger age structure, would have increased the share of the minority population from 28% in 1998 to 39% by 2050 (Pollard & O'Hare, 1999).

Members of ethnic minorities and recent immigrants in particular show distinct socioeconomic and residence patterns. They are known to settle predominantly in the major urban centers of California, Hawaii, New Mexico, and Texas and to create communities quite distinct from the mainstream counterparts in terms of cultural background, social norms, and family structure, as well as recreation participation patterns (Alba & Nee, 1997). In 1990, four minority groups made up at least one half of the residents of Honolulu, Los Angeles, Miami, San Antonio, and several other metropolitan areas. In recent years, the spatial distribution of minorities in the United States has been changing rapidly. By 2000, states such as Arkansas, Colorado, Georgia, Nebraska, Nevada, North Carolina, Tennessee, and Utah saw the number of immigrants more than double. This rapid increase in the minority population in nontraditional states has caused major strains on local resources (ranging from housing to public education) and on the willingness of the local populations to absorb culturally distinct newcomers. At the same time, while many minorities have enjoyed a degree of emancipation and an increased economic and political power, some groups remain largely disfranchised. A recent study by the Center for Immigration Studies (Camarota, 2001) indicated immigrants in the United States still lag behind native-born Americans in terms of income and home ownership rates. Furthermore, it suggested the economic position of immigrants steadily deteriorated during the recent decades.

Rapid growth in minority populations has a profound influence on the racial and ethnic makeup of the countries' schools, workplaces, and neighborhoods. Many businesses target their products to specific ethnic groups, as they recognize the increasing purchasing power of minority populations. Aspects of minority culture, such as art, food, music, dress styles, and leisure patterns, are being adopted throughout American society (Pollard & O'Hare, 1999). In the next two decades, given that Whites are likely to be outnumbered by minorities in many states, Caucasians may lose their monopoly on defining what is considered mainstream and what falls outside of the cultural norm (Pollard & O'Hare, 1999). Such changes are beginning to be noticed by leisure researchers, who pay increased attention to issues of ethnic minority groups. A testimony to this may be the special issues devoted to leisure of ethnic and racial minorities published by two main journals in our field, *Journal of Leisure Research* and *Leisure Sciences*. The literature on ethnicity and immigration developed so far in our field primarily tackled the effect of assimilation on leisure behavior (Carr & Williams, 1993a, 1993b; Floyd & Gramann, 1993; Floyd, Gramann & Saenz, 1993; Gramann, Shaull & Saenz, 1995; Shaull & Gramann, 1998), the use of parks and natural areas by minority groups (Bass, Ewert & Chavez, 1993; Cordell, Betz & Green, 2002; Gobster, 2002; Gobster & Delgado, 1993; Gramann, 1996; Payne, Mowen & Orsega-Smith, 2002; Tinsley, Tinsley & Croskeys, 2002), culture-specific meanings of and motivations for leisure (Carr & Williams, 1993a; Virden & Walker, 1999), and postimmigration adaptation patterns (Juniu, 2000; Stodolska, 2000; Tirone & Pedlar, 2000; Tirone & Shaw, 1997). While studies that specifically focus on the leisure constraints experienced by ethnic minority members and immigrants are still rare (Stodolska, 1998; Tsai & Coleman, 1999), the very nature of the life experience of minorities and immigrants makes it difficult to overlook the significance of constraints as a factor defining their leisure. In fact, one may argue any study of minorities' and immigrants' leisure would be incomplete without acknowledging the effects of the constraints that they face.

Ethnicity

To explore how ethnicity and immigration status constrain people's leisure, we need to clarify how ethnicity can be conceptualized. The issue of conceptualization of ethnicity is particularly important if one considers a major limitation of the existing literature on the leisure of ethnic and racial minorities can be traced to the fact that it tends to disregard distinctions among the concepts of race, ethnicity, and generational tenure. While it is difficult to argue the individual role of each of these three factors can always be isolated in a meaningful fashion, one should recognize these concepts are not interchangeable and they may affect the leisure of minorities in different ways and through different causal mechanisms. Cultural (ethnic) or racial differences can have a significant effect on constraints on leisure experienced by minorities. It can be argued constraints related to language or distinct cultural norms are clearly a function of ethnicity. Discrimination, on the other hand, may be triggered not only by manifestations of cultural distinctiveness, but also by mere differences in physical appearance.

According to the traditional, strictly physical, "essentialist" definition, race is considered a biological fact and a physical attribute of individuals—a set of genetically determined physical characteristics, such as skin color or stature (Anderson & Frideres, 1981). In contrast to the biologically oriented "essential" approaches, more recent definitions of race assert that race is a "social" category. According to Omi and Winant (1994), race is a matter of both "social structure" and "cultural representation." Race is described as

> a concept which signifies and symbolizes social conflict and interest by referring to different types of human bodies. Although the concept of race invokes biologically based human characteristics (so-called "phenotypes"), selection of these particular human features for purposes of racial signification is always and necessarily a social and historical process. (p. 55)

Depending on the field of study, the definition of race is usually extended to cover a variety of additional factors, but the physical component of race is almost always present.

In contrast to race, ethnicity is always described as a culturally based concept. While the term "ethnicity" appeared in the English language for the first time only in the 1950s, the adjective "ethnic" has been used as a synonym for "gentile" in the English language since the Middle Ages (Hutchinson & Smith, 1996). As a result, in the United States, the usage of the term ethnic tends to depend on the dichotomy between a nonethnic "us" and ethnic "others." Although the term ethnic has been applied not only to minorities or immigrants, but also to the majority or the host society, in the United States and Canada it is likely to be associated with minority groups (Hutchinson & Smith, 1996). In 1959 Berry proposed an early definition of an ethnic group, as a group of people

> possessing ties of cultural homogeneity; a high degree of loyalty and adherence to certain basic institutions such as family patterns, religion,

and language; distinctive folkways and mores; customs of dress, art, and ornamentation; moral codes and value systems; patterns of recreation; some sort of object to which the group manifests allegiance, such as a monarch, a religion, a language, or a territory; a consciousness of kind, a we-feeling; common descent (perhaps racial), real or imagined; and a political unit. (Berry, cited in Anderson & Frideres, 1981, p. 36)

According to Lewin (1948), ethnic identity is a "manner in which persons, on account of their ethnic origin, locate themselves psychologically in relation to one or more social systems, and in which they perceive others as locating them in relation to those systems" (as cited in Isajiw, 1990, p. 35). Isajiw identified external aspects (e.g., use of ethnic langue, maintaining ethnic traditions, maintaining ethnic networks, participation in voluntary organizations such as clubs and societies, as well as in functions sponsored by the ethnic community such as dances, picnics and concerts), and internal aspects (e.g., cognitive, moral, and affirmative dimension) of ethnic identity. He maintained internal factors are interconnected with external behavior, but stressed it should not be assumed the two types always depend on each other.

While Isajiw's (1990) external and internal aspects of ethnic identity focused on the level of an individual, Conzen, Gerber, Morawska, Pozzeftta, and Vecoli's (1992) concept of ethnicization focused more on the social and historical contexts of ethnic group formation. Adopting the social constructionist perspective, Conzen et al. (1992) argued ethnicity is not a stable attribute assigned to an individual, but is being reinvented by minorities in their daily interactions with the mainstream society. The invention of ethnicity has characteristics of "contextuality" and "periodicity." It is a process taking place within a specified and concrete historical context and its saliency fluctuates along a certain time continuum. Nagel (1994) also considered ethnicity as a dynamic, constantly evolving property of both individual identity and group organization. According to Nagel, every individual carries a portfolio of ethnic identities that are more or less salient in various situations and vis-à-vis various audiences. Ethnic identity is the result of a dialectical process involving internal and external opinions and processes, as well as the individual's self-identification and outsiders' ethnic designations. It is both optional and mandatory, since individual options are limited by the ethnic categories available at a particular time and place. While some people have many ethnic categories available to them (e.g., American vs. Irish American), for others (e.g., African Americans), the range of available ethnic categories may be extremely conscribed and constraining (Nagel, 1994). According to Nagel (1994), "identity" and "culture" are two fundamental factors of ethnicity and are essential to the central projects of ethnicity: the construction of boundaries and the production of meaning.

Problems With Research on Constraints to Leisure Among Ethnic Minorities and Immigrants

Research on the leisure constraints experienced by ethnic minorities and immigrants involves certain inherent problems that may be difficult to overcome for mainstream researchers. First, a question arises as to whether outsiders are fully capable of understanding the problems faced by ethnic and racial minorities and how well they are equipped to conduct research among ethnically enclosed communities. Furthermore, mainstream researchers are often vulnerable to accusations of exploitation and manipulation of these disfranchised groups, and their work may be perceived as an attempt to impose cultural constructs of the dominant group on minority populations (Gramann & Allison, 1999; Henderson, 1998). However, research conducted by members of ethnic or racial minorities is not immune to problems either. While it might be easier for insiders to study ethnically enclosed populations, their research is often perceived as lacking objectivity or being inherently biased (Henderson, 1998; Rehman, 2002). Research on constraints on leisure experienced by ethnic minorities is particularly prone to bias, as the researcher's cultural background can easily affect the way in which he or she interprets the leisure behavior of people from distinct ethnic groups. It may be tempting to label as "constraints" factors present in the lives of ethnic minorities they themselves do not perceive as barriers to their leisure (Stodolska & Livengood, 2003). Recently it has been argued some White researchers studying constraints experienced by ethnic and racial minorities have been approaching the issue from an ethnically or racially insensitive perspective and have not paid enough attention to the unique preferences of ethnic minority members (Kivel, in press; Stodolska, in press). Moreover, researchers studying constraints on leisure are open to criticism they assume the existence of certain desired levels of participation to which minorities should aspire and constraints are responsible for "underrepresentation" of minorities in their "desired," "White" activities.

Regardless of the cultural background of the researcher, work on the leisure of minorities and immigrant groups involves some universal difficulties. Members of minority populations are often difficult to access and may be quite reluctant to participate in research projects (Cannon, Higginbotham & Leung, 1991; Henderson, 1998). This problem is particularly evident when researchers attempt to tackle sensitive issues, such as constraints to participation related to low socioeconomic status, discrimination, and problems associated with establishment in the host country. Problems with translations, differences in the meaning of certain words or concepts, as well as the lack of cultural compatibility between the researchers and the populations being studied are also likely to become significant obstacles for this type of research (Henderson, 1998; Juniu, 1999; Livengood & Stodolska, in press; Mâsse et al., 1998; Stodolska, 1998; Stodolska & Jackson, 1998).

One of the main problems affecting research on the leisure behavior of ethnic and racial minorities, including their constraints on leisure, is the implicit assumption of homogeneity of minority populations (Sasidharan, 2002). The majority of the existing literature uses very broad generalizations and all-inclusive labels, such as White, Black, Hispanic, or Asian, without much concern for any heterogeneity in terms of race, ethnicity, and social class that might be present within those groups (Gramann & Allison, 1999). For instance, Hispanics (a term that itself is debated and criticized) encompasses individuals of Mexican, Cuban, Puerto Rican, Colombian, or Peruvian descent who are likely to differ in terms of culture, lifestyle, leisure preferences, and constraints on leisure. While Latino populations have certain common cultural traits, it is difficult to argue that second-generation Cubans share many experiences with recent refugees from Salvador, temporary migrants from Mexico, or graduate students from Colombia, Argentina, or Chile. A similar argument can be applied to so-called Asians who include people of Chinese, Korean, Japanese, Vietnamese, Pakistani, and Hindu descent and who do not even share a common language, not to mention other cultural features. In addition to issues of national origin, differences in generational tenure introduce yet another dimension of intergroup heterogeneity that simply cannot be ignored. While first-generation immigrants are likely to experience constraints related to their lack of English language proficiency, lack of knowledge of the existing surroundings, or postsettlement economic and social difficulties (Stodolska, 1998, 2000; Stodolska & Alexandris, 2002), second- or third-generation minorities are likely to be largely immune to these barriers. Conversely, it has been argued some descendants of immigrants are affected by their disillusionment related to lack of advancement of people from their ethnic group, persistent discrimination, and lack of prospects for upward mobility (Gans, 1992).

Assuming homogeneity of the "mainstream" population is often equally as deceiving as the lack of attention given to heterogeneity within minority groups. Most research on the leisure of ethnic groups defines the "mainstream" solely in terms of physical race (i.e., the White mainstream) with complete disregard for its ethnic heterogeneity. Hence, all Caucasian ethnic groups are automatically included in the mainstream category regardless of their cultural characteristics. By adopting such broad definitions, we not only distort our perception of what "mainstream" really means, but also perpetuate the misconception that race is somehow more important than culture. There are many examples of White ethnic groups that exhibit more profound cultural differences from the Anglo-Saxon norm than do certain well-established racial minorities. Yet, such White ethnic groups continue to be regarded as "mainstream" solely on the basis of their race. By downplaying the importance of ethnic diversity within the non-Hispanic White population we prevent ourselves from appreciating the constraints on leisure faced by many members of this group. Moreover, by focusing solely on "visible" ethnic minorities, we make it more difficult to distinguish the effects of "ethnicity" from the effects of "race" on leisure behavior and on leisure constraints.

Theoretical Approaches to Studying Ethnicity and Leisure

In her 1998 article, Stodolska postulated constraints could be divided into two broad categories based on their temporal nature. Some constraints, such as discrimination or lack of access to resources, exhibit *static* characteristics. Others, such as child care responsibilities, language proficiency, or lack of familiarity with the surroundings are more *dynamic* and clearly evolve with time. While no constraints are absolutely static (if one were to exclude factors such as disability or permanent poverty), the strength of certain constraints experienced by a particular individual clearly changes with the passage of time. For members of ethnic minorities, those dynamic constraints have a tendency to vary along with the level of establishment in the host country. The dynamic nature of constraints experienced by ethnic minorities has been modeled using different adaptation theories. Static constraints, such as cultural differences and socioeconomic position, have been approached from the marginality/ethnicity (subcultural) perspective. In this section we review the adaptation theories used in research on leisure constraints. Application of the marginality/ethnicity/discrimination framework to the study

of leisure constraints will be the focus of a subsequent section.

Over the last 50 years, a number of theories have been developed in the fields of sociology, social psychology, geography, and ethnic studies that describe the processes of adaptation of immigrants to the new social and economic environment of the host country (Barth, 1998; Gans, 1992, 1994; Glick Schiller, Basch & Blanc-Szanton, 1992; Gordon, 1964; Keefe & Padilla, 1987; LeVine & Campbell, 1972; Portes 1984, 1997; Portes & Zhou, 1993; Warner & Srole, 1945; Waters, 1994). The assimilation framework has been most often applied theory of ethnic change to study intraethnic/racial differences in recreation participation (Floyd & Gramann, 1993, 1995; Floyd, Gramann & Saenz, 1993; Shaull & Gramann, 1998; Stodolska, 1998). *Assimilation* was defined as the process of reduction of differences in values and behavioral practices between minorities and the mainstream society that leads to their acceptance by the mainstream population and facilitates their success within the mainstream economy (Gordon, 1964). It was perceived to be an irreversible, linear process in which immigrants progressed through various stages, such as acculturation, structural assimilation, amalgamation, and identificational assimilation (Gordon, 1964; Portes & Borocz, 1989). *Identificational assimilation* is defined by Gordon (1964) as "the taking on of a sense of [American] peoplehood" (p. 70). It was assumed that the process of assimilation affected most aspects of minorities' leisure behavior, including their participation patterns, motivations, and constraints on leisure. Moreover, the level of attachment to ethnic leisure pursuits was expected to decrease with increasing levels of assimilation to the mainstream society (Floyd & Gramann, 1993, 1995; Floyd, Gramann & Saenz, 1993).

An example of the empirical applications of cultural assimilation (acculturation) theory is a study of Chinese immigrant adolescents by Yu and Berryman (1996). They used the acculturation model developed by Padilla (1980) to investigate relationships between constraints and factors such as self-esteem, acculturation level, and recreation participation among recent teenage immigrants. Their findings suggested perceived importance of certain constraints—including language problems, inability to find leisure partners, lack of money, and lack of awareness of existing opportunities—negatively related to self-esteem levels. Yu and Berryman (1996) found students with higher levels of acculturation participated significantly more often in recreation activities, especially in sports, and they affiliated more often with organizations for recreation.

In 1998, Stodolska employed Gordon's (1964) assimilation framework to study constraints on leisure experienced by first-generation immigrants to Canada from

Poland. She discovered the perceived importance of certain leisure constraints was negatively associated with assimilation level. In particular, the study showed the behavioral receptional assimilation (related to the perceived level of discrimination) significantly influenced many types of constraints, while acculturation level had a significant effect only on a single dimension of constraints. She concluded the leisure of immigrants was most severely constrained immediately after their arrival and some of the constraints declined in significance as people adapted to the new environment. Stodolska argued given the speed of assimilation inversely related to the duration of residence, constraints tended to undergo the most profound changes during the postarrival period. However, barriers on participation immigrants experience continue to evolve at a slower pace for long periods following the arrival. This finding was confirmed in a study by Stodolska and Alexandris (2002), who found recreational sport participation among immigrants was severely constrained during the first establishment period, but the circumstances usually changed when immigrants became better adjusted to life in the United States.

Similarly, a study by Stodolska (2000) found many constraints experienced by immigrants in the initial periods after their arrival were transitory, and immigrants were able to take advantage of new opportunities and to quickly expand their leisure repertoires. Findings of this study conducted on first-generation immigrants also allowed for the detection of patterns that could be applied to the leisure behavior of the mainstream population. It was observed activities in which people participate in certain lifestages depend not only on their wants, needs, and constraints currently experienced, but also on the constraints they experienced in preceding periods of their life. In other words, the removal of constraints often triggers people's leisure participation (see Jackson, this volume). Moreover, under certain circumstances, constraints experienced at one point in time may serve as motivations for future participation. It was postulated that barriers to participation that people experience increase the scarcity and thus the perceived value of the desired object or activity. Thus, subsequent removal of such barriers may trigger participation even among people who would otherwise be unlikely to engage in a given activity.

In recent years leisure researchers have begun to look beyond the traditional framework of assimilation and to embrace more contemporary approaches of ethnic adaptation and change. While the classic models focused on the assimilation processes expected to guide the adjustment of immigrants, more recent theories pointed out generational "returns" exist in the assimilation process, and minorities often retain selected elements of their culture, promote ethnic group solidarity, maintain boundaries of their respective communities, or even foster transnational ties with their home countries. For instance, selective acculturation—a variation of the assimilation theory developed by Keffe and Padilla (1987) that asserted minorities assimilate with respect to critical traits that further their socioeconomic success, but retain certain cultural elements, including leisure behavior— was frequently utilized in leisure studies research (Carr & Williams, 1993a). Portes (1984) and Barth (1998) also questioned the underlying assumptions behind the assimilation theory and observed that despite years and even generations of residence in the United States, many minority groups resisted assimilation tendencies and retained their distinct cultural traits. In his *boundary maintenance* theory, Barth (1998) emphasized cultural differences and ethnic boundaries can persist despite interethnic contact and interdependence. He observed groups articulate their in-group cohesiveness and simultaneously emphasize boundaries between themselves and the larger society through factors such as cultural traits (e.g., language, traditions, dress, and leisure activities), historical traditions, and political movements. In 1984, Portes put forth the concept of *ethnic resilience* and stressed the awareness of racial and cultural differences and the social solidarity based on them and *not* assimilation is the key to minorities' success in the host country.

The concepts of selective acculturation, ethnic resilience, and boundary maintenance surfaced clearly in Stodolska and Livengood's (2003) research on the effects of Islam on the leisure behavior of Muslim immigrants. As the study showed, ethnic minority members consciously used leisure as a tool to prevent acculturation, to promote ethnic resiliency, and to ensure preservation of the ethno-religious group. The perception of constraints seemed to be dependent on the age at arrival, the relative position of a person within the social group, and the degree of retention of their traditional customs. While individuals who emigrated at an older age, who held prominent positions within their families and communities, and who retained significant elements of their heritage did not perceive certain impositions of their culture as constraining (e.g., the requirement of life with the extended family or subordination to senior family members), younger immigrants more exposed to the influences of the western culture were likely to perceive the same factors as barriers to their leisure.

In their 1993 article, Portes and Zhou noted the "new immigrants" who settled in the United States since the passage of the Hart–Cellar Act of 1965 distinguished themselves from their predecessors in terms of their more diverse ethnic and social composition and different economic opportunities in the United States (the so-called "hourglass economy"). Portes and Zhou (1993) argued these differences caused the new immigrants and their descendents to go through diverse paths of *segmented assimilation*. While some immigrants acculturate, adopt mainstream values and expectations, and become integrated into the American middle class, others assimilate the values and attain substandard economic levels of the American underclass, or conversely, preserve their ethnic traits and promote their in-group solidarity (Portes & Zhou, 1993). One can argue the diverse adaptation paths followed by ethnic minorities may have a significant impact on the leisure constraints they experience in the host country. While minorities who choose the difficult path of assimilation into the mainstream society may face severe barriers in the initial adaptation period, or even social exclusion from the culture they aspire to and their own ethnic community, their subsequent socioeconomic advancement may release them from some of the economic barriers experienced by those who follow the route of assimilation to the American underclass (Wiley, 1967). On the other hand, we may postulate those who decide to remain entrenched in their ethnic enclaves will experience fewer constraints related to underdeveloped social networks or to outright social exclusion, but will be more noticeably affected by barriers related to their lack of participation in the mainstream culture and economy (e.g., thwarted economic mobility, lack of language skills, lack of access to certain recreation resources). It needs to be acknowledged that according to the alternative theories (Portes & Bach, 1985; Portes & Jensen, 1992; Portes & Zhou, 1992, 1993; Wilson & Portes, 1980) the immigrants who choose to foster links within their ethnic communities might be more economically successful than those who attempt to compete in the mainstream economy (the so-called "enclave economy" hypothesis).

During the last decade, *transnationalism*—a new approach to understanding issues of adaptation of immigrants—gained significant popularity in the fields of sociology, geography, and migration studies (Portes, 1997). The concept of transnationalism is based on the premise that contemporary immigrants do not "assimilate" in the traditional sense, but instead maintain social, political, and cultural links to their countries of origin. Members of transnational ethnic communities contribute economically to more than one country and maintain social and cultural ties with both the sending and the host country (Nagel, 2002). These new immigrants are often bilingual, they frequently maintain homes in two countries, and they easily move across cultural and national borders (Portes, 1997; Portes, Guarnizo & Landolt, 1999). Although the concept of constraints typical to "new" transnational migrants remains largely unexplored, it is difficult to overlook the fact that the "new" ethnic communities of the 21st century face an entirely different set of circumstances, which have their roots in the global economy. Their mobility patterns distinguish them from the previous immigration waves of the 19th and 20th century. While the transnational migrants may range from highly mobile employees of the high-tech industry who earn substantial salaries and maintain residence in more than one country, to temporary agricultural migrants from Mexico, it is quite possible that they share similar sets of constraints on leisure. One may expect that their mobility patterns, lack of long-term residence in one country, and severe strains on their families and social networks are likely to put them in a unique position in terms of the leisure constraints they experience.

It needs to be stressed that ethnic groups in contemporary North America are themselves characterized by much diversity. They include individuals with different personal histories, goals, and distinct social endowments and who follow different trajectories when it comes to their adaptation in the host country (Alba & Nee, 1997; Keefe & Padilla, 1987; Riccio, 2001; Waters, 1994). Such different trajectories not only have a profound impact on their lives in general and their leisure behavior in particular, but also likely have a strong effect on constraints on leisure that they face. The next section will focus on different approaches to study static constraints on leisure experienced by ethnic minority members. First, constraints related to the marginality theory will be reviewed, followed by constraints associated with distinct cultural backgrounds of ethnic groups, and lastly discrimination they face.

The Marginality/Ethnicity/Discrimination Framework and Its Applicability to Research on Constraints of Ethnic Minorities

Marginality

Interest in constraints on the leisure of ethnic and racial groups can be traced back to Washburne's (1978) marginality/ethnicity thesis, and as some authors argue, can be attributed to discrimination responsible for the existence of intergroup differences in leisure (Blahna & Black, 1993; Philipp, 1993; Taylor, 1992; West, 1989).

According to the marginality thesis, the history of inequality in resource allocation is an important factor constraining the recreation pursuits of Black Americans as well as other ethnic and racial minorities. While this framework has been traditionally employed to analyze barriers to participation experienced by African Americans only (Johnson, Bowker, English & Worthen, 1998; Klobus-Edwards, 1981; West, 1989; Woodard, 1988), it can be readily adapted to tackle constraints on leisure among ethnic groups. Although many ethnic minority members have achieved remarkable success in North America, ethnic minorities are still predominantly clustered in lower-status occupations, and many continue to face discrimination in hiring and promotion. In general, minority populations in the United States are younger, poorer, and less educated; tend to earn less than Whites even after accounting for differences in education; and live in larger households (Martin & Midgley, 2003). The poverty rate for most minority groups is higher than the rate for the mainstream White population. In 1999, 22.8% of Hispanics were living in poverty, compared to 7.7% of non-Hispanic Whites (Therrien & Ramirez, 2000). Even Asian Americans, who have higher median household incomes than non-Hispanic Whites ($45,400 per year versus $40,600 per year in 1997) are more likely than Whites to live below the poverty line (Pollard & O'Hare, 1999). Ethnic minorities are also overrepresented among the poorest of the poor—more than one half (57%) of those with incomes less than one half the official poverty line are minorities (Pollard & O'Hare, 1999). Since many ethnic groups lag behind the mainstream in terms of education, income, and wealth, the marginality explanation is potentially useful for studying the leisure constraints of ethnic populations.

Low level of discretionary income is not the only factor likely to affect the leisure choices of ethnic minority members. The lack of time associated with the low wage, strenuous employment minorities are compelled to accept may further restricts their leisure options. Evidence suggests the types of jobs minorities undertake directly relate to their leisure choices. As the results of a study by Crespo (2000) indicated, minorities in general and Hispanics in particular are more likely to be employed in occupations that require higher energy expenditures compared to their White counterparts, which can potentially explain their lower rates of participation in physical activities during leisure time. While subcultural preference for more sedentary, family-oriented pastimes (Chavez, 1991, 1996; Hutchison, 1987; Hutchison & Fidel, 1984) can also contribute to these nonactive leisure patterns, lack of stamina related to physically demanding employment can act as a constraining factor for those who might exhibit a preference for active leisure (Stodolska & Alexandris, 2002). Moreover, in his study of the recreation patterns of minority users of Chicago's Lincoln Park, Gobster (2002) observed Latino and Asian recreationists were constrained by physical distance and transportation problems when it came to accessing well-developed and well-maintained parks in downtown neighborhoods. He noted distance to the park can restrict access for large, family-oriented groups of minorities. Since ethnic minorities are less likely to reside in upscale neighboring communities, they are forced to travel by car and to rely on expensive parking in downtown areas.

Residential segregation is still one of the key features that distinguishes ethnic minorities from mainstream society, and one that also exacerbates the constraints to leisure they face (Massey & Denton, 1993). Average living costs tend to be higher in cities and in geographic regions where minority groups are concentrated, worsening the economic burden they tend to experience. For instance, most Asians live in large cities of the West or Northeast where living costs are relatively high, thus reducing the discretionary income that can be devoted to leisure. Moreover, minorities make up a disproportionately large share of residents of the central cities that form the core of metropolitan areas (Pollard & O'Hare, 1999). For instance, in 1997, 88% of minorities lived in metropolitan areas compared with 77% of non-Hispanic Whites, and the gap continued to increase despite the recent move of more affluent ethnics to suburban areas (Paral, 2000; Pollard & O'Hare, 1999). Low-income neighborhoods where most ethnic minorities reside differ in terms of the quality of schools, facilities, and services and the likelihood of being affected by crime (Pollard & O'Hare, 1999). Not only are the locations where minorities reside and recreate known to lack well-maintained parks and recreation facilities (Blahna & Black, 1993; Gobster & Delgado, 1993), but also fear for personal safety in public spaces has been proven to disproportionately affect their participation in leisure activities (Crespo, 2000). Safety issues are likely to be particularly constraining for minority women living in neighborhoods with high poverty and above-average crime rates (Crespo, 2000; Henderson & Ainsworth, 1999). For instance, a study of an Arab ethnic community in Chicago suggested the majority of Arab immigrants negatively perceived the overall conditions in their neighborhoods, complained about lack of security, and feared harassment by the general public and the local police (Cainkar, 1999). Crime, gang activity, and the prevalence of drugs also contributed to the neighborhood's negative perception. Since the neighborhood was seen as a hostile environment, parents demanded their children, especially girls, stayed close to home and limited their own out-of-home, leisure-related outings (Cainkar, 1999).

Ethnicity

The volume of evidence suggesting ethnicity, or cultural characteristics, may be responsible for determining constraints on leisure faced by minorities is probably even more extensive than that supporting marginality. In contrast to the marginality theory, the ethnicity thesis disregards the effects of resource constraints on leisure participation patterns. It suggests instead differences in leisure styles result from variations in norms and values in ethnic/racial groups (Washburne, 1978). While the importance of resource constraints is downplayed in this approach, other types of constraints are not necessarily excluded, at least as partial determinants of the observed behavioral differences. Beginning with the original study by Washburne (1978), who noted there might have existed "powerful forces within community that discourage participation in *White* activities" (p. 178), a number of studies have mentioned cultural characteristics as possible constraints on leisure. These culture-related factors creating constraints on leisure among ethnic minorities have included, among others, child care functions of women and young girls, subordination of youth, gender segregation in leisure, emphasis on family-oriented recreation, and preferences for recreation incompatible with facility design (Alvirez & Bean, 1981; Clark, 1979; Hutchison, 1987; Irwin, Gartner & Phelps, 1990).

For instance, in his 1987 study on the use of Chicago's public parks, Hutchinson pointed out excessive crowding and utilization of recreation facilities beyond their capacity resulting from Hispanics' family-oriented style of participation hindered the leisure pursuits of members of this minority. Similarly, Irwin, Gartner, and Phelps (1990) and Gobster (2002) found Hispanics tended to recreate in larger groups, and given the design of most American campgrounds and park facilities, the group size itself could be a factor constraining their recreational behavior. Similar findings were obtained by Stodolska and Livengood (2003), who observed recreation participation of American Muslim immigrants was constrained by the lack of family-oriented facilities that could accommodate large groups of recreationists, lack of large outdoor recreation spaces designed to accommodate their communal meetings, lack of single-sex facilities where men and women could spend their free time separately, and lack of private locations in recreation places and tourist resorts where Muslims could perform their daily prayers.

Hutchison (1987) observed Hispanics were more likely than either Whites or Blacks to spend their free time within mixed-age family groups often composed solely of females. He concluded this participation pattern could be related to child care functions of mothers and older girls expected to provide care for their younger siblings. Certain demographic characteristics of the Hispanic population, such as younger average age at marriage, higher fertility rates, or higher likelihood of living in family households with dependent children, may contribute to a differentiation in the patterns of constraints on leisure experienced by Hispanics in general and by Hispanic women in particular. In 1998, nearly two thirds (64%) of Hispanic family households included children under the age of 18, compared to less than 50% of non-Hispanic Whites (Pollard & O'Hare, 1999). Thus, the culture-based and demographically propelled family responsibilities of Hispanics may reinforce the constraints on leisure they experience.

Cultural traditions and economic difficulties also can affect people's living arrangements. The tendency among Asian households to include extended family members or the greater tendency of young Hispanics, especially women, to live with their parents until marriage is well-documented in the ethnic studies literature (Alvirez & Bean, 1981; Clark, 1979). Such living patterns may be even more pronounced among recent immigrants, who are more likely to adhere to traditional values, or who may be less able to afford a home of their own (Pollard & O'Hare, 1999). Living in households with extended family members is likely to exacerbate the constraints related to lack of privacy and lack of decision making power when it comes to spending free time or resources on leisure (Stodolska & Livengood, 2003; Stodolska & Yi, 2003). On the other hand, as the literature on some ethnic groups (Rublee & Shaw, 1991) pointed out, the *lack* of extended kin networks among immigrants and the perception of cultural insensitivity on the part of mainstream day care providers may constitute factors constraining the leisure of young immigrant mothers.

Besides the emphasis on family-oriented recreation commonly found among Hispanics, other ethnic characteristics of this group could also be responsible for their distinct participation patterns and possibly act as constraining factors. Both Alvirez and Bean (1981) and Clark (1979) pointed out factors such as *machismo* or male dominance, emphasis on respect for elders, subordination of youth, gender segregation of activities, and restrictions on social contacts of unmarried females as important characteristics of the Hispanic minority. One can argue such cultural characteristics can modify the leisure behavior of ethnic groups, and in certain circumstances create or reinforce constraints on leisure.

Similarly, culturally determined group-oriented behavior, strict hierarchy within the group, and respect for the elderly can act as constraining factors for more assimilated Asian immigrants from Korea, who find the Confucian values of their communities to be too restrictive in the American environment (Stodolska & Yi, 2003). A study by Stodolska and Alexandris (2002) on the role of recreational sport participation in the assimilation and retention of ethnic identity among immigrants from Korea, Mexico, and Poland detected yet another culture-determined constraint of leisure. They attributed the relatively low participation of middle-class Koreans in active leisure pursuits to a stereotype pervasive in the Korean culture that associates physical strength and interest in sports with the lack of intellectual capabilities. According to traditional Korean beliefs, people are expected to value their minds more than their bodies, adults should be composed and well-mannered, and any physical pursuits should be reserved for men (Kim, 1999). Such values can act as interpersonal (or perhaps intrapersonal) constraints, preventing those who desire to participate in sports from engaging in their favorite leisure pursuits (Crawford, Jackson & Godbey, 1991).

A series of studies conducted on the leisure and recreational behavior of South Asians, and Muslims in particular, provided an interesting picture of culture-determined constraints. According to Walseth and Fasting (2003), the main barriers to recreational sport participation of women imposed by Islam are related to their use of the veil, gender segregation, the concept of "excitement," and the power relationship between men and women. In their study on the influence of Islam on the recreational sport participation of women they noted that the requirement of wearing a veil called *hijab* (and sometimes a full body and face covering of *nikab*) made women's participation in any active recreation pursuits "almost impossible." Women wearing more traditional head and body coverings (*nikabs* or *krimars*) were compelled to participate in active recreation in the confines of their homes or in sex-segregated "training studios." Moreover, Walseth and Fasting (2003) observed the fact that Islam prohibited women from making movements that could be considered sexually suggestive, in the presence of men, severely constrained their sport participation. Not only aerobic activities, but also jogging and running were found by some to be unacceptable according to their religious doctrine. In general, most of the barriers detected in this study were related to Islam's view of women's sexuality. According to Islam, women are viewed as less moral, more seductive, and more prone to temptations as compared to men. Thus, participation in physically active recreation by women

can easily create *fitna* (chaos and temptation) in the society. In Islamic cultures, women are also perceived to be less capable of making decisions, including deciding about their own leisure activities, thus legitimizing men's control over their lives. Walseth and Fasting (2003) also observed different interpretations of Islam produce different constraints on leisure. For women who adhered to more "modern" interpretation of Islam, primary constraints were related to patriarchy (i.e., the prominent role of men in Muslim families; men were to decide whether women should be allowed to participate in certain leisure activities). Those women who followed more traditional interpretations of Islam were stricter in their definitions of "excitement" and more constrained by their strict dress codes.

Similarly, Stodolska and Livengood (2003) focused on the effects of Islam on the leisure behavior of Muslim immigrants. Their findings indicated Muslims experienced constraints related to their inability to spend time in mixed-gender company, to date, to attend parties, to eat certain foods, and to drink alcohol. Such restrictions affected their social interactions with mainstream Americans and leisure activities, such as family BBQs, proms, and after-work outings. Muslim women were not allowed to travel without a male escort for long distances and their specific dress requirements affected their participation in active leisure pursuits. It has to be stressed, however, that many women indicated these restrictions imposed by their faith were not perceived by them as constraints per se, but rather as understandable requirements of their religious doctrine. Many of them learned how to maximize their leisure participation and enjoinment of leisure by devising certain negotiation techniques, such as ordering alternative foods in mainstream restaurants, wearing inventive clothing that facilitated their sport participation, and organizing single-sex parties. Obstacles to their leisure participation were also addressed by local mosques that rented recreation facilities, such as pools, to allow Muslim women to participate in isolation from male onlookers.

Results of the study by Tirone (1999, 2000) on second-generation South Asian youth in Atlantic Canada also indicated minority teenagers experienced severe constraints to their sport and leisure participation. Lack of sensitivity on the part of coaches to the fact that Muslim students are required to fast during the month of Ramadan led some teenagers to withdraw from sporting competitions. Moreover, religion prevented Muslim girls from wearing shorts required during physical education classes. Preliminary results of a longitudinal study conducted on the same population suggested the leisure of South Asian teens was also constrained by the pressures from parents to remain at home and to conform to traditional cultural practices (S. Tirone, personal communication, February 16, 2003). Students of other religious faiths had more freedom to pursue their favorite activities and their families seemed to be more tolerant of their desire to make decisions regarding friends and marriage partners.

Research on leisure constraints among South Asian youth conducted in the United Kingdom during 1980s confirmed South Asian girls were severely constrained in their leisure pursuits by lack of parental approval for out-of-home activities and for sports participation in particular, strict dress codes, inadequate availability of single-sex facilities, and by their religious beliefs (Carrington, Chievers & Williams, 1987; Glyptis, 1985; Taylor & Hegarty, 1985). At the same time, boys, who enjoyed more freedom from such restrictions, were more likely to experience racial discrimination that interfered with their leisure pursuits (Carrington et al., 1987).

Discrimination

Regardless of their ethnic background, race-related characteristics, immigrant status, or generational tenure, members of many minority groups are subjected to various forms of mistreatment in leisure settings. While some research suggests members of White ethnic groups experience different forms of discrimination or discrimination of different intensity than members of "visible" ethnic or racial minorities (Driedger & Mezoff, 1981; Stodolska & Jackson, 1998), the constraining effects of discrimination on leisure behavior are equally serious and troubling. Discrimination, or even the expectation of discrimination, has been shown to alter the leisure behavior of ethnic minorities (both in terms of activities chosen and the location and composition of the group), impose additional constraints on participation, and diminish the satisfaction derived from leisure. Severe forms of discrimination are likely to involve physical violence and may lead to the displacement of some groups and their nonuse of recreation resources (Gobster, 2002). So far, while the majority of research on discrimination in leisure studies has focused on experiences of African Americans and to some extent Hispanic Americans, studies on discrimination against ethnic Whites have been conspicuously rare.

Discrimination against ethnic groups is not a new phenomenon. In fact, Asian Americans faced severe discrimination even 150 years ago, during their first years of settlement in America. For instance, legislation enacted in 1790 excluded Asians and other non-White immigrants from obtaining U.S. citizenship by limiting

citizen rights to "free Whites." This racial requirement for citizenship formed the basis for excluding non-Whites from many activities and rights. Until Asian immigrants became eligible for U.S. citizenship in 1952, some states could legally keep them from owning land or businesses, attending school with White students, or living in White neighborhoods (Pollard & O'Hare, 1999). Discrimination against Mexican Americans also has a long history, and even today manifests itself in violent attacks, killings, denial of jobs, and exclusion from recreational activities and recreational spaces (Chavez 1991, 1993; Gobster, 2002). Similarly, White ethnics, such as Italians, Irish, Jews, or Eastern Europeans have long endured exclusion and resentment on the part of the Anglo Saxon mainstream in many areas of life, including sports and recreation (Harney, 1985; Mormino, 1982; Wilcox, 1994).

After African Americans, experiences with discrimination in leisure settings among Latinos have been most often researched in our field. In their 1995 study, Floyd and Gramann tested how cultural assimilation, primary structural assimilation, and socioeconomic assimilation among Mexican Americans affected their perception of discrimination in recreational settings. Their results suggested less assimilated Mexican Americans were more inclined to report discrimination in leisure, while those with higher education levels were less likely to report experiencing encounters with racism. Floyd and Gramann concluded the perception of ethnic-based discrimination is greater among those who exhibit low socioeconomic mobility and acculturation. In the study of visitor's perception of crowding and discrimination in California's national forests Chavez (1991, 1993) reported almost a third of all Hispanic and Mexican Americans perceived themselves as having been victimized by an act of discrimination. Racist acts were perpetrated both by other forest visitors and by law enforcement officers. In Gobster's (2002) study, only more African Americans reported discrimination in Chicago's Lincoln Park than Latinos and Asians. Discrimination was reported to originate from other users, police, and staff. The discriminatory acts encountered in this park setting included verbal harassment, physical gestures or assaults, and "nonverbal messages resulting in a feeling of discomfort" (p. 152). Recreationists also complained about being treated unequally by the police and unequal distribution of facilities in predominantly White versus predominantly minority areas of the park. Similarly, results of the study on recreation preferences of ethnic minority students in Chicago by Blahna and Black (1993) indicated racism was an important barrier to park and forest visitation, particularly for African Americans and Hispanics. Racism was identified as the third most common barrier to recreation among Hispanic Americans. Blahna and Black (1993) identified six forms of racism that restricted park use of minorities:

1. on-site experiences of racism from other recreationists.

2. on-site experiences of racism from professional staff.

3. differential upkeep and management of sites.

4. fear of expected or potential racism.

5. socialization resulting from historical racism.

6. social effects of past economic discrimination.

In a study on the influences of racism on the outdoor recreation opportunities and experiences of Native Americans conducted as a follow-up to Blahna and Black's (1993) project, McDonald and McAvoy (1997) confirmed the existence of five previously identified types of racism. In particular, Native Americans experienced on-site discrimination from both fellow recreationists and professional staff. People recounted frequent stares and rude comments, as well as being singled out, checked, and hassled by the state DNR staff. Experiences with racism forced Native Americans to look for secluded places, to participate in recreation on the reservation, to recreate only with other members of their family and Native American friends, and to avoid contact with non-Native park users.

Stodolska and Jackson (1998) also determined discrimination to be an important constraining factor that affected White ethnic immigrants' participation in and enjoyment of leisure activities. They found patterns of discrimination experienced by White ethnic groups differed from those of well-established visible minorities both in terms of the types of discriminatory treatment and the locations where such treatment took place. In particular, White ethnic groups experienced markedly less discrimination in leisure settings than they did at work, at school, or in some public places. This finding was attributed to difficulties associated with identifying members of White ethnic groups in leisure, as well as the lesser importance of language skills in informal situations. While ethnic jokes, language ridicule, and name calling were the most often reported forms of discrimination; serious discriminatory actions such as physical attacks and vandalism were rare. Similar findings were obtained by Driedger and Mezoff (1981), who observed ethnic Whites were discriminated against less frequently than members of visible minorities and discriminatory acts perpetrated against Whites usually did not involve violence.

Tirone's (1999, 2000) study of South Asians provided many examples of racism endured by adolescents in schools, community recreation programs, YMCAs, summer camps, and competitive sport activities. Racist acts experienced by study participants included name calling, taunting, teasing, and cruel racist remarks related to their distinct skin color, clothing, hair styles, and head covering. While most serious and violent discriminatory attacks were perpetrated against Sikh boys, Muslim girls were often ridiculed and verbally abused by their peers. Experiences with discrimination made some of the younger students feel ashamed of their culture, reject their traditions, and even move into different areas. Others felt the need to excel in their activities, including sports, to "prove" they could be better than their White counterparts.

In their study on the effects of discrimination and constraints negotiation on the leisure behavior of American Muslims in post-September 11 America, Livengood and Stodolska (in press) discovered most of the discrimination experienced by Muslim Americans was of a nonviolent nature, and included bad looks, verbal abuse, and social isolation. The discrimination affected the leisure of Muslim immigrants directly through experiences in leisure-related settings and while engaged in leisure activities by restricting the range of available leisure options and coparticipants, by affecting their willingness to participate in leisure activities, and by restricting their freedom of movement, travel, timing, and location of activities. American Muslims have been found to employ certain negotiation strategies to adapt to their new environment, such as being vigilant and conscious about their surroundings, walking in groups, blending in, restricting travel, or modifying travel patterns.

Livengood and Stodolska's study (in press) confirmed not only *actual* discrimination, but also the *expectation* of discrimination severely constrained the recreation of minorities. Blahna and Black (1993), who indicated the expectation of racism and general fear or discomfort due to potential discrimination may have acted as constraints on leisure, obtained similar findings. They argued the expectation of discrimination might not necessarily be based on actual experiences with negative treatment, but may have its roots in rumors, myths, experiences of friends, media accounts, or other secondary sources of information. Young Sikhs in Tirone's (1999, 2000) study even mentioned minorities forming gangs, as they claimed, to provide protection for those Sikh teens harassed for wearing turbans. Cainkar's (1999) study of an Arab ethnic community in Chicago suggested the majority of Arab immigrants perceived their neighborhoods as unsafe and feared harassment on the part of the general public and the local police. Such perceptions constrained the out-of-home activities of minority members and of minority women in particular and were partly blamed for their sedentary lifestyles.

It needs to be stressed that ethnically based conflict in recreational spaces and during recreational activities is not limited to the "top-down" discrimination in which White recreationists, park operators, or law enforcement officers discriminate against ethnic minority members. Instances where conflict in leisure occurs *between* members of different minority groups and *within* ethnic populations are beginning to be documented. For instance, Chavez (1991, 1993) indicated part of the mistreatment received by Hispanic recreationists in California's national forests originated from other Hispanics. Juniu (2000) noted the resentment of middle class Latinos toward their countrymen of lower socioeconomic class. Similarly, Stodolska and Yi (2003) recorded negative feelings of middle class Polish teenagers toward their less assimilated counterparts. Interethnic animosities are probably even more common than conflicts within ethnic groups. Stodolska and Yi's (2003) study reported after-school fights between Mexican American and African American students. Tirone (1999, 2000) recorded serious animosities between Indian and Pakistani immigrants in Eastern Canada that resulted in exclusion, fights, and cancellation of recreational events. Reports also indicated ethnic gathering places in parks were clearly delineated, and some of the Chicago parks witnessed violent confrontations over the use of recreational space between Puerto Ricans, Mexicans, Whites, and African Americans (Gobster, 2002).

Feelings of resentment can be directed not only at specific ethnic minority groups, but also at immigrants in general. In fact, it has been asserted that while American and British sociologists are more inclined to embrace the concept of racism, French and German schools recognize the differences between racism and xenophobia (Banton, 1996). In particular, in Germany the term *Rassismus* has been so closely associated with the Nazi era many felt compelled to distinguish the "old racism" from the more contemporary hostility toward foreigners. While *racism* has been described as actions by which persons assigned to another group are kept at a distance because they are considered racially inferior, *xenophobia* denotes actions or feelings by which people are kept at a distance because they are considered different (Banton, 1996). The recent worldwide resurgence of militant nationalism, neo-Nazi movements, and fundamentalist intolerance has put the issues of violence and xenophobia at the center of social science research and theory (McLaughlin, 1996). Research on those issues has been particularly salient in the European context in light of far-right and recent anti-Semitic movements in countries such as Austria, France, and Germany, and the unification policies whose aim, as some people claim, is the creation of pan-European identity (Shore, 1993). These themes, however, are yet to find their way into the mainstream of leisure research.

Constraints of Immigrants

Constraints Experienced by Immigrants

While the leisure behavior of ethnic minority members is likely to be constrained by their distinct cultural traits, marginal position in the society, or experiences of discrimination, immigrants' leisure also can be affected by additional factors related to their resettlement patterns. Immigration is associated with profound changes in an individual's life—changes that can only be compared with major lifestage transitions, such as marriage, birth of the first child, or retirement (see Jackson, this volume). The initial transitional shock, imperfect language skills, separation from family and friends, need to regain economic stability, and lack of familiarity with basic institutions of the host country may often lead to very dramatic changes in a person's lifestyle. Leisure is not immune to these changes—the new environment may open some opportunities for certain leisure activities and at the same time create constraints on others. It can be argued immigrants are likely to experience significantly more constraints than native born members of the same ethnic group, because immigration-related constraints will become superimposed on those related to ethnic origin and culture.

Evidence suggests immigrants experience certain unique types of constraints related both to their minority status and to the postarrival adaptation processes they undergo. These constraints include language difficulties, being unfamiliar with the new ways of life in the host country, and social isolation (Carrington et al., 1987; Rublee & Shaw, 1991; Stodolska, 1998; Tirone & Shaw, 1997; Yu & Berryman, 1996). Besides immigration-specific constraints, immigrants may experience common types of constraints, such as lack of time and lack of money, differently from their mainstream counterparts. For instance, in her 1999 study of recent immigrants from Latin America, Juniu reported their leisure was severely constrained by the lack of time, being overworked, family responsibilities, and general changes in their life. Lack of time appeared to be a particularly salient barrier for immigrants not only in Juniu's study, but also in other research on the leisure of immigrant populations (Stodolska & Yi, 2003; Tsai & Coleman, 1999). A common reason behind immigration is the desire to improve one's standards of living and to secure a stable future for one's children. Such a strong emphasis on economic success and providing their children with a good education makes most recent immigrants work long hours and sacrifice the leisure sphere of their lives, at least during the initial three- to four-year establishment period. Only after the first several years have passed and immigrants obtain stable employment and desired living conditions do they begin to reestablish their leisure lives (Stodolska & Alexandris, 2002).

Establishment struggles of immigrants are also associated with severe monetary constraints. Because many newcomers have to build their careers anew, take the least desirable employment available, and make additional purchases associated with establishment in the new place, discretionary income available for leisure is often extremely limited. Moreover, many immigrants are known to channel monetary remittances to their families still living in their home countries, which puts an additional burden on their meager financial resources. The finding that time and money are the most salient constraints among recent immigrants has been supported by the results obtained by Stodolska (1998, 2000), Stodolska and Jackson (1998), Stodolska and Yi (2003), Tirone and Pedlar (2000), Tirone and Shaw (1997), and Tsai and Coleman (1999). It is interesting to note these two constraints are also the most often reported barriers among the general population. The new environment after settlement, however, makes their presence even more burdensome for recent immigrants. Stodolska and Alexandris (2002) also pointed out while analyzing constraints of recent immigrants one should not discount the effects of environmental factors that influence their life. While more mobile ethnic minority members often settle in middle-class American communities, recent immigrants are still overrepresented in low-income, inner-city ethnic enclaves. The leisure participation of immigrants residing in ethnically enclosed communities is significantly restricted by the lack of facilities, open spaces, quality natural environment, and safety problems.

Lack of English skills is another powerful factor limiting the leisure pursuits of recent immigrants. As Juniu (1999, 2000) reported, lack of language proficiency prevented Latino immigrants from establishing social interactions with mainstream Americans and individuals from other ethnic groups. Rublee and Shaw (1991), who studied Latin American refugee women in Atlantic Canada, also stressed the negative impact of lack of language skills on the leisure lives of recent immigrants. They suggested the lack of community involvement due to language difficulties and new societal norms, combined with the reduced opportunity for socialization in church and neighborhood settings, made the life of refugee women more home-oriented, passive, and focused on child-care-related activities.

Postarrival social isolation and lack of established social networks have also been identified as constraints detrimental to the leisure pursuits of recent immigrants (Rublee & Shaw, 1991; Stodolska, 1998, 2000). Interpersonal factors, including inability to find leisure coparticipants, were also salient in the 1999 study of Chinese immigrants to Australia conducted by Tsai and Coleman. Stodolska's (2000) findings suggested many immigrants emphasize the importance of shattered social networks as a factor limiting their leisure participation following immigration. Given that newcomers get separated from most of their relatives and childhood friends, certain types of leisure, such as socializing, may become severely constrained. Severe postarrival depression caused by the lack of language skills, fear of the new environment, and lack of social networks induced immigrants in Stodolska's study to abandon many of their old pastimes, and at the same time prevented them from acquiring new ones. Similarly, Stodolska and Yi (2003) observed broken social networks, more formal social interactions, and more structured leisure environment in the United States restricted the leisure activities of Mexican and Polish teenagers. Rublee and Shaw (1991) also identified lack of overall orientation to Canadian everyday life and environmental differences as having a particularly detrimental effect on the leisure of Latin American refugee women. Stodolska (2000) also suggested immigration is associated with a need to adapt to a different social and physical environment in the new country. Certain leisure activities are no longer available in the country of settlement, while others become too expensive or too time-consuming, or no longer fit the new lifestyles of immigrants.

It has to be noted while immigration does create new constraints on leisure, it may also eliminate constraints on certain activities, particularly if these activities were highly constrained in the home country (Stodolska, 2000). For instance, in Stodolska's (2000) and Stodolska and Alexandris's (2002) studies, middle-class individuals, particularly those who engaged in recreational sports in their former countries or those who desired to participate but were prevented from participation by certain constraining factors, increased their sport participation after having passed through the strenuous period of initial adaptation. While in Stodolska and Alexandris's

(2002) study Korean immigrants visibly increased their participation in golf and tennis—activities severely constrained by exceptionally high prices in Korea—middle-class Poles in Stodolska's (2000) study took on physically active leisure constrained by interpersonal factors in their former country.

Factors Affecting Constraints of Immigrants

While immigrants of different backgrounds are likely to share some experiences, they differ significantly in terms of many important "modes of incorporation" (Portes & Borocz, 1989; Portes & Zhou, 1993). These differences can have a significant effect on the types and the intensity of constraints on leisure they experience.

The national origin of immigrants is probably the most obvious determinant of the constraints on leisure they experience. One may anticipate newcomers from areas relatively similar to the host country in terms of culture and particularly in terms of language (e.g., England or Ireland) will experience a lesser degree of immigration-related constraints than their counterparts from countries more culturally distant (e.g., India, China, or Korea).

Another important characteristic likely to affect the type and level of constraints experienced by immigrants is the composition of the emigration party and the level of support immigrants receive from the ethnic community in their place of settlement. Immigrants who arrive alone and who settle in areas with a very low density of their respective ethnic group face barriers on leisure markedly different from those who emigrate with extended families and who can benefit from help of their more established counterparts.

The socioeconomic status of immigrants, including their educational endowment, personal wealth, age at arrival, and compatibility of qualifications, plays a significant role in determining the life of immigrants after their settlement in the host country, including their constraints on leisure activities (Stodolska, 1998; Stodolska & Alexandris, 2002). Given the importance of socioeconomic factors, it is likely constraints on leisure will differ for members of different immigration waves from the same country. Changes in the numbers of emigrants from a given country, as well as in their preferred final destinations, closely associate with the economic and political situation in both the home and host countries, the immigration policy of the host country, and certain major global or regional events. Consequently, profound differences in terms of the socioeconomic profile are often present between various immigration waves (Heydenkorn, 1990; Li, 1987). For instance, Chinese immigrants who came to Canada in the late 19th century and found employment in coal mines or in railroad construction faced markedly different problems than the highly educated, typically young, independent Chinese immigrants of today (Li, 1987; Yu, 1987). Similarly, farmers from Eastern Europe who settled in the United States and Canada at the end of the 19th and in the early 20th century faced different problems than Eastern Europeans who arrived from Displaced Persons camps following World War II, or those who immigrated in the 1960s and the 1980s escaping political persecution in their home countries (Charon, 1989; Heydenkorn, 1990).

Constraints on leisure experienced by immigrants also depend on the immigration policy of the host country at the time of their arrival (e.g., level of government support), as well as on other factors, such as

- place of settlement (e.g., regional differences).

- prevailing societal attitudes.

- level of tolerance of the local population and their willingness to accept or to assimilate the newcomers.

- economic situation, including job market at the time of immigration.

- size of immigrant community.

Personal preferences and decisions regarding the desired speed and degree of integration into the mainstream society and the intensity of interactions with the respective ethnic group also play an important role in immigrants' everyday life, including leisure choices and constraints on leisure. Immigrants who make a conscious choice to learn the mainstream language, to acquire mainstream customs, and to quickly assimilate to the new way of life are likely to face different barriers than those who choose to live within the bounds of their ethnic community.

Evidence suggests constraints experienced by immigrants are closely linked to their preferences and ultimately to the type of activities that they engage in. First, immigrants face certain constraints on participation in mainstream activities, including being unfamiliar with existing opportunities, lack of time, lack of money, and the fact that some mainstream forms of leisure are not compatible with their cultural norms (Carrington et al., 1987; Glyptis, 1985; Matejko & Matejko, 1974; Stodolska, 1998). Moreover, as suggested by Philip (1999), mainstream Americans may consider certain activities inappropriate for minorities, which may lead to discrimination against immigrants who fail to play by the rules (Philip, 1999; Stodolska, 1998; Stodolska & Jackson, 1998). Second, immigrants who want to take part in certain traditional ethnic activities may face especially strong constraints on their preferred leisure. Lack of ethnic clubs and organizations, lack of facilities and equipment, shattered social networks, lack of other participants of the same ethnic background, and expectation of discrimination often act as effective barriers that prevent immigrants from engaging in their chosen ethnic pastimes (Carrington et al., 1987; Heydenkorn, 1990).

The leisure of immigrants, including constraints on leisure they experience, is likely to be affected by their status of permanent immigrants as opposed to temporary migrants. While this factor has been largely overlooked in leisure research, it is quite plausible significant differences in leisure constraints will exist between temporary migrants who relocate to the host country for short periods in search of employment and those who choose to make it their permanent home.

Conclusions

Despite growing interest in issues of minority populations in recent years, research on the leisure constraints of ethnic minorities and immigrants is still underdeveloped. Not only is the volume of literature on the subject modest, but also the existing research is troubled by methodological problems and lack of a strong connection to the general theory of constraints and ethnic change. The discontinuance between the broader field of constraints research and its application to the study of ethnic (and racial) minorities is particularly striking. The majority of research that tackles issues of constraints among ethnic groups focused on identifying barriers experienced by specific groups of minorities (e.g., women, Muslims, refuges, immigrants) and failed to move beyond its descriptive phase. Moreover, past research suffered from the lack of attention given to variability within specific ethnic populations and treated them as monoliths suitable for convenient comparisons with the "White mainstream." Leisure researchers have only recently begun to acknowledge intragroup heterogeneity among recreationists (Gobster, 2002). Lack of attention to specific modes of incorporation, such as place of settlement, prevailing societal attitudes, level of tolerance of the local population, and size of immigrant community, among others, constitutes a significant drawback of the existing research.

It is likely, however, that given the increased importance of minority groups in the American and Canadian societies, research on determinants of their leisure behavior will expand in the near future. Several issues deserve more in-depth attention from leisure researchers. In particular, the issue of discrimination acting as a constraint on leisure is not well-understood. It would be worthwhile to explore how acts of discrimination and the expectation of discrimination affect the leisure choices of visible minorities and ethnic Whites and the implications of discrimination for their leisure behavior. Second, the relationship between constraints and adaptation patterns of minorities needs to be tackled. While theories developed in the fields of sociology and ethnic and migration studies have made enormous strides in modeling the postimmigration adaptation patterns of newcomers, their effect on leisure is still largely unknown. Also, the evolution of constraints among different generations of minorities is a topic that requires more attention on the part of leisure researchers.

The share of ethnic minorities in the social and economic life of the United States and Canada has been steadily growing and is likely to continue to do so in the decades to come. In fact, according to the most recent Census projections, minorities will soon surpass the White population of the United States, thus redefining the notions of the "mainstream" and "standard" forms of behavior, including people's leisure. Consequently, it is reasonable to anticipate the focus on leisure behavior of ethnic minorities, and their constraints in particular, is going to gain importance and prominence in the field of leisure research.

References

Alba, R. and Nee, V. (1997). Rethinking assimilation theory for a new era of immigration. *International Migration Review, 31,* 826–874.

Alvirez, D. and Bean, F. D. (1981). The Mexican American family. In C. H. Mindel and R. W. Habenstein (Eds.), *Ethnic families in America.* New York, NY: Elsevier.

Anderson, A. B. and Frideres, J. S. (1981). *Ethnicity in Canada: Theoretical Perspectives.* Toronto, Ontario, Canada: Butterworths.

Banton, M. (1996). The cultural determinants of xenophobia. *Anthropology Today, 12,* 8–12.

Barth, F. (1998). *Ethnic groups and boundaries.* Prospect Heights, IL: Waveland Press.

Bass, J. M., Ewert, A., and Chavez, D. J. (1993). Influence of ethnicity on recreation and natural environment use patterns: Managing recreation sites for ethnic and racial diversity. *Environmental Management, 17,* 523–529.

Blahna, D. and Black, K. (1993). Racism: A concern for recreation resource managers. In P. Gobster (Ed.), *Managing urban and high use recreation settings: Selected papers from the 4th North American Symposium on Society and Natural Resource Management* (GTR NC-163; pp. 111–118). St. Paul, MN: USDA Forest Service.

Cainkar, L. (1999). The deteriorating ethnic safety net among Arab immigrants in Chicago. In M. W. Suleiman (Ed.), *Arabs in America building a new future* (pp. 192–206). Philadelphia, PA: Temple University Press.

Camarota, S. A. (2001). *The slowing progress of immigrants: An examination of income, home ownership, and citizenship, 1970–2000.* Report prepared for the Center for Immigration Studies. Retrieved from http://www.cis.org/articles/2001/back401.html

Cannon, L. W., Higginbotham, E., and Leung, M. L. A. (1991). Race and class bias in qualitative research on women. In M. M. Fonow and J. A. Cook (Eds.), *Beyond methodology: Feminist scholarship as lived research* (pp. 107–118). Bloomington, IN: Indiana Press.

Carr, D. S. and Williams, D. R. (1993a). Understanding the role of ethnicity in outdoor recreate on experiences. *Journal of Leisure Research, 25,* 22–38.

Carr, D. S. and Williams, D. R. (1993b). Understanding diverse recreationists: Beyond quantitative analysis. In P. Gobster (Ed.), *Managing urban and high use recreation settings: Selected papers from the 4th North American Symposium on Society and Natural Resource Management* (GTR NC-163; pp. 101–106). St. Paul, MN: USDA Forest Service.

Carrington, B., Chievers, T., and Williams, T. (1987). Gender, leisure and sport: A case study of young people of South Asian descent. *Leisure Studies, 6,* 265–279.

Charon, M. (1989). *Words apart: New immigrant voices.* Dunvegan, Ontario, Canada: Cormorant Books.

Chavez, D. J. (1991). Crowding and discrimination: Unwelcome guests in wildland recreation. *Proceedings of the 1991 Society of American Foresters National Convention* (pp. 425–430), San Francisco, CA.

Chavez, D. J. (1993). *Visitor perceptions of crowding and discrimination at two national forests in southern California* (Research paper PSW-RP-216). Albany, CA: Pacific Southwest Research Station, USDA Forest Service.

Chavez, D. J. (1996). Leisure experiences of Hispanic families. *Proceedings of the 1996 NRPA Leisure Research Symposium* (p. 96). Kansas City, MO.

Cheeseman Day, J. (1996). Population projections of the United States by age, sex, race, and Hispanic origin: 1995 to 2050. *Current Population Reports* (P25-1130). Washington, DC: U.S. Government Printing Office.

Clark, M. (1979). Mexican-American family structure. In G. Henderson (Ed.), *Understanding and counseling ethnic minorities.* Springfield, IL: Charles C. Thomas.

Conzen, K. N., Gerber, D., Morawska, E., Pozzeftta, G. E., and Vecoli, R. J. (1992). The invention of ethnicity: A perspective from the U.S.A. *Journal of American Ethnic History, 12,* 3–41.

Cordell, H. K., Betz, C. J., and Green., G. T. (2002). Recreation and the environment as cultural dimensions in contemporary American Society. *Leisure Sciences, 24,* 13–41.

Crawford, D. W., Jackson, E. L., and Godbey, G. (1991). A hierarchical model of leisure constraints. *Leisure Sciences, 13,* 309–320.

Crespo, C. (2000). Encouraging physical activities in minorities: Eliminating disparities by 2010. *The Physician and Sports Medicine, 28,* 1–12.

Driedger, L. and Mezoff, R. A. (1981). Ethnic prejudice and discrimination in Winnipeg high schools. *Canadian Journal of Sociology, 6,* 1–17.

Floyd, M. F. and Gramann, J. H. (1993). Effects of acculturation and structural assimilation in resource-based recreation: The case of Mexican Americans. *Journal of Leisure Research, 5,* 6–21.

Floyd, M. F. and Gramann, J. H. (1995). Perceptions of discrimination in a recreation context. *Journal of Leisure Research, 27,* 192–199.

Floyd, M. F., Gramann, J. H., and Saenz, R. (1993). Ethnic factors and the use of public outdoor recreation areas: The case of Mexican Americans. *Leisure Sciences, 15*, 83–98.

Gans, H. J. (1992). Second-generation decline: Scenarios for the economic and ethnic futures of the post-1965 American immigrants. *Ethnic and Racial Studies, 15*, 173–192.

Gans, H. J. (1994). Symbolic ethnicity and symbolic religiosity: Towards a comparison of ethnic and religious acculturation. *Ethnic and Racial Studies, 17*, 577–592.

Glick Schiller, N., Basch, L., and Blanc-Szanton, C. (1992). *Towards a transnational perspective on migration: Race, class, ethnicity and nationalism reconsidered.* New York, NY: New York Academy of Science.

Glyptis, S. (1985). Women as a target group: The views of the staff of Action Sport–West Midlands. *Leisure Studies, 4*, 347–362.

Gobster, P. H. (2002). Managing urban parks for a racially and ethnically diverse clientele. *Leisure Sciences, 24*, 143–159.

Gobster, P. H. and Delgado, A. (1993). Ethnicity and recreation use in Chicago's Lincoln Park: In-park user survey findings. In P. Gobster (Ed.), *Managing urban and high use recreation settings: Selected papers from the 4th North American Symposium on Society and Natural Resource Management* (GTR NC-163; pp. 75–81). St. Paul, MN: USDA Forest Service.

Gordon, M. M. (1964). *Assimilation in American life.* New York, NY: Oxford University Press.

Gramann, J. J. (1996). *Ethnicity, race, and outdoor recreation: A review of trends, policy, and research* (Miscellaneous paper R-96-1). Vicksburg, MS: U.S. Army Corp of Engineers.

Gramann, J. H. and Allison, M. T. (1999). Ethnicity, race, and leisure. In E. L. Jackson and T. Burton (Eds.), *Leisure studies: Prospects for the twenty-first century.* State College, PA: Venture Publishing, Inc.

Gramann, J. H., Shaull, S. L., and Saenz, R. (1995, October). *Cultural assimilation and the importance of family-related and nature-related recreation experience among Hispanic Americans in California.* Paper presented at the NRPA Leisure Research Symposium, San Antonio, TX.

Harney, R. F. (1985, Spring/Summer). Homo ludens and ethnicity. *Polyphony: The Bulletin of the Multicultural History Society of Ontario, 7*(1).

Henderson, K. A. (1998). Researching diverse populations, *Journal of Leisure Research, 30*, 157–170.

Henderson, K. A. and Ainsworth, B. E. (1999). *Enablers and constraints to walking for older African American and American Indian women: The cross-cultural activity participation study.* Paper presented at NRPA Leisure Research Symposium, Nashville, TN.

Heydenkorn, B. (1990). *Many faces of Canada. Memoirs of Polish immigrants 1981–1989.* Toronto, Ontario, Canada: Canadian Polish Research Institute.

Hutchison, R. (1987). Ethnicity and urban recreation: Whites, Blacks, and Hispanics in Chicago's public parks. *Journal of Leisure Research, 19*, 205–222.

Hutchison, R. and Fidel, K. (1984). Mexican-American recreation activities: A reply to McMillen. *Journal of Leisure Research, 16*, 344–349.

Hutchinson, J. and Smith, A. D. (Eds.). (1996). *Ethnicity.* Oxford, England: Oxford University Press.

Irwin, P. N., Gartner, W. C., and Phelps, C. C. (1990). Mexican-American/Anglo cultural differences as recreation style determinants. *Leisure Sciences, 12*, 335–348.

Isajiw, W. W. (1990). Ethnic-identity retention. In Isajiw, W.W. (Ed.), *Ethnic identity and equality.* Toronto, Ontario, Canada: University of Toronto Press.

Johnson, C. Y., Bowker, J. M., English, D. B. K., and Worthen, D. (1998). Wildland recreation in the rural South: An examination of marginality and ethnicity theory. *Journal of Leisure Research, 30*, 101–120.

Juniu, S. (1999, October). *Leisure experience of Latino women immigrants.* Paper presented at NRPA Leisure Research Symposium, Nashville, TN.

Juniu, S. (2000). The impact of immigration: Leisure experience in the lives of South American immigrants. *Journal of Leisure Research, 32*, 358–381.

Keefe, S. E. and Padilla, A. M. (1987). *Chicano Ethnicity.* Albuquerque, NM: University of New Mexico Press.

Kim, D-K. (1999, January). *Viewing modern sports world from a political perspective.* Paper presented at the 35th SSPS Seminar, Yeong-San, Korea.

Kivel, B. D. (2005). Examining racism, power, and white hegemony in Stodolska's conditioned attitude model of individual discriminatory behavior. *Leisure Sciences, 27*, 21–27.

Klobus-Edwards, P. C. (1981). Race, residence, and leisure style: Some policy implications. *Leisure Sciences, 4*, 95–112.

LeVine, R. A. and Campbell D. T. (1972). *Ethnocentrism: Theories of conflict, ethnic attitudes, and groups behavior.* New York, NY: John Wiley & Sons, Inc.

Lewin, K. (1948). *Resolving social conflicts: Selected papers on group dynamics.* New York, NY: Harper and Row.

Li, P. S. (1987). The economic cost of racism to Chinese-Canadians. *Canadian Ethnic Studies, XIX*, 102–113.

Livengood, J. S. and Stodolska, M. (2004). The effects of discrimination and constraints negotiation on leisure behavior of American Muslims in the post-

September 11 America. *Journal of Leisure Research, 36*, 183–208.

Martin, P. and Midgley, E. (2003). Immigration: Shaping and reshaping America. *Population Bulletin, 58*, 3–46.

Mâsse, L. C., Ainsworth, B. E., Tortolero, S., Henderson, K. A., Fulton, J., and Mayo, K. (1998). Measuring physical activity in mid-life, older, and minority women: Issues and recommendations from an experts' panel meeting. *Journal of Women's Health, 7*, 1–10.

Massey, D. S. and Denton, N. A. (1993). *American apartheid: Segregation and the making of the underclass.* Cambridge, MA: Harvard University Press.

Matejko, J. and Matejko, A. (1974). Polish Canadians. In B. Heydenkorn (Ed.), *Past and present* (pp. 37–60). Toronto, Ontario, Canada: Canadian–Polish Research Institute.

McDonald, D. and McAvoy, L. (1997). *Racism, recreation and Native Americans.* Paper presented at the 1997 Leisure Research Symposium, Salt Lake City, UT.

McKinnon, J. (2003). The Black population in the United States: March 2002. Current Population Reports. Retrieved from http://www.census.gov/prod/2003pubs/p20-541.pdf

McLaughlin, N. (1996). Nazism, nationalism, and the sociology of emotions: Escape from freedom revisited. *Sociological Theory, 14*, 241–261.

Mormino, G. R. (1982). The playing fields of St. Louis: Italian immigrants and sports, 1925–1941. *Journal of Sport History, 9*, 5–19.

Nagel, C. R. (2002). Geopolitics by another name: Immigration and the politics of assimilation. *Political Geography, 21*, 971–987.

Nagel, J. (1994). Constructing ethnicity: Creating and recreating ethnic identity and culture. *Social Problems, 41*, 152–176.

Omi, M. and Winant, H. (1994). *Racial formation in the United States from the 1960s to the 1990s* (2nd ed). New York, NY: Routledge.

Padilla, A. M. (1980). *Acculturation: Theory, models and some new findings.* Boulder, CO: Westview Press.

Paral, R. (2000). *Suburban immigrant communities. Assessment of key characteristics and needs.* Report prepared for The Fund for Immigrants and Refugees.

Payne, L. L., Mowen, A. J., and Orsega-Smith, E. (2002). An examination of park preferences and behaviors among urban residents: The role of residential location, race, and age. *Leisure Sciences, 24*, 181–198.

Philipp, S. F. (1993). Racial differences in the perceived attractiveness of tourism destinations, interests and cultural resources. *Journal of Leisure Research, 25*, 290–304.

Philipp, S. F. (1999). Are we welcome? African American racial acceptance in leisure activities and the importance given to children's leisure. *Journal of Leisure Research, 31*, 385–403.

Pollard, K. M. and O'Hare, W. P. (1999). America's Racial and Ethnic Minorities. *Population Bulletin, 54*, 1–48.

Portes, A. (1984). The rise of ethnicity: Determinants of ethnic perceptions among Cuban exiles in Miami. *American Sociological Review, 49*, 383–397.

Portes, A. (1997). Immigration theory for a new century: Some problems and opportunities. *International Migration Review, 31*, 799–825.

Portes, A. and Bach, R. L. (1985). *Latin Journey: Cuban and Mexican immigrants in the United States.* Berkeley, CA: University of California Press.

Portes, A. and Borocz, J. (1989). Contemporary immigration: Theoretical perspectives on its determinants and modes of incorporation. *International Migration Review, 23*, 606–630.

Portes, A., Guarnizo, L. E., and Landolt, P. (1999). The study of transnationalism: Pitfalls and promise of an emergent research field. *Ethnic and Racial Studies, 22*, 217–237.

Portes, A. and Jensen, L. (1992). Disproving the enclave hypothesis. *American Sociological Review, 57*, 418–420.

Portes, A. and Zhou, M. (1992). Gaining the upper hand: Economic mobility among immigrant and domestic minorities. *Ethnic and Racial Studies, 15*, 491–522.

Portes, A. and Zhou, M. (1993). The new second generation: Segmented assimilation and its variants. *Annals AAPSS, 530*, 74–82.

Ramirez, R. B. and de la Cruz, G. P. (2003). The Hispanic population in the United Status: Population characteristics. Current Population Reports. Retrieved from http://www.census.gov/prod/2003pubs/p20-545.pdf

Reeves, T. and Bennett, C. (2003). The Asian and Pacific Islander population in the United States: March 2002. Current Population Reports. Retrieved from http://www.census.gov/prod/2003pubs/p20-540.pdf

Rehman, L. A. (2002). Recognizing the significance of culture and ethnicity: Exploring hidden assumptions of homogeneity. *Leisure Sciences, 24*, 43–57.

Riccio, B. (2001). From 'ethnic group' to 'transnational community'? Senegalese migrants' ambivalent experiences and multiple trajectories. *Journal of Ethnic and Migration Studies, 27*, 583–599.

Rublee, C. and Shaw, S.M. (1991). Constraints on the leisure and community participation of immigrant women: Implications for social integration. *Loisir et Sociètè, 14*, 133–150.

Sasidharan, V. (2002). Special issue introduction: Understanding recreation and the environment within the context of culture. *Leisure Sciences, 24*, 1–11.

Shaull, S. L. and Gramann, J. H. (1998). The effect of cultural assimilation on the importance of family-related and nature-related recreation among Hispanic Americans. *Journal of Leisure Research, 30,* 47–63.

Shore, C. (1993). Inventing the 'people's Europe': Critical approaches to European community 'cultural policy.' *Man, 28,* 779–800.

Statistics Canada (2003). Immigrant population by place of birth and period of immigration. Retrieved March 9, 2004, from http://www.statcan.ca

Stodolska, M. (1998). Assimilation and leisure constraints: Dynamics of constraints on leisure in immigrant populations. *Journal of Leisure Research, 30,* 521–551.

Stodolska, M. (2000). Changes in leisure participation patterns after immigration. *Leisure Sciences, 22,* 39–63.

Stodolska, M. (2005). A conditioned attitude model of individual discriminatory behavior—A rejoinder. *Leisure Sciences, 27,* 49–57.

Stodolska, M. and Alexandris, K. (2002, October). *The role of recreational sport in the assimilation process and in the retention of ethnic identity among immigrants.* Paper presented at the 2002 NRPA Leisure Research Symposium, Tampa, FL.

Stodolska, M. and Jackson, E. L. (1998). Discrimination in leisure and work experienced by a white ethnic minority group. *Journal of Leisure Research, 30,* 23–46.

Stodolska, M. and Livengood, J. S. (2003, October). *The effects of Islam on leisure behavior and the use of community recreation resources by American Muslim immigrants.* Paper presented at the NRPA Leisure Research Symposium, St. Louis, MO.

Stodolska, M. and Yi, J. (2003). Impacts of immigration on ethnic identity and leisure behavior of adolescent immigrants from Korea, Mexico and Poland. *Journal of Leisure Research, 35,* 49–79.

Taylor, D. (1992). *Identity in ethnic leisure pursuits.* San Francisco, CA: Mellan Research University Press.

Taylor, M. J. and Hegarty, S. (1985). The best of both worlds...? A review of research into the education of pupils of South Asian origin. Windsor, England: NFER-Nelson.

Therrien, M. and Ramirez, R. R. (2000). The Hispanic population in the United States: March 2000 (P20-535). Washington, DC: U.S. Census Bureau. Retrieved from http://www.census.gov/population/www/socdemo/hispanic/ho00.html

Tinsley, H. E. A., Tinsley, D. J., and Croskeys, C. E., (2002). Park usage, social milieu, and psychological benefits of park use reported by older urban park users from four ethnic groups. *Leisure Sciences, 24,* 199–218.

Tirone, S. (1999). *Racism, indifference and the leisure experiences of South Asian Canadian teens.* Paper presented at the 1999 CCLR 9 Conference at Acadia University, Wolfville, Nova Scotia, Canada.

Tirone, S. (2000). Racism, indifference and the leisure experiences of South Asian Canadian teens. *Leisure: The Journal of the Canadian Association of Leisure Studies, 24*(2).

Tirone, S. and Pedlar, A. (2000). Understanding the leisure experiences of a minority ethnic group; South Asian teens and young adults in Canada. *Loisir et Sociètè, 23,* 145–169.

Tirone, S. and Shaw, S. M. (1997). At the center of their lives: Indo Canadian women, their families and leisure. *Journal of Leisure Research, 29,* 225–244.

Tsai, E. H. and Coleman, D. J. (1999). Leisure constraints of Chinese immigrants: An exploratory study. *Loisir et Sociètè 22,* 243–264.

U.S. Census Bureau. (2000). Current Population Survey, March 2000, Ethnic and Hispanic statistics branch, population division. Internet Release Date: March 6, 2001.

U.S. Census Bureau. (2003). Table 1: United States—Race and Hispanic origin, 1790 to 1990. Retrieved from http://www.census.gov/population/documentation/twps0056

Virden, R. J. and Walker, G. J. (1999). Ethnic/racial and gender variations among meanings given to, and preferences for, the natural environment. *Leisure Sciences, 21,* 219–239.

Walseth, K. and Fasting, K. (2003). Islam's view on physical activity and sport. *International Review for the Sociology of Sport, 38,* 45–60.

Warner, W. L. and Srole, L. (1945). *The social systems of American ethnic groups.* New Haven, CT: Yale University Press.

Washburne, R. F. (1978). Black under participation in wildland recreation: alternative explanations. *Leisure Sciences, 1,* 175–189.

Waters, M. C. (1994). Ethnic and racial identities of second-generation black immigrants in New York City. *International Migration Review, 28,* 795–820.

West, P. C. (1989). Urban region parks and black minorities: subculture, marginality, and interracial relations in park use in the Detroit metropolitan area, *Leisure Sciences, 11,* 11–28.

Wilcox, R. (1994). The shamrock and the eagle: Irish Americans and sport in the nineteenth century. In G. Eisen and D. Wiggings (Eds.), *Ethnicity and sport in North American history* (pp. 55–75). London, England: Greenwood Press.

Wiley, N. F. (1967). The ethnic mobility trap and stratification theory. *Social Problems, 15*, 147–159.

Wilson, K. L. and Portes, A. (1980). Immigrant enclaves: An analysis of the labor market experiences of Cubans in Miami. *American Journal of Sociology, 86*, 295–319.

Woodard, M. D. (1988). Class, regionality, and leisure among urban black Americans: The post-civil rights era. *Journal of Leisure Research, 20*, 87–105.

Yu, M. (1987). Human rights, discrimination, and coping behavior of the Chinese in Canada. *Canadian Ethnic Studies, XIX*, 114–124.

Yu, P. and Berryman, D. L. (1996). The relationship among self-esteem, acculturation, and recreation participation of recently arrived Chinese immigrant adolescents. *Journal of Leisure Research, 28*, 251–273.

Chapter 5

A Developmental Approach to Understanding Constraints to Adolescent Leisure

Linda L. Caldwell (The Pennsylvania State University) and Cheryl K. Baldwin (Aurora University)

We thank Dr. Rainer Silbereisen and Dr. Reed Larson for their comments and support of our earlier draft.

Why is it important to examine leisure constraints among adolescents? Meaningful leisure participation is one way adolescents effectively engage with their environments. Certainly among industrialized or developed nations, if not all nations, leisure is an important developmental context for youth and adolescents (e.g., Kleiber, 1999; Larson, 2000). The experience of leisure is critical to one's being and humanity, and while empirical evidence is lacking, leisure participation may also contribute to socioemotional and civic competence and societal well-being (Canadian Policy Research Networks/Canadian Council on Social Development, 2001). Thus, the extent to which leisure is constrained on an ongoing, everyday basis is problematic to adolescents' personal development and well-being, as well as to future societal and civic competence. At a less problematic level, leisure that is occasionally constrained, a common occurrence, is also worthy of discussion in that important human experiences are denied.

Research on adolescence, leisure, and constraints is necessarily intertwined with the developmental issues and contexts of the age. Lifespan frameworks and developmental concerns have helped researchers to understand factors that influence leisure participation and to complement and extend current models of leisure constraints. Building on that work, this chapter will use contemporary developmental models to theoretically frame and examine how developmental processes and issues underlie and intersect with constraints to adolescent leisure behavior and experience.

The goals of this chapter are to introduce and to discuss the concept of adolescent leisure constraints from a developmental systems perspective, to summarize research on adolescent leisure constraints, and to identify how future research could use this framework to build on and to extend constraints research. We begin by introducing a developmental systems theoretical framework, and then review the evolution of adolescent leisure constraints research. The second part of the chapter discusses salient issues in the literature related to constraints and adolescent developmental tasks and illustrates the implications of developmental systems theories for future research. We end with a brief description of what organized recreation programs can do to help adolescents overcome constraints.

Constrained leisure is a salient component to a developmental model of leisure, as it directs attention to factors that may intervene and modify interest development, choice, participation, and experience. On a general level, the perspective taken in this chapter requires that constraints are viewed not as something that act on the adolescent to prevent or constrain participation or enjoyment. Rather, the perception of constraint and the ability to adapt and negotiate constraints is a reciprocal and iterative process that involves personal and environmental factors. This perspective allows examination of diverse youth in diverse contexts and does not fall prey to the reductionism of "one size fits all" in explaining behavior and experience.

Developmental Systems Theories and Adolescence

A fertile family of developmental systems theories emphasizes the coactional nature of human development (see Lerner & Walls, 1999, for a review) and offers insight into the factors that may encumber an adolescent's ability to develop interests, to exercise choice of preferences, to participate, and to positively experience leisure. These theories all assert an active, self-constructing approach to life produces healthy and engaged individuals. When initiative, interest development, self-regulation, and autonomous functioning are thwarted or underdeveloped, adolescents are less likely to develop in a healthy and productive manner. From the developmental systems family, the bioecological model (Bronfenbrenner, 1995; Bronfenbrenner & Morris, 1998), developmental contextualism (Lerner, 1999), the metatheory of selective optimization with compensation (SOC; Lerner, Freund, De Stefanis & Habermas, 2001), and initiative development (Bronfenbrenner & Morris, 1998; Larson, 2000) provide the basis for our discussion. Other theories essential to our discussion include intrinsic motivation and self-determination (Deci & Ryan, 1985; Ryan & Deci, 2000), as well as theories of optimal arousal (e.g., boredom; Csikszentmihalyi, 1990). We focus on the conceptual tenets common to the family of developmental systems theories in general, while we use particular theories to highlight various content areas and processes relevant to adolescent leisure constraints.

Adolescence is a period of the lifespan characterized by both normative and nonnormative changes and transitions. These changes and transitions occur in all adolescents in all cultures and revolve around biological, cognitive, and social domains (Steinberg, 1996). The abundance of developmental tasks creates a period of almost constant change throughout adolescence. Characteristic normative changes in adolescents' evolution to adulthood include the transition to middle school, "driving age," and attaining legal adult status at the departure of high school. These transitions roughly coincide with Elliott and Feldman's (1990) work that subdivides the period of adolescence into early (age 10 to 14), middle (age 15 to 17), and late (age 18 into the middle 20s). These normative changes do not presuppose a singular pathway through adolescence, because development is also influenced by a series of nonnormative events (e.g., parental divorce or chronic illness).

Developmental systems theories conceptualize individual functioning as the result of reciprocal interactions between an active individual and biological, social, and environmental forces (Bronfenbrenner, 1979, 1995; Bronfenbrenner & Morris, 1998). Thus, leisure constraints implicate various factors and processes that influence behavior and experience from the intrapersonal to sociocultural level. There are two main areas of interest here. First, it is important to understand the way people interact with, and are acted on by, their environments. Second, it is also important to understand behavior and consequent development are the result of not only reciprocal interaction among forces (e.g., personal, interpersonal, community, and institutional), but also the pattern or configuration of those forces at any given time (Lerner, 1999).

Although predominantly used to explain successful aging in older adults (see McGuire & Norman, this volume), selective optimization with compensation (SOC) is well-suited for understanding how adolescents negotiate the myriad changes of their lives (Lerner et al., 2001). SOC provides a perspective for understanding how people manage change and life events to maintain desired activities across the lifespan (e.g., Baltes, 1997; Freund & Baltes, 1998, 2000). These changes (e.g., decrease in physical ability) occur at different contextual levels (e.g., person, social, community, cultural) and require personal flexibility and adaptability to manage them. Presaging this chapter, Lerner et al. (2001) advised:

> we may study how a youth decides what "to do," how he or she "does" (what is selected), and how he or she may either "keep at it" or identify alternative routes to healthy functioning in the face of failure or loss. Thus, selection, optimization, and compensation denote processes of goal-selection, goal-pursuit, and goal-maintenance/alternation, respectively. (p. 32)

In keeping with the developmental systems perspective, selection, optimization, and compensation operate together but are unique processes to constrain optimal leisure experiences. (See Lerner et al., 2001, for more detail.)

Our view of adolescent leisure and constraints intersects constructs related to developmental tasks associated with the predominant domains of adolescent life and multilevel influences on behavior. **Figure 5.1** represents our conceptualization of how these components interact. The left side represents the multiple person in context levels that influence behavior. The right side reflects the domains, tasks, and transitions that characterize the developmental processes of adolescence. Optimal leisure functioning is situated between these and demonstrates that constraints may influence leisure interest, choice, participation, and experience. Whether these constraints are present or successfully negotiated determines whether leisure is stressful and risky or healthy, meaningful, and self-determined.

Each component of the diagram represents a fertile area of discussion. Equally important are the processes by which these components combine to influence behavior and experience, and particularly constraint. Here is where the idea of a developmental systems theory approach contributes to understanding how the influence of each of these components, as well as aspects within each component, mutually and dynamically influence and respond to each other. This is represented in the messy middle of the diagram, as well as in the reciprocal arrows that reflect the interrelationship between components. Lerner and Walls (1999) termed this "coaction." Developmental systems theories suggest the patterns of how constructs or elements within these components combine influence behavior.

As illustrated on the right side of Figure 5.1, perceived or actual constraints may relate to a variety of issues and tasks that occur during adolescence. The development of identity, autonomy (self-regulation), initiative, sexuality, intimacy, competence (achievement), the acquisition of life skills (e.g., planfulness), and the way new relationships are forged with parents as a result of growing up all interact to affect constraints. Furthermore, the degree to which an adolescent evolved in terms of regulation of self also bears on perception of constraints. These issues and tasks of adolescence will be discussed more fully in a later part of this chapter in terms of how they may influence constraints to leisure. Other factors that affect constraint include structural issues of age (e.g., not driving until a certain age) and resource availability (e.g., no skate park nearby, parents too busy to take adolescent to volunteer at a nature center), as well as cultural issues (e.g., in our community, leisure is only for the elite few).

As suggested in Figure 5.1, the way each of these plays out in the leisure context is multifaceted.

Figure 5.1 represents a highly complex and ambitious perspective. In this chapter, we cannot cover all possibilities implied in this model, but we will address several main areas and research questions pertinent to the constraint of adolescent leisure.

To summarize so far, developmental systems theories frame the conceptualization of constraints in several ways. Developmental systems theories take a process and interaction view of human functioning and development. Theoretically grounding the study of constraints in one of the developmental systems theories such as initiative (Larson, 2000), intrinsic motivation and self-regulation (Ryan & Deci, 2000), or SOC (Lerner et al. 2001) provides a basis for the operationalization of leisure and the factors that support or constrain it. This perspective generates research questions that extend beyond identifying and describing constraints on adolescent leisure to developing hypotheses concerning the developmental consequences of constrained leisure, how factors operate conjointly to constrain leisure, and the process of leisure constraints negotiation.

Before proceeding with a discussion that examines leisure constraints from a developmental theories perspective, we first review literature on leisure constraints of adolescents. These studies not only provide an important

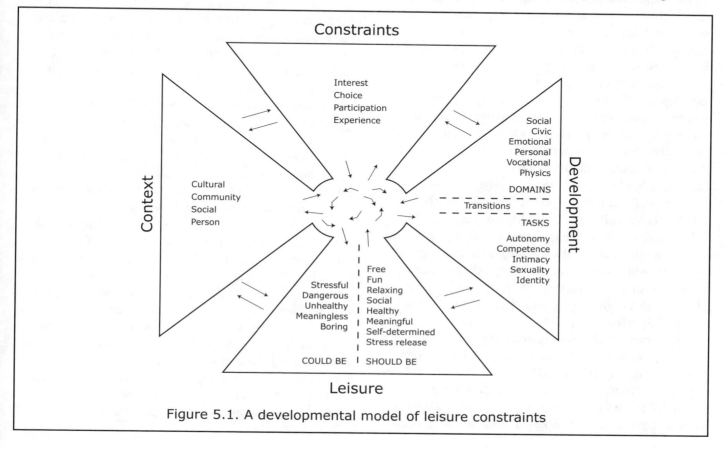

Figure 5.1. A developmental model of leisure constraints

place to begin to examine adolescent constraints to leisure, but also serve as examples in our subsequent discussion.

Existing Literature on Adolescent Constraints

Research on adolescent leisure constraints, like the more general research on adolescent leisure, has been somewhat fragmented and largely descriptive. Nevertheless, current research contributed important preliminary evidence that enhanced understanding of salient types and forms of adolescent leisure constraints. A number of these studies have used inductive and qualitative designs and are particularly relevant, as they identify multiple ways in which leisure constraints are perceived and negotiated.

The early research on adolescent leisure constraints largely mirrors concerns evident in the broader constraints literature focused on adult populations. Several studies (Hultsman, 1992, 1993b; Jackson & Rucks, 1993) examined whether leisure constraint was an internally homogenous construct—that is, do the same constraints apply equally to all processes of activity engagement, such as initiating activity or ceasing activity? Findings from these investigations suggested the types of constraints inhibiting the initiation of a new activity are not the same as those influencing the decision to cease participation. Within each of these respective nonparticipation conditions (e.g., failure to start a new activity and ceasing activity), however, adolescents' viewed the relative importance of the constraint in a similar manner.

The question of ceasing or initiating activities is particularly salient in early adolescence, as participation in agency-sponsored, structured activities (e.g., after-school programs or sports) tends to drop notably at about the seventh grade, or approximately age 13 (Carnegie Council on Adolescent Development, 1992). At the same time, there has been a decrease in physical activity (Caspersen, Pereira & Curran, 2000), particularly among females (Gordon-Larsen, McMurray & Popkin, 1999; Robinson & Godbey, 1993). James (2000) described this decline in sport participation among girls and women to be a worldwide phenomenon. Among other concerns, the decline in participation in physical activity has been attributed to the increasing obesity rates in the United States (Caspersen et al., 2000).

Hultsman (1992) investigated early adolescents' perceptions of constraints to joining and reasons for dropping out of desired organized activities. Reasons for not joining an activity were cost, parents disallowed participation, lack of transportation, and not being old enough. Reasons for ceasing participation were lost interest, ac-

tivity no longer offered, not offered at convenient time, and moving. Hultsman (1993a) further investigated the influence of parents, significant other adults, and peers as barriers to continuing participation and initiating new engagement in organized recreation activities. Program leaders were associated with adolescents ceasing participation, while parents were cited as reasons for not joining an organized activity.

Hultsman's (1992, 1993a, 1993b) work suggested types of constraints varied by context (e.g., sports, nonsports, school-based nonsports, and community-based nonsports). Additionally, parents, other adults, and peers were differentially perceived as constraining to participation, providing evidence that constraints are not internally homogenous across contexts. From a developmental systems framework, this observation is consistent with the expectation that the characteristics of the context are an important influence on behavior.

While the Hultsman (1992, 1993a, 1993b) studies examined constraints associated with the theoretical understanding of early adolescence, Raymore and colleagues (Raymore, Godbey & Crawford, 1994; Raymore, Godbey, Crawford & von Eye, 1993) investigated a hierarchical model of leisure constraints (Crawford, Jackson & Godbey, 1991) among 12th grade students. Raymore et al. (1993) tested the measurement model and factorial validity of a scale developed to assess constraints affecting adolescents' decisions to begin a new leisure activity. In addition, they examined the proposed sequential and hierarchical structure of intrapersonal, interpersonal, and structural constraints. The measurement model and factorial validity of intrapersonal, interpersonal, and structural constraints as three distinct but intercorrelated facets was supported. There was mixed support for the sequential proposition of the model.

In a related article using the same data, Raymore et al. (1994) examined the relations between intrapersonal, interpersonal, and structural constraints with self-esteem, gender, and socioeconomic status. Based on the hierarchical model, adolescents with low self-esteem were hypothesized to experience greater intrapersonal constraints, which inhibit the development of preference. Raymore et al. found a significant negative relation between self-esteem and the perception of intrapersonal, interpersonal, and total constraint, but found no significant relationship with structural constraints. As expected, there were gender differences in self-esteem, with girls reporting lower levels than boys. Moreover, gender moderated the influence of self-esteem on constraint. Girls with lower self-esteem reported higher levels of intrapersonal and total constraints. There was also a negative relationship between socioeconomic status (SES) and intrapersonal constraints: those with higher incomes perceived fewer constraints. There was no relationship between SES and interpersonal and structural constraints.

Because early research provided evidence that constraints were not internally homogeneous and support for examining constraints negotiation grew, a number of researchers employed qualitative methods to study specific populations, activity domains, and the process of negotiating constraints (Culp, 1998; Jackson & Rucks, 1995; James, 2000; McMeeking & Purkayastha, 1995). Two qualitative studies focused specifically on adolescent girls' experience of constraint in outdoor recreation settings (Culp, 1998) and swimming pools (James, 2000). Both studies provided descriptive accounts of differential perceptions of constraint and strategies for dealing with constraints. These studies address girls' confrontations of gender stereotypes, body image, general and physical self-concept, and safety.

McMeeking and Purkayastha (1995) investigated structural constraints focusing on issues of location and access to spaces for adolescents to independently pursue leisure interests. Cotterell (1993), who explored gender difference in the use of public leisure places, conducted a creative study of spatial influence on perceived constraints of adolescent girls. Gender differences in the use of space were not as prevalent as anticipated, but girls did differ from boys in their evening use of a festival site and participation with parents.

Jackson and Rucks (1995) focused specifically on the concept of negotiating constraints among a sample of 7th to 12th grade adolescents. Using qualitative data to build quantitative measures of negotiation strategies, the researchers demonstrated some consistency between the types of constraints encountered and the strategies used to manage them. Strategies included modifying time use, building skills, or modifying aspirations. This study advanced an understanding of the constraints negotiation processes underlying participation.

The literature reviewed provides a description of the kinds of leisure constraints perceived by adolescents. While negotiation strategies are described, this area is ripe for further study. The constraints described in these studies are typically constraints to participation, and to some degree the ability to choose desired activities and develop interests. This chapter extends the existing work to more deeply embed perceptions and negotiations surrounding constraints in an ecological and developmental perspective, and we call attention to constraints on interest development and leisure experience.

Adolescent Leisure Constraints: A Developmental Systems Perspective

In the next section we describe a number of developmental and contextual factors (as depicted in Figure 5.1) that may constrain an adolescent's ability to form leisure-related interests, to make consequent choices, to participate, and to have positive experiences. The theories of selective optimization with compensation (SOC) and motivation and self-determination are highlighted and applied using the developmental systems framework. The role of gender and sexual development is briefly discussed after that.

Constraints and Selective Optimization With Compensation

From the perspective of SOC, leisure engagement is a process of acquiring and sustaining lifelong leisure pursuits in the face of changing abilities and life conditions. SOC suggests at each step in the engagement process, the ability to analyze situations and to adapt to social and environmental conditions are important aspects of selection, optimization, and compensation. Lerner et al. (2001) stated: "...the regulation by individuals of their relations with their complex and changing context is the key problem for successful development across life" (p. 30). Adolescents devoid of self-regulated, meaningful leisure interests are not likely to be meaningfully engaged with their environment. Negative experiences, such as stress and boredom, which often co-occur with leisure that is not self-regulated or meaningful, are also counterproductive to optimal experience and related to unhealthy behavior. Therefore, research needs to address the consequences of constrained leisure as well as the conditions of leisure that make leisure developmentally beneficial.

Conceptualizing leisure engagement as a process comprised of goal identification and selection (i.e., interest), and goal pursuit (i.e., choice and participation) is consistent with the concept of negotiated constraint and with the expansion of the types of criterion variables used in constraints research (Jackson & Scott, 1999). That is, constraints may influence the formation of interests or preferences, level of enjoyment during engagement, or specialization in particular types of leisure. Additionally, intrapersonal, interpersonal, and sociocultural variables may differentially impact these distinct aspects of leisure choices. Thus, counter to the sequential and hierarchical view of constraints, variables from each of these levels may need to be jointly considered, resulting in representing individuals in a multivariate array of variables (Magnusson, 1998). Research should address ways intrapersonal, interpersonal, and structural factors combine to support or inhibit interest, choice, participation, and quality of experience. This perspective suggests perhaps something other than a sequential hierarchical model should be explored that would examine how factors at each level intertwine to influence pertinent leisure engagement (i.e., interest, choice, participation, and experience). Henderson and Bialeschki (1993) had similar concerns and suggested an alternative, nonhierarchical model, and Hutchinson and Kleiber (this volume) make similar arguments.

The concept of selection indicates interest development is requisite to making informed choices. The process of interest development requires knowledge and awareness of leisure opportunities, the ability to select an activity of meaning, and the means to participate in that activity (choice and participation). Forming an interest requires more than simply indicating a preference; it incorporates maintaining an active orientation to the pursuit and a period of experimentation or trial and error that enables interest to be something more than a fleeting desire. Once one has determined leisure interests, the ability or freedom to choose when, where, how, and with whom one will engage are important aspects of the self-regulation of time, acquisition of skills and resources, and negotiation with others necessary for participation.

Particularly salient at adolescence are the developmental tasks and processes of identity and autonomy development, which involve the ability to differentiate oneself from others while at the same time learning to integrate and assimilate the values and beliefs of one's peers, parents, and society. The extent to which an adolescent is actively involved in the process of differentiation and integration is important to healthy development of one's core self (Ryan, 1993). It is logical to assume adolescents' identities are shaped by, among other things, the leisure interests and choices they pursue, and the way their peers, parents, and other adults constrain or contribute to them. Lerner et al. (2001) suggested adolescents must interact with the environment in a self-regulatory (or autonomous) manner to select an appropriate peer group (or modify an existing one) so their identity and goal (in this case leisure interest) are optimally facilitated. Research that identifies interactions and forces surrounding leisure interest developments that are supportive or constraining to the expression of true interests of youth is needed, although two studies on constraints and adolescents recently explored the process of socialization into and support for leisure (Culp, 1998; James, 2000).

Culp (1998) was interested in understanding constraints to girls' participation in outdoor recreation. Many of the girls and women in her study described instances of both positive and negative types of influence. In some cases, girls were inhibited from participating in outdoor recreation activities because of negative peer reaction. In this case, interests were not supported and peer pressure dominated. Conversely, some respondents recognized the important support and encouragement of their peers and family. With that support, some girls and women developed interests and did participate in outdoor recreation activities. In Culp's study, the influence of the peer group was compounded by gender, which will be discussed later.

The tensions between adult control and adolescent autonomy are often played out in the leisure context. Kleiber (1999) referred to this as the "contested terrain." In some contexts, the ability to autonomously choose and participate in activities is lacking. For example, some parents choose adolescents' activities for them, because they do not believe their child is responsible or capable of choosing and selecting for himself or herself. When this happens, adolescents may feel too controlled by their parents. This constraint on choice and activity may lead to less positive experiences (e.g., boredom or stress) and behaviors (e.g., substance use; Caldwell & Smith, 1995). Adolescents with disabilities are often overprotected in their choice and participation in activities, but the outcomes of that overprotection have not been well-documented. As well, youth who live in restricted environments (e.g., group homes or correctional facilities) have similar constraints placed on their leisure. We will return to the issue of overcontrol in the following section on constraints and motivation.

SOC theory champions the importance of a deliberate selection process, and suggests adolescents must learn to optimize what exists personally, interpersonally, and environmentally, and compensate when conditions are not ideal for pursuit of desired interests. A good example that documents this process is provided by James (2001). Her study of adolescent females led her to conclude the following:

> In all three areas studied [basketball courts, public swimming pools, and bedrooms], girls appeared to make their recreational choices based on a complex interaction of factors. While some girls were active in courts and pools, many girls weighed up the possible negative impacts of the audience against the potential enjoyment of an activity and their desire to be included. (p. 86)

Thus, selecting an interest also depends on structural opportunities (see McMeeking & Purkayastha, 1995) in addition to one's cognitive and affective evaluation of the situation and the desire and ability to achieve an optimal experience (Prenzel, 1992). Youth who can make sure all the elements are in place—the right friends, equipment, and setting—are less likely to be constrained in their leisure experience. Future research needs to identify and to describe the behavioral skills and social–cognitive orientations of youth successfully engaged in meaningful leisure (see Jackson & Rucks, 1995). Again, there is a clear link between the processes of optimization and compensation and the latest conceptualizations of negotiated constraint or negotiation strategies.

There are a couple of other miscellaneous points to be made about interest development. The SOC process of *selection* suggests a need for greater understanding of the goals (e.g., leisure interests) adolescents pursue in their leisure and how these goals may evolve through early, middle, and late adolescence. Although choosing meaningful and developmentally productive interests to pursue is very important, too many goals (overselection) or too few goals (underselection) are problematic (Lerner et al., 2001). Both overselection and underselection of interests to pursue are constraining. Finding the optimal number of meaningful interests to pursue is an important task of adolescent leisure. Too few interests, whether from lack of opportunity or amotivation, can lead to long-term boredom and apathy. Too many interests, even if all internally compelled, can be stressful and interfere with other aspects of life (e.g., maintaining relationships with family and friends). Furthermore, a youth with a variety of interests spanning physical, creative, and social activities is less susceptible to experiencing later constraints due to change in life circumstance or environmental factors (e.g., knee problems or closing of skate park). Adolescents who foreclose on one activity (e.g., basketball; the adolescent would be on the basketball team, regularly play pick up basketball, read basketball magazines, regularly participate in basketball practice) may face more severe future constraints (e.g., difficulty adapting and compensating) if that activity is no longer possible, or if they choose to quit for some reason.

Constraints and Motivation

While understanding leisure engagement is enhanced by applying SOC, it is also profitably and compatibly understood using the lens of self-determination theory (SDT) and intrinsic motivation (Deci & Ryan, 1985; Ryan & Deci, 2000). Furthermore, a number of scholars suggested the study of leisure constraints can profit from exploring the link with motivation (Jackson, Crawford & Godbey, 1993; Jackson & Rucks, 1995; Raymore, 2002). Jackson

et al. (1993) posited motivation is a crucial part of the negotiation hypotheses and presented a model formalizing that link. The lens of motivation helps to further understand the dynamic coaction of personal characteristics (e.g., cognitions and affect), peers, and parents, but does so from a more ecological perspective than SOC. That is, SDT is an explanatory framework that applies across activity domains and addresses the processes and behaviors associated with autonomous forms of self-regulated behavior and motivation. SDT also addresses the role of socializing agents and contextual factors that support or inhibit the expression of more internally motivated behaviors that underlie positive human development. To the extent one's interests are intrinsically derived, the quality of the experience is enhanced. That is, the interests are likely to be more authentic to the self, psychologically rewarding, and experienced "as one's own doing" (Ryan, 1993, p. 10).

Research using the SDT framework examined the conditions that either enhance or deter the expression of internally motivated behavior within given contexts, such as classrooms (Ryan & Deci, 2000), competitive sports (Vallerand & Fortier, 1998), or physical activities (Biddle, 1999). Thus, the influence of conditions that deter the formation of more internally oriented types of motivation would be viewed as constraints. Conditions that support or enhance internal types of motivation would be means for persistence and constraint negotiation. Internally motivated behaviors are characterized by persistence and effort and are supported by informational feedback and actions that support competence and relatedness. This framework provides the tools to model factors that impact optimal forms of engagement.

SDT also provides an explanatory framework for understanding motivational orientations associated with less than optimal engagement. Of particular concern is amotivation, which results when youth do not actively engage their environments or engage without meaning. Amotivation is a potential constraint to interest development, choice, participation, and experience. Although an unexamined empirical question, it is likely feelings of amotivation negatively affect each of the aspects of leisure we consider in this chapter—in particular interest development and positive experience of leisure. Caldwell, Darling, Payne, and Dowdy (1999) found youth who participated in activities because there was "nothing else to do" were more bored than their peers who "wanted to do" an activity. Amotivation may be due to a number of personal, social, community, or cultural factors. For example, lack of cognitive ability, community resources, or hope for the future may individually influence motivation, or combine to do so. There is some preliminary evidence parental structure and guidance, however, can offset the constraint of amotivation and propel an adolescent into taking more initiative and being more self-regulated (Hutchinson, Caldwell & Baldwin, 2002).

When action is pursued as a result of external compulsions and not attributed to the self, even if it is intentional, it will be less valid to the person and produce inferior quality experiences. Returning to our previous discussion of parental control, valuable questions to ask include

1. What is the range of strategies that parents use to manage what the adolescent "wants to do" and "has to do"? (Hutchinson, Baldwin & Caldwell, 2003).

2. What is the outcome of those strategies on adolescent well-being?

SDT would suggest strategies that support the adolescent's autonomy, even if in a structured way, are associated with positive parenting and have good outcomes for adolescents (Grolnick, Deci & Ryan, 1997). That is, through autonomous supportive structure adolescents can learn to become responsibly self-determined and to make good leisure choices. Moreover, the structure and guidance provided by parents often helps adolescents to think through how to overcome constraints to their desired participation, thus enabling the adolescent to become a good problem solver (or constraints negotiator) in the future.

Another example of when participation in an activity is not internally compelled is when an adolescent may decide to join the debate team because his or her best friends have joined, even though he or she is not particularly interested. In this case, he or she has joined volitionally, but from an external force. Only if and when action is internally driven will interest evolve, resulting in more meaningful engagement. While some adolescents may be purely externally controlled in their pursuit of leisure interests, it is more likely they have begun to internalize some of the expectations of others and to use their own internal controls to influence leisure choices. This is, of course, a double-edged sword in that internalization of some activities leads to positive and productive choices (e.g., choosing to spend time working on a hobby), and some to more negative or problematic choices (e.g., substance use).

To complicate matters, the internalization process is multifaceted and internal beliefs can become constraining and problematic to interest development if they are driven by guilt or stereotypes. Ryan (1993) suggested:

People's internalized ideals, standards, "shoulds," and "have tos" often seem to enslave them and pressure them at least as powerfully as any external agent could. These same internalized controls often appeared to be inimical to further development, killing *intrinsic interest* [italics added], rigidifying values, and foreclosing alternative directions for growth and change. (p. 26)

Last, not much has been said about the need for competence and achievement, two important aspects of intrinsic motivation. In general, the most positive type of internal motivation is associated with experience that enhances an adolescent's sense of competence, autonomy, and relatedness. Naturally youth develop interests because they think they can be good at whatever they choose. Information (e.g., feedback from a coach) perceived as useful rather than constraining tends to support internal forms of motivation (Ryan & Deci, 2000). Lack of confidence in one's ability, on the other hand, can undermine interest development, as expressed by the girls and women in Culp's (1998) study.

In sum, adolescents' motivation or self-determination levels interact with developmental issues. Considering the developmental tasks of autonomy, intimacy, sexuality, and identity, it is easy to see why adolescents may be constrained in their ability to develop self-determined interests driven by internal desires. The dominant need for social connectedness among most adolescents compels youth to join peers in activities just to be with their friends. According to intrinsic motivation theory, if adolescents allow peer pressure to overly control their activity pursuits, their leisure activity will be less than optimal—apathy, disinterest, and boredom may ensue.

Gender and Sexual Development

For many adolescents, developing their sexuality seems to become a large part of their leisure (e.g., spending hours in the bathroom or in front of the mirror, reading teen magazines, talking about girls). Issues surrounding developing one's sexuality may influence being constrained in leisure. For example, included in sexuality and intimacy are issues surrounding body image. Girls typically have a more severe body image of themselves than do boys (Frederick & Shaw, 1995; James, 2000). James posited because girls in her study spent a great deal of time in the bedroom so that they could "be themselves" (p. 82), when they were in public they felt less authentic. Extending that supposition, it is possible developing one's sexual view of oneself and developing intimate relationships with others may be constraining to the development of interests if an adolescent is not comfortably autonomous in his or her actions. Doing what one's boyfriend or girlfriend wants can, at least temporarily, constrain the development of other interests during the "boy crazy" or "girl crazy" phases. At least during early adolescence, it is enough of a challenge to negotiate intimate relationships without having the added pressure of simultaneously negotiating shared interests. In this case, leisure important to oneself (either alone or with friends) is often subordinate to being with "my boyfriend" or "my girlfriend."

Gender is often cited as a constraint to participation (e.g., Canadian Policy Research Network/Canadian Council on Social Development, 2001), and although the girls and women in Culp's (1998) study described no blatant discrimination, they felt "gender roles functioned as a 'subtle undermining'" of interest (p. 366). This form of constraint was cited as the strongest of all constraints that challenged girls' participation in outdoor recreation and is but one example of how gender roles and stereotypes might constrain interest development. While developing long-term interests that endure over time is central to positive development (Bronfenbrenner & Morris, 1998; Larson, 2000), sometimes an intense period of trial and error is needed to choose interests compatible with self, ability (competence), peers, and other contextual aspects of life. Unfortunately, many adolescents do not have the opportunity or support to engage in such trial and error due to an initial thwarting of interest development based on gender. The coaction of gender and culture will be further elaborated in the next section.

Other aspects of gender and sexual development may have equally constraining effects on interest development as well as on enjoyment of the experience. If an adolescent reaches puberty at a late age, he or she will likely be constrained in the ability to participate in sports in the same way his or her more pubertally advanced peers are. Boys, in particular, may be embarrassed if their development is slower than their peers, perhaps leading to more isolated leisure pursuits. On the other hand, early pubertal onset often compels one to participate in sports, again especially for boys. While this is usually a positive experience, it is possible the participation in sports is not congruent with one's true or authentic interests, and therefore is a constraint of sorts to the quality of the experience. This might be more problematic if sports participation takes time away from other, more intrinsically interesting activities.

Sociocultural and Structural Constraints and Opportunities

Interest development, choice, participation, and experience may be constrained by various aspects of the environment. We have already described some issues related to how peers, parents, and families interact with the developing adolescent to constrain or to support leisure engagement, but the more distal ecological influences are also important to consider. These influences raise questions about the opportunity structures and cultural norms that support and influence interest development, expanding the traditional meaning of structural constraints to include the more macrolevel influences associated with Bronfenbrenner's (1979) multilevel model of ecological systems (reflected in the left side of Figure 5.1).

Sociocultural and Structural Constraints

In the literature, structural constraints include accessibility of facilities, cost of participation, knowledge and awareness, mobility and transportation, money, time, and commitment (McMeeking & Purkayastha, 1995). However, factors such as sociocultural influences, as well as community and social structures, need further exploration. Increasingly, units of analysis such as the neighborhood are being considered as influences on adolescent functioning (Zeldin & Price, 1995). While gender received the most attention, research on the role of race (Philipp, 1995) and other cultural patterns has not been explored.

When examining constraints to leisure, it is important to recognize and to explore how gender and culture interact. For example, in some cultures, girls are not encouraged and are even discouraged from participating in leisure (Caldwell, Perkins, Adubra, Adubra & Smith, 2002), creating and reinforcing deep cultural norms and internalized perceptions (e.g., girls should not play rugby, it is only for boys) that work against even developing an interest in participation. Others also noted opportunity for participation is inequitably distributed due to sociocultural characteristics and gender. Patterson, Pegg, and Dobson-Patterson (2000) found rural Australian females were much more bored in their free time than urban youth or rural boys and attributed this to lack of opportunity. They posited that boys had sports, but no such opportunity for sports or an alternative existed for girls. James (2000) contended boys dominated public spaces in Australia, making it uncomfortable for girls to participate. Similarly, Møller (1991) reported on the high incidence of leisure boredom among South African males, again attributing this to lack of services for those youth, possibly as a residual effect of apartheid.

In Culp's (1998) study, the girls and women interviewed reported that next to constraining gender roles, lack of opportunity to participate in outdoor recreation was their biggest problem. It was not clear whether or not lack of opportunity related to gender. Although lack of an accessible facility is a problem, a more subtle opportunity problem relates to the type of opportunity or setting of the opportunity. Youth need physically and psychologically safe places to gain the maximal optimal experience. Essential elements of recreational spaces for youth include opportunities to try out gender roles, to experiment with an identity, and to hang loose and relax in a "safe" place. From feminist perspectives, a number of authors have recently advocated for "girl friendly" spaces, structures, and institutional processes (e.g., type of leadership) to increase optimal participation among female adolescents (Culp, 1998; James, 2001; King, 2000). Lack of such places not only can be constraining to optimal experience, but also can cause a decline in or halt to participation (e.g., King, 2000).

Lesbian, gay, and transgendered youth, or youth who are questioning their sexual identities, have additional challenges, because their feelings and desires run counter to the dominant society (Caldwell, Kivel, Smith & Hayes, 1998). As well, youth with physical and mental challenges are equally, but differently, challenged to find supportive and safe spaces for their leisure. The literature on leisure constraints among adolescents has far to go in exploring these power, cultural, and gendered constraints.

Program Structure, Leadership, and Constraint

One of the predominant themes in the literature addressing constraints is targeted and deliberately constructed programs can alleviate the impact of structural constraints. Because structured recreation opportunities may have the "greatest potential for the widest range of developmental impacts" (Kleiber, 1999, p. 68), alleviating constraints to interest development, selection, participation, and experiences associated with these contexts is a critical concern. The topic of organized leisure and recreation contexts raises theoretical and programmatic concerns.

Some research has already addressed this need. For example, the participants in Culp's study were asked to reflect on ways outdoor recreation programming could be more facilitative of their interests and participation. Respondents' answers were categorized into program philosophy, structure, and gender composition. One interpretation of Culp's data was the program type (as well as family and peer expectations and gender identification) could constrain the ability to fully express oneself in leisure if the only programs offered reinforce cultural stereotypes (Culp, 1998). For example, in the outdoor recreation program, if girls were steered in the direction

of learning cooking skills, they may be constrained from learning other outdoor skills.

Another programming issue that can potentially constrain positive experience (as well as participation) is the amount and type of adult structure and supervision. The concept of youth voice is gaining currency and recognition as an important facet of youth involvement in structured recreation programs (Ellis, 2001). To the extent youth can "control" their own spaces and have a say in what goes on, their experiences will be better and more developmentally productive. In fact, there is some evidence when youth no longer have a say in their own leisure, they cease participation (King, 2000). Opportunities for youth voice and youth leadership, however, must be guided by experienced leaders. Poorly run youth centers that encourage youth voice without guidance are equally problematic.

A good example of the need for leadership and program structure is a set of studies that examined youth participation in structured (organized) activities versus unstructured participation (Koutakis, 2002; Mahoney & Stattin, 2000). These studies compared youth regularly involved with Swedish Youth Recreation Centers (SYRC) to those who participated in structured, organized activities, such as sports, scouting, and church leisure. The SYRCs first appeared in the 1900s in response to concerns over lack of leisure opportunities for youth to spend their free time in the evening and were an alternative to spending time on the streets. Currently, these centers are not well-staffed, there is high staff turnover, and staff does not provide much guidance or structure (Koutakis, 2002.). These studies found youth regularly involved with the SYRC were more antisocial and reported more fights, property offenses, substance use, and police arrests. Although the authors noted the programs should not be shut down, they did suggest a reorganization of staff and program structure was needed to maximize youth experience.

Conclusion

Adolescent leisure constraint is a multifaceted, complex topic, in large part because of the developmental issues of the period of adolescence. As mentioned at the beginning of the chapter, we were not able to cover all aspects of constraint to adolescent leisure; however, we hope the reader gained some insight into the myriad issues of adolescent leisure. It is important to acknowledge while many of the issues and constraints discussed in this chapter can be applied to youth in other countries our discussion stemmed primarily from a western nation perspective.

The literature on youth development provided a consistent message since at least the 1980s (e.g., Silbereisen & Eyferth, 1986): Youth must be active agents in their interactions with their environments for maximal development (e.g., Bronfenbrenner & Morris, 1998; Larson, 2000; Lerner et al., 2001; Pittman, Irby, Tolman, Yohalem & Ferber, 2001; Silbereisen & Todt, 1994). Leisure, over most any other context, offers the best chance for youth to be intrinsically motivated and engage in authentic experience—a concept Larson (2000) terms initiative. For leisure engagement to contribute to initiative and development, activity must happen on a regular basis over time, youth must be actively engaged, and challenges to continued participation must be met and overcome (Bronfenbrenner & Morris, 1998; Larson, 2000).

Constraints to these fully engaged leisure experiences are many and complex, and more research is needed to untangle the numerous ways leisure engagement is both constrained and meaningful. While this chapter identified and discussed numerous constraints from a developmental systems perspective, many more constraints could have been identified.

Future research needs to specify the exact mechanisms that constrain and support leisure engagement of adolescents. It is not enough to say the adolescents are motivated or can overcome constraints. It is also not enough to identify, for example, the external constraints to leisure engagement. We have made a number of suggestions for future research throughout the chapter and argued that a number of developmental theories provide guidance on the conceptualization of the processes involved with the pursuit of leisure. There is a descriptive base for the conceptualization of varying types of constraints and empirical evidence of the process of constraint negotiation. An important next step is to examine whether constraints and negotiation strategies are predictive of constructive and optimal forms of adolescent leisure.

From a developmental systems theory perspective, it is important for the next generation of research to examine the specific linkages across the various personal, social, environmental, and cultural factors that influence behavior, as well as to understand how these factors intersect with developmental processes. The more precisely these processes are modeled, the better the field will be able to develop interventions and management strategies that support positive leisure engagement.

At the same time, the question of "for whom and under what conditions" must be addressed. There is great value in broadly generalizable research, because there are certainly processes common to many people, even across cultures. But it is also desirable and necessary to revisit the notion of generalizability (Tolan, 1999) and to examine the specific ways certain processes play out in more focused samples. The knowledge of which processes are broadly generalizable and which are more specific to certain groups (e.g., females, preteens, Asian Americans, or youth living in poverty) will further shape interventions and management strategies.

We chose to take a broad view of adolescents and constraints in this chapter, thus ignoring our own advice in the previous paragraph. It would have been difficult to focus on specific "groups" or "types" of youth and still discuss the general ideas we put forth. Nevertheless, a brief mention of vulnerable youth and the role of leisure constraint and engagement in prevention efforts seems warranted in terms of suggesting future research. From a prevention perspective, which has been embraced by the U.S. Department of Health and Human Services, preventing risky behaviors, promoting physical activity, and preventing diseases such as obesity are critical to the nation's health. For example, on September 18, 2003, U.S. Department of Health and Human Services Secretary Tommy G. Thompson announced 12 grants totaling $13.7 million under the "Steps to a Healthier U.S." initiative administered by the Centers for Disease Control and Prevention to encourage community initiatives to promote better health and prevent disease (U.S. Department of Health and Human Services, 2003). Leisure researchers have yet to adequately address the role leisure can play in prevention and health promotion efforts for adolescents (and for all persons). As advocated previously, research is needed to specify the ways in which leisure engagement (e.g., individual styles of leisure, negotiation constraint strategies, motivations) and the leisure context can serve as protective or risk factors. To do this, questions such as "Can constraints to leisure (e.g., imposed by parents or peer pressure) be a protective factor, and under what conditions?" must be asked. Another question might be "When are constraints to leisure engagement so powerful that they become risk factors, and what are those risks?"

Finally, we end with a brief comment on the study of constraints and adolescent leisure research. While this chapter was on constraints to adolescent leisure, it was also about adolescent development and adolescent leisure in general. The boundaries among these areas are permeable and not well-defined, as illustrated in the center of the diagram in Figure 5.1. The usefulness of the term "constraint" may be still yet to be determined fully, perhaps through the kinds of prevention research that links leisure styles and skills with protection and risk previously mentioned. We hope readers are inspired to conduct relevant research that reduces constraints to adolescent leisure, while at the same time promotes positive engagement.

References

Baltes, P. B. (1997). On the incomplete architecture of human ontogeny: Selection, optimization, and compensation as foundations of developmental theory. *American Psychologist, 52*, 366–380.

Bronfenbrenner, U. (1979). *The ecology of human development*. Cambridge, MA: Harvard University Press.

Bronfenbrenner, U. (1995). Developmental ecology: Through space and time—A future perspective. In P. Moen, G. H. Elder, and K. Luscher (Eds.), *Examining lives in context: Perspectives on the ecology of human development* (pp. 619–647). Washington, DC: American Psychological Association.

Bronfenbrenner, U. and Morris, P. A. (1998). *The ecology of developmental processes*. In W. Damon (Series Ed.) and R. M. Lerner (Vol. Ed.) *Handbook of child psychology, Vol 1. Theoretical models of human development* (pp. 993–1028). New York, NY: Wiley.

Biddle, S. (1999). Adherence to sport and physical activity in children and youth. In S. J. Bull (Ed.), *Adherence issues in sport and leisure* (pp. 111–144). New York, NY: John Wiley.

Caldwell, L. L., Darling, N., Payne, L., and Dowdy, B. (1999). "Why are you bored?" An examination of psychological and social control causes of boredom among adolescents. *Journal of Leisure Research, 31*, 103–121.

Caldwell, L. L., Kivel, B. D., Smith, E. A., and Hayes, D. (1998). The leisure context of adolescents who are lesbian or gay: An exploratory study. *Journal of Leisure Research, 30*, 341–355.

Caldwell, L. L., Perkins, D., Adubra, E., Adubra, L., and Smith, E. (2002). *Youth capacity building in rural Togo: A community analysis*. Technical report submitted to the Children, Youth, and Family Consortium, The Pennsylvania State University, University Park, PA.

Caldwell, L. L. and Smith, E. A. (1995). Health behaviors of leisure alienated youth. *Loisir et sociètè/Society & Leisure, 18*, 143–156.

Canadian Policy Research Networks/Canadian Council on Social Development. (2001). *Four hypotheses about the public policy significance of youth recreation: Lessons from a literature review and a data analysis on "learning through recreation."* Ottawa, Ontario, Canada: Author. Retrieved from http://www.cprn.com/en/doc.cfm?doc=383

Carnegie Council on Adolescent Development. (1992). Task force on youth development and community programs. *A matter of time: Risk and opportunity in the nonschool hours*. Washington, DC: Author.

Caspersen, C. J., Pereira, M. A., and Curran, K. M. (2000). Changes in physical activity patterns in the United States, by sex and cross-sectional age. *Medicine and Science in Sport and Exercise, 32*, 1601–1609.

Cotterell, J. L. (1993). Do macro-level changes in the leisure environment alter leisure constraints on adolescent girls? *Journal of Environmental Psychology, 13*, 125–136.

Crawford, D. W., Jackson, E. L., and Godbey, G. (1991). A hierarchical model of leisure constraints. *Leisure Sciences, 13*, 309–320.

Csikszentmihalyi, M. (1990). *Flow: The psychology of optimal experience*. New York, NY: Harper and Row.

Culp, R. H. (1998). Adolescent girls and outdoor recreation: A case study examining constraints and effective programming. *Journal of Leisure Research, 30*, 356–379.

Deci, E. L. and Ryan, R. M. (1985). *Intrinsic motivation and self-determination in human behavior*. New York, NY: Plenum.

Elliott, G. R. and Feldman, S. S. (1990). Capturing the adolescent experience. In S. S. Feldman and G. R. Elliott (Eds.), *At the threshold: The developing adolescent* (pp. 1–14). Cambridge, MA: Harvard University Press.

Ellis, J. M. (2001). *Youth-directed recreation: A model of voice and community attachment*. Unpublished masters thesis, The Pennsylvania State University, University Park, PA.

Frederick, C. J. and Shaw, S. M. (1995). Body image as a leisure constraint: Examining the experience of aerobic exercise classes for young women. *Leisure Sciences, 17(2)*, 57–73.

Freund, A. M. and Baltes, P. B. (1998). Selection, optimization, and compensation as strategies of life management: Correlations with subjective indicators of successful aging. *Psychology and Aging, 13*, 531–543.

Freund, A. M. and Baltes, P. B. (2000). The orchestration of selection, optimization, and compensation: An action-theoretical conceptualization of a theory of developmental regulation. In W. J. Perrig and A. Grob (Eds.), *Control of human behavior, mental processes, and consciousness: Essays in honor of the 60th birthday of August Flammer* (pp. 35–58). New York, NY: Erlbaum.

Gordon-Larsen, P., McMurray, R. G., and Popkin, B. M. (1999). Adolescent physical activity and inactivity vary by ethnicity: The national longitudinal study of adolescent health. *Journal of Pediatrics, 135*, 301–306.

Grolnick, W. S., Deci, E. L., and Ryan, R. M. (1997). Internalization within the family: The self-determination theory perspective. In J. E. Grusec and L. Kuczynski (Eds.), *Parenting and children's internalization of values: A handbook of contemporary theory* (pp. 135–161). New York, NY: John Wiley & Sons.

Henderson, K. A. and Bialeschki, M. D. (1993). Negotiating constraints to women's physical recreation. *Leisure & Society, 16*, 389–412.

Hultsman, W. Z. (1992). Constraints to activity participation in early adolescence. *Journal of Early Adolescence, 12*, 280–299.

Hultsman, W. Z. (1993a). The influence of others as a barrier to recreation participation among early adolescents. *Journal of Leisure Research, 25*, 150–164.

Hultsman, W. Z. (1993b). Is constrained leisure an internally homogeneous concept? An extension. *Journal of Leisure Research, 25*, 319–334.

Hutchinson, S., Baldwin, C. K., and Caldwell, L. L. (2003). Differentiating parent practices related to adolescent behavior in the free time context. *Journal of Leisure Research, 35*, 396–422.

Hutchinson, S., Caldwell, L. L., and Baldwin, C. K. (2002, October 18). *That extra push: The moderating influence of parents on adolescent initiative.* Leisure Research Symposium, National Recreation and Parks Association, Tampa, FL.

Jackson, E. L., Crawford, D. W., and Godbey, G. (1993). Negotiation of leisure constraints. *Leisure Sciences, 15*, 1–11.

Jackson, E. L. and Rucks, V. C. (1993). Reasons for ceasing participation and barriers to participation: Further examination of constrained leisure as an internally homogeneous concept. *Leisure Sciences, 15*, 217–230.

Jackson, E. L. and Rucks, V. C. (1995). Negotiation of leisure constraints by junior-high and high-school students: An exploratory study. *Journal of Leisure Research, 27*, 85–105.

Jackson, E. L. and Scott, D. (1999). Constraints to leisure. In E. L. Jackson and T. L. Burton (Eds.), *Leisure studies: Prospects for the twenty-first century* (pp. 299–321). State College, PA: Venture Publishing, Inc.

James, K. (2000). "You can feel them looking at you": The experiences of adolescent girls at swimming pools. *Journal of Leisure Research, 32*, 262–280.

James, K. (2001). "I just gotta have my own space!": The bedroom as a leisure site for adolescent girls. *Journal of Leisure Research, 33,* 71–90.

King, K. (2000). From the precipice: Recreation experiences of high risk girls. *Journal of Park and Recreation Administration, 18,* 19–34.

Kleiber, D. A. (1999). *Leisure experience and human development: A dialectical interpretation.* New York, NY: Basic Books.

Koutakis, N. (2002, 3–7 September). *Leisure time as a risk vs. protective factor.* Paper presented at the Conference of the European Association for Research on Adolescence, Oxford, England.

Larson, R. (2000). Toward a psychology of positive youth development. *American Psychologist, 55,* 170–183.

Lerner, R. M. (1999). Developmental contextualism, and the further enhancement of theory about puberty and psychosocial development. In R. E. Muuss and H. D. Porton, *Adolescent behavior and society: A book of readings* (5th ed.; pp. 22–33). New York, NY: McGraw-Hill.

Lerner, R. M., Freund, A. M., De Stefanis, I., and Habermas, T. (2001). Understanding developmental regulation in adolescence: The use of the selection, optimization, and compensation model. *Human Development, 44,* 29–50

Lerner, R. M. and Walls, T. (1999). Revisiting individuals as producers of their development: From dynamic interactionism to developmental systems. In J. Brandtstädter and R. M. Lerner, *Action in self-development: Theory and research through the life span* (pp. 3–36). Thousand Oaks, CA: Sage Publications.

Magnusson, D. (1998). The logic and implications of a person-oriented approach. In R. B. Cairns, L. R. Bergman, and J. Kagan (Eds.), *Methods and models for studying the individual* (pp. 33–64). Thousand Oaks, CA: Sage.

Mahoney, J. L. and Stattin, H. (2000). Leisure activities and adolescent antisocial behavior: The role of structure and social context. *Journal of Adolescence, 23,* 113–127.

McMeeking, D. and Purkayastha, B. (1995). "I can't have my mom running me everywhere": Adolescents, leisure, and accessibility. *Journal of Leisure Research, 27,* 360–378.

Møller, V. (1991). Lost generation found: Black youth at leisure. Youth Centre Project and Indicator Project. *Indicator South Africa Issue Focus,* 1–63.

Patterson, I., Pegg, S., and Dobson-Patterson, R. 2000. Exploring the links between leisure boredom and alcohol use among youth in rural and urban areas of Australia. *Journal of Park and Recreation Administration, 18*(3), 53–76.

Philipp, S. F. (1995). Race and leisure constraints. *Leisure Sciences, 17,* 109–120.

Pittman, K. J., Irby, M., Tolman, J., Yohalem, N., and Ferber, T. (2001). Preventing problems, promoting development, encouraging engagement: Competing priorities or inseparable goals? The Forum for Youth Investment. Retrieved November 14, 2002, from http://www.forumforyouth investment.org/reswork. htm

Prenzel, M. (1992). The selective persistence of interest. In A. K. Renninger, S. Hidi, and A. Krapp (Eds.), *The role of interest in learning and development,* (pp. 71–98). Hillsdale, NJ: Lawrence Erlbaum Associates, Inc.

Raymore, L. A. (2002). Facilitators to leisure. *Journal of Leisure Research, 34,* 37–51.

Raymore, L. A., Godbey, G. C., and Crawford, D. W. (1994). Self-esteem, gender, and socioeconomic status: Their relation to perceptions of constraint on leisure among adolescents, *Journal of Leisure Research, 26,* 99–118.

Raymore, L. A., Godbey, G. C., Crawford, D. W., and von Eye, A. (1993). Nature and process of leisure constraints: An empirical test. *Leisure Sciences, 15,* 99–113.

Robinson, J. and Godbey, G. (1993). Sport, fitness and the gender gap. *Leisure Sciences, 15,* 291–307.

Ryan, R. M. (1993). Agency and organization: Intrinsic motivation, autonomy, and the self in psychological development. In R. Dienstbier and J. Jacobs (Series Eds.), *Developmental perspectives on motivation, Vol. 40 of the Nebraska Symposium on Motivation* (pp. 1–56). Lincoln, NE: University of Nebraska Press.

Ryan, R. M and Deci, E. L. (2000). Self-determination theory and the facilitation of intrinsic motivation, social development, and well-being. *American Psychologist, 55,* 68–78.

Tolan, P. H. (1999, June 25). *Methodological issues in a developmental–ecological perspective on substance abuse.* Presented at the Society for Prevention Research Annual Conference, New Orleans, LA.

Steinberg, L. (1996). *Adolescence* (4th ed.). New York, NY: McGraw-Hill.

Silbereisen, R. K. and Eyferth, K. (1986). Development as action in context. In R. K. Silbereisen, K. Eyferth, and G. Rudinger (Eds.), *Development as action in context: Problem behavior and normal youth development* (pp. 3–16). New York, NY: Springer-Verlag.

Silbereisen, R. K. and Todt, E. (1994). *Adolescence in context: The interplay of family, school, peers, and work in adjustment.* New York, NY: Springer-Verlag.

U.S. Department of Health and Human Services. (2003). HHS awards $13.7 million to support community programs to prevent diabetes, asthma, and obesity. Retrieved March 22, 2004, from http://www.hhs. gov/news/press/2003pres/20030918.html

Vallerand, R. J. and Fortier, M. S. (1998). Measure of intrinsic and extrinsic motivation in sport and physical activity: A review and critique. In J. L. Duda (Ed.), *Advances in sport and exercise psychology measurement* (pp. 81–101). Morgantown, WV: Fitness Information Technology.

Zeldin, S. and Price, L. A. (1995). Creating supportive communities for adolescent development: Challenges to scholars. *Journal of Adolescent Research, 10,* 6–14.

Chapter 6

The Role of Constraints in Successful Aging: Inhibiting or Enabling?

Francis McGuire and William Norman (Clemson University)

It is helpful to provide a framework for examining and evaluating constraints to leisure. Within an aging perspective, the impact of constraints on "successful aging" appears to be an effective framework. Rowe and Kahn (1998) defined successful aging as the ability to maintain three essential behaviors:

1. low risk of disease or disease-related disability.

2. high mental and physical functioning.

3. active engagement with life.

Any factor interfering with the pursuit of successful aging, such as poor health or lack of opportunities for active engagement, may be viewed as a constraint. The impact of these constraints will be aging that falls short of the possibilities open to older people. In that sense constraints not only restrict or limit leisure involvement, but also prohibit successful aging. However, this perspective of successful aging, while reinforcing to those in the leisure service profession, reflects a value system that may not mirror all possible approaches to later life. The premise involvement is better than uninvolvement and social activity is better than solitary activity may not be accurate for all individuals. There may be circumstances supporting inactivity, or at least the curtailment of some activity, as a successful approach to later life. For example, declining health not only requires reduction in activity but also may be improved by conserving energy through reduced efforts to engage in activities. This chapter will explore the possibility constraints may not only inhibit successful aging, but also in some cases contribute to it.

One of the difficulties in examining leisure constraints in later life is the presumption underlying much of the constraints literature that engagement is preferable to disengagement and therefore the presence of constraints is somehow damaging to the individual. Within a gerontological context the issue of what constitutes "successful aging" relates to the perspective one takes on constraints. Constraints become those factors blocking the path to success in later life. And what defines success? Typically success is defined within an activity perspective, with physical activity and social contacts identified as predictors of successful aging (Phelan & Larson, 2002). It is possible successful aging does not inherently require high levels of activity. Phelan and Larson (2002) documented a failure to ask older individuals what successful aging is to them. It may be differences in health alter perspectives on successful aging. For example, an individual experiencing severe functional losses may not view success within an engagement context. Rather, success may be viewed as retention of remaining abilities. Within such a context constraints may be allies in successful aging. Katz (2000) suggested just such an alternative perspective, questioning the assumption activity is associated with well-being in old age:

> Most gerontological and policy discourses pose activity as the "positive" against which the "negative" forces of dependency, illness, and loneliness are arrayed. However, retired older people understand that the expectations for them to be active present a more complex issue than that suggested by the typical positive/negative binarism inherent in the activity programs and literature. (p. 147)

Katz's concern is nonstop activity may become the antithesis to personal growth. Those older individuals preferring their "inner" world to others' "external" world may be pressured to remain actively engaged. In such a case constraints may actually provide refuge from a pervasive activity perspective.

Tornstam (1992) stated the concern gerontologists derive theory from their own biases and presuppositions:

"We place our own theoretical cap over the heads of old people without thinking that our points of departure for assessment are relative" (p. 223). The danger of this relativism when examining leisure constraints in the elderly is clear. Our activity preference translates into a search for whatever prevents active engagement. Again, Tornstam's words say it best: "'passive' pensioners who do not share a 'normal' interest in career work, leisure-time activities, and keep-fit measures are regarded as problematic and *in need of activation*" [italics added] (p. 323). Tornstam's proposal for a different worldview is called "gerotranscendence."

Others also allowed for the possibility constrains may be positive in some circumstances. Elster (2000) suggested in some cases constraints might be a necessary and positive force in life. He coined the term "beneficial constraints" to suggest there may be times when individuals want to limit their freedom of choice and use self-imposed constraints as a mechanism for doing so. Later in this chapter we will discuss why older individuals may want to limit their range of possible behaviors. Shogan (2002) also pursued the theme of "enabling constraint" which actually make participation possible. For some older people, constraints may form a barrier to support a disengagement from life congruent with physical, emotional, cognitive, or financial losses. For example, an individual who has retired and is living on a fixed income may identify lack of money as a constraint to involvement in activities. The assumption may then be made that negotiating this constraint will open a range of previously constrained leisure activities. However, it may be that the individual does not have the physiological capacity for engagement and the restriction of activities is a desirable state.

The Aging of the North American Population

Most readers are probably familiar with the headlines ballyhooing the aging of our society. Clearly the number of individuals aged 65 or over is rising dramatically. The aging of the so-called baby boomers will assure this rapid increase in the number of individuals age 65 and over will continue. The statistics tell part of the story of the aging of North America. There are approximately 35 million individuals in the United States 65 or older. This is 12.4% of the population—one in every eight Americans. There is a net increase of 650 people in the 65 and over population every day. At the same time, the composition of the aging population points toward its heterogeneity. For example, the older population has more females than males—143 women for every 100 men. In addition, the proportion of the older population composed of minorities, currently 16.4%, is increasing. The profile of the aging population itself is also changing, with an increasing population age 85 years or older. The number of individuals age 65 to 74 grew eight-fold between 1900 and 2000. Over the same period of time the 75 to 84 population was 16 times larger in 2000 than in 1900 and the 85-plus population was 34 times larger (Administration on Aging, 2002).

The Canadian population is also aging. There were approximately 3.9 million Canadians 65 years of age or older in 2001, representing nearly 13% of the total population. The trend in Canada is also toward increasing numbers of older residents as a result of the aging of the baby boomers. There was a 10% increase in the number of individuals aged 65 or over between 1996 and 2002. By the year 2016, it is estimated nearly 16% of the population of Canada will be at least 65 years of age. The oldest old, those 80 and over, increased by 41.2% from 1991 to 2002, a proportion expected to expand by another 43% by 2011, when there will be 1.3 million Canadians age 80 or over (Statistics Canada, 2001).

Although individuals 65 or older are as unique as those in any other age group, examining some of the shared characteristics of members of this population can provide suggestive evidence of constraints experienced in later life, particularly in areas such as money, health, and companionship. For example, lack of money is frequently identified as a constraint. Approximately 10% of the 65 and over population were below the poverty level in 2000. Some groups of elderly experience poverty at higher levels. Over 20% of older individuals living alone were below the poverty level—22.3% of elderly African Americans, and 38% of Hispanic women living alone. In addition, health-related factors function as constraints. The older an individual becomes the more likely he or she will experience health-related problems. For example, in 1999 approximately 25% of older Americans assessed their health as fair or poor. This is significantly higher than among the total population (9.2%). Among older African Americans approximately 41% viewed their health as either fair or poor. This health assessment was matched by limitations in activities. Data from 1998 indicated 28.8% of Americans between the ages of 65 and 74 experienced limitations on activities as a result of a chronic health condition. Among those 75 or over, 50% experienced limitation in activities because of chronic health problems (Administration on Aging, 2002). The living arrangements of older adults indicate why lack of companionship may be a problem, particularly among older women. The percentage of older women living alone is the same as the percentage living with a spouse, 41%. To the extent a spouse may be a primary leisure companion, that may be a severe limitation on leisure engagement. However, the data also indicate the older population is changing in positive ways. For example, evidence shows the proportion of individuals with chronic disabilities is decreasing (Recer, 2003). In addition, the aging of the baby boomers will result in higher levels of education and income in the older population.

Perspectives on the very nature of the elderly population are also changing. Some gerontologists are shifting their focus from viewing old age as a period of decline and disability to a growth model. Advances in the medical field make it more likely people will live healthy lives well into the ninth decade of life. As a result, the notion life ends at 65 is no longer accurate, and probably never was. The later years are an opportunity for continued growth and development. Elsewhere (McGuire, Boyd & Tedrick, 1999) we have used the concept of Ulyssean living, originally discussed by John McLeish (1976) as a model for this type of aging. McLeish stated:

> To gain entry to the country and company of the Ulyssean people no passport is required….Membership has nothing to do with whether one is physically well or dogged by ill-health, whether one is personable or plain, well-traveled or confined to a limited area….It is a process, not a state; a process of becoming, and great practitioners of the Ulyssean way would certainly describe themselves as voyagers, not inhabitants. (p. 285)

A large part of the older population has the potential for a Ulyssean lifestyle, marked by engagement and growth. Indeed, two of the crucial determinants of leisure, time and freedom, may be more present in post-retirement years than at any other point in life. Later life may be the leisure golden years. However, that is not necessarily the case, at least not if the golden years require engagement in a large number of activities. The reason may be found in the constraints experienced in later years.

The Literature on Leisure Constraints and Aging

Some of the concomitants of aging may themselves function as constraints. For example, decline in visual acuity may result in the loss of the ability to drive and therefore lack of transportation may become problem-

atical. Similarly, reduced income resulting from retirement and reliance on social security as a major source of finances may magnify the effects of not having enough money. In addition, some constraints may shift in meaning in later life. For example parental responsibility may be a barrier to desired participation in early adulthood. Having and caring for children may intrude on choices. However, in later life the presence of children may or may not be a constraint. Utz, Carr, Nesses, and Wortman (2002) specifically identified having no living children as a constraint to social participation by elderly widows. Their rationale was children might encourage parents to remain engaged.

Unlike some of the other populations discussed in this book, there is not a dearth of research examining constraints in the later years. This is probably a result of the perspective on aging in this country. Because later life is frequently viewed as a period of loss and decline, it is natural a great deal of effort focused on studying the extent to which these losses limit involvement in daily life, particularly in areas such as social participation, physical activity, and activities of daily living. The increasing age of the older population points toward an increase in constraints affiliated with physical and cognitive decline. It is more likely an 85-year-old individual will be restricted from participating in physical activities than a 65-year-old.

There have been many "single-item" studies examining the impact of loss of some aspect of behavior. For example, Bruce, Devine, and Prince (2002) examined the relationship between fear of falling and recreational physical activity levels. According to Bruce et al., fear of falling may impact up to 30% of the elderly, and frequently results from frailty, poor balance, and immobility that accompany old age. The authors queried older women about their extent of involvement in sports or regular physical exercise. They also asked participants whether they were afraid of falling and whether they had limited their outside the home activities because of a fear of falling. They found fear of falling to be associated with a sedentary lifestyle and concluded, "even in high-functioning, healthy older women, fear of falls is common and strongly associated with restriction of recreational physical activity" (p. 88). Murphy, Williams, and Gill (2002) found similar linkages between fear of falling and activity restriction. Clearly, fear of falling, when it causes reductions in activity levels, can be viewed as a constraint. Similar studies examined factors such as income, transportation availability, health, and specific diseases or debilitating conditions in limiting activity levels.

Another approach to examining constraints in later life is to examine activity-specific constraints. Perhaps the largest area of such study has been exercise. Exercise is recognized as a crucial factor in health in the later years. As a result, exercise programs—many designed for older people, such as mall walking or water aerobics—have become common and research efforts have examined why more people do not participate in physical activity. Grant (2001) identified factors such as childhood socialization, limited early life opportunities, physical and social vulnerability (particularly among women), fear of injury, and cultural values, such as perceptions of what is age-appropriate, as potential constraints to involvement in physical activities by older people.

As older people are recognized as a potential market for a variety of leisure service providers, there will be a growing effort to examine factors, including constraints, shaping their involvement in many areas of behavior. For example, Fleisher and Pizam (2002) explored tourism constraints among older Israelis, recognizing the senior market is important to many countries. They surveyed Israelis 55 years of age and over and found the decision to take a vacation depended on two variables: self-assessed health and income. Age did not matter. However, income, health, past vacation experience, and age (where the relationship is not linear but rather increases and then decreases over time) influenced the length of a vacation. Fleisher and Pizam's study supported the findings of most of the literature on leisure constraints in later years: income and health are critical factors in facilitating or limiting engagement in leisure.

Some of the earliest works on constraints to leisure included older people in their samples (Buchanan & Allen, 1983; McGuire, 1984; Witt & Goodale, 1981). For example, McGuire, Dottavio, and O'Leary (1986) used data from the 1982–1983 nationwide recreation survey to identify constraints to participation in outdoor recreation across the lifespan. Constraints were identified as either limitors (factors reducing participation below desired levels) or prohibitors (constraints responsible for the cessation of activities). The primary limitors experienced by older adults aged 61 to 75 were lack of time, health reasons, and lack of companions. Respondents 75 years of age and over identified the same three constraints as limitors, although health increased in prevalence while time and companionship decreased. Poor health and lack of companions were the primary prohibitors to individuals aged 61 to 75. Health and safety concerns were prohibitors to the 75 years of age and older respondents.

More recent work also examined constraints on leisure in later life (Iso-Ahola, Jackson & Dunn, 1994;

Jackson, 1993; Jackson & Witt, 1994; Rogers, Meyer, Walker & Fisk, 1998). For example, Rogers et al. (1998) used focus group interviews to assess constraints in the daily lives of 59 healthy older individuals, ranging in age from 65 to 88. They addressed the following four issues:

1. In what ways do older adults encounter constraints in everyday life?

2. What is the source of the constraints?

3. How do older adults respond to constraints?

4. Can human factors research help to minimize constraints?

The focus groups began with participants being asked to discuss the last time "you really got frustrated trying to use something" and concluded with participants being asked to review a list of everyday activities (e.g., transportation, new technologies, using the library, remaining healthy, consumer-related issues, hobbies and entertainment, communication, cooking and eating, money management, home maintenance, and housekeeping) and to discuss problems related to each area. The results indicated constraints could be sorted into motor-related problems (e.g., problems with bending, balance, and walking), fine motor difficulties, visual and auditory problems, cognitive limitations (including memory and procedural knowledge), external limitations (e.g., fear of crime and dependence), and general health limitations. The most common areas where these limitations were problems included leisure activities, transportation, housekeeping, and locomotion.

The study also examined responses to limitations. The most common response to constraints was activity cessation, with nearly half of all responses being curtailment of task performance. It is particularly noteworthy that physical limitations were the cause for cessation in a variety of leisure activities, including walking, swimming, reading, dining out, traveling, library use, visiting family and friends, and dancing. Perseverance, often marked by reduced speed or accuracy in performance, was another response to constraints. The study participants also used compensation as a strategy to overcome limitations. This approach included using a tool to assist in task completion, changing the environment, or changing the steps in the task. A final approach to negotiating limitations was self-improvement. For example, rehabilitating after a stroke, concentrating more to accommodate memory loss, or learning a new skill such as how to use a computer, were identified as self-improvement mechanisms. The final purpose of the study was to identify interventions that ergonomics (i.e., human factors) professionals could use to help reduce constraints. The authors found that approximately half of the identified problems were not correctable through training or redesign. Of the half open to remediation, a number could be addressed through training (e.g., information on how to exercise safely) or redesign (e.g., providing lightweight tools for gardening).

Although Strain, Grabusic, Searle, and Dunn (2002) did not specifically address constraints in their longitudinal study of continuing and ceasing activity in later life, their findings related to correlates of continuing engagement provide at least an indication of limiting factors. The longitudinal approach in this study makes it particularly significant. Strain et al. examined changes in leisure activity from 1985 to 1993 among 308 individuals who were at least 60 years of age at the initiation of the study. Their examination included eight activities: shopping, dining out, walking, travel, outdoor yard work, church services/activities, playing cards, and theater/movies/spectator sports. In general, the younger one was the more likely to continue participation in an activity. Self-rated health, change in functional ability, educational level, gender, and not losing a marital partner were also related to continuation in some of the activities. The implication of these findings is factors such as health, age, gender, and companionship may function to facilitate or limit activity engagement.

Jackson and Witt (1994) completed another study examining change over time. They used data from the 1988 General Recreation Survey and the 1992 replication to determine the magnitude of changes in constraints over a four-year period, the extent to which the changes resulted from variations in samples and populations, and the stability of the relationships of constraints to socioeconomic variables, including age, over time. We will look only at the stability and change in the relationship of age to constraints. The pattern of the five constraints studied was consistent between 1988 and 1992. Admission fees and charges and being too busy with work were less important to respondents aged 65 or over than to younger respondents. Lack of physical ability increased in importance. No opportunity close to home showed little variation across the ages studied, and being too busy with family was distributed in an inverted U-shaped pattern, with higher importance in middle age and lower importance early and later life. Only one constraint, lack of physical ability, was significantly different from 1988 to 1992 among the age 65 and older participants, increasing in importance over time.

There have been several studies that included age as a variable in their analysis. For example, Jackson (1993) focused on comparing varying ways of manipulating constraints data: leisure constraint categories derived from cluster analysis, item-by-item analysis, a total constraint score, and factor analysis. Part of the analysis examined the relationship of age, using six categories (18 to 21, 22 to 28, 29 to 36, 37 to 43, 51 to 65, and over 65), to the constraints identified within each analysis. Data came from the 1988 General Recreation Survey conducted by Alberta Recreation and Parks. Respondents' age was related to constraints based on the item-by-item analysis for all five of the constraints discussed. Family commitment displayed an inverted U-shaped relationship, with relatively few older and younger respondents identifying it as a constraint. The oldest and youngest respondents were more like to identify lack of partners as a constraint than the middle-age respondents. Lack of physical ability was more likely to be a constraint for the oldest respondents than for the other age groups, whereas being too busy with work was least prevalent among the oldest participants. Jackson also found a significant, but weak, decline in the overall intensity of constraints as the age of the respondents increased. The factor analysis yielded six factors and age was significantly related to five. Cost and accessibility declined with age. The young and old respondents more frequently identified social isolation as a constraint, whereas time commitment was lower within those two groups than among the middle aged groups. The factor labeled "personal reasons" increased with age. Jackson's final analysis was based on a cluster analysis. He found variations in cluster membership varied significantly based on the respondent's age. There was little variation in the "costs," "time, costs, and accessibility," and the "costs, facilities, and awareness" clusters. The "time" cluster exhibited an inverted U-shaped distribution across the age group studies and the "accessibility and awareness" cluster showed a U-shaped distribution. The percentage of respondents within each age group in the "relatively unconstrained" cluster increased with age.

More recently, Clayton (2002) used a concept mapping approach to study leisure constraints experienced by several groups, including college students, wilderness first responders, and older individuals. Concept mapping is an approach to developing a conceptual framework based on participant-generated data (Trochim, 1989). Clayton began his examination of constraints by asking a group of five residents in a leadership role in their retirement community to generate a list of constraints. Respondents were told "a leisure constraint is anything that gets in the way of your participation in leisure. A constraint can be something that prevents participation, or some obstacles that can be overcome in order to participate." The participants generated a list of 51 items. These were then sorted by each participant into categories based on shared perceived similarities of items. Multi-dimensional scaling and cluster analysis were then used to create categories of constraints emerging from the 51 items. Clayton reports on all possible cluster solutions. However, we will limit our review to his eight-cluster solution, the median number of all possible cluster solutions. The eight leisure constraint categories generated from the responses of the retiree group were as follows:

1. responsibility, including items related to not wanting to take a leadership role.
2. facility management, defined by a poor coordination of activities.
3. cost, including constraints related to costs.
4. too many choices, typified by lack of motivation and inability to do all desired activities.
5. adverse effects of participation, such as fear of injury, crime, and failure to enjoy activities.
6. lack of ability and skills.
7. lack of availability, including items related to location, transportation, and weather.
8. rules/resources involving laws and legal restrictions as well as lack of partners.

Clayton concluded the nature of constraint categories varied based on the group being studied, concomitants of the aging process, and the constraints identified by the retirees reflected their role in the community, and each was active in planning activities for the community.

The research examining constraints in later life yielded expected results. Factors viewed as concomitants of aging, such as reduced income, physical decline, loss of friends, and uncertainty over the ability to keep up, function as brakes on behavior. Although these studies are of interest and provide foundations for further work, it is also useful to look elsewhere for insight into the leisure/aging/constraint link.

Gerontological Theory and Constraints

Various aspects of the aging process have been analyzed from a multitude of perspectives and an ever-expanding number of theoretical frameworks. However, there have been few, if any, attempts to integrate gerontological theory into the study of constraints in later life. Theories of aging provide opportunities to speculate about the role of constraints in explaining successful aging. They also illustrate how one's view of the world shapes how constraints may be conceptualized. We will examine several theories of aging and speculate about the implications of each for leisure constraints.

Theorizing about aging has resulted in many models. Articles by Schroots (1996) and Lynott and Lynott (1996) summarized many of these. The three most enduring theories in social gerontology are activity theory, disengagement theory, and continuity theory. According to Utz, Carr, Nesse, and Wortman (2002), these three are among the most prominent theories; the authors used them as a springboard to their discussion of the effect of widowhood on social participation. Similarly, the theories provide a starting point to examine constraints. We will also discuss three more recent theories: selective optimization with compensation, socioemotional selectivity theory, and gerotranscendence. Finally we examine the political economy of aging theory, because it shifts the perspective from the individual to the society and therefore provides a different perspective on the link between aging and constraints.

Early Theories

Theoretical perspectives on aging expanded in recent years. Nevertheless, the early theories presented here continue to have a presence in the literature. In addition, they provide a commonsense view of aging. Each matches up with popular conceptualizations of aging and each has merits, providing insight into potential mechanisms for successful aging. Therefore, they provide a starting point for looking at theoretical perspectives on aging.

Activity Theory

Activity theory is one of the earliest and most intuitively attractive aging theories. Its origins may be traced back to Havighurst and Albrecht (1953), although a more formal statement of the theory did not appear until 1972 (Lemon, Bengston & Peterson, 1972). At the heart of activity theory is the link between engagement in meaningful activity and life satisfaction. Successful aging is based on the ability to maintain involvement in activities. If an activity is lost (e.g., through retirement), the individual must find a replacement activity. At the core of activity theory is the importance of roles and role performance as a vehicle for retaining a sense of self. We judge ourselves on *how* we are doing, and this in turn depends, at least partly, on *what* we are doing. Because aging is accompanied by role loss resulting from retirement, death of a spouse, or children leaving home, it is crucial other roles be adopted. Activity theory suggests the more active an individual is then the higher his or her level of life satisfaction. Further, activities requiring interpersonal interaction are especially powerful in increasing life satisfaction (Lemon et al., 1972).

The theory certainly is attractive to individuals in the aging field. In spite of limited support, it still appears in the literature and continues to drive popular thinking about aging. Although activity theory is overly simplistic as an explanation for successful aging, it does provide a useful perspective on aging. Indeed there are individuals who exemplify an activity approach to later life. The popularity of programs such as Elderhostel, Senior Olympics, and community centers supports an activity perspective.

The activity theory supports the traditional perspective and approach to constraints. A constraint is anything either inhibiting or preventing the replacement of lost activities, or roles, by other activities. Constraints would influence not only activity engagement but also psychological well-being. They are also linked to low self-esteem, negative self-concept, and negative affect. The activity perspective would view constraints as age-related factors, such as decreasing physical ability, as well as socially constructed factors, such as ageism and negative stereotypes. Within this perspective, constraints such as money, time, health, and facilities might also be present.

Disengagement Theory

Disengagement theory (Achenbaum & Bengston, 1994; Cumming & Henry, 1961) sprung from an aging perspective built around social disconnection and based primarily on the social system. Its central premise is a process of disengagement is inevitable in later life. As people age it is functional for them to gradually withdraw from roles, other people, and activities. This withdrawal is mutual (the individual withdraws from society and society withdraws from the individual) and desirable. As people age, they disengage from roles and social relationships. This disengagement is permanent and beneficial. This model does seem to explain some individuals' approach to later life. Constricting life space and restricting social interaction does appear to be a successful approach to later life for some individuals.

Disengagement theory provides an interesting perspective on leisure constraints. In some ways it is a paradoxical perspective to much of our understanding of constraints. It would suggest constraints to successful aging are things prohibiting or limiting the reduction of engagement in activities. Since disengagement theory indicates less is better, studying constraints would require examining factors that force individuals to stay active. This certainly has not been the constraint perspective commonly used. An alternative perspective would be to view constraints as positive forces in life. Disengagement implies we may welcome constraints because they limit involvement at the point in life when involvement needs to be limited.

Continuity Theory

Continuity theory, also identified as personality theory, attempted to reconcile the apparently contradictory activity and disengagement theories. Successful aging within the continuity perspective is contingent on the individual's ability to adapt to change and to use coping mechanisms developed throughout life. Neugarten, Havighurst, and Tobin (1968) identified various patterns of aging (reorganizer, focused, disengaged, achievement oriented, holding on, constricted, succorance seeking, apathetic, and disorganized). In addition they identified four personalities (integrated, armored–defended, passive–dependent, and unintegrated) within which the patterns are expressed. Continuity requires individuals "preserve continuity of attitudes, dispositions, preferences, and behaviors throughout their life course" (Utz et al., 2002, p. 523). Successful aging depends on adjusting and adapting, using previously successful mechanisms.

Within the continuity perspective successful aging would be limited by factors intervening in the ability to use resources and compensatory mechanisms that have been effective throughout life. Constraints would be anything intervening on the prolongation of coping mechanisms. Factors traditionally examined in constraint research might operate within this realm. However, the "criterion variable" (Nadirova & Jackson, 2000) would be different under the continuity model. Rather than focusing on activity engagement (the criterion variable would be inability to start new activities, continue engagement, participate more) the continuity perspective would require viewing constraints as factors intruding upon an individual's ability to continue lifelong patterns of coping. For example, rather than asking whether "not having anyone to do the activity with" is a factor in limiting participation, a constraint question would be framed as "What limits your ability to call friends when you need assistance?" (assuming this has been a coping mechanism).

Theories Based on an Individual Perspective

Three theories—selective optimization with compensation, socioemotional selectivity theory, and gerotranscendence—are built on the notion successful aging evolves from what Baltes and Carstensen (1999) identified as a "redistribution of resources" by older people. They acknowledge losses as concomitants of aging, but also acknowledge the importance of older individuals reacting to these losses and not being "bullied" by them. They provide a unique perspective on losses of aging by viewing losses as counteracted by gains. As Baltes and Smith (1999) wrote, "conditions of loss, limitation, or deficit could also play a catalytic role for positive change." This paradoxical view frames constraints as necessary for true freedom since they provide the impetus for change (see the chapters by Jackson and Hutchinson & Kleiber, this volume).

Selective Optimization With Compensation

The selective optimization with compensation (SOC) theory was developed by Baltes (Baltes & Carstensen, 1996; Freund & Baltes, 1998, 2002) to reflect a process needed for continued growth in the later years. Within the SOC perspective individuals seek simultaneously to maximize gains while minimizing losses over time. Successful aging is defined as the minimization of loss and the maximization of gains. This is accomplished through the interplay of three mechanisms: selection, optimization, and compensation. SOC is based on the assumption the three processes underlie behavior and "in their orchestration, they generate and regulate development and aging" (p. 218).

Selection is the process of narrowing the range of possible activities to a smaller set and the "restriction of life domains as a consequence or in anticipation of changes in personal and environmental resources" (Baltes & Carstensen, 1996). Lang, Rieckmann, and Baltes (2002) viewed selection as the process of reducing the number of domains, goals, or activities in which one is engaged to allow an increased focus on the things most important to one's life. They illustrate selection using a leisure example: "We argue that in the context of aging, selection relates to reducing the diversity of activities (e.g., playing tennis or jogging) by excluding other activities within a domain of goal-relevant leisure activities (e.g., physical activity)" (p. 502). Selection may be as comprehensive as avoidance of an entire realm of behavior and as restricted as limited engagement in tasks within a single domain (Baltes & Carstensen, 1999). The result is the individual is able to focus energy and effort on fewer activities.

Optimization follows selection by allowing an individual to optimize engagement in a more limited activity set through utilizing remaining abilities at the highest level possible. Optimization may include focusing attention, persisting in movement toward a goal, practicing skills, acquiring new resources or skills, and devoting more time or effort to a specific activity.

Finally, *compensation* is the process of adapting activities and skills to shape them to meet goals. Compensation can occur through the use of external aids, increased effort, or prosthetic devices. It involves using alternative ways to reach desired goals once losses are experienced. Individuals with many resources are more able to successfully compensate for loss (Lang et al., 2002) and effectively reach desired goals.

Baltes and Baltes (1998) provided an example of SOC in their discussion of pianist Arthur Rubenstein. Rubenstein was asked how he was able to remain such a good concert pianist in his ninth decade of life. He responded that he played fewer pieces and practiced more. In addition he used variations and contrasts in speed to generate the impression of faster play. Rubenstein was reflecting selection (reducing the number of pieces he played), optimization (allowing more practice time on those pieces) and compensation (using an alternative approach to compensate for the loss of finger agility and psychomotor coordination). Baltes and Baltes (1998) summarized, "By careful selection, optimization, and compensation we are able to minimize the negative consequences from losses that occur with old age and to work on aspects of growth and new peaks of success, albeit in a more restricted range" (p. 17).

SOC implies older individuals make choices to maximize opportunities for Ulyssean living in later life. As Baltes and Smith (1999) wrote, "In late adulthood, because of the basic architecture of the life course, selection and especially compensation become increasingly important to maintain adequate levels of functioning and permit advances in select domains of functioning" (p. 162). Within the SOC perspective there would be choices made about losses. Some would be accepted as inevitable, irreversible, and non-negotiable. For example, failing eyesight and reaction time might render driving impossible. Inability to drive will remain a constraint and there may be necessary restrictions in the freedom to come and go as one pleases. However, an SOC approach would indicate the possibility of riding with a friend, but doing so on a limited basis to not overdo it. Rather than seeking ways to retain the status quo, the SOC model requires seeking maximization of a progressively shrinking life space. Bates and Baltes concluded: "Making smaller territories of life larger and more beautiful is at the core of *savoir vivre* in old age" (p. 19).

Constraints might be viewed from two different perspectives within the SOC theory. First would be the traditional view of constraints as those things intruding on the ability to select and to engage in activities after the process of selection, optimization, and compensation occurred. However, constraints may also limit the ability to engage in the SOC process. Evidence suggests (Freund & Baltes, 1998) using selection, optimization, and compensation may become more difficult in advanced old age, because SOC-related behaviors require resources, including efforts, skills, and organizational metastrategies, that may be lost with increasing age. Constraints, therefore, may be defined as those factors making it difficult to narrow one's activity focus, to optimize engagement in activities, or to effectively compensate for loss. The nature of constraints shifts from factors making it difficult to participate in a wide range of activities to factors inhibiting the ability to select, optimize, and compensate.

An alternative view of constraints would view them as positive factors in successful aging, because they force individuals to initiate the SOC process required for successful aging. Constraints are the catalyst to SOC and therefore allow individuals to make smaller territories from their larger early life. In this sense constraints set older individuals free.

Socioemotional Selectivity Theory

The socioemotional selectivity theory focuses on social interaction and how it decreases as age increases. According to Baltes and Carstensen (1999):

> the reduction in the breadth of older people's social networks and social participation reflects, in part, a motivated redistribution of resources by the elderly person, in which engagement in a selected range of social functions and a focus on close emotional relationships gives rise to meaningful emotional experience. (p. 215)

A process similar to that identified in the selective optimization with compensation theory occurs within socioemotional selectivity, with a focus on social relationships. The goal in social relationships becomes emotional support—more peripheral relationships not providing this support are curtailed. The theory views reduction in social circles as an efficacious approach to successful aging, or as Carstensen (1993) wrote, "as I pursued a line of research initially aimed at identifying the psychopathological concomitants of social inactivity in the very old, I became increasingly convinced of the adaptive value of reduced social activity" (p. 210). She describes socioemotional selectivity as a choice by older individuals, rather than as an imposition by society,

to narrow one's social environment by reducing social contacts.

According to Carstensen (1993) social contact becomes less important to many older individuals for three reasons. First, as age increases, need for the transmission of knowledge and information through social interaction decreases. This occurs because the amount of information an individual has increases with age and therefore "information rich" contacts are less likely to occur. In addition, individuals acquire skills needed to gain information through other means, such as reading. The second reason older individuals may seek fewer social interactions is they have a decreasing need to develop a sense of self, a process requiring exposure to a wide circle of people, and an increased focus on maintaining the already established sense of self, requiring more selectivity in partners, because affirmation and support is necessary. As a result the focus shifts from seeking the widest variety of social contacts possible to seeking affirmation from a smaller circle of significant others. The final reason for socioemotional selectivity is older individuals increasingly seek social contacts because of their affective quality. The result is a preference for contact with people already known rather than seeking novel interaction. Carstensen cautions this may not be related to age per se, but rather the perceived nearness of death. The result of all this is a reduction of social interaction accompanied by an increase in interaction with close friends and loved ones, since they are more likely to provide what is needed from social interaction. Carstensen (1993) concluded:

> It may well be that old age, more than any other period in life, liberates people from the need to pursue social contacts devoid of emotional rewards, in which complex emotions dominate the affective sphere and a final integration of meaning and purpose in life can be achieved. (p. 244)

Baltes and Carstensen (1999) hinted at the relationship of socioemotional selectivity to constraints. They wrote:

> By molding social environments, constructing them in a way that maximizes the potential for positive affect and minimizes the potential for negative affect, older people increase the odds that they will regulate the emotional climate, which, at the end of life, may represent the supreme social goal. (p. 216)

The ultimate outcome of socioemotional selectivity is a decrease in the size of an individual's social circle. New friendships are less likely than earlier in life, primarily friendships lacking depth and emotional payoffs.

Constraints within this framework can serve a positive purpose by allowing individuals to limit their social circle because of health, time, and money. From a more traditional view, constraints within this theory would also be those things inhibiting the creation of a small circle of supportive friends.

Gerotranscendance

An alternative view of aging is provided in a theory called gerotranscendence (Jonson & Magnusson, 2001; Lewin, 2001; Tornstam, 1992). Gerotranscendence posits a redefinition of the self as individuals age. According to Jonson and Magnusson (2001), the theory was developed by Tornstan based on a belief that gerontological theorizing viewed activity as good and inactivity bad. He viewed this as a western perspective in that productivity was valued, whereas weakness and dependency were to be avoided. According to Jonson and Magnusson, "Tornstam set out to outline an alternative and phenomenologically inspired theory of aging where performance-oriented human qualities of the productive sphere were replaced by alternative qualities such as rest, relaxation, comfortable laziness, play, creativity and 'wisdom'" (p. 318). The process of gerotranscendence is marked by a shift in perspective from a material one to a more cosmic and transcendent one. The transcendent individual sees the world from a new perspective, marked by decreased preoccupation with the self and material things. The link with earlier generations is strengthened. However, general social interactions may lose importance. Solitude increases in importance, as does altruism. Material things may lose importance, with this loss counterbalanced by an understanding of the freedom of asceticism. The changing worldview experienced as gerotranscendence frees the individual from traditional ways of viewing life.

From the perspective of this theory, constraints might be viewed very differently from our more traditional model. Constraints may be positive forces in developing the transcendent perspective. Decreased functional levels may make it easier to shift from egoism to altruism. Decreased financial resources may hasten the realization that material goods are not significant in successful aging. The loss of friends may enhance intergenerational appreciation. The gerotranscendent approach to the later years is a framework that causes us to reevaluate the role of constraints. A life free of constraints, with unlimited resources and unlimited time, would prevent a person from reaching the transcendent state that Tornstam viewed as a requirement for successful aging.

Theory Based on an Institutional Perspective

A very different perspective on aging and older individuals is provided by the political economy of aging perspective. McMullin (2000) viewed this perspective as shifting focus when examining problems of the aging population from the individual and his or her declining capacities to social structures. Quadagno and Reid (1999) stated the political economy approach views public policy as an "outcome of the social struggles and dominant power relations of the era, which are not merely components of private sector relationships but also are adjudicated within the state" (p. 348). Factors such as social policy and the social structure are explanations for the problems faced by older individuals. For example, decisions about medical care, retirement benefits, transportation, and food stamps programs are based on political ideology, and these decisions impact older individuals. The focus of the political economy perspective shifts from the individual's ability to change and adapt over time, as seen in selective compensation with optimization and socioemotional selectivity, to an examination of how institutions impact well-being in the later years (Quadagno & Reid, 1999). Within this perspective constraints arise from forces outside the individual and are imposed by political structures and entities. As Quadagno and Reid wrote, political economy "emphasizes that the analysis of social policy must not only consider political, social, and economic consequences of policy provisions but also the underlying processes that create structural barriers to equality" (p. 355). The focus on constraint research within this model would be at the policy level, examining how social policies, including funding decisions, as well as the social construction of old age, create inequalities and result in constraints on individuals. It is noteworthy that few efforts to examine constraints have revolved around the examination of social policy and how policies are determined and implemented.

Alternative Perspectives on Later Life Constraints

Most constraints research starts with a question implying, or directly stating, the presumed impact of constraints. Simply put, previous research typically started with the presumption constraints negatively impact participation, although some research (Shaw, Bonen & McCabe, 1991) found otherwise. This approach is not surprising, because a primary requirement for leisure is perceived freedom and therefore anything impinging on this freedom is viewed as deleterious. The leap from constraints to restricted freedom is easy to make and seems logical.

Recently, Nadirova and Jackson (2000) called for a broadening of the criterion variables against which we measure the impact of constraints. However, their underlying perspective on constraints was illustrated in the first question they asked study participants: "Do you feel the amount of your leisure time or the type of recreation activities that you want to do are constrained (restricted or inhibited) in any way?" A "yes" response required participants to indicate whether these constraints resulted in activities they wanted to start but could not, ceasing participation in activities they would have liked to continue, participation at less frequency than desired, and/or decreased enjoyment of activities. However, the exploration of aging theory and the role of constraints points toward an additional criterion variable: a welcome decrease in the range of activity options and reduced need to make decisions. It may be that the presence of some constraints free individuals to pursue other activities, or to remain blissfully inactive. In a sense a red light on roads may serve as a metaphor for this type of constraint. The red light limits travel. We are not free to move as we might like, as the light controls the flow of traffic. Many might indeed identify the light as a constraint to their driving behavior. However, most would probably not want the light removed, recognizing the resulting anarchy would ultimately restrict driving even further. We suggest that when examining constraints in later life there may be similar "red lights" serving to limit participation at the most elementary level, but on deeper examination allowing a lifestyle more suited to one's desires.

Fully understanding leisure constraints in later life is a challenging task. The realities of aging, such as loss of health, decreased income, loss of friends, and physical and cognitive decline, would seem to indicate the number and severity of constraints will increase as one moves further along the aging path. Much research supports this conclusion. Nevertheless, a complete representation of constraints in old age may require a shift in perspective, and an acknowledgment that in some circumstances constraints may, paradoxically, assist in successful aging. Coincidentally, the political economy perspective also calls for expanding the examination of constraints in later life. Since older individuals are among the most marginalized of groups, the search to understand constraints should expand beyond viewing them solely as individual phenomena and include a search for institutional factors resulting from inequalities in the social system.

Conclusion

Our examination of leisure constraints in the later years supports the need to expand research efforts examining leisure constraints. The possibility a category of constraints may be beneficial to successful aging and optimum leisure involvement is intriguing. We suggest expanding the conceptualization of constraint categories to include beneficial constraints and to initiate the process of determining whether it is valid. In this chapter we focused on the existence of beneficial constraints in the later years. However, it may be that others also experience beneficial constraints. For example, the presence of children may constrain leisure involvement by young couples, but may also be crucial in facilitating family bonding through leisure. Adolescents' leisure may be constrained by their parents, but parental intervention may also protect youth from engaging in risky behavior. It is possible factors limiting some leisure behaviors may facilitate other leisure behaviors. Most previous research focused on what was lost as a result of constraints—perhaps it is time to examine what is gained.

Our argument also supports the utility of examining leisure constraints from a more theoretical perspective than has happened to date. Placing constraints within a selective optimization with compensation, gerotranscendence, or political economy of aging framework provides fresh insights into the nature of constraints. It is possible a multitude of other theories, such as exchange theory and self-determination theory, could provide insights into leisure constraints. The reverse may also be true: examining constraints may provide insight into the theory.

Like others before us, we also suggest future research expand the examination of constraints beyond their link to leisure participation. We used a successful aging perspective to anchor our examination of constraints. It would be beneficial to link constraints to other outcomes, such as quality of life, family interaction, community satisfaction, or social networks. The present state of research about constraints, leisure, and aging is incomplete. The approach taken in this chapter will, it is hoped, be a catalyst to further research, designed to achieve a more detailed mosaic of the importance and role of constraints in later life.

References

Achenbaum, W. A. and Bengston, V. L. (1994). Re-engaging the disengagement theory: On the history and assessment of theory development in gerontology. *The Gerontologist, 34,* 756–763.

Administration on Aging. (2002). *A profile of older Americans.* Washington, DC: Author. Retrieved from http://aoa.gov/prof/statistics/profile/profiles2002.asp

Baltes, M. M. and Carstensen, L. L. (1996). The process of successful aging. *Aging and Society, 16,* 397–422.

Baltes, M. M. and Carstensen, L. L. (1999). Social-psychological theories and their applications to aging: From individual to collective. In V. L. Bengston and K. W. Schaie (Eds.), *Handbook of theories of aging* (pp. 209–226). New York, NY: Springer.

Baltes, P. B. and Baltes, M. M. (1998). Savior vivre in old age: How to master the shifting balance between gains and losses. *National Forum, 78*(2), 13–18.

Baltes, P. B. and Smith. J. (1999). Multilevel and systemic analyses of old age: Theoretical and empirical evidence for a fourth age. In V. L. Bengston and K. W. Schaie (Eds.), *Handbook of theories of aging* (pp. 153–173). New York, NY: Springer.

Bruce, D. G., Devine, A., and Prince, R. L. (2002). Recreational physical activity levels in healthy older women: The importance of fear of falling. *The Journal of the American Geriatrics Society, 50,* 84–89.

Buchanan, T. and Allen, L. (1983). *Barriers to participation among the urban elderly.* Paper presented at the 1983 Society of Park and Recreation Educators Leisure Research Symposium, Kansas City, MO.

Carstensen, L. L. (1993). Motivation for social contact across the life span: A theory of socioemotional selectivity. In J. E. Jacobs (Ed.), *Developmental perspectives on motivation: Nebraska Symposium on Motivation, Volume 40* (pp. 209–254). Lincoln, NE: University of Nebraska Press.

Clayton, L. (2002). *The use of concept marring to evaluate the isomorphism of the hierarchical leisure constraint model.* Unpublished doctoral dissertation, Clemson University, Clemson, SC.

Cumming, E. and Henry, W. E. (1961). *Growing old: The process of disengagement.* New York, NY: Basic Books.

Elster, J. (2000). *Ulysses unbound.* Cambridge, England: Cambridge University Press.

Fleisher, A. and Pizam, A. (2002). Tourism constraints among Israel seniors. *Annals of Tourism Research, 29,* 106–123.

Freund, A. M. and Baltes, P. B. (1998). Selection, optimization, and compensation as strategies of life management: Correlations with subjective indicators of successful aging. *Psychology and Aging, 13,* 531–543.

Freund, A. M. and Baltes, P. B. (2002). Life-management strategies of selection, optimization and compensation: Measurement by self-report and construct validity. *Journal of Personality and Social Psychology, 82,* 642–662.

Grant, B. C. (2001). 'You're never too old': Beliefs about physical activity and playing sport in later life. *Aging and Society, 21,* 777–798.

Havighurst, R. J. and Albrecht, R. (1953). *Older people.* New York, NY: Longmans.

Iso-Ahola, S. E., Jackson, E. L., and Dunn, E. (1994). Starting, ceasing, and replacing leisure activities over the human lifespan. *Journal of Leisure Research, 26,* 227–249.

Jackson, E. J. (1993). Recognizing patterns of leisure constraints: Results from alternative analyses. *Journal of Leisure Research, 25,* 129–140.

Jackson, E. L. and Witt, P. A. (1994). Change and stability in leisure constraints: A comparison of two surveys conducted four years apart. *Journal of Leisure Research, 26,* 322–336.

Jonson, H. and Magnusson, J. A. (2001). A new age of old age? Gerotranscendence and the re-enhancement of aging. *Journal of Aging Studies, 15,* 317–331.

Katz, S. (2000). Busy bodies: Activity, aging, and the management of everyday life. *Journal of Aging Studies, 14,* 135–152.

Lang, F. R., Rieckmann, N., and Baltes, M. M. (2002). Adapting to aging losses: Do resources facilitate strategies of selection, compensation, and optimization in everyday functioning. *Journal of Gerontology: Psychological Sciences, 57B,* 501–509.

Lemon. B. W., Bengston, V. L., and Peterson, J. A. (1972). An exploration of the activity theory of aging: Activity types and life satisfaction among in-movers to a retirement community. *Journal of Gerontology, 27,* 511–523.

Lewin, F. A. (2001). Gerotranscendence and different cultural settings. *Aging and Society, 21,* 395–415.

Lynott, R. J. and Lynott, P. P. (1996). Tracing the course of theoretical development in the sociology of aging. *The Gerontologist, 36,* 749–760.

McGuire, F. A. (1984). A factor analytic study of leisure constraints in advanced adulthood. *Leisure Sciences, 6,* 313–326.

McGuire, F. A., Boyd, R. K., and Tedrick, R. E. (1999). *Leisure and aging: Ulyssean living in later life* (2nd ed.). Champaign, IL: Sagamore Publishing.

McGuire, F. A., Dottavio, D., and O'Leary, J. T. (1986). Constraints to participation in outdoor recreation across the life span: A nationwide study of limitors and prohibitors. *The Gerontologist, 26,* 538–544.

McLeish, J. (1976). *The Ulyssean adult: Creativity in middle and later years.* Toronto, Ontario, Canada: McGraw-Hill/Ryerson.

McMullin, J. A. (2000). Diversity and the state of sociological aging theory. *The Gerontologist, 40,* 517–530.

Murphy, S. L., Williams, C. S., and Gill, T. M. (2002). Characteristics associated with fear of falling and activity restriction in community-living older persons. *Journal of the American Geriatrics Society, 50,* 516–520.

Nadirova, A. and Jackson, E. L. (2000). Alternative criterion variables against which to assess the impact of constraints to leisure. *Journal of Leisure Research, 32,* 396–405.

Neugarten, B. L., Havighurst, R. J., and Tobin, S. S. (1968). Personality and patterns of aging. In B. L. Neugarter (Ed.), *Middle age and aging* (pp. 173–177). Chicago, IL: University of Chicago Press.

Phelan, E. A. and Larson, E. B. (2002). Successful aging—Where next? *Journal of the American Geriatric Society, 50,* 1306–1308.

Quadagno, J. and Reid, J. (1999). The political economy perspective in aging. In V. L. Bengston and K. W. Schaie (Eds.), *Handbook of theories of aging* (pp. 344–358). New York, NY: Springer.

Recer, P. (2003). Study: Elderly enjoying more vigorous old age. In H. Cox (Ed.), *Annual editions: Aging* (15th ed.). Guilford, CT: McGraw-Hill/Dushkin.

Rogers, W. A., Meyer, B., Walker, N., and Fisk, A. D. (1998). Functional limitations to daily living tasks in the aged: a focus group analysis. *Human Factors, 40,* 111–126.

Rowe, J. W. and Kahn, R. L. (1998). *Successful aging.* New York, NY: Pantheon Books.

Schroots, J. F. (1996). Theoretical developments in the psychology of aging. *The Gerontologist, 36,* 742–748.

Shaw, S. M., Bonen, A., and McCabe, J. F. (1991). Do more constraints mean less leisure? Examining the relationship between constraints and participation. *Journal of Leisure Research, 23,* 286–301.

Shogan, D. (2002). Characterizing constraints of leisure: a Foucaultian analysis of leisure constraints. *Leisure Studies, 21,* 27–38.

Statistics Canada (2001). Profile of the Canadian population by age and sex: Canada ages, 2001 census (Analysis series, 2001 census). Retrieved September 5, 2003, from http://www.statcan.ca

Strain, L. A., Grabusic, C. C., Searle, M. S., and Dunn, N. J. (2002). Continuing and ceasing leisure activities in later life: A longitudinal study. *The Gerontologist, 42,* 217–223.

Tornstam, L. (1992). The quo vadis of gerontology: On the scientific paradigm in gerontology. *The Gerontologist, 32,* 318–325.

Trochim, W. M. K. (1989). A introduction to concept mapping for planning and evaluation. *Evaluation and Program Planning, 12,* 1–16.

Utz, R. L., Carr, D., Nesse, R., and Wortman, C. B. (2002). The effect of widowhood on older adults' social participation: An evaluation of activity, disengagement, and continuity theories. *The Gerontologist, 42,* 522–533.

Witt, P. A. and Goodale, T. L. (1981). The relationships between barriers to leisure enjoyment and family stages. *Leisure Sciences, 4,* 29–49.

Chapter 7

Fear of Violence: Contested Constraints by Women in Outdoor Recreation Activities

M. Deborah Bialeschki (University of North Carolina–Chapel Hill)

On a warm early summer day, two women were brutally murdered while backpacking in a well-known national park. They were experienced hikers on a five-day vacation that ended tragically when a man decided that they deserved to die because of who they were, and where they were, and what they were doing. This event sent shock waves through the outdoor community as people struggled to comprehend this type of danger in outdoor activities. While many women outdoor enthusiasts were outraged, most women recognized that the fear of physical violence with which they have learned to live on a daily basis was merely made visible yet again—just a different scenario.

The issue of fear in recreation activities is rarely considered when examining perceptions of constraints held by an individual. When fear has emerged as a consideration, the focus has generally centered on fears arising from the outdoor environment or safety issues related to personal skill development (Ewert, 1989; Holyfield & Fine, 1997; Little, 2002; Pohl, Borrie & Patterson, 2000). For women, however, a different type of fear is often present: the fear of physical violence. In the few studies of leisure that explored the issue of fear of violence, the findings suggested this constraint exists within many aspects of women's lives and is manifested in varied forms (Bialeschki, 1999; Bialeschki & Hicks, 1998; Coble, Selin & Erickson, 2003; Frances, 1997; James & Embrey, 2001; Mustaine & Tewksbury, 1998; Shaw & Whyte, 1996; Whyte & Shaw, 1994). As suggested by Green, Hebron, and Woodward (1987) and Frances (1997), fear can be used as a form of social control even though the woman may not have directly experienced a violent incident herself. However, researchers found some women confront these fears and resist their control in ways that allow them to continue to participate in outdoor activities (Bialeschki & Hicks, 1998; Day, 1997; Henderson & Bialeschki, 1993).

The purpose of this chapter is to explore perceptions of fear of physical violence as a potential constraint for women. Within this exploration of fear as a constraint, social control obtained through levels of acceptance as well as instances of resistance by women are addressed. The context is primarily centered on outdoor recreation activities and the social construction of outdoor spaces. The chapter analyzes fear from a social interactionism perspective and proposes a model that explores how women confront fear of violence engaged in outdoor recreation activities. This type of analysis was suggested by Valentine (1992) when she called for more research to examine how women's experiences that run contrary to a woman's geography of fear affect perceptions of vulnerability.

The Construction of Fear of Violence

Before fear can be considered a potential constraint, we must understand how fear has been socially constructed. Fear seems, on the surface, to be an elementary concept with little need of explanation, but when viewed from a gendered perspective, the complexities begin to emerge.

The social construction of fear can be seen in women's lives as something "constantly trying to break the courage" (Koskela, 1997, p. 311). The ideology of fear is supported by crime news, violence in film and fiction, and security education that reminds women they need to be prepared for something violent to happen (Gardner,

1990). Warr and Stafford (1983) pointed out fear is an affective response quite distinct from judgments of victimization risk, and perceived risk has a potent influence on fear. Thus, one must distinguish between fear and perceived risk. Within the literature on fear, it is widely understood perceived risk is a necessary, but not sufficient, cause of fear. However, perceived risk is a significant influence on all forms of fear with incivility being the substantial basis (Ferraro, 1996). For example, I may decide to take a run alone during the day in my neighborhood. I am aware of a risk in this choice but am not particularly fearful. However, if I hear "cat calls" from a bystander as I run by him, my perception of risk may increase dramatically and result in a more fearful attitude for the rest of my run.

When confronted with the possibility of a crime of physical violence, the two primary reactions are fear and constrained behavior (Ferraro, 1996). Constrained behavior generally centers on adjustments in activities thought to lower the risks. This constrained behavior has two domains: avoidance behavior and defensive behavior. These two behaviors provide a continuum along which to manage the degree of fear experienced and the perception of risk accepted in a particular activity. However, Ferraro (1996) and Liska, Sanchirico, and Reed (1988) found although people intended to lower their fear by constraining behavior, their fear usually rose by such actions so that constrained behavior increased fear but not vice versa. For example, a woman may be interested in taking a walk in a local natural park but may be so fearful for her personal safety she decides she just can't risk it; in effect her avoidance of the park renders this area a "dangerous" place for her where she does few if any activities. As an alternative, this same woman could decide to go for her walk but take along pepper spray to "protect" her from a potential attacker. As suggested by the previous research, she may be more aware of the pepper spray she is carrying and her heightened sense of wariness of the happenings around her to the point her defensiveness and fear block all opportunities for any enjoyment of her time in the park.

Fear reflects the gendered power relations in society, especially when viewed as a product of systematic structural violence rather than actual attacks (Koskela, 1997). Even though young men are more likely to be victims of personal violence, women are the ones more fearful of physically violent crimes, because they perceive a unique and severe threat rarely felt by men: sexual violence (Baumer, 1978; Ferraro, 1995, 1996; Karmen, 1991; Liska, Sanchirico & Reed, 1988; Pain, 1997; Valentine, 1992; Warr, 1985). Rape has been called the "ever present terror" (Stanko, 1985, p. 34) and the "fe-

male fear" (Gordon & Riger, 1989). Sexual assault may actually "shadow" other types of victimization among women. Rape seems to operate like a "master offense" among women, especially younger women who have the highest rate of rape, which heightens fear reactions for other offenses. One study found controlling for the fear of rape eliminated the gender differences in fear of crimes to the point where the findings suggested men were more fearful than women of murder and assault (Ferraro, 1996).

Theories abound as to why rape and sexual violence against women are so ubiquitous (Baron & Straus, 1989; Bourque, 1989; Hollander, 2004; Stanko, 1985), yet no definitive answer exists. Gender inequality, pornography, social disorganization, and cultural acceptance of violence have been suggested as partial explanations that seem rooted in patriarchal attitudes. As hooks (1994) stated:

> We live in a culture that condones and celebrates rape. Within a phallocentric patriarchal state, the rape of women by men is a ritual that daily perpetuates and maintains sexist oppression and exploitation. We cannot hope to transform "rape culture" without committing ourselves fully to resisting and eradicating patriarchy. (p. 109)

Women's fears about physical assault center on the violent act (i.e., rape) as well as the stigma that accompanies the action (Gordon & Riger, 1989). An unsympathetic society, and often the woman herself, may feel she somehow "asked for it" through her dress, location, or activity. The media often interpret attacks as some responsibility of the woman, because she placed herself in areas where she was at risk. Women too often place responsibility on the victim as a way to convince themselves they will not be victimized, because they would not put themselves in the same place. The media generally place a disproportionate focus on attacks in public places rather than on the more common domestic violence, because these sensationalized public attacks sell and create an interesting human interest angle. The reality is that women are most at risk for sexual violence in their own homes from men they know (Pain, 1997). Ironically, the media do not tell women to stop dating or living with men if they are abused by a male partner; rather, they encourage women to transfer their threat appraisal from men (known and strangers) to public places (Valentine, 1992).

Violence against women has become so normalized that incidents are almost invisible (Wolf, 1991; Wood, 1994). This acceptance may be an indication of the way fear can be used as a form of social control even on women who have not personally experienced a violent incident (Frances, 1997; Green, et al., 1987; Mehta & Bondi, 1999). Social contact becomes the key method of spreading information about fear of violent personal crime (Skogan & Maxfield, 1981). For many women, their fear of violence (especially sexual violence) is therefore forged on personal experiences (i.e., their own experiences and the experiences of women close to them) of intimidating and/or violent sexual behavior as well as feelings of personal vulnerability. The result of all of these messages is that women are often perceived as sexualized objects of violence, allowing the aggressor to view them as "Other."

This process of "Othering" women may be a key element in the victimization of women through sexual assault and may indirectly contribute to constraints on women's outdoor experiences and leisure. "Othering" is the process of constructing the Other by "defining where you belong through a contrast with other places, or who you are through a contrast with other people" (Rose, 1995, p. 116). Characterized by dualisms, this process inevitably defines norms and deviants, centers and margins, cores and peripheries, the powerful and the powerless. Three fundamental relationships exist within this process of "Othering." First, the construction of the Other is dependent on a simultaneous construction of "the same," or something from which to be Other to. Second, this relationship is one of power whereby that defined as "same" is accorded greater power and status from that defined as Other. Third, the Other is accorded a gender and this gender is always feminized (Aitchison, 2000). In contemporary feminism, then, the concept of women as Other involves the central claim that Otherness is "projected on to women by, and in the interests of, men, such that we are constructed as inferior and abnormal" (Wilkinson & Kitsinger, 1996, pp. 3–4). This "Othering" opens the door for the construction of a perception that women involved in outdoor experiences are viewed as less powerful objects, are deviant and on the fringe of acceptable behaviors, and are therefore "fair game" for whatever may befall them.

Recognizing the way women as Other have been socially constructed illustrates the need to have men accept accountability for the ways in which masculinity and patriarchy contribute to this perspective. Male assailants who view women as Other depersonalize them in a way that the women become mere dehumanized objects. This dehumanizing process has led feminists to acknowledge that reconstruction and transformation of male behavior and masculinity are a necessary and essential part of the feminist agenda (Anderson & Umberson, 2004; hooks, 1989). Since the fear of physical violence is almost exclusively linked to male violence against women, this constraint for women involved in outdoor activities is intrinsically tied to a societal mandate with the onus on men. However, women have to devise a way to live with this reality of "the Other" until that transformation occurs.

The threat of violence to women is a "fact of life" ingrained in most girls and women at an early age (Buchwald, 1993; Herman, 1991). Almost every little girl is warned to "not talk with strange men and never ever accept a ride from them." Girls are often more supervised and restricted in play, especially in the outdoors. Valentine (1992) found the gender division of space becomes a reality for most children around age 11, when parental restrictions on boys' spatial ranges are relaxed but are restricted increasingly for girls with an emphasis on their physical vulnerability to sexual attack. For many girls adolescence is the turning point marked by a bold moment of defiance against parental warnings or a phase of accumulating uncertainty and fear (James & Embrey, 2001; Koskela, 1997). Most girls find themselves believing protective parents who instilled a sense of vulnerability in public space into their daughters that consequently affects their behavior and use of space (Valentine, 1992). These parents often actively encourage girls to seek the protection of one man from all men (e.g., father or husband as promoted by an ideology of family), which sets the stage for a disconnect between the reality of a geography of fear and the geography of violence. This geography of fear is constructed when girls and women are taught to see the private sphere of the home as the safe haven and the male partner as the protector, while the public sphere of outdoor spaces is to be constructed as dangerous environments of strange males with unpredictable occurrences of male violence (Ferraro, 1996; Pain, 1997; Valentine, 1992). However, statistics show women are most vulnerable to sexual assault in their own home with men they know, thus the reality of the "geography of violence" is in direct opposition to the socially constructed "geography of fear" (Koskela, 1997; Mehta & Bondi, 1999; Pain, 1997; Valentine, 1989, 1992).

The social construction of any social concept is complex and fraught with opposing interpretations and explanations. The deconstruction of women's fear of physical violence, particularly centered on rape, raises important questions about structured power relations and social constructions of masculinities and femininities. These personal images of fear are dynamic. They develop over time and space and vary in strength at different times in women's life cycles. As suggested by Aitchison (2000), analyses that address the sociocultural nexus of leisure relations therefore require the theorization of both structural and cultural power of material and symbolic power. A "geography of fear" sets the stage for examining more closely the roles of the physical environment, power, and the ways they affect outdoor recreation behaviors of women.

The Social Construction of Outdoor Environments

Findings from previous studies of constraints, violence, and women's leisure raised issues related to the way space, particularly outdoor space, has been socially defined (Bialeschki & Hicks, 1998; Day, 1997; Henderson & Bialeschki, 1993; Shaw & Whyte, 1996; Woodward, Green & Hebron, 1989). The association of outdoor recreation activities and environments has historically been with males (Henderson & Bialeschki, 1990/1991; Valentine, 1989, 1992). As mentioned in the previous section, a geography of fear describes public places as constructions of gendered space that privilege men, establishes a heterosexual scenario where a woman's interests and protection are represented by a man (Valentine, 1992), and is a spatial expression of patriarchy. This conception of public outdoor space combined with women's sense of physical vulnerability to men (Dobash & Dobash, 1992) established a framework of constraints built on the foundation of women's fear of violence in the outdoors. This perception allows women to be blamed and to be held responsible for being in "inappropriate" places. It acts as a warning to other women when something happens to a woman who does not heed the societal message and perpetuates a sexualized social representation of outdoor settings. The outcome seems to fit precisely the previously described process that constructs women involved in outdoor recreation as "the Other" (Aitchison, 2000; De Beauvoir, 1953; Wilkinson & Kitsinger, 1996).

The processes by which women develop images of certain environmental contexts as dangerous must be articulated if we are to understand women's use of spaces. An intertwining of women's common experiences of public space along with an ideology of the family and the gendered division of space, media hype of sexual assault, and social contact with friends, neighbors, and work associates have resulted in many outdoor recreation sites and activities fitting women's images of dangerous environments (Valentine, 1992). Many women ground instances of violence in space and time and reassure themselves they can stay safe by avoiding those places and times associated with danger. Information about attacks related to women's own lifestyles (geographically and socially) levels a strong impact on images of dangerous places because of the ease with which

a woman can imagine the same thing happening to her. For example, a woman who considers a greenway a safe place to bike during the day can suddenly have second thoughts when an evening broadcast carries a story about an attempted rape of a woman jogging along that same path earlier that afternoon.

The result of women's fear of physical violence and sexual assault is often seen as a limitation of women's mobility and a cause of restricted access to public spaces. Since public space can be understood as a medium for constructing identities and producing strategies for managing the self (Koskela, 1997; Ruddick, 1996), male domination and female victimization further subordinate women by limiting their construction of identity (Massey, 1994). Valentine's (1996) findings that access to some public places is limited based on gender implies everyday spaces are actively produced and bound into various and diverse dynamics of power and subjectivity (Koskela, 1997; Rose, 1993). As a consequence, resistance to constraints arising from these spatial relations has the potential to become a test of equality and a parameter of empowerment. As suggested by Koskela (1997), the question of fear and courage—women's ability to use public space—is a question of (re)defining and (re)producing space as well as managing the self.

Some women accept the challenge of reclaiming the outdoors and asserting their right to belong in that environment. Outdoor recreation settings and activities become sites for resistance and boldness. This boldness is associated with freedom, equality, and a sense of control over and possession of space. While fear of violence may undermine some of women's confidence, we know fear is a socially constructed state. That acknowledgement allows for the possibility that some women may redefine fear in ways that allow for a reemergence of confidence and possession of those outdoor environments. Some worry that women may actually place themselves in danger, because they defiantly resist following precautions that may alter the experience, or they exhibit naivetè concerning their vulnerability (Colasduro, 1997; Whyte & Shaw, 1994). However, these challenging women may see their actions as emancipatory. Despite the risks, these women demonstrate their agency over their own lives in a way that actively produces, defines, and reclaims space (Alcoff, 1996). These examples of resistance to constraints of violence support the new cultural geographies that suggest sexuality and gender must be considered as we find people beginning to redefine place in terms of their own negotiations of constraints.

New cultural geography provides a different context from which to analyze the role of violence in women's outdoor experiences. It places greater emphasis on agency rather than structure and is critical of researchers who "celebrate" place without problematizing space and place in relation to gender and sexuality (Aitchison, 1999). The literature suggests a discussion of spaces needs to acknowledge the diversity and plurality of agencies, particularly those aspects previously defined as marginal or peripheral, as well as to recognize the microsocial and cultural phenomena in shaping spatial relations (Aitchison, 1999; Giddens, 1984). As cultural geography emerged, it became a part of sociological and cultural studies analyses that focus on the multiplicity of behaviors, meanings, and identities constructed in and through leisure. This approach considers gender and sexuality as key cultural constructs in the social construction of space (Aitchison & Jordan, 1998). Through cultural geography we have a tool to investigate the multiplicities of behaviors, meanings, and identities constructed in and through leisure, and we can give attention to the relative and symbolic nature of space and place. With place viewed not as a fixed concept, but as a result of struggles of power and resistance, we have a powerful way to examine women's fear of violence in outdoor recreation activities and spaces.

A Model to Challenge the Dominant Paradigm of Fear and Outdoor Recreation

Background of the Model

The focus of a model is simply to tell a story of relationships. The story for the model presented in this chapter is one of how some women resist socially constructed behavioral controls as they negotiate their personal fear of violence when engaged in outdoor recreation experiences. Rather than adopt either a structuralist perspective that relies on resistance as a direct challenge to hegemonic structured power relations, or a postmodernist and poststructuralist perspective that focuses on a diffusion of power and a rejection of structural relations of power (Shaw, 2001), a social interactionist perspective underpinned the analyses of data on which this model of constraint and resistance was constructed. The model (**Figure 7.1**, p. 108) illustrates the melding of individual microlevel experiences and subjectivities with a macrolevel analysis of structured relations of power as suggested by Shaw (2001).

Bialeschki and Hicks (1998; see also Bialeschki, 1999) derived the model from studies of women's

fear of violence, although studies by Whyte and Shaw (1994), Delamere (1998), Day (1997), James and Embrey (2001), and Pohl, Borrie, and Patterson (2000) were also considered for their perspectives. A brief summary of key findings from past studies follows to provide a basic understanding for the fundamental elements of the proposed model. These findings are from Bialeschki and Hicks (1998; see also Bialeschki 1999, 2002) unless otherwise referenced.

When asked about participation in outdoor recreation activities, most women identified their fear about physical violence while engaged in outdoor activities as a major constraint for them. Women and girls often voiced concern and frustration similar to the following quotes:

> The only thing I worry about as far as being a woman is male human predators. There have been women attacked while hiking. That is what I fear most.

> It's just frustrating. I think it would be a lot of fun to go camping by myself...even simply walking at the lake is something I used to do on a regular basis. I still hesitate because I hear of these attacks you know. And that I just think is sad.

These women outdoor enthusiasts also added these fears rarely stopped them from participating in their favorite outdoor pursuits. They felt the benefits from these activities far outweighed the fear of potential violence. These benefits included health and well-being, their love of the outdoors and their favorite activities, shared social opportunities as well as valued time alone, and a sense of autonomy, independence, and freedom. Their refusal to let their fear control their actions spoke to the importance of these values gained through outdoor activities. As one woman stated:

> I wouldn't just deliberately do something and say "I dare you to come and get me," but part of me refuses to lock myself in my house and never go out, because there is evil out there...try not to be stupid about the things I do. When you have been raised and all your life you have felt free to do things that you felt like doing, it is real hard to give that up. You can get real resentful about not feeling safe. Some of it is just stubbornness.

These women were clear that while they respected their feelings of fear of physical violence, they did not feel it was a paranoid reaction. They often talked about taking precautions, being frank in their admission of the possibilities for "something to happen," and using common sense. As one woman stated:

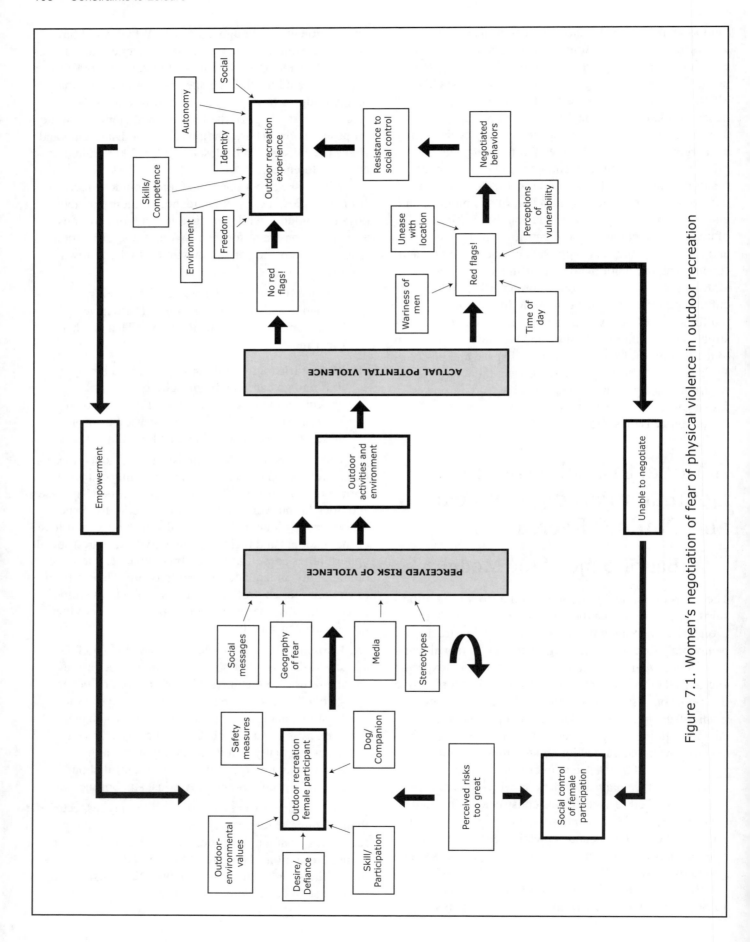

Figure 7.1. Women's negotiation of fear of physical violence in outdoor recreation

I hate to use the word "fear." It's not really fear—it's more like being cautious. It's not being fearful. It is just not being naïve. I will try to prevent a situation from happening by keeping myself out of it rather than doing it and being paranoid.

Most women outdoor enthusiasts mentioned an awareness of their personal "red flags" or danger signals. Some of these signals were similar to the ones found by Whyte and Shaw (1994) that centered on location, time of day, and being alone. One of the most prevalent warning signals underlined the women's general wariness of men when outdoors and the need to "keep your guard up." This quote illustrates the concern women had about men in these spaces:

When I am in the outdoors doing stuff, I am more afraid of guys. I know I shouldn't be, but it seems like a male can do more harm than a female even if you're with a small group. Just first impression, usually I would be more apt to be frightened of a male than a female.

Other signals directly or indirectly linked to men centered on uncomfortable feelings of vulnerability and intimidation when subjected to behaviors such as yelling or "wolf calling," cruising, hanging out (especially if drinking), acting suspicious or out of place, and encountering young all-male groups.

When the women discussed their personal danger signals, they often talked about strategies they used before and during their outdoor activities to reduce their fears about personal violence. Many of their strategies centered on taking precautions and planning ahead. The women developed techniques and behaviors such as telling others where they were going, developing skills and competencies in their outdoor activities, and planning their activities to avoid "stupid" mistakes. Comments such as, "I think I view myself differently because I have a lot of experience...I have had a lot of training that makes it comfortable for me" illustrated the value of experience to them. They talked about not wearing headphones while outside, carrying a whistle or perhaps pepper spray, and being sure to tell a friend where they were going. As one woman stated, "I just make sure I plan ahead. I make sure I know my safety guidelines or rules." Other strategies focused on the location and the time of day in which the women did outdoor activities, participating with other companions, and taking along a dog, particularly if going alone. Every woman had her own rationale for how these varied strategies reassured her and helped her feel more in control of her personal safety.

An interesting component about these red flags and strategies is they appeared to be fluid and continually reassessed, adapted, or discarded in response to the environment encountered while engaged in their outdoor activities. The women seemed to have a primary plan, a backup ("plan B"), and a variety of other options should any number of conditions change while involved in their outdoor activities. Strategies used to feel safe at the beginning of an outdoor experience did not guarantee feeling safe from personal violence during the entire experience. The women constantly were alert for red flags and the possibility of continual negotiations of threatening situations, but refused to let the potential for violence control their outdoor behaviors. Only when the potential for danger became a perceived risk with very real possibilities did most women alter their outdoor experiences.

Elements of the Model

The basic premise of the model is that women who want to engage in outdoor activities have varied constraints related to physical violence that must be negotiated at multiple critical incidences. The following example will help us to move through the model and to explore relationships that may exist for women and how we deal with the potential for physical violence.

Imagine a woman who wants to be involved in an outdoor experience, particularly something like running, which she enjoys doing alone. As an outdoor recreation participant, she has been and continues to be influenced by her past experiences. She may have strong environmental values and a developed sense of place that drives her to be engaged in the outdoors. Over time she develops a repertoire of outdoor skills, as well as varied safety schemes that help her feel comfortable in the outdoors. Her desire to "be outside" may be the platform from which she appears deviant and unwilling to succumb to messages of fear. She may agree to participate with other friends or take along her dog as a safety precaution, but her desire and motivation for being outdoors and engaged in activities she likes is high.

As she readies for her run, she must first address her individual perceptions of risk of violence (Stage 1). These perceptions are mediated by her experiences and values as just described, but she must also consider the impact of past media and socially constructed stereotypes as discussed earlier in this chapter. As this act of personal cost–benefit occurs, some women may not be able to move beyond fear-inspiring perceptions, so they succumb to the social controls that restrict them from certain outdoor experiences.

A woman who decides to step beyond these initial perceived risks and to enter into the actual experience may or may not encounter occasions of actual risks of violence (Stage 2). At this point, she again chooses a particular course of action for continued participation (Stage 3). If no red flags appear, she enjoys varied benefits, such as increased outdoor skills and competencies, freedom, autonomy, new environmental values, a sense of place, and possibly a different sense of identity—all associated with the outdoor experience. The woman appears to have no sense of being socially controlled and may actually experience a heightened sense of personal empowerment that may strengthen her feelings of desire and competence the next time she considers her outdoor activities.

However, if our runner perceives warning red flags during her activity, such as unease with a location, unknown men loitering, feelings of vulnerability, and concern for time of day, she may have a different set of constraints to negotiate. She may use strategies (often developed in Stage 1 for potential use later on) to reduce or eliminate the perceived danger. If successful with these strategies, she continues on in her run with the same potential for benefits from the experience as if she had encountered no red flags. The argument can be made that women who have to do additional negotiations are subjected to a partially controlled experience, particularly if their negotiation of potential violence continues to place limitations on their behaviors.

If our woman runner is unable to handle the danger signals safely and has to end her run prematurely, she is similar to women in Stage 1 who were unable to overcome their fears around the perceived potential for violence. Her threatening experiences encountered in the outdoors will be added to her collective perceptions regarding outside activities and spaces and potentials for violence directed toward her. The extent of social control felt by women will be interpreted within their own frame of reference of perceived and actual risk of violence, past experiences, social messages, and values associated with these outdoor activities and spaces.

Discussion

The model raises some interesting issues related to resistance, empowerment, agency, and social control through constructed social structures. Most women see their participation mainly as an expression of their love of the outdoors and particular outdoor activities. Their resistance to social control of their access to the outdoor environment or the activities usually consists of individual acts. However, one could argue they are also collective in that they directly resist a socially constructed ideology of femininity, male-defined outdoor space, and violence. Their individual acts could be perceived as operating in "the margin" where social change is created (hooks, 1996). The outcomes of women engaging in outdoor activities could result in personal empowerment, but could also result in potential for social change. For example, women who engage in these outdoor experiences would be seen by other women who may then be encouraged to participate in similar "resistive behaviors" or at least question the societal assumptions about femininity, outdoor spaces, and activities, and women as objects of violence. As suggested by Shaw (2001), this questioning or participation in behavioral challenges can extend to larger dominant ideologies about gender behavior, appearance expectations, and gendered inequalities in opportunities for and provision of activities.

The intentionality of women's resistance is another point that deserves attention. While each woman may have her own reasons for participating in outdoor activities, which range along a continuum of deliberate and conscious acts of ideological challenge to nonintentional acts that merely reflected a personal interest, the outcomes can still be seen to empower individuals and challenge dominant views. However, the interaction is further complicated when resistance strategies must be continually evaluated with the possibility initial acts may not continue in the same manner. Women find themselves once again feeling socially controlled in outdoor activities where perceived risks eventually outweigh the benefits. The model illustrates this interaction and provides a basis from which to analyze how the process of resistance may work for certain women with high values on outdoor recreation experiences.

The process in the model parallels what Wearing (1998) suggested about the importance of personal space for leisure when she said, "leisure spaces can provide possibilities for women...to rewrite or resignify women's subjectivities so they are no longer inferiorized" (p. 145). Rojek (1990) suggested ambiguity and hyperreality of a postmodern world run counter to the lived reality of many people that is often other-determined. As suggested by Kiewa (2001), a narrative of self as victim may inspire resentment and a desire to resist. I suggest that the process used by women outdoor recreationists is a model for resisting that other-determined, victimized life. These postmodern women would have a "new self-confidence to challenge the givens of their existence, to resist what they have been told they are and to reach toward what they could be" (Wearing, 1998, pp. 144–145). Perhaps women who address their fears of physical violence while involved in outdoor activities are practically and symbolically rejecting the label of victim and asserting their freedom to choose to resist (Foucault, 1983; McHoul & Grace, 1993).

The use of public space as a site of resistance to dominant discourses on womanhood and femininity has been recognized by many researchers (Burgess, 1998; Valentine, 1989, 1992, 1996; Wearing, 1998; Wilson, 1989). As suggested by Wearing (1998), these public spaces offer opportunities to develop the self that go beyond incremental resistance to male power. Outdoor activities may be important enough to some women to risk physical violence, even rape that attaches a social stigma to the victim, so they can construct their own meanings in relation to themselves. The simplistic description of the model as a negotiation of fear in outdoor activities may operate at a deeper level, which describes the use of space for discovering and becoming one's sense of self. The self that leaves these outdoor spaces is rarely the same as the self that enters (Wearing, 1998).

Ultimately, the model is one attempt to provide an interpretation of how women consider activities in contested environments, assess perceptions of risks and constraints, and make choices that result in personal as well as collective outcomes. The outcomes from these confrontations can range from personal restrictions and social control that reinforce dominant ideologies to personal empowerment and broad social change that enhance the lives of women. Perhaps this model illustrates what Wearing (1998) and Foucault (1986) discussed as "heterotopia."

I suggest both physical and metaphorical leisure spaces can act as heterotopias for struggle against and resistance to domination of the self and inferiorized subjectivities. They also provide a space for reconstituting the self and rewriting the script of identity. In this sense, for women, leisure is a "heterotopia," a personal space for resistance to domination, a space where there is room for the self to expand beyond what it is told it should be. Woodbury (cited in Wearing, 1998) took this idea a bit further in this conclusion:

Women need safe outdoor leisure and recreation settings for the spaces within to be inhabitable. It is relation to the exterior that the individual shatters, carves up and landscapes—or seascapes— the self. It is relation to others that the individual cuts through the boundaries of personal identity and recreates the interior. (p. 141)

The ways in which women address their fear of violence in outdoor recreation activities raise a dilemma in our current patriarchal society. In a world that demands male dominance and female dependence, outdoorswom-en who transgress these boundaries and resist socially constructed views of outdoor spaces risk blame if violence befalls them. From a feminist viewpoint, women who resist the societal messages seem to create a world based on their realities and ideals (i.e., outdoor heterotopias). A radical feminist perspective brings visibility to the controlling of women's sexuality by men (Tuana & Tong, 1995) and demonstrates the power of men over women arises from the pervasiveness of male sexual violence against women (MacKinnon, 1995).

Distinct, irreconcilable understandings of space underscore the cultural mappings of the contemporary (Keith & Pile, 1993). A different sense of place is being theorized where the margins are simultaneously real and metaphorical. Hooks (1996) calls this alternative spatiality "radical openness...a margin—a profound edge. Locating oneself there is difficult yet necessary. It is not a 'safe' place. One is always at risk. One needs a community of resistance" (p. 149). Perhaps women who love the outdoors and the activities they do there, even in the face of societal sanction and personal danger, are such a community of resistance. Perhaps this margin becomes their location of radical openness, possibility, and their response to domination. Again as hooks suggested (1996):

We are transformed, individually, collectively, as we make radical creative space, which affirms and sustains our subjectivity, which gives us a new location from which to articulate our sense of the world. (p. 153)

The proposed model tells a story of women faced with issues of violence and patriarchy, social control and resistance, and identity through leisure. I believe these women found a margin from which to articulate a different world. I hope they force us not to be sidetracked so much by their behaviors on the margins as much as raise discomfort with what rests at the center.

References

Aitchison, C. (1999). New cultural geographies: The spatiality of leisure, gender and sexuality. *Leisure Studies, 18*, 19–39.

Aitchison, C. (2000). Poststructural feminist theories of representing others: A response to the 'crisis' in leisure studies' discourse. *Leisure Studies, 19*, 127–144.

Aitchison, C. and Jordan, F. (1998). *Gender, space, and identity: Leisure, culture and commerce*. Eastbourne, England: Leisure Studies Association.

Alcoff, L. M. (1996). Feminist theory and social science: New knowledge, new epistemologies. In N. Duncan (Ed.), *Bodyspace: Destabilizing geographies of gender and sexuality* (pp. 13–27). London, England: Routledge.

Anderson, K. L. and Umberson, D. (2004). Gendering violence: Masculinity and power in men's accounts of domestic violence. In S. N. Hesse-Biber and M. L. Yaiser (Eds.), *Feminist perspectives on social research* (pp. 251–270). New York, NY: Oxford University Press.

Baron, L. and Straus, M. (1989). Four theories of rape in American Society. New Haven, CT: Yale University Press.

Baumer, T. (1978). Research on fear of crime in the U.S. *Victimology, 3*, 254–267.

Bialeschki, M. D. (1999). *Fear of violence, freedom, and outdoor recreation: A feminist viewpoint*. Paper presented at the 9th Canadian Congress on Leisure Research, Acadia University, Wolfville, Nova Scotia, Canada.

Bialeschki, M. D. (2002). *Are we having fun yet?: Resistance and social control of women's outdoor experiences as a contested area of constraints*. Paper presented at the Canadian Conference for Leisure Research, Edmonton, Alberta, Canada.

Bialeschki, M. D. and Hicks, H. (1998). *I refuse to live in fear: The influence of fear of violence on women's outdoor recreation*. Paper presented at the Leisure Studies Association 4th International Conference, The Big Ghetto: Gender, sexuality, and leisure, LEEDS Metropolitan University, England.

Bourque, L. B. (1989). *Defining rape*. Durham, NC: Duke University Press.

Buchwald, E. (1993). Raising girls for the 21st century. In E. Buchwald, P. Fletcher, and M. Roth (Eds.), *Transforming a rape culture* (pp. 179–200). Minneapolis, MN: Milkweed Editions.

Burgess, J. (1998). "But is it worth taking the risk?" How women negotiate access to urban woodland: A case study. In R. Ainley (Ed.), *New frontiers of space, bodies, and gender* (pp. 115–128). London, England: Routledge.

Coble, T. G., Selin, S. W., and Erickson, B. B. (2003). Hiking alone: Understanding fear, negotiation strategies and leisure experiences. *Journal of Leisure Research, 35*, 1–22.

Colasduro, N. (1997, March, 21–22). Is being strong making us stupid? *Women's Sports and Fitness, 19*(2).

Day, T. (1997). *The fear of violence as a leisure constraint to women participating in solo wilderness trips*. Unpublished honors thesis, Lakehead University, Thunder Bay, Ontario, Canada.

De Beauvoir, S. (1953). *The second sex*. New York, NY: Knopf.

Delamere. F. M. (1998). *A critical examiniation of fear of violence as a form of social control and the impact of this fear on women's leisure experience*. Paper presented at the 9th Canadian Congress on Leisure Research, Acadia University, Wolfville, Nova Scotia, Canada.

Dobash, R. E. and Dobash, R. P. (1992). *Women, violence, and social change*. London, England: Routledge.

Ewert, A. (1989). Managing fear in the outdoor experiential education setting. *Journal of Experiential Education, 12*, 19–25.

Ferraro, K. F. (1995). *Fear of crime: Interpreting victimization risk*. Albany, NY: SUNY Press.

Ferraro, K. F. (1996). Women's fear of victimization: Shadow of sexual assault? *Social Forces, 75*, 667–690.

Foucault, M. (1983). The subject and power. In H. Dreyfus and P. Rabinow (Eds.), *Michel Foucault: Beyond structuralism and hermeneutics* (pp. 208–220). Chicago, IL: Chicago University Press.

Foucault, M. (1986, Spring). Of other spaces. *Diacritics*, 22–27.

Frances, S. L. (1997). Leisure as a tool for social control: The role of leisure in the lives of women during and after involvement in abusive relationships. In J. Hultsman and M. D. Bialeschki (Eds.), *Abstracts from the 1997 Symposium on Leisure Research* (p. 36). Ashburn, VA: National Recreation and Park Association.

Gardner, C. B. (1990). Safe conduct: Women, crime and self in public places. *Social Problems, 37*, 311–328.

Giddens, A. (1984). *The constitution of society: Outline of a theory of structuration*. Cambridge, England: Polity Press.

Gordon, M. T. and Riger, S. (1989). *The female fear*. New York, NY: Free Press.

Green, E., Hebron, S., and Woodward, D. (1987). *Leisure and gender: A study of Sheffield women's leisure experience*. London, England: The Sports Council and Economic and Social Research Council.

Henderson, K. A. and Bialeschki, M. D. (1990/1991). Ecofeminism. *Leisure Information Quarterly, 17*(1), 1–5.

Henderson, K. A. and Bialeschki, M. D. (1993). Negotiating constraints to women's physical recreation. *Loisir et Societe/Society and Leisure, 16*, 389–412.

Herman, D. (1991). The rape culture. In J. W. Cochran, D. Langston, and C. Woodward (Eds.), *Changing our power: An introduction to women's studies* (2nd ed.; pp. 276–289). Dubuque, IA: Kendall/Hunt Publishing Co.

Hollander, J. A. (2004). Vulnerability and dangerousness. In S. N. Hesse-Biber and M. L. Yaiser (Eds.), *Feminist perspectives on social research* (pp. 296–319). New York, NY: Oxford University Press.

Holyfield, L. and Fine, G. A. (1997). Adventure as character work: The collective taming of fear. *Symbolic Interaction, 20*, 343–363.

hooks, b. (1989). *Talking back: Thinking feminist, thinking black*. Boston, MA: South End Press.

hooks, b. (1990). *Yearning: Race, gender, and cultural politics*. Boston, MA: South End Press.

hooks, b. (1994). *Outlaw culture: Resisting representations*. New York, NY: Routledge.

James, K. and Embrey, L. (2001). "Anyone could be lurking around!": Constraints on adolescent girls' recreational activities after dark. *World Leisure, 43*(4), 44–52.

Karmen, A. A. (1991). Victims of crime. In J. F. Sheley (Ed.), *Criminology: A contemporary handbook* (pp. 165–186). Belmont, CA: Wadsworth.

Keith, M. and Pile, S. (1993). Introduction Part I: The politics of place. In M. Keith and S. Pile (Eds.), *Place and the politics of identity* (pp. 1–21). New York, NY: Routledge.

Kiewa, J. (2001). Control over self and space in rock-climbing. *Journal of Leisure Research, 33*, 363–382.

Koskela, H. (1997). "Bold walk and breakings": Women's spatial confidence versus fear of violence. *Gender, Place, and Culture, 4*, 301–319.

Liska, E., Sanchirico, A., and Reed, M. (1988). Fear of crime and constrained behavior: Specifying and estimating a reciprocal effects model. *Social Forces, 66*, 827–837.

Little, D. E. (2002). Women and adventure recreation: Reconstructing leisure constraints and adventure experiences to negotiate continuing participation. *Journal of Leisure Research, 34*, 157–177.

MacKinnon, K. (1995). Sexuality, pornography, and method: "Pleasure under patriarchy." In N. Tuana and R. Tong (Eds.), *Feminism and philosophy: Essential readings in theory, reinterpretation, and application* (pp. 134–161). Boulder, CO: Westview Press, Inc.

Massey, D. (1994). *Space, place, and gender*. Cambridge, England: Polity Press.

McHoul, A. and Grace, W. (1993). *A Foucault primer*. New York, NY: University Press.

Mehta, A. and Bondi, L. (1999). Embodied discourse: On gender and fear of violence. *Gender, Place, and Culture, 6*(1), 67–84.

Mustaine, E. E. and Tewksbury, R. (1998). Victimization risks at leisure: A gender-specific analysis. *Violence and Victims, 13*, 231–249.

Pain, R. (1997). Whither women's fear? Perceptions of sexual violence in public and private space. *International Review of Victimology, 4*, 297–312.

Pohl, S. L., Borrie, W. T., and Patterson, M. E. (2000). Women, wilderness, and everyday life: A documentation of the connection between wilderness recreation and women's everyday lives. *Journal of Leisure Research, 32*, 415–434.

Rojek, C. (1990). Baudrillard and leisure. *Leisure Studies, 9*, 7–20.

Rose, G. (1993). *Feminism and geography. The limits of geographical knowledge*. Minneapolis, MN: University of Minnesota Press.

Rose, G. (1995). Place and identity: A sense of place. In D. Massey and P. Jess (Eds.), *A place in the world? Places, cultures and globalisation* (pp. 87–132). Milton Keynes, England: Open University Press.

Ruddick, S. (1996). Constructing difference in public spaces: Race, class and gender as interlocking systems. *Urban Geography, 17*, 132–151.

Shaw, S. (2001). Conceptualizing resistance: Women's leisure as political practice. *Journal of Leisure Research, 33*, 186–201.

Shaw, S. M. and Whyte, L. B. (1996). An analysis of the hierarchical model of leisure constraints: Using fear of violence as a case study. In D. Dawson (Ed.), *Proceedings from the 8th Canadian Congress on Leisure Research* (pp. 245–249). Ottawa, Ontario, Canada: University of Ottawa.

Skogan, W. G. and Maxfield, M. G. (1981). *Coping with crime: Individual and neighborhood reactions*. London, England: Sage Publications.

Stanko, E. A. (1985). *Intimate intrusions: Women's experience of male violence*. London, England: Routledge and Kegan Paul.

Tuana, N. and Tong, R. (1995). Preface. In N. Tuana and R. Tong (Eds.), *Feminism and philosophy: Essential readings in theory, reinterpretation, and application* (pp. xi–xii). Boulder, CO: Westview Press, Inc.

Valentine, G. (1989). The geography of women's fear. *Area, 21*, 385–390.

Valentine, G. (1992). Images of danger: Women's sources of information about the spatial distribution of male violence. *Area, 24*, 22–29.

Valentine, G. (1996). Renegotiating the "heterosexual street": Lesbian production of space. In N. Duncan (Ed.), *Bodyspace: Destabilizing geographies of gender and sexuality* (pp. 146–155). London, England: Routledge.

Warr, M. (1985). Fear of rape among urban women. *Social Problems, 32*, 238–250.

Warr, M. and Stafford, M. (1983). Fear of victimization: A look at the proximate causes. *Social Forces, 61*, 1033–1043.

Wearing, B. (1998). *Leisure and feminist theory.* London, England: Sage Publications.

Whyte, L. B. and Shaw, S. M. (1994). Women's leisure: An exploratory study of fear of violence as a leisure constraint. *Journal of Applied Recreation Research, 19*(1), 5–21.

Wilkinson, S. and Kitzinger, C. (1996). *Representing the Other: Feminism and psychology.* London, England: Sage Publications.

Wilson, E. (1989). Sex, politics, and society. London, England: Longman.

Wolf, N. (1991). *The beauty myth: How images of beauty are used against women.* New York, NY: William Morrow and Co.

Wood, J. T. (1994). *Gendered lives: Communication, gender, and culture.* Belmont, CA: Wadsworth Publishing Co.

Woodward, D., Green, E., and Hebron, S. (1989). The sociology of women's leisure and physical recreation: Constraints and opportunities. *International Review for the Sociology of Sport, 24*, 121–136.

Chapter 8

Impacts of Life Transitions on Leisure and Constraints to Leisure

Edgar L. Jackson (University of Alberta)

For the majority of people, most of the time daily life consists largely of routine—what the novelist John O'Hara (1984, p. 130) called "day-to-day, unepisodic living." We do not consciously, every day, decide whether to drive, bus, or walk to work or what route to take, when to eat supper, or how we will spend our free time. Most of our everyday behavior, including leisure, probably arises more from the unconscious reaffirmation and repetition of past decisions taken within a structured personal, family, social, economic, political, and environmental context, and from a relatively unconscious adaptation to evolving personal circumstances, than it does from immediate, overt new choices. How, then, does leisure change? The premise I develop in this chapter is *leisure changes most at transitional points in people's lives*. This happens partly if not entirely because it is precisely at transitional points that new leisure opportunities become available or foreclosed, new leisure constraints disappear or emerge, and new strategies to negotiate leisure constraints are perceived and adopted or rejected. In other words, it is at transitional points the unconscious becomes conscious. Elaborating on this perspective should address some of the concerns raised elsewhere in this book, and in the wider constraints literature—namely that we know very little about the processes associated with how people encounter and adapt to leisure constraints over time.

Leisure Constraints, Negotiation, and Transitions

Constraints and Transitions

One of the key ideas for this chapter is constraints are not static, insurmountable obstacles to leisure participation and enjoyment, but instead are negotiable. This idea represented a new view in the early 1990s that challenged prevailing assumptions about constraints (Jackson & Scott, 1999). The alternative framework originated in the late 1980s (Crawford & Godbey, 1987) was stimulated by a set of papers that hinted at the idea of negotiation (e.g., Kay & Jackson, 1991; Scott, 1991; Shaw, Bonen & McCabe, 1991) and was more formally stated and extended in a series of conceptual articles in the 1990s (Crawford, Jackson & Godbey, 1991; Henderson & Bialeschki, 1993; Jackson, Crawford & Godbey, 1992, 1993). The authors of several chapters in this book also extended these ideas. Two distinct but interrelated aspects of the new perspective included

1. the hierarchical model, in which intrapersonal, interpersonal, and structural constraints were proposed to be arrayed and encountered in a predictable sequence.

2. the thesis that people negotiate (or "navigate," as some authors would have it) sequentially through these categories of constraints to accomplish their leisure goals.

Both of these themes received some empirical investigation in the 1990s (see Crawford & Jackson, this volume, as well as Jackson & Scott, 1999). However, little if any attention was paid to the question of whether there are particular circumstances or points in people's lives when leisure constraints are especially acute, prompting people to search for and to adopt new strategies to negotiate constraints. One exception was a study reported by McQuarrie and Jackson (1996), in which the authors used an account of the "leisure careers" (Stebbins, 1992, 1999) of adult amateur ice skaters to draw inferences concerning connections between serious leisure and the negotiation of constraints. McQuarrie and Jackson found new constraints tended to emerge at transitional points between stages in the serious leisure career, and progression to the next stage depended, at least partly, on the successful negotiation of these new constraints. Indeed, McQuarrie and Jackson went so far as to suggest a transitional point in a serious leisure career can be viewed, not simply as occurring coincidentally with new constraints and negotiation strategies, but as actually defined by changes in these. In summary, McQuarrie and Jackson concluded, "constraints may be particularly pertinent at transition points in the leisure career and that strategies to negotiate constraints may be crucial in making such a transition" (1996, pp. 476–477).

In this chapter I use McQuarrie and Jackson's observation as the foundation for exploring the role that many kinds of transitions play in people's leisure generally and in shaping the experience of and response to constraints specifically. In this context, the chapter should enhance our understanding of leisure across the lifespan (Freysinger, 1999) in that, to date, more attention has been paid to the nature and characteristics of leisure *within* life stages than to how leisure changes during transitions *between* stages. Moreover, to the extent that the leisure research literature has dealt with transitions and leisure, each individual study tended (1) to select a single transition and (2) to focus on the impacts of leisure on that transition, typically emphasizing the therapeutic value of leisure in helping people cope with a negative life event. This is the consistent with the approach taken by Hutchinson and Kleiber (this volume), and is a theme in much of Kleiber's work on negative life experiences and leisure. (See, for example, Kleiber, 1999, especially chapter 6, *Personal Experiences and the Transcendence of Negative Life Events*.)

I adopt an alternative perspective here, in which the emphasis is placed on the impacts on leisure of transitions (as opposed to a single transition), with particular focus on transition-related changes in constraints and negotiation as part of this process. Moreover, most work that investigated transitions concentrated on those that occur over the lifecycle. This study broadens that parameter by including other personal transitions, such as movement through the stages of a leisure career and emigration and immigration. Thus, the review is simultaneously wider in scope than most traditional studies and reverses the typical emphasis in the relationship between transitions and leisure.

The Nature of Transitions

Many types of transitions can influence and perhaps even fundamentally alter the course of people's lives and leisure. They include but are not confined to adolescence and menopause, illness and accident, marriage and divorce, birth of a child and loss of a spouse, and emigration and immigration. They share many attributes in common but may differ in others. For example, they may be

- "positive," such as the welcome birth of a child, or "negative," such as the trauma of a loved one being killed in an accident.

- anticipated, such as leaving home for university, or unexpected, such as a new employment opportunity.

- part of almost everyone's experience, such as entering junior high school, or confined to a few, such as contracting a rare disease.

- virtually instantaneous in occurrence (e.g., the split second of a crippling accident), or spread out over some time (e.g., menopause).

Moreover, the antecedents and experience of, as well as adaptation to, a given transition will likely vary among individuals. Part of this variation has to do with how people react to the transition (see Walker & Virden, this volume), which in turn creates difficulties for assigning positive and negative as objective or absolute descriptors to a given transition. For example, it could be argued that no transition, however traumatic, is entirely absent of benefits—what one person views as negative another may experience as positive. As is repeatedly documented in the next chapter (Hutchinson & Kleiber), victims of cancer or accidents, while they would obviously not wish to repeat the experience, frequently find life-affirming benefits in it. Similarly, the death of an ill spouse or elderly parent may suddenly create new freedoms if a person's previous life has been committed to caregiving. In the opposite direction, marriage or the birth of a child may create new commitments and reduce the time and money available for previously enjoyed leisure activities.

Objectives of the Chapter

Despite the obvious differences among transitions, an essential premise of this chapter is that they all share a sufficient number of attributes to permit the development and application of a generic concept of "transition." This generic notion can then be used to establish linkages among apparently dissimilar events, and then to capitalize on the idea to establish a framework for investigating relationships among transitions, leisure, and the experience and negotiation of constraints.

Before proceeding, it is important to recognize I am not making overly ambitious claims for the perspective offered here. I should like to note what I am trying to do in this chapter. First, I do not mean to imply continuity and change between stages bounded by transitions can be explained only by constraints. Obviously, many other factors have an effect. However, my argument is constraints and their interactions with other factors should be systematically investigated at transitional points and in studies of continuity and change. Second, I do not intend to imply constraints are important only at transitions; this is clearly not so. I do wish to argue, however, constraints may change, become acute, and be more a part of people's conscious experience at transitional points than between them, after which they become internalized and part of the everyday routine. If my reasoning is sound, then the investigation of constraints at transitions should help us to understand, in ways not previously recognized or examined, how people experience and respond to constraints—a research need identified by the authors of several other chapters in this book.

Key Concepts

For its theoretical background, the chapter draws on several conceptual frameworks both from within and outside leisure studies, including

1. concepts related to lifespan, continuity, and change.

2. negative life experiences.

3. "punctuated equilibrium" as an expression of adaptation and adjustment to changing events and circumstances (Gersick, 1988, drawing on a ecological concept developed by Eldrege and Gould, 1972).

According to Gersick:

> systems progress through an alternation of stasis and sudden appearance—long periods of inertia, punctuated by concentrated, revolutionary periods of quantum change. Systems' histories are expected to vary because situational contingencies are expected to influence significantly the path a system takes at its inception and during periods of revolutionary change, when systems' directions are formed and reformed. (1988, p. 16)

Further, Gersick suggested, "Punctuated equilibrium paradigms direct attention to periods of stability and to change processes, provoking questions about what happens...during the short periods of time when systems are especially plastic and labile" (1988, p. 36).

The concepts listed in the preceding paragraph are interrelated in the sense that life stages, characterized

both by continuity and change in leisure from previous stages (Freysinger, 1999), can be thought of as periods of balance or equilibrium between passages (Gersick, 1988). Within each stage, little conscious thought may be given to constraints (indeed, to leisure decisions more generally). Equilibrium may be upset, however, at transitional points, precisely because new leisure constraints and opportunities occur or fade, prompting adaptation and adjustment in the form of new leisure behaviors.

Rather than including an extensive review of these concepts, I have elected to interweave key ideas from the relevant literature into a critical examination of quantitative findings previously published about the experience of constraints, in particular as this experience varies across the lifespan. The assumptions the analysis and display of such data contain are also discussed, and I propose an alternative interpretation of the process of changes in constraints and leisure through transitional points in people's lives.

Strategy of Analysis

Having established this background, the chapter then goes on to examine seven distinct transitions. In each instance, a single article or pair of articles is used as the foundation for the review. My purposes are to establish connections among different transitions, to develop a generic concept of transitions, and to use this concept as a framework for understanding the impacts of transitions on leisure and the role of constraints to leisure during transitions. The intention is not so much to dwell on the details of each transition but rather to learn something of a more general nature about how leisure and constraints change at crucial points in people's lives.

Instead of conducting a comprehensive literature-based review of everything known about each transition, the strategy I elected to follow in preparing this chapter was to draw on one or two articles on each transition. In each instance I summarized the authors' objectives and findings, noted the specific changes and challenges encountered by people who experience that transition, established the role of leisure in the transition as identified by the author(s) of each article, and summarized what, if anything, the authors had to say—and what I could deduce—about leisure constraints. In each instance, I then wrote an initial summary of and commentary on the article and mailed it to the author(s) involved, requesting their comments on and approval of the summary as an accurate representation and constraints-related interpretation of the article. All authors replied favorably and in some cases provided additional comments helpful in making minor revisions to produce the versions included here. As a concluding step, general inferences related to the impacts of the transition on leisure and the role of constraints were developed and summarized together.

Alternative Perspectives on How Constraints Change Over the Life Cycle

The Conventional Perspective

To develop an understanding of how people come to experience and to adapt to constraints, and to provide the foundation for introducing new ideas related to the impact of transitions in people's lives on the experience and impacts of constraints, it is helpful to begin with an idealized summary of the conventional wisdom about how constraints to leisure appear to evolve over the lifespan. The composite graph shown in **Figure 8.1** is a good example of the kinds of quantitative data that typically emerge from questionnaire surveys, in which respondents are asked to rate the importance of varying numbers of constraints items (e.g., being too busy with their family, the costs of participating) in relation to aspects of constrained leisure (criterion variables). Criterion variables might include desiring but being unable to participate in an activity, or quitting a previously enjoyed activity. (For the most recent study of how the choice of criterion variables affects constraints scores, see Nadirova & Jackson, 2000.)

Figure 8.1 also represents a fairly conventional product of the ways in which survey-based data about leisure constraints are analyzed and displayed. (See, for example, the sequence of figures in Jackson & Henderson, 1995.) In most empirical leisure constraints research, specific items are usually not analyzed or presented individually, but instead are grouped into categories ("dimensions") derived either from a conceptual classification or, more commonly, an empirical–statistical method, such as factor analysis. (See Jackson, 1993, and Mannell & Iwasaki, this volume, for discussions of empirical, data-based classifications of constraints.) This grouping procedure not only is more parsimonious from the standpoints of data analysis, display, and interpretation, but also helps to uncover more general patterns that otherwise might be obscured when presenting a large amount of item-by-item data in a single table, or as a large number of lines on a single graph or series of graphs. The five dimensions of constraints shown in Figure 8.1 are

1. the costs of participating, such as admission fees and equipment costs.

2. time and commitments, such as being too busy with work or family.

3. lack of facilities or poor facilities.

4. "isolation," which in factor analysis sometimes separates out into "social isolation" (e.g., absence of people with whom to participate, shyness), and "geographic isolation" (e.g., difficulties with accessibility, problems with transportation).

5. absence or insufficiency of the required physical skills and abilities.

With minor variations, these dimensions are representative of the kinds of empirical groupings commonly reported in quantitative analyses of constraints items and scales.

When analyzed and presented at this level of generality, some interesting—and quite robust—patterns emerge about apparent changes in constraints across the life cycle. Moreover, each category of constraint not coincidentally exhibits a distinct pattern of association with age. Thus, a lack of skills and abilities, although consistently rated as the least important category of constraints among every age group when averaged across a survey sample, gradually increases in importance as the life cycle progresses. In contrast—both in terms of the relative importance of the constraint and the direction of the

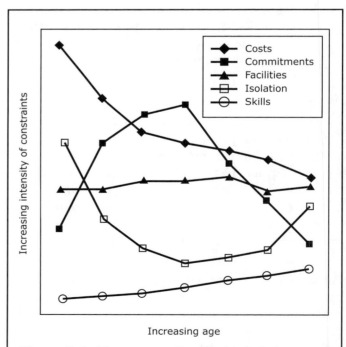

Figure 8.1. The conventional view of changes in constraints

relationship—costs as a negative influence on participation decline with advancing age (once again, it is important to point out, when the results are aggregated across samples). Perhaps not surprisingly, because the category of constraints may be viewed as "external" to the individual (see Jackson, 1988, for a discussion of problems with the internal–external dichotomy), most studies have shown the amount and quality of facilities as a constraint to leisure do not vary with age.

As far as the remaining two categories are concerned, isolation is typically characterized by a U-shape relationship with age, meaning it is most important in the early stages of the life cycle, declines until early middle age, and increases once again in the later stages of life. In dramatic contrast, commitments and time constraints are usually characterized by a very strong inverted U-shape relationship. These two trends are intuitively obvious and presumably may be accounted for by "marker events," such as leaving high school, entering the work force, marriage, the birth of children, the child-rearing years, employment change and/or promotion, the empty nest, retirement, and the many circumstances that tend to be associated with old age, often including solitude. The two trends are probably also interrelated: young people may have more time for leisure but less disposable income, whereas people in early middle age may have achieved employment and income security but also work longer hours and, in many instances, are also constrained by family commitments.

This brings us to the first of two major advantages of this type of analysis and display, namely that for each category of constraints empirical support is provided for what we may have suspected and likely could have predicted. Thus, findings of this kind, while interesting in and of themselves, are important not so much because they explain anything about constraints, but because they provide the starting point for further exploration and understanding of the roles that leisure constraints play in people's lives. They help us to focus on and to questions what it is about the circumstances associated with a particular age or life stage that somehow translates into the exacerbation or alleviation of constraints.

The second major advantage is Figure 8.1 is a composite graph. As such, it dramatically draws attention to the distinct and contrasting ways in which categories of constraints typically vary across the life cycle. But a composite diagram of this kind also draws attention to another key aspect of constraints, namely that each stage of life is characterized by its own unique combination of constraints, resulting from the absolute and relative decline of some categories of constraints over the lifespan, while others increase in intensity or stabilize. For ex-

ample, early middle age may be accompanied for many people, particularly those in the middle class, by increasing financial security and the establishment of family and social networks, thus serving to relax the effects of intrapersonal and structural constraints, such as the costs of participating and the interpersonal constraints of a family and social milieu within which to enjoy leisure. However, early middle age also appears to be precisely the stage in life when other pressures on leisure choices emerge, experienced most notably in terms of commitments to work and family, and frequently expressed in the almost universal reason (or excuse) for just about everything in life, including leisure: "I don't have the time" (see also Godbey, and Mannell & Iwasaki, this volume). In summary, the diagram suggests the experience of constraints is not only an ongoing process of *change* over the life cycle, but also—and equally importantly—a process of *exchange*, of one combination of constraints for another. (The idea it is combinations of constraints changing together over the life cycle, as opposed to isolated and disconnected changes in each category of constraints separately, has been explored using cluster analysis and other multivariate statistical methods; see, for example, Jackson, 1993, and Hultsman, 1995.)

Problems With the Conventional Perspective

Having identified the two major advantages of analyzing and displaying data about constraints in the manner shown in Figure 8.1, it is also important—not only for the sake of balance but also to develop an alternative perspective on what triggers new constraints to leisure and how in turn they might affect people's leisure behavior and experience—to acknowledge several disadvantages and limitations. From the standpoint of the theme of this chapter, some of these disadvantages are less important, but there is at least one that may have fundamentally guided and influenced the ways in which researchers have thought about constraints in the past. Only by recognizing and addressing it can an alternative perspective emerge.

The first and least important disadvantage is the data are usually derived from quantitative scales administered in questionnaire surveys; they rarely tell us much about how constraints are experienced and how people react to them. Moreover, the types of constraints embodied in the items usually included in leisure constraints questionnaire surveys have tended to concentrate on ones more easily measured (e.g., time, costs, facilities), while omitting types of constraints that have more often been revealed in qualitative, usually gender-based research. The latter have included ethic of care, lack of a sense of entitlement to leisure, body image, and fear of violence (e.g., Henderson & Allen, 1991; Henderson & Bialeschki, 1991; Frederick & Shaw, 1995; Whyte & Shaw, 1994; plus the chapters by Shaw & Henderson and Bialeschki, this volume). Connected with the survey-based orientation of research, studies of the type referred to here have also focused more on constraints to participation than on other aspects of leisure. As a consequence, they have also tended to focus on structural constraints rather than intrapersonal and interpersonal constraints, which are more closely related to leisure preferences and the meaning and quality of the leisure experience than to participation. Indeed, this cluster of interconnected problems (survey research that focuses on measurable, structural constraints in relation to participation) has been the most frequent focus of criticism of constraints research by leisure scholars, most notably Samdahl (Samdahl & Jekubovich, 1997a, 1997b; see also Samdahl, this volume). The overall orientation can be traced to the dominant social psychological, quantitative, agency-based methodological paradigm, which until the emergence of alternative paradigms and new methodologies in recent years dominated leisure research in North America. (See Jackson & Scott, 1999, for a discussion in relation to constraints research, and Samdahl, 1999, for a counter-perspective and a discussion of the limitations of this approach.)

Stemming in part from the foregoing, a second and more serious limitation is that when the data are displayed in a manner such as Figure 8.1, by definition they represent an averaging of the lives of large numbers of individuals but do not necessarily apply to any given individual. It may well be, as social scientists and popular writers alike have assumed, that biological age is in part associated with other characteristics and marker events. However, the presence or absence of these events, the sequence in which they occur, the general and specific circumstances within which they take place, variations in the ways in which they are experienced, differences in personal resiliency and adaptability, and the effects on people's lives will vary tremendously from person to person. These variations are obscured when reduced to a series of deceptively simple mean scores for questionnaire items, and in the categories, points, and lines on a quantitative, survey-based graph, such as that shown in Figure 8.1.

Related to all of this, of course, is a third limitation: data and diagrams of this kind are cross-sectional. While it is tempting to draw developmental-like inferences from them, we should be extremely wary of assuming the experience of constraints among, say, people in the 44 to 50 age group will—when they reach a later stage—duplicate those of people who are currently in the 66 and over age group. (See Freysinger, 1999, for a leisure-related review of cross-sectional and developmental research and the underlying assumptions associated with each type of research.)

The most serious drawback of the points-and-line type of display shown in Figure 8.1, however, has to do with the possibly misleading perceptions of and assumptions about constraints to leisure that may be inadvertently set up in the researcher's mind, in particular in relation to the process of change in leisure constraints over the course of people's lives. In a nutshell, expressing mean scores for each age group on each dimension of constraints, and then joining the points on the graph with lines, tends to encourage—and therefore fix in the researcher's mind—the assumption that the process of change in leisure constraints over the life course is continuous, gradual, and smooth. However, the diagram may be inherently deceptive, because it may be more appropriate to think of the emergence or disappearance of constraints as a series of steps separated by abrupt changes—"punctuated equilibrium," to use the term employed by Gersick (1988). What is needed, therefore, is an alternative perspective that not only more accurately models constraints in people's lives, but also generates new ideas about how constraints to leisure emerge and are dealt with.

An Alternative Perspective

In the alternative perspective proposed here, change in leisure constraints is conceived of not as a smooth process, but rather as a sequence of distinct stages, each characterized by a relatively stable prechange period, followed by a (usually short) period of transition and adjustment (or adaptation), and concluded by the achievement of a new balance, or relatively stable postchange period. This then becomes the precursor for a possible but not inevitable subsequent transition. Thus, more realistically than is implied in Figure 8.1, we may think of people's lives, from a constraints-based perspective, as a series of stages in each of which there is relatively little change (equilibrium), punctuated from time to time with frequently predictable but sometimes unanticipated events and changes. At these points new constraints appear and disappear, as do new leisure opportunities. This alternative perspective is summarized in **Figure 8.2**, which for the sake of clarity is restricted to just one category of constraints: time commitments. In this alternative histogram display of the same kind of data as in

Figure 8.1 (but with categories added to reflect stages in the lifespan rather than age groups), the average intensity of constraints associated with each stage in the lifecycle is shown as a column instead of as a point. This serves to accentuate the idea that a transitional point is associated with a more abrupt change in leisure constraints than the gradual and continuous process implied when points are joined by lines, as in Figure 8.1.

Problems remain, however—the data represent scores on scales derived from survey data and averaged across a sample and they are cross-sectional. Nevertheless, the bar graph type of display in Figure 8.2 is still useful, because we can now adapt it and turn to the level of the individual. We can also adopt the kind of thinking associated with Figure 8.2 into a speculation of how an individual person (**Figure 8.3**, p. 122) might experience transitions and encounter new constraints or benefit from the relaxation or disappearance of previous ones. (It should be noted, at this level the possibilities for exemplifying transitions and constraints are enormous if not infinite. Thus, the diagram shown in Figure 8.3 is intended as illustrative rather than comprehensive.)

The key features of Figure 8.3 are as follows. First, the horizontal axis is defined by marker events between life stages instead of biological age categories. Second, a constraint is assumed to undergo an abrupt transition-related change at each transitional point. Such change might involve the appearance or disappearance, exacerbation, or alleviation of constraints; Figure 8.3 shows only an intensification. Third, from the standpoint of

people's response to constraints, the change will likely engender some form of adjustment, or what has been referred to in the leisure constraints literature as a new "negotiation strategy." Fourth, between transitions, a person adapts to new circumstances and a new equilibrium is maintained in terms of the experience of constraints and the relative stability of leisure behavior.

In summary, while it is not without its own limitations, the alternative view of changes in constraints, how people react to them, and therefore how leisure behavior is characterized by both continuity and change, provides a more realistic picture of changes in constraints in people's lives and how they adjust to them than the conventional perspective summarized here. It is also a useful framework to bear in mind when reading the following research-based accounts of transitions and leisure.

A Review of Seven Transitions

Based on the foregoing relatively abstract ideas, we now turn our attention to particular transitions and what various leisure researchers have discovered with respect to these transitions and the constraints associated with them. The seven transitions summarized are as follows:

- Parry and Shaw (1999) on women's experiences of menopause and midlife.

- Bialeschki and Michener (1994) on transition within the role of motherhood.

- Patterson and Carpenter (1994) on the death of a spouse.

- Crawford and Huston (1993) on the transition to parenthood.

- Raymore (1995) on the transition from adolescence to young adulthood.

- Stodolska (1998, 2000) on immigration.

- McQuarrie and Jackson (1996) on stages within a serious leisure career.

The Role of Leisure in Women's Experiences of Menopause and Midlife

Parry and Shaw (1999) conducted a qualitative study among five women from southern Ontario currently experiencing menopause. Using a feminist framework, their objective was to explore menopause and midlife,

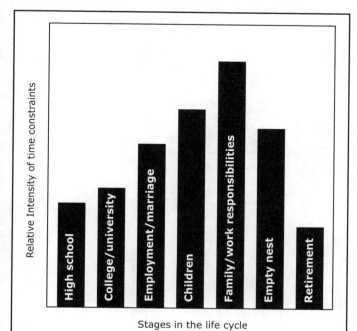

Figure 8.2. Abrupt changes in constraints associated with transitions

(Y-axis: Relative Intensity of time constraints)
(X-axis: Stages in the life cycle — High school, College/university, Employment/marriage, Children, Family/work responsibilities, Empty nest, Retirement)

and the role of leisure during these simultaneous transitions. In contrast to the widespread emphasis on medical research and what the authors label the "medicalization" of menopause, Parry and Shaw argued menopause is not only a complex psychological and physiological experience, but also socially constructed and contextual. Further, several other changes frequently occur at this stage in life, such as sickness or death of a parent, children leaving home, or personal health problems. These often simultaneous changes "may cause women to re-examine their total life situations, including their work, their relationships, and their family obligations, as well as their reactions to socially imposed gender-role expectations" (p. 206).

While recognizing leisure may have negative as well as positive consequences, Parry and Shaw focused on the beneficial, or therapeutic, effects of leisure on the experience of menopause and midlife. The two main sets of problems encountered by the women they interviewed were emotional challenges and the realization of aging. Leisure played an important part in helping to cope with both of these challenges and changes: "without exception, the women felt that their leisure activities were having a positive effect on their lives, and that

leisure provided benefits for them with respect to the challenges faced in their everyday lives" (pp. 210–211). This tended to occur in two ways. First, leisure enhanced health, physical well-being, and emotional well-being (e.g., positive self-attitude). Second, it became a vehicle to achieve a sense both of continuity and change. Some activities provided a feeling of familiarity, security, and continuity while life was changing—others allowed the women to develop new interests, to focus on themselves, and to improve their self-attitudes. In summary, Parry and Shaw demonstrated transitions are complex and interconnected. Transitions stimulate a heightened awareness, which may translate into new behaviors while at the same time reinforcing previous ones. New opportunities emerge, new constraints may appear, and others may become less pertinent or acute. Together, these are both the stimuli for and the consequences of change at transitional points in people's lives.

Four general inferences emerged from this article. First, the emphasis of the study was on the impacts of leisure on menopause and midlife transitions, rather than the impacts of the transitions on leisure. Nevertheless, we can infer that both continuity and change in leisure activities, as well as the desire for these and the leisure

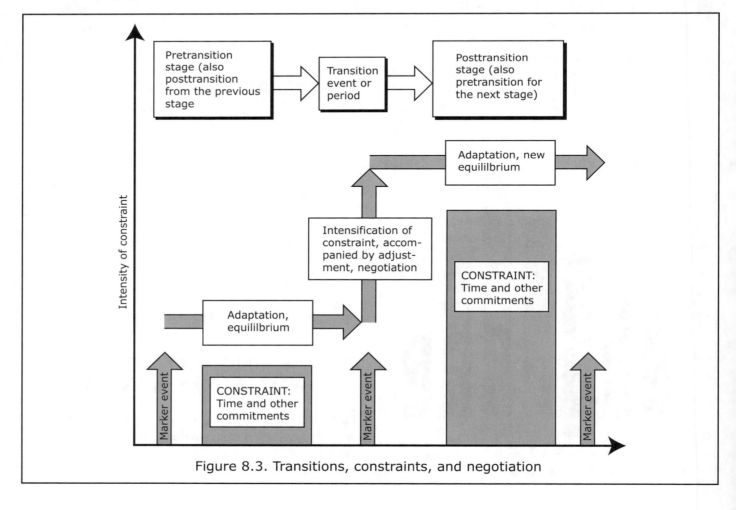

Figure 8.3. Transitions, constraints, and negotiation

preferences that ensue, also depend on the transitions; they are prompted by heightened awareness, reflection, and self-perception during menopause and midlife. Thus, while leisure plays a role in ameliorating a transition, it is simultaneously affected by it, partly by reinforcing past decisions (continuity) but also by stimulating new needs and interests (change).

Second, one of the important contributions of the study is its demonstration that a single transition is not necessarily experienced in isolation, but that two or more transitions may occur at the same time. However, the complexity of these changes means it is often difficult, both for the people experiencing them and for the researchers who want to understand them to disentangle the causes and effects of the several transitions that may be occurring simultaneously.

Third, while menopause and midlife are seemingly specific concepts, "the women in this study all had different and unique experiences" in relation to them (p. 209). Thus, the study demonstrates while a transition common to many other people may be encountered by an individual, how it actually plays out in that person's life may be quite different from another person's experience. From this perspective, then, even something as apparently specific as menopause is still a label given to a collection of diverse experiences, and so could be seen as a generic concept. This point can be taken a step further, to argue for the validity and value of "transition" as a generic concept that enables us to perceive and capitalize on linkages among seemingly quite different phenomena and events.

Fourth, while constraints to leisure were not explicitly investigated in the interviews nor emerged as a theme in Parry and Shaw's findings, there is something to be learned from this study about the role of constraints during transitions. For example, it would appear, for the women in this study at least, constraints to leisure may decline at menopause and midlife (which would be consistent with the survey-based findings summarized previously). This appears to occur largely because of increasing amounts of discretionary time available for self and for leisure as children become less dependent and subsequently leave home (see the summary of Bialeschki and Michener's study for further elaboration).

Reentering Leisure: Transition Within the Role of Motherhood

There are close connections between a study conducted by Bialeschki and Michener (1994) and the investigation reported by Parry and Shaw (1999), in that the focus of the former study—the relationship between leisure and motherhood among women reaching the end of active mothering—may occur at midlife and close to menopause, if not simultaneously with it. Moreover, some of the transition-related changes touched on by Parry and Shaw are also described in detail by Bialeschki and Michener. However, in the latter case, unlike most of the other studies reviewed here, the emphasis is on changes in leisure that occur because of or in conjunction with a transition, rather than on the beneficial effects of leisure in experiencing and coping with a transition.

Based on a series of qualitative interviews with 53 mothers "reaching the end of active mothering roles needed by dependent children, commonly known as the 'launching' phase within the family cycle" (p. 61), Bialeschki and Michener's purpose was to examine how "changing role demands affect leisure" and how "women in varying life situations perceive changes in leisure and family across the life span" (p. 57). Drawing on Kelly (1983), they argued, "certain transitions may require radical adaptation in behavior and in role identities. These shifts in role demands can be accompanied by changes in leisure expectations." Three main sets of questions were addressed:

1. the meaning and importance of leisure.

2. the influence of the family on the woman's leisure.

3. what the woman would do differently if she were to go through motherhood again.

Four distinct themes emerged from the interviews:

1. the way in which leisure was described as a focus on the self.

2. the concept of "full circle" leisure.

3. limitations imposed on mothers due to socialized gender roles.

4. the dichotomous influence of the ethic of care on the women's leisure.

Each of these interrelated changes illustrates, directly or indirectly, the important part changes in constraints played for these women over what we might call the "parenting life course"—becoming more intense at some points, less so at others. Thus, becoming a mother and the associated growing importance of the ethic of care leads to what Bialeschki and Michener refer to as "leisure shifts" (p. 59), involving sublimation of the primary meaning of leisure (focus on self), changes in available leisure time, and long-term interruption of leisure preferences and activities (cf. the account of Crawford & Huston's article). In the authors' words, "the leisure experiences of the women which focused on self and autonomy were often suppressed or even abandoned when the women married and became mothers. This leisure interruption remained for most of the mothers until their children left home" (p. 65). Transition at the end of the mothering period appears to be accompanied by a reduction in constraints, recapturing of the meaning of leisure, and full-circle leisure:

> Similar to interruption of career as a result of the birth of children, leisure experiences that originally met the self-oriented needs of the women were often suspended during active mothering but returned to a self focus when the children became independent....[A]s the women separated themselves from family roles, they engaged in leisure activities that once again could focus on self. (pp. 64–65)

The lessons of the Bialeschki and Michener study are consistent with several of the general inferences drawn from other studies included in this review. In addition, however, we note the following conclusions, which arise specifically from Bialeschki and Michener's article. First, a transition can be "received"; it does not necessarily occur as the result of a physiological or other type of change to oneself, but rather because of a transition that another person, such as a spouse or a child, is going through. Second, some transitions that occur during a later stage in the life cycle may be thought of as "mirror images" of earlier ones. In cases like this, changes in leisure may include a return to previous aspirations, experiences, and activities. From the perspective of constraints to leisure, such a transition may result in the alleviation or removal of one or more constraints that emerged during another transition experienced at an earlier stage in the life cycle. Third, a transition may involve choosing to set a new balance among competing needs and aspirations, motivations, and constraints. Thus, constraints-induced changes in leisure do not necessarily occur as a result of uncontrollable external influences but because of a conscious decision to forgo some needs in exchange for others. In this sense, a constraint may be "voluntarily accepted" during a transition rather than imposed from outside.

Participation in Leisure Activities After the Death of a Spouse

According to Patterson and Carpenter (1994), "the death of a spouse has been identified as the single most stressful life event that occurs to an individual" (p. 105). In addition to the devastating loss of a long-term, intimate companion, widowhood usually results in sudden changes in lifestyle and associated roles, followed by a recovery phase, which may take a considerable period of time, perhaps up to several years.

As in Parry and Shaw's investigation of menopause and midlife, the article by Patterson and Carpenter focused largely on one direction in the reciprocal relationship between transitions and leisure, namely the beneficial role leisure may play in helping people to cope with the changes brought about by the transition. Two main themes were addressed:

1. Do widows and widowers who participate more frequently in leisure activities adapt more successfully to widowhood?

2. Do they report significantly higher morale than widows and widowers who participate less frequently?

Using a theoretical framework derived from the literature on leisure and stressful life events, Patterson and Carpenter viewed leisure as a moderator of life stress. Based on qualitative interviews and quantitative scales administered to 60 recently bereaved widows and widowers living independently in a state capital in Australia, Patterson and Carpenter found respondents typically confined their leisure to home-based activities and socializing with family and friends; participation in outdoor recreation and more "public" forms of socialization were not popular. Leisure was regarded as important for some people, helping to ameliorate the shock of their loss; for others there was a reduction in leisure activity, coupled with a lack of purpose or motivation to become involved in leisure activities. Overall, no relationship was found between successful adjustment to widowhood and frequency of leisure participation, but the latter was positively related to levels of morale following bereavement.

A significant contribution of this study has to do with the context of transitions, specifically that a transition such as the death of a spouse may be experienced in different ways by different people—its impacts being moderated by a host of personal and situational factors. Thus, with respect to adapting to widowhood, several factors, acting singly or in combination, will likely determine the impact of and response to the loss. These include but are not confined to the importance placed on the support of family and friends, the depth of religious faith, the ability to keep busy, whether the death was sudden or occurred after a long illness, and perception of the happiness or unhappiness of the marriage.

Despite the primary directional focus of the paper, Patterson and Carpenter also demonstrate leisure can and frequently does change significantly after the death of a spouse, most commonly with a lowered frequency of participation for up to two years. The authors identify two main reasons for this: (1) shock of the loss and lack of incentive to become involved in leisure during the early stage of the grieving process, and (2) ensuing stress, resulting in health problems which in turn lead to restricted leisure involvement. Further, some of their findings can be interpreted as reflecting the influence of changes in the nature and role of constraints—an interpretation recognized by the authors themselves (p. 112). For example, Patterson and Carpenter cite several instances of the ways in which the absence of a former leisure companion (an interpersonal constraint) resulted in the loss of interest in certain activities or even in leisure as a whole (an intrapersonal constraint). Incidentally, this is an interesting reversal of the "normal" sequence in the experience of constraints predicted in the hierarchical and negotiation models (Crawford et al., 1991; Jackson et al., 1993).

In conclusion, the following general inferences pertinent to the theme of this chapter emerge from Patterson and Carpenter's article. First, leisure frequently undergoes a major change during a transitional period. Second, how people experience a transition, as well as how they subsequently adjust and adapt to it, varies among individuals and is moderated by a range of personal, social, and situational factors. Third, new constraints may emerge during a transition. Some are "antecedent" (intrapersonal and interpersonal constraints which modify leisure interest and preferences), others are "structural" or "intervening" (modifying the abilities to participate in activities for which an interest of preference exists). Fourth, if a transition involves a change in interpersonal circumstances and relationships, then the driving force in the predicted sequence of experiencing constraints may be reversed, with interpersonal constraints becoming more proximal and salient than during normal, everyday life. Finally, a transition may occur over a long period of time, consist of an ordered sequence of events and responses, and be subdivided into a set of substages.

The Impact of the Transition to Parenthood on Marital Leisure

While Bialeschki and Michener investigated transitions experienced by mothers at a late stage in the parenting cycle, Crawford and Huston (1993) addressed aspects of the transition to parenthood encountered by both partners in recent marriages. Also, while the former study was qualitative, Crawford and Huston took a quantitative approach consisting of a sequence of questionnaires and structured interviews. The purpose of the study was to examine "whether the transition to parenthood affects the amount of time spouses pursue leisure activities—both together and apart—and the degree to which they pursue leisure activities they particularly enjoy" (p. 39). Three main aspects of changes in leisure were examined:

1. how much time was available for and spent in leisure.

2. whether the activities in which each spouse participated were liked or not.

3. whether the activities were done together or apart.

It is important to note the authors did not explicitly address issues related to the experience, impacts, or negotiation of constraints to leisure, although the study does appear to have been based on the implicit assumption that newly emerging constraints, in particular those related to time, are mainly responsible for the changes in leisure new parents frequently experience.

Crawford and Huston adopted an innovative and complex design by conducting a longitudinal study of people experiencing the transition to parenthood, together with a comparison group of couples who did not become parents. This strategy permitted the authors to disentangle parenthood-related changes from those that ordinarily occur over time in marriage. The study was initiated one year after the marriages of 69 couples, 46 of whom remained childless, and was conducted in three phases: when the couples were newlyweds, after one year (all were still childless), and after a second year (by which time 23 couples were now parents). The four main elements of the findings were as follows:

1. the new parents and childless couples did not differ in the amount of time they spent in leisure activities both spouses liked.

2. parenthood reduced the amount of time new fathers engaged in leisure activities independently.

3. parenthood increased the amount of time couples pursued activities together liked by the wife but not by the husband.

4. parenthood reduced the amount of time wives pursued leisure activities they disliked but their husbands liked.

Crawford and Huston are careful to point out the finding concerning the apparent realization of wives' rather than husbands' leisure preferences—counter to much of the conventional wisdom about leisure and gender (e.g., Bella, 1989; Henderson & Bialeschki, 1999; Shaw, 1999)—must be placed in the broader context of spouses' lives as a whole and not simply the leisure domain. The authors observed:

the shifts in the correspondence between wives' leisure preferences and their leisure activities are small compared with the shifts that take place in the domain of household work. Thus, the changes in instrumental roles that result from the transition to parenthood are not entirely balanced by the changes that occur within the leisure domain....[T]he activity patterns that make up the day-to-day life of the couple are still more consistent with the husband's preferences than the wife's. (p. 45)

This important point about the context of transitions and of the changes in leisure that may occur during them is a crucial element of Crawford and Huston's article, and one touched on in several other ways. For example, it is predictable the majority of couples will likely experience a decrease in the amount of time for leisure and in the range of activities in which they participate once they become new parents. However, the choice of liked versus disliked activities and the extent to which leisure is independent or companionate will be predicated on the nature and strength of spouses' values toward gender-based role responsibilities and expectations, which in turn shape the potential for accord or conflict. Other aspects of context that affect the transition include whether the wife is employed outside the home and whether the child was planned or unplanned.

Crawford and Huston's article makes several additional contributions to a general understanding of transitions and constraints. First, the authors argued, despite constraints the impacts of a transition are not entirely negative. For example, "it is possible...parenthood brings with it pleasures with regard to the use of leisure time that counterbalance the burdens of parenthood" (p. 40). In turn this suggests balancing the positives and negatives of a transition may be a conscious and deliberate process and not necessarily a passive response to constraints. Second, the period over which the impacts of a transition are experienced and assimilated will likely vary—what the authors describe as "adjustment problems" may be "minimal and short-term for some couples, but for others they make create a major upheaval that persists over time" (p. 39). Third, the finding one spouse or another may be encouraged or obliged to participate in activities he or she might not otherwise choose suggests new circumstances may lead an individual into becoming constrained *into* a leisure activity and not simply *out* of one, as is most commonly assumed in the leisure constraints literature. (See Jackson, 1988, and Shaw, 1994, 1999, for further discussion of constraint into leisure.)

In summary, while Crawford and Huston did not explicitly address the issue of constraints during the transition to parenthood, their article nonetheless offers findings that can be interpreted from the standpoint of current knowledge about constraints, and generates insights which either support or complement those derived from the other articles summarized here. In particular, Crawford and Huston's study supports the notion transitions and their impacts on leisure are complex, two or more transitions may occur simultaneously, changes are not always negative even when new constraints emerge, and above all acknowledging context is crucial for enhancing our understanding of transitions, leisure, and constraints.

Leisure Behavior and the Transition From Adolescence to Young Adulthood

Although essential and frequently unavoidable parts of the lives of large numbers of people and proportions of the population, not all of the transitions summarized here are experienced universally: menopause as it is commonly understood is confined to women, less than half the population experience the death of a spouse, and only a small proportion of people leave their home country to emigrate to a new one. Assuming that they reach adulthood, however, everyone goes through the transition from adolescence to young adulthood, the focus of a theoretical review article by Raymore (1995).

Using Kelly's (1983) framework of continuity and change, complemented by other theoretical perspectives, Raymore suggested three crucial questions need to be addressed to understand how leisure patterns evolve at this crucial life stage (p. 204):

1. What types of individuals maintain a particular focus of leisure interests across the transition, and why?

2. What types of individuals increase their range of interest or switch focus?

3. What types of individuals decrease their leisure interests?

She also noted the transition from adolescence to young adulthood is not a simple or single change, but is usually accompanied by a wide variety and combination of events, which include but are not confined to leaving home, beginning work or attending university, marriage, and first parenthood. Moreover, Raymore argued to understand a transition and its impacts on and implications for leisure, each stage—adolescence and young adulthood in this instance—must be described and understood independently, on which basis inferences may be drawn about changes in leisure during the transition. She also implied leisure at each stage should be understood as a complex of interacting factors, both individual and contextual, such as needs and aspirations, activities (including what, where, when, and with whom), anticipated and realized benefits, constraints, socially defined gender expectations, and so on. A transition, then, represents simultaneous and interactive "organic" change in all of these factors. Further, investigating differences in such interactions can help us to understand variations in the nature of and response to the transition, both among individuals as well as between groups, such as males and females. Above all, the message of Raymore's article is transitions and their effects are not simply individual and psychological, but also profoundly contextual. Therefore, they cannot be understood without trying "to capture the influence of contextual changes which accompany life transitions" (p. 213). Raymore also argued forcefully for the use of longitudinal studies to overcome the limitations of cross-sectional comparisons and research based on recall (pp. 212–213).

As far as constraints during transitions are concerned, this aspect of leisure receives more attention in Raymore's article than in some of the others summarized here, although the treatment occurs more "in passing" than as a systematic focus of the account. Raymore noted, for example, how going to a university not only presents new resources and opportunities, but also may involve a decrease in constraints, such as parental supervision and control. Also, while marriage may not necessarily bring new constraints (although leisure will undoubtedly change at this point), the birth of a child unquestionably affects people's (especially women's) leisure, largely if not exclusively as a result of limited choices and especially limited time. Further reflection on the nature and role of constraints, however, leads to the suggestion it may be more useful to think of constraints not just as changing individually or independently, but instead as undergoing a process of "exchange." Thus, for example, while going to a university may indeed relax parental influence as a constraint on leisure choices, it may also be accompanied by new ones, such as time pressures, financial problems, and changing role expectations and responsibilities.

On the basis of Raymore's article we may draw the following inferences about the nature of transitions, leisure during transitions, and the role of constraints. First, some transitions are effectively universal while others are confined to certain individuals or identifiable subgroups of the population. Second, a transition is not necessarily a single event but may consist of a set of events occurring simultaneously or in close sequence (although not always in the same order for everyone). Third, transitions may be investigated in two complementary ways, directly or indirectly, by describing conditions before and after the transition and on this basis drawing inferences about change during the transition. Fourth, changes in leisure during a transition should not be described simply in terms of activities, but reflect a complex interaction of individual and social factors. Fifth, changes in constraints over a transition do not necessarily occur independently or in isolation of one another, but frequently in the form of an exchange of one set of constraints for another.

Changes in Leisure Participation Patterns After Immigration

Immigration is a transition only a relatively small proportion of the population undergoes, but for those who do move from the country of their birth to a new home, its impact on their lives, including their leisure, can be profound. As Stodolska (2000, p. 40) commented, "the immigration process may magnify and temporally cluster certain undesirable or traumatic life experiences, such as separation from family or a major downward shift in social status."

Stodolska (1998) conducted a combined qualitative and quantitative study of solidarity-wave emigrants from Poland who moved to Canada after 1979. Several articles emerged from this project, two of which are particularly helpful for our understanding of transitions, leisure, and constraints. In the more recent of the two articles, Stodolska (2000) focused on the first part of the immigration process, describing and analyzing how leisure patterns changed after members of her sample left Poland and arrived in Canada. In the other article Stodolska (1998), tracked postimmigration experiences to assess how changes in constraints to leisure are associated with assimilation into the host society. This division of the research material into two articles is an overt recognition that the general transition of immigration is a complex phenomenon consisting of at least two distinct subtransitions.

As far as changes in leisure over the first part of the immigration process are concerned, the quantitative portion of Stodolska's study included data about leisure activities ceased on leaving Poland and those taken up after arrival in Canada. Patterns of change in leisure behavior were analyzed both at the level of specific activities and types of activities, as well in the context of a more general framework of leisure continuity and change. The analysis was also conducted controlling for age on arrival, and for activities, "to isolate the immigration-related changes from those characteristic of a certain age group or activity type" (p. 49). Interpretation of the quantitative data was enhanced by using information about motivations and constraints derived from in-depth, qualitative interviews.

At the activity level of analysis, Polish immigrants to Canada most often ceased participating in outdoor recreation activities, typical Polish activities, and home-based recreation. Activities started consisted mainly of new forms of outdoor recreation not possible or widespread in Poland and exercise-oriented pursuits. More general patterns of continuity and change were measured using Jackson and Dunn's (1988) framework developed for a study of the host community, Alberta, to which Stodolska's sample of Poles had immigrated. Data about activities ceased and started were used in combination to create a four-part classification of quitters, adders, replacers, and continuers. Stodolska (2000) discovered general patterns of leisure change among her sample were almost identical to those of the host community—surprising, given the divergent nature of the two populations. However, she makes the important point that it can be misleading to focus solely on the superficialities of activities. While many immigrants continued former leisure pursuits, both the meaning they attached to these activities and the reasons why they continued to participate in them changed radically, often being chosen because they now provided a sense of comfort, connection with the past, and a buffer against problems connected with life in a foreign country:

> certain activities...had been transformed so dramatically in terms of their meaning that they might play a completely different role in immigrants' leisure experience....For instance, quantitative results indicate that not very many immigrants had stopped [socializing] following their settlement. Yet the interview material points out the fact that the ways in which immigrants socialize in Canada can be different from those back in Poland. In particular, the inability to socialize with extended family and childhood friends often completely transforms the meaning of this activity. (pp. 54–55)

More broadly, Stodolska demonstrates how immigrants' postarrival leisure is shaped both by prior circumstances and by the new environment:

> all immigrants bring with them baggage of their culture, which includes distinct leisure-participation patterns. Both the very fact of immigration and the subsequent processes associated with getting established in the new environment can effectively redefine many aspects of immigrants' lives, including their work and living arrangements, family relations, and leisure experience. Changes that immigrants introduce into their leisure behavior can be attributed not only to the different physical and social environment of the new country but also to other immigration-related factors, such as altered family and friendship networks or shifts in socio-economic position. Although such changes may appear to be quite profound, most immigrants do retain significant elements of their ethnic heritage. In particular, despite certain postarrival changes in the participation style and the leisure repertoire itself, the leisure behavior of immigrants still is influenced heavily by the values and customs of the old country. (pp. 39–40)

Having identified how leisure changes after immigration, Stodolska then continued with a detailed and persuasive interpretation of the patterns she observed. She showed how leisure is influenced by a variety of factors, including the need to adapt to a different social and physical environment in the new country, shattered social networks, postarrival depression, availability of new opportunities (coupled with growing awareness of them over time), and leisure being viewed as a relatively quick and pleasant way of assimilating into the new society (pp. 50–53). Finally, she reduced the explanation to three main themes. First is relaxation or removal of constraints to activities for which there was latent demand in the country of origin:

> activities in which people participate in certain life stages depend not only on people's wants, needs, and constraints currently experienced, but also on the constraints they experienced in preceding periods of their life. In other words, it is the removal of constraints that triggers participation. (p. 58)

Second is the "forbidden fruit effect," similar to latent demand but different in that there may have been no previous intrinsic desire because an activity was forbidden or culturally unacceptable. Third is encountering new opportunities, summarized in the "demonstration effect," which occurs when people suddenly become exposed to "culturally alien" activities not embedded in the previous culture and/or not considered prestigious, and for which people therefore did not develop a prior preference.

Although the three elements in the explanation of changes in leisure over the immediate immigration process appear to reflect, for the most part, the relaxation of constraints that used to be experienced in the home country prior to emigrating, constraints to leisure do continue and can be quite acute after immigration (see also Rublee & Shaw, 1990; Tirone & Shaw, 1997; Yu & Berryman, 1996). In the second of her two articles, Stodolska (1998) investigated connections between aspects of assimilation and the nature and intensity of constraints to leisure. She showed how constraints experienced by immigrants are both different from and similar to those of the general population. With respect to differences, immigrants may experience a number of barriers related both to their minority status and to problems with adaptation to the new cultural and economic environment, including language difficulties, being unfamiliar with ways of life in the host country, and discrimination. All of these can have significant effects on the leisure decisions and experiences of newcomers. In addition, immigrants tend to experience the "usual" constraints associated with age, occupation, gender, or family status in the mainstream population, such as problems related to time, costs, social isolation, and skills and abilities. However, these are likely to be exacerbated for immigrants by postarrival stress, depression, anxiety, alienation, and often a sense of loss. Equally important for our purposes, constraints change over time as immigrants become assimilated into the host population. Although the details of these changes and their associations with distinct components of assimilation are complex, all are consistent with Stodolska's finding:

> the perceived importance of constraints tended to decrease along with the increasing assimilation level. Thus...the leisure of immigrants is most severely constrained immediately after their arrival and...some of these constraints have a tendency to decline in significance as people adapt to the new environment. (p. 543)

While one might somewhat cynically observe that researchers who look for evidence of constraints in their investigations of leisure are likely to find them (the premise underlying a critique by Samdahl and Jekubovich, 1997a), there can be no doubt, on the basis of Stodolska's work and parallel studies, the impacts of immigration on leisure are intimately intertwined with the experience of constraints and changes in these. It is also clear from Stodolska's research immigration is an unusually pertinent example of how transitions are associated with changes in leisure and constraints. Thus, several key inferences emerge from Stodolska's articles in addition to those that support or amplify inferences derived from the other studies reviewed here.

First, Stodolska's study affirms a transition can be a multistage process, each substage being distinct but sequentially linked with the others and representing a specific minitransition within an overall larger one. Each substage is associated with reasonably predictable changes in leisure behavior, which in turn are associated with changes in leisure opportunities, motivations, and constraints.

Second, a transition is characterized by both continuity and change in leisure. Focusing merely on activities and patterns of change through a transition at the superficial behavioral level, however, can be misleading, because such changes are also likely to be accompanied by changes in leisure meanings and motivations.

Third, transitions and leisure must be viewed and investigated "contextually." Although each individual experiences a transition and its impacts in his or her own way, these experiences are filtered through and shaped by an individual's past history and culture, as well as the new "culture" into which he or she passes as a result of undergoing the transition.

Fourth, a transition creates its own combination and sequence of constraints to leisure. Some constraints may be unique to the transition, while others, encountered more universally, are experienced in distinct ways by people progressing through the transition. Conversely, the distinct combination of leisure constraints associated with a transition is unlikely to be experienced in the same way by people who are not undergoing that transition. Thus, while there may indeed be considerable internal variation in the experience of and response to constraints by people who share a given transition, they also have sufficient in common to distinguish them from nontransitional people.

Fifth, leisure constraints may change during a transition, as part of the process of adapting to new circumstances and developing strategies to negotiate constraints.

Sixth, while new constraints encountered during and after a transition may impose limits on fulfilling leisure aspirations, other constraints, experienced prior to the transition, may be alleviated or disappear entirely. Consequently, prior latent demand now becomes expressed demand. In extreme cases, relaxation of a pretransitional constraint may serve as a motivation for leisure in the posttransitional stage.

Connections Between Negotiation of Leisure Constraints and Serious Leisure

A set of transitions of a seemingly quite different kind from the aforementioned is considered in an article by

McQuarrie and Jackson (1996), namely those that occur during the course of a serious leisure career (Stebbins, 1992, 1999). However, one reason for including this "different" type of transition here is to solidify the point that much can be gained by adopting a generalized perspective that treats transitions as similar from an abstract point of view, focusing more on what they have in common than dwelling on their differences. Another is the conclusions emerging from McQuarrie and Jackson's study offer certain insights into leisure, transitions, and constraints not touched on in the other articles reviewed here but which, when incorporated into a composite list of inferences, can be generalized back to other specific transitions.

Stebbins's (1992, 1999) concepts of "serious leisure" and "leisure career" explicitly pointed toward notions of transitions. By definition, a leisure career is characterized by several distinct stages and the transitions that occur between them. It involves "long-term commitment to and involvement with a leisure activity, centered on acquiring its special skills, knowledge, and experience, and shaped by its own *special contingencies, turning points,* and *stages of achievement or involvement* [italics added]" (Stebbins, cited in McQuarrie & Jackson, 1996, p. 465). McQuarrie and Jackson chose adult amateur ice skating as the leisure activity to be investigated because it exhibits the attributes of serious leisure and the experience and impacts of constraints: "successful participation in adult amateur ice skating frequently requires that a complex sequence of constraints must be negotiated" (p. 461).

McQuarrie and Jackson's primary purpose was to enhance understanding of the concepts of serious leisure and the negotiation of leisure constraints by identifying linkages between these two subfields of leisure studies. The authors argued, although they had not previously been studied systematically, connections between serious leisure on the one hand and leisure constraints and their negotiation on the other hand are plain, and can fruitfully be explored to the benefit of both fields of research. The essential premise was several of the theoretical qualities of serious leisure defined by Stebbins (1992, 1999) implied not only the presence of constraints to achieving leisure-related goals, but also the demand of conscious efforts to achieve these goals. This would be labeled "adoption of leisure constraints negotiation strategies" in the language of leisure constraints research, if not the terminology used by Stebbins, who wrote instead of "the occasional need to persevere" and "a significant personal effort" (Stebbins, 1999, pp. 72–73).

Adapting Stebbins's framework, McQuarrie and Jackson identified five stages in an adult amateur ice skater's serious leisure career:

1. becoming a potential participant.

2. beginning in the sport.

3. development.

4. establishment

5. decline or exit from the sport.

They then described each stage in considerable detail, paying particular attention to its unique combination of constraints and the strategies of negotiation typically adopted to overcome them. For example, despite an initial interest in the sport, people might be constrained from entering Stage 1, not only by a lack of facilities, but also by interpersonal and intrapersonal constraints, such as the absence of role models, lack of companions, or negative self-perceptions. Similarly, reaching and progressing through the development stage may be inhibited by barriers to specialization, such as a lack of training opportunities, or inconvenient timing or location of the training facilities and programs that do exist. Other constraints at this level include lack of appropriate coaching, coupled with an emphasis on grooming children for competition to the neglect of coaching adults for noncompetitive participation.

Decline in participation in adult amateur ice skating or exit from the sport may take place at any time during the career, not necessarily or only after Stage 4 (establishment). McQuarrie and Jackson pointed to several reasons for this, including costs, changes in the availability of opportunities, changes in outside commitments, and discouragement. The important point to be drawn from the account of decline and exit is if one or more of these kinds of constraints becomes particularly acute, not only will a change in participation occur (e.g., its nature, timing, frequency, or location), but also the skater will progress to a different stage. Thus, in this instance at least, the transition may not just occur simultaneously or coincidentally with new or increasingly powerful constraints, but actually be prompted by them. In other words, the transition is grounded in constraints.

The important general inference to be drawn from McQuarrie and Jackson's study is a transition—at least in the context of progression through the stages of a serious leisure career and perhaps in other transitions as well—is initiated and shaped not just by changing opportunities, skills, and interests, but also by constraints. With particular reference to the development stage, for example, the authors noted, "paradoxically, at the time the adult's interest in skating increases, the opportunities for advancement radically decrease; thus, constraints to specialization, as opposed to participation, begin to take effect" (p. 468). This suggests a transition is defined as much by emerging constraints as by anything else. In summary, McQuarrie and Jackson's study leads to the crucial conclusion—from the standpoint of the present chapter—"constraints may be particularly pertinent at transition points...and that strategies to negotiate constraints may be crucial in making such a transition" (pp. 476–477).

Inferences From the Review of Seven Transitions

The purposes of the preceding summary reviews were to examine seven distinct and (on the surface at least) dissimilar transitions, and to draw out a number of general inferences concerning the ways in which constraints to leisure evolve over a transition and are intimately interconnected with observable, stable, and predictable changes in leisure. Each transition, as well as others which could have been selected for examination, is distinct if not unique. However, the value of approaching them as specific examples of a more generic phenomenon or concept has been the opportunity to identify attributes and processes sufficiently general to apply, within limitations, to all of them, even if specific inferences were not identified by the researchers who investigated a particular transition. These may now be summarized and integrated in three themes:

1. the nature of transitions.
2. transitions and leisure.
3. transitions, leisure, and constraints.

The Nature of Transitions

- Some transitions are effectively universal, while others are confined to certain individuals or identifiable subgroups of the population.

- Each specific and apparently unique transition is best thought of as a more general phenomenon for which the antecedents, experience, impacts, and aftermath will likely vary substantially among individuals. Thus, transitions such as menopause, marriage, divorce, and parenthood are umbrella terms in which a single, generic label masks a variety of phenomena. Conversely, despite these variations, there is value in thinking of each specific transition generically.

- The notion of each type of transition as generic prompts a further abstraction to a more general concept of transition. This permits the establish-

ment of connections between diverse events—such as menopause, death of a spouse, marriage, immigration, and progression through the stages of a serious leisure career—in turn leading to deeper understanding of transitions and constraints and connections between them.

- A transition is not necessarily a single event but may occur in a stable and predictable sequence of substages. Thus, a transition can be a *multistage process*, each substage being distinct but sequentially linked with the others and representing a specific transition within an overall larger and more general one. Alternatively, a transition may consist of a set of events occurring simultaneously, although not necessarily in the same combination for everyone.

- People do not necessarily experience a single transition in isolation. Two or more interconnected transitions may be experienced simultaneously.

- Variations in the impacts of and adaptation to the events occurring during a transition are modified (ameliorated or exacerbated) by personal and situational characteristics. Thus, transitions must be viewed and investigated contextually. Although each individual experiences a transition and its impacts in his or her own way, these experiences are filtered through and shaped by an individual's past history and culture, as well as the new culture into which he or she passes as a result of undergoing the transition.

- A transition can be received—it does not necessarily occur as the result of a physiological or other type of change to oneself, but may be because of a transition that another person, such as a spouse or a child, is going through.

- Transitions and their impacts may be investigated in two complementary ways, directly or indirectly, by describing conditions before and after the transition and on this basis drawing inferences about change during the transition.

Transitions and Leisure

- Transitions are characterized by both continuity and change in leisure.

- Understanding change and continuity in leisure can be enhanced, not only by comparing key aspects of leisure between or among stages, but also by explicitly investigating changes in leisure during transitional periods between the stages.

- Changes in leisure that occur during a transition cannot be fully understood in isolation, but must be placed in a more general context of people's lives, such as work, family, and spousal relations.

- In addition to its beneficial or therapeutic role in helping people to cope with and to adapt to transitions, leisure is likely to be impacted by transitional events and stages in people's lives. Thus, the relationship between transitions and leisure is not unidirectional, but reciprocal.

- Impacts of transitions on leisure may be positive as well as negative, even when new constraints emerge.

- Changes in leisure may be prompted by heightened awareness, reflection, and self-perception, as well as by the exposure to new opportunities triggered by transitions.

- Changes in leisure during a transition should not be described simply in terms of activities, but reflect a complex interaction of individual and social factors that shape the meaning and experience of leisure, even if the activities themselves do not change. Conversely, the activity may change but provide the same meanings and experiences associated with previous activities in which participation no longer occurs.

Transitions, Leisure, and Constraints

- Changes in leisure during transitions may be prompted by changes in constraints. Some constraints may become relaxed or disappear altogether; others may emerge or become more intense.

- Constraints may not only change at transitional points, but also be particularly acute at these times.

- If a transition consists of two or more substages, then constraints and their impacts will not remain static, but will change over these substages.

- Some transitions that occur during a later stage in the life cycle may be thought of as mirror images of earlier ones. In such cases, changes in

leisure may include a return to previous aspirations, experiences, and activities. From the perspective of constraints to leisure, such a transition may result in the alleviation or removal of one or more constraints that emerged during a transition experienced at an earlier stage in the life cycle.

- A transition may involve setting a new balance among competing needs and aspirations, motivations, and constraints. Thus, constraints-induced changes in leisure do not necessarily occur as a result of uncontrollable external influences but because of a conscious decision to forgo some needs in exchange for others. In this sense, a constraint may be voluntarily accepted during a transition rather than imposed from outside.

- Balancing the positive and negative aspects of a transition may be a conscious and deliberate process and not necessarily a passive response to constraints. In a sense this is part of the process of negotiating leisure constraints.

- A transition may create new circumstances that lead an individual into becoming constrained into a leisure activity and not simply out of one, as is most commonly assumed in the leisure constraints literature.

- Changes in constraints over a transition do not necessarily occur independently or in isolation of one another, but frequently occur in the form of an "exchange" of one set of constraints for another. Thus, a transition creates its own combination and sequence of constraints to leisure. Some constraints may be unique to the transition, while others, encountered more universally, are experienced in distinct ways by people progressing through the transition. Conversely, the distinct combination of leisure constraints associated with a transition is unlikely to be experienced in the same way by people not undergoing that transition.

- If a transition involves a change in interpersonal circumstances and relationships, then the "driving force" in the predicted sequence of experiencing constraints may be reversed, with interpersonal constraints becoming more proximal and salient than during normal, everyday life when—as proposed in the hierarchical model of constraints—intrapersonal constraints are the most proximal and salient.

- Strategies to negotiate constraints may be crucial for the successful progression through a transition from one stage to another.

Discussion and Conclusions

In this chapter, I attempted to provide a fresh perspective on constraints to leisure that extends previous thinking on concepts such as negotiation, while dealing with some of the difficulties inherent in conventional ways in which data about constraints have been collected, analyzed, displayed, and interpreted. The ideas offered here can also potentially address two additional problems. The first is our lack of understanding of processes whereby constraints enter into people's lives and the steps people take to adjust to them. The second is the criticism that, because people don't think in terms of constraints, and because constraints are not part of their overt decision making on a day-to-day basis, the concept of constraints is an artificial construct invented by researchers but with little if any relevance to how people make choices about their leisure behavior (e.g., Samdahl & Jekubovich, 1997a). However, the idea most leisure behavior is the product of inertia, an ongoing equilibrium that is punctured perhaps only occasionally by marker events or the kinds of transitions described and interpreted in this chapter, neatly sidesteps this problem.

To a considerable extent, and as argued earlier in this chapter, much of the difficulty associated with "leisure constraints"—empirical, conceptual, theoretical, and methodological—stems from the fact that, until recently, with the more widespread adoption of qualitative methods, the predominant data collection tool in leisure constraints research has been the questionnaire survey. As touched on previously, and as explored by the authors of several other chapters in this book, there are many reasons for the dominance of surveys, and they are not always good ones, nor are their effects always desirable.

As far as the leisure constraints research field is concerned, perhaps the two most significant effects have been (1) to produce a picture of constraints as static and invariant over time—something that people either experience or do not—leading to the assumption that it makes little difference as to the timing of when researchers ask them questions about constraints, and (2) this, in turn, attenuated our in-depth understanding of the impacts constraints have on people's lives in general and their leisure lives in particular. In a sense, because of our social scientific desire to isolate and focus on specific phenomena, we have tended, perhaps inadvertently, to compartmen-

talize leisure and constraints and separate them from the rest of people's lives.

Thus, we typically asked people to rate how constraints relate to some facet of their leisure, measured using an array of social psychological items. What we have also effectively done, however, is produce a picture of constraints that says very little if anything about the rest of people's lives, except indirectly and at an aggregate level by using statistical methods to correlate constraints with various socioeconomic and demographic variables. In short, much constraints research is bereft of context, whether this be at the personal, familial, or societal levels. It is almost as if we have said to our survey respondents, "Tell us about your leisure and constraints, but don't tell us about anything else important in your life." This state of affairs reminds me of the isolated, uniform plain (no topography, no rivers or lakes, no forests and so on) that the geographer Walther Christaller (1933/1996), in his development of central place theory, assumed to be able to see and explain regularities in a hexagonal pattern of human settlement expressed in regions characterized by a hierarchy of hamlets, villages, towns, cities, and metropolises.

From the standpoint of social scientific procedure, in which the goal is to promote a general understanding of phenomena at an abstract and theoretical level, the assumptions we make, the methods we use to collect data, and the boundaries we set around our investigations are all perfectly acceptable—without them we would not be able to proceed at all. They are set, in part, by the level of generality at which we choose to conceive our questions and conduct our research. The loss of detail and context are the costs we are willing to incur in exchange for being able to enjoy insights that otherwise would be difficult or even impossible to gain at either a finer or coarser level of detail, just as Christaller was able to deduce some powerful central place principles precisely because he assumed away the physical geography of the regions he studied. However, the downside is a picture of constraints as static, and, apart from correlative analyses, passive. When we ask a person a question such as rating the importance of "being too busy with my family" as a constraint on leisure choices, we rarely if ever ask when and how that constraint emerged and was first experienced, or if and how its nature and effects have increased or decreased over time.[1]

The notion constraints are not invariant over time is, of course, an inherent and unavoidable assumption in age-based analyses of leisure behavior and leisure constraints—at least if we permit ourselves to draw developmental-like inferences from cross-sectional data.

This is not unreasonable, because otherwise we would be forced to view survey data as unique snapshots of human perceptions and behavior defined purely by when they were collected and that have no temporal (or cultural or spatial for that matter) relevance or generalizability. But the issues of how constraints change over time, and what the implications are for people's leisure, are not well-understood. Investigations of transitions, leisure, and constraints offer one of several opportunities to enhance this understanding.

References

Bella, L. (1989). Women and leisure: Beyond androcentrism. In E. Jackson and T. Burton (Eds.), *Understanding leisure and recreation: Mapping the past, charting the future* (pp. 150–180). State College, PA: Venture Publishing, Inc.

Bialeschki, M. D. and Michener, S. (1994). Re-entering leisure: Transition within the role of motherhood. *Journal of Leisure Research, 26*, 57–74.

Christaller, W. (1996). Die zentralen Orte in Süddeutschland [Central Places in Southern Germany] (C. W. Baskin, Trans.). Princeton, NJ: Prentice Hall. (Original work published 1933)

Crawford, D. W. and Godbey, G. (1987). Reconceptualizing barriers to family leisure. *Leisure Sciences, 9*, 119–127.

Crawford, D. W. and Huston, T. L. (1993). The impact of the transition to parenthood on marital leisure. *Personality and Social Psychology Bulletin, 19*, 39–46.

Crawford, D. W., Jackson, E. L., and Godbey, G. (1991). A hierarchical model of leisure constraints. *Leisure Sciences, 13*, 309–320.

Eldrege, N. and Gould, S. J. (1972). Punctuated equilibria: An alternative to phyletic gradualism. In T. J. Schopf (Ed.), *Models in paleobiology* (pp. 82–115). San Francisco, CA: Freeman, Cooper and Co.

Frederick, C. J. and Shaw, S. M. (1995). Body image as a leisure constraint: Examining the experience of aerobic exercise classes for young adults. *Leisure Sciences, 17*, 57–89.

Freysinger, V. J. (1999). Life span and life course perspectives on leisure. In E. Jackson and T. Burton (Eds.), *Leisure studies: Prospects for the twenty-first century* (pp. 253–270). State College, PA: Venture Publishing, Inc.

Gersick, C. J. G. (1988). Time and transition in work teams: Toward a new model of group development. *Academy of Management Journal, 31*, 9–41.

Henderson, K. A. and Allen, K. (1991). The ethic of care: Leisure possibilities and constraints for women. *Loisir et Sociètè, 14*(1), 97–113.

Henderson, K. A. and Bialeschki, M. D. (1991). A sense of entitlement to leisure as constraint and empowerment for women. *Leisure Sciences, 13*, 51–65.

Henderson, K. A. and Bialeschki, M. D. (1993). Exploring an expanded model of women's leisure constraints. *Journal of Applied Recreation Research, 18*, 229–252.

Henderson, K. A. and Bialeschki, M. D. (1999). Makers of meanings: Feminist perspectives on leisure research. In E. Jackson and T. Burton (Eds.), *Leisure studies: Prospects for the twenty-first century* (pp. 167–176). State College, PA: Venture Publishing, Inc.

Hultsman, W. Z. (1995). Recognizing patterns of leisure constraints: An extension of the exploration of dimensionality. *Journal of Leisure Research, 27*, 228–244.

Jackson, E. L. (1988). Leisure constraints: A survey of past research. *Leisure Sciences, 10*, 203–215.

Jackson, E. L. (1993). Recognizing patterns of leisure constraints: Results from alternative analyses. *Journal of Leisure Research, 25*, 129–149.

Jackson, E. L., Crawford, D. W., and Godbey, G. (1992). *The process of negotiating leisure constraints*. Paper presented at the NRPA Symposium on Leisure Research, Cincinnati, OH.

Jackson, E. L., Crawford, D. W., and Godbey, G. (1993). Negotiation of leisure constraints. *Leisure Sciences, 15*, 1–11.

Jackson, E. L. and Dunn, E. (1988). Integrating ceasing participation with other aspects of leisure behavior. *Journal of Leisure Research, 20*, 31–45.

Jackson, E. L. and Henderson, K. A. (1995). Gender-based analysis of leisure constraints. *Leisure Sciences, 17*, 31–51.

Jackson, E. L. and Scott, D. (1999). Constraints to leisure. In E. Jackson and T. Burton (Eds.), *Leisure studies: Prospects for the twenty-first century* (pp. 299–321). State College, PA: Venture Publishing, Inc.

Kay, T. and Jackson, G. (1991). Leisure despite constraint: The impact of leisure constraints on leisure participation. *Journal of Leisure Research, 23*, 301–313.

Kelly, J. R. (1983). *Leisure identities and interactions*. London, England: Allen and Unwin.

Kleiber, D. (1999). *Leisure experience and human development: A dialectical interpretation*. New York, NY: Basic Books.

McQuarrie, F. and Jackson, E. L. (1996). Connections between negotiation of leisure constraints and serious leisure: An exploratory study of adult amateur ice skaters. *Loisir et Société, 19*, 459–483.

Nadirova, A. and Jackson, E. L. (2000). Alternative criterion variables against which to assess the impacts of constraints to leisure. *Journal of Leisure Research, 32*, 396–405.

O'Hara, J. (1984). *Collected stories of John O'Hara*. New York, NY: Random House.

Parry, D. C. and Shaw, S. M. (1999). The role of leisure in women's experiences of menopause and midlife. *Leisure Sciences, 21*, 197–212.

Patterson, I. and Carpenter, G. (1994). Participation in leisure activities after the death of a spouse. *Leisure Sciences, 16*, 105–117.

Raymore, L. (1995). Leisure behaviour and the transition from adolescence to young adulthood. *Leisure Studies, 14*, 202–226.

Rublee, C. B. and Shaw, S. M. (1990). Constraints on the leisure and community participation of immigrant women: Implications for social integration. *Loisir et Société, 14*(1), 133–150.

Samdahl, D. (1999). Epistemological and methodological issues in leisure research. In E. Jackson and T. Burton (Eds.), *Leisure studies: Prospects for the twenty-first century* (pp. 119–133). State College, PA: Venture Publishing, Inc.

Samdahl, D. and Jekubovich, N. (1997a). A critique of leisure constraints: Comparative analyses and understandings. *Journal of Leisure Research, 29*, 430–452.

Samdahl, D. and Jekubovich, N. (1997b). A rejoinder to Henderson's and Jackson's commentaries on "A critique of leisure constraints." *Journal of Leisure Research, 29*, 469–471.

Scott, D. (1991). The problematic nature of participation in contract bridge: A qualitative study of group-related constraints. *Leisure Sciences, 13*, 321–336.

Shaw, S. M. (1994). Gender, leisure, and constraint: Towards a framework for the analysis of women's leisure. *Journal of Leisure Research, 26*, 8–22.

Shaw, S. M. (1999). Gender and leisure. In E. Jackson and T. Burton (Eds.), *Leisure studies: Prospects for the twenty-first century* (pp. 271–281). State College, PA: Venture Publishing, Inc.

Shaw, S. M., Bonen, A., and McCabe, J. F. (1991). Do more constraints mean less leisure? Examining the relationship between constraints and participation. *Journal of Leisure Research, 23*, 286–300.

Stebbins, R. A. (1992). *Amateurs, professionals, and serious leisure*. Montreal, Quebec, Canada: McGill-Queen's University Press.

Stebbins, R. A. (1999). Serious leisure. In E. Jackson and T. Burton (Eds.), *Leisure studies: Prospects for the twenty-first century* (pp. 69–79). State College, PA: Venture Publishing, Inc.

Stodolska, M. (1998). Assimilation and leisure constraints: Dynamics of constraints on leisure in immigrant populations. *Journal of Leisure Research, 30*, 521–551.

Stodolska, M. (2000). Changes in leisure participation patterns after immigration. *Leisure Sciences, 22*, 39–63.

Tirone, S. and Shaw, S. M. (1997). At the center of their lives: Indo Canadian women, their families and leisure. *Journal of Leisure Research, 29*, 225–244.

Whyte, L. B. and Shaw, S. M. (1994). Women's leisure: An exploratory study of fear of violence as a leisure constraint. *Journal of Applied Recreation Research, 19*, 5–21.

Yu, P. and Berryman, D. L. (1996). The relationship among self-esteem, acculturation, and recreation participation of recently arrived Chinese immigrant adolescents. *Journal of Leisure Research, 28*, 251–273.

Endnote

1. These remarks should not be interpreted as being critical only of leisure constraints research conducted by others. Looking back over the 20-plus years of my own involvement in the field, I realize that much of the work I myself have produced is equally vulnerable to this kind of criticism.

Chapter 9

Leisure, Constraints, and Negative Life Events: Paradox and Possibilities

Susan L. Hutchinson (Dalhousie University) and Douglas A. Kleiber (The University of Georgia)

Life is often determined by the unexpected—sometimes pleasantly, often unpleasantly. In contrast to the previous chapter, which addresses the ways leisure changes with and is constrained by various predictable life transitions (e.g., marriage, birth of children), this chapter focuses on those life events that are unexpected, unwanted, and often traumatic. The death of a loved one, the unexpected termination of a job, a traumatic injury, or the onset of chronic illness differ significantly in many respects, but they share the experience of disruption and loss to which the individuals (and their friends and families) must learn to adjust.

We begin this chapter by presenting a phenomenological perspective on negative life events. To understand the paradoxical nature of leisure in the context of trauma or loss, we draw on our own work with adults who have experienced a traumatic injury or illness (Hutchinson, 2000; Hutchinson, Loy, Kleiber & Dattilo, 2003; Kleiber, Brock, Lee, Dattilo & Caldwell, 1995; Kleiber, Dattilo, Loy & Hutchinson, 2001) as well as autobiographical "survivor" stories of people who have experienced cancer and physical attacks (Tocher, 2002; Van Tighem, 2000). These stories capture not only the experience of trauma, but also its effects on people's everyday lives, including their leisure. Our intent is to contextualize the meaning and experience of unexpected negative or traumatic life events. Some life events, such as a divorce or the death of a spouse, may actually provide relief to one who has been in an abusive relationship or has endured the burden of caring for an ailing loved one through a protracted and terminal illness. However, our focus here is on those events that result in *unwanted* disruptions to valued roles, relationships and preferred activities. In this context, we consider the various constraints to leisure that follow from such events

and how leisure meanings are reconstructed to personal advantage in their aftermath.

Constraints to leisure are inevitably created by the occurrence of traumatic events, though the factors that affect subsequent leisure engagement have more widespread effects as well. For example, while loss of money and the ensuing alienation that result from losing one's job may restrict an individual's freedom to engage in his or her preferred leisure, it also clearly constrains other aspects of life as well (e.g., family life). Nonetheless, leisure is likely to be implicated rather immediately in the problems associated with almost every negative life event (e.g., Kleiber et al., 1995). The challenge is typically negotiating or accommodating the constraint created.

After considering predictable responses to loss and ensuing leisure constraints in the first part of this chapter, we will provide evidence of improvement in perspective and experience as a result of negative life events. Researchers have begun to document the conditions under which negative events lead to "post traumatic growth" (Tedeschi, Park & Calhoun, 1998). According to Tedeschi et al., the positive changes that commonly occur after a traumatic life event include changed perceptions of self (e.g., survivor vs. victim) and changed interpersonal relationships (e.g., more emotionally expressive and compassionate). Such changes are also likely to reflect a greater appreciation of the smaller things in life and a desire to make the most of moments available. From this perspective it seems reasonable to look at the ways leisure may be used to create the conditions that foster coping and personal growth.

In the final part of the chapter we examine the ways in which managing and overcoming leisure constraints parallel the coping process itself. Again, drawing on our own work with illness/injury survivors, as well as other first-person accounts, we explore what we see as the possibilities for leisure as a resource in coping with and adjusting to negative life events. To that end, we suggest ways the work on negotiation of leisure constraints may be informed by theory and research evidence on the subject of coping.

The Phenomenology of Loss

The experience of intense disruption to the normalcy of everyday life is typical of most accounts of loss or trauma. Physical and social losses following trauma may be evident to others, but psychological responses of shock, confusion, anxiety, or depression, which are not always obvious, inevitably follow traumatic life events (Updegraff & Taylor, 2000). In extreme cases, posttraumatic stress disorder (PTSD) can result. Based on years of research with trauma victims, Janoff-Bulman (1992) suggested people typically maintain an "illusion of invulnerability" that leads them to believe bad things will not happen to them, and that for the most part the world is safe and they are worthy, "good" individuals. As a result of a negative life event, these fundamental assumptions are "shattered." As Janoff-Bulman wrote:

> The assault on fundamental assumptions is massive. These traumatic events do not produce the psychological equivalent of superficial scratches that heal readily, but deep bodily wounds that require far more in the way of restorative efforts. The injury is to the victim's inner world. Core assumptions are shattered by the traumatic experience. (p. 53)

People who have experienced trauma, whether as a result of a disabling injury or disease or at the hand of others (e.g., rape, abuse, war), consistently describe feeling violated and filled with a sense of vulnerability, a feeling that could no longer rely on and feel secure in their own lives and bodies. For many, a profound sense of loss of power and control is especially difficult to overcome.

Michelle Tocher's (2002) retelling of women's experiences of breast cancer, *How to Ride a Dragon: Women with Breast Cancer Tell Their Stories,* exemplifies the range of emotions and thoughts that are typical responses to trauma or loss. Tocher recounted one woman's first thoughts after finding out she was diagnosed with breast cancer: "I thought I was so strong and invincible. This news knocked the wind right out of my sails. I couldn't breathe" (p. 39). Another woman also described this loss of control: "They could cut my hair, they could cut my body parts, but to take away my ability to be in control of my life was unbearably painful" (p. 56).

Although these are typical initial responses to loss and trauma, descriptions of chronic stressors are also common. These chronic stressors arise from permanent changes that follow the sudden onset of a chronic illness, disease, or accident, or other unexpected and unwanted life events. For example, the ongoing effects of pain or fatigue or having to live with tightly controlled health regimens often become chronic sources of stress that may continue indefinitely after the acute onset of some illnesses or injuries. In our study of people with spinal cord injuries, many of the people we interviewed spoke of their frustration and sadness about the loss of independence that resulted from their injury (Hutchinson et al, 2003; Kleiber et al., 2001). In addition, they expressed guilt over asking family members to do things they would have done on their own previously.

Physical disability or disfigurement may even threaten one's sense of femininity or masculinity in the wake of a traumatic injury or illness. Not feeling attractive can be profoundly challenging to peoples' sense of personal worth and self-identity. Likewise, disruptions to work or the ability to contribute productively to household management tasks or child care can become ongoing sources of conflict or stress in relationships and undermine a person's sense of self-worth. These changes in functioning affect not only the individual himself or herself, but others, such as children or spouses. Coping with the ongoing challenges associated with the uncertainties and realities that follow a traumatic life event becomes a "family affair." These chronic stressors are typically manifested as constraints to maintaining previously valued activities, role and relationships, including those in leisure contexts.

Leisure Constrained

Descriptions of various constraints to leisure are now prevalent in the leisure studies literature (e.g., Crawford & Godbey, 1987; Crawford, Jackson & Godbey, 1991; Jackson, 1988; Jackson & Henderson, 1995; Whyte & Shaw, 1994), including this volume. As one set of constraints, disability and injury are immediately constraining to many kinds and aspects of leisure, and may even define the experience of illness and disability (Kleiber et al., 1995). The constraints to leisure that result from losses associated with an event's occurrence fall into all three of the categories commonly used for the classification of leisure constraints: intrapersonal, interpersonal and structural.

Intrapersonal Constraints to Leisure

In studies of traumatic injury and illness, loss of leisure-based abilities is frequently among the first things recognized as concomitants of the illness. Skills cultivated and taken for granted in the creation of pleasure and enjoyment now become problematic. In our earlier studies (Kleiber et al., 1995), interview subjects identified the sudden inability to throw, play, sing, swim, dance, and fish as immediately prominent in their sense of loss. Perceptions of stigma (along with concern for being " a burden") also seem to impose additional and sometimes even more significant constraints to people who have experienced illness or injury. Several of the people we interviewed in our more recent research spoke about magnified perceptions of self-consciousness and disability in some social leisure contexts (Hutchinson et al., 2003; Kleiber et al., 2001). One woman said, "When I go out somewhere I always feel like everybody is looking and everybody is watching." For her and others we interviewed, these perceptions of stigma led to avoiding social situations or places where they would be subject to public scrutiny. While this provided temporary relief, it also made people feel increasingly isolated. Likewise, people who lost a spouse expressed self-consciousness going alone to public places, such as restaurants, thus potentially limiting these forms of leisure engagement. These descriptions of public self-consciousness were less visible in the accounts of cancer survivors where clothes could partly hide scars or a missing breast, at least in public situations.

Other traumatic events impose further intrapersonal constraints to leisure. For example, fear for personal safety following an attack may lead to feelings of vulnerability that make certain leisure activities, such as spending time in the outdoors, threatening. Similarly, the inability to engage in leisure activities in a manner that would have been previously enjoyable may be a constraint to participation. One young woman with a spinal cord injury we interviewed noted she did not enjoy going shopping anymore, because it is now a painful reminder of her past self and life: "Shopping for cute clothes and stuff. That kind of depresses me in a way too because I can't wear all the stuff I want to wear." Likewise, she now avoids going out with her friends because she "can't dress up" like she used to. Although her physical limitations impose structural constraints to certain activities, more salient are her interpretations of the meaning of these constraints for her experiences in leisure. In such cases the ability to engage in the activity may not be constrained, or may have been restored in some way, but the individual may choose not to participate because the intrinsic meanings of the activity have been altered.

Interpersonal Constraints to Leisure

While a negative life event may happen to one person, its effects are spread throughout all personal relationships. Coping with lost or altered leisure affects spouses, siblings, children, parents, and friends of the individual who are likely coparticipants. Although, as mentioned previously, death or divorce may be perceived as "for the best" in some respects, there is nonetheless a recognition in most cases that shared (mutually enjoyable) leisure activities and leisure companionship have been lost. A back injury that keeps a father from playing with his daughter has the potential for distancing them from each other and making other kinds of leisure interaction more difficult.

Most negative life events remove people from their social networks in various ways. A woman who loses her job, for example, usually has limited contact with coworkers who were likely coparticipants in activities; coworkers and the unemployed woman may be mutually reluctant to contact each other. A disabling accident or illness that limits physical function typically reduces the number of available activities, and thus reduces the circle of coparticipants. The disposition of former recreation partners to do other things with the person who is ill or impaired depends on the strength of the relationship, because it often requires them to alter their own leisure behavior and manage whatever discomfort they have about interacting with their former playmate/partner. Even when individuals or families try to resume previously enjoyed activities, in many situations change in the meaning and form of the shared leisure activity results. Children of divorce, for example, have expressed their disappointment about not being able to have their "family" together for special family trips or vacations, in spite of the one parent's efforts to reproduce the trip as it was before the divorce (Hutchinson & Golish, 2003).

Structural Constraints to Leisure

Lack of time, physical inaccessibility, and inadequate financial resources are among the more common structural constraints to leisure, and negative life events are likely to exacerbate all three. With respect to time scarcity, while loss of a job might actually increase available time, most other losses (physical and social) create conditions that result in greater time needs (e.g., for activities of daily living, transportation if not able to drive; Kleiber et al., 2001). In interviews with individuals with a spinal cord injury, several people described how much they missed the experience of enjoyment that used to be associated with house, garden, and car maintenance lost as a result of the extra time and effort required to do even the most basic of activities. In addition, several people described how their diminished physical mobility limited their enjoyment of physically expressive activities such as dancing. We heard this repeatedly in people's accounts of their leisure following injury. Although they could still dance, or garden, or go to a pool to swim, many questioned whether the benefits to doing were worth the extra costs—in terms of effort and energy and time—required to continue with the activity in question.

A Blurring of Boundaries

Arguably, the aforementioned leisure constraints categories are only heuristically useful; they tend to blend together, as suggested elsewhere (Kleiber, Wade & Loucks-Atkinson, this volume). We see this blurring in the description of "lost leisure" described by Patricia Van Tighem (2000) after a vicious bear attack, which left her and her husband permanently disfigured:

> I can wish it never happened but it did. I will cry about it and feel sorry for myself. I will cry for Trevor [her husband] and the distortion his face now wears. I will cry over the changes in our relationship. And I will be angry that I can never feel the same way about hiking in the Rockies, grieve the loss of that shared love. (p. 141)

Fear (an intrapersonal constraint) of being in the wilderness is the result of real threats to safety from future animal attacks (a structural constraint).

In the same way, although we can argue that public self-consciousness and perceived stigma may be intrapersonal constraints to leisure for men and women with disabilities, these perceptions arise from actual interactions with people in public or social spaces, from which interpersonal constraints result. Likewise, the limited financial resources available to a person who has lost his job will likely be an issue for him and for potential coparticipants, defining both individual comfort (intrapersonal constraint) and ease of interaction (interpersonal constraint) around decision making related to what is ostensibly a structural constraint.

Those who live with the results of victimization (e.g., abuse, rape, attack) may suffer more from internal trauma that inhibits self-expressive leisure activity than the lack of suitable companions. Loss of psychological safety and grief are thus more clearly "intrapersonal" constraints to leisure. However, this is problematic, because it makes recovering feelings of safety an individual problem to overcome. The same can be said of the constraints imposed from the adoption of societal or cultural ideologies associated with femininity/masculinity, or even grieving, for which strict social rules or expectations for acceptable behavior are implicitly imposed. In these cases leisure or being seen in public having fun may be unacceptable.

Although the boundaries between intrapersonal, interpersonal, and structural constraints to leisure are not clear cut, for all victims of traumatic life events appraisals of leisure constraints are interconnected with and influenced by perceptions of event-related stressors and changes, appraisals of one's coping resources, and appraisals of leisure itself. From this we can conclude although leisure constraints may exist following a life event, they should not be considered in a unitary and static way. As we saw in the last chapter, changes that occur throughout the life span lead to ongoing reappraisals, even without traumatic events, that can alter the perceptions people have of their leisure—both how it is constrained and what it offers by way of opportunity. In spite of these constraints, and even because of them in some cases, people seek out leisure in various forms to cope with daily stressors, to reconnect, and to sustain hope for the future.

Trauma and Loss as Opportunities for Change and Growth

Overwhelmingly consistent in "survivor" accounts are descriptions of a renewed appreciation for life, a stronger sense of self, stronger ties with friends and family, and new life priorities as a result of their experiences (Calhoun & Tedeschi, 2001; Tedeschi & Calhoun, 1995; Updegraff & Taylor, 2000; Wortman & Silver, 1987). These findings are reflected in autobiographical accounts as well as studies of various traumatic life events, including war (Frankl, 1963; Riolli, Savicki & Cepani, 2002; Shapiro, 2002; Tedeschi, 1999), bereavement (Raphael & Dobson, 2000; Tedeschi & Calhoun, 1995), cancer (Cordova, Cunningham, Carlson & Andrykowski, 2001; Leedham & Meyerowitz, 2000; Taylor, 1983; Weiss, 2002), sexual assault (Frazier, Conlon & Glaser, 2001; Yaffe, 1996), and chronic illness (Thompson & Kyle, 2000), such as HIV/AIDS (Cadell, 2001; Schwartzberg, 1993; Updegraff, Taylor, Kemeny & Wyatt, 2002).

In our interviews with people who acquired a spinal cord injury, some described "enjoying life" more since their injuries and a renewed appreciation for their relationships (Kleiber et al., 2001). This renewed appreciation for friends and family was often manifested in people making more time to spend together than they had before being injured. Although there have not been published research studies that document responses to the September 11th terrorist attacks, journalistic accounts that followed in the days and weeks after the event have been dominated by stories of people describing how their life priorities had changed, with a particular emphasis on putting family first. These stories provide testimony of the renewed appreciation some people have of the small things in life in the aftermath of such traumatic losses, particularly the new or renewed emphasis on spending time with friends and family.

In *Flow: The Psychology of Optimal Experience,* Csikszentmihalyi (1990) referred to several examples of such personal transformations as "cheating chaos." He pointed to work in Milan, Italy, with individuals who lost the use of limbs in accidents who identified their accidents as being both the most negative and the most positive events in their lives. Csikszentmihalyi related this reaction to the "focusing" effect of a tragic event. The limitations of the handicap become the new focus of attention for applying effort and skill. Goals are clarified and contradictory alternatives are reduced in the face of the demands of just coping. Learning to live again in a new way, focusing on what the environment affords, and developing the skills necessary becomes a source of enjoyment and pride in many cases.

When a crisis becomes a juncture for reappraising one's self, life, values, and goals, it often culminates in greater openness to and appreciation of experience and other people. Janoff-Bulman and Berger (2000) pointed out people do not make such changes "in spite of their losses and sense of vulnerability, but because of them" (p. 39) and named this phenomenon the "psychology of appreciation." The following statement by one woman after her cancer diagnosis is illustrative of the benefits some people extract from adversity:

> In some ways I feel fortunate. I know that may sound silly, but so many positive things have happened to me since my diagnosis. I have gained a deeper understanding of myself. Several of my friendships have strengthened and I have developed some wonderful new friendships. I have become an advocate for the Breast Cancer Foundation... (Tocher, 2002, p. 140)

Researchers on posttraumatic growth (Tedeschi et al., 1998) have concerned themselves primarily with the personality attributes that predispose a person to positive reappraisal (much as leisure researchers have done in charting the leisure–coping relationship) or with the changes in the individual as a result of the experience. Relatively little attention has been given to the dynamics of positive reappraisal itself and the coping mechanisms that foster it. It seems reasonable to think that leisure, as

a context for spending time with friends and family, and as a focus of altered priorities (e.g., in place of work), may be important in the processes of reappraisal and appreciation.

Support for this thesis can be found in the stress–coping literature. Working with caregivers of people diagnosed with AIDS, Folkman and her colleagues (Folkman, 1997; Folkman & Moskowitz, 2000) documented the importance of positive events (e.g., laughter, enjoyment, pleasurable insights, uplifting messages) for precipitating positive reappraisal and thus sustaining coping efforts in the face of high levels of ongoing stress. While such experiences may not actually be regarded as leisure at the time, they are significant in demonstrating the importance of positive affect in the coping process and in suggesting one of the ways leisure experience may serve as an important coping resource.

Coping, Negotiating, and Navigating in Leisure

Although enjoyable and personally meaningful leisure may be a large part of what is lost following a negative life event, leisure may also serve as a resource in coping in the aftermath of the crisis. Many times, leisure activities are chosen for their ability to help people to reframe the way they view their present situation as well as the future. This positive reappraisal is important to sustain coping efforts and to generate hope for the future.

In an interview with Tocher (2002), a woman explained how she had used an expressive activity—painting—to transform the way she viewed her cancer. By seeing herself in a different relationship to the cancer, she was able to feel she had more control and hope in the face on ongoing challenges:

> I can change my reality by changing the image. It's magic in a way. It is a way to keep me grounded. Doing something of value keeps me connected to a normal life. When I am painting, I feel normal. (p. 88)

Although diversionary activities have often been noted in the literature outside leisure studies as less than ideal forms of coping, several of the people we spoke with described how important different forms of leisure activities—often those requiring lower levels of mental or physical engagement—were as a mental distraction to avoid their problems, even momentarily. Another breast cancer survivor explained, in addition to relying on family members and friends for support, a special television program was also important:

One other person whom I relied on heavily throughout my treatment was J. R. Ewing. Reruns of *Dallas* began simultaneously with my treatments. Every day, no matter what, I stopped what I was doing in order to watch my show. Everyone knows not to call between 10 a.m. and 11 a.m. It was a perfect escape. (Tocher, 2002, p. 93)

Likewise, several of the people we interviewed following their spinal cord injury talked about the value of enjoyable activities, such as reading, watching television and movies, and taking a bath, for their usefulness as a mental distraction from their worries. For example, one young woman commented, "I like movies because they are just a total escape. You know, it's like you are somebody else for a little while. You are in their world, you don't have to think anything about yourself and your problems..." She also talked about daydreaming or being in the bath as an "escape from everyday life."

Support, including leisure-based support, seemed critical to all survivors of injury or illness. Friends who "made" the cancer or injury survivor go back into the public domain and return to social situations, were cited as pivotal in reclaiming one's life. For example, one young woman who had cancer described to Tocher (2002) how a friend of her brother's "made her" go for a beer with friends:

> He "ordered" me to get a grip and to put on make up, dress up, make my bed and start being active. My brother's friends convinced me to come along with them. I agreed....I took a shower, put on my leather pants, my bra with a temporary prosthesis (so what, it did the job!), a nice knitted camisole and my leather "rocker" jacket. A naked head. I actually looked great! And I had fun doing it!...We drank beer and sangria, and my brother's friends all thought I looked gorgeous! My brother was so happy to see me smile again. Even though I did not believe my brother's friends, their compliments made me feel like a woman again. My feminine aura was back!...For the first time in a very long time, I felt alive again. I was a woman again. Wow! (pp. 112–113)

Several of the spinal cord injury survivors we interviewed mentioned the importance of a shared interest, not a shared disability, for helping them redefine themselves following their injury (Hutchinson et al., 2003). However, for others, particularly those who struggled with perceptions of stigma and public self-consciousness, opportunities to be with others who were also wheelchair users were liberating.

Leisure-based support networks can be instrumental in defining not only a sense of belonging, but also a sense of purpose. The turning point several people with cancer and those we interviewed described often occurred in the context of an anticipated or real leisure activity. Tocher (2002) summed this up in the context of dragon boat[1] racing for cancer survivors: "Dragon boating became a lifeline for the survivors. It helped them to recover physically, it provided their emotional support group and it was a symbol of their new identity, their new life" (p. 156). For many breast cancer survivors the opportunity to be a dragon boat member provided the sense of common experience as well as common goal that honored their struggles and survivorship. Engagement in this shared leisure pursuit provided a context for the women to symbolically battle their cancer. This is exemplified in one woman's description:

> When I enter the boat I take on a persona that doesn't appear in my everyday life. I become somewhat ruthless and aggressive in my attempt to win the race. I push myself to the limit, all to show this breast cancer dragon that it can't push me or my friends around. It gives me a sense of control over my life. (Tocher, 2002, pp. 105–106)

The team itself not only provides profound support, but also recognizes they are providing hope and support to others, including other women dealing with breast cancer and inspiration.

Several people described their injury or illness as a turning point—a wake-up call to pursue dreams formerly neglected. Often these dreams are oriented around valued leisure pursuits. Women cancer survivors described taking up creative writing or painting, going back to school, learning to fly an airplane, and taking action on their newfound commitment to themselves (Tocher, 2002). This commitment to oneself, expressed most often through different forms of expressive activity, speaks to the transformative potential of leisure. Leisure's transformative potential, particularly in the face of traumatic losses, is evidenced in many of the cancer survivors' stories. One woman reflected on her first dragon boat race:

> I fully realized, fully, how totally alive and strong I *still* was. I think a part of me had died previously and suddenly I felt whole again....It's incredible how quickly the change took place. Acceptance washed over me....This new world has a better focus with a sense of acceptance, power and beauty, both within and outside myself. I don't hate my own disfigurement like I did before. (Tocher, 2002, pp. 148–149)

In the next section we consider these accounts in relation to recent theoretical propositions regarding leisure's role in coping with and adjusting to negative life events.

Leisure as a Resource in Coping With and Adjusting to Negative Life Events

Recent research on the significance of leisure in coping with stress (e.g., Coleman & Iso-Ahola, 1993; Iso-Ahola & Park, 1996; Iwasaki, 2001; Iwasaki & Mannell, 2000) suggested a variety of ways in which leisure may serve as a resource in dealing with negative life events. Kleiber, Hutchinson, and Williams (2002) introduced several propositions for the ways in which leisure is used to provide self-protection, self-restoration, and personal transformation following negative life events. These propositions are the basis of this next section. Hutchinson et al. (2003) found support for these propositions in interviews with people who experienced serious injury or chronic illness. For present purposes, we group these influences into those that have a buffering effect, those that sustain coping efforts, those that restore a sense of self, and those that lead to change.

Leisure as a Buffer From the Immediacies of Stress

As noted earlier, the impact of a negative life event is often overwhelming. Therefore the first task is to create some stability and control by reducing, deflecting, and managing the distress. Distracting activities and relationships often serve that function. Subsequently, positive events and experiences may have a buoying effect, raising optimism and courage about the prospects for taking control and finding solutions to the problems directly. Both positive and negative forms of leisure activity enable one to avoid or to create distance from stressful circumstances. Watching television, listening to music, using drugs and alcohol, sleeping, playing with video games, playing with a pet, exercising, eating, shopping, engaging in sex, and other forms of diversion are emotion-focused strategies used to keep one's mind off the problem and reduce the negative feelings associated with negative life events and resulting stressors. These strategies are particularly salient in the context of dealing with situations in which people perceive themselves to have little control over the situation. As Houston (1987) suggested, what all of these have in common is that they divert one's attention from negative feelings and their cause, and supplant them with neutral or positive feelings, which may in time stimulate reinterpretation of the situation in question. While these activities may not be experienced as "pure" leisure (e.g., self-determined, intrinsically motivated) there is relative freedom in the ability to experience some choice and control, if even only to create a temporary separation from the stressors associated with the negative life event. This temporary suspension of attention is palliative in generating positive emotions, and in distancing one's self from the losses associated with the event (Folkman & Moskowitz, 2000; Iwasaki & Mannell, 2000; Lazarus, Kanner & Folkman, 1980).

Leisure as a Resource to Sustain Coping Efforts

From our interviews with spinal cord injury survivors, as well as the first-person accounts described previously, it seems leisure has the power to restore hope for one's future in spite of dire circumstances. Enjoyable experiences that require little risk are often encouraging; a brighter future with new opportunities is more readily imagined. As Lazarus et al. (1980) put it, "Positively toned emotions reinforce successful new activities and, by virtue of their intrinsic pleasurable nature, help put the person in a different, more optimistic 'state of mind'" (p. 212). In our own work, we found evidence of leisure's potential to sustain effort and generate hope in the face of disruptions associated with illness or disability (Hutchinson et al., 2003). In addition to the previously noted examples from our study of spinal cord injury survivors, involvement in evening "diversionary" activities (e.g., going to the mall or listening to music) and other leisure activities (e.g., card playing or pool playing) came to symbolize possibilities for the future for individuals receiving therapeutic recreation services in a rehabilitation hospital (Hutchinson, 2000). For example, a woman with multiple sclerosis noted attending an evening of musical entertainment was "so encouraging...it made me feel like I was part of the world again."

For most people leisure brings the expectation of enjoyment (e.g., Iso-Ahola, 1989; Kleiber, 1999; Shaw, 1985). Turning one's attention to sources of enjoyment in times of stress not only provides some relief and escape from the negative emotions in the palliative sense of providing a breather, but also opens up the realm of possibilities (see also Kleiber et al., this volume). The suggestion here is positively toned experiences create both an emotional uplift *and* an opening up for cognitive reappraisal. Beyond simple distraction, such experiences allow for the consideration of "possible selves" (cf. Markus & Nurius, 1986) in an imaginative, hopeful sense, prior to taking any action. Activities that are captivating but excessively challenging may leave too little space for the reflective process. This may explain in part why Zuzanek, Robinson, and Iwasaki (1998) found physically active participation to contribute to higher rather than lower levels of stress following negative life events, while more "leisurely" activities such as relaxation, resting, and socializing with friends showed more beneficial effects (p. 270). Nevertheless, leisure activities may provide a context for connecting with others, or for engaging in personally meaningful and enjoyable activities that generate optimism and hope for the future.

Leisure as a Resource for Self-Restoration

Although coping continues to be an ongoing response to situational stressors associated with a negative life event, over time people begin to come to terms with the event and even seek to integrate it somehow with the personal narrative written before it happened. Achieving a sense of coherence and a continuity of self involves reconciling changes (whether bodily changes or role losses) and making sense of personal experiences in relation to one's past and hoped-for future. Personally expressive leisure activities from the past are particularly important in recovering meaning and direction. Such activities are also likely to nurture perceptions of competence, control, and freedom (Hutchinson et al., 2003), qualities thought to moderate the impact of stress on well-being (Coleman & Iso-Ahola, 1993).

Picking up the story from the past is not always possible or desirable. In situations where people have been abused, or made lifestyles choices they subsequently regretted (e.g., that led to a critical, traumatic juncture such as jail or an alcohol-related injury), the event becomes a defining moment for reappraising one's self and life. But, for many people who experience a traumatic life event, and perhaps most, return to some semblance of normalcy means focusing efforts on returning, if only symbolically, to the past. Understanding that "all is not lost" following a traumatic life event often requires some level of acceptance of one's circumstances and self, and a recognition that possibilities exist to extend one's self through and because of the experience. Leisure, in this situation, provides a way for people to get back to "normal."

Some forms of leisure provide the social space to reconnect with others in familiar activities that restore a sense of continuity. Resumed involvement in familiar leisure, such as playing pool or going out for dinner, thus serves to affirm one's identity and to reinforce valued

aspects of one's previous life. Whether it is a return to a style of interacting or to an activity itself, establishing continuity with the past is often the priority in the aftermath of traumatic loss. Experiencing a sense of competence and independence within an activity becomes important for feeling like one's self. At times, leisure provides a way for people to demonstrate their abilities and to affirm and express valued self-attributes. Leisure can be a context for having a shared experience that transcends disability, enabling people to feel accepted for who they were and who they are.

Leisure as a Resource for Personal Transformation

The value of reestablishing former leisure activities as seamlessly as possible after a negative life event can be contrasted with using the event as a symbolic jumping off point for transforming one's previous existence in ways unimagined before the event. The word "transformation" applies to such changes, and leisure often plays a central role in this process. It has become almost axiomatic for midlife men suffering heart attacks to review their lifestyles, to reassess life for what it offers, and to reconsider what is most important. A reduced workload and more exercise often follows, but being with one's family is typically still more important. The metaphor of a "phoenix rising from the ashes" is often used in such cases (cf. Csikszentmihalyi, 1990), but even with less traumatic cases, the disintegration caused by such events creates the conditions for reorganization and makes individuals more open to change in priorities. In these situations, as indicated earlier, people often come to a greater appreciation of the "smaller things" in life (Tedeschi et al., 1998).

As described earlier, studies of posttraumatic growth demonstrated many trauma survivors report a renewed appreciation for life, a stronger sense of self, stronger ties with friends and family, and new life priorities as a result of their experiences (Tedeschi & Calhoun, 1995; Updegraff & Taylor, 2000; Wortman & Silver, 1987). As a context of relative openness and freedom of expression, leisure is ideally suited for facilitating such effects. Implicit in leisure is a receptivity to life's possibilities—including the small things in life—and a recognition that engaging in leisure activities can enhance one's quality of life. The cliché that people on their deathbed will never say that they wished they had worked more is relevant for considering the way leisure strengthens one's sense of self. By engaging in personally meaningful leisure, people can affirm these newfound values and beliefs (and resurrect those deeply held but previously neglected values and beliefs) about who they are and what is important in life. Finally, leisure becomes a context for connecting with family and friends and taking action on one's new life priorities. We all know the story of how Scrooge becomes transformed through the spirits visiting him on Christmas Eve but enacts this newfound awareness in the years that follow through time spent with Tiny Tim. By embracing their mortality, people seem to make a commitment to using their time better in a more worthwhile ways. And by living life in ways more consistent with personal beliefs and values, people feel better about themselves because they are taking better care of the only "self" they have.

Negotiating and Navigating Leisure Constraints

Embedded in research on leisure constraints is the recognition people can and often do engage in leisure activity in spite of obvious obstacles (cf. Kay & Jackson, 1991; Scott, 1991; Shaw, Bonen & McCabe, 1991). Leisure constraints negotiation implies "participation is dependent not on the absence of constraints (although this may be true for some people) but on negotiation through them. Such negotiation may modify rather than foreclose participation" (Jackson, Crawford & Godbey, 1993, p. 4).

Leisure constraints negotiation refers to people's efforts to confront constraints and to make adaptations through cognitive or behavioral strategies that facilitate participation (Jackson et al., 1993; Jackson & Rucks, 1995). Behavioral strategies include actions such as gathering information or developing skills. Cognitive strategies include things like changing the way one perceives an activity so it becomes less important, or perceiving greater benefits despite the "costs" involved. Behavioral and cognitive strategies can involve modifications to leisure (e.g., duration or intensity) or nonleisure (e.g., chores or work) aspects of one's life. However, as Jackson and Rucks concluded, "While not all strategies of leisure constraints negotiation involve modifications to leisure, *all modifications of leisure may be interpreted as ways in which people negotiate leisure constraints*" (p. 103).

Over the last decade, research on leisure constraints demonstrated the various ways people negotiate constraints to leisure in their everyday lives (see Alexandris & Carroll, 1997; Hubbard & Mannell, 2001; Jackson & Rucks, 1995; Nadirova & Jackson, 2000) and in response to adverse life circumstances, such as disability (Henderson, Bedini, Hecht & Schuler, 1995). In the study done by Henderson et al. (1995), for example,

women with disabilities revealed while they often faced constraints to leisure (e.g., lack of energy, time shrinkage, lack of opportunities, dependence on others) they used negotiation strategies, such as resisting gender role expectations, balancing the costs with the benefits of participation, and modifying their preferences to enable them to continue to participate in leisure activities despite perceived constraints. All of these strategies have been reflected in our interviews with people with spinal cord injury and the onset of chronic illness (Hutchinson et al., 2003; Kleiber et al., 2001).

In an effort to seek greater conceptual specification of the constraints negotiation construct, Samdahl and Hutchinson (1999) used the analogy of traveling down a river to suggest many actions to overcome leisure constraints are not negotiation but rather navigation around or accommodation to the constraint. From this perspective, the constraint remains static and the person must navigate around it. In keeping with this perspective, we consider negotiation of constraints to leisure to refer to people's efforts to change a situation to seek compromise or resolution to a problem. From this perspective, it seems accommodation to a constraint (e.g., moving around it) may not be appropriately identified as a matter of negotiation, whereas acts of negotiation may result in new meanings (within an individual or between people) in relation to broader social contexts.

It may be argued that taking the constraint at face value—that is, not to try to change or minimize it, but rather moving away from it, around it, or over it—is consistent with emotion-focused coping strategies identified in the stress-coping literature (e.g., Lazarus & Folkman, 1984). In situations often seen as uncontrollable, people undertake actions to minimize the distress associated with the stressor. For example, we see some forms of leisure as vehicles for distraction in the coping process (e.g., watching television, taking a bath), providing people a way to distance or buffer themselves from the stressor and thereby eschewing activities now constrained in other ways (e.g., for lack of money, absence of companions, fear of the night). In these situations there is no attempt to change the meaning of the situation, or to take control of it through action, but rather to simply avoid it. For example, people often turn to home-based activities in the face of structural barriers to participating in preferred leisure activities, such as when a physical disability prevents shopping or loss of a spouse prevents dining out. "Going along with" the activity choices of others, even though they may not be one's choice, is another example of accommodation to what is otherwise an interpersonal constraint to preferred leisure engagement.

On the other hand, coping strategies that involve some change in the meaning of the situation, or change in the situation itself, can be considered examples of leisure constraint negotiation as we defined it earlier (e.g., as efforts to change a situation to seek compromise or resolution to a problem). As previously mentioned, we have abundant evidence of the ways people reframe (reappraise) the meaning of a situation to better understand its place in their lives, or of the ways they resist social expectations or other-imposed constraints to pursue valued leisure interests. In contrast to emotion-focused coping, this problem-focused coping strategy is evidence of constraint negotiation—the person is negotiating the meanings of the activity or the situation to create some sense of control or to engage in higher priority interests. We can think of the "turning points" that follow in the aftermath of a traumatic event as examples of negotiation, wherein they altered the meaning of the situation—or their own values—to connect with previously neglected activities or relationships. This proposition is consistent with the recent work of Hubbard and Mannell (2001), who suggested perceived efficacy in the face of leisure constraints (which they termed "negotiation self-efficacy") may be important in determining whether or not people attempt these negotiation strategies and that factors, other than the desire to overcome/negotiate constraints to leisure, may be at work. This is certainly consistent with our thinking that positive reappraisal following a negative life event may actually facilitate engagement in leisure that may have been constrained due to lack of time or other factors prior to the event's occurrence.

Reappraisal of an activity (or one's priorities) may result in it no longer being selected, rather than seeing it constrained in the same way. Even when people are able to resume a previously enjoyed leisure activity, the value people may have originally ascribed to it may have changed, and the activity is no longer as important as before. For example, although someone may have been able to return to a favored individual sport, reappraised priorities may lead the person to conclude she or he would rather spend time with family. In these cases, the constraint may no longer exist because of the way priorities have been reorganized.

In terms of the earlier propositions, then, constraints are typically navigated around when leisure choices are made to avoid the stress that would be generated in doing certain activities. But taking a small step to reengage in leisure may provide a sense of possibility or hope that encourages the negotiation of constraints through both cognitive and behavioral strategies. Restoration of previous activities becomes more likely as constraints are negotiated, and the envisioning of new possibilities may include the negotiation or navigation of concomitant constraints.

Conclusion

Negative life events typically result in constraints to many aspects of life, including leisure. Loss of companionship, financial resources, accessibility to resources, and even self-confidence erode many of the prospects for preferred leisure experiences. But leisure often emerges in important ways in the aftermath of a negative life event. The course of coping and adjustment may involve periods of escapist activity—especially in the absence of social support—that are emotionally necessary if not personally meaningful. When some simple activities and events are recognized as pleasant, they may have the effect of turning a mere distracting experience into an occasion for hope and optimism, shaping personal meaning around old loves and new possibilities. And whether meaningful activity involves reconnecting with the self temporarily "lost," reorganizing the self around old interests, setting directions for a new self, or perhaps some combination of those, it may be the single most important process in enabling one to carry on with hope and appreciation for life itself. In this context, constraints negotiation allows for expanding beyond past interests and activities to explore new ways to enjoy leisure, despite ongoing stressors in the aftermath of the event. There seems to be some interesting, albeit tentative, parallels between leisure-based coping strategies and leisure constraints negotiation worthy of further investigation.

The evidence we have from our own work, as well as autobiographical accounts of injury and illness, reveals the ways people rely on enjoyable and personally meaningful activities—both alone and with others—to buffer stressors associated with the immediacies of their situation and to sustain ongoing efforts to cope with changes to everyday living as a result of the trauma. Although the range of examples is limited to living with a disability, these findings are nonetheless consistent with previous writings about leisure's role in coping (Iwasaki & Mannell, 2000), and emotion-focused and problem-focused strategies to cope with stress (Lazarus & Folkman, 1984). Nevertheless, there are numerous limitations to the interpretation of leisure constraints and constraints negotiation presented in this chapter. Most of our illustrations for this chapter were from examples of individuals who incurred physical accidents or serious disease. The literature outside leisure studies suggests comparable patterns with people who suffer the loss of a spouse or child, the loss of a job, and other significant negative life events. Coping with chronic stress is also no doubt different in some respects from coping with finite and circumscribed events. Still, we feel confident that leisure is an important resource for coping with stress, whatever its source.

It was of interest to us to consider the leisure-based coping strategies that have been the basis of our research as indications of different forms of leisure constraints negotiation. By differentiating constraints negotiation from accommodation of a constraint, we were able to delineate different patterns of coping with the constraint. To the extent people maintain belief systems or patterns of action in the face of constraints, a behavioral strategy is required to overcome or accommodate the constraint. In this pattern, values and beliefs and past patterns of activity participation remain unquestioned. However, to the extent people reappraise their own values and beliefs, then actively seek ways to make changes within their relationships or environment (although not necessarily in themselves), negotiation strategies are being used in the face of leisure constraints. Further investigation of this distinction between negotiation versus accommodation of leisure constraints is required. Research to elaborate the relationship between leisure constraints negotiation (and accommodation) and the ways leisure is used to cope with and adjust to the occurrence of a negative life event is also needed.

In sum, although constraints to leisure are common in accounts following a traumatic life event, there is also some evidence of the ways leisure can serve as a context for coping, for expressing and affirming valued aspects of one's self, for connecting with important people, and at times for personal growth. Thus, in leisure we see both paradox and possibility. Although constraints to leisure typically result from the occurrence of a negative life event, our interest is in the possibilities that leisure affords people (see also Kleiber, Loucks-Atkinson & Wade, this volume), particularly in the face of ongoing stressors associated with the event's occurrence. While the opportunity to return to a previously enjoyed leisure pursuit may be lost following a negative life event, other opportunities—for connecting with others, for resurrecting important values, and for exploring new priorities and interests—may not only provide temporary relief but also be part of a positive reconstruction of life.

References

Alexandris, K. and Carroll, B. (1997). Demographic differences in the perception of constraints on recreational sports participation: Results from a study in Greece. *Leisure Studies, 16*, 107–125.

Cadell, S. (2001). The sun always comes out after it rains: Exploring the experience of AIDS caregivers. *Dissertation Abstracts International Section A: Humanities and Social Sciences, 61*(10-A).

Calhoun, L. G. and Tedeschi, R. G. (2001). Posttraumatic growth: The positive lessons of loss. In R. Neimeyer (Ed.), *Meaning reconstruction & the experience of loss.* Washington, DC: American Psychological Association.

Coleman, D. and Iso-Ahola, S. E. (1993). Leisure and health: The role of social support and self-determination. *Journal of Leisure Research, 25*(2), 111–128.

Cordova, M. J., Cunningham, L., Carlson, C. R., and Andrykowski, M. A. (2001). Posttraumatic growth following breast cancer: A controlled comparison study. *Health Psychology, 20*(3), 176–185.

Crawford, D. W. and Godbey, G. (1987). Reconceptualizing barriers to family leisure. *Leisure Sciences, 9,* 119–127.

Crawford, D. W., Jackson, E. L., and Godbey, G. (1991). A hierarchical model of leisure constraints. *Leisure Sciences, 13,* 309–320.

Csikszentmihalyi, M. (1990). *Flow: The psychology of optimal experience.* New York, NY: Harper Perennial.

Folkman, S. (1997). Positive psychological states and coping with severe stress. *Social Science and Medicine, 45*(8), 1207–1221.

Folkman, S. and Moskowitz, J. T. (2000). Positive affect and the other side of coping. *American Psychologist, 55*(6), 647–654.

Frankl, V. E. (1963). *Man's search for meaning.* New York, NY: Washington Square Press.

Frazier, P., Conlon, A., and Glaser, T. (2001). Positive and negative life changes following sexual assault. *Journal of Consulting and Clinical Psychology, 69*(6), 1048–1055.

Henderson, K. A., Bedini, L. A., Hecht, L., and Schuler, R. (1995). Women with physical disabilities and the negotiation of leisure constraints. *Leisure Studies, 14,* 17–31.

Houston, B. K. (1987). Stress and coping. In C. R. Snyder and C. E. Ford (Eds.), *Coping with negative life events* (pp. 373–397). New York, NY: Plenum Press.

Hubbard, J. and Mannell, R. C. (2001). Testing competing models of the leisure constraint negotiation process in a corporate employee recreation setting. *Leisure Sciences, 23,* 145–163.

Hutchinson, S. L. (2000). *Discourse and the construction of leisure meanings in the context of therapeutic recreation.* Unpublished dissertation, University of Georgia, Athens.

Hutchinson, S. L. and Golish, T. (2003). *Coping with divorce: What's leisure got to do with it?* Paper presented at the National Park and Recreation Society Congress, Leisure Research Symposium, St. Louis, MO.

Hutchinson, S. L., Loy, D., Kleiber, D. A., and Dattilo, J. (2003). Leisure as a coping resource: Variations in coping with traumatic injury and illness. *Leisure Sciences, 25,* 1–19.

Iso-Ahola, S. E. (1989). Motivation for leisure. In E. L. Jackson and T. L. Burton (Eds.), *Understanding leisure and recreation: Mapping the past, charting the future.* State College, PA: Venture Publishing, Inc.

Iso-Ahola, S. E. and Park, C. J. (1996). Leisure-related social support and self-determination as buffers of stress–illness relationship. *Journal of Leisure Research, 28*(3), 169–187.

Iwasaki, Y. (2001). Contributions of leisure to coping with daily hassles in university students' lives. *Canadian Journal of Behavioral Science, 33*(2), 128–141.

Iwasaki, Y. and Mannell, R. C. (2000). Hierarchical dimensions of leisure stress–coping. *Leisure Sciences, 22,* 163–181.

Jackson, E. L. (1988). Leisure constraints: A survey of past research. *Leisure Sciences, 10,* 203–215.

Jackson, E. L., Crawford, D. W., and Godbey, G. (1993). Negotiation of leisure constraints. *Leisure Studies, 15,* 1–11.

Jackson, E. L. and Henderson, K. A. (1995). Gender-based analysis of leisure constraints. *Leisure Sciences, 17,* 31–51.

Jackson, E. L. and Rucks, V. C. (1995). Negotiation of leisure constraints by junior-high and high-school students: An exploratory study. *Journal of Leisure Research, 27,* 85–105.

Janoff-Bulman, R. (1992). *Shattered assumptions: Towards a new psychology of trauma.* New York, NY: The Free Press.

Janoff-Bulman, R. and Berger, A. R. (2000). The other side of trauma: Toward a psychology of appreciation. In J. H. Harvey and E. D. Miller (Eds.), *Loss and trauma: General and close relationship perspectives.* Philadelphia, PA: Brunner-Routledge

Kay, T. and Jackson, G. (1991). Leisure despite constraint: The impact of leisure constraints on leisure participation. *Journal of Leisure Research, 23,* 301–313.

Kleiber, D. A. (1999). *Leisure experience and human development: A dialectical interpretation.* New York, NY: Basic Books.

Kleiber, D. A., Brock, S. C., Lee, Y., Dattilo, J., and Caldwell, L. (1995). The relevance of leisure in an illness experience: Realities of spinal cord injury. *Journal of Leisure Research, 27*(3), 58–68.

Kleiber, D. A., Dattilo, J., Loy, D., and Hutchinson, S. L. (2001). *The influence of leisure engagement in adjustment of individuals with spinal cord injury.* Report prepared for the American Association of Spinal Cord Injury Psychologists and Social Workers, University of Georgia.

Kleiber, D. A., Hutchinson, S. L., and Williams, R. (2002). Leisure as a resource in coping with negative life events: Self-protection, self-restoration, and personal transformation. *Leisure Sciences, 24*(2), 219–235.

Lazarus, R. S. and Folkman, S. (1984). *Stress, appraisal, and coping.* New York, NY: Springer.

Lazarus, R. S., Kanner, A. A., and Folkman, S. (1980). Emotions: A cognitive–phenomenological analysis. In R. Plutchik and H. Kellerman (Eds.), *Emotion: Theory, research and experience (Vol. 1), Theories of emotion* (pp. 189–217). New York, NY: Academic Press.

Leedham, B. and Meyerowitz, B. (2000). Loss, adjustment, and growth after cancer: Lessons from patients' children. In J. H. Harvey and E. D. Miller (Eds.), *Loss and trauma: General and close relationship perspectives.* Philadelphia, PA: Brunner-Routledge.

Markus, H. R. and Nurius, P. (1986). Possible selves. *American Psychologist, 41,* 954–969.

Nadirova, A. and Jackson, E. L. (2000). Alternative criterion variables against which to assess the impacts of constraints to leisure. *Journal of Leisure Research, 32,* 396–405.

Raphael, B. and Dobson, M. (2000). Bereavement. In J. H. Harvey and E. D. Miller (Eds.), *Loss and trauma: General and close relationship perspectives.* Philadelphia, PA: Brunner-Routledge.

Riolli, L., Savicki, V., and Cepani, A. (2002). Resilience in the face of catastrophe: Optimism, personality and coping in the Kosovo crisis. *Journal of Applied Social Psychology, 32*(8), 1604–1627.

Samdahl, M. D. and Hutchinson, S. L. (1999). *Navigating constraints? A critical commentary on negotiation in leisure studies.* Paper presented at Ninth Canadian Congress on Leisure Research, Wolfville, Nova Scotia, Canada.

Schwartzberg, S. S. (1993). Struggling for meaning: How HIV-positive gay men make sense of AIDS. *Professional Psychology: Research and Practice, 24,* 483–490.

Scott, D. (1991). The problematic nature of participation in contact bridge: A qualitative study of group-related constraints. *Leisure Sciences, 13,* 321–336.

Shapiro, E. R. (2002). Family bereavement after collective trauma: Private suffering, public meanings, and cultural contexts. *Journal of Systematic Therapies, 21*(13), 81–92.

Shaw, S. (1985). The meaning of leisure in everyday life. *Leisure Sciences, 13,* 33–50.

Shaw, S. M., Bonen, A., and McCabe, J. F. (1991). Do more constraints mean less leisure? Examining the relationship between constraints and participation. *Journal of Leisure Research, 23,* 286–300.

Taylor, S. E. (1983). Adjustment to threatening events: A theory of cognitive adaptation. *American Psychologist, 38,* 1161–1173.

Tedeschi, R. G. (1999). Violence transformed: Posttraumatic growth in survivors and their societies. *Aggression and Violent Behavior, 4*(3), 319–341.

Tedeschi, R. G. and Calhoun, L. G. (1995). *Trauma and transformation: Growing in the aftermath of suffering.* Thousand Oaks, CA: Sage.

Tedeschi, R.G., Park, C. L., and Calhoun, L.G. (Eds.). (1998). *Posttraumatic growth: Positive changes in the aftermath of crisis.* Mahwah, NJ: Lawrence Erlbaum Associates, Inc.

Thompson, S. C. and Kyle, D. J. (2000). The role of perceived control in coping with the losses associated with chronic illness. In J. H. Harvey and E. D. Miller (Eds.), *Loss and trauma: General and close relationship perspectives.* Philadelphia, PA: Brunner-Routledge.

Tocher, M. (2002). *How to ride a dragon: Women with breast cancer tell their stories.* Toronto, Ontario, Canada: Key Porter Books.

Updegraff, J. A. and Taylor, S. E. (2000). From vulnerability to growth: Positive and negative effects of stressful life events. In J. H. Harvey and E. D. Miller (Eds.), *Loss and trauma: General and close relationship perspectives.* Philadelphia, PA: Brunner-Routledge.

Updegraff, J. A., Taylor, S. E., Kemeny, M. E., and Wyatt, G. E. (2002). Positive and negative effects of HIV infection in women with low socioeconomic resources. *Personality and Social Psychology Bulletin, 28*(3), 382–394.

Van Tighem, P. (2000). *The bear's embrace: A true story of surviving a grizzly bear attack.* Vancouver, British Columbia, Canada: Greystone Books.

Weiss, T. (2002). Posttraumatic growth in women with breast cancer and their husbands: An intersubjective validation study. *Journal of Psychosocial Oncology, 20*(2), 65–80.

Whyte, L. and Shaw, S. (1994). Women's leisure: An exploratory study of fear of violence as a leisure constraint. *Journal of Applied Recreation Research, 19,* 5–21.

Wortman, C. B. and Silver, R. C. (1987). Coping with irrevocable loss. In G. R. Van den Bos and B. K. Bryant (Eds.), *Cataclysms, crises, and catastrophes: Psychology in action.* Washington, DC: American Psychological Association.

Yaffe, R. (1996). *Leisure and adjustment to date rape.* Unpublished doctoral dissertation, University of Georgia, Athens.

Zuzanek, J., Robinson, J. P., and Iwasaki, Y. (1998). The relationships between stress, health, and physically active leisure as a function of life-cycle. *Leisure Sciences, 20,* 253–275.

Endnote

1. A dragon boat is a large dug-out canoe in the Native American Indian tradition. At the helm of the boat is one person whose drumming sustains the rhythm and pace of the dragon boaters—in this case, a team of 12 women, all cancer survivors.

Section 3

New Approaches to the Study of Constraints

Chapter 10

Leisure Constraints Theory: Dimensions, Directions, and Dilemmas

Duane W. Crawford (Texas Tech University) and Edgar L. Jackson (University of Alberta)

One way to think about any scientific discipline is in terms of the overarching abstractions—better known as theories and models—that have originated within it or have been adapted from other fields of study, and the extent to which they have guided a related line of research. Conversely, it is also useful to examine the ways in which empirical efforts have prompted revisions or modifications to the abstractions to which they are allied. Whether one is inclined to think deductively or inductively about conceptual issues, however, we contend priority be given to abstractions over empirical research in scientific inquiry, in that the latter can never rise above the quality of the abstractions that direct it.

In this context, we take the opportunity in this chapter to discuss theories and models related to leisure constraints for which we have been partly responsible. These theories are themselves discussed within a theoretical framework—a "theory of theory," if you will. Taking this approach enables us to do several things more or less simultaneously: recapitulate the thinking that lay behind the development of the models and propositions we developed a decade ago, draw attention to some of the critical issues ignored or sidestepped by those who have criticized these formulations, and begin a tentative agenda for leisure constraints research based explicitly on the recognition of the fundamental importance of adopting a theoretical approach.

We will begin by briefly reminding the reader of the origins and current status of the constraints conceptualizations with which we are most concerned for the present purposes. The core of our presentation will then

1. consider the many different, yet acceptable, perspectives and orientations that theories may adopt regarding a number of fundamental evaluative dimensions, locating constraints theory along these continua as we go.

2. review the objectives to which theories aspire as we summarize the characteristics of "good" theory, following which we assess constraints theory in light of these criteria.

3. examine what we see as some of the central issues confronting this line of investigation.

A number of these issues take the form of questions that require answers before we advance our understanding of leisure constraints much beyond its current state (and here we boldly presume it is worthwhile to do so). We regard these questions, however, with some trepidation, given that in our view they clearly lead to no easy answers.

Before proceeding, two points of clarification are appropriate. First, neither speculation about leisure constraints nor their systematic investigation is a recent phenomenon. As Goodale and Witt (1989) reminded us in one of the first integrative summaries of this subfield of leisure studies, constraints to leisure have been an implicit part of both recreation programming and the social scientific study of leisure from the beginning, making their appearance in the research literature on leisure in a variety of guises. These include, for example, early studies of social class and workplace influences on leisure participation. Some lines of leisure research continue this tradition more or less independently of constraints conceptualizations, most notably regarding the systematic gender differences in leisure interests and involvement documented over the past few decades, and more recently ethnic and racial differences (see Shaw & Henderson, this volume; Shinew & Floyd, this volume; Stodolska, this volume). Among the traditional foci of leisure research have been individuals' actual participation in leisure activities and the factors that deter such participation. Hence, the attention devoted to constraints on leisure is not of recent origin, but rather as old as the scientific study of leisure itself.

Second, we would be the last to claim the ideas we offered over the last couple of decades are the "best"—still less the only—way to think about and conduct research on constraints to leisure. Both the field itself and the concepts and approaches we have previously suggested, however, have on occasion been met with scepticism if not scorn. Thus, one of the purposes of this chapter is to recapitulate our previous work and to place it in the context of what we believe is the essence of how to approach the development of a theoretical perspective to enhance the growth of research on leisure constraints in the future.

Constraint Conceptualizations

Historical Development

The historical antecedents of current constraints models are well-known, and as a result we are not inclined to discuss them at length. (For a recent and comprehensive overview, see Jackson & Scott, 1999.) The conceptual lineage of the models and theories with which we are most concerned for the purposes of this discussion is as follows: from Crawford and Godbey (1987); to Crawford, Jackson, and Godbey (1991); to Jackson, Crawford, and Godbey (1993); and finally, with many other examples of research articles along the way, to Hubbard and Mannell (2001), an article notable not only for its quality, but also for the success with which it combines conceptual analysis with theoretical reasoning to produce what we consider to be the most significant theoretical advances in the field in the last 10 years.

To briefly recap, the 1987 model proposed by Crawford and Godbey—which first posited the existence of intrapersonal, interpersonal, and structural constraints—had as one of its principal goals the extension of our thinking about leisure constraints to include those not of the intervening or structural sort. This theoretical development was due in large part to the fact that such "barriers" accounted for so little of the observed variance in the relationship between leisure activity preferences and their subsequent pursuit. Shortly thereafter, Crawford et al. (1991) united the three earlier and largely unrelated constraint types into a single hierarchical system that proposed a specific sequencing of their effects. Jackson et al. (1993) further speculated negotiation strategies facilitate the pursuit of leisure despite the presence of constraints, and thus impact the extent to which individuals are able to surmount the constraints they encounter. Finally, Hubbard and Mannell's (2001) recent examination of four possible models of the negotiation process sug-

gests several very important, and largely unconsidered, issues for further study.

Before we consider the research inspired by these conceptualizations, we would like to note it is inaccurate to believe these conceptualizations themselves began essentially materializing out of thin air in the late 1980s and early 1990s. Much of the requisite groundwork, the real heavy lifting, that foreshadowed the development of these models occurred in the 1970s and early 1980s. In addition to chapters in Wade's (1985) edited volume, *Constraints on Leisure*, this earlier work consisted of a string of studies (e.g., Boothby, Tungatt & Townsend, 1981; Chase & Cheek, 1979; Francken & van Raaij, 1981; Godbey, 1985; Howard & Crompton, 1984; Kelly, 1973; McGuire, 1984; Romsa & Hoffman, 1980; Searle & Jackson, 1985; Witt & Goodale, 1981). Three other articles that appeared around the time we were contemplating the hierarchical model should also be acknowledged. Shaw, Bonen, and McCabe (1991) reported the controversial finding that leisure participation was not necessarily inhibited by constraints, and indeed under some circumstances was inversely proportional to the intensity of the constraints people experience. Kay and Jackson (1991) independently but simultaneously uncovered results similar to those of Shaw et al., which they characterized as representing "leisure despite constraint," and suggested several strategies that people adopt to side-step—"negotiate," in subsequent language—these problems. Scott's (1991) seminal article based on qualitative research on participation in contract bridge was the first to introduce the concept and terminology of negotiation into the leisure constraints literature. Along with the two others mentioned here, it was fundamentally influential in our thinking about constraints models and processes in general, and in the development of our propositions about the experience of constraints and the process of leisure constraints negotiation.

Individually and collectively, these articles laid the foundation for the constraints conceptualizations that followed—conceptualizations that continue to attract most of the attention, both good and bad. Nevertheless, without the work of these investigators and others, the development of the conceptualizations with which we are familiar would have been impossible. We believe those of us working on the conceptual end of things were privileged to have had such earlier efforts at hand to directly or indirectly suggest especially promising avenues of investigation.

Contemporary Status

We now briefly turn to our attention to where we currently stand regarding the progress (or lack thereof) made in the area of constraints conceptualizations. Borrowing Berscheid's (1986) analogy, early cartographers fashioned maps of the known world bordered with fearsome creatures and the legend, "Here be monsters." Given the extent of our current understanding of the known constraints world, it strikes us as a good idea to fix our current position for a variety of reasons, not the least of which being the monsters about which we have been warned almost certainly occupy the territory that we covet. Most of the conceptualizations for which we just provided an overview are actually getting on in years and, with the exception of Hubbard and Mannell (2001), it seems that little has been done conceptually in the last decade to move the frontier much beyond these early efforts (although, inevitably, various refinements are offered in one way or another in some of the chapters in this book: see, for example, Figure 13.1 (p. 202) and the accompanying text in Walker & Virden's chapter on constraints and outdoor recreation). We always assumed these earlier models eventually would have to give way to newer conceptualizations as they arose. Unexpectedly, however, they are still prominent in the leisure literature. There may be some very understandable reasons for this state of affairs, some of which may be reflected in the questions that we pose later. Empirically, the main focus of research on leisure constraints is still on intervening constraints, and we would observe most of the questions posed by Jackson et al. in 1993 remain largely unanswered: What negotiation strategies are adopted, and by whom? What is the impact of these strategies on participation and on constraints? How do constraints and motivations interact to impede or promote leisure and recreation participation? What other variables are systematically related to the perception and adoption of successful and partly successful strategies?

The study of leisure constraints, not surprisingly, finds itself struggling with some basic issues, not the least of which is the development of an adequate descriptive language for thinking about and studying constraints. Constraints researchers relatively recently have begun to test some of the ideas embodied in earlier conceptualizations (models), thereby necessarily and inevitably generating, in the process, true theory. Examples of this work include studies by Alexandris (Alexandris, Tsorbatzoudis & Grouios, 2002; Carroll & Alexandris, 1997), Hawkins (Hawkins, Peng, Hsieh & Eklund, 1999), Henderson (Henderson & Bialeschki, 1993), Mannell (Hubbard & Mannell, 2001; Mannell & Zuzanek, 1991), McQuarrie (McQuarrie & Jackson, 1996), Shaw (Shaw, Bonen & McCabe, 1991), Jackson (Jackson & Rucks, 1995), Kay & Jackson (1991), Scott (1991), and Raymore (Raymore, Godbey & Crawford, 1994; Raymore, Godbey, Crawford & von Eye, 1993).

A second issue, particularly in the literature that attacked the fundamental construct of constraints, as well as the approaches we have taken for understanding them, is confusion over the distinction between "models" and "theories." This difference is not trivial, and although we tend to use the terms interchangeably, we would like to remind the reader technically they do not mean the same thing. Reese and Overton (1970), among others, cautioned social scientists many years ago that models and theories are quite different sorts of abstractions—the most important implication of this assertion being that model terms are not theory terms (i.e., constructs operationalizable as variables). In other words, models, which typically take the form of analogies ("the solar system is like a wheel") or metaphors ("all the world's a stage") are not in and of themselves testable. It is only when we translate our models into theories, by defining constructs (and interdefining them in testable theoretical statements or propositions), that research may proceed. The important point to be made here is one cannot directly test a model. Although models may serve heuristic purposes, only theories can be tested. When claiming to test a model, investigators are in fact testing a theory they deduced from the metatheoretical model in which they are interested. Thus, much unacknowledged theory construction actually occurs in the course of testing constraints propositions; this is, in essence, "where the rubber meets the road," and is a topic to which we will return shortly.

Theoretical Perspectives and Properties

We think it worthwhile at this juncture to consider several topics concerning the nature of scientific theory as a means of illuminating what theory is—and, perhaps as importantly, what it is not—as well as to serve as a vehicle for the discussion of some features of contemporary constraints theory that strike us as particularly important. For those readers familiar with the philosophy of science this will seem redundant, yet it may prove useful to those who are not. We do not wish to produce a treatise on theory construction here, as the task would be too long and renowned philosophers of science have already accomplished this task far beyond our ability. Accordingly, the reader is directed to some of the classic works in the field for a more thorough and sophisticated overview of the issues that we touch on next (e.g., Braithwaite, 1953; Kaplan, 1964; Kuhn, 1970; Nagel, 1961; Popper, 1959, 1962; Stinchcombe, 1968). In the section that follows we rely heavily on the guidance of several of these authors, and that of Rychlak (1968) in particular, in discussing dimensions of theory in general, and constraints theory in particular, following which we describe the characteristics of "good" theory.

Dimensions of Theory

Abstractedness

All theories regarding social behavior may be arrayed in terms of their *abstractedness*. This dimension is often identified by several labels, namely the distinctions typically drawn between macrolevel and microlevel analyses, between molar and molecular inference levels, and so on. Thus, when one begins the process of "abstracting" one's theoretical constructs, one begins to describe a phenomenon by leaving out progressively more detail. Such abstractions range from first-order abstractions, which can be defined by pointing to physical "things," to higher-order abstractions, which have no physical referent. This "ladder of abstraction" (Rychlak, 1968) has no top or bottom; it is always possible to make another abstraction about an abstraction (e.g., to observe that an individual is prevented from pursuing water-based leisure activities by denoting one's specific "fear of water" as "generalized anxiety," and then generalizing to a type of constraint, and ultimately to the generic concept of constraint). It is at these higher levels of inference, those at which the phenomenon of interest cannot be seen by the naked eye, that theoretical assumptions become important in the conceptualization process. (More on this in the next section, wherein we discuss the delimiting capacity of theory.) In this vein, we would observe constraints theory is really quite abstract in nature, perhaps surprisingly so to those of us who tend to view it as highly concrete and closely tied to the level of sheer description. Indeed, "constraint" is likely among the most abstract constructs in leisure research, subsuming all sorts of constraints, both those previously identified and others yet to be named. This may have created some of the confusion among those who routinely think about leisure constraints in that, for some, existing constraints theory is "too abstract"—that is, not closely enough tied to the first-order, observable world around them. We would argue, however, the value of constructs and models lies less in how closely their appearance and components resemble some aspect of the real world; rather, they should be judged against the yardstick of the new insights and research questions that emerge from their use and that would be difficult, perhaps impossible, to attain in their absence. For example, the elements and relationships in $E = mc^2$ may not be intuitively obvious, but it would be foolish to dismiss the equation on these grounds and forgo the insights into the nature of the universe that have resulted from this most fundamental of formulations. Thus, theories and their constituent constructs may be cast at whatever level of abstraction suits the theorist and enhances his or her understanding of a phenomenon. It therefore follows that scholars are not condemned to follow our precedent in their use.

Probably no issue related to theory is more salient and contentious than the much-dreaded accusation of reductionism, usually leveled in a pointedly pejorative fashion. Unfortunately, many times the debate regarding a theory's level of abstraction inappropriately confounds reductionistic tendencies with other perfectly legitimate ways of discussing a theory's scope (e.g., as genuine levels of analyses, or arrayed as proximal versus distal influences). Strictly speaking, reductionism is merely the doctrine that higher-order phenomena may be explained by reference to lower-level phenomena. For example, the operation of leisure constraints may be fully explained by purely cognitive psychological processes, at which point constraints theory—at least on this issue—would have to give way entirely as a more fundamental set of descriptors swallows up those invoking higher-order processes. At such time as this may happen, the law of parsimony will demand that, in effect, the simpler explanation is preferable to that which is more complex. The caveat in our desire for parsimony, of course, is counterbalanced by our awareness that we must still abstract a sufficient number of constructs to provide a complete accounting of the phenomena in question. In other words, one must not multiply constructs beyond their necessity, but may also not use fewer than are necessary.

At this point it becomes evident levels of analysis explanations differ from those that emphasize reductionism in that each analytic level—individual, dyadic, group, institution—may offer its own unique and equally plausible explanations of the same basic phenomenon. For instance, an individual's intrapsychic feelings that certain leisure activities are inappropriate at one level may be linked with—that is, partially, although not entirely, deduced from—more macrolevel factors associated with traditional sex-role socialization; it simply depends on the theorist's intentions at the moment. We will consider a related issue next, but would suggest that we believe this is one point at which our earlier constraints theory—wherein we attempted to simultaneously span several such levels—was misconstrued. Accordingly, one way to view the theoretical orientation of these earlier efforts is as levels-of-analysis formulations, wherein the system of influences on leisure decision-making processes ranges from more proximal microlevel (intrapersonal) elements through social-relational influences (interpersonal) to yet other, more distal, macrolevel social and environmental factors (structural). Finally, although our concern in this chapter is with conceptual issues, at some point conceptual and methodological issues converge, and it would be remiss of us to neglect to point out this is one of the points at which quite common methodological problems often arise, ordinarily in the form of constructs that are conceptualized at one level of analysis yet operationalized and measured at another.

Introspective–Extraspective

Another important way to think about theoretical perspective is along an *introspective–extraspective* dimension (Rychlak, 1968). Quite simply, this dimension refers to whether theoretical constructs are generated vis-à-vis the point of view of the object of study (an introspective position) versus the point of view of the observer (an extraspective posture). For the sake of completeness, we emphasize this is a dimension, and the orientation of any theorist may reside at either pole (although probably rarely are they so pronounced) as well as any place between them. Neither of these bipolar stances, nor any point between them, is intrinsically more valid than another; again, a theorist's viewpoint simply reflects how the theorist is reasoning at the moment and the purposes for which the theoretical scheme is being developed. As such, it is fair to say most of us in the social sciences sometimes lean toward one pole of this dimension and sometimes the other, always depending on the goals we have set for ourselves in our work. Moreover, on occasion a theorist may begin reasoning in a certain direction simply for curiosity, and at this point it is clear the origins of theory often include speculation and analogy in addition to the more well-respected modes of deduction and induction. Indeed, theories must admit of any influence that derives from humans thinking, and all ideas, whatever their source, become fair game at this point. The behaviorist school in psychology probably holds the record regarding the most extreme adoption of an extraspective theoretical stance, in that the behaviorists did not care how their rats, primates, or college sophomores viewed the stimulus materials, whereas the more phenomenological and interpretive schools within the social sciences clearly inhabit the antithesis of it via their introspective position.

It strikes us that many, perhaps most, leisure scholars traditionally have studied leisure behavior in a largely extraspective way, although significant variance exists in the approaches brought to bear. With respect to constraints theory, we suggest constraints theory has been the casualty of misinterpretation on this score as well

by our more vocal detractors (Samdahl & Jekubovich, 1997), who apparently prefer their theory more introspectively oriented and who appear to have concerns about the fundamental concepts underlying leisure constraints research, because, to paraphrase, "people don't think in terms of constraints." From the standpoint of extraspective theory, however, this criticism is, quite bluntly, irrelevant. It denies the ability of the social scientist to think in abstract, generalist, and theoretical terms when trying to understand a phenomenon. As observed elsewhere (Jackson, 1997), the fact that you or I may not overtly proceed through an evaluative comparison of competing shops in conjunction with the relative importance of the square of the distance from home to all possible destinations when popping over to the convenience store to buy a jug of milk in no way invalidates the use of the gravity model and the principles of spatial interaction when geographers investigate human spatial behavior. (This is not to argue that these approaches are immune from criticism; they are not. But our point is that the kind of criticism we have referred to here is misguided and unproductive.)

Thus, when we constructed our models, our strategy was to reason in an extraspective way and see how far it took us. The point we want to stress is both are legitimate ways to proceed in the process of theory construction. Having said that, we would like to propose those who gravitate to the introspective pole take it on themselves to construct an introspectively oriented theoretical system rather than issue periodic philosophical criticism. Following this, of course, such a theory will need to be put to an empirical test, and thus subjected to the grave danger of refutation, something that cannot be done to esoteric censure. Research, not opinion, is the truth criterion for theory, and we would remind our readers leisure scholars do not comprise a debating society, but rather a scientific community wherein research is the rule of law. Theory without research is philosophy, and while we clearly recognize the importance and value of philosophy, we note such contributions rightfully occur in departments of philosophy, not science.

Objectivity Versus Subjectivity

Closely related to the introspective–extraspective dimension is denoting the relative *objectivity* versus *subjectivity* of any theory's perspective. Unfortunately, as Rychlak (1968) astutely observed, this dimension has quite often been confounded with the introspection–extraspection continuum, so much so that being subjective now has become largely isomorphic with being introspective. This is a complex issue and we do not wish to take up the matter in its entirety here. Suffice it to say theoretical objectivity simply denotes the extent to which a theory's constructs—both their definition and by extension the logical rigor of their interdefinition as theoretical statements and logical syllogisms—can be understood and agreed on by a class of individuals who possess similar scientific training. Sometimes the term "intersubjective" is used in this way. Such definitions do not have to be shared, only comprehended to an extent that permits their use in theoretical and empirical practice. Being subjective, on the other hand, indicates the individual theorist is reasoning in a way entirely personal, exclusive, and undisclosed, and thus incapable of being communicated to—and thus shared by—(scientifically) significant others, or at least the abstractions of the theorist are not (yet) widely understood (e.g., early versions of Freudian theory). Social scientists who formulate their constructs in such a uniquely idiosyncratic way produce abstractions inaccessible to others in the field, and therefore are not useful in scientific endeavors as we conceive of them here.

Formal Versus Informal Endpoints

Yet another dimension on which theories may be arrayed is *formal endpoints* and *informal endpoints*. Formal theory is the prototype to which most social scientists were likely first exposed and in which they were first indoctrinated, wherein formalized assumptions, axioms, and theoretical statements (propositions, hypotheses) are brought together into a unified whole (thereby earning its pseudonym of "axiomatic theory"). Formal systems of mathematics are likely the best examples to be found of theory of this sort. Informal theory has not yet been consolidated in the explicit ways in which we see formal theoretical presentations—wherein, for example, one may see axioms and postulates and so forth—and often appears so discursive it occasionally is quasi-conversational in tenor.

A potentially more insidious or subversive connotation of informality, however, involves the extent to which ideas are "hidden," often in the form of unarticulated or unexplicated assumptions that nonetheless exert unrecognized influences on the theoretical presentation of which they are a part. (As we noted previously, early "barriers research" contained several hidden assumptions subsequently revealed and rejected.) Such ideas are almost invariably better presented as either explicit assumptions or as hypotheses tested rather than assumed away. It is certainly the case, however, that at other times these implicit premises assume much greater importance, particularly when they bear on veiled proclivities (or, for

that matter, disinclinations) in theoretical perspective. For example, it is not difficult to discern many authors' unacknowledged biases regarding the relative desirability or importance of certain theoretical stances, and we simply observe that the field would benefit from a more forthright depiction of these unavoidable biases. Repeating our earlier caution, we would remind the reader that, being a continuum, it is possible for a theory to lie anywhere between these two poles, and some occupy ground close to the center of it. Again, all are permissible ways of proceeding, insofar as at some point their constructs can be operationalized and their interdefinition or association empirically tested. Such methodological considerations are the point at which scholarly altercations usually erupt, as interested individuals debate what type of evidence derived from what class of respondents gathered by what sort of methods would constitute a valid test of the hypotheses deduced from any particular theory. We now once again risk going too far afield, as we are approaching the boundary between theory and methods, but the point we wish to reiterate is theories, whether relatively more formal or informal, must, by their definition, permit some form of empirical scrutiny.

How Does Constraints Research Measure Up?

The current state of constraints theory, in our opinion, reflects an emphasis on formal theory—or at least theory that leans toward that end of the spectrum—although it seems that many latent theoretical ideas lurk within other more informal works, waiting to be extracted and tested. In addition, and before the reader assumes we prefer formal theory to the more informal sort, it is indisputably the case that some of the most interesting, suggestive, and important social–behavioral investigations ever conducted had great affinity with the informal, discursive, and qualitative end of this dimension (e.g., Becker, 1963; Berger & Luckmann, 1966; Henry, 1971; Hess & Handel, 1959; Laing & Esterson, 1964). Although these informal qualitative treatises seem to have fallen from favor in the last few decades, such highly informal modes of analysis are not only theoretically permissible, but also desirable, being richly decorated with more theoretical ideas than any group of scholars could ever hope to test in a lifetime. Consequently, legitimate theory exists in all forms—the only indispensable quality being the ability of the theorist to think creatively and clearly about the issues at hand and for such thinking to at least hold the possibility of being put to the test. Although it need not yet have undergone such a test, it absolutely must, in principle, be capable of being so tested. To belabor the point a bit, if the vehicle of all scientific understanding is theory, we need to increase our awareness that theoretical questions cannot be settled by fiat, assertion, or indignant declaration; only research will suffice.

To sum up to this point, we submit contemporary constraints theory is quite abstract in its scope, calling into play a wide variety of mentalistic phenomena (e.g., motivations, perceptions, traits, states, attitudes, values, and a host of other predispositions). Moreover, constraints theory in its current form is infused with elements of both introspection and extraspection via its use of a levels-of-analysis framework that takes the form of a proximal–distal array of influences and thus positions the theory somewhere toward the center of this theoretical dimension. These two countervailing perspectives occasionally intermingle uneasily at the interpersonal level, and caution must be exercised in the face of both conceptual and methodological threats. Finally, constraints theory tends to be formal in its presentation, as evidenced by the prevalence of explicit theoretical statements in the conceptual and empirical work appearing in the 1990s, which took the form of propositions and hypotheses, respectively.

Attributes of Good Theory

We now turn our attention to other qualities of theory in general and constraints theory in particular, namely those that taken together comprise desirable characteristics of theory. As such, the following discussion does not focus on the range of legitimate perspectives (even biases) theorists may adopt, but rather considers more specifically the attributes of valid, useful, and otherwise "good" theory.

The Descriptive Function of Theory

One of the most basic, and in principle easiest to achieve, goals of theorizing is the *descriptive* function. Thus, theories—or more precisely, their classification systems, categorizations, typologies, taxonomies, and so forth—must describe as completely as possible the phenomenon for which the theory was designed. This appears perfectly reasonable as a first step on the road to theory. Such an exercise, however, is rarely as simple as it sounds—imagine the sad straits in which leisure scholars find themselves when they cannot agree on a definition of "leisure," or the embarrassing position inhabited by family scholars when they cannot define a concept as basic to the discipline as "family" to the satisfaction of

all interested parties. Thus, intersubjectivity often enters the fray at this point as scholars strive to determine others' use of construct labels and the extent to which they define the constructs in the same way (and, moreover, attempting to sort out the attendant difficulties when it becomes apparent they do not). As a result, it comes as no surprise to seasoned researchers that creating suitable descriptions can be devilishly difficult in practice (a fact quite disconcerting to those new to the endeavor, in that when it is discovered the supposed simplest element in the theoretical enterprise is, at least occasionally, actually quite difficult, the relatively uninitiated find the prospect of proceeding on to the development of true theory truly daunting). It seems to us that much of the disagreement about constraints theory stems from the contention that the theory has done an inadequate job of designating the nature and operation of leisure constraints (i.e., it has done an insufficient job of covering the descriptive conceptual waterfront). This may be the case, but how are we to proceed in tackling ostensibly the easiest but in reality the most fundamental theoretical task before us?

The problem posed by this question does not suggest it is impossible or inordinately difficult to generate nominal representations of anything, material or nonmaterial, but on the contrary that a quasi-infinite number of descriptions may be generated with respect to practically any object of study. After all, rocks may be classified by size, color, hardness, weight, and so on, and the same may be said about the multiple taxonomies in existence for leisure activities. Fortunately, and at the risk of redundancy, we note assessments regarding the "goodness of fit" of descriptive frameworks do not involve opinions, but rather rely on established criteria. In this instance, Reynolds (1971) and Wallace (1971) come to our rescue by proposing only two such criteria: exhaustiveness and mutual exclusiveness. The first pertains to the stipulation that all of the phenomena under study must find a place in the typology (i.e., nothing is left unassigned), whereas the second criteria restricts each item to be classified to only one place within the classification system (i.e., any given item can be designated as part of one, and only one, category).

On this score, constraints theory could be argued to fare less well, and were we inclined to launch an attack on our own theory, it likely would come from this quarter. In our view, the exhaustiveness of current constraints descriptions poses no real problems, although—as several authors in this book argue—there may be some lingering issues regarding mutual exclusiveness. In some ways, it may simply be too soon to tell. Part of the problem most likely bridges over into research methods, but some of the issues that inhere in the assignment of a construct's level of analysis (to go back to an earlier point) may be unresolved, or at least constitute a trap for the unwary. For example, are sex-role attitudes as they are linked to leisure activity preferences and involvement an intrapersonal or structural constraint? Probably the most accurate answer is both, depending on how they are conceptualized (and subsequently measured). Such norms may be thought of as structural constraints in that they exist on a macrolevel, yet also seen as intrapersonal in that they are translated into more microlevel individual psychological traits. The difference is not trivial, as norms are never perfectly so translated. Thus, although most women and men may be likely to identify specific leisure activities—or classes of activities—that are more and less appropriate for them, not all women and men will do so identically. In essence the issue involves the difference between requesting that respondents provide their own views regarding an issue versus asking them to report on (admittedly still their view) the consensus among society's members concerning the same issue (e.g., the differences between asking any given male respondent how much he enjoys sewing versus asking him how much he believes, on average, most men in general like to sew, or how society overall sees the appropriateness of sewing for men). The correlation between these two items may reflect an overall index of the extent to which broad social norms are experienced at the individual level (i.e., as an index of "successful" sex-role socialization), but the important point is they represent two distinct—although perhaps related—constructs, each of which occupies a different analytic level. Some constructs, then, are multiordinal and may be specified and measured at multiple levels of generality, each one of the researcher's choosing, but it is usually at this stage of the game that conceptual ambiguity and/or misspecification nearly inevitably produce measurement misfortune. Suffice it to say we believe constraints theory may have been the focus of no little misunderstanding on this score as well, and at the end of the day experienced investigators appreciate that the road between theory and research (or practice) is often bumpy and best traveled carefully.

Explanation and Prediction

Closely related to the descriptive level, yet more ambitious, are the goals of *explanation* and *prediction*. We take them together for the simple reason that, except for the time element involved, explanation and prediction are essentially the same operation if the concepts and statements are abstract (i.e., time and space independent). Here we are using the term "abstract" as we did earlier, and now the reason for our earlier insistence on

abstractedness becomes clear: theoretical constructs, and their interdefinition in the form of theoretical statements, must be abstract to allow their use across time and space. Such is the case principally for reasons of efficiency—that is, so new disciplines must not essentially be recreated in every global location and in each and every epoch, and what is learned in one place, ideally, informs science at others (although this is likely more true of physical phenomena that are the province of the natural sciences than those studied in the social sciences, which tend to vary, sometimes dramatically, via the influences of culture). Some explanations appear nonabstract in their substance and thus historically bound to a particular period in time. (They are, not surprisingly, known as "historical explanations.") It is not uncommon to hear such arguments regarding some of the classic works in the study of family and human development in this way. For instance, Elder's (1974) *Children of the Great Depression* is sometimes politely regarded as an interesting investigation of the effects of an infamous historical event, but little more. Such arguments are actually quite facile, however, in that it is a simple matter to abstract concepts from such work that span time and space (e.g., to view Elder's analysis as providing more general lessons about the effects of social change—in this case, widespread unemployment—on both family roles and the long-term development outcomes of the children therein). We think it somewhat obvious that constraints theory is currently engaged in the business of prediction as evidenced by the amount of research being conducted that by necessity generates predictive theoretical statements in the form of hypotheses.

Theory and Delimitation

Another characteristic of good theory is that it be *delimited*—in other words, the theorist should place limits or bounds around the phenomena the theory is to describe, explain, and predict. No theory, in any branch of science, can explain everything, and any theory that attempted to do so would simply collapse under the weight of the demands posed by the earlier criteria (e.g., although quantum mechanics brought all of the known universe under the sweep of one mathematical equation, it nonetheless cannot explain and otherwise help us understand the leisure activity preferences of the average adolescent). Among the social sciences, those theories initially posed as "grand theories"—the functional formulations of Durkheim (1933) and Parsons (1937), or the conflict schemes of Marx (1932) and Simmel (1955)—ultimately buckled under the enormous explanatory and predictive burden dictated by such an attempt. Probably the best examples of such grand theoretical formulations are the well-known theoretical systems of mathematics or physics, and Einstein's theory of relativity in the natural sciences (the latter, not incidentally, having been found inadequate for the description of physical phenomena heretofore considered fundamental and which serves as a source of some satisfaction for those social scientists admonished for decades that their theoretical creations do not resemble those in the classical physical sciences after which they should be modeled).

Again we merely observe our detractors have somehow misinterpreted our original theoretical aim, in that constraints theory was never intended to explain all of social behavior or even the entirety of leisure behavior—as is sometimes seemingly asserted—but was only proposed as one way out of the spectrum of potential ways to think about the factors that deter leisure involvement or detract from its enjoyment. Thus, in many respects it often feels as if we are being criticized for not doing what we never said we were going to do in the first place. We believe that largely appropriate boundaries have been established around constraints theory at this early stage, although at its outer reaches it has always shown some potential to escape and run amok when the inquiry shifts to progressively macroscopic levels of analysis. We may, finally, speak of acquiring knowledge when we understand why our predictions were empirically confirmed or disconfirmed after our study is complete.

The Integrative Nature of Theory

Another desirable characteristic of theory is that it be *integrative*—that it bring together its constructs and statements in a coherent fashion. This term is occasionally also used, however, to highlight the possibility that "good" theories have the capacity to attract other theories or subtheories into their orbits. Such a possibility was, in fact, the entire rationale behind Merton's (1949) famous recommendation that the construction of multiple midrange theories—those more modest and less ambitious in scope—offered the greatest promise in the pursuit of "grand" theory in the social sciences, in essence arguing for an inductive rather than deductive theory-building plan. These midrange theories, then, would on some happy future day be assimilated or integrated into "grand" theory, an eventuality not realized. It is on this score that theoretical eclecticism occasionally gets one into some difficulty, as theoretical constructs from antithetical metatheoretical families (e.g., organicist versus mechanistic worldviews) may be uncritically ripped from their theoretical contexts and inadvisably lumped together, a fact that disregards their fundamen-

tal theoretical incompatibility. In any event, we think it entirely possible—to turn the process around for a moment—constraints theory itself may some day be completely swallowed up by future theoretical developments, an event that would underscore both the integrative function of theory and the role of theory in science.

The Generative Function of Theory

The *generative* function of theory closely relates to the issue of empirical relevance—or the fact that theory must be testable—a topic we take up next. It is perhaps in this area current constraints theory has been most conspicuous in the past decade, engendering an increasing number of articles appearing in the professional literature. The ability to generate a more or less steady stream of empirical efforts is one of the basic characteristics of "good" theory, and such research typically illustrates the areas in which the theory is largely valid in addition to advancing ideas for revision which are, in their turn, put to the test. On occasion, theories that initially show great promise eventually succumb to their inability to sustain an expanding body of research. It is this relationship between theory and research that gives science its cumulative character, one wherein this symbiotic relationship results in an escalating spiral of scientific output. Moreover, we are optimistic it will continue to do so, paradoxically enough, as accumulated empirical results disconfirm predictions deduced from it from it, thereby illustrating where the theory gathers support as well as areas in which further work is needed.

The parallels between this process and the early research into physical matter strike us as particularly apt, a process wherein models were the initial vehicle in the conceptualization of unknown phenomenon, as Robert Oppenheimer (1956) clearly recognized:

> At each point the first scientists have tried to make a theory like the earlier theories, light like sound, as a material wave; matter waves like light waves, like a real, physical wave; and in each case it has been found one had to widen the framework a little, and find the disanalogy which enabled one to preserve what was right about the analogy. (p. 131)

To systematically (in)validate theories is an arduous process—and sometimes one with seemingly little imminent payoff—but it is also an indispensable one, relying as it does on the recognition it is the cumulative character of the interplay between theory and research that results in the pyramiding or stairstepping effect that is so conspicuous in emergent and viable areas of inquiry

(Meehl, 1978). To short-circuit this approach results in a routine disturbingly similar to Meehl's (1978) devastating description:

> I consider it unnecessary to persuade you that most so-called "theories" in the soft areas of psychology (clinical, counseling, social, personality, community, and school psychology) are scientifically unimpressive and technologically worthless....In the developed sciences, theories tend either to become widely accepted and built into the larger edifice of well-tested human knowledge or else they suffer destruction in the face of recalcitrant fact and are abandoned....But in fields like personology and social psychology, this seems not to happen. There is a period of enthusiasm about a new theory, a period of attempted application to several fact domains, a period of disillusionment as the negative data come in, a growing bafflement about inconsistent and inexplicable empirical results, multiple resort to ad hoc excuses, and then finally people just sort of lose interest in the thing and pursue other endeavors. (pp. 806–807)

Theory Must Be Falsifiable

Finally, then, the stipulation that theory be *testable*, and thus *falsifiable*, is the most important among all of its attributes, although by this time the reader will likely feel we have reinforced this view to the point at which to say much more is unnecessarily repetitious. To sum up, we will only comment that without the prospect of testability all of science would devolve into endless wrangling over whose vision of reality is more correct, in effect arguing over the metatheoretical assumptions of a theory rather than the extent to which the theoretical statements themselves (i.e., propositions and hypotheses), which are derived from it, can withstand empirical inspection. This appears to be the tactic of choice of the critics of constraints theory; that is, rather than do the necessary research to suggest modifications in the scheme (or perhaps even its total abandonment), they apparently prefer the less fatiguing role of critical bystanders. As we have repeatedly noted, the truth criterion for theory is research. To chronically debate the relative merits of any theoretical system amounts to little more than theoretical silliness, needlessly postponing the necessary and admittedly more difficult and less entertaining task of rolling up our sleeves and getting to work collecting the evidence required to support, refute, or revise the theory at hand. Like "good" theory, "good" research can take a variety of forms (witness the traditional di-

chotomy between qualitative and quantitative research), none of which is, in and of itself, intrinsically better than any other. Without exception, however, the selection of methods depends on the theoretical questions for which the investigator seeks answers.

The Modern "Paradigmatic Revolution"

To recapitulate, we contend contemporary constraints theory is largely consistent with the demands of "good" theory, although there is doubtless much yet to be done and many pathways down which such work could profitably proceed (some of which we will suggest shortly). The reader may object that we have presented theory "by the book," in keeping with the positivistic heritage. Recognizing the postpositivistic reproaches to such an orientation, we would nevertheless maintain we see no currently available alternative to positivism. Postpositivism, as a basis for true scientific thought, seems to us to have a grim and joyless future, being much more akin to philosophy or religion than science. Echoing Berscheid's (1986) concerns, we would observe, for example, the relatively recent commotion in the social sciences concerning the desirability of "adopting a systems perspective" has yielded few, if any, benefits, and this state is unlikely to change (e.g., a systems solution for some fairly basic questions in physics unhappily results in more interaction terms than particles in the universe). The simple reason for this is systems orientations—and all other such postpositivistic explanations, to the best of our knowledge—essentially amount to nothing more than "explanation in principle," which is nothing at all like the early researchers had envisioned when beginning the task of constructing social scientific theory. With such a strategy, the researcher/theoretician is in the personally enviable—but scientifically untenable—position of being able to deal himself or herself a full house every time, since any explanation can be offered to account for any event after it has happened if rigorous and objectively verifiable evidence is not required (e.g., alien abduction as an explanation for missing work yesterday, a faith in the efficacy of voodoo in creating zombies and assorted upper-level university administrators, or the unwavering belief that Elvis is holed up in Edmonton).

In short, such explanations—and we do not say predictions here, because for these and other reasons none ever appear—can never be disconfirmed, and therefore fail Popper's (1959) stipulation of falsifiability as the crucial requisite in scientific investigation. Relatedly, we have absolutely no idea, frankly, what decent progress in the social sciences looks like, nor the rate at which we may expect such progress to occur. It took chemistry, mathematics, and physics thousands of years—and a seemingly similar number of cumulative failures—to arrive at their current imperfect state, yet we have been pursuing explanations for social phenomena for something like a century and a half at this point, and for leisure behavior for far less. As Berscheid (1986) noted, we in the social sciences may have actually made incredibly swift progress in our investigations, but when was the last time one of our colleagues stood and loudly announced this possibility at a national conference? At any rate, it seems premature to throw in the towel on "science" at this time, particularly if it is the only way we know to proceed at this early stage in our efforts. To be sure, later scholars may regard us as the "new alchemists," on the direct ancestral line of the ancient ones who vainly attempted to transform lead into gold, but that is the risk regardless of one's stance on scientific thought. Lest the reader think us naïve, we acknowledge the limits of positivistic thinking—which have become the liturgy of the postpositivists—but, alas, we think it the only game in town at present.

Directions and Dilemmas

Turning to our final theme, we see several important and unresolved clusters of issues associated with constraints conceptualizations and the research they have encouraged—issues that simultaneously constitute future empirical and theoretical directions as well as, regrettably, the real monsters lurking around the fringes of our domain. Many of the issues we identify in this section have been raised by Hill and Mattessich (1979) with respect to human development research, in general, but we see them as equally salient for leisure constraints research.

First, to what extent do the constraints experienced—and negotiation strategies employed—vary *systematically* across the individual life course, across the family life course, by gender, by socioeconomic status, by geographical region, by historical epoch, and so on? Unless we want to argue constraints effects are purely random, and thus entirely coincidental and arbitrary, we need to begin to think about them systematically over time (both individual time and family time, and perhaps over social and historical time and space as well). If they do show patterns of systematic variation, then we have overlooked a major source of variance in the leisure restrictions of real people in the real world. Moreover, does the impact of the different types of constraints more or less lawfully vary over time, individuals, and groups (e.g., are structural constraints more or less potent early in the life course of individual and families vis-à-vis intrapersonal and interpersonal ones)?

Further, groups of individuals as well as individuals themselves need to be studied much more thoroughly than has been the case to date. Most pertinent constraints research has been conducted at a primarily individual levels of analysis, but the constraints theory with which we are acquainted was not cast at that level. If it had been, a category of interpersonal constraints would have made no sense. Many interpersonal phenomena targeted by those who study marriage and family life, when considered dyadically, constitute constraints on leisure experience, either by family members together or independently (e.g., Crawford, Houts, Huston & George, 2002). For example, when wives and husbands hold quite dissimilar leisure activity preferences—and thus are to some extent incompatible on an interpersonal level—they may be less likely to pursue activities together and more likely to do so apart. Such activity patterns, in turn, may have profound consequences for both marital hostility and harmony. Thus, much of the research conducted on both individuals (e.g., adolescents, the aged) and groups of both related and unrelated individuals (e.g., families, peer groups) implicitly concerns itself with leisure constraints, although it may not explicitly do so.

Second, on an individual level are the experiences of constraints and negotiation tactics (and motivations) essentially cumulative and linear (i.e., the older individuals get, the more/less constraints, or certain kinds of constraints, they endure)? Or do such experiences reflect periods of comparative stability punctuated by discrete changes ushered in (e.g., by age-graded status transitions to adolescence, adulthood, retirement)? In other words, are the longitudinal experiences of constraints and negotiation tactics relatively *continuous* or *discontinuous*? (See Jackson, this volume, for a discussion that promotes the latter view.) Such trajectories also raise important questions regarding family development over time, as families experience quasi-predictable changes in size and composition from wedding to widowhood. Taken together, both levels of development—individual and family—call into play what are for some developmental scholars the essential principal components of development: roles, relationships, and activities. Leisure and constraints to leisure figure prominently in these developmental "building blocks," yet their function has never been widely appreciated or systematically investigated. This issue begins to encroach on one of the points we raise shortly, and it also highlights the inherent weakness of relying nearly exclusively on cross-sectional research designs, reinforcing the idea we will absolutely need longitudinal data on the same respondents if we are to achieve a valid perspective of systematic change over time. Further, even assuming more valid research designs, we will also need to be sure we acquire valid data. It is possible, after all, to use good designs and get poor data. The development of measures is perhaps the most pressing need right now, and this development will logically require both qualitative and quantitative efforts, perhaps most usefully in some sort of sequence (e.g., qualitative focus groups leading, on occasion, to the development of standardized paper-and-pencil instruments).

Third, and related to our second point, constraints have never been assumed to be essentially stable over time; on the contrary, we think instability may very well be expected to normatively occur for a number of reasons. For example, one form of analysis might emphasize the typical changes in leisure interests, competencies, and so on, which may be associated with various individual developmental pathways or trajectories. As mentioned previously, other constraints may or may not vary predictably over the life course of salient social groups (e.g., family, peer networks). On a family level, these constraints would likely be closely linked to both socioemotional aspects of family members' interaction as well as the structural features of families, such as the plurality pattern of any given family—that is, main effects for number of children, spacing of children, and gender of children, as well as all possible interactions between these variables. From a slightly different perspective, instability might also be the result of the impact of constraints that closely resemble psychological *states* (e.g., inherently unstable psychological moods, such as anxiety, arousal, and stress) and those which are more akin to relatively enduring or persistent psychological *traits* (e.g., introversion and stimulus-seeking). Thus, the extent to which individual's or groups of individuals' preferences for leisure activities are stable over time is entirely open to speculation. This is not an insignificant point, for if we measure preferences at one point in time and assess participation rates at subsequent multiple intervals, we assume—perhaps inappropriately—preferences are largely fixed or stable. The numerous implications of this idea at both the empirical and applied levels seem fairly obvious. Concerning the latter, for instance, if activity preferences are more fluid than heretofore presumed, we may be expending considerable time and money on facilities few people now desire to the degree they expressed a few months or years ago. The underlying question, then, in some ways mirrors the age old trait–state question in psychology: to what extent do preferences for specific leisure activities—or groups of activities—reflect relatively enduring psychological dispositions (trait-like attributes) and, alternatively, to what degree do they resemble the ephemeral phenomena of fleeting moods and other largely transitory psychological qualities (more state-like in nature)? We would be wise to find out before we assume away what is in reality an empirical question, and one of the most proper and important points of inquiry.

Fourth, many years ago Robert Havighurst (1953) identified "developmental tasks," some of which were leisure-oriented, associated with each level or "stage" of individual development. Is the locus of these tasks (and, by extension, the negotiation of the constraints associated with them) *internal* (individual–developmental) or *external* (social norms, expectations linked to age-graded developmental norms), or both? In other words, are constraints largely (but not exclusively) the product of social processes (e.g., socialization) or are they largely internal to the individual (e.g., psychological), and thus so qualitative and idiosyncratic they will defy quasi-lawfulness? On a similar track, are constraints, motivations, and negotiation strategies most properly thought of as emergent in the sense they arrive relatively "out of the blue," are not reducible to prior experience (or individual maturation), and thus represent qualitatively different responses to, perhaps, the same constraints? In other words, to what extent do the number and strength of constraints and negotiation strategies vary *qualitatively* and/or *quantitatively* over time?

Fifth, is the nature of individual (or family) differences in the experience of constraints and negotiation tactics *classical* (an invariant sequence, related to points made earlier as well as social markers such as age norms) or *differential* (whereby individuals and groups get sorted into subgroups based on some attribute or set of attributes, such as Henderson, Bedini, Hecht & Schuler's [1995] tripartite classification of achievers vs. attempters vs. passive responders)? Along the same lines, to what extent is it reasonable to assume some degree of *universality* (although, of course, not perfect universality) in the experience of constraints versus thinking about constraints in a more *relativistic* way? One can opt for heavily relativistic models, at their extreme, only if one is willing to adopt a reactive (i.e., behavioristic) model of human behavior, in that relativism essentially posits that individual behavior (human or rat) develops uniquely because individuals are shaped by external stimuli and they experience uniquely different stimuli. If one leans toward the universalistic pole of this dimension, the question involves the extent to which people who occupy similar social niches (again, via gender, socioeconomic status, and so on) are in turn sufficiently similar to allow us to proceed with identifying constraints and individuals' or groups' modal patterns of dealing with them. This is an empirical question and no amount of arguing will settle it, a point which we made earlier.

Sixth, and very importantly, another significantly underresearched area involves the importance of motivations *for* leisure, quite clearly called for by Crawford and Godbey (1987) and Jackson et al. (1993), and which recently has been the subject of one of the best constraints investigations conducted over the past decade (Hubbard & Mannell, 2001). Thus, constraints are only one force or valence that impacts leisure pursuits, and eventual behavioral choices are, oftentimes, the not completely satisfying compromise between attraction and restraint (Levinger, 1976; Lewin, 1951).

Conclusions

We believe many issues—both descriptive and predictive—confront the advancement of constraints knowledge. Chief among these are critically important questions involving longitudinal (e.g., stability vs. change) and interpersonal (e.g., social influences of many types) issues that will likely occupy center stage in the years to come. Moreover, it seems likely constraints conceptualizations will be more fruitfully linked to other areas of leisure scholarship in the near future, such as attractions and motivations for leisure in addition to those factors that operate to constrain it. These attractants may, in turn, come to shed more light on the intrapersonal constraints, or those individual dispositional factors that induce individuals to undertake, or make it difficult for them to undertake, leisure pursuits of various types, both independently as well as with others. We may ultimately come to the realization that one of the major issues this line of work faces is not that it has been too brazen, but that it may not have been adventurous enough. Why not be daring and speculate imaginatively now, at this relatively early stage?

The question, then, is not why have those interested in factors that promote and deter the pursuit of leisure activities tried to do so much, but rather why is the field in general satisfied with so little? It is quite possible the scholars involved in research regarding leisure constraints as one aspect of leisure behavior will not achieve their ultimate goals—after all, theories are sometimes like dry wells and one is left with no alternative but to pull up stakes and prospect elsewhere. So far as we know, however, the only means of finding out whether such is the case is by trying. Thus, only subsequent research will reveal whether we have pursued a useful line of inquiry and whether the monsters that prowl our realm are even capable of being slain, or whether we will be induced to die of fright simply from the prospect of confronting them.

References

Alexandris, K., Tsorbatzoudis, C., and Grouios, G. (2002). Perceived constraints on recreational sport participation: Investigating their relationship with intrinsic motivation, extrinsic motivation and amotivation. *Journal of Leisure Research, 34*, 233–252.

Becker, H. (1963). *Outsiders: Studies in the sociology of deviance.* New York, NY: Free Press.

Berger, P. and Luckmann, T. (1966). *The social construction of reality: A treatise in the sociology of knowledge.* Garden City, NY: Doubleday.

Berscheid, E. (1986). Mea culpas and lamentations: Sir Francis, Sir Isaac, and "The slow progress of soft psychology." In R. Gilmour and S. Duck (Eds.), *The emerging field of personal relationships* (pp. 267–287). Hillsdale, NJ: Lawrence Erlbaum Associates, Inc.

Boothby, J., Tungatt, M., and Townsend, A. (1981). Ceasing participation in sports activity: Reported reasons and their implications. *Journal of Leisure Research, 13*, 1–14.

Braithwaite, R. (1953). *Scientific explanation.* London, England: Cambridge University Press.

Carroll, B. and Alexandris, K. (1997). Perception of constraints and strength of motivation: Their relationship to recreational sport participation in Greece. *Journal of Leisure Research, 29*, 279–299.

Chase, D. and Cheek, N., Jr. (1979). Activity preferences and participation: Conclusions from a factor analytic study. *Journal of Leisure Research, 11*, 92–101.

Crawford, D. and Godbey, G. (1987). Reconceptualizing barriers to family leisure. *Leisure Sciences, 9*, 119–127.

Crawford, D., Houts, R., Huston, T., and George, L. (2002). Compatibility, leisure, and satisfaction in marital relationships. *Journal of Marriage and the Family, 64*, 433–449.

Crawford, D., Jackson, E., and Godbey, G. (1991). A hierarchical model of leisure constraints. *Leisure Sciences, 13*, 309–320.

Durkheim, E. (1933). *The division of labor in society.* New York, NY: MacMillan.

Elder, G., Jr. (1974). *Children of the great depression: Social change in life experience.* Chicago, IL: University of Chicago Press.

Francken, D. and van Raaij, W. (1981). Satisfaction with leisure time activities. *Journal of Leisure Research, 13*, 337–353.

Godbey, G. (1985). Non-participation in public leisure services: A model. *Journal of Park and Recreation Administration, 3*, 1–13.

Goodale, T. L. and Witt, P. A. (1989). Recreation non-participation and barriers to leisure. In E. L. Jackson and T. L. Burton (Eds.), *Understanding leisure and recreation: Mapping the past, charting the future* (pp. 421–449). State College, PA: Venture Publishing, Inc.

Havighurst, R. (1953). *Human development and education*. New York, NY: Longmans & Green.

Hawkins, B. A., Peng, J., Hsieh, C.-M., and Eklund, S. J. (1999). Leisure constraints: A replication and extension of construct development. *Leisure Sciences, 21*, 179–192.

Henderson, K., Bedini, L., Hecht, L., and Schuler, R. (1995). Women with physical disabilities and the negotiation of leisure constraints. *Leisure Studies, 14*, 17–31.

Henderson, K. and Bialeschki, D. (1993). Exploring an expanded model of women's leisure constraints. *Journal of Applied Recreation Research, 18*, 229–252.

Henry, J. (1971). *Pathways to madness*. New York, NY: Random House.

Hess, R. and Handel, G. (1959). *Family worlds: A psychosocial approach to family life*. Chicago, IL: University of Chicago Press.

Hill, R. and Mattessich, P. (1979). Family development theory and life-span development. In P. Baltes and O. Brim (Eds.), *Life-span development and behavior* (Vol. 2; pp. 161–204). New York, NY: Academic Press.

Howard, D. R. and Crompton, J. L. (1984). Who are the consumers of public park and recreation services? An analysis of the users and non-users of three municipal leisure service organizations. *Journal of Park and Recreation Administration, 2*, 33–48.

Hubbard, J. and Mannell, R. (2001). Testing competing models of the leisure constraint negotiation process in a corporate employee recreation setting. *Leisure Sciences, 23*, 145–163.

Jackson, E. L. (1997). In the eye of the beholder: A comment on Samdahl and Jekubovich, "A critique of leisure constraints: Comparative analyses and understandings." *Journal of Leisure Research, 29*, 458–468.

Jackson, E., Crawford, D., and Godbey, G. (1993). The negotiation of leisure constraints. *Leisure Sciences, 15*, 1–11.

Jackson, E. and Rucks, V. (1995). Negotiation of leisure constraints by junior-high and high-school students: An exploratory study. *Journal of Leisure Research, 27*, 85–105.

Jackson, E. and Scott, D. (1999). Constraints to leisure. In E. L. Jackson and T. L. Burton (Eds.), *Leisure studies: Prospects for the twenty-first century* (pp. 299–321). State College, PA: Venture Publishing, Inc.

Kaplan, A. (1964). *The conduct of inquiry*. San Francisco, CA: Chandler.

Kay, T. and Jackson, E. (1991). Leisure despite constraint: The impact of leisure constraints on leisure participation. *Journal of Leisure Research, 23*, 301–313.

Kelly, J. (1973). Three measures of leisure activity: A note on the continued incommensurability of oranges, apples, and artichokes. *Journal of Leisure Research, 5*, 56–65.

Kuhn, T. (1970). *The structure of scientific revolutions* (2nd ed.). Chicago, IL: University of Chicago Press.

Laing, R. and Esterson, A. (1964). *Sanity, madness, and the family*. New York, NY: Basic Books.

Lewin, K. (1951). *Field theory in social sciences*. New York, NY: Harper.

Levinger, G. (1976). A social psychological perspective on marital dissolution. *Journal of Social Issues, 32*, 21–47.

Mannell, R. and Zuzanek, J. (1991). The nature and variability of leisure constraints in daily life: The case of the physically active leisure of older adults. *Leisure Sciences, 13*, 337–351.

Marx, K. (1932). *Capital: The communist manifesto and other writings*. New York, NY: The Modern Library.

McGuire, F. A. (1984). A factor analytic study of leisure constraints in advanced adulthood. *Leisure Sciences, 6*, 313–326.

McQuarrie, F. and Jackson, E. L. (1996). Connections between negotiation of leisure constraints and serious leisure: An exploratory study of adult amateur ice skaters. *Loisir et Sociètè, 19*, 459–483.

Meehl, P. (1978). Theoretical risks and tabular asterisks: Sir Karl, Sir Ronald, and the slow progress of soft psychology. *Journal of Consulting & Clinical Psychology, 46*, 806–834.

Merton, R. (1949). *Social theory and social structure*. New York, NY: Free Press.

Nagel, E. (1961). *The structure of science*. New York, NY: Harcourt, Brace & World.

Oppenheimer, R. (1956). Analogy in science. *American Psychologist, 11*, 127–135.

Parsons, T. (1937). *The structure of social action*. New York, NY: MacMillan.

Popper, K. (1959). *The logic of scientific discovery*. New York, NY: Basic Books.

Popper, K. (1962). *Conjectures and refutations: The growth of scientific knowledge*. New York, NY: Basic Books.

Raymore, L., Godbey, G., and Crawford, D. (1994). Self-esteem, gender, and socioeconomic status: Their relations to perceptions of constraint on leisure among adolescents. *Journal of Leisure Research, 26,* 99–118.

Raymore, L., Godbey, G., Crawford, D., and von Eye, A. (1993). Nature and process of leisure constraints: An empirical test. *Leisure Sciences, 15,* 99–113.

Reese, H. and Overton, W. (1970). Models of development and theories of development. In L. Goulet and P. Baltes (Eds.), *Life span developmental psychology: Theory and research* (pp. 115–145). New York, NY: Academic Press.

Reynolds, P. (1971). *A primer in theory construction.* Indianapolis, IN: Bobbs-Merrill.

Romsa, G. and Hoffman, W. (1980). An application of non-participation data in recreation research: Testing the opportunity theory. *Journal of Leisure Research, 12,* 321–328.

Rychlak, J. (1968). *A philosophy of science for personality theory.* Boston, MA: Houghton Mifflin.

Samdahl, D. and Jekubovich, N. (1997). A critique of leisure constraints: Comparative analyses and understandings. *Journal of Leisure Research, 29,* 430–452.

Scott, D. (1991). The problematic nature of participation in contract bridge: A qualitative study of group-related constraints. *Leisure Sciences, 13,* 321–336.

Searle, M. S. and Jackson, E. L. (1985). Socioeconomic variations in perceived barriers to recreation participation among would-be participants. *Leisure Sciences, 7,* 227–249.

Shaw, S., Bonen, A., and McCabe, J. (1991). Do more constraints mean less leisure? Examining the relationship between constraints and participation. *Journal of Leisure Research, 23,* 286–300.

Simmel, G. (1955). *Conflict and the web of group affiliation.* Glencoe, IL: Free Press.

Stinchcombe, A. (1968). *Constructing social theory.* New York, NY: Harcourt, Brace, & World.

Wade, M. (Ed.). (1985). *Constraints on leisure.* Springfield, IL: Charles C. Thomas.

Wallace, W. (1971). *The logic of science in sociology.* Chicago, IL: Aldine.

Witt, P. and Goodale, T. (1981). The relationships between barriers to leisure enjoyment and family stages. *Leisure Sciences, 4,* 29–49.

Chapter 11

Cultural Constraints on Leisure

Garry Chick and Erwei Dong (The Pennsylvania State University)

In 1869, the Victorian poet Matthew Arnold described culture as "the best which has been thought and said in the world" (p. 4). When used in this sense, culture refers to art, music, drama, and other trappings of an elite, even aristocratic, element of society otherwise known as "high culture." As such, culture can be thought of as progressive, with lower (i.e., mundane) and higher, (i.e., better) forms. Arnold's definition underpins, at least in part, current academic fields, such as cultural studies and forms of literary theory, which address cultural issues. A second, and generally scientific, as opposed to Arnold's humanistic, conceptualization of culture originated with E. B. Tylor's 1871 definition as "that complex whole which includes knowledge, belief, art, morals, law, custom, and any other capabilities and habits acquired by man as a member of society" (p. 1). This definition, while much modified in detail over the last 130 years, articulates the modern anthropological understanding of culture as something (a) learned and (b) shared. In this chapter, we will limit our consideration of culture to Tylor's definition and its descendents.

In its anthropological sense, culture is humanity's great enabler. With it, we compensate for our lack of specialized physical tools, such as speed, size, strength, protective coloration, claws, or wings, which members of other species use to make their livings. Human culture is made possible, however, by physical attributes we seem to possess in much greater degree other animals, namely our large and sophisticated brains, our marvelously dexterous hands, and our upright posture that frees our hands from locomotion. Although recent research suggests a variety of other mammals, including chimpanzees, orangutans, dolphins, whales, elephants, and perhaps even some birds, have rudimentary cultures (e.g., de Waal, 2001; Whiten et al., 1999) theirs are far less sophisticated than ours. In addition, archaeological evidence suggests the cultures of earlier human forms, such as the Neanderthal, were much simpler than those of roughly contemporaneous modern humans. There is little evidence to indicate, for example, the Neanderthals had art, body decoration in the form of jewelry, funerary rites, or complete control of fire. Their tool kits were far simpler than those of the anatomically modern Cro-Magnon (Klien, 2003) people of perhaps 40,000 years ago. On the other hand, the Neanderthals, who disappeared around 30,000 years ago, had thick torsos and relatively short but powerful arms and legs and appeared to have been physically adapted to the cold climates that characterized their habitats. Modern humans living in artic climates also exhibit similar physical features, but despite the fact that they often live in even colder areas than did the Neanderthals, the features are much less pronounced (Klein, 2003). Instead, modern arctic dwellers have adapted culturally rather than physically. Our cultural adaptations are such that no other living thing, so far as we know, has gone where we have gone and done what we have done. Culture is, in the words of biologist Richard Dawkins (1982), part of humanity's "extended phenotype."

The flip side of enablement, however, is constraint. While we are enabled by our cultures, we are also constrained by them. Culture constrains in at least two distinguishable, but related, ways.[1] First, all cultures both prescribe and proscribe behaviors, including leisure activities. Second, limited research suggests leisure activities must be integrated into the cultures of which they are part, although the extent to which that integration occurs, or must occur, is unclear at present. Hence, it seems reasonable to assert that leisure coevolves with other aspects of culture. Both of these types of constraints relate to the fact that cultures differ in the complexity of their content and organization. That is, when thought of as stores of information, cultures vary greatly in terms of size, elaboration, and how cultural information is interrelated. While all cultures contain the basic information needed for production, or making a living, and reproduction, or raising a family (in the environment wherein they are located), some contain much more information than others in an absolute sense. Therefore, individual cultures differ in the *ways* they can enable and in *what* they can enable. Cultures of more or less similar levels of elaboration may also prescribe and proscribe differently. That is, members of different cultural groups agree—though generally far from perfectly—on which behaviors are allowed and which are prohibited. Permission and prohibition typically extends to beliefs, values, and other ideological traits, as well. Therefore, based on these two features, what is available or acceptable in some cultures may be unavailable or unacceptable in others. This applies to both the utilitarian and the expressive aspects of life.

The purpose of this chapter is to explore the ways in which cultures, largely through differences in prescriptions and proscriptions (i.e., norms) and integration of traits, enable and constrain leisure in its extent, form, function, and meaning. First, however, it is necessary to provide some background on the concepts of leisure constraints, culture, and leisure as culture.

Cultural Constraints on Leisure

To understand how culture constrains leisure, we will first define what we mean by constraints and culture. These have been defined numerous times and we will not attempt to define any of them anew. However, we will indicate the definitions we are using so the concepts integrate coherently in this chapter. The majority of the research we cite denotes leisure in the sense of certain kinds of activities. We regard these activities as "expressive" in nature in that they are not, under most circumstances, related to immediate survival needs. We also touch on research that addresses the notion of leisure as free time and note only that both leisure activities and free time definitions of leisure imply it also has an existential quality that distinguishes it from other states of mind or being.

What Are Constraints?

Leisure constraints "limit the formation of leisure preferences and...inhibit or prohibit participation and enjoyment in leisure" (Jackson, 1991, p. 279). While Jackson (1983) initially cautioned against classifying constraints, he acknowledged later (1988) considerable effort in doing so had already been accomplished and there are both analytical and conceptual reasons for developing dimensions of constraints. As Jackson (1988) also noted, researchers investigated many types of constraints and developed several constraint classification systems. He divided the classification systems into those basically conceptual and those empirically derived. The former includes systems such as internal/external, where constraints are due to personal attributes of individuals or characteristics of the environment. Jackson and Searle (1985) discussed "blocking" and "inhibiting" constraints, with the former precludes participation while the latter only restrains participation, perhaps depending on contexts. In their conceptual system, Crawford and Godbey (1987) divided constraints into three categories:

1. intrapersonal constraints (e.g., psychological issues, such as stress or depression; "I wouldn't be caught dead doing that").

2. interpersonal constraints (e.g., lack of suitable partners for leisure; "Nobody will do that with me").

3. structural constraints (e.g., lack of time, money, or other resources; family life cycle; "I don't have the time or money to do that").

These categories of constraints have been tested in a variety of studies and have been found to have varying degrees of support.

Empirical methods, such as factor analyses of survey-type results, have provided additional typologies and dimensions of constraints. As Jackson (1988) noted, however, the factors derived from such studies explicitly depend on the questions asked in the first place. None of the studies reviewed by Jackson included a "culture" dimension. This is not surprising, however, as virtually all constraint studies are grounded in social psychology and questions asked have not addressed cultural prescriptions and proscriptions, per se.

The model of hierarchical constraints—developed by Crawford, Jackson, and Godbey (1991) and based on the earlier Crawford and Godbey (1987) categories—seems to have gained some ascendancy among constraints classification systems. In this model, individuals must attend to a sequential ordering of constraints wherein the sequence reflects importance (Crawford et al., 1991). That is, intrapersonal constraints must first be overcome, followed by interpersonal and, lastly, structural constraints. Where does culture fit into Crawford et al.'s hierarchical model?[2] Arguably, culture is present in intrapersonal, interpersonal, and structural constraints (G. Godbey, personal communication, January 15, 2003). To an anthropologist, however, these three constraint categories seem too individualistically oriented. Human beings, after all, are highly social animals and our social groups have systems of laws, rules, norms, and so on—cultures, to be more precise—that guide both intrapersonal and interpersonal relationships. Moreover, these systems of information about what people should and should not do are superordinate to individual agency and interpersonal relationships. Culture also may be superordinate to some structural variables as well, in the sense that systems of class, caste, gender, ethnicity, and race are culturally constructed, but often also legitimate who can or cannot have access to valued resources.

For example, Crawford et al. (1991) discussed a situation wherein Godbey's daughter wanted to wrestle when in the sixth grade. They indicated most girls did not "want" to wrestle for it was something that girls "ought" not to do (p. 313). They suggested the first constraint she faced was intrapersonal; that is, an internal psychological state based, perhaps, on reference group attitudes, prior socialization, or subjective evaluation of the appropriateness of the activity. To us, this seems to be equivalent to saying that the intrapersonal constraints were the result of culture. Once her intrapersonal constraints were successfully negotiated, Godbey's daughter then faced some interpersonal constraints (e.g., With whom would she wrestle?). This problem was solved when the physical education teacher "identified a few smaller, lighter sixth-grade boys willing to wrestle with a girl." This situation was surely influenced by culture, as well. Our culture, in general, says boys do not wrestle with girls. Adolescent boys' culture probably has an even stronger prohibition against such an activity. What if one lost to a girl, for example? Boys do not enhance their reputations among peers by losing wrestling matches to girls.[3] Nevertheless, the fact that Godbey's daughter was able to negotiate through the various constraints indicates that these, at least, are not fully deterministic in our culture. However, in many other cultures, the idea of a girl not only wanting to wrestle, but wrestling with boys, is all but inconceivable. In a traditional Muslim community in Saudi Arabia or Afghanistan, for example, would the constraints to a girl wrestling with boys be intrapersonal, interpersonal, or structural? See Brooks, 1995, for an in-depth look at Muslim women's feelings about their lives in Islamic cultures. These categories seem deeply artificial in the face of what is clearly a cultural prohibition that, in turn, influences both intrapersonal and interpersonal constraints and some structural constraints, as well. Wrestling facilities for sixth grade girls are not culturally prescribed, even in the United States, and are therefore rare or nonexistent. Such facilities for girls would be inconceivable in some parts of the world.

To us, this example, along with other evidence to be presented next, suggests culture is logically prior to intrapersonal, interpersonal, and certain structural constraints (although not others, such as season, climate, or related environmental factors) as defined by Jackson (1991). Moreover, we feel culture, as a construct with a significant history in social science thought, can usefully be separated out from Crawford and Godbey's (1987) classification scheme wherein it seems to be inconspicuously spread among their three categories. We will return to this issue after reviewing additional evidence for cultural constraints on leisure.

What Is Culture?

Though Tylor's characterization is still useful, the number of definitions of culture has proliferated since his day. Kroeber and Kluckhohn (1963), for example, catalogued 164 definitions and many more have appeared in the last 40 years. Nearly all of these have common threads, however, and a minimal definition would be culture is information (often described as beliefs and values) learned from and shared with others. Cultural information exists in three forms (see Chick, 1997, for an extended discussion of the ways in which culture has been defined). First, and foremost, it exists in the heads of people. Second, it may exist in behaviors and behavior patterns highly characteristic of certain groups. Similarly, it may exist in artifacts associated with particular peoples (e.g., boomerangs with aboriginal Australians and igloos with the Inuit, even though these occur among other cultures as well). However, many anthropologists now regard behaviors and artifacts to be manifestations of information stored in the heads of members of the various cultures (e.g., D'Andrade, 1981; Roberts, 1951, 1964; Romney & Moore, 1998; Romney, Weller & Batchelder, 1986; Swartz, 2001). As noted previously, this permits culture to be used as an explanatory variable for both behavior and artifacts. Hence, we will conceptualize culture here based on the work of Roberts (1964), who wrote, "It is possible to regard all cultures as information and to view any single culture as an 'information economy' in which information is received or created, retrieved, transmitted, utilized, and even lost" (p. 438).

Anthropologists use the term culture in two distinct but related ways (Goodenough, 1996). First, culture can refer to a phenomenal order. That is, the term is used to distinguish among groups or communities who differ in their ways of life, or sets of patterned beliefs, behaviors, and artifacts. In this sense, culture is a group characteristic and distinct cultures presumably can be distinguished one from another. Indeed, for much of the history of anthropology, cultures were treated as monoliths that could be clearly differentiated, even from near neighbors. Moreover, presumably distinct cultures were usually treated as internally homogenous. While traditional names, such as the Hopi, the Wolof, the Yanomamo, the

Bedouin, or the Hmong are still commonly used, anthropologists now recognize that cultures, especially when they are near neighbors, usually share many characteristics. Anthropologists now are very concerned with intra-cultural variability, as it is obvious cultural knowledge is shared differentially among members of even the least populous and technologically simplest of groups. Still, referring to "cultures" in the phenomenal sense is a useful shorthand, and we will do so here while reminding readers that this usage is, to some extent, only a handy fiction.

The second way in which anthropologists use culture is ideational (Goodenough, 1996). That is, culture is "what members of a human group have to know in order to function acceptably as members of that group in the activities in which they engage" (Goodenough, 1996, p. 293). When conducting ethnographic research, anthropologists typically examine culture in its phenomenal sense so they can understand it in its ideational sense. Unfortunately, some theorists conflate the phenomenal and ideational orders with the result being they include both artifacts and behaviors, along with ideas, in their definitions of culture. That renders culture impotent as an independent variable in the effort to account for behavior (or artifacts), because such an explanation would be a tautology.

Finally, for heuristic purposes, it is useful to (roughly) divide culture into its instrumental aspects, or the information that people use to make a living, and its expressive aspects, or the information that people use to make their lives meaningful. To explore culture's enabling and constraining aspects, we will examine some of the instrumental and expressive features of culture as well as characteristics of the "expressive array."

Instrumental and Expressive Culture

The instrumental/utilitarian components of culture encompass what, in Marxian terms, would be called forces of production and forces of reproduction. The former deals with how individuals, as members of particular cultural groups, go about making their livings. The latter addresses kinship and family life. Expressive culture refers to the search for meaning in life and its expression in thought, behavior, and artifacts. Instrumental and expressive culture cannot be thought of as distinct, but instead as blending into one another. Their division is best regarded as more heuristic than real. Still, some things in life are more instrumental than expressive (e.g., a claw hammer) while others are clearly more expressive than instrumental (e.g., going to a movie). Moreover, what is instrumental to one person (or group of people)

may be expressive to others. This often occurs with respect to producers versus consumers. For example, for professional baseball players, the game is a way of making a living though it surely has expressive aspects for them, as well. For fans, it is largely expressive, although treating business associates to a game has instrumental aspects. Hence, the instrumental and expressive aspects of human activities should not be thought of as ends of a continuum so much as two, related, zero-sum dimensions. Some things are both highly instrumental and highly expressive (e.g., the now-defunct Concorde supersonic passenger plane) while others rate rather low in both regards (e.g., a Ford Pinto). Others change with time and use. We very commonly restore and preserve old, formerly utilitarian items, such as automobiles, trains, furniture, toys, and scores of other "collectibles" either as a genuine leisure pursuit (hobby) or otherwise for their now expressive qualities. In various parts of the United States, for example, it is possible to take recreational rides on trains pulled by wood or coal fired steam locomotives. At one time these were almost purely instrumental, now they are almost purely expressive.

As an additional heuristic, expressive culture can be divided (again with fuzzy boundaries and much overlap) into the arts on one hand and entertainment on the other. Religion is a third major form of expressive culture, but one so important a comprehensive discussion of its effects on leisure and leisure constraints would require a separate chapter, if not a book. We will not discuss religion further here except to note some of the examples of cultural constraints we provide are basically religious in nature.

The arts include the plastic and graphic arts, music, drama, dance, written and oral narrative, crafts, and much more. Entertainment encompasses play, games, sport, recreation, and leisure. As with instrumental and expressive culture, what is art in one context can be entertainment in another, and vice versa. Like the instrumental/expressive culture distinction, art and entertainment are probably best not though of as ends of a continuum but as two zero-sum qualities. A painter may derive a great deal of entertainment in the creation of her work of art, for example. On the other hand, some expressive activities (e.g., the first author's golf game) are neither very artistic nor terribly entertaining (except perhaps to others). Anthropologists have spent much more time and effort studying instrumental culture than expressive culture, and within the domain of expressive culture they directed far more attention to art than to entertainment (Chick, 1998a; Chick & Donlon, 1992). Nevertheless, we know some cultures have much more elaborate expressive repertoires than others. The size of expressive repertoires correlates with several factors but probably most strongly with cultural complexity (Chick, 1998a).[4]

The Expressive Array

Cultures offer different arrays of expressive opportunities to their members, depending on a variety of factors, including physical environment, complexity, size, and history. That is, they have different "expressive arrays." These arrays include the various forms of arts and entertainments (and religious activities) extant in cultural communities. In keeping with the general lack of interest in expressive culture, the expressive arrays of different cultures remain far less studied than their instrumental counterparts. However, while the arts have received more attention than entertainment, the study of games is an exception. Systematic scholarship on games dates to the second half of the 19th century under the leadership of pioneers such as Edward B. Tylor and Stuart Culin. Tylor felt apparent similarities in games found in different parts of the world were evidence of early culture contacts (e.g., Tylor, 1879). Culin attempted to show games are an important and integral part of human culture, publishing at least 17 books and articles on games, including the encyclopedic *Games of the North American Indians* in 1907. That book remains the standard on Native American games. Other researchers (e.g., Firth, 1930; Gini, 1939; Kroeber, 1920; Stern, 1949) provided ethnographic information on games during the first half of the 20th century, but the major breakthrough in terms of how games relate to and are integrated with the rest of culture came with the 1959 article by Roberts, Arth, and Bush, "Games in Culture." Roberts et al. (1959) showed, among other things, that game types did not vary randomly cross-culturally and were integrated with other features of the cultures wherein they were found.

Integration of the Expressive Array With Other Aspects of Culture

Anthropologists have long debated the degree to which cultures are integrated. That is, are cultures "things of shreds and patches," to use a famous description by the American anthropologist Robert Lowie in 1920 (p. 441)? Or must the individual components of culture be closely matched to each other in functional relationships? To use an analogy, all spring-driven, wind-up clocks have much in common, but that does not mean that their parts are interchangeable. Parts from a grandfather's clock will not interchange with those from a railroader's pocketwatch. Similarly, can expressive activities from one culture be adopted unproblematically by members of another culture?

In one sense, the answer is obvious. Members of societies with simple technologies cannot engage in the sorts of activities found in technologically complex societies. It is not possible to play video games, watch TV, or listen to CDs without having the technological means to do so. You cannot engage in leisure activities not in your expressive array. But would the members of technologically simple cultures play video games even if they had access to them? The answer to that question seems mostly, but not universally, to be yes. Although some 19th century cultural evolutionists held that individual cultures must pass through all of a series of linear stages before attaining "civilized" status, the fact is that some cultural groups have acquired modern technology without transitioning through the stages previously thought to be necessary. There are exceptions, however. Some groups, such as the Amish, fiercely avoid the use of most modern technologies and are often largely, though not always completely, successful despite living in close contact with such technologies. In addition, environment must always be considered. Tribal people of the Amazon basin are as unlikely to take up snow skiing as the Bedouins of the deserts of the Middle East are to go waterskiing.

In "Games in Culture," Roberts et al. (1959) developed a definition and a classification scheme for games that remain the standards in anthropology. They defined a game as "a recreational activity characterized by (1) organized play, (2) competition, (3) two or more sides, (4) criteria for determining the winner, and (5) agreed-upon rules" (p. 597). They added, "other recreational activities which do not satisfy this definition, such as noncompetitive swimming, top-spinning, and string-figure making, are considered 'amusements'" (p. 597). They based their classification of games on the factors important in determining outcomes (i.e., winning or losing). Some kinds of games require physical skill, others require strategy, and still others rely on luck. Most games involve combinations of two (but not often all three) of these attributes. It is hard to think of a game or sport that involves physical activity but not strategy, for example, while most card games involve strategy and chance. There are pure types, however. Chess and checkers are examples of games of pure strategy while nearly all casino games (the major exceptions being blackjack, baccarat, and poker) are games of pure chance.

Roberts et al. also tested several hypotheses with a cross-cultural sample of 50 societies drawn from the ethnographic literature. Of these, 44 had games of physical skill, 19 had games of chance, and 19 had games of strategy. Though six societies were reported as having no games (according to Roberts et al.'s definition), Roberts later came to believe this was due either to ethnographic error or societies that originally had games later lost them. Roberts et al.'s most important hypothesis was that games of strategy simulate social systems. Chess, for example, with its hierarchically organized system of pieces, models a military organization. Indeed, with its two opposing sides, chess rather transparently models warfare. When Roberts et al. correlated the presence or absence of games of strategy with an index of social system complexity, they found a significant association between the two. Recently, Chick (1998b) replicated Roberts et al.'s study with a much larger sample (172 societies). He found the presence of games of strategy correlated relatively strongly with both the degree of political integration and the degree of social stratification of the societies in the sample (Spearman's rho = .494 for the former and .464 for the latter), thus supporting Roberts et al.'s hypothesis. Of the 11 societies in the sample that lacked any multicommunity organization, none of them had games of strategy, while only 5 of the 63 societies that lacked any form of social stratification had games of strategy. We should note technological sophistication is not needed for the presence of games of strategy. Mancala, the well-known African game of strategy, can be played with stones of two colors and an array of holes in the ground. Tick-tack-toe, the simple children's strategy game, can easily be played with a stick and a bare patch of dirt.

Roberts maintained games of strategy not only model hierarchical social structures, but also function as socialization and learning devices. Moreover, for each society, there is a fit between the array of games present and the culture in general. Roberts and Sutton-Smith (1962) developed the "conflict–enculturation hypothesis of model involvement" as the formalization of this position. They claimed expressive models, such as games, "provide a form of buffered learning through which the child can make enculturative step-by-step progress toward adult behavior" (p. 184). Roberts and Cosper (1987) found individuals whose occupations have formal ranks, such as police officers, played more kinds of games of strategy than did individuals employed in occupations that have either fewer or less formal ranks, such as factory workers or auto mechanics.

Roberts and Barry (1976) related game-type combinations to cultural complexity. They hypothesized games of physical skill are the first to develop in simple societies. Then, as cultures become more complex, games of chance and, finally, games of strategy are added to expressive arrays. Moreover, they found societies with

all three types of games are low in the inculcation of self-reliance to children while obedience to authority and self-restraint are strongly inculcated. Societies with only one game-type (those of physical skill) have the opposite profile while those with two game-types fall in between. The key element here appears to be whether or not societies have games of strategy. Games of physical skill are so ubiquitous in human cultures they comprise a constant (though, naturally, larger and more complex societies have more kinds of such games). The presence of games of chance seems to be unrelated to cultural complexity, but this is not true for games of strategy. Chick (1998b) found the presence or absence of games of strategy strongly related to Murdock and Provost's (1973) index of cultural complexity (gamma = .649) using a sample of societies from the Human Relations Area Files[5] (n = 172). Other research (Heider, 1977; Maccoby, Modiano & Lander, 1964) showed competitive games introduced from the outside may either disappear or be modified so as to no longer involve competition in societies where competition is either unknown or unimportant.

Art, music, and other activities provide additional examples of the relatedness of culture and expressive behavior. Early cross-cultural comparative studies by Barry (1957), Fischer (1961), and Robbins (1966) sought relationships between expressive forms, particularly art styles, and other aspects of culture. Barry (1957) found a correlation between the complexity of art and cultural complexity as measured by the degree of social stratification present. Robbins (1966) proposed art styles, in terms of the use of straight versus curved lines, may be reflected in house shape. House shapes themselves reflect other social variables—hunter–gatherers tend to live in impermanent round houses, while people in relatively complex small-scale societies tend to have houses with rectangular floor plans and multiple rooms. Fischer (1961) hypothesized art designs that repeat several relatively simple elements in symmetrical designs should characterize egalitarian societies, while the art of hierarchically organized societies should integrate a number of unlike elements in asymmetrical designs. While each of these authors found support for their hypotheses, their studies were substantially flawed in terms of sampling.

Dressler and Robbins (1975) examined Greek painted pottery from different historical periods characterized by different levels of social stratification, finding support for Fischer's (1961) hypotheses. That is, periods of low social stratification were characterized by pottery decoration with simple designs with open figures. Painted pottery produced during periods of high stratification tended to have complex designs with enclosed figures. In a 1987 paper, Merrill coded art from the Shoshone of the western Great Basin (on 1–7 scales) as simple or complex; enclosed figures as prominent or absent, symmetrical or asymmetrical; and space as crowded or empty. She summed these scales as representative of "complexity of art." She compared these data with changed levels of sociopolitical complexity at different reservation periods (1870–1901 and 1973–1983). She coded sociopolitical complexity as either "low" or "high" in terms of social stratification, political integration, fixity of settlement, community leadership, and local political succession. She found art forms were much less complex in terms of the individual scales as well as a sum of all of the scales during the earlier, less complex reservation period.

In a major cross-cultural comparative study involving data from 233 societies, Lomax (1968) found songs and performance styles, in terms of text wordiness, melodic intervals, and rhythmic freedom, also reflect cultural complexity. Lomax, Bartenieff, and Pauley (1968) showed that movement in dance models common everyday movements found in the culture of the dancers, and dances in more complex cultures tend to involve more body parts than those in simpler cultures. Finally, Roberts and Forman (1971) found the presence of riddles in cultures relates to the presence of games of strategy, higher levels of childhood responsibility training, and the presence of a jurisdictional hierarchy.

So, it appears art, music, and dance styles, as well as riddling, like games of strategy, do not flourish where they do not "fit," but are appropriate under the right cultural conditions. Particular expressive forms appear to develop only where culturally relevant. For example, if games of strategy model stratified social systems and function as mechanisms through which individuals learn about such systems, it is not likely such games would develop in societies that lack social stratification. Both Roberts et al.'s (1959) original study and Chick's (1998b) replication support this contention. So, it may be that culture acts not so much as a constraint than as an indicator of relevance—games of strategy are not relevant in societies where what they model does not exist. Hence, it might be worthwhile to think of differences in elements of expressive arrays based on cultural integration in terms of Jackson and Searle's (1985) categorization of constraints as either "blocking" or "inhibiting."

Additional Evidence for Cultural Constraints on Leisure Activities

While few other studies address the direct influence of culture on leisure participation and nonparticipation, some do exist. Roberts and Chick (1984) and Chick, Roberts, and Romney (1991) described how the small group culture in a recreational billiards league influenced players either to continue or to quit. While neither the league nor individual teams had explicit rules regarding player skill levels or match attendance, those who lost more often than they won were "urged," although generally not openly, to show up late for matches, after the match pairings had been assigned. They would then play only if too few players (less than 15) were in attendance before their arrival. They could then participate in the ancillary activities of the league (e.g., drinking, socializing) but would only play when not enough of the better players showed up. In addition, players who failed to attend matches, unless they had a good reason (e.g., work schedule, illness), were often shunned into dropping out of the league, except if they were especially good players. Again, these were cultural rules, in the sense of being learned, shared beliefs and values, rather than written team or league rules (which, of course, are also cultural). Chick (1991) showed how cultural changes in communities in the Tlaxcala–Puebla Valley of Mexico resulted in major changes in festivals in those communities in terms of who organized and administered them, who attended them, and the nature of festival activities themselves. Specifically, the process of secularization taking place in the valley resulted in festival leadership moving from ecclesiastical to secular hands. The festivals themselves were redesigned to attract tourists from the outside, whereas they had previously been directed at demonstrating and maintaining religious commitment within communities. Chick and Dong (2003) compared and contrasted leisure constraints in China and Japan. Dong conducted interviews in two cities in each country. While informants mentioned constraints that fit the Crawford and Godbey (1987) model, they also noted other constraints that clearly involve culture. Several excerpts from interviews follow.

> I live in a traditional Japanese residential area. Most people who live in this area are old people. They think women should stay at home to take care of their kids and do housework. So traditional Japanese culture constricts my leisure activities and makes me give up some leisure activities. (Japanese businessperson, female, 50s)

> We have to take care of my grandchildren every day. In traditional Chinese culture, mothers should be responsible for taking care of their grandchildren. We are very old and we also have chronic illnesses, but we have to do this. This is an obligation. (Retired Chinese couple, 70s)

> Now, we have three long holidays: Spring Festival, Labor Day and National Day. I may tell

my parents I have to get some rest at home or visit my friends or travel during Labor Day and National Day. But I have to see my parents and stay with them during the Spring Festival, which is a cultural symbol of family gathering. Chinese parents cannot accept that their children don't visit them and traditional culture also doesn't allow me to engage in my leisure activities instead of visiting my parents during the Spring Festival. (Chinese male, 20s)

I just got married last year. Traditionally, in Japan, after women got married, they had to visit their husbands' parents during the New Year Holiday (usually January 1st). I have to visit my husband's parents during the New Year holiday because our culture doesn't allow me to do leisure activities instead of visiting my parents-in-law. (Japanese female, 20s).

The informants themselves used the terms "culture" and "tradition" to describe constraints on their leisure. We feel there is virtue in using their own categories to classify constraints if we want to understand how they believe their leisure is constrained. Indeed, if we accept Goodenough's (1996) definition of ideational culture, quoted earlier, it is evident culture is a distinct constraint category.

Other Characteristics of the Expressive Array

Expressive Persistence

Things that have long outlived their instrumental value are often rescued from cultural extinction by their transfer to the expressive array. Pottery making is an example. It is possible to buy pots at a local department store that are both much less expensive and much better for utilitarian use than those formed by hand on a potter's wheel. Nevertheless, many people devote considerable time and energy to designing, throwing, and firing clay pots. By being transferred to the expressive array, obsolete artifacts or behaviors can persist for very long periods of time, far longer than their utility would merit.

Collecting things often involves expressive persistence. Collecting antiques is an example. Modern substitutes are almost always available for antique artifacts and are usually, but not always, functionally superior to them. For example, agricultural fairs and festivals held throughout the United States permit collectors to exhibit antique farm equipment, such as steam-powered tractors. These tractors, as well as other tools, are commonly used in demonstrations of plowing, harvesting, and other activities, but few would argue they are in any way superior to their modern counterparts. Such fairs often also include demonstrations of domestic activities, such as food preparation and storage (e.g., hand churning butter, canning fruits or vegetables), quilting, and clothing making. Cultural information is preserved by these activities. But, in the past, plowing with a steam tractor or a team of oxen was a chore, as was creating a quilt. Now they are fun.

Why are some things are collected while others are not? What makes something a "collectible"? While some truly bizarre collections exist, the situation is analogous to that of the preservation of species around the world. Most everyone wants the panda to survive but few would mourn the loss of the mosquito. So collectibles typically are eye-catching and exhibit variety. They are not usually annoying or dangerous. On one hand, cultures define what is collectible and what is not (e.g., in the United States it is illegal to collect machine guns unless one obtains a license to do so), while on the other we tend to collect things that preserve some part of a culture or cultures. So, collecting stamps or coins is popular and met with approval. Other sorts of collections, such as pornographic films or magazines, may also be quite common but can engender cultural disapproval of varying degrees. Both approved and disapproved collections preserve cultural information, but we are more tolerant of the former than the latter.

Expressive Intolerance

Depending on our cultural or subcultural roots, we are often intolerant of the expressive activities of others. Music is a simple and close-to-home example. The first author's parents and members of their generation were not tolerant of the popular music of his youth (e.g., the Beatles, Bob Dylan, Chuck Berry, the Temptations, the Rolling Stones) and now many of the first author's generation find themselves to be fairly intolerant of the music preferred by their children. People in many parts of the world find baseball to be tedious and American football to be incomprehensible. Many Americans find soccer (football, outside of North America), the world's most popular sport, to be stunningly boring. Professional wrestling is one of the most popular spectator "sports" in North America but is regarded with distain, or worse, by nonfans. Expressive intolerance can range from mild disapproval to execution of the practitioners of certain activities by authorities. For example, religious intolerance through the ages has led to the demise of untold numbers of individuals who did not believe or practice what more powerful groups felt was appropriate.

While it could be argued, with some merit, that expressive intolerance is based on individual preferences, there is also a clear cultural component to it. The Amish, for example, are intolerant of bright colors in their clothing and elaborate ritual in their churches. Other cultural groups prescribe these things. Female participation in many kinds of leisure activities and sports is forbidden in fundamentalist Muslim cultures. Indeed, females may need permission from a father or husband to merely leave their houses without escort. Visitors to Amsterdam will find that the level of expressive intolerance directed at prostitution, pornography, and drug use is far below what one would find in a typical midwestern city in the United States. Expressive intolerance is a major cultural obstacle to leisure, probably in all cultures around the world, but virtually no research effort has been directed at it.

Cultural Constraints on Free Time

How much free time individuals and members of cultural communities have, on average, directly relates to the environments where they live and to the subsistence methods they use to exploit those environments. For the overwhelming majority of human existence, we extracted our livings by collecting food from the environment, rather than producing it. The onset of food production in the so-called Agricultural Revolution, which took place at varying times in different parts of the world but first began around 10,000 years ago, marked a dramatic turning point in cultural evolution. Franz Boas (1940), generally acknowledged as the founder of American anthropology, and V. Gordon Childe (1951), the great British archeologist, believed that leisure, when conceived as free time, has a major role in cultural evolution. They felt the adoption of sedentary agriculture provided an increase in the food supply that permitted larger settlements, craft specialization, and extra leisure time that could be devoted to invention. In turn, the technological developments that resulted from this newfound leisure provided increased agricultural productivity, even larger settlements, greater craft specialization, and even more leisure.

This so-called "surplus theory" of cultural evolution and change was important in anthropology through the 1950s and is still cited in other fields, including leisure studies (e.g., Ibrahim, 1991; Shivers, 1981; Shivers & deLisle, 1997). In the late 1950s, however, anthropologists working among the Bushmen of the Kalahari Desert

of southwest Africa found, contrary to expectations, the people living even in this harsh environment spent relatively little time in the food quest and, in consequence, had abundant free time. Other evidence suggested that sedentary agriculture does not, in fact, provide either a more dependable or a more nutritious diet than food collecting and that increases in free time are used mostly for rest, rather than thinking and invention (Just, 1980). The anthropologist Lauriston Sharp already published similar information about the Yir Yiront, an Australian Aboriginal group, in 1952. Sharp (1952, p. 82) wrote:

> Any leisure time the Yir Yiront might gain by using steel axes or other Western tools was invested, not in "improving the conditions of life," and certainly not in developing aesthetic activities, but in sleep, an art they had thoroughly mastered.

More recently, Johnson (1978) compared the time use patterns of the French with those of the Machiguenga—a hunting, gathering, and simple horticultural society of the upper Amazon River basin. Johnson found Machiguenga men and women had more free time than French men and women. There is little merit for food collectors to acquire resources beyond their immediate needs if they have no way of storing or transporting them. Hence, many seem to have abundant time left over after the food quest is satisfied, a situation that anthropologist Marshall Sahlins (1972) referred to as "Zen affluence."

This sort of information led Just (1980) to speculate leisure might be instrumental in cultural elaboration and evolution in a way opposite to that indicated by the surplus theory. As cultures become more complex, the amount of free time available decreases. Free time becomes scarce, and as such takes on economic value. In turn, things that have economic value are to be used wisely. Hence, economically valuable free time should be used to advance technologies that would create more free time. Like the surplus theory, this "time scarcity" theory proposes a system of positive feedback, but one where cultural evolution results from efforts to better utilize constantly declining, rather than increasing, free time.

The difficulty with the time scarcity theory is not that it is based on incorrect data, but that the data used in its formulation were incomplete. The comparison of the French and the Machiguenga (Johnson 1978) is an example of a study that looks at societies at nearly opposite ends of the scale of cultural complexity (commonly used as a measure of degree of cultural evolution) while disregarding those in between. Munroe et al. (1983) compared measures of time spent in productive labor for !Kung San, Machiguenga, Canchino, Kikuyu, Logoli, and American women. Traditionally, the !Kung

San are hunter–gatherers of the Kalahari Desert in southwestern Africa, the Canchino are horticulturalist–herders of southern Peru, the Kikuyu are central Kenyan horticulturalist–herders, the Logoli of southern Kenya practice horticulture, animal husbandry, and some wage labor, and the American sample was taken from middle-class households of suburban Los Angeles. Munroe et al. found the amount of time spent in productive labor for the three horticultural societies (the Canchino, Kikuyu, and Logoli) is considerably higher than for the hunter–gatherers (the !Kung and the Machiguenga) or the urban–industrial group (the Americans). Munroe et al. suggested the relationship between the amount of time spent working is curvilinear, with cultures of low and of high complexity having relatively more time free from work than cultures of medium complexity. Johnson (1980) and Burch (1970) reported similar findings.

Others indicated no relationship between patterns of time use and cultural complexity. Hill, Kaplan, Hawkes, and Hurtado (1985) maintained when time spent in food processing and miscellaneous chores is added to the time spent in food acquisition, estimates of the total amount of time spent working by hunter–gatherers increases sharply. They concluded no significant differences can be found between hunter–gatherers and subsistence horticulturalists in the amount of time spent on subsistence work.

Chick (1986) reviewed these perspectives on time use and availability and developed a cross-cultural sample of 55 different societies to test them empirically. Since leisure itself could not be coded due to the paucity of information on the topic, Chick (1993) operationalized it as the amount of time left over after work. He coded societies selected from the Standard Cross-Cultural Sample (Murdock & White, 1969) for hours of productive labor per day (for males only; the ethnographic record for female activities is very poor) and these data were compared with previously coded data on cultural complexity by Murdock and Provost (1973). Chick assessed the relationship between hours of labor and cultural complexity through the use of second order polynomial regression to determine whether the data were best fit by a straight line or a parabola. While societies at the lower ranges of cultural complexity seemed to have somewhat fewer hours of labor than those at the upper range, a straight line fit the data nearly as well as a parabola. Societies of midrange cultural complexity exhibited only marginally longer hours of work than societies of either lower or higher complexity. This result seems to favor the time scarcity theory, although it provides no evidence free time is used wisely or otherwise.

Chick (1993) then tested two other hypotheses and these proved to be more promising. First, if free time is a scarce but valuable commodity, it can be increased in

several ways. Laborers could be hired or slaves kept, for example, but neither of these options is common except in already relatively stratified and complex societies. On the other hand, children are inexpensive sources of labor if their net output exceeds the net input required to keep and raise them. Hence, where there are high levels of adult subsistence labor, children may be able to contribute to the labor pool. In addition, the children may be put to productive labor at earlier ages where free time is scarce for adults. Hence, data were also coded for the number of children (who reach the age of economic productivity) born per female and for the age at which children begin to contribute to household production. Chick (1986) hypothesized female fertility should be lower at both low and high levels of cultural complexity than for societies of midrange complexity and children should begin productive labor later in societies of either high or low cultural complexity than for those in between. Plots for these data were best fit by parabolic curves, supporting the hypotheses. Indeed, ethnographic reports of hunter–gatherers (e.g., Lee & DeVore, 1968) indicated they tend to have relatively low levels of fertility and that children and adolescents tend to contribute little productive labor. Similarly, families in modern industrial societies have relatively low fertility and adolescence is extended. Even in recent western history, however, working class children began productive labor at early ages and spent long hours on the job. Thus, the availability of free time seems to be closely related to subsistence technology, which in turn relates to cultural complexity.

Rubin, Flowers, and Gross (1986) looked at leisure time, leisure activity, and culture in a somewhat different way in a study of the time allocation patterns of four native Amazonian cultures: the Kanela, the Bororo, the Xavante, and the Mekranoti. These four groups are linguistically and culturally similar and live in similar habitats in central Brazil. All subsist largely on slash-and-burn horticulture as well as some hunting and fishing. The first two groups live in areas that suffer from substantial habitat degradation, while the environments of the second two are relatively pristine. Rubin et al. suggested the leisure of the four groups might provide evidence of adaptation to their habitat conditions through adjustment of consumption patterns. They defined leisure as activities that did not directly contribute to either production or reproduction. They also noted some leisure activities consume more energy than others; vigorous play or dancing is more energy intensive than quiet rest or sleep. The question is whether high or low energy leisure is culturally favored as an adaptive response to habitat conditions. Rubin et al. hypothesized low energy cost leisure should increase as the return rate of subsistence activities declines.

Rubin and his colleagues found two patterns of leisure consumption among the four groups. Though adults in the four groups all spend roughly equal amounts of time in subsistence activities, the way in which labor is allocated among these activities differs. More important for the purposes here, the groups spend their free time differently. The Xavante and the Mekranoti, groups living in relatively abundant habitats, spend nearly twice as much of their leisure time in active, high energy, activities (47.4% and 48.6%, respectively) than either the Kanela or the Bororo (25.3% and 33.4%, respectively). This pattern is most apparent in children under 15. Kanela children spend more than twice as much time sleeping and resting as they do in active play. Similarly, Bororo children spend somewhat more time in inactive than active play. Xavante and Mekranoti children, on the other hand, spend substantially more time playing actively than resting or sleeping. Thus, the intensity of leisure activities, rather than amount of time devoted to leisure, appears to be adjusted according to the degree of effort required to obtain adequate nutrition from the habitat. Moreover, rather than working harder to maintain a higher level of caloric intake, the groups living in degraded habitats adjust their activity levels downward so that they require fewer calories. A similar strategy has been observed among primates living in degraded habitats. In such circumstances, the animals spend little, if any, time in play but use their energy resources in the food quest (Baldwin & Baldwin, 1972). Rubin et al. noted the ways in which individuals in the four groups studied experience leisure does not need to be a matter of conscious choice. Cultural prescriptions and proscriptions are "natural"; once learned, they are not kept constantly in mind.

Though interesting in their own right, Rubin et al.'s results also suggested a possible interpretation for the results of the study of cultural complexity and time use by Chick (1993). Chick hypothesized the relationship between cultural complexity and time spent in productive labor would be curvilinear; that did not turn out to be the case. Working hours were slightly higher in complex than in simple societies, but the relationship was basically linear. Rubin et al. found individuals in each of the four societies they studied worked essentially the same number of hours, regardless of the richness or poverty of their habitats. They managed the resulting differences in caloric intake by adjusting the degree of energy cost of their leisure. It may be this is true cross-culturally—that is, that people work pretty much the same amount of time everywhere and compensate for differences in the caloric output of their work by other means. These other means may include enlarging the family work force by adding children, putting children to work early in life,

or adjusting nonwork activity energy use levels. These adjustments need not be—and almost certainly are not—the result of conscious and rational decisions, but rather the result of peoples' gradual but constant adaptation to their habitats.

Culture as an Enabler and a Constraint: Summary

Just as the study of leisure and expressive culture has remained a backwater in anthropology, the role of culture in constraining leisure, although often implicit, has received little direct attention in leisure studies. We feel this is due, at least in part, to the strong paradigmatic basis in social psychology for leisure research. Moreover, we feel the disregard of culture as an independent variable in the study of leisure constraints is itself highly constraining. Since cultures vary, and if we believe culture influences behavior, then it is only reasonable to consider it in cross-cultural comparative research on leisure. One reason that culture has not been taken into account in the great majority of leisure research is very little cross-cultural comparative research of any kind has been undertaken in the field of leisure studies up to now. Moreover, culture is also typically disregarded in within-culture leisure research because it is assumed to be homogenous; that is, a constant, rather than a variable. We argue that culture, varies substantially within what are generally assumed to be "cultures" along the lines of gender, age, race, class, and other social and demographic parameters. We would argue, for example, that the "red" and "blue" voting patterns of Americans in the 2004 presidential election were primarily the result of cultural issues, (i.e., differences in learned and socially transmitted beliefs and values).

We provided evidence that games, art, music, dance, and probably other forms of leisure and expressive activities appear to be strongly enough integrated with culture that some forms occur while others do not depending, especially, on the complexity of the culture in question. But, in some cases, complexity is not the only key. Expressive persistence and expressive intolerance dictate, to some extent, what forms of leisure will continue to exist in cultural communities, what new forms will be introduced, and what forms will be rejected even when complexity is held constant. Moreover, we have shown evidence that how we think about and what we do with free time is strongly influenced by culture. The problem we face is constructs, such as cultural integration, expressive persistence, expressive intolerance, and even the balance between instrumental and expressive culture are poorly understood (but see Chick, in press, for a discussion of the instrumental/expressive balance in culture). We advocate a new line of research wherein culture is used as an independent variable in both intracultural and cross-cultural comparative studies of leisure and leisure constraints. Unfortunately, culture has been notoriously difficult to operationalize. Cultural complexity, on the other hand, has been operationalized in several related (and, in general, highly correlated) ways and has been shown to be significantly associated with many other variables, some discussed previously (see also Chick, 1997; Levinson & Malone, 1980)

Differences in cultures are often expressed in terms of technology. Indeed, most of the early discussions of cultural evolution and cultural complexity hinged on technology. That is, increases in cultural complexity, often taken to represent cultural evolution, have commonly been indexed by technological elaboration (e.g., Morgan, 1877; Murdock & Provost, 1973; Tylor, 1871). Since biology presents a constraint on leisure and expressive behavior, we have used technology to make up for our physical shortcomings. For example, no human can fly like a bird for entertainment, but technology has made a variety of forms of recreational flying commonplace. The same is true of many other activities for which we are biologically unsuited (e.g., transporting ourselves at high speed on the ground or across water, staying underwater for extended periods, sliding safely down snow covered mountains). And technology is part and parcel of human culture. In this sense culture is enabling. But it can also be constraining in that culture prescribes and proscribes the way we think about ourselves, the world around us, and the ways in which we behave toward other humans, other living things, and the inanimate world. Our prescriptions and proscriptions with respect to some leisure activities, some uses of time, and some ways of thinking often carry legal consequences or even the threat of supernatural retribution. In sum, our cultures provide us with rules for both our instrumental and our expressive lives. We may not always, or even often, be aware of them when we make leisure choices. Some of these rules are far more flexible than others at any point in time and all evolve over time. They differ from culture to culture. Nevertheless, they are always there, informing us about what we should and what we should not do.

References

Arnold, M. (1869). *Culture and anarchy*. New York, NY: Macmillan.

Baldwin, J. D. and Baldwin, J. I. (1972). The ecology and behavior of squirrel monkeys (Saimiri oerstedi) in a natural forest in western Panama. *Folia Primatologica 18*, 161–184.

Barry, H., III. (1957). The relationship between child training and the pictorial arts. *Journal of Abnormal and Social Psychology, 54*, 380–383.

Boas, F. (1940). *Race, language and culture*. New York, NY: Macmillan.

Bowden, E. (1972). Standardization of an index of sociocultural development for precivilized societies. *American Anthropologist, 74*, 1122–1132.

Burch, W. R., Jr. (1970). Recreation preferences as culturally determined phenomena. In B. L. Driver (Ed.), *Elements of outdoor recreation planning* (pp. 61–87). Ann Arbor, MI: University of Michigan Press.

Chick, G. (1986). Leisure, labor, and the complexity of culture: An anthropological perspective. *Journal of Leisure Research, 18*, 154–168.

Chick, G. (1991). Acculturation and community recreation in rural Mexico. *Play & Culture, 4*, 185–193.

Chick, G. (1993). Leisure and the evolution of culture: Cross-cultural tests of several hypotheses. In G. Cushman, P. Jonson, and T. Veal (Eds.), *Leisure and tourism: Social and environmental change* (pp. 293–300). Sydney, Australia: WLRA/University of Technology, Sydney.

Chick, G. (1997). Cultural complexity: The concept and its measurement. *Cross-Cultural Research, 31*, 275–307.

Chick, G. (1998a). Leisure and culture: Issues for an anthropology of leisure. *Leisure Sciences, 20*, 111–133.

Chick, G. (1998b). Games in culture revisited: A replication and extension of Roberts, Arth, and Bush (1959). *Cross-Cultural Research, 32*, 185–206.

Chick, G. (in press). Case studies in cultural control: John M. Roberts' Four southwestern men. *Cross-Cultural Research*.

Chick, G. and Donlon, J. (1992). Going out on a limn: Geertz's "Deep play: Notes on the Balinese cockfight" and the anthropological study of play. *Play & Culture 5*, 233–245.

Chick, G. and Dong, E. (2003, April 6–8). *The possibility of refining the hierarchical model of leisure constraints through cross-cultural research*. Presented at the annual meeting of the Northeastern Recreation Research Symposium, Bolton Lake, NY.

Chick, G., Roberts, J. M., and Romney, A. K. (1991). Conflict and quitting in the Monday nite pool league. *Leisure Sciences, 13*, 295–308.

Childe, V. G. (1951). *Man makes himself.* New York, NY: Mentor Books.

Crawford, D. and Godbey, G. (1987). Reconceptualizing barriers to family leisure. *Leisure Sciences, 9*, 119–127.

Crawford, D., Jackson, E., and Godbey, G. (1991). A hierarchical model of leisure constraints. *Leisure Sciences, 13*, 309–320.

Culin, S. (1907). *Games of the North American Indians* (24th Annual Report, Bureau of Ethnology). Washington, DC: U.S. Government Printing Office.

D'Andrade, R. G. (1981). The cultural part of cognition. *Cognitive Science, 5*, 179–195.

Dawkins, R. (1982). *The extended phenotype.* Oxford: Oxford University Press.

de Waal, F. B. M. (2001). *The ape and the sushi master.* New York, NY: Basic Books.

Dressler, W. W. and Robbins, M. C. (1975). Art styles, social stratification, and cognition: An analysis of Greek vase painting. *American Ethnologist, 2*, 427–434.

Firth, R. (1930). A dart match in Tikopia: A study in the sociology of primitive sport. *Oceania, 1*, 64–96.

Fischer, J. L. (1961). Art styles as cultural cognitive maps. *American Anthropologist, 63*, 79–93.

Gini, C. (1939). Rural games in Libya (Berber baseball and shinny). *Rural Sociology, 4*, 283–299.

Goodenough, W. H. (1996). Culture. In D. Levinson and M. Ember (Eds.), *Encyclopedia of cultural anthropology* (Vol. 1; pp. 291–299). New York, NY: Henry Holt and Company.

Heider, K. G. (1977). From Javanese to Dani: The translation of a game. In P. Stevens, Jr. (Ed.), *Studies in the anthropology of play* (pp. 72–81). West Point, NY: Leisure Press.

Hill, K., Kaplan, H., Hawkes, K., and Hurtado, A. M. (1985). Men's time allocation to subsistence work among the Ache of eastern Paraguay. *Human Ecology 13*, 29–47.

Ibrahim, H. (1991). *Leisure and society: A comparative approach.* Dubuque, IA: Wm C. Brown.

Jackson, E. L. (1983). Activity-specific barriers to recreation participation. *Leisure Sciences, 6*, 47–60.

Jackson, E. L. (1988). Leisure constraints: A survey of past research. *Leisure Sciences, 10*, 203–215.

Jackson, E. L. (1991). Leisure constraints/constrained leisure: Special issue introduction. *Journal of Leisure Research, 23*, 279–285.

Jackson, E. L. and Searle, M. S. (1985). Recreation nonparticipation and barriers to participation: *Loisir et Sociète, 8*, 693–707.

Johnson, A. (1980). Comment on 'Does labor time decrease with industrialization? A survey of time-allocation studies' by W. Minge-Klevana. *Current Anthropology 21*, 292.

Johnson, A. (1978). In search of the affluent society. *Human Nature, 1*, 50–59.

Just, P. (1980). Time and leisure in the elaboration of culture. *Journal of Anthropological Research, 36*, 105–115.

Klein, R. G. (2003). Whither the Neanderthals? *Science, 299*, 1525–1527.

Kroeber, A. L. (1920). Games of the California Indians. *American Anthropologist, 22*, 272–277.

Kroeber, A. L. and Kluckhohn, C. (1963). *Culture: A critical review of concepts and definitions.* New York, NY: Vintage.

Lee, R. B. and DeVore, I. (Eds.). (1968). *Man the hunter.* Chicago, IL: Aldine.

Levinson, D. and Malone, M. J. (1980). *Toward explaining human culture.* New Haven, CT: HRAF Press.

Lomax, A. (Ed.). (1968). *Folk song style and culture.* Washington, DC: American Association for the Advancement of Science.

Lomax, A., Bartenieff, I., and Pauley, F. (1968). Dance style and culture. In A. Lomax (Ed.), *Folk song style and culture* (pp. 222–247). Washington, DC: American Association for the Advancement of Science.

Lowie, R. (1920). *Primitive society.* New York, NY: Liveright.

Maccoby E. E., Modiano, N., and Lander, P. (1964). Games and social character in a Mexican village. *Psychiatry, 27*, 150–162.

Merrill, E. B. (1987). Art styles as reflections of sociopolitical complexity. *Ethnology, XXVI*, 221–230.

Morgan, L. H. (1877). *Ancient society.* New York, NY: Holt.

Munroe, R. H., Munroe, R. L., Michelson, C., Koel, A., Bolton, R., and Bolton C. (1983). Time allocation in four societies. *Ethnology, XXII*, 355–370.

Murdock, G. P. and Provost, C. (1973). Measurement of cultural complexity. *Ethnology, 12*, 379–392.

Murdock, G. P. and White, D. R. (1969). Standard cross-cultural sample. *Ethnology, 8*, 329–369.

Naroll, R. and Divale, W. T. (1976). Natural selection in cultural evolution: Warfare versus peaceful diffusion. *American Ethnologist, 58*, 687–715.

Robbins, M. C. (1966). Material culture and cognition. *American Anthropologist, 68*, 745–748.

Roberts, J. M. (1951). *Three Navaho households: A comparative study in small group cultures*. Papers of the Peabody Museum of American Archaeology and Ethnology, Harvard University (Vol. XL, No. 3). Cambridge, MA: Peabody Museum.

Roberts, J. M. (1964). The self-management of culture. In W. H. Goodenough (Ed.), *Explorations in cultural anthropology* (pp. 433–454). New York, NY: Mc-Graw-Hill.

Roberts, J. M., Arth, M. J., and Bush, R. R. (1959). Games in culture. *American Anthropologist, 61*, 597–605.

Roberts, J. M. and Barry, H., III. (1976). Inculcated traits and game-type combinations. In T. T. Craig (Ed.), *The humanistic and mental health aspects of sports, exercise and recreation* (pp. 5–11). Chicago, IL: American Medical Association.

Roberts, J. M. and Chick, G. (1984). Quitting the game: Covert disengagement from Butler County eight ball. *American Anthropologist, 86*, 549–567.

Roberts, J. M. and Cosper, R. S. (1987). Variations in strategic involvement in games for three blue collar occupations. *Journal of Leisure Research, 19*, 131–148.

Roberts, J. M. and Forman, M. L. (1971). Riddles: Expressive models of interrogation. *Ethnology, X*, 509–533.

Roberts, J. M. and Sutton-Smith, B. (1962). Child training and game involvement. *Ethnology, I*, 166–185.

Romney, A. K. and Moore, C. C. (1998). Toward a theory of culture as shared cognitive structures. *Ethos, 26*, 314–337.

Romney, A. K., Weller, S. C., and Batchelder, W. H. (1986). Culture as consensus: A theory of culture and informant accuracy. *American Anthropologist, 88*, 313–339.

Rubin, J., Flowers, N. M., and Gross, D. R. (1986). The adaptive dimensions of leisure. *American Ethnologist, 13*, 524–536.

Sahlins, M. (1972). *Stone age economics*. Chicago, IL: Aldine-Atherton.

Sharp, L. (1952). Steel axes for stone age Australians. In E. H. Spicer (Ed.), *Human problems in technological change: A casebook* (pp. 69–90). New York, NY: Russell Sage.

Shivers, J. S. (1981). *Leisure and recreation concepts: A critical analysis*. Boston, MA: Allyn & Bacon.

Shivers, J. S. and deLisle, L. J. (1997). *The story of leisure: Context, concepts, and current controversy*. Champaign, IL: Human Kinetics.

Stern, T. (1949). *The rubber ball games of the Americas*. Seattle, WA: University of Washington Press.

Swartz, M. J. (2001). On the substance and uses of culture's units. *Cross-Cultural Research, 35*, 179–200.

Tylor, E. B. (1871). *Primitive culture*. London, England: J. Murray.

Tylor, E. B. (1879). On the game of patolli in ancient Mexico and its probable Asiatic origin. *Journal of the Royal Anthropological Institute of Great Britain and Ireland, 8*, 116–131.

Whiten, A., Goodall, J., McGrew, W. C., Nishida, T., Reynolds, V., Sugiyama, Y., et al. (1999). Cultures in chimpanzees. *Nature, 399*, 682–685.

Endnotes

1. This sentence sounds like we are reifying culture; that is, making it something real that has agency of its own. We are not. We create and use culture. So, when we say "culture constrains" we mean only that we, as members of social groups, have agreed (and not necessarily consciously) on sets of prescriptions and proscriptions, variously enforced, that we expect ourselves and others to conform to under most circumstances. We use the turn of phrase only for ease of presentation.

2. For an attempt to do this, see Figure 16.1 in chapter 16 (Walker & Virden) and the accompanying text.

3. Adult males may be concerned about this, as well. Vijay Singh, then the world's second ranked male golfer, expressed concern about playing in the 2003 Colonial Golf Tournament in Fort Worth, Texas, if Annika Sorenstam, the number one ranked female golfer in the world, was permitted to enter. Similarly, Greg Norman, a former number one ranked male golfer, opposed Laura Davies's participation in the 2003 ANZ Championship in Port Stephens, Australia.

4. Cultural complexity has never been indisputably defined but the various operationalizations and measurements of the concept have usually involved technological elaboration of one form or another (Chick, 1997). So, in the phenomenal sense, a complex culture is technologically more elaborate than a simple culture. When culture is operationalized in its ideational sense, the size of the largest settlement in a society appears to be an excellent proxy for complexity (Bowden, 1972; Chick, 1997; Naroll & Divale, 1976). This makes intuitive sense in that a larger agglomeration of people requires more complex systems for production, reproduction, and expression.

5. The Human Relations Area Files provide coded ethnographic data on approximately 400 societies, past and present, gleaned from anthropological and other sources. Twenty universities from around the world have copies of the original paper files while many others have the files on microfiche. Recently, Human Relations Area Files, Inc., the nonprofit organization that now distributes the files, developed a web-based version along with a powerful search engine that makes cross-cultural comparative research much easier and more powerful than before.

Chapter 12

Time as a Constraint to Leisure

Geoffrey Godbey (The Pennsylvania State University)

Time constrains our lives and our leisure. We are changed and controlled by time more than we change and control it. In the modern and postmodern worlds, time is often thought of as the primary constraint to leisure. Time constrains how long we live and every aspect of participation in leisure activity, including time to undertake an activity, how often it can be done, how much time can be devoted to it during each occasion, when it can be done, the pace at which it is done, and how much time can be spent preparing for it or recovering from it. Time may also constrain our ability to experience leisure as a state of mind. Feeling rushed, feeling that everything is "necessary," and the inability to let go and drift in the direction the world takes us are assuredly constraints, perhaps of a more severe nature. The poet W. H. Auden (1939, p. 69) wrote:

> Time will say nothing but I told you so.
> Time only knows the price we have to pay;
> If I could tell you I would let you know.

What time doesn't know is the role it plays in making leisure possible. Time is a device to stop everything from happening at once (Anonymous). Time constraints are not necessarily a problem, unless one would like to be God. Time constraints make intentionality necessary, and without intention there can be no leisure. It is the very fact of temporal constraint that makes leisure possible. Leisure involves choice: the willing sacrifice for that which might be desirable for that which clearly, intuitively, is desirable. Leisure demands sacrifice, as does all free choice. Constraints of time are therefore both constraints to leisure and a necessary condition for leisure to occur. When this is not understood, there is no leisure.

Concepts of Time

The ways in which time constrains leisure directly relate to how time is conceived. Every living thing on earth has its own sense of time as a part of its genetic endowment. At a cellular level, there is a point at which spermatozoa become capable of making their incredible dark journey toward an unfertilized egg and another when nutrition can no longer be metabolized. The way humans think about time, however, is based largely on their way of life and how they view the world. Although all notions of time relate in some way to change, vastly different concepts historically conditioned the individual to behave in a certain way and affected his or her understanding of others.

Our very definition of a situation is directly shaped by how we view time. If a resident of Manhattan and one from Mexico City are both standing at a bus stop, one may define the situation as "waiting" for a bus which is "13 minutes late" while the other one is "being" there for a bus which is "coming." In some cultures, rushing is a sign of rudeness and poverty of spirit, while in others it is a sign of intelligence and importance. Arriving on time for dinner at a neighbor's house may be considered necessary or an unthinkable insult. A rural Turk might invite you to dinner "this evening," while for a resident of Boston a term like "this evening" contains insufficient temporal information.

The Chinese have historically had a preference for organic naturalism in which time and nature are conceived as aspects of dynamic, living systems to be qualitatively explored. Both the Hindu judgment of time as unimportant and the Chinese preference for thinking of time in natural, qualitative terms, however, are systematically changed when a culture begins to "modernize." If "modern" means anything, it means our sense of time becomes more ordered by human activity than by the acts of nature.

Thus, time is a diverse concept redefined in each culture and by each individual. There are, of course extremes. As a homeless man said, "I don't think there's any such thing as time." At the other extreme, a psychologist I knew calculated how many hours of his life he would spend tying his shoes and putting on a belt and, having decided the investment was too great, henceforth wore only shoes which could be closed with a Velcro fastener and bought pants which were "Sansabelt."

Living in a Circle

In ancient and traditional societies, time had to do with the ebb and flow of tides, the orbits of sun and moon, and the passing of seasons. It was marked by thinning light, the gradual thawing of ice or the birth of lambs in the endlessly recurring seasons. Time was a circle within which humans lived. Not only was there an element of recreation in the economic activities of most preindustrial cultures, but also in many the amount of time available for leisure appears to have been as great as or greater than our own. Anthropologists Allen and Orna Johnson (1978) studied the Machiguenga Indians of Peru for 18 months and found this to be the case. These Indians survive by growing food in gardens, hunting, fishing, and collecting wild foods. "They are self-sufficient; almost everything they consume is produced by their own labors using materials that are found close at hand."

When the Johnsons divided the time of the Machiguenga into production time (work), consumption time (using consumer goods for pleasure, eating), and free time (idleness, rest, sleep, chatting), and then compared these time expenditures to those in current French society, they discovered that the Machiguenga's free time surpassed that of the French by more than four hours a day. The pace of life for the Peruvian Indians was leisurely; daily activities never seemed hurried or desperate. Anthropologists have found that many hunter–gatherer societies, such as the Australian aborigines, require only three or four hours of work per day to provide the material requirements for their simple way of life (Sahlins, 1972). Thus, there are two ways to reach affluence: our own way, which is to produce more, or to be satisfied with less.

Even when mechanical means began to be used to measure time many centuries ago, it did not signal drastic changes in the organization of society. Early devices such as the sundial, hourglass, water clock, and timing candle or lamp were operated independently of any standardized time. There was no fixed moment to which the hourglass could be synchronized. Precision in the use of time was rare, and if rain rendered the sundial useless it didn't matter.

Church and Commerce

Concepts of time that were circular and less precise gradually changed to linear ones in the western world. Time became a straight line with a fixed beginning and a fixed end. Early emperors such as Alexander or Augustus declared that year one began with their rule. Judaism replaced the reoccurring events of nature as a basis for conceiving time with specific nonreoccurring events, thus constructing a past, present, and future.

History no longer repeated itself. "The Creation," which started time, was thought to be the work of a single god. The passage of time was marked by the events of humans rather than nature. In Judaism and Christianity as well, there was an imagined end of time—a Day of Judgment, of potential salvation. Individual behavior would shape the outcome. Thus, our notion of "free will" was born and with it the measurement of time in terms other than nature's.

For Christians, the linear progression of history from the fall of Adam and Eve in the Garden of Eden, to the birth, death, and resurrection of Christ, and from there to the last judgment, became the foundation of Christian faith. Ancient Hebrews preferred to believe in linear progress—progress toward the Promised Land. Time became a line of finite but indeterminate length.

Mechanical measurement of time by clocks reinforced the linear concept of time. It allowed more accurate measurements of time to be made and shared among people. This was necessary as people began to earn their living in ways other than hunting and gathering, farming, or individual production of goods. Mechanical measurement of time was to pave the way for industrialization and the splitting of the day into segments of work and leisure.

Viewing time as a line with a beginning and an end made it a finite commodity. As an expert in the study of time, philosopher J. T. Fraser (1987, p. 48) pointed out:

> With the meteoric advance of science and technology—made possible by the linear view of time and history—the relationship between God-the-timer and man-the-timed has changed. In our epoch, carrying out the promise of salvation history became a responsibility of the created and not the Creator.

Eventually "man-the-timed" was timed more closely, not only by God, but also by employers, schools, stoplights, parking meters, and stopwatches. By the actuarial tables of insurance companies and the whistles of referees in sporting events, by the regularity with which the ghost images of television appeared, dancing in another world. By sex manuals, by aerobic dance instructors, by the coming and going of planes and trains, by digital clocks spread throughout the household, by the beep of cell phones and pagers, and finally by the precise unfolding of events as various as the firing of nuclear missiles to the cooking of French fries made possible by the computer's rhythms.

The Industrialization of Work

Little by little, humans became runners on the straight line of time. From the Middle Ages through industrialism, the pace of life began an unprecedented process of speeding up, not only the speedup of work in factories but also related changes that reflected the new values of speed and efficiency: standardization of hours which pubs could be open, mass production of watches, imposition of laws against loitering. While the idea of democracy had caught hold in Europe and North America, rejecting the tyranny of humans, there was increased willingness to accept the tyranny of the clock. Slowly, time became the ultimate organizing mechanism of the modern world—the ultimate scarce commodity.

Industrial capitalism brought about not only a small "leisure class," which had both time and money, but also a class of workers forced into a new kind of labor and eventually enticed into a model of open-ended consumption. While a Luddite movement developed, which sought to destroy the machines introduced into the work place (until its leaders were shot, hanged, and deported into submission), such protest groups were mistaken in their attacks. What really changed and came to rule their lives was not the machines on the shop floor but what hung over them from the ceiling: the clock.

Prior to the factory system, the work of peasants and life in general was less time-bound and organized. The clock, which made industrial work possible, fundamentally changed the shoemaker's work, making time scarce. In the 17th century, when clocks began to be considered more than a bauble for the rich, the poet Ciro di Pers (quoted by De Grazia, 1962, p. 310), understood they make time scarce:

> Noble machine with toothed wheels
> Lacerates the day and divides it in hours
> Speeds on the course of the fleeing century.
> And to make it open up,
> Knocks every hour at the tomb.

By the late 1800s, inexpensive Swiss-made and then U.S. watches were lacerating the day for millions. By 1888 the Waterbury Company in Connecticut was selling 500,000 watches a year. While earliest clocks had only an hour hand, the minute hand was added as time became more precious, then a sweeping second hand that moved in endless circles as if time were still a circle of seasons. Seconds were divided by the stopwatch, first into tenths and then hundreds. Ultimately, the computer

was to provide a further division of time beyond human perception—the nanosecond—one billionth of a second.

Scientific Management

While industrialization and the clock profoundly altered life and sped up its pace dramatically, Frederick Taylor, the creator of scientific management, may have been responsible more than anyone else for the time famine in American culture. In 1899, Taylor established a company whose product was advice on how to make enterprises more efficient. Among Taylor's services were time-and-motion studies of workers on the shop floor. He called his system the "piece-rote" system: each man performed by rote in the most efficient (usually meaning fastest) way. Taylor's techniques controlled each of six temporal dimensions on the shop floor—sequence, duration, schedule, rhythm, synchronization, and time perspective—stripping the individual worker of control of the processes of work and making him a servant of the machine. As the late Daniel Bell (1975) observed:

> If any social upheaval can ever be attributed to one man, the logic of efficacy as a mode of life is due to Taylor. With scientific management as formulated by Taylor in 1895, we pass the old rough computations of the division of labor and move into the division of time itself. (p. 55)

The ultimate impact of scientific management was not only to wrest control of the processes of work from the worker, but also to make the worker more efficient. In doing so, Taylor unwittingly reshaped the use of time in every aspect of our lives. Modern homemaking began to reflect these values and processes: kitchens were designed in increasingly standardized ways based on the same time-and-motion studies that Taylor helped introduce. The methods of coaching many sports became indistinguishable from the methods employed by Henry Ford to produce the Model T. Largely because of the economic success of scientific management in the workplace, time and attitudes toward time have slowly been reorganized in the rest of life, with the ultimate result being a general scarcity of time.

The Industrialization of Free Time

As work became more ordered and time became the ordering device, for many the rest of life became "free time"—an empty container that could no longer be filled with the old forms of play and holy days, which characterized peasant life. New work patterns, the emergence of capitalism and the urban environment, largely an unplanned phenomenon accompanying the factory system, made former ways of life and leisure obsolete.

If the factory system was a catastrophe for peasant culture, peasant culture was initially a catastrophe for the factory system. Peasants often preferred idleness, drink, working when the mood struck them, and the pleasures of the body over the pleasures of the mind. In both Europe and North America, gambling and drinking either accompanied or had been the source of most leisure activity of adult males and some females. Such preferences led to a series of attempts to reform the leisure of the peasants, since employers and managers believed it was necessary to change such habits for industrialism to succeed. Many, including Charles Dickens, also recognized leisure time was the only arena for the "re-creation" of the physical and psychological capacity to work.

By the 1830s, reformers understood new work patterns deprived members of society of the means of expressing their religious and family values. The "rest of life," in many senses, had to be reinvented. Leisure was thought by such reformers to be the best place to promote the personal values essential for a growing commercial economy: self-control, family values, and respectability. The various reform movements wanted not only to suppress various leisure behaviors considered evil, but also to transform leisure behavior, replacing play that was public, inconclusive, and improvised with play that was more highly ordered and planned. In doing so, the intent was to make the working class more "respectable, more predictable, less dangerous to others, and more amenable to industrial working conditions" (Kanigel, 1997). In all such change, the ability to treat time as a scarce resource was critical.

The means of achieving these ends were as diverse as the promotion of reading, choral societies, structured sport experiences, adult education, and a variety of other nonwork experiences. The nature of many such efforts was an offshoot of the techniques of industrial work. Modern sport, for instance, was born during the 19th century during the transformation of work to the industrial system. In Britain, sports such as track and field, swimming, rowing, and soccer became regulated contests with techniques drawn from industrial production and from the unfolding world of capitalistic market relationships. Athletics were increasingly measured, timed, specialized, and synchronized in ways that would have made Taylor proud.

To reform the habits of working class women, the "rational domesticity" movement featured visits to their homes by upper-class females to teach ways of improving housework, handicrafts, and childrearing; increasing

hygiene; and becoming more efficient, punctual, and productive. The transformation of work caused the transformation of leisure. Free time became industrialized. Many traditions of preindustrial life were lost forever.

The Further Ordering of Time

Time became not only more ordered in the daily lives of those in individual communities, but also standardized throughout the world. Historically, different communities had set their own time based on tradition, their local economy, or nature as late as the beginning of the 20th century. In 1870, a rail passenger traveling from Washington to San Francisco would have traveled through roughly 200 different time systems on the journey (Rifkin, 1987). The British, however, had set a standardized time system for their railroads and soon countries with large rail systems also wanted to do so. An International Conference on Time held in Paris in 1912 ratified the agreement of an earlier conference in which Greenwich, England became the timekeeper for the world: the prime meridian. Thus, the entire world became, to some extent, subject to a uniform system of time, a system that was removed from nature and based completely on utilitarian considerations. The stage was set for the time to become a new form of tyranny, an unrecognized imperialism.

Today the computer has joined the clock as the new time-allocating device. Computer programs predetermine how the future will unfold and control the sequence, duration, tempo, and coordination of activities. The computer differs from a clock as a teller of time. While clocks are set in terms of sequence, duration, and rhythm, a computer can manipulate these by changing the program. Time is no longer a single fixed reference point that exists external to events. It is no longer bound in any way to the rhythms of the natural world, but rather a mathematical abstraction that separates us from the natural world.

While time has always been equated with change and more recently equated with money (as Ben Franklin observed), it is now equated with information as well. The rate at which such information is calculated, the nanosecond, speeds up the rate of change exponentially. Thus, we dance faster and faster just to stay in place. Computers have not so much become "user friendly" as we have had to become "computer friendly."

If the computer increasingly defines and controls time in whatever capacity it is used, it may reshape our inner sense of time. All of us experience time in psychological terms, making qualitative judgments about it. For instance, if you enjoy reading this book, 45 minutes spent reading seems to pass more quickly than if you do not enjoy reading it. Psychological time or inner time is our perception or inner sense of the passage of events. In this sense, time can be judged only in terms of personal meaning. As we shall see later, our inner sense of time has been fundamentally reshaped by a computerized world.

Time may now be thought of as a relative concept rather than an absolute one, not only because of the computer's ability to "program" time in any way we wish, but also because of parallel changes in theoretical physics. Einstein's special theory of relativity assumes space and time are relative and related concepts rather than constant, absolute, and separate. While the speed of light is a constant throughout the universe, our perceptions of time are shaped by how fast we are moving. Nothing is at absolute rest. If we moved at the speed of light away from a clock tower that said 12 o'clock and continued to view the clock, it would always say 12 o'clock, since the light that carried the image of the clock would be traveling at the same speed we were. Even looking at a wristwatch produces a little lag, since light must carry the image to our eyes and then our brain. Thus, there is no universal "present." People experience events differently depending on where they are on the planet and how fast they and what they observe are traveling. Perhaps the psychological equivalent of Einstein's theory is that our world and the events we perceive in it seem to be traveling faster and faster. Americans may perceive time differently from those in other countries, because both we and the events we observe are moving faster and faster.

Every culture, of course, is haunted by something seemingly beyond its control: weather, war, disease, religious prejudice, boredom, starvation. Presently, our own society is starving, not the starvation of Somalis or other traditional cultures, who die for lack of food, but the ultimate scarcity of the postmodern world: time. Starving for time does not result in death; it results, as ancient Athenian philosophers observed, in never having begun to live. Examples of time scarcity surround us:

- The condensation of birthday parties into restaurant meals at which the wait staff assemble to sing a quick chorus of "Happy Birthday," perhaps accompanied by a cupcake with a lit candle, extinguished within 20 seconds.

- Running red lights; risking life and limb to save a few seconds.

- Gulping food at meals too quickly to savor the flavor; such habits may be a major factor in obesity.

- Drive-through windows in "fast food" restaurants. You drive through throwing money at them while they throw grease, salt, and sugar back at you.

- "Quickies."

- Parents' talk about "quality time" with children, which simply means doing more with them in less time.

- Museum curators report that visitors rarely spend more than 30 seconds in front of an exhibit.

- Retired couples who complain of always feeling rushed even though there is almost nothing they have to do.

- A friend who wrecked his car while driving, talking on the telephone, listening to a taped lecture, and eating lunch out of a McDonald's bag.

- Perverse games of "communication tag," made worse by call waiting, fax machines, and voice mail.

- The new social taboos: being late, taking too long to get to "the point" in a conversation, waiting (for anything).

- The increasing resort to guns and violence as a quick way to resolve conflicts.

- The massive evidence of the decline of patience in everyday life—except for those who are "patients" in hospitals—but even patients are getting impatient.

The qualities of leisure experience have changed dramatically as life has gotten faster. Consider a simple trip to the zoo, in the foggy past and now:

The kids talked about the trip for several weeks. Mom packed a lunch the night before and instructed her children about what clothes to wear—their good clothes. Next day the entire family drove to the zoo, or took a bus, and once their destination was reached spent all morning just roaming around. After a leisurely lunch on the grass, the father perhaps snoozed a bit, the mother cleaned up and the kids wandered off to see their favorite animals. Once alone, the mother and father might even have talked to each other in hushed tones while slowly pulling blades of grass or staring at the clouds. Lying on their backs, hands folded behind their heads, the couple slowly came to realize that a distant cloud bank looked like dreaming elephants bound for home. They watched other people with a passive receptiveness that once in a while led to insights about the world and one's life in it. The children returned. A few arguments were partially settled. The animals were discussed with great enthusiasm as the remains of the picnic basket were depleted. Perhaps blades of grass were pulled from the father's cupped hands to determine who got the last half of a brownie—the shortest blade winning. They returned home as the sun set, tired and full of wonder.

Today the same trip might go as follows:

Mom or Dad, not both, throws the kids in the car and gets on the interstate and drives at 75 miles an hour to Animal Safari Park where they pay $12.00 per person and drive through taking snapshots with a throwaway camera through rolled up windows. Within 45 minutes they are back on the interstate looking for a fast food place.

What Does It Mean to Rush?

To "rush" is a bit more sinister than we might suspect. In a particularly rushed culture this may be hard to discern, because it takes lots of unrushed reflection to recognize what rushing means. The word "rush" has many related meanings. It may be either a swift advance or an attack or charge." To rush means "to move, act, or progress with speed, impetuosity, or violence" (*Random House College Dictionary*, 1988). Thus, to rush may mean not only speed of action or progression, but also rash or unthinking action or an injurious, rough, or destructively forceful action. The range of synonyms for rushing is great and includes the following: speed, race, hasten, hie, hurry, run, dash, tear, scramble, dart, hustle, scurry, scamper, speed up, accelerate, dispatch, expedite, perform hastily, finish with speed, work against time, hurry, spur, whip, urge, goad, drive, pressure, push, press, keep at, go carelessly, go headlong, act thoughtlessly, leap, plunge, precipitate oneself, attack suddenly, storm, charge, descend upon, have at, dash, sprint, haste, and urgency (*Random House Thesaurus, College Edition*, 1989). In most of these meanings, there is the quality of aggression. Aggression is a widely admired trait in our culture—from business to sport to politics to matters of the heart, aggression is encouraged. There is also the quality of violence in rushing—it is no accident that the high-speed train system in Japan is called the "bullet train." There is rushing in football, in dating, and in fraternities. In many cases, rushing indicates going after some objective independent of the feelings of others.

If you move slowly, though, the other individuals involved have time to consider what you are doing and to make judgments about it. If you rush, they may not.

Among the antonyms one finds are walk, crawl, slow, dawdle—and leisure. Leisure requires an absence of rushing, tranquility, an end to hurrying, a letting go. Thus, questions of amounts of "free time" in a society may not tell us much about the extent to which that society experiences leisure.

Rushing, then, is a complex term. It is easy to see situations in which rushing would be worthwhile and functional. If your house is on fire, you should rush out of the building; if a mugger is chasing you, rush away; if the wind blows your hat across the field, rush after it. As a way of life, however, rushing doesn't sound very inviting or even functional.

Effortless speed, of course, is something very different from rushing. The leopard does not "rush" after its prey. Mozart did not rush to create music; it simply poured out. One who is a "quick study" does not have to necessarily "rush" for answers, and a savant seems to receive his or her magical skills as a gift from God. Indeed, much of what we can do quickly without rushing appears to be God's gift. Barry Sanders, formerly of the Detroit Lions, was remarkably gifted at "rushing," yet, like most highly talented running backs, he never seemed in a hurry. Rushing, then, is something different from speed; it is an attempt at greater control, often after control seems to have been lost. If you stomp an anthill with your boot, the ants will rush around. Perhaps our culture has become one big stomped anthill.

Of Time Pressure Good and Bad

Not all time pressures, of course, are unnatural or dysfunctional. All living things are subject to daily (diurnal) and annual cycles and processes. Humans are not exempt from such processes. All the organs of the human body are subject to the influences of the biological diurnal clock. These biological cycles are not caused by the alternation of sleeping and waking. Rather, just as sleeping and waking, they are an expression of our genetic make-up. A large body of research shows our performance ability is greatly influenced by the time of day. With industrial workers, for instance, performance reaches its first peak in the morning and then another slightly lower one in the afternoon, following a midday low. Performance in the evening drops off quickly and reaches a pronounced low in the early hours of the morning. This pattern applies to both day shift and night shift workers. Other examples abound. Alcohol is absorbed into the bloodstream faster at some times of the day than others. Suicide rates, the conception of illegitimate children, the number of books loaned by libraries, even the effects of exercise vary by the time of year.

There is also a social element to time pressures, which is highly desirable for humans. Being "unemployed" means not only lack of income, but also, even where income is provided by government, it is the destruction of a temporal routine. The absence of a succession of events and "intentionality of action" makes workless days forgettable and destructive for many of the unemployed (Cross, 1993). As historian Gary Cross (1993, p. 176) observed about the Depression, "To the jobless male, in particular, unemployment destroyed the oppositional character of time: it obliterated the division between public 'obligation,' which justified the individual with a wage, and private freedom, where men displayed themselves as chums and providers." Those who cope with unemployment successfully generally establish new routines with new time pressures around which the rest of life can unfold.

All of these examples demonstrate we are shaped by time and time pressures, which are part of our make-up. This time pressure is a good thing:

> Temporal pressure is constricted, but it is also the framework within which our personality is organized. When it is absent we are disoriented. There is nothing to bind the sequence of activities: we are alone. Human equilibrium is too precarious to do without fixed positions in space and regular cues in time. (Fraisse, 1964, p. 141)

There are, in other words, advantages to time pressure. It is a natural and healthy part of our lives. There are also time patterns in the natural world, which shape us because we are a part of nature. More recently, however, time pressures have intensified to the point where millions of Americans are starving for time.

Time Deepening

How do we explain the time famine? Economist Staffan Linder theorized the speed-up of the pace of life in America occurred as follows. An equilibrium existed between the work and leisure of Americans in terms of what they accomplished during each period of life. As output per worker increased, the time of each worker became more valuable and therefore thought of as more scarce. This destroyed the balance between work and leisure, since people had increased the "yield" on their work but not their leisure. People then began to attempt to increase the "yield" on their leisure both by speeding up their participation in various activities and by combining given activities with additional material goods. This caused a shift away from leisure activities that could not be sped up or easily combined with additional

material goods, such as contemplation, singing, dancing, or writing poetry; it increased time spent in activities which could be sped up and combined with material goods, such as driving a car for pleasure, shopping, and tourism. Linder (1969) argued this situation led to a general perceived scarcity of time. Burns (1993) gave several examples of this principle in action, such as why people prefer cats to dogs (because they are less time-intensive) and why people buy orange juice made from concentrate rather than frozen juice (because it doesn't have to be thawed and mixed).

The response to the time famine has been "time deepening" behavior. Time deepening assumes that, under pressure of expanded interest and compulsion, people are capable of higher rates of "doing." Rather than thinking of human behavior in "either–or" terms, in which a person either does one activity or another, some people develop the capability of doing both activity A and activity B. Time deepening occurs in four ways:

1. Attempting to speed up a given activity: bringing the relief pitcher in from the bull pen in a golf cart; visiting a national park without getting out of your car; telling a date your life story in under two minutes.

2. Substituting a leisure activity which can be done more quickly for one which takes longer: phoning for home-delivered fast food instead of cooking it yourself; playing a game of racquetball or squash instead of tennis.

3. Doing more than one activity at once: watching television while reading the newspaper and eating dinner; eating, drinking, doing your income taxes, and watching a movie while traveling in an airplane.

4. Undertaking a leisure activity with more precise regard to time, perhaps planning an evening of cocktails, dinner, and attending the theater with friends with only a five-minute tolerance in the schedule.

Time deepening is more likely to occur among upwardly mobile middle or upper class Americans. While it may have some advantages in terms of accomplishment, it has many disadvantages. First, it produces great stress. It additionally means that, during leisure, many Americans never experience anything fully; they never live in the moment. They may also avoid leisure activities that require a long time to learn the necessary skills.

The desire to speed things up extends even to sexual activity. Pornography is, in effect, a sped-up substitute for more time-intensive forms of sexual involvement.

Prostitutes operate in alleys or out of parked cars for "quickies." The practice of taking a mistress, as Linder observed, is dying out simply because men don't have sufficient unaccounted for time to develop such a relationship. Even the increase in sexual intercourse outside of marriage may represent, not so much a change in morals, but rather an attempt to obtain the only type of intimacy that may be realized quickly. Social or spiritual intimacy is hopelessly time-consuming.

Work activities, of course, have been sped up as well. Yesterday's average typist used to average about 30,000 keystrokes per hour, while today's VDT (video display terminal) operator is expected to attain about 80,000 keystrokes in the same amount of time (Rifkin, 1987). The fax machine, electronic mail, cell phones, pagers, and the information highway make communication faster and faster, although rarely more thoughtful. Computers speed up the process of analyzing information. Sony and Panasonic have marketed a variable speech control cassette tape recorder, which allows the human voice to be sped up without sounding like a chipmunk. Over one million people have already become speed listeners.

Americans also substitute quicker activities for more time-consuming ones. The Nautilus machine can replace more time-demanding exercise forms. People debate if they really want to "invest the time" in learning ballroom dancing or organic gardening. Candidates interviewing for many jobs are shuttled from interview to interview, with trips to the bathroom planned into the schedule.

Americans have become more proficient at devising and adapting to such behaviors during the last few decades. In multinational time-diary studies, Americans were more likely to record multiple activities in their diaries than respondents from other nations. As German sociologist Erwin Scheusch (1972) observed about the landmark 12-nation time-diary study of 1965:

> A main problem in recording the use of time derives from the fact that many people during a large part of the day do more than one thing at one time. Our pretests suggest that the more a person is part of an industrial society with a very high density of communication, the more educated a person, the more likely he is to do a number of things simultaneously.

It is hard to remember that prior to television people sat by the radio and listened, doing nothing else. A child might sit, staring through the window at the darkening trees, hearing only the Lone Ranger's voice and the hooves of horses in the canyon. Today radio is almost exclusively a secondary activity, something we listen to while doing something else. Television is beginning to go the same route as radio: at least a third of TV viewing is combined with other activities. Those who don't do something else while watching can "graze" on the video menu, switching from channel to channel every few seconds.

Such behavior may be described in terms of "the more... the more..." a pattern initially described by Meyersohn (1968). Rather than either playing tennis or squash, those who do one are more likely to do the other as well. Rather than choosing between working longer hours and participating in lots of active leisure pursuits, those who work longer hours show more active participation. Rather than joining one club or another, those who join one are more likely to join others. Rather than hold a part-time job or spend time studying, those who hold part-time jobs are often more likely to spend longer hours studying. While "the more... the more..." does not always hold true, enough of it seems to that we must consider that people have different rates of "doing." Rather than thinking of time as a given—a rope tied around our activities—it is more like a mysterious rubber band which binds us but which can be stretched and stretched almost infinitely. When we stretch it, the stress created is often transferred to us. Those who use time deepening techniques keep stretching that rubber band to see where the breaking point is.

Speeding up the pace of life, history and our perception of reality is a dangerous thing. Things that go faster and faster have less margin for error. Many of us are flying blind at mach speed—we know not where.

Some Reasons for Increased Time Constraints to Leisure

Exponential and Discontinuous Change

The pace of change in the world is at an all-time high. History is speeding up. With little warning the Soviet Union collapsed, cell phones reshaped the form and extent of human communication, animals were cloned and animal organs transplanted into humans, Whites became a minority group in the biggest state in the United States, a higher portion of women than men went to college, the planet rapidly warmed, and littering became a problem in outer space. Both exponential change and discontinuous change, such as the sudden appearance of AIDS or laptop computers, reshape daily life. Such change requires massive adjustment on the part of individuals.

As the economic basis of the world rapidly moves from hunting and gathering to agriculture to mercantilism to industry to a service economy to an information and leisure experience-based economy, knowledge has become the central resource. By 1990 there was "no developed country where traditional workers making and moving goods account for more than one-sixth or one-eighth of the work force" (Drucker, 1993, p. 167). To obtain the advances in productivity that the postcapitalist society will need, all organizations will have to embrace rapid changes in both teaching and learning. Knowledge will have to be made more productive, and organizations will have to cope with change by serving as destabilizing agents more than their traditional role of stabilizing. What a person needs to know will change every four or five years, making learning a way of life rather than a period of life. Everyone, to some extent, is playing catch-up with reality. This produces the mindset that there is not enough time.

From Specialists to Generalists

People are in the process of moving from being "specialists" in regard to time use (e.g., taking care of children and a household, or working at a given occupation, or pursuing a single form of leisure expression) to becoming generalists. In the core theme of sociology, modernization, specialization is assumed to play a key role. The sociologist Linton (1937) assumed a society's culture could be divided into three elements:

1. universals (habits, ideas, and conditioned emotional responses shared by everyone).

2. specialties (elements of culture shared by certain socially recognized categories of individuals but not the whole population).

3. alternatives (traits shared by certain individuals but not common to all members of any one of the socially recognized categories of society).

In the ideal male-provider household, housekeeping is the specialty of women and earning the family's income is the specialty of men (Van den Broek, 1998). Watching TV is a customary pattern of all people, while pastimes such as going to the theater are alternative activities.

In the past few decades, in most modern societies, the percentage of people who undertake both paid work and housework is increasing. So, too, is the percentage of people doing alternative activities, such as going to the theater.

As a consequence of these trends towards greater universality of daily activities, growing numbers of people are involved in growing numbers of activities. With respect to both tasks and leisure, the degree of specialization is being reduced. Task combination and the combination of cultural with leisure activities are on the rise. In their respective domains, both combinations imply a time squeeze....Dispersion of the available leisure time over a greater number of pastimes means that the involvement per pastime is cut down. At the level of specific leisure pursuits, this implies that one more often is a passer-by rather than a participant. (Van den Broek, 1998, p. 21)

Thus, people may both have more free time and feel more rushed. In the period of industrialization, people became specialists. "Professionalism" was built on such specialization. The medical profession emerged in Britain, for instance, out of a period in which being a doctor was a moral calling, something worth doing but not something that you could earn a living from. Women, at least middle-class women, often specialized in domestic life and childcare. They could bake, sew, decorate, and undertake the extraordinarily demanding task of caring for children.

Specialization in the use of time is declining. Today, many people are taking on more roles than they knew existed. Males are learning something about cooking, caring for their clothing, taking care of children and pets, and community life. Women are learning about mutual funds, careers, competitive sport, international politics, shooting firearms, and plumbing.

In summary, how those in modern nations use time is changing as is the way such individuals feel about time. The irony of modern life is that free time is increasing, but, to a large section of the population, it feels like there is never enough time.

The Saturated Self

The increasing amount of communication in society may have literally "saturated" us, changing our concepts of self in the process. As a mass culture is replaced with a more diverse and individualized culture in which the amount of sensory input we get grows and grows, we think about ourselves differently. The romantic and modern notions of self are largely being replaced with postmodern ones. Psychologist Kenneth Gergen (1991, pp. 7–8) explains what has happened as follows:

Cultural life in the twentieth century has been dominated by two major vocabularies of the self. Largely from the nineteenth century, we have inherited a romantic view of the self, one that attributes to each person characteristics of personal depth: passion, soul, creativity, and moral fiber. This vocabulary is essential to the formation of deeply committed relationships, dedicated friendships and life purposes. But since the rise of the modernist worldview beginning in the early twentieth century, the romantic vocabulary has been threatened. For modernists, the chief characteristics of the self reside not in the domain of depth, but rather in our ability to reason—in our beliefs, opinions and conscious intentions. In the modernist idiom, normal persons are predictable, honest and sincere. Modernists believe in educational systems, a stable family life, moral training and rational choice of marriage partners....[B]oth the romantic and modern beliefs about the self are falling into disuse, and the social arrangements that they support are eroding. This is largely a result of the forces of social saturation. Emerging technologies saturate us with the voices of mankind, both harmonious and alien. As we absorb their varied rhymes and reasons, they become part of us and we of them. Social saturation furnishes us with a multiplicity of incoherent and unrelated languages of the self. For everything we "know to be true" about ourselves, other voices within respond with doubts and even derision. The fragmentation of self-conceptions corresponds to a multiplicity of incoherent and disconnected relationships. These relationships pull us in myriad directions, inviting us to play such a variety of roles that the very concept of an "authentic self" with knowable characteristics recedes from view. The fully saturated self becomes no self at all.

In the postmodern era, according to Gergen, the very concept of personal essences is thrown into doubt. People exist in a state of construction and reconstruction, placing the absolute answers provided by science, moral authority, and the law into question. The saturated self constantly changes and does so based on an ever-widening array of relationships and communication.

Part of this saturated self comes from new costs of coordination. As society becomes more complex, as we become more interdependent, and as our ability to harm each other increases, planning and regulating our society become more important and more difficult. Additionally, the necessity of interacting with increasing numbers of people and a greater number of social situations is necessary, and to facilitate that more travel is needed. Such coordination is not the prerogative of an elite but is necessary for everyone so that our own cars, chemicals, and radioactive wastes do not kill us.

Finally, of course, is the factor of time—the ultimate scarcity for those who wish to consume and to experience at a historically unprecedented rate. How shall we view this ironic situation? What an extraordinary luxury to have, as a problem, a perceived scarcity of time not tied to economic production. The desire to experience all things pleasurable, to be needed and involved in as many sets of human experiences as possible is, in many respects, the ultimate greed, the greed of a small frog who tries to swallow the sun. Two things must be said about this greed for experience. First, it springs directly from the mentality and processes of economic capitalism, where competition for goods and the production process are divorced from need. It is natural that this progression has taken place. Capitalism may be defined as

an economic system based upon the accumulation and investment of capital by private individuals who then become the owners of the means of production and distribution of goods and services. Capitalism is also characterized by economic motivation through private profit, competition, the determination of prices and wages primarily through supply and demand, an extensive system of credit, freedom of contract and a free labor market. (Theodorson & Theodorson, 1969, pp. 36–37)

In similar terms, the accumulation and investment of time by individuals in diverse pleasurable activity has taken place as a means of self-actualization. It has become a competition with time the scarce resource to find out who we are—literally, to re-create ourselves, experientially.

The 24-Hour Economy

Work is increasingly "portable"—that is, it can be done in many different places, and at any time. As most workers become involved in services, and the production of information becomes important to providing such services, the computer and other digital devices of communication make the location of many people's work more and more flexible. This has led to the "outsourcing" of work to people in other countries or locations within a country. Examining insurance claims, word processing, filling orders for a product, and processing airline tickets are increasingly done by people in remote locations.

Also, more people are now working in their homes. Since over one half of American workers use a computer as part of their job (U.S. Census Bureau, 2000), the potential to further decentralize working hours is enormous. Between 1991 and 1997, the number of people working at home in the United States rose from 7.2 million to 9.5 million in 1997 and continues to rise. Today about 10% of all workers work at home (Stainback & Donato, 1998). Working at home is often done to coordinate work schedules with personal and family needs. As it becomes common for both the male and female in a household to work "full-time," working at home may provide the opportunity for work to be combined with family and personal needs. For all dual-worker households, it may be a way of providing more control over ones' lives.

As manufacturing becomes more automated and a service/knowledge economy dominates, the day may come when a large segment of the working population works at home, or wherever they want to. This has already happened to the extent that distinctions between weekdays and weekends are minimal in terms of time use (Robinson & Godbey, 1999). Opposition to the 24-hour economy will increasingly come from more fundamentalist sects of Christianity, Judaism, and Islam, but the rationalization of economies and time flexible nature of occupations are likely to keep the 24-hour economy in place.

The 24-hour economy and flexible working arrangements will be increasingly necessary as the roles of females continue to change dramatically. Much of the standardized weekday–weekend work and leisure cycle implied a male head of household who got most of the formal education and worked full-time and a wife who stayed home and took care of children and household. Such assumptions are now obsolete. Consider the following:

> There is cultural lag in Americans' perception of the educational attainment and achievements of girls and boys. While the feeling persists that girls are ignored in public school, remain passive, have low self-esteem, etc., girls are far higher achievers in public schools than boys and they are more likely to go to college. According to the U.S. Department of Education, girls get better grades in public schools, are slightly more likely to enroll in higher level math and science courses and outnumber boys in student government, honor societies, school newspapers and debating teams. Girls read more books than boys, outperform them on tests for artistic and musical ability, and are more likely to study abroad. Boys are more likely to be suspended from school, held back, drop out, or be involved in crime, alcohol or drugs. Boys are more than three times more likely to receive a diagnosis of attention deficit hyperactivity disorder. While

> girls are more likely to attempt suicide, boys are more likely to succeed in killing themselves by a ratio of more than five to one. In 1996 there were 8.4 million women but only 6.7 million men enrolled in college and the projections are that by 2007, women will outnumber men in college even more substantially: 9.2 million women and 6.9 million men. (Sommers, 2000, p. 60)

As women gain educational advantage over men, flexible working arrangements are increasingly necessary for women to pursue both careers and motherhood.

In the 21st century, technological change is being organized around biological models, and biology operates on the principle that difference is better. While many modern societies are still organized around the pretense of treating people equally, the organizing principle is changing to treating them appropriately. Treating people equally makes no sense in a decentralized society, because we are not interchangeable parts. Treating people appropriately will make more sense as we become even more diverse. Treating people appropriately occurs only when you know a lot about their needs.

In all these changes, the simple divisions of work and free time, weekday–weekend, home and workplace blur into obscurity. So, too, does the simple notion of attempting to treat people equally. The logistics of life become more complex, the intrusion of work into the night, the weekend, the holiday and the distant location makes time feel scarce.

Efficiency as A Dominant Value

Efficiency has slowly become the most important American value since Fredrick Taylor's scientific management revolutionized the factory floor. Using time and motion study, Taylor sought to reduce the time needed to undertake every physical task in a factory. Slowly, this mentality spread to the rest of life. Homemaking experts began to apply Taylor's principles, breaking down each step in baking biscuits into the number of seconds needed for each task. Taylor's influence extended to public education as well: "Journals and lecture platforms were soon littered with the likes of 'The Principles of Scientific Management Applied to Teaching Music in the Public Schools'" (Kanigel, 1997, p. 13). Gradually, the value of efficiency spread to leisure activity. Sport went from being playful to being efficient and work-like. Time and motion studies were applied as much to football or track and field as making automobiles. Restaurants such as McDonald's were organized on efficiency principles. Even sexual behavior was rethought, as was tourism.

The current rationalization of the workplace, which pushes the worker to work even faster (if not longer), seems to have no upper limit. Workers who must do things faster, sooner, and "just in time" carry such values into the rest of life. In effect, the service worker has been caught in the same open-ended model of efficiency as Taylor imposed on steelworkers and other manufacturing workers. The knowledge worker, too, appears to be subject to Taylorism. University faculties, for instance, are held to the principle that more research and faster research is always better. They then write "cut and paste" journal articles from such rushed endeavors. Journalists have story quotas that increase in number so rapidly they often must settle for "sound bites." In all these changes, the open-ended desire for efficiency harms quality while increasing quantity, harms tranquility while increasing stress. Indeed, many efficiency experts in Japan speak of "stressing the system." If you speed it up enough, you find out what is inefficient and it dies.

Efficiency, of course, is no friend of leisure or of play. Leisure requires the absence of the necessity of being occupied (De Grazia, 1962); play is inherently limited in its objectives (Huizinga, 1950). The cult of efficiency that now pervades every aspect of American life may be said to have "denatured" leisure—and constrained it.

Increasing Sense of the Necessary

The more principles of scientific management were applied to every aspect of daily life, the more could be done. Simultaneously, rising expectations about what could be accomplished produced an increasing sense of what was "necessary." Home economist Katherine Walker (1969), for instance, found that most laborsaving devices in households produced rising expectations about what it was necessary to do. More efficient airplanes redefined where it was necessary to go. The open-ended application of efficiency has meant notions of what is necessary continue to increase and, as this happens, time becomes a bigger constraint even as we do more.

"Needs," of course, are also introduced by advertising. The rather monstrous scope of advertising is such that today the average child views 30,000 commercials each year ("Children and Advertising," 1998). As a result, it is not surprising that definitions of the necessary increase continuously. It is becoming "necessary" to have an all-wheel-drive car; it will soon be "necessary" to have an onboard navigation system. It is "necessary" to take vitamin E and a huge variety of diet supplements, and to drink a "sports" drink, bottled water, double lattes. The ability of advertising to continuously raise the

ante on definitions of necessary means one is always behind in achieving and obtaining the necessary.

The Paradox of More Time, More Time Constraint

It is paradoxical that people in modern societies have more free time compared to 100 years ago but feel more time constraints. Additionally, work is taking a smaller and smaller fraction of the hours of one's life. An analysis of British citizens, for instance, found

> although the average career length has remained around 40 years, the total life hours worked shrank from 124,000 hours in 1856 to 69,000 in 1983. The fraction of disposable lifetime hours spent working declined from 50 percent to 20 percent. (Ausubel & Grubler, 1994, p. 195)

The portion of our lives devoted to both paid work and housework is decreasing, and it appears that such declines are predicted by rising economic standards of living within a country. Gershuny (1992, p. 18), after a meta-analysis of time use in 15 countries, drew this conclusion and added, "there is no basis, theoretical or empirical, for thinking that we are 'running out of time.'"

It should be noted some researchers have argued Americans work longer hours than previously. Harvard economist Juliet Schor (1991) has made the most widely noted argument that Americans are working longer, arguing that the average employed person worked an additional 163 hours more per year in 1987 compared to 1969. Such analyses, however, rest on people's reported hours of work and, as time diary studies show, people overreport how long they work. Most people don't have much idea how long they actually work and overestimation is the common response to this uncertainty (e.g., Robinson & Godbey, 1999). Additionally, such analyses do not consider the total hours of people's lives, only those in the workplace. Americans enter the labor force later and live longer after leaving it than a few decades ago.

Even if we have not achieved a society of leisure, we have gained free time, not only on a daily basis but also as a percentage of our total lives. Free time is increasing in a wide range of countries and the increases of free time positively relate to increased Gross Domestic Product. Time, however, as mentioned previously, has many aspects: sequence, duration, schedule, rhythm, synchronization, and time perspective. As sequences of time use become more complex, synchronization more difficult to achieve, rhythm or pace accelerating, and time perspective one which increasingly values time as a commodity, time seems to become more scarce even as we work a smaller fraction of our life's hours. The dilemma faced is similar to that of a waterflea:

> The wish to live as intensely as possible has subjected humans to the same dilemma as the waterflea, which lives 108 days at 8 degrees Centigrade, but only 26 days at 28 degrees, when its heartbeat is almost four times faster, though in either case its heart beats 15 million times in all. Technology has been a rapid heartbeat, compressing housework, travel, entertainment, squeezing more and more into the allotted span. Nobody expected that it would create the feeling that life moves too fast. (Zeldin, 1994, p. 62)

When people are asked about constraints to leisure in survey research, "lack of time" is often the number one answer given to explain why one hasn't participated in some activity. Such an answer, unfortunately, has a number of meanings, none of which the researcher can be sure. It may mean the individual has little or no control over their paid work, household work, or social obligations. It may mean a scheduling difficulty (synchronization), it may mean the pace of life is so fast they are reluctant to add one more activity, or it may simply mean they aren't interested enough in the activity to do it. When I asked students in an undergraduate class why they hadn't visited a museum of art on the Penn State campus, a popular response was "lack of time." Those same students, when they kept a one-week time diary, showed an average of 45 hours of free time. Perhaps a more realistic answer would have been that weren't very interested in the museum of art.

The range of meanings to a response that one was constrained from doing some leisure activity due to lack of time include the following:

- scheduling conflict (e.g., "I can't do A because it must be done at a time which conflicts with B.").

- perception of too many obligated events within one's daily life to add additional activity.

- perception of a comparatively low cost–benefit ratio from adding the activity and dropping something else.

- perception of being too rushed if the activity were added.

- perception that friends or other potential participants don't have enough time to participate.

- insufficient interest in the activity.

This range of meanings prevents simple "lack of time" responses to be precisely interpreted in ways useful to leisure service professionals or for academic purposes. Unfortunately, respondents are rarely quizzed further about what lack of time means. The failure to undertake such inquiry often means little is known about temporal constraints to leisure. What does it mean when a respondent says that lack of time prevents them from visiting a park more frequently than he or she does? It could mean they would rather watch TV, it could mean they don't have friends whose schedules would allow them to go, it could mean the respondent feels overwhelmed with their daily routine. As a practical matter, however, the researcher doesn't know what it means.

Minimizing Time Constraints

If all time constraints disappeared, the world would descend into chaos. Parks would overflow with people, museums would be jammed, the meaningfulness of much activity that springs directly from its limitedness would disappear. The millionth beer party or softball game would lack meaning. If time constraints were somewhat minimized, however, the world might be a better place. I have simplistically suggested that this might be done by owning less, doing less, and saying "no" more often. While many Americans and others in modern nations are in a position to do this, in general, it appears they don't want to. Americans, in particular, still want to own even bigger cars and houses; do more things; and consume, experience, and achieve more.

There is, however, some evidence to the contrary. With regard to values, U.S. citizens can now be classified into three major groups: Moderns, Traditionals, and Cultural Creatives. Moderns and Traditionals are easily recognized but today there are 50 million Cultural Creatives, providing the potential for a cultural revolution—one already underway (Ray & Anderson, 2000). The Moderns are currently dominant, making the rules, controlling the civil service, the military, the courts, the media, and some multinational corporations. Moderns believe in a technological economy and dismiss other cultures and ways of life as inferior. They accept the commercialized urban–industrial world without looking for alternatives. Growth is considered essential. Traditionals, generally an older segment of the population, tend to believe that patriarchs should again dominate family life; family, church, and community are where you belong; customary freedom to carry arms is essential; and familiar ways of life should be maintained. Angry about the destruction of the world they remember, many are pro environment and anti big business. Traditionals tend to be older, poorer, and less educated than others in the United States. As they die off, they are not being replaced.

The big news in terms of values is that there are now 50 million Cultural Creatives in the United States, and their numbers are growing. According to Ray and Anderson (2000), their values are such that they

- love nature and are deeply concerned about its destruction.

- are strongly aware of the problems of the whole planet and want to see action to curb them, such as limiting economic growth.

- would pay more taxes or higher prices if you knew the money would go to clean up the environment and stop global warming.

- give a lot of importance to developing and maintaining relationships.

- place great importance on helping other people.

- volunteer for one or more good causes.

- care intensely about psychological or spiritual development.

- see spirituality and religion as important, but are concerned about the role of the religious right in politics.

- want more equality for women at work and want more women leaders in business and politics.

- are concerned about violence and the abuse of women and children everywhere on earth.

- want politics and government to emphasize children's education and well-being, the rebuilding of neighborhoods and communities, and creation of an ecologically sustainable future.

- are unhappy with both left and right in politics and want a new way that is not the mushy middle.

- tend to be optimistic about the future and distrust the cynical and pessimistic view offered by the media.

- want to be involved in creating a new and better way of life in our country.

- are concerned about what big corporations are doing in the name of profit: exploiting poor countries, harming the environment, and downsizing.

- have their finances and spending under control and are not concerned about overspending.

- dislike the modern emphasis on success, "making it," and wealth and luxury goods.

- like people and places that are exotic and foreign, and enjoy experiencing and learning about other ways of life.

Cultural Creatives are not defined by particular demographic characteristics—they are accountants and social workers, waitresses and computer programmers, hair stylists and lawyers, chiropractors, truck drivers, photographers, and gardeners. The large majority of them are very mainstream in their religious beliefs. They are no more liberal or conservative than the U.S. mainstream, although they tend to reject left–right labels. Really, their one distinguishing demographic characteristic is that 60% of them are women, and most Cultural Creatives tend to hold values and beliefs that women have traditionally held about issues of caring, family life, children, education, relationships, and responsibility. In their personal lives, they seek authenticity, meaning that they want their actions to be consistent with what they believe and say. They are also intent on finding wholeness, integration, and community. Cultural Creatives are quite clear that they do not want to live in an alienated, disconnected world. Their approach to health is preventive and holistic, though they do not reject modern medicine. In their work, they may try to go beyond earning a living to having "right livelihood" or a vocation.

> In the twenty-first century, a new era is taking hold. The biggest challenges are to preserve and sustain life on the planet and find a new way past the overwhelming spiritual and psychological emptiness of modern life. Though these issues have been building for a century, only now can the Western world bring itself to publicly consider them. The Cultural Creatives are responding to these overwhelming challenges by creating a new culture. (Ray & Anderson, 2000, p. 19)

With new businesses, new management styles, new technologies, new forms of social organization (e.g., leasing products such as carpets and refrigerators, to consumers instead of selling them to make sure they are recycled), and new decision-making techniques (e.g., the precautionary principle), the Cultural Creatives are constructing a new world, largely ignored by the media (Ray & Anderson, 2000).

If time constraints to leisure are going to be minimized, it is likely this segment of society that will do so. For the dominant moderns, time constraints, to both work and leisure, will remain a way of life and a penalty willingly, if grudgingly, paid.

Closing Time

What can be concluded from the previous? Perhaps the most important conclusion is that time as constraint to leisure has multiple meanings. It is both blessing and curse; dialectic in nature. Its interpretation is highly political. Are rushed people who sometimes work long hours slaves to a rationalized economy and right-wing capitalism, or are they greedy individuals who want money and possessions more than tranquility and simplicity? The fact that higher income and education individuals are more likely to report feeling rushed than those with lower ones (Godbey & Graefe, 1993) is also subject to multiple interpretations.

What does seem clear is the distinctions between work and free time have been minimized for many. The industrial separation of fast, long work time and slow, short free time has come apart. Postmodernity has produced a way of life in which time is perceived as the most valuable commodity and efficiency as the most prevalent value. Is it any wonder, then, that the most privileged society that has thus far existed feels time as the primary constraint to leisure, even as the amount of free time increases?

Note

Parts of this chapter were quoted with permission from

Robinson, J. and Godbey, G. (1999). *Time for life: The surprising ways Americans use their time* (Rev. ed.). University Park, PA: Penn State Press.

References

Auden, W. H. (1939). *Selected poems of W. H. Auden.* New York, NY: The Modern Library.

Ausubel, J. and Grubler, A. (1994). *Working less and living longer: Long-term trends in working time and time budgets* (Working paper 94-99). Laxenburg, Austria: International Institute for Applied Systems Analysis.

Bell, D. (1975, September 8). The clock watchers: Americans at work. *Time*, 55.

Burns, L. (1993). Busybodies—Why our time-obsessed society keeps us running in place. New York, NY: Norton.

Children and advertising. (1998, February). *Consumer Reports*, 9.

Cross, G. (1993). *Time and money—The making of consumer culture.* London, England: Routledge.

DeGrazia, S. (1962). *Of time, work, and leisure.* New York, NY: Twentieth Century Fund.

Drucker, P. (1993). *Post-capitalist society.* New York, NY: Harper Business.

Fraisse, P. (1964). *The Psychology of time.* London, England: Eyre and Spottiswoode.

Fraser, J. T. (1987). *Time—The familiar stranger.* Redmond, WA: Microsoft Press.

Gergen, K. (1991). *The saturated self—Dilemmas of identity in contemporary life.* New York, NY: Basic Books.

Gershuny, J. (1992, January/February). Are we running out of time? *Futures*, 1–18.

Godbey, G. and A. Graefe. (1993, April). Rapid growth in rushin' Americans. *American Demographics*, 26–27.

Huizinga, J. (1950). *Homo ludens: A study of the play element in culture.* Boston, MA: Beacon Press.

Johnson, A. and O. Johnson. (1978, September). In search of the affluent society. *Human Nature*, 50–59.

Kanigel, R. (1997). *The one best way: Fredrick Winslow Taylor and the enigma of efficiency.* New York, NY: Viking.

Linder, S. (1969). *The harried leisure class.* New York, NY: Columbia University Press.

Linton, R. (1937). The study of man: An introduction. New York, NY: Appleton.

Meyersohn, R. (1968). Television and the rest of leisure. *Public Opinion Quarterly*, 32, 102–112.

Random House College Dictionary. (Rev. ed). (1988). New York, NY: Random House.

Random House Thesaurus, College Edition. (1989). New York, NY: Random House.

Ray, P. and Anderson, S. (2000). *The cultural creatives*. New York, NY: Harmony Books.

Rifkin, J. (1987). *Time wars—The primary conflict in human history*. New York, NY: Henry Holt.

Robinson, J. and Godbey, G. (1999). *Time for life: The surprising ways Americans use their time* (Rev. ed.). University Park, PA: Penn State Press.

Sahlins, M. (1972). *Stone age economics*. New York, NY: Aldine Atherton.

Scheusch, E. (1972). The time budget interview. In A. Szalai (Ed.), *The use of time*. The Hague, The Netherlands: Mouton.

Schor, J. (1991). *The overworked American*. New York, NY: Basic Books.

Sommers, C. May, (2000). The war against boys. *Atlantic Monthly*, 60.

Stainback, M. and Donato, K. (1998, September). Going to work but never leaving home. *Population Today, 26*(9), 3.

Theodorson, G. and Theodorson, A. (1969). *Modern dictionary of sociology*. New York, NY: Thomas Y. Crowell.

U.S. Census Bureau. (2000). Retreived December 9, 2004 from http://www.census.gov/Press-Release

Van den Broek, A. (1998, August 1). *From specialists to generalists? Despecialization in daily life in the Netherlands, 1975–1995*. International Sociological Association Conference, Montreal, Quebec, Canada.

Walker, K. (1969, October). Homemaking still takes time. *Journal of Home Economics, 61*, 621–624.

Zeldin, T. (1994). *An intimate history of humanity*. New York, NY: Harper Perennial.

Chapter 13

Constraints on Outdoor Recreation

Gordon J. Walker (University of Alberta) and Randy J. Virden (Arizona State University)

Although both constraints research and outdoor recreation research have their origins in the U.S. Outdoor Recreation Resources Review Commission (ORRRC) reports of the early 1960s (Jackson & Scott, 1999), to date there has been relatively little conceptual cross-fertilization between these two areas. Rather, the studies that examined constraints on outdoor recreation tended to be more descriptive than explanatory. Thus, although we do briefly describe some of these studies, this chapter focuses on how constraints research and outdoor recreation research have the potential to contribute conceptually to each other, as well as how outdoor recreation research could contribute to three dimensions of constraints research that need to be addressed. These research challenges, based in part on suggestions for constraints research proposed by Jackson (2000), include the need

1. to investigate intrapersonal and interpersonal constraints and simultaneously adopt a more sociologically informed perspective.

2. to broaden the range of variables related to structural constraints.

3. to investigate processes of leisure constraints negotiation.

First, however, we provide a brief overview of the different types of leisure constraints and introduce the outdoor recreation constraints model that guides this chapter.

According to Crawford and Godbey (1987), it is useful to think of three types of constraints:

1. *intrapersonal* constraints—individual psychological qualities that affect the formation of leisure preferences (e.g., anxiety, perceived lack of skill).

2. *interpersonal* constraints—social factors that affect the formation of leisure preferences (e.g., friends or family members who prefer similar or other activities).

3. *structural* constraints—factors that occur after leisure preferences are formed but before actual leisure participation takes place (e.g., lack of time, lack of money).

Crawford, Jackson, and Godbey (1991) contended these three types of constraints are hierarchical in nature, with intrapersonal constraints being the most proximal and powerful (p. 314). Although we are in general agreement, we believe the more complex model on which this chapter is based may better explain constraints on outdoor recreation specifically and potentially constraints on leisure generally (see **Figure 13.1**, p. 202).

Our rationale for the left side of this model is based in part on Jackson and Scott's (1999) contention that motivations, along with intrapersonal and interpersonal constraints, affect leisure preferences. Because some individually oriented factors also affect leisure preferences either directly or indirectly through motivations and intrapersonal and interpersonal constraints or both, an antecedent microlevel construct is now included. Similarly, because some socioeconomic, sociocultural, and sociostructural factors affect leisure preferences either directly, or indirectly through motivations and intrapersonal and interpersonal constraints or both, an antecedent macrolevel construct is included as well. Furthermore, based on sociological social psychology (Cook, 1995; House, 1995), we hold that these two constructs act in a reciprocal manner. In addition, we believe both microlevel and macrolevel factors affect setting affordances—that is, "social and physical environmental conditions that are conducive to leisure behavior" (Mannell & Kleiber, 1997, p. 345). Finally, underlying the entire model is the recognition that outdoor recreation involves an interaction with the environment. Consequently, one's perception of both affordances and constraints is influenced, and tempered, by personal experience.

Our rationale for the right side of the model is based on Jackson and Scott's (1999) contention that both interpersonal and structural constraints intervene between leisure preferences and actual participation. However, because the decision to participate is a distinct act that occurs between leisure preferences and actual leisure participation, this intervening variable has been added. Consequently, constraint negotiation (i.e., how people try to ameliorate or alleviate the effects of constraints) is now seen as a two-stage process, which initially takes place as part of the decision-making process (thus mitigating intrapersonal and interpersonal constraints), and then takes place once again after structural constraints come into play (thus mitigating interpersonal and structural constraints). Additionally, constraint negotiation is affected by microlevel factors and, in a reciprocal manner, setting affordances. Furthermore, setting affordances affect not only leisure preferences but also the decision process and most directly actual participation. Finally, after actual participation occurs, does not occur, or occurs to a lesser degree or in a different way, the recreationist evaluates his or her experience. This feedback, in turn, affects his or her perceptions of the intrapersonal, interpersonal, and structural constraints he or she has just encountered, the success or failure of the constraint negotiation strategies he or she has just employed, and what the setting may afford the next time he or she participates. In addition, this feedback also affects the recreationist's original motivations for participating as well as some of the microlevel factors (e.g., his or her experience use history) antecedent to the aforementioned.

Based on the model described, we begin our discussion by describing some of the key variables that affect outdoor recreation preferences. We then review the various structural constraints found to affect outdoor recreation participation before we identify four new structural constraint categories. Finally, we examine how constraints on outdoor recreation may be negotiated, before concluding with a brief section on implications for management and for future research.

Outdoor Recreation Preferences

Motivations, Preferences, and Constraints

As shown in Figure 13.1, microlevel and macrolevel factors, along with intrapersonal constraints, interpersonal constraints, and motivations have a cumulative effect on leisure preferences. While in no way diminishing the importance of these two types of constraints for leisure preferences, in this section we attend to the role motivations may play, because doing so could help to demonstrate how outdoor recreation research might contribute to constraints research. In the remainder of this section, we focus on the role certain microlevel and macrolevel factors may play, in response to Jackson's (2000) recommendation for more sociologically informed research.

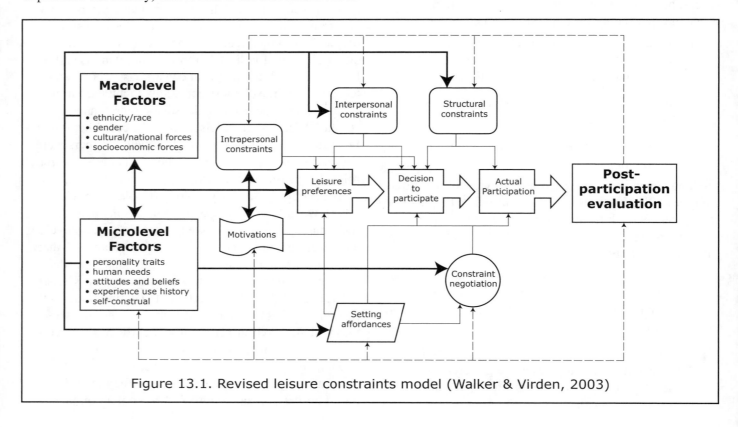

Figure 13.1. Revised leisure constraints model (Walker & Virden, 2003)

Motivations have often been characterized as emerging from human need theory or as an interaction between needs and the environment (Csikszentmihalyi, 1975; Maslow, 1964). Leisure motivations are diverse, as is the range of needs identified by need theorists (Lawler, 1973; Lewin, 1935; Ryan, Sheldon, Kasser & Deci, 1996; White, 1959). Unfortunately, an in-depth discussion of leisure motivations is beyond the scope of this chapter, and therefore readers are encouraged to pursue this topic elsewhere (e.g., Iso-Ahola, 1999; Mannell & Kleiber, 1997). Having stated this, however, it should be noted that over the past 30 years Driver and his colleagues spent considerable effort examining outdoor recreationists' motivations, culminating in the development of the Recreation Experience Preference (REP) scales. According to Manfredo, Driver, and Tarrant (1996):

> The REP scales are linked, theoretically, to the experiential approach and are intended to measure the types of goal states desired by recreationists. They can be usefully applied when attempting to determine motivations for or the psychological outcomes desired from leisure. In this regard, the scales have been used to determine ...activity-specific motivations (i.e., why people engage in a particular activity). (pp. 204, 207)

Based on the last statement in this passage, it would appear the REP scales could provide great insight into how motivations affect outdoor recreation preferences, particularly when the comprehensiveness of this inventory is taken into account. (The REP consists of 19 domains, with some of these domains being further divided into two to seven subdomains.) Moreover, because motivations may "balance out" the effect intrapersonal and interpersonal constraints have on leisure preferences (Jackson, Crawford & Godbey, 1993), greater understanding of exactly how this process occurs could result. However, because motivations also influence a person's leisure preferences in a certain direction, they may simultaneously limit or constrain them in other directions. Thus, the effect motivations may have on leisure preferences may be much more complicated than originally thought. Those who wish to begin to address this complexity may want to first peruse the extensive literature that already exists on outdoor recreation motivations.

In contrast with the amount of research conducted on outdoor recreation motivations, and despite the early interest in the relationship between outdoor recreation and the microlevel factor of personality traits (e.g., Driver & Knopf, 1977), very few studies have been conducted in this area recently. In part this may be because leisure research, in general, has not examined the relationship between personality traits and leisure preferences or participation. For example, Mannell and Kleiber (1997) noted, "in recent years the study of personality has been able to reduce the vast array of personality characteristics to five fundamental factors: extroversion, agreeableness, conscientiousness, neuroticism, and openness to experience" (p. 156); yet, when they go on to describe how each of the "Big Five" may affect leisure, Mannell and Kleiber are often forced to make suppositions and speculations concerning these potential relationships, rather than draw on empirical evidence from existing research.

There are, however, some exceptions. In a study of sensation seeking (a facet of extroversion), Freixanet (1991) assessed the personalities of alpinists, mountaineering-related sportsmen (i.e., climbers and skiers), nonmountain risk sportsmen (e.g., scuba divers, parachutists), and individuals who did not do any risk activities (i.e., a control group). Using seven personality measures, including the multidimensional Sensation Seeking Scale (SSS; Zuckerman, Eysenck & Eysenck, 1978) and the Eysenck Personality Questionnaire (EPQ; Eysenck & Eysenck, 1975), Freixanet found all three risk recreation groups differed significantly from the control group in terms of the Thrill and Sensation and Emotional Stability dimensions of the SSS, the overall SSS, and the Extraversion dimension of the EPQ. In addition, the mountain-related sportsmen also scored significantly higher than the nonmountain risk sportsmen on the Thrill and Sensation and Emotional Stability dimensions of the SSS as well as the overall SSS. These findings suggest, at least for Spanish males, a relationship between extroversion and sensation seeking and participation in some outdoor recreation activities.

Research also suggests absorption, "defined as a characteristic of the individual that involves an openness to experience emotional and cognitive alterations across a variety of situations" (Roche & McConkey, 1990, p. 92), may be linked to the desire to engage in outdoor recreation. Brown and Katcher (1997) found, for example, absorption was significantly correlated with a Nature Attachment Index composed of items, which included "spending time in parks, feeling emotions while in nature, preferences for living around trees, gardens, and open spaces, and preferring to take vacations by the sea or mountains" (p. 126). These findings imply that there is a relationship between openness to experience and absorption and preferences for, and participation in, outdoor recreation activities. Taken together with Freixanet's (1991) findings, this suggests that the microlevel factor of personality traits could have a positive effect on certain leisure preferences for some people while having a negative effect on certain leisure preferences for others.

The development of outdoor recreation preferences can also be affected by another microlevel factor—an individual's attitudes toward the activity and the natural environment in which it takes place. Bixler and Floyd (1997) concurred, noting, "the perception of the physical environment in which a specific activity takes place plays a role in preference for that activity. If the environment is negatively perceived, activities that occur within it may also be avoided" (p. 445; see also Coble, Selin & Erickson, 2003). Bixler and Floyd used three variables to represent negative reactions to natural environments:

1. fear expectancy (e.g., getting lost, seeing a snake).

2. disgust sensitivity, ranging from mild (e.g., getting itchy from bug bites) to strong (e.g., accidentally stepping in animal scat).

3. comfort range, subdivided into indoor comforts (e.g., access to hot water) and outdoor comforts (e.g., having a sleeping bag).

A series of regression analyses using these independent variables found preference for participation in wildland activities (e.g., hiking or backpacking in the woods, canoeing or boating on lakes) was negatively associated with strong disgust, indoor comforts, and fear expectancy, while preference for participation in consumptive wildland activities (e.g., hunting, fishing) was negatively associated only with strong disgust. These findings led Bixler and Floyd to state, "whereas travel distance and economic barriers may limit access to wildlands for some, negative perceptions of wildland environments also lower the appeal of a wide range of [outdoor recreation] activities" (p. 464).

Similarly, Wright and Goodale (1991) found attitudes toward hunting were a significant predictor of interest and/or participation in this activity, and as a result inclusion of this variable could help segment constraint categories. Ajzen and Driver (1991, 1992) also found attitude toward a behavior, along with subjective norm and perceived behavioral control (i.e., the theory of planned behavior or TPB; Ajzen, 1987) were often significant predictors of the intention to participate in a variety of outdoor recreation activities, including spending time at the beach, jogging or running, mountain climbing, boating, and biking. The role of the latter two variables is particularly noteworthy, since both appear to be closely associated with constraint theory (Mannell & Kleiber, 1997), with subjective norm referring to "the perceived social pressure to perform or not to perform the behavior" (Ajzen & Driver, 1992, p. 208) and perceived behavioral control referring to "the perceived ease or difficulty of performing the behavior...assumed to re-

flect past experience as well as anticipated impediments and obstacles" (Ajzen & Driver, 1992, p. 208). Thus, it would appear attitudes and perceived behavioral control could both be considered microlevel intrapersonal factors that affect outdoor recreation preferences, while subjective norms may be seen more as an interpersonal, rather than an intrapersonal, constraint.

In part the theory of planned behavior's popularity may be due to its parsimonious nature, although it should be noted Ajzen (1991) stated additional predictors should be examined "if it can be shown that they capture a significant proportion of the variance in intention... after the theory's current variables have been taken into account" (p. 199). Two such variables found to increase the TPB's predictive ability are motivation and previous experience. Perugini and Bagozzi (2001) found motivations (or what they prefer to call "desires") affected intention to diet and to exercise. Bozionelos and Bennett (1999) found past exercise behavior was the most predictive variable for intention to exercise in the future, and Fekuda and Kraft (2001) found past condom experience was a significant predictor of intention to use condoms in the future. Based on these findings, we now discuss how childhood socialization and recreation specialization, two aspects of the microlevel factor of experience use history, may affect outdoor recreation preferences.

Leisure socialization has been defined as a process by which basic leisure knowledge, attitudes, values, skills, and motivations are learned and internalized (Iso-Ahola, 1980). Iso-Ahola's model of leisure socialization identifies three major influences:

1. social and cultural forces.

2. social agents (e.g., parents, relatives, peers).

3. one's repertoire of individual experiences.

During the 1970s a considerable body of leisure research examined the influence childhood/adolescence leisure experience (and key social agents) had on adult leisure participation (Kelly, 1974, 1977; Sofranko & Nolan, 1972; Yoesting & Burkhead, 1973). These studies suggested up to 50% of adult leisure activities are learned through childhood and adolescent experiences, while the remaining 50% are learned during adulthood.

The type and amount of individual experience has also been an area of interest in outdoor recreation research. Schreyer and Lime (1984) introduced the concept of experience use history (EUH) as a means of exploring the relationships between internal states (e.g., attitudes, motivations, preferences) and recreation behavior. The authors' underlying hypothesis, based on cognitive theory and how mental schemas develop over time (Neisser, 1976), was that different amounts and types of past experience (i.e., EUH categories) serve as indicators for how recreationists cognitively structure information and the types of motivations, attitudes, and preferences they exhibit.

Another area of outdoor recreation research that recognized the importance of both past experience and leisure socialization is Bryan's (1977, 1979) concept of recreation specialization. (Constraints research also recognized the potential value of Bryan's concept, albeit not to the same degree; cf. Crawford et al., 1991.) *Recreation specialization* is defined as a continuum of behavior, ranging from novices at one end to specialists at the other end. Bryan argued where an individual may be placed along a continuum is a reflection of his or her experience, skill, equipment usage, and value orientation. He suggested a recreationist evolves into a more specialized leisure subculture through personal experience in a recreation activity.

Recreation specialization has also been empirically and conceptually linked to a variety of behavioral variables, including motivation, conflict perception, and physical setting and management preferences. For example, research on the effect recreation specialization has on motivation includes studies by Chipman and Helfrich (1988), Graefe and Kauffman (1987), and Wilde and Ditton (1994). Similarly, Wellman, Roggenbuck, and Smith (1982) found highly specialized recreationists were more sensitive to disruptive behavior, and that this behavior had a greater negative impact on the recreation experience of highly specialized canoeists. Virden and Schreyer (1988) found recreation specialization was an indicator of environmental preference, such that highly specialized backcountry hikers were less likely to prefer intensive management and more likely to prefer rugged terrain and opportunities for solitude.

In summary, the research suggests a recreationist's experience use history plays an important role in forming his or her predisposition to certain leisure attitudes, motivations, preferences, and ultimately participation. Because a certain predisposition leads a person toward preferred states, settings, and/or activities, it also limits or constrains other states, settings, and/or activities. As noted, an adult who does not have a strong use history, or who has not been socialized into a subculture that values wildland experiences and places, may be constrained by the social and cultural forces that shape his or her life. And, finally, some constraints are more likely to be associated with a novice or a less experienced recreationist, such as lack of information, lack of companions, lack of equipment, or lack of skills and abilities.

Moreover, a microlevel factor, such as experience use history, not only affects leisure preferences, but also can be affected by a macrolevel factor, such as subculture. In the remainder of this section, therefore, we examine other examples of this phenomenon, beginning with a brief discussion of how the macrolevel factors of ethnicity/race and gender may affect a person's attitudes toward the natural environment and, consequently, his or her outdoor recreation preferences. (Readers interested in this topic are referred to other authors in this text, including Shaw & Henderson, chapter 2, on gender; Shinew & Floyd, chapter 3, on race; Stodolska, chapter 4, on ethnicity and immigration; and Bialeschki, chapter 18, on women and outdoor recreation). We then move on to a more in-depth discussion of how the macrolevel factor of culture, through the microlevel factor of self-construal, may affect an individual's motivations and, subsequently, his or her outdoor preferences, as well as how the macrolevel factor of nationalism (and, possibly, an associated variable, romanticism) may affect preferences for outdoor recreation, through the microlevel factor of self-identity.

Race, Gender, Culture, and Nationalism

The development of outdoor recreation preferences can be affected by a person's ethnicity/race, gender, or both through his or her attitudes toward both the activity and the natural environment in which it takes place. For example, Floyd, Outley, Bixler, and Hammitt (1995) examined 1,200 Black and White, male and female, middle and high school students and found higher preference for wildland environments was associated with higher preference for wildland activities. Whites rated wildland activities higher than Blacks, and boys rated wildland activities higher than girls. (There were no significant interaction effects.) In a second analysis of covariance, Floyd et al. found a significant race by gender interaction effect, with Black female students expressing greater preference for nonwildland social activities. The authors also found higher scores on fear expectancy and desire for urban environments were positively related to nonwildland social activity preference.

In one of the few other studies that looked at how ethnicity/race and gender affect attitudes toward the natural environment, Virden and Walker (1999) found White university students considered a forest environment to be more pleasing and safe than Black students, who viewed forests as more annoying and threatening. White students also considered forests to be less threatening than Hispanic respondents. Virden and Walker believe that these results may be due to the following:

1. Blacks, compared with Whites, being more apprehensive about the possibility of encounters with undesirable or dangerous animals.

2. Blacks and Hispanics, compared with Whites, being more apprehensive about the possibility of unpleasant encounters with other humans.

In regard to the first proposition, Taylor (1989) contended one reason Blacks may be fearful of forest environments is because African American mythology often depicts animals in exaggerated forms (e.g., giant elephants). A study conducted by Wallace and Witter (1992) with Black focus group participants also supports this proposition, as many of the group members stated their lack of interest in natural environments was a consequence of their anxiety about the possibility of encountering bears, snakes, and other animals. Potentially, this fear of wildlife may be less important for Hispanic individuals because, although their worldview considers humans to be part of nature (Gramann, 1996), it also accepts that humans have limited control over nature (Simcox, 1993).

At the same time, however, greater uneasiness does exist for both Hispanics and Blacks, although it may have more to do with the threat of other people rather than other species (i.e., the second proposition). Taylor (1989), for example, described numerous pre–World War II cases of Blacks and Mexican Americans being attacked because they visited "White" outdoor recreation areas. In an *Outside* magazine article about his experience as a black outdoorsman, Eddy Harris offers one explanation of Blacks' relationship to the outdoors:

> The point, of course, is that historically bad things have happened to black people in the outdoors. If we choose to conjure them up, our associations with the woods can easily run in the direction of bloodhounds, swinging hemp ropes, and cracker Wizards in Klan bedsheets. And those associations, I think, play a large though largely unspoken role in this whole question. (Harris, 1997, p. 177)

In other words, the freedom associated with wildland forest environments may also imply the lack of a social structure where the human inhabitants (most commonly White) of these forest environments are not under society's norms or control (i.e., the absence of societal restraint). It is perhaps not surprising, therefore, to note both Blacks and Hispanics find forest environments to be more threatening than do Whites (see also Blahna & Black, 1993).

Virden and Walker (1999) also found female students felt a forest environment was more threatening than did their male counterparts. The sense of feeling less safe in a forest environment could be derived from either fear of natural threats (e.g., wild animals, remoteness, rivers, weather, the elements, or the unknown), or fear of potential physical violence. Women, for example, report significantly more fear of crime than men (Riger & Gordon, 1981), and at least in terms of urban public spaces, this fear is often a factor in what discretionary activities women chose to do and how they chose to do them (Gordon, Riger, LeBailly & Heath, 1981; see also Bialeschki, this volume). Whyte and Shaw (1994) found the fear of violence was more salient in leisure settings where women participated in solitary activities, such as walking or running alone, as compared to participating in similar activities with others (either men or women). Furthermore, Henderson (1996) contended western European folklore (e.g., Goldilocks, Little Red Riding Hood) has traditionally transmitted negative messages about the danger girls may encounter in natural settings. Henderson also stated these myths, in conjunction with the rising violence against women, serve to "mitigate the possible positive values that might be associated with the outdoors" (p. 156). Thus, it appears, at least in the case of forest and wildland environments, it is White males who have the most positive attitudes toward such settings, and as a consequence they are also the group members most likely to prefer outdoor recreation activities.

In addition to ethnicity/race and gender, the macrolevel factor of culture may also affect outdoor recreation preferences (see Chick & Dong, this volume). Simcox (1993), for example, describes how Western, Eastern, Hispanic, and Latin American cultures' leisure preferences, behaviors, and environmental orientations vary due to differences in

1. worldview (i.e., how a culture views the relationship between humans and nature).

2. time orientation (i.e., if a culture emphasizes the past, present, or future, or has a linear vs. cyclical perspective).

3. activity orientation (i.e., doing, being, or being-in-becoming; Kluckhohn & Strodtbeck, 1961).

4. the primary type of relationship between self and others (i.e., individualism or collectivism).

Based on these four characteristics, Simcox believes people from western cultures are likely to exhibit

> highly individual pursuit of leisure activities; a need for a wide range of activities; an emphasis on personal testing and dominance over nature; a focus on future activities; and a tendency toward initiative and making this happen. (p. 276)

In comparison, people from eastern cultures are more apt to have

> a strong social orientation toward leisure with a deemphasis on individual leisure pursuits; a desire for tranquil and contemplative experience; a focus on tradition; an emphasis on aesthetics, and the practice of a harmonic relationship with nature. (p. 277)

People from Hispanic and Latin American cultures will have

> a social orientation toward leisure with the family as the dominant social unit; a focus on relaxation, tranquility, and a celebration of life, concentration on present events rather than past experiences or an uncertain future; and an environmental orientation that reinforces nature appreciation even though humans have little ability to control the forces of nature. (p. 277)

Simcox admits these cultural patterns are extremely broad; however, his framework does provide a starting point for understanding the relationship between a culture's characteristics and an individual's attitudes, preferences, and behaviors, including his or her attitudes toward, preferences for, and behaviors involving nature, leisure, and nature-based leisure.

One of Simcox's (1993) cultural characteristics may be particularly important when trying to understand outdoor recreation preferences: What is the primary type of relationship between self and others—what Markus and Kitayama (1991) have called "self-construal"? According to Markus and Kitayama, individuals in or from Western Europe and North America are more likely to have "independent" self-construals, while individuals in or from Asia, Africa, Latin America, and Southern Europe are more likely to hold "interdependent" self-construals. Markus and Kitayama also contended independent selves value being unique, expressing themselves, and promoting their own goals, while interdependent selves value belonging, fitting in, and promoting others' goals. It must be noted, however, "interdependent selves do not attend to the needs, desires, and goals of *all* others. Attention to others is not indiscriminate; it is highly selective and will be most characteristic of relationships with 'in-group' members" (Markus & Kitayama, p. 229). In addition, Markus and Kitayama also believe the type of self-construal an individual holds affects his or her thoughts, feelings, and motivations.

Walker, Deng, and Dieser (2001) examined how Chinese and Euro-North Americans' outdoor recreation motivations differed due to culture, and more importantly due to the mediating variable of self-construal. Results of their study indicated

1. culture does affect both types of self-construal.

2. culture does affect four outdoor recreation motivations directly, although this relationship is usually, but not always, mediated by self-construal.

3. culture does affect four other recreation motivations indirectly, either through the interdependent self-construal or through both types of self-construal.

4. with Chinese respondents, acculturation did affect one recreation motivation directly and, through the independent self-construal, two other motivations indirectly.

Based on these findings, therefore, we would also anticipate that differences in self-construal would affect the development of a person's outdoor recreation preferences, through his or her motivations.

It is also worth noting the microlevel factor of self-construal may affect the development of leisure preferences not only through motivations, but also through other processes. For example, as stated earlier, an individual's attitudes have been found to be a predictor of his or her leisure preferences (Wright & Goodale, 1991) along with the variables of subjective norm and perceived behavioral control (e.g., Ajzen & Driver, 1991, 1992). Recent research suggests the significance of these variables differs across cultures, likely due to differences in self-construal. For example, a study by Abrams, Ando, and Hinkle (1998) suggested subjective norms associated with certain relationships (e.g., one's partner, family members) were more influential on Japanese workers' intentions to leave a company than on British workers' intentions. Abrams et al. believe this finding is due to Japanese (and other Asians) having interdependent self-construals while most Western Europeans (and North Americans) have independent self-construals. Thus, it would seem worthwhile to include the variable of self-construal when examining the effect of social norms (or using theories, such as the theory of planned behavior, which include this variable), or when examining culture, intrapersonal constraints (and possibly interpersonal constraints), and leisure preferences.

Additionally, the macrolevel factor of nationalism (and possibly an associated variable, romanticism) could affect the microlevel factor of self-identity, and as a consequence, outdoor recreation preferences. According to Nash (2001), nationalism can be traced back to the emergence of national states in Europe and the rise of the Industrial Revolution, with the Romantic Movement occurring around the same time. Environmental historians such as Nash and others (e.g., Runte, 1997) argued

19th century Americans combined both romantic and nationalistic feelings to explain American concern for, and protection of, natural resources, forests, and parks. Runte contended:

> Unlike the Old World, the new nation lacked an established past, particularly as expressed in art, architecture, and literature. In the romantic tradition nationalists looked to scenery as one form of compensation....America's incentive for the national park idea lay in the persistence of a painfully felt desire for time-honored traditions in the United States. (p. 7)

Nash concurred, stating:

> The nation's short history, weak traditions, and minor literary and artistic achievements seemed negligible compared to those in Europe. But at least in one respect Americans sensed that their country was different: wilderness had no counterpart in the Old World. (p. 67)

Nash (2001) and Runte (1997) also pointed out these romantic and nationalistic tendencies helped to create a set of American frontier cultural and historical heroes and folklore (e.g., Daniel Boone, Davy Crockett), while American artists (e.g., Thomas Cole, Thomas Moran) and writers (e.g., James Fennimore Cooper, Henry David Thoreau, John Muir) assigned certain types of values and meanings (e.g., awe, the sublime, primitivism) to natural settings. Potentially, because these traditions, values, and meanings are most relevant for Euro-Americans' self-identity and much less relevant for non-Euro-Americans' self-identity, preferences for outdoor recreation also differ between these two groups.

It should be noted the relationship between nationalism and outdoor recreation preference, through the microlevel factor of self-identity, is not unique to the United States. Benidickson (1997), for example, contended the canoeing vacation has often been seen as being a "typically Canadian" holiday. Additional support for this relationship can also be found in a famous, albeit somewhat facetious, statement made by populist historian Pierre Burton, who said, "a Canadian is someone who knows how to make love in a canoe" (Brown, 1973, p. 3).

But as Cook (1995) and others (e.g., House, 1995) recognized, the relationship between macrolevel and microlevel factors is reciprocal. In the case of canoeing, for example, it is not surprising to find this outdoor activity also played an important role in helping to define not only what Canada is, but also how Canadians feel about their country. Two specific passages from Benidickson's (1997) book illustrate this proposition, the first being from an early 20th century magazine called *Rod and Gun*:

> There is a secret influence at work in the wild places of the North that seems to cast a spell over the men who have once been in them. One can never forget the lakes of such wonderful beauty, the rivers, peaceful or turbulent, and the quiet portage paths, or the mighty forest of real trees. It is really getting to know Canada, to go where these things are. After having made camps along the water routes, one feels a proud sense of ownership of that part of the country, which must develop into a deeper sense of patriotism in regard to the whole land. (Bocking, 1915, p. 580)

The second example comes from a famous 1944 essay written by Canada's future prime minister Pierre Elliott Trudeau, which describes his love of canoeing and concludes with the following statement: "I know a man whose school could never teach him patriotism, but who acquired that virtue when he felt in his bones the vastness of his land, and the greatness of those who found it" (Bendickson, 1997, p. 244).

In addition, it is not only the activity that affects one's sense of nationalism, but where the activity takes place. For example, a recent survey found that over 70% of respondents identified national parks as icons of national identity (Parks Canada Agency, 2000), while 76% of people responding to another poll reported that nature strongly strengthened their attachment to Canada (the highest rated factor, and over twice the percentage for bilingualism; "Bilingualism Bottoms Out," 2001, A4).

Thus, it appears not only can nationalism affect outdoor recreation preferences through self-identity, but also participation in outdoor recreation can affect a person's sense of national identity and, further, if this happens with a large portion of the population, this microlevel factor could, in turn, affect the macrolevel factor of nationalism.

Structural Constraints on Outdoor Recreation

Expanding the Range of Constraints on Outdoor Recreation

To establish an empirical and summative base of the common constraints that emerged from outdoor recreation research, constraints data from four relatively recent studies are presented in **Table 13.1**. The data from all four studies (presented alphabetically) were based on large provincial or statewide samples from the general public.

The Alberta study was conducted by mail in May and June of 2000 and represented data from 2,719 households (Alberta Community Development, 2000). The Arizona Study was initially collected in the fall of 1991 from a statewide telephone sampling 1,236 households. A total of 683 of those respondents completed a subsequent mail survey (Virden & Yoshioka, 1992). The Florida study consisted of 3,610 Florida residents and was conducted via telephone in the spring of 2001 (Holland, Pennington-Gray & Thapa, 2001). The final study was conducted in 1998 and included responses about outdoor recreation participation and constraints of 3,000 Texas residents (Scott & Kim, 1998). All four studies utilized random sampling techniques. Also, the scales in each study were different, so for comparison purposes the individual constraint items were assigned a high, medium, or low value based on that item's mean score relative to the other items within that study. A value of high indicates the constraint item was in the strongest group of constraints relative to that study.

The summary data indicate outdoor recreation is similar to other leisure activities, in that time or "busy with other activities" is the strongest constraint (all four exhibited high ratings). It should be noted time may have a more constraining impact on outdoor recreation and tourism because of the travel requirements associated with visiting natural resource locations. Consequently, much outdoor recreation requires larger commitments of time than local-based or at home leisure pursuits. While these four studies did not use exactly the same constraint items, the table data suggest other potentially strong (high) outdoor recreation constraints include the following:

- outdoor recreation areas are too far away (3).

- areas that are too crowded (3).

- lack of information (2).

Table 13.1. Findings from four outdoor recreation structural constraint studies

Type of Constraint	Alberta (1998)	Arizona (1992)	Florida (2001)	Texas (1998)
Too busy with other activities, work, or leisure	High	High	High	High
Lack of time	---	High	High	High
Lack of information about parks or outdoor recreation areas	---	---	High	High
Too busy with family responsibilities	High	---	---	High
Family members in poor health	---	---	---	High
Companions prefer other things	---	---	High	---
Parks and outdoor recreation areas are too far away	Medium	High	High	High
Areas are too crowded	High	High	High	Medium
Don't have the money; too expensive to visit	High	High	Medium	Medium
Don't know where parks are	Medium	High	---	Medium
Poorly maintained areas/facilities	Medium	Medium	---	Medium
Don't have the equipment	---	Medium	Medium	---
Fear of crime	---	---	Medium	---
The areas are unsafe	---	Medium	---	---
Weather conditions	---	Low	Medium	High
Admission fees too high	High	---	---	Low
Camping fees too high	---	---	---	Low
Don't have companions or people to go with	---	Medium	Low	Low
I'm in poor health or physically unable	Low	Low	Medium	---
Don't have transportation	Low	Low	Low	Low
Don't have the skills or physical abilities	Low	Low	Low	---
Lack of interest in outdoor recreation activities	---	---	Low	Low
Don't approve of others behaviors or activities	---	---	---	Low
Afraid of getting hurt or being attacked	---	---	---	Low
Lack of family interests	---	---	Low	---

- too expensive (2).

- family commitments (2).

- family members in poor health (1).

- companions prefer other things (1).

The constraints that demonstrated medium or moderate strength include the following: don't know where the parks are, poorly maintained areas and facilities, don't have the equipment, fear of crime, areas are unsafe, weather conditions, and admission fees are too high. Lack of transportation and lack of skills were consistently rated low.

In general, these findings suggest outdoor recreation may be more influenced by time availability, trip costs, and geographic accessibility than other types of nonoutdoor recreation activities (although these effects may differ depending on the type of outdoor activity; see Jackson, 1994). Moreover, the limited amount of research to date on outdoor recreation constraints is, in itself, somewhat of a constraint on making many pronouncements, because there may be other structural constraints on outdoor recreation participation that have not yet been examined. In the next sections, therefore, we propose four new categories:

1. natural environment structural constraints.

2. social environment structural constraints.

3. territorial structural constraints.

4. institutional structural constraints.

Natural Environment Structural Constraints

The finding that weather was one of the structural constraints affecting people's probable participation in nature-based tourism/outdoor recreation points to the importance the environment can have as a limiting factor on outdoor recreation. Mitchell (1983), for example, noted accurate weather predictions are of critical importance in mountaineering, with climbers scanning newspapers, calling the Weather Bureau, and watching televised weather reports (p. 10). Weather can also cause the occurrence of other environmental constraints—or the possibility thereof, which can be just as limiting—including avalanches, flash floods, unnavigable or uncrossable rivers, and the lack/excess of snow. And weather, of course, is also a function of the seasons, with many outdoor-recreation activities being impossible to engage in at certain times of the year in certain places (Hinch & Jackson, 2000).

The environmental setting (natural and managerial) can present a variety of other related constraints. For example, topography and landscapes can present barriers related to mountains, hills, trails (or lack of trails), the presence or absence of water features, the type or size of water bodies, forested settings, and desert environments. Access to these landscapes may also be limited by other non-weather-related environmental constraints, including the lack of accurate maps or the potential interaction with dangerous animals (e.g., bears, wolves). In addition, because the same outdoor activity (e.g., backpacking) can take place in two completely different types of natural areas (e.g., deserts vs. mountains), a recreationist who feels completely comfortable in one may feel totally unprepared (and consequently constrained) in the other. It is important to recognize, however, that while the environment may present setting features perceived as being a constraint to one person (e.g., rugged terrain or the presence of wildlife), the very same setting features could be perceived as being an affordance to another (Virden & Schreyer, 1988). In sum, a variety of structural constraints associated with the natural environment may affect participation in outdoor recreation.

Social Environment Structural Constraints

If structural constraints are defined as those factors that intervene between leisure preference and participation (Crawford & Godbey, 1987), conditions in the social environment, such as crowding, activity style, and perceived conflict may also constrain outdoor recreation participation and enjoyment. Crowding is one area of outdoor recreation research that received considerable attention (Manning, 1999). Crowding is perhaps more commonly associated with the quality of the on-site experience, rather than influencing the choice to participate. However, the fear or dislike of crowding can influence a person's decision to either participate in an activity or to visit a particular site. Schreyer (1986) identified crowding as one of the "subtle" constraints that can impact outdoor recreation participation. Much of the crowding literature examines the influence of crowding on experience satisfaction with the common assumption being that higher levels of crowding lead to lower quality experiences.

Crowding can be viewed as one type of specialized recreation conflict, as well as a constraint on leisure. Jacob and Schreyer (1980) defined conflict as goal interference attributed to another person or group. Common examples of recreation conflicts would include seeing too many people, hearing loud music, the presence of motorized vehicles, fear of other people, and not being able to obtain a permit to enter a desired recreation area. All of these examples could also be viewed as structural constraints on the recreation experience. And while they may not prevent participation, they can degrade or decrease the quality of the recreation engagement.

According to Jacob and Schreyer (1980), conflicts can originate from differences in recreation activity styles, environmental relations, mode of experience, and lifestyle tolerance. For example, activity style refers to a specific orientation to the meaning and expression of a leisure activity. Recreation vehicle (RV) camping and backcountry camping represent two distinct activity styles whose orientations or values could potentially clash. Perhaps more classic is the conflict between motorized and nonmotorized activity styles that can often lead to on-site conflict (especially for nonmotorized recreationists). A bad experience attributed to such a conflict occurrence can feed back into one's experience use history, and, therefore affect the next round of decision making for these recreationists. Specifically, the decision to recreate will then be influenced in a negative way (i.e., an intrapersonal constraint) by the desire to avoid conflict with an on-site person or group who might obstruct enjoyment, just as the actual recreation engagement can be influenced by actual contact with a conflicting person or group. Consequently, an individual's beliefs or perception of the probability of on-site structural constraints can have an impact on their decision to participate and ultimately, through the feedback loop, will become an intrapersonal constraint on future activity participation or in visiting certain recreation settings.

This feedback loop has been recognized by previous constraint researchers and is important in understanding the dynamic nature of the revised leisure constraints model presented in this chapter (Crawford et al., 1991). Experiencing structural constraints prior to and during the recreation engagement contributes to the development of one's experience use history and internal schema (Neisser, 1976). This also raises the issue of specialized or experienced recreationists possessing greater skill to take advantage of affordances and to negotiate constraints in ways that lead to more satisfying recreation experiences (Bryan, 1977). Over time, these microlevel factors complete the feedback cycle by influencing not only the perception of constraints, but also the tools and features in the setting that can be used to overcome them. (See Wade, Kleiber & Loucks-Atkinson, this volume, for more on affordances.)

Territorial Structural Constraints

Outdoor recreation differs from other forms of recreation because of its dependence on access to specific types of places (i.e., "natural" settings). But while the process of determining who gets access to outdoor recreation areas is often assumed to be value-free, there may, in fact, be aspects of "territoriality" (Sack, 1986) involved in this planning and management process. Territoriality entails "setting places aside and enforcing degrees of access...[whereby] individuals and groups have removed some activities and people and places and included others" (Sack, p. 26). In regard to outdoor recreation, for example, Lee (1972) reported that an Asian man "said of a large city park 'I don't go to that park—that's a white man's park'" (cited in West, 1993, p. 111).

But in addition to ethnicity/race being a basis for limiting access (see Floyd & Shinew, this volume), social class may also be a factor in whose access is constrained, and just as importantly who determines who will have access to a natural setting. In the case of designated wilderness, for example, Walker and Kiecolt (1995) argued this type of natural setting has been territorialized by members of what Wright (1978) referred to as the semi-autonomous class. Unlike proletarians, semi-autonomous employees "control *how* they do their work and have at least some control over *what* they produce" (Wright 1978, p. 81). Thus, highly educated craft and professional–technical wage earners, such as research scientists and university professors, are members of this group. This description, Walker and Kiecolt contended, is also an accurate description of both past wilderness users, who sought wilderness experiences as a means of emulating the upper classes while distancing themselves from the proletariat, and present wilderness users, who seek the autonomy they lack in their workday world (i.e., relative deprivation) as well as the desire to do so with similar others (e.g., Knopf, 1987). Members of the semi-autonomous class were ideally suited to take control of wilderness because of their ability to impose specific meanings on landscapes (e.g., Greider & Garkovich, 1994), a process which continues to this day through their participation in organizations such as the Sierra Club and the Wilderness Society and their active role in the development and implementation of government regulations (Wildavsky, 1979). In summary, wilderness and other natural areas are often contested spaces and constraints research must take into account how this can act as a structural barrier to leisure participation. (See also Bialeschki, this volume, on this topic in terms of women's outdoor recreation participation.)

Institutional Structural Constraints

In regard to the aforementioned structural constraint categories, the natural resource agency also plays a critical role based on institutional practices or biases (see Scott, this volume). Institutional or management constraints can be intentional or unintentional. For example, it is through the agency staff areas are zoned as "closed" due to the presence of bears or as "restricted" to certain types of recreationists (e.g., nonmotorized users or visitors with a permit). These types of intentional constraints are often conceived and implemented so that equity and communication issues are addressed.

However, institutional policies and practices can be a more subtle and unacknowledged form of constraint, but just as restrictive. For example, when natural resource agency managers allow visual resource degradation, crowding, and chronic user conflicts to persist, the impact on the quality of the recreation experience can discourage visitors from returning. These sorts of on-site problems can lead to a compromised experience, spatial displacement (where a substitute site is found), or the search for other leisure pursuits. Institutional discrimination may also occur in the types of outdoor opportunities offered to minorities or women (Floyd, 1999). Floyd uses the example of park agencies developing historical or other themes not relevant to minority groups. Providers of recreation opportunities also disseminate and market information about recreation attractions and opportunities. To the extent an agency, community, or business is ineffective or inattentive to the need to communicate to visitors about available outdoor recreation opportunities, it will contribute to the subtle structural constraint of a lack of information. Additionally, use restrictions and direct management techniques that limit choice can serve to unintentionally demotivate future visits to such areas (Manning, 1999; Schreyer, 1986).

Institutional structural constraints can also be extended to the local communities and tourism-related businesses that share in the provision of outdoor recreation opportunities with the natural resource agency. Proponents of the Benefits Approach to Leisure (BAL) argued the delivery of recreation opportunities needs to be shared (Driver & Bruns, 1999). To the extent that these entities are synergistic and work collaboratively, the more opportunities and information are available to visitors and local residents to maximize personal, social, economic, and environmental benefits. On the other hand, local communities and tourism-related businesses that do not facilitate such experiences can constrain outdoor recreation just as much as a natural resource agency can.

Summary

As noted earlier, most of the research on leisure constraints generally, and outdoor recreation constraints specifically, focused on structural constraints. To date, research suggests available time, trip costs, and geographic accessibility are the key structural constraints for outdoor recreation, although we contend other categories, such as the natural environment, social environment, institutional, and territorial structural constraints, should be examined more fully in the future. Additionally, we also put forth, at least in the case of outdoor recreation, future research in this area should include not only constraints that affect participation in a preferred activity, but also constraints on the preferred setting for the activity and constraints on the preferred social conditions.

Outdoor Recreation and the Negotiation of Leisure Constraints

As Jackson and Scott (1999) stated, much remains to be done in terms of "explaining (as opposed to identifying and describing) the negotiation of leisure constraints," including "why some people choose (or are obliged to follow) one set of strategies rather than another" (p. 310). Arguably, in outdoor recreation, much of the research in this area focused on behavioral negotiation strategies (Jackson et al., 1993), such as activity and setting substitutability (cf. Manning, 1999), although Shelby and Vaske (1991) also identified other substitution strategies (e.g., temporal, where the person participates in the same activity but at a different time). In this section, therefore, we focus on how five additional concepts could potentially help researchers better understand how individuals decide which type and kind of strategy they will employ, both in terms of outdoor recreation specifically and leisure generally:

1. attitudes (specifically, the theory of planned behavior).

2. place attachment and sparing.

3. primary and secondary control.

4. self-construal theory.

5. capitalizing on setting affordances.

Earlier in this chapter we discussed how attitudes toward both nature and activities that occur in nature can be examined in terms of subsequent behavior. We also believe, however, this research could be used to examine the negotiation of constraints. For example, in terms of outdoor recreation, an understanding of attitudes toward both the type of constraint (e.g., quotas) and the perceived source of the constraint (e.g., the natural resource agency responsible for managing the area) may provide insight into how an individual interprets and responds to a specific barrier (see **Figure 13.2**). In this example, three different attitudinal and behavioral responses may occur. With response A, the outdoor recreationist will likely readily accept imposition of the constraint and may, in fact, internalize it (Deci & Ryan, 1991). With responses B and C, the outdoor recreationist will likely view imposition of the constraint as a "necessary evil." And with response D, the outdoor recreationist will likely reject imposition of the constraint, and potentially, may chose to behave in exactly the opposite manner the agency desires (e.g., sneaking into the restricted area without a permit).

In addition to one's attitude toward the type of constraint and the perceived source of the constraint, another variable associated with the theory of planned behavior may also shed light on negotiating leisure constraints. Specifically, Gollwitzer (1993) stated *intending* to behave in a certain manner is separate and distinct from *planning* to behave in a certain manner, as the latter involves deciding exactly when and where one will do so. Gollwitzer calls these plans *implemental intentions*. According to Orbell, Hodgkins, and Sheeran (1997, p. 946), doing so may be particularly valuable when either a chronic intention (i.e., a long-standing decision to pursue a particular goal has never been acted on) or a postponed intention (i.e., a decision to act sometime in the future) is involved. Typically, studies that examine implemental intentions utilize an experimental group that, in response to an intervention, writes down when and where they will carry out the intended behavior. These results are then compared with those of a control group not exposed to the intervention. Results of such studies found significant differences. For example, Gollwitzer and Brandstatter (1997) discovered three times as many students in an experimental group completed a self-perceived "difficult" goal intention over a holiday period than did those in a control group. Moreover, in regard to leisure as a type of activity rather than as a type of time, Orbell et al. (1997) stated the use of implementation intentions could increase the likelihood of someone taking up exercising or playing the piano, or, we would add, potentially participating in an outdoor recreation activity they prefer.

One of the characteristics of outdoor recreation (and outdoor recreation constraints) that make it unique is the importance placed on the "natural" setting. Moreover, outdoor recreationists' relationship with such settings often occurs at a level of complexity that includes, but is not limited to, one's positive or negative feelings toward such spaces. Specifically, spaces where outdoor recreation takes place may, for a variety of reasons, become embedded with meaning, and in the process become "places" for a recreationist. In an early conceptualization of place and placelessness, Relph (1976) proposed the places people are most attached to engender a sense of commitment and responsibility, or what Heidigger referred to as sparing:

> letting things, or in this context places, be the way they are; it is a tolerance for them in their own essence....Sparing is a willingness to leave places alone and not to change them causally or arbitrarily, and not to exploit them. (Heidigger, as cited in Relph, 1976, p. 39)

Based on Relph's proposition, a positive relationship may exist between attachment to a place and pro environmental behaviors toward that place, including, for example, deciding to reduce, or even to stop completely, recreating at that place. A recent study suggests outdoor recreationists may indeed self-constrain themselves under certain circumstances. Specifically, Walker and Chapman (2003) found sense of place—through feelings of empathy induced by a perspective-taking intervention—indirectly affected outdoor recreationists' intention to either decrease their visits to, or stop visiting altogether, places perceived as being environmentally impacted by such visitations. Thus, an outdoor recreationist may self-constrain himself or herself in terms of participating in an activity, or visiting a setting, or both, to preserve

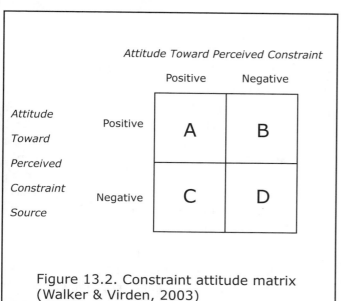

Figure 13.2. Constraint attitude matrix (Walker & Virden, 2003)

and protect a place—behaviors that suggest when examining how constraints are negotiated it may be important to take into account the role altruistic feelings toward a place may play.

Potentially, a person's perception of control may also affect the negotiation process. In a paper by Weisz, Rothbaum, and Blackburn (1984), these authors contended there are two distinct types of control:

1. primary control, where "individuals enhance their rewards by influencing existing realities (e.g., other people, circumstances, symptoms, or behavior problems" (p. 955).

2. secondary control, where "individuals enhance their rewards by accommodating to existing realities and maximizing satisfaction or goodness of fit with things as they are" (p. 955).

Although Weisz et al.'s conceptualization was originally developed to describe differences between America and Japan, and the two types of control were dichotomous, Scherl (1989) recognized Australian outdoor recreationists, who were likely more inclined to use primary control in their everyday world often used secondary control during their wilderness visits. As Scherl stated, "in wilderness, even if one's knowledge about the particular environment is considerable, there is still nothing one can do to alter that environment" (p. 127). Moreover, Scherl contended such self-control has distinct psychological benefits because attention is shifted inward and different domains of self-consciousness are subsequently enhanced. Regardless of the potential benefits, however, because wilderness can be conceived as a nonresponsive environment (Wohlwill, 1983), it may be necessary to reexamine how outdoor recreationists perceive and respond to at least some constraints (e.g., natural environment structural constraints), and further, for researchers in general to reevaluate the role secondary control may play in the negotiation of constraints.

In addition to a looking at a person's attitude, sense of place, and type of control when trying to understand constraint negotiation, a fourth concept, already discussed in some detail earlier, may also be of importance: self-construal. As described earlier, according to Markus and Kitayama (1991) independent selves value being unique, expressing themselves, and promoting their own goals, while interdependent selves value belonging, fitting in, and promoting others' goals. Potentially, these differences in self-construal may affect how people interpret and subsequently react to a leisure constraint. For example, in the case of interdependent selves, research suggests these individuals place a high priority on maintaining harmony with others (Oyserman, Coon

& Kemmelmeier, 2002) as well as fulfilling their obligations and duties (Bontempo, Lobel & Triandis, 1990). In both cases, this sense of self-constraint results in highly positive feelings, possibly because such actions have been internalized by the individual (Bontempo et al., 1990). As a consequence, it is important for researchers to understand even though the response to a constraint may be cessation, the etiology for this behavior may differ considerably between independent and interdependent selves.

Finally, one other concept that may contribute to our understanding of leisure contstraints is capitalizing on setting affordances. For example, a recreationist who finds a crowded backcountry campsite appalling may choose to hike over the next ridge to take advantage of an uncrowded setting opportunity. In contrast, an experienced or specialized backcountry hiker would likely not have chosen the original crowded setting to begin with. This suggests experienced or specialized recreationists may be more adept at capitalizing on opportunities afforded by recreation settings than novice or less specialized recreationists.

Conclusion

Due in part to the need to synthesize research from two areas—outdoor recreation and leisure constraints—that have, heretofore, been conceptually independent, this chapter emphasized breadth over depth. As a consequence, we recognize some topics may not have received the attention they deserve and merit future research; yet, at the same time, we believe many of the ideas put forth in this chapter deserve the same attention.

Implications for Research

We recommend the following for future research on outdoor recreation constraints:

- First, it is important not only to broaden the range of structural constraints by including the new categories identified by us, but also to begin developing a standardized set of structural constraint scale items which demonstrate high levels of validity and reliability (similar in this respect to the work done by Driver and colleagues with the Recreation Experience Preference scales).

- Second, because of the changing demographics of Canada and the United States, specifically in terms of the growing number of immigrants from cultures likely to have interdependent self-construals, future research on constraints on outdoor recreation, as well as future research on leisure constraints and on leisure in general, should consider incorporating ideas, concepts, and theories from cross-cultural research. In particular, we need to develop a better understanding of how different ethnic/racial groups feel about outdoor recreation and perceive nature and wildland environments.

- Third, while gender-based research is well-established in the leisure literature, a gendered understanding of leisure socialization, participation patterns, constraints, nature aversion, and wildland meaning in outdoor recreation is needed. Furthermore the possibility of an interaction effect between gender and ethnicity/race may be an area ripe for future inquiry.

- Fourth, research is needed on how other micro-level and macrolevel factors affect leisure preferences, as well as the effect setting affordances have overall.

- Fifth, we know very little about how recreationists perceive agency and management practices and to what extent institutional constraints influence outdoor recreation behavior. More research is needed to understand how managers can increase the quality of the outdoor recreation experience by removing or reducing structural constraints.

- Sixth, the various relationships described in this chapter's revised leisure constraints model should be examined using both qualitative and quantitative methodologies, and ideally using multiphase or longitudinal approaches.

- Finally, from a much broader perspective, we recommend that future studies on constraints, outdoor recreation, or both, borrow liberally from the other area for conceptual cross-fertilization to occur.

Implications for Practice

In addition to these future research recommendations, we believe there are also some implications for natural resource agencies and their employees. An understanding of the constraints that operate in outdoor recreation settings and influence outdoor recreation decision making and participation is important if natural resource planners and managers are to be effective. As our knowledge about the cultural forces, social psychological forces, and types of constraints that influence outdoor recre-

ation behavior increases, managers will have more tools and more knowledge about where to apply those tools. Table 13.1 (p. 209) provides a descriptive summary of the kinds of common constraints or barriers many outdoor recreation planners and managers are familiar with. For example, time constraints may mean that people want more opportunities for a quick experience close to home. Providing information and marketing recreation opportunities broadly through a variety of media is one way to reduce information and knowledge constraints. Knowing that visitors perceive "poorly maintained areas and facilities" as a constraint or that people "don't know where the parks are" can suggest concrete management actions that can serve as either as interventions or proactive management.

Structural constraints like lack of time, lack of money, and inadequate transportation have a particularly strong influence on outdoor recreation because of the distance from home required to participate, especially for national park, forest, and nature-based tourism. These constraints are especially strong for lower income households, ethnic/racial minorities, the elderly, and persons with disabilities (as are many other constraints). Management strategies such as quotas and direct/indirect management techniques, and management concepts such as carrying capacity are also clearly types of (institutional) structural constraints and should be seen as such. Implementing these management interventions constrains the choices of recreationists and impacts the quality of the visitor experience. However, it should also be recognized not all structural constraints result in negative consequences. For example, by limiting use or restricting behavior, benefits to the natural resource can occur. By doing so, these variables become linked to constraints research and can be put in a much broader context.

Many natural resource agencies and managers have discovered the value of doing visitor surveys to monitor activity and setting preferences, perceived management problems, recreation satisfaction, and visitor demographics. The data from these studies are commonly used to plan and to provide visitor and public input into management decisions. However, it is less common that visitor studies examine recreation constraints. Part of the problem is awareness on the part of natural resource agencies as to the importance of monitoring or examining constraints; the other part is most of the most constrained public does not show up to participate in visitor studies (see Scott, this volume).

Structural constraint categories, such as social environment and institutional structural constraints, are less apparent to natural resource managers. Even more hidden from managers are the influences of macrolevel factors such as culture, ethnicity/race, and gender. Many natural resource agencies and managers would not even include such forces or issues as areas of agency concern. The representativeness of outdoor recreation participation is more likely a policy concern than a management concern at this point. Two questions thus arise:

1. Should public natural resource recreation agencies be striving to serve a representative population of visitors?

2. If so, how would that be accomplished?

In conclusion, we hope this chapter provided the reader with a better understanding of constraints on outdoor recreation. We leave the last word, however, to an earlier nature writer who also knew of both constraints and constraint negotiation:

> Let us spend one day as deliberately as Nature, and not be thrown off the track by every nutshell and mosquito's wing that falls on the rails. Let us rise early and fast, or break fast, gently and without perturbation; let company come and let company go, let the bells ring and the children cry—determined to make a day of it. (Thoreau, 1854/1960, p. 70)

References

Abrams, D., Ando, K., and Hinkle, S. (1998). Psychological attachment to the group: Cross-cultural differences in organizational identification and subjective norms as predictors of workers' turnover intentions. *Personality and Social Psychology Bulletin, 24,* 1027–1039.

Alberta Community Development. (2000). *2000 Alberta recreation survey.* Edmonton, Alberta, Canada: Sport and Recreation Branch.

Ajzen, I. (1987). Attitudes, traits, and actions: Dispositional prediction of behavior in personality and social psychology. In L. Berkowitz (Ed.), *Advances in experimental social psychology* (Vol. 20; pp. 1–63). New York, NY: Academic Press.

Ajzen, I. (1991). The theory of planned behavior. *Organisational Behavior and Human Decision Process, 50,* 179–211.

Ajzen, I. and Driver, B. (1991). Prediction of leisure participation from behavioral, normative, and control beliefs: An application of the theory of planned behavior. *Leisure Sciences, 13,* 185–204.

Ajzen, I. and Driver, B. (1992). Application of the Theory of Planned Behavior to leisure choice. *Journal of Leisure Research, 24,* 207–224.

Benidickson, J. (1997). *Idleness, water, and a canoe: Reflections on paddling for pleasure.* Toronto, Ontario, Canada: University of Toronto Press.

Bilingualism bottoms out. (2001, August 1). *National Post,* p. A4.

Bixler, R. and Floyd, M. (1997). Nature is scary, disgusting, and uncomfortable. *Environment and Behavior, 29,* 443–467.

Blahna, D. and Black, K. (1993). Racism: A concern for recreation managers? In Paul Gobster (Ed.), *Managing urban and high-use recreation settings* (General Technical Report NC-163; pp. 111–118). Washington, DC: U.S. Department of Agriculture.

Bocking, W. (1915). A canoe trip. *Rod and Gun, 17,* 580.

Bontempo, R., Lobel, S., and Triandis, H. (1990). Compliance and value internalization in Brazil and the U.S. *Journal of Cross-Cultural Psychology, 21,* 200–213.

Bozionelos, G. and Bennett, P. (1999). The Theory of Planned Behavior as predictor of exercise: The moderating influence of beliefs and personality variables. *Journal of Health Psychology, 4,* 517–529.

Brown, D. (1973, December 22). It was a very good year. *Canadian Magazine,* 3.

Brown, S. and Katcher, A. (1997). The contribution of attachment to pets and attachment to nature to dissociation and absorption. *Dissociation: Progress in the Dissociative Disorders, 10,* 125–129.

Bryan, H. (1977). Leisure value systems and recreation specialization: The case of trout fisherman. *Journal of Leisure Research, 9,* 174–187.

Bryan, H. (1979). *Conflict in the great outdoors: Towards understanding and managing for diverse user preferences.* Tuscaloosa, AL: University of Alabama, Bureau of Public Administration.

Chipman, B. D. and Helfrich, L. A. (1988). Recreational specializations and motivations of Virginia River Anglers. *North American Journal of Fisheries Management, 8,* 390–398.

Coble, T., Selin, S., and Erickson, B. (2003). Hiking alone: Understanding fear, negotiation strategies, and leisure experience. *Journal of Leisure Research, 35,* 1–22.

Cook, K. (1995) Social relationships and group processes. In K. Cook, G. Fine, and J. House (Eds.), *Sociological perspectives on social psychology* (pp. 203–208). Boston, MA: Allyn & Bacon.

Crawford, D. and Godbey, G. (1987). Reconceptualizing barriers to family leisure. *Leisure Sciences, 9,* 119–127.

Crawford, D., Jackson, E., and Godbey, G. (1991). A hierarchical model of leisure constraints. *Leisure Sciences, 13,* 309–320.

Csikszentmihalyi, M. (1975). *Beyond boredom and anxiety.* San Francisco, CA: Jossey-Bass.

Deci, E., and Ryan, R. (1991). A motivational approach to self: Integration in personality. In R. Dienstbier (Ed.), *Nebraska Symposium on Motivation: Vol. 38. Perspectives on motivation* (pp. 237–288). Lincoln, NE: University of Nebraska Press.

Driver, B. and Bruns, D. (1999). Concepts and uses of the benefits approach to leisure. In T. Burton and E. Jackson (Eds.), *Leisure studies: Prospects for the twenty-first century.* State College, PA: Venture Publishing, Inc.

Driver, R. and Knopf, B. (1977). Personality, outdoor recreation, and expected consequences. *Environment and Behavior, 9,* 169–193.

Eysenck, H. and Eysenck, S. (1975). *Manual of the Eysenck Personality Questionnaire.* London, England: Hodder & Stoughton.

Fekuda, Z. and Kraft, P. (2001). Self-identity in planned behavior perspective: Past behavior and its moderating effects on self-identity-intention relations. *Social Behavior and Personality, 29,* 671–686.

Floyd, M. F. (1999). Race, ethnicity and use of the national park system. *Social Science Research Review, 1,* 1–24.

Floyd, M. F., Outley, C. W., Bixler, R. D., and Hammitt, W. E. (1995). Effect of race, environmental preference and negative affect on recreation preferences. *Abstracts from the 1995 National Recreation and Park Association Symposium on Leisure Research.* Arlington, VA: National Recreation and Parks Association.

Freixanet, M. (1991). Personality profile of subjects engaged in high physical risk sports. *Personality and Individual Differences, 12,* 1087–1093.

Gollwitzer, P. (1993). Goal achievement: The role of intentions. In P. Gollwitzer and J. Bargh (Eds.), *The psychology of action: Linking cognition and motivation to behavior* (pp. 287–312). New York, NY: Guildford Press.

Gollwitzer, P. and Brandstatter, V. (1997). Implementation and effective goal pursuit. *Journal of Personality and Social Psychology, 73,* 186–199.

Gordon, M. Y., Riger, S., LeBailly, R. K., and Heath, L. (1981). Crime, women and the quality of urban life. In C. R. Stimpson, E. Dixler, M. J. Nelson, and K. B. Yatrakis (Eds.), *Women and the American city* (pp. 141–157). Chicago, IL: University of Chicago Press.

Graefe, A. R. and Kauffman, R. B. (1987, September). *Recreation specialization among canoeists and climbers: a comparative analysis.* Paper presented at the Tenth Annual NRPA Symposium on Leisure Research, New Orleans, LA.

Gramann, J. H. (1996). *Ethnicity, race, and outdoor recreation: A review of trends, policy, and research.* (Miscellaneous paper R-96-1). Vicksburg, MS: U.S. Army Corp of Engineers.

Greider, T. and Garkovich, L. (1994). Landscapes: The social construction of nature and the environment. *Rural Sociology, 59,* 1–24.

Harris, E. L. (1997). Solo faces: A black outdoorsman takes a wilderness census, and finds it disturbingly light. *Outside Magazine, 22*(12), 106–110, 177–178.

Henderson, K. (1996). Feminist perspectives, female ways of being, and nature. In B. L. Driver, D. Dustin, T. Baltic, G. Elsner, and G. Peterson (Eds.), *Nature and the human spirit: Toward an expanded land management ethic* (pp. 153–162). State College, PA: Venture Publishing, Inc.

Hinch, T. and Jackson, E. (2000). Leisure constraints research: Its value as a framework for understanding tourism seasonality. *Current Issues in Tourism, 3,* 87–107.

Holland, S., Pennington-Gray, L., and Thapa, B. (2001). [Outdoor recreation needs assessment for Florida]. Unpublished raw data.

House, J. (1995). Social structure, relationships, and the individual. In K. Cook, G. Fine, and J. House (Eds.), *Sociological perspectives on social psychology* (pp. 387–395). Boston, MA: Allyn & Bacon.

Iso-Ahola, S. (1980). *The social psychology of leisure and recreation*. Dubuque, IA: Wm. C. Brown.

Iso-Ahola, S. (1999). Motivational foundations of leisure. In E. Jackson and T. Burton (Eds.), *Leisure studies: Prospects for the twenty-first century* (pp. 35–51). State College, PA: Venture Publishing, Inc.

Jackson, E. (1994). Constraints on participation in resource-based outdoor recreation. *Journal of Applied Recreation Research, 19*, 215–245.

Jackson, E. (2000). Will research on leisure constraints still be relevant in the twenty-first century? *Journal of Leisure Research, 32*, 62–68.

Jackson, E., Crawford, D., and Godbey, G. (1993). Negotiation of constraints. *Leisure Sciences, 15*, 1–11.

Jackson, E. and Scott, D. (1999). Constraints on leisure and recreation. In E. Jackson and T. Burton (Eds.), *Leisure studies: Prospects for the twenty-first century*. State College, PA: Venture Publishing, Inc.

Jacob, G. and Schreyer, R. (1980). Conflict in outdoor recreation: A theoretical perspective. *Leisure Sciences, 3*, 129–154.

Kelly, J. (1974). Socialization toward leisure: A developmental approach. *Journal of Leisure Research, 6*, 181–193.

Kelly, J. (1977). Leisure socialization: Replication and extension. *Journal of Leisure Research, 9*, 121–131.

Kluckhohn, F. and Strodtbeck, F. (1961). *Variations in value orientations*. Evanston, IL: Row, Peterson.

Knopf, R. C. (1987). Human behavior, cognition, and affect in the natural environment. In D. Stokols and I. Altman (Eds.), *Handbook of environmental psychology* (pp. 783–826). New York, NY: John Wiley and Sons.

Lawler, E. III. (1973). *Motivation in work organizations*. Monterey, CA: Brooks/Cole Publishing.

Lewin, K. (1935). *A dynamic theory of personality*. New York, NY: McGraw-Hill.

Manfredo, M. J., Driver, B. L., and Tarrant, M. A. (1996). Measuring leisure motivation: A meta-analysis of the recreation experience preference scales. *Journal of Leisure Research, 28*, 188–213.

Mannell, R. and Kleiber, D. (1997). *A social psychology of leisure*. State College, PA: Venture Publishing, Inc.

Manning, R. (1999). *Studies in outdoor recreation* (2nd ed.). Corvallis, OR: Oregon State.

Markus, H. and Kitayama, S. (1991). Culture and the self: Implications for cognition, emotion, and motivation. *Psychological Review, 98*, 224–253.

Maslow, A. (1964). *Motivation and personality*. New York: Harper-Row.

Mitchell, R. (1983). *Mountain experience: The psychology and sociology of adventure*. Chicago, IL: University of Chicago Press.

Nash, R. (2001). *Wilderness & the American mind* (3rd ed.). New Haven, CT: Yale.

Neisser, U. (1976). *Cognition and reality: Principles and implications of cognitive psychology*. San Francisco, CA: W.H. Freeman.

Orbell, S., Hodgkins, S., and Sheeran, P. (1997). Implementation intentions and the Theory of Planned Behavior. *Personality and Social Psychology Bulletin, 9*, 945–954.

Oyserman, D., Coon, H., and Kemmelmeier, M. (2002). Rethinking individualism and collectivism: Evaluation of theoretical assumptions and meta-analyses. *Psychological Bulletin, 128*, 3–72.

Parks Canada Agency. (2000). *Unimpaired for future generations? Protecting ecological integrity with Canada's National Parks. Volume 1, A call to action*. Ottawa, Canada: Minister of Public Works.

Perugini, M. and Bagozzi, R. (2001). The role of desires and anticipated emotions in goal-directed behaviors: Broadening and deepening the theory of planned behaviour. *British Journal of Social Psychology, 40*, 79–98.

Relph, E. (1976). *Place and placelessness*. London, England: Pion.

Riger, S. and Gordon, M. T. (1981). The fear of rape. *Journal of Social Issues 37*, 71–93.

Roche, S. and McConkey, K. (1990). Absorption: Nature, assessment, and correlates. *Journal of Personality and Social Psychology, 59*, 91–101.

Runte, A. (1997). *National parks: the American experience* (3rd ed.). Lincoln, NE: University of Nebraska.

Ryan, R., Sheldon, K., Kasser, T., and Deci, E. (1996). All goals are not created equal. In P. Gollwitzer and J. Bargh (Eds.), *The psychology of action: Linking cognition and motivation to behavior* (pp. 7–26). New York, NY: Guilford.

Sack, R. (1986). *Human territoriality: Its theory and history*. Cambridge, England: Cambridge University Press.

Scherl, L. (1989). Self in wilderness: Understanding the psychological benefits of individual–wilderness interaction through self-control. *Leisure Sciences, 11*, 125–135.

Schreyer, R. (1986). Motivation for participation in outdoor recreation and barriers to that participation—A commentary on salient issues. In *A literature review: the President's Commission on Americans Outdoors.* Washington, DC: U.S. Government Printing Office.

Schreyer, R. and Lime, D. W. (1984). A novice isn't necessarily a novice: The influence of experience use history on subjective perceptions of recreational participation. *Leisure Sciences, 6,* 131–149.

Scott, D. and Kim, C. (1998). *Outdoor recreation participation and barriers to involvement* (Texas Parks and Wildlife Department Tech. Rep.). Retrieved from http://www.rptsweb.tamu.edu/tpwd/scott.pdf

Shelby, B. and Vaske, J. (1991). Resource and activity substitutes for recreational salmon fishing in New Zealand. *Leisure Sciences, 13,* 21–32.

Simcox, D. E. (1993). Cultural foundations for leisure preference, behavior, and environmental orientation. In A. W. Ewert, D. J. Chavez, and A. W. Magill (Eds.), *Culture, conflict, and communication in the wildland–urban interface* (pp. 267–280). Boulder, CO: Westview Press.

Sofranko, A. J. and Nolan, M. F. (1972). Early life experiences and adult sports participation. *Journal of Leisure Research, 4,* 6–18.

Taylor, D. E. (1989). Blacks and the environment: Toward an explanation of the concern and action gap between blacks and whites. *Environment and Behavior, 21,* 175–205.

Thoreau, H. (1854/1960). *Walden and civil disobedience.* New York: New American Library.

Virden, R. J. and Schreyer, R. (1988). Recreation specialization as an indicator of environmental preference. *Environment and Behavior, 20,* 721–739.

Virden, R. J. and Walker, G. J. (1999). Ethnic/racial and gender variation among meanings given to, and preferences for, the natural environment. *Leisure Sciences, 21,* 219–239.

Virden, R. J. and Yoshioka, C. (1992). *The 1992 Arizona outdoor recreation needs survey* (Arizona State Parks Board Tech. Rep.). Tempe, AZ: Arizona State University.

Walker, G. J. and Chapman, R. (2003). Thinking like a park: The effects of sense of place, perspective-taking, and empathy on pro-environmental intentions. *Journal of Park and Recreation Administration, 21,* 71–86.

Walker, G. J., Deng, J., and Dieser, R. (2001). Ethnicity, acculturation, self-construal, and motivations for outdoor recreation. *Leisure Sciences, 23,* 263–283.

Walker, G. J. and Kiecolt, K. J. (1995). Social class and wilderness use. *Leisure Sciences, 17,* 295–308.

Wallace, V. K. and Witter, D. J. (1992). Urban nature centers: What do our constituents want and how can we give it to them? *Legacy 2*(2), 20–24.

Weisz, J., Rothbaum, F., and Blackburn, T. (1984). Standing out and standing in: The psychology of control in America and Japan. *American Psychologist, 39,* 955–969.

Wellman, J. D., Roggenbuck, J. W., and Smith, A. C. (1982). Recreation specialization and norms of depreciative behavior among canoeists. *Journal of Leisure Research, 14,* 323–340.

West, P. (1993). The tyranny of the metaphor: Interracial relations, minority recreation, and the wildland–urban interface. In A. W. Ewert, D. J. Chavez, and A. W. Magill (Eds.), *Culture, conflict, and communication in the wildland–urban interface* (pp. 109–115). Boulder, CO: Westview Press.

White, R. (1959). Motivation reconsidered: The concept of competence. *Psychological review, 66,* 297–333.

Whyte, L. B. and Shaw, S. M. (1994). Women'a leisure: An exploratory study of fear and violence as a leisure constraint. *Journal of Applied Recreation Research, 19*(1), 5–21.

Wilde, G. and Ditton, R. (1994). A management-oriented approach to understanding diversity among largemouth bass anglers. *North American Journal of Fisheries Management, 14,* 34–40.

Wildavsky, A. (1979). Using public funds to serve private interests: The politics of the new class. In B. Bruce-Briggs (Ed.), *The new class?* (pp. 147–153). New Brunswick, NJ: Transaction Books.

Wohlwill, J. (1983). The concept of nature: A psychologist's view. In I. Altman and J. Wohlwill (Eds.), *Human behavior and environment* (Vol. 6; pp. 5–37). New York, NY: Plenum.

Wright, B., and Goodale, T. (1991). Beyond nonparticipation: Validation of interest and frequency of participation categories in constraints research. *Journal of Leisure Research, 23,* 314–331.

Wright, E. (1978). *Class, crisis, and the state.* New York, NY: Schocken Books.

Yoesting, D. and Burkhead, D. (1973). Significance of childhood recreation experience on adult leisure behavior: An exploratory analysis. *Journal of Leisure Research, 5,* 25–36.

Zuckerman, M., Eysenck, S., and Eysenck, H. (1978). Sensation seeking in England and America: Cross-cultural, age, and sex comparisons. *Journal of Consulting and Clinical Psychology, 46,* 139–149.

Chapter 14

Why Don't People Do What's "Good" for Them? Cross-Fertilization Among the Psychologies of Nonparticipation in Leisure, Health, and Exercise Behaviors

Roger C. Mannell (University of Waterloo) and
Angela Loucks-Atkinson (University of Georgia)

Prescriptions for health and wellness have increasingly included recommendations that people engage in behaviors that prevent ill health, allow the detection of potentially unhealthy conditions, and promote positive health and wellness. These prescriptions are often packaged as "healthy" lifestyle choices, and today people are inundated with information about activities and behaviors, including leisure, that are "good" for them. The foods people eat, the manner in which they prepare it, how active they are, the entertainment and leisure they select, the work they do, and how they raise their children all define lifestyle and are seen as determining well-being. These lifestyle choices have increasingly come under scrutiny to determine the nature of those activities that are socially, psychologically, and physically good or beneficial for people.

Paradoxically, although a considerable amount of information is available about the activities that are good for people, and people seem to be interested in leading healthy lifestyles, many do not do so. Consequently, the study of nonparticipation in beneficial activities and behaviors has been undertaken by health psychologists and exercise scientists, and more recently by leisure researchers to better understand *why people don't do what is supposedly good for them.* The term "nonparticipation" is typically used to refer not only to the complete absence of participation, but also to less than desired or modified participation (Brawley, Martin & Gyurcsik, 1998; Jackson & Scott, 1999). Recreation practitioners and leisure researchers have tended to see leisure behavior as beneficial or good for people, and nonparticipa-

tion has traditionally been considered a problem to be addressed with leisure services (Goodale & Witt, 1989). Consequently, models of leisure constraint that distinguish types of constraint and the role of factors such as motivation and negotiation (e.g., Jackson, Crawford & Godbey, 1993) have been developed to better understand why people do not engage in desired and beneficial leisure activities.

Interestingly, many of the models and theories used or developed in the health and exercise behavior fields have also included the construct of barriers or constraints or some such analogous idea (Brawley et al., 1998). However, researchers concerned with nonparticipation or low levels of participation in leisure, health, or exercise behavior have had only limited contact with each other's ideas. In this chapter, the models and theoretical approaches used in the leisure, exercise, and health behavior fields are compared. In particular, common underlying social psychological principles and the possibility of theoretical cross-fertilization will be examined to further our understanding of the leisure constraint process from a social cognitive perspective.

What Is Constrained? The Idea of "Good" or "Beneficial" Leisure Activities

Though leisure tends to be seen as good by leisure researchers and service providers, there also is recognition some activities with which people choose to structure their free time are better than others (Mannell, 1993). Presumably, then, there are good and bad leisure choices, activities, and lifestyles. For example, Stebbins (2001) demonstrated serious leisure activities provide a variety of benefits and can be good for people. However, under some conditions leisure can be viewed as deviant (Rojek, 1999). Even certain types of much touted leisure, such as family leisure, may have their dark sides (Shaw, 1997). Social scientists belong to two camps concerning the appropriateness of making these types of judgments about the worth of leisure activities (Kando, 1980). On the one hand are those who feel the leisure behavior of individuals and groups is simply a difference in lifestyle reflecting social values and choices, and social scientists should remain value-free and not make value judgments of what is good and bad. As Csikszentmihalyi and Kleiber (1991) pointed out, this view is often accompanied by the belief it is important to allow "people their freedom, even if its exercise leads to 'wasting' time or to personal harm" (p. 97). On the other hand are those who argue certain types of leisure behavior are better because they are superior in engendering quality of life and other benefits (see Mannell & Kleiber, 1997).

Given research efforts to identify the nature of good leisure activities and the conditions under which they are beneficial (Driver & Bruns, 1999), it is not surprising, then, that nonparticipation in leisure activities, programs, and services has been seen as problematic. While some benefits, such as fun, enjoyment, and relaxation, have been considered somewhat transient and suspect as positive outcomes, other more enduring psychological benefits, such as personal development and self-actualization, have been viewed as quite important (Mannell & Kleiber, 1997). Leisure behavior also has been seen to have community, societal, economic, and environmental benefits (Driver, Brown & Peterson, 1991). Recently, increased research attention has been focused on the physical and mental health benefits of leisure activities (Iso-Ahola, 1997; Iwasaki & Mannell, 2000; Iwasaki & Schneider, 2003; Kleiber, Hutchinson & Williams, 2002). This growing concern is likely to stimulate even greater efforts to understand leisure constraints, and to develop interventions to assist people in overcoming them.

Efforts to promote wellness and health also have led researchers in the fields of health and exercise psychology to develop models to help practitioners and policymakers better understand the factors that influence nonparticipation in those activities thought to prevent ill health and those that positively contribute to healthy lifestyles and well-being. These health-related activities involve behaviors that provide for the early detection of symptoms, prevention of illness, coping with stressors, and promotion of positive health. Nonparticipation has been referred to as noncompliance and nonadherence to health-related behaviors, such as regular exercise, and following prescribed medical treatments, medication regimens, and recommended eating practices. Health promotion efforts involve interventions to overcome or mitigate factors that prevent or limit these types of behaviors (cf. Baum, Revenson & Singer, 2001).

Nonparticipation Theories and Common Underlying Social Cognitive Processes

Health and Exercise Models

A variety of theories—health belief model (Janz & Becker, 1984; Rosenstock, 1974), protection motivation theory (Prentice-Dunn & Rogers, 1986; Rogers, 1983), health locus of control (Wallston, 1992; Wallston, Wallston & Devellis, 1978), habit theory (Ronis, Yates & Kirscht, 1989), and transtheoretical model (Marcus & Simkin, 1994; Prochaska & DiClemente, 1982)—have been developed to specifically predict nonparticipation and participation in health and exercise behaviors. Also, more general social psychological theories, such as self-efficacy theory (Bandura, 1986) and the theories of reasoned action and planned behavior (Ajzen, 1991; Fishbein & Ajzen, 1975), have been used to inform the development of specific health models and to explain nonparticipation.

Though diverse, these models are based on an underlying social cognitive approach (Maddux, 1993). Social cognitive theory is an approach to understanding human cognition, action, motivation, and emotion that assumes people are capable of self-reflection and self-regulation and are active "shapers" of their environments rather than passive "reactors" (Bandura, 1986). These assumptions suggest the following:

1. environmental events, personal factors, and behavior interact.

2. people think, create mental models of the way their worlds work, develop strategies for taking action, and test the effectiveness of these strategies.

3. people move toward their goals by anticipating events and planning.

4. people are capable of self-regulation by exerting direct control over their own behavior by choosing or altering environmental conditions that, in turn, influence their behavior (Bandura, 1986).

To understand these processes and social cognitions, "the individual in the social context...is viewed as one who is virtually always engaged in some form of information processing" (Hamilton, Devine & Ostrom, 1994, p. 3), whether reminiscing about last year's summer vacation, flirting, coping with a child's illness, or deciding whether to go to a movie. As Maddux (1993) pointed out, the basic underlying assumptions of social cognitive theory are implicit in most health and exercise models and suggest that they provide "compatible rather than competing" (p. 119) perspectives.

Leisure Models

Although there are a number of alternative models of nonparticipation in the health and exercise areas, there are few leisure behavior nonparticipation models. The *hierarchical constraint model* (Crawford, Jackson & Godbey, 1991), and its extension (Jackson, Crawford & Godbey, 1993), is widely recognized as the major leisure nonparticipation theory, although it can be argued the theory of *recreation substitutability* (Hendee & Burdge, 1974; Iso-Ahola, 1986) also is a nonparticipation theory (Jackson & Rucks, 1995; Mannell & Kleiber, 1997). Shelby and Vaske (1991) and Brunson and Shelby (1993) extended the idea of recreation substitutability by suggesting tactics (temporal, resource, and strategic) other than "the replacement of one activity with another" describe and explain the ways people react when a preferred leisure activity is no longer available to them. These ideas are parallel to the ideas of constraint and negotiation. However, research stimulated by these developments has been relatively limited.

Concerns have been raised about the scope of the hierarchical constraint model. On the one hand, leisure constraint theory has been criticized as inappropriately becoming a general theory of leisure behavior (Samdahl & Jekubovich, 1997). On the other hand, constructs such as *affordances* (Mannell & Kleiber, 1997; also see Kleiber, Wade & Loucks-Atkinson, this volume) and *facilitators* (Hubbard & Mannell, 2001; Raymore, 2002) have been proposed that may be useful in conceptualizing factors that fall outside the reach of constraint theory. However, leisure constraint theory continues to stimulate considerable research attention, and it has undergone a number of changes since it was first proposed that continue to make it an interesting and viable theory (see Crawford & Jackson, this volume; Jackson & Scott,

1999). Research findings that suggested constraints do not always prevent or reduce participation (Kay & Jackson, 1991; Scott, 1991; Shaw, Bonen & McCabe, 1991) led Jackson et al. (1993) to extend the hierarchical constraints model by developing propositions about the role of negotiation and motivational processes. Researchers have tested the hierarchical nature of the model (Raymore, Godbey, Crawford & Von Eye, 1993), identified the negotiation resources and strategies used by people (e.g., Henderson, Bedini, Hecht & Schuler, 1995; Jackson and Rucks, 1995), examined the role of motivation in the constraint process (Carroll & Alexandris, 1997), and more fully specified the constraint–negotiation process by testing a variety of models of the interrelationships among motivation, constraint, negotiation, and participation (Hubbard & Mannell, 2001). In effect, as a consequence of these developments and research efforts, leisure constraint theory has been evolving almost "unaware" into a social cognitive theory that now goes well beyond being a stimulus–response model of barriers causing nonparticipation. In particular, the negotiation and motivation constructs that are part of the theory would seem to be based on social cognitive assumptions that suggest people set participation goals, develop an understanding of the constraints they encounter and their cause, develop and plan the use of strategies, experiment with their use, and attempt to exert control over their environment and behavior to achieve their leisure goals.

As noted earlier, most health and exercise behavior models have been based to varying degrees on social psychological theory, in particular, the social cognitive approach. Although social psychological theories such as self-efficacy and the theories of reasoned action and planned behavior have been used to explain and predict various types of leisure behavior (e.g., Ajzen & Driver, 1991), they have not been formally applied to the development of leisure nonparticipation models (but see Walker & Virden, this volume). There has been some speculation about social psychological theories that might prove helpful in understanding the operation of constraints, such as learned helplessness, locus of control, reasoned action (Iso-Ahola & Mannell, 1985), cognitive dissonance, and self-efficacy (Henderson & Bialeschki, 1993; Hubbard & Mannell, 2001; Jackson et al., 1993). However, these theories have not been used to extend thinking or to develop empirical tests of the social cognitive processes of constraint and constraint–negotiation. Until recently, Iso-Ahola's (1986) development of a system of formal propositions based on psychological reactance theory to explain the psychological processes involved in successful recreation substitution could be seen as one of the few exceptions.

Health/Exercise Models and Leisure Models

The hierarchical leisure constraint model as it is evolving has a number of structural and process characteristics in common with health and exercise social cognitive nonparticipation theories. Research on nonparticipation and nonadherence to exercise activity, like that on leisure nonparticipation, began as an attempt to simply identify and describe the various "barriers" that prevent people from participating (Dishman, 1988). Also, the health belief model and the theory of planned behavior use constructs similar to the concept of constraint. Even the lack of self-efficacy has been seen as a type of barrier (e.g., Devellis, Alfieri & Ahluwalia, 1995). In the case of the health belief model (Rosenstock, 1974), the construct of "perceived barriers" includes factors that would be labeled interpersonal and structural constraints in leisure constraint theory, and in the case of the theories of reasoned action and planned behavior (Ajzen, 1991; Fishbein & Ajzen, 1975), the notion of "subjective norms" has some similarity to interpersonal constraints. In research on leisure, there has been more of a focus on classifying and developing categories of constraint, though various exercise behavior researchers have distinguished between internal and external, behavioral, cognitive, and environmental barriers (Brawley et al., 1998). However, there appears to have been less emphasis on the categorization of barriers and more focus on the operation of obstacles to specific and more narrowly defined behaviors than in the leisure literature—for example, exercise and health behaviors, such as cardiovascular exercise (Verhoef & Love, 1994) and obtaining a mammogram (Champion, 1995). Motivational constructs are also common to most models, such as motivation to participate (e.g., leisure constraint theory), self-protection (e.g., health belief model, protection motivation theory), and evaluation (e.g., theories of reasoned action and planned behavior).

Motivational processes and a number of other common processes are assumed to operate in most nonparticipation models. Based on the view that people are "active shapers" of their behavior and experience, processes that account for when and how people go about overcoming barriers to participation or initiating participation have been proposed. In leisure constraint theory this process has come to be called "negotiation." In health and exercise models, this process has been designated with terms such as *strategies*, *resources*, *self-efficacy*, *behavior control*, and *coping*. Health and exercise researchers generally have not been interested in identifying the actual strategies people use for dealing with constraints or barriers, but have focused more on the amount of control people feel they have over participation, and their level of confidence in being able to participate in spite of barriers.

Social Cognitive Perspectives and Leisure Constraint Theory

As argued earlier, leisure constraint theory is evolving into a psychological process model with a number of features in common with social cognitive–based models of general behavior as well as health and exercise behavior. However, there are a number of features found in these models that may be worth further consideration, perhaps even expropriation, for their potential contributions to leisure constraint theory. General and leisure stress coping process models that conceptualize coping as a dynamic and "transactional" process also would appear to be useful frameworks for the further development of constraint theory. Ideas that appear useful include the following:

1. maintaining the level of generality and specificity of key variables in leisure constraints models.

2. including expectancy-value constructs and processes to account for the saliency or importance of participation outcomes.

3. extending the notion of negotiation beyond strategies and resources to include behavior control and self-efficacy.

4. conceptualizing the constraint-negotiation process as somewhat analogous to transactional coping processes to help in describing the dynamic links among the various structural components of constraints models.

5. examining the constraint-negotiation process as an ongoing and evolving process that may operate differently for different stages of participation, such as adoption and early participation in an activity and later participation adherence.

Level of Generality and Specificity of Variables in Constraints Models

The prediction of level of participation in the face of constraints might be improved if the level of generality and specificity of measures of constraints, negotiation strategies, motives, and participation were similar. This lesson has been made clear by research based on the attitude-behavior theories of reasoned action and planned behavior (Ajzen, 1991; Fishbein & Ajzen, 1975). A long tradition of empirical research demonstrated the link between attitudes and behavior is far from automatic (see Eagly & Chaiken, 1993). Having a negative attitude toward television viewing does not mean that people do not watch television. Conversely, holding positive attitudes toward spending more leisure time with family, exercising regularly, or traveling to exotic places does not necessarily mean that people do these things. A number of conditions have been identified in which attitudes are linked to behavior, and these conditions would seem to be relevant for predicting nonparticipation and participation based on knowledge of the constraints people encounter and the negotiation resources they have available. For the attitude-behavior relationship, one key factor is the level of generality and specificity of the attitude and behavior of interest. Attitudes are strongly predictive of behavior only when the scope of the attitude closely matches the scope of the behavior (Ajzen, 1991). For example, attitudes may be used to predict whether people will visit an art gallery sometime within the next six months. Attitudes might be measured with a series of questions ranging from very general (e.g., "How do you feel about art galleries?") to very specific (e.g., "How do you feel about visiting your community art gallery during the next six months?"). Because the latter type of question is more specific and matched to the behavior in question, people's answers to it likely would be more predictive of actual art gallery visiting behavior. With respect to constraint theory, it is quite likely that if factors such as constraint, motivation, and negotiation influence leisure behavior, this influence is more likely to be demonstrated if greater care is taken to ensure that the level of specificity of the variables in a constraint study matched.

This matching of levels of specificity could be accomplished in several ways. As with the attitude-behavior examples, greater predictability is likely to be achieved if the constraints examined are specific to the particular leisure behavior in question. Rather than attempt to predict nonparticipation or participation in leisure activities in general, a more successful approach might involve examining participation in specific or more narrowly defined types of leisure activities matched with the constraints likely to be operating during the same timeframe and in similar social and physical contexts. For example, to determine the affect of constraints on level of attendance at an onsite employee fitness facility, a more complete picture could be expected to emerge if both the constraints encountered by employees and their attendance during a specific period of time were examined. Efforts also could be made to ensure the constraints examined were relevant and specific to attendance at the fitness facility during the same time period rather than general leisure constraints not anchored to the specific context of interest—in this case an employee fitness facility. A review of the leisure constraint literature suggests researchers varied widely in the extent to which they have attempted to match the level of specificity-generality of leisure constraints and behavior.

This matching of level of specificity can also be applied to the other components in leisure constraints models. Congruence between the specific constraints people encounter and the negotiation strategies or resources they have available and use may be an important factor in their likelihood of participating. For example, it might be expected that the negative impact of structural constraints involving lack of time would be mitigated to a greater extent by time management negotiation strategies than other types. Jackson and Rucks (1995) found "there was a general consistency between the type of constraint encountered and the *specific* strategy adopted" (p. 100) by the adolescents they studied. However, they were quick to note there were exceptions and the adolescents were creative and sometimes did "tackle problems in a tangential manner rather than head-on"—that is, using negotiation strategies that were not congruent with the constraints encountered. Research focused on better understanding this aspect of the constraint negotiation process would likely contribute to the further development of a social cognitive theory of leisure nonparticipation.

Another lesson that can be learned from attitude-behavior theory and research is the potential value of measuring people's intentions to participate. In leisure constraints research, researchers often determine whether those people studied were interested in participating, the reasons (constraints) that they did not participate, and their level of participation. However, rarely, if ever, are participants asked if they actually intended or intend to participate. Attitude research has shown the best predictors of behavior are people's intentions to participate, and that attitudes, in turn, are better predictors of intentions than behavior. Perhaps, the inclusion of the variable *intention to participate* as a mediating process variable might allow researchers to better determine the impact of constraints on nonparticipation and participation.

Expectancy-Value Constructs

Another feature of social cognitive–based theories that could be incorporated more fully into leisure nonparticipation models is an expectancy-value component.

Terms such as motive, reason, benefit, and psychological outcome have been used to describe the outcomes people expect as a consequence of engaging in a particular behavior. These outcomes are seen to have values that can be costs or benefits. The value of the outcomes of participation has been found to be an important factor in predicting the occurrence of participation. This expectancy-value process is a motivational process that represents the strength of people's desire to engage in a behavior. For example, the theory of planned behavior suggests attitudes that influence behavior are a function of the beliefs people hold about the outcomes a particular behavior will produce and how much they value those outcomes (Ajzen, 1991). The "perceived benefits" and "health value" variables specified by the health belief model (Janz & Becker, 1984) and the protection motivation theory's (Rippetoe & Rogers, 1987) "perceived vulnerability" variable are also examples of expectancy-value constructs.

Jackson et al. (1993) introduced the psychological construct of *motivation* into the hierarchical constraint model in the form of a "balance proposition," which stated "both the initiation and outcome of the negotiation process are dependent on the relative strength of, and interactions between, constraints on participating in an activity and motivations for such participation" (Proposition 6, Jackson et al., 1993, p. 9). Motivation has been widely used to explain leisure behavior (see Iso-Ahola, 1999) but research on the role of motivation in the constraint negotiation process has been neglected and rarely assessed in studies of constraint. Exceptions are studies reported by Carroll and Alexandris (1997), who asked their respondents to indicate the reasons they participated in recreational sport activities, and Hubbard and Mannell (2001), who assessed the extent to which their study participants were motivated to participate in employee recreation programs for enjoyment and health reasons. In both studies, motivation was found to be an important factor in the response to constraints. Carroll and Alexandris found higher levels of motivation were associated with higher levels of participation and lower levels of perceived constraint. While Hubbard and Mannell found no relationship between motivation and perceived constraint, motivation appeared to be strongly related to participation through its strong positive influence on efforts to negotiate the constraints encountered by the participants as proposed by their constraint-effects-mitigation model (**Figure 14.1**). The conceptualization of this expectancy-value or motivational process deserves greater attention in constraint theory and research.

People as Active Shapers or Agents of Their Behavior

The idea of constraint negotiation is consistent with the social cognitive view that people actively respond to conditions that impede their goals rather than passively accept them. For example, Hubbard and Mannell (2001) found although encounters with constraints had a negative effect on participation in employee recreation programs, these constraints also triggered greater efforts to negotiate which, in turn, mitigated the effects of the constraint and led to higher levels of participation (see the constraint-mitigation model in Figure 14.1). A number of researchers have attempted to identify the actual negotiation strategies or resources people use to circumvent leisure constraints (e.g., Henderson & Bialeschki, 1993; Henderson et al., 1995; Jackson & Rucks, 1995). In partial support of this proposition, researchers have found that people, when asked, are able to describe specific resources or strategies that they use to help them deal with constraints. For example, the women studied by Henderson and Bialeschki (1993) and Henderson et al. (1995) felt they were successful at becoming or staying involved in leisure activities based on the use of negotiation strategies that allowed them to resist gender role expectations, to respond actively rather than passively to constraints, and to balance the benefits and costs of participation. High school students reported using a variety of approaches when faced with constraints that Jackson and Rucks (1995) classified as cognitive strategies (e.g., push themselves harder, ignore parents) and behavioral strategies (e.g., better organize their time, take lessons). Frederick and Shaw (1995) found young women participating in aerobic exercise classes reported using negotiation strategies that involved minimizing their concerns with their physical appearance, a factor that may have acted as a constraint. Based on an analysis of their interview data, Samdahl and Jekubovich (1997) identified several approaches that enabled the adults in their study to use their leisure as they wished. Although they discussed the advantages of interpreting their findings within a nonconstraint framework, the researchers recognized that these approaches (making time for self, coordinating time with others, compromising on activity, and sharing leisure with others) could be interpreted as negotiation strategies depending on the perspective adopted.

While health and exercise nonparticipation theories and general social psychological theories do not focus on strategies as much, constructs have been developed that attempt to explain when and under what conditions people will attempt to engage in behaviors that will allow them to overcome barriers to their participation.

The attitude theory of planned behavior (Ajzen, 1991) and self-efficacy theory (Bandura, 1986) suggest the importance of understanding how confident people are (behavior control and self-efficacy, respectively) in their abilities to perform the behavior in question. The protection motivation theory of health behavior (Rippetoe & Rogers, 1987) incorporates the notion of self-efficacy, and the health belief model (Rosenstock, 1974) specifies a variable called health locus of control to account for individual differences in the amount of control people feel they have for engaging in a particular health behavior. A fuller understanding of the negotiation process and its success could likely be gained by assessing negotiation efficacy—that is, the confidence people have in their ability to successfully use negotiation strategies (Hubbard & Mannell, 2001). Similar ideas have been developed and used to predict adherence in the face of barriers to exercise behavior (Poag-DuCharme & Brawley, 1993). In an attempt to explore the usefulness of the self-efficacy idea, Loucks-Atkinson (2002) developed a measure of negotiation efficacy and extended the constraint-mitigation model proposed by Hubbard and Mannell. She found that the people in her study who had high negotiation efficacy—that is, confidence in their ability to use the negotiation resources and strategies they had available—were both more motivated to participate in active leisure and more likely to negotiate (see **Figure 14.2**, p. 228). It would appear to be productive to pursue the development of theory and research that extends thinking and knowledge about the negotiation process and those factors that influence it.

Constraint and Nonparticipation Process Models

Social cognitive theories are comprised of structural components, such as motives, beliefs, attitudes, appraisals, and self-efficacy, and they also specify the links and intervening processes that exist among these constructs. With respect to leisure constraint theory, Jackson et al. (1993) developed a series of propositions that begin to articulate a social cognitive model that describes the relationships among motivation, constraint, negotiation, and participation. Given that a number of alternative sets of interrelationships, each describing a somewhat

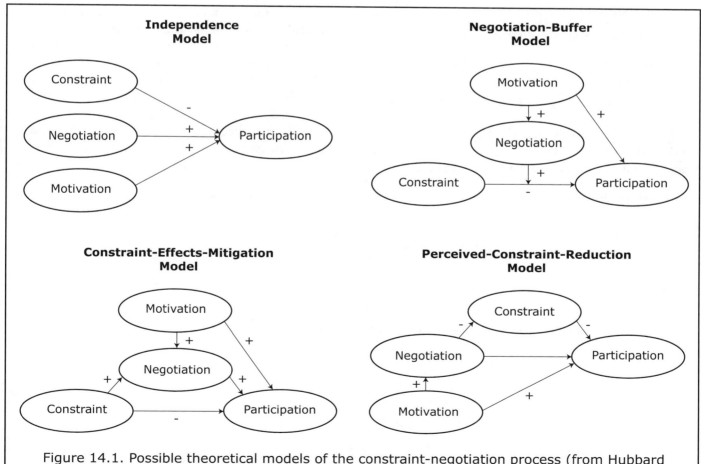

Figure 14.1. Possible theoretical models of the constraint-negotiation process (from Hubbard & Mannell, 2001, p. 148)

different constraint negotiation process, are possible within the framework of these propositions, there still is room for further theoretical development of Jackson et al.'s constraint theory. To this end, Hubbard and Mannell (2001) argued the relationships among the constructs of constraint, negotiation, and participation have some parallels to relationships hypothesized to exist among the constructs of stress, coping, and health, respectively, by a variety of social cognitive stress coping and health models. Wheaton (1985) and Ensel and Lin (1991) discussed a number of possible models that suggest different links among these latter constructs, and these models could provide a useful framework for developing and testing competing models of the constraint-negotiation process. For example, the effect of constraint on leisure participation, like that of stress on health, is conceptualized as being negative, and negotiation can be seen to be a process analogous to coping. Based on this type of thinking, Hubbard and Mannell proposed and tested four constraint-negotiation models that specified different links between motivation, constraint, negotiation, and participation:

- independence model.

- negotiation-buffer model.

- constraint-effects-mitigation model.

- perceived-constraint-reduction model (see Figure 14.1).

They found the strongest support for the constraints-effects-mitigation model.

Transactional process models of general stress coping (Lazarus, 1995) and leisure stress coping (Iwasaki & Mannell, 1999–2000) also suggest additional ideas for

the development of social cognitive constraint models. To understand the mediating role of coping strategies in the stress-health relationship, a variety of other cognitive and behavioral factors, such as event appraisal, coping outcomes, and emotions have been identified as possible mediators. Relative to understanding the dynamic nature of the constraint process likely influenced by transactions between persons and contexts over time, researchers need to conceptualize and assess mediating factors in addition to negotiation. The importance or undesirability of the constraint (constraint appraisal), negotiation strategies, and negotiation outcomes (the extent to which people feel that their negotiation strategies are effective, they are satisfied with their negotiation outcomes, and they feel that their constraint levels are reduced) might all be useful process variables to consider in addition to the inclusion of the variable intention to participate that was mentioned earlier (see **Figure 14.3**).

Constraint Models and Stages of Participation

A final suggestion that might prove useful in the development of constraint theory is to conceptualize constraint and negotiation as ongoing and evolving processes that may operate differently for the adoption of an activity and later participation adherence. Researchers have given some attention to understanding the stages of exercise adoption and adherence, and the characteristics of people at these various stages (Brawley et al., 1998). The transtheoretical model of health behavior change (Prochaska, Redding, Harlow & Rossi, 1994) has a similar focus. A key premise of this latter model

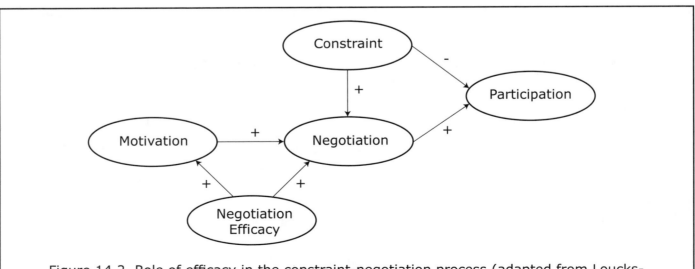

Figure 14.2. Role of efficacy in the constraint-negotiation process (adapted from Loucks-Atkinson, 2002, p. 197)

is that people go through various stages of change in adopting and maintaining a health behavior. According to Prochaska et al. (see also Prochaska & Marcus, 1994) constructs such as self-efficacy can be integrated into the transtheoretical model. A few leisure researchers have examined the process by which people become initiated, eventually committed, and sometimes drop out of leisure activities (e.g., Stebbins, 2001), but little leisure constraint research has been carried out to determine the role of constraints in this process. An exception is a study reported by McQuarrie and Jackson (1996). They examined changes in the negotiation strategies used as adult amateur ice skaters progressed through this serious leisure "career." It may prove profitable to assess over time the situation-specific and context-specific reactions and adjustments people make to start new leisure activities, increase levels of activity, or maintain their current activity level when confronted with constraints.

Development and Value of Nonparticipation Models of Leisure Behavior

The present discussion suggested models developed in the leisure, health, and exercise fields to explain nonparticipation and to help in developing interventions are either evolving to become social cognitive theories or have been consciously developed with the use of formal social cognitive theories. There is considerable similarity in the constructs that comprise these models and the processes hypothesized to link them with participation. However, in spite of these similarities, there is good potential for additional cross-fertilization. While considerable cross-fertilization has occurred in health and exercise with the application of formal social psychological theory, nonparticipation models of leisure behavior have been more isolated in their development.

However, in spite of this potential for the development of nonparticipation models, is there a need for specialized theories of nonparticipation such as leisure constraint theory? Social science theories attempt to explain human behavior, including level of participation. Is not nonparticipation just the "flip-side" of participation? The value of singling out and labeling some factors that influence participation "constraints" is still a topic of debate, particularly if the definition of constraint becomes so broad as to allow any factor influencing participation to be seen as a constraint. For example, if a favorable attitude toward partying or having an extroverted personality trait is related to participation in this activity, having a negative attitude or an introverted personality trait could be considered a constraint. How much farther does identifying all factors that influence participation as constraints go toward helping researchers and practitioners understand participation and nonparticipation?

Samdahl and Jekubovich (1997), in their critique of leisure constraints, raised a similar issue. They argued that constraint theory, particularly the concept of negotiation, was a framework that could limit researchers' efforts to develop a comprehensive understanding of the factors that influence the leisure choices people make and how they construct their leisure lifestyles. If the concept of negotiation is used so loosely and generally to refer to any factor that facilitates participation, leisure constraint theory may appear to explain all leisure behavior without any real improvement in researchers' understanding of the phenomena. In the case of the negotiation process, Hubbard and Mannell (2001) suggested it may be important to distinguish between the *facilitatory* and *negotiatory* functions of factors that influence leisure participation. It could be argued that factors are negotiatory only if they are triggered by encounters with constraint. It is likely many of the resources and strategies used to negotiate constraints are also general factors that can facilitate participation whether constraints are encountered or not (e.g., having friends with whom to do

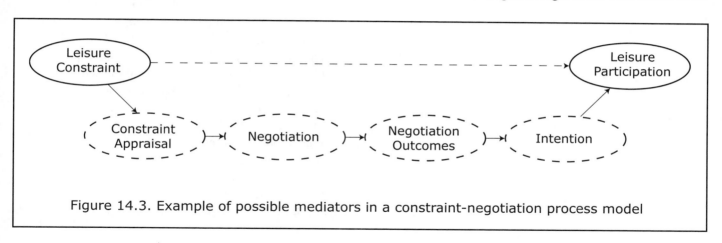

Figure 14.3. Example of possible mediators in a constraint-negotiation process model

things or being a person who likes to learn new skills). Some further thought needs to be given to determining when factors that influence participation are best treated as constraints, general facilitatory influences, or negotiation resources.

From a practical perspective, there is little doubt nonparticipation models are useful heuristic devices that direct and focus policymakers' and service providers' attention on the factors that restrict participation in the "good" behaviors they are trying to promote, possibly leading to more focused and specific interventions. These models have what Brawley (1993, p. 100) has called "theory practicality." In leisure studies the constructs of barriers and constraints first came about as a consequence of a concern with the external factors that kept people from using parks (Jackson, 1988). The development of models on preventative, detection, and coping health behavior also seems to have been utilization-focused for the benefit of policymakers and practitioners. This focus on *why people don't do what is good for them* appears to be an important and continuing concern in leisure studies and services.

References

Ajzen, I. (1991). The theory of planned action. *Organizational Behavior and Human Decision Processes*, *50*, 179–211.

Ajzen, I. and Driver, B. L. (1991). Prediction of leisure participation from behavioral, normative and control beliefs: An application of the theory of planned behavior. *Leisure Sciences*, *13*, 185–204.

Bandura, A. (1986). *Social foundations of thought and action: A social cognitive theory*. Englewood Cliffs, NJ: Prentice Hall.

Baum, A., Revenson, T. A., and Singer, J. E. (Eds.). (2001). *Handbook of health psychology*. Mahwah, NJ: Lawrence Erlbaum Associates, Inc.

Brawley, L. R. (1993). The practicality of using social psychological theories for exercise and health research and intervention. *Journal of Applied Sport Psychology*, *5*, 99–115.

Brawley, L. R., Martin, K. A., and Gyurcsik, N. C. (1998). Problems in assessing perceived barriers to exercise: Confusing obstacles with attributions and excuses. In J. L. Duda (Ed.), *Advances in sport and exercise psychology measurement* (pp. 337–350). Morgantown: WV: Fitness Information Technology, Inc.

Brunson, M. W. and Shelby, B. (1993). Recreation substitutability: A research agenda. *Leisure Sciences*, *15*, 67–74.

Carroll, B. and Alexandris, K. (1997). Perception of constraints and strength of motivation: Their relationship to recreational sport participation in Greece. *Journal of Leisure Research*, *29*(3), 279–299.

Champion, V. (1995). Development of a benefits and barriers scale for mammography utilization. *Cancer Nursing*, *18*, 53–59.

Crawford, D. W., Jackson, E. L., and Godbey, G. C. (1991). A hierarchical model of leisure constraints. *Leisure Sciences*, *13*, 309–320.

Csikszentmihalyi, M. and Kleiber, D. A. (1991). Leisure and self-actualization. In B. L. Driver, P. J. Brown, and G. L. Peterson (Eds.), *Benefits of leisure* (pp. 91–102). State College, PA: Venture Publishing, Inc.

Devellis, R. F., Alfieri, W. S., and Ahluwalia, I. B. (1995). The importance of careful measurement in health education research, theory and practice. *Health Education Research, 10*, i–vii.

Dishman, R. K. (1988). Behavioral barriers to health-related physical fitness. In L. K. Hall and G. C. Meyer (Eds.), *Epidemiology, behavior change, and intervention in chronic disease* (pp. 49–83). Champaign, IL: Life Enhancement Publications.

Driver, B. L., Brown, P., and Peterson, G. L. (1991). *Benefits of leisure*. State College, PA: Venture Publishing, Inc.

Driver, B. L. and Bruns, D. H. (1999). Concepts and uses of the benefits approach to leisure. In E. L. Jackson and T. L. Burton (Eds.), *Leisure studies: Prospects for the twenty-first century* (pp. 349–369). State College, PA: Venture Publishing, Inc.

Eagly, A. H. and Chaiken, S. (1993). *The psychology of attitudes*. Fort Worth, TX: Harcourt, Brace and Company.

Ensel, W. M. and Lin, N. (1991). The life stress paradigm and psychological distress. *Journal of Health and Social Behavior*, 32, 321–341.

Fishbein, M. and Ajzen, I. (1975). *Belief, attitude, intention, and behavior: An introduction to theory and research*. Reading, MA: Addison-Wesley.

Frederick, C. J. and Shaw, S. M. (1995). Body image as leisure constraint: Examining the experience of aerobic exercise classes for young women. *Leisure Sciences, 17*, 57–73.

Goodale, T. L. and Witt, P. A. (1989). Recreation non-participation and barriers to leisure. In E. L. Jackson and T. L. Burton (Eds.), *Understanding leisure and recreation: Mapping the past, charting the future* (pp. 421–449). State College, PA: Venture Publishing, Inc.

Hamilton, D. L., Devine, P. G., and Ostrom, T. M. (1994). Social cognition and classical issues in social psychology. In P. G. Devine, D. L. Hamilton, and T. M. Ostrom (Eds.), *Social cognition: Impact on social psychology* (pp. 1–13). New York, NY: Academic Press.

Hendee, J. C. and Burdge, R. J. (1974). The substitutability concept: Implications for recreation research and management. *Journal of Leisure Research, 6*, 157–162.

Henderson, K. A., Bedini, L. A., Hecht, L., and Schuler, R. (1995). Women with physical disabilities and the negotiation of leisure constraints. *Leisure Studies, 14*, 17–31.

Henderson, K. A. and Bialeschki, M. D. (1993). Negotiating constraints to women's physical recreation. *Society and Leisure, 16*, 389–412.

Hubbard, J. and Mannell, R. C. (2001). Testing competing models of the leisure constraint negotiation process in a corporate employee recreation setting. *Leisure Sciences, 23*, 145–163.

Iso-Ahola, S. E. (1986). A theory of substitutability of leisure behavior. *Leisure Sciences, 8*, 367–389.

Iso-Ahola, S. E. (1997). A psychological analysis of leisure and health. In J. T. Haworth (Ed.), *Work, leisure and well-being* (pp. 131–144). New York, NY: Routledge.

Iso-Ahola, S. E. (1999). Motivational foundations of leisure. In E. L. Jackson and T. L. Burton (Eds.), *Leisure studies: Prospects for the twenty-first century* (pp. 35–51). State College, PA: Venture Publishing, Inc.

Iso-Ahola, S. E. and Mannell, R. C. (1985). Social and psychological constraints on leisure. In M. G. Wade (Ed.), *Constraints on leisure* (pp. 111–151). Springfield, IL: Charles C. Thomas.

Iwasaki, Y. and Mannell, R. C. (1999–2000). The effects of leisure beliefs and coping strategies on stress–health relationships: A field study. *Leisure/Loisir, 24*, 3–57.

Iwasaki, Y. and Mannell, R. C. (2000). Hierarchical dimensions of leisure stress coping. *Leisure Sciences, 22*, 163–181.

Iwasaki, Y. and Schneider, I. E. (2003). Leisure, stress, and coping: An evolving areas of inquiry. *Leisure Sciences, 25*(2/3), 207–230.

Jackson, E. L., Crawford, D. W., and Godbey, G. (1993). Negotiation of leisure constraints. *Leisure Sciences, 15*, 1–12.

Jackson, E. L. and Rucks, V. C. (1995). Negotiation of leisure constraints by junior-high and high-school students: An exploratory study. *Journal of Leisure Research, 27*, 85–105.

Jackson, E. L. and Scott, D. (1999). Constraints to leisure. In E. L. Jackson and T. L. Burton (Eds.), *Leisure studies: Prospects for the twenty-first century* (pp. 299–321). State College, PA: Venture Publishing, Inc.

Janz, N. K. and Becker, M. H. (1984). The Health Belief Model: A decade later. *Health Education Quarterly, 11*, 1–47.

Kando, T. M. (1980). *Leisure and popular culture in transition*. Toronto, Ontario, Canada: The C.V. Mosby Company.

Kay, T. and Jackson, G. (1991). Leisure despite constraint: The impact of leisure constraints on leisure participation. *Journal of Leisure Research, 23*, 301–313.

Kleiber, D. A., Hutchinson, S. L., and Williams, R. (2002). Leisure as a resource in transcending negative life events: Self-protection, self-restoration, and personal transformation. *Leisure Sciences, 24*, 219–235.

Lazarus, R. S. (1995). Theoretical perspectives in occupational stress research. In R. Crandall and P. L. Perrewe (Eds.), *Occupational stress: A handbook* (pp. 3–14). Washington, DC: Taylor and Francis.

Lazarus, R. S. and Folkman, S. (1987). Transactional theory and research on emotions and coping. *European Journal of Personality, 1*, 141–169.

Loucks-Atkinson, A. (2002). Role of self-efficacy in the constraint negotiation process: The case of individuals with fibromyalgia syndrome. In E.L. Jackson (Ed.), *Proceedings of the tenth Canadian congress on leisure research* (pp. 196–198). Edmonton, Alberta, Canada: Canadian Association for Leisure Studies.

Maddux, J. E. (1993). Social cognitive models of health and exercise behavior: An introduction and review of conceptual issues. *Journal of Applied Sport Psychology, 5*, 116–140.

Mannell, R. C. (1993). High investment activity and life satisfaction among older adults: Committed, serious leisure and flow activities. In J. R. Kelly (Ed.), *Activity and aging* (pp. 125–145). Newbury Park, CA: Sage Publications.

Mannell, R. C. and Kleiber, D. A. (1997). *A social psychology of leisure*. State College, PA: Venture Publishing, Inc.

Marcus, B. H. and Simkin, L. R. (1994). The transtheoretical model: Applications to exercise behavior. *Medicine and Science in Sports and Exercise, 26*, 1400–1404.

McQuarrie, F. and Jackson, E. L. (1996). Connections between negotiation of leisure constraints and serious leisure: An exploratory study of adult amateur ice skaters. *Society and Leisure, 19*, 459–483.

Poag-DuCharme, K. A. and Brawley, L. R. (1993). Self-efficacy theory: Use in the prediction of exercise behavior in the community setting. *Journal of Applied Sport Psychology, 5*, 178–194.

Prentice-Dunn, S. and Rogers, R. W. (1986). Protection motivation theory and preventive health: Beyond the health belief model. *Health Education Research: Theory and Practice, 1*, 153–161.

Prochaska, J. O. and DiClemente, C. C. (1982). Transtheoretical therapy: Toward a more integrative model of change. *Psychotherapy: Theory, Research and Practice, 19*(3), 276–288.

Prochaska, J. O. and Marcus, B. H. (1994). The transtheoretical model: Application to exercise. In R. K. Dishman (Ed.), *Advances in exercise adherence* (pp. 161–180). Champaign, IL: Human Kinetics.

Prochaska, J. O., Redding, C. A., Harlow, L. L., and Rossi, J. S. (1994). The transtheoretical model of change and HIV prevention: A review. *Health Education Quarterly, 21*, 471–486.

Raymore, L. A. (2002). Facilitators to leisure. *Journal of Leisure Research, 34*, 37–51.

Raymore, L., Godbey, G., Crawford, D., and von Eye, A. (1993). Nature and process of leisure constraints: An empirical test. *Leisure Sciences, 15*, 99–113.

Rippetoe, P. A. and Rogers, R. W. (1987). Effects of components of protection–motivation theory on adaptive and maladaptive coping with a health threat. *Journal of Personality and Social Psychology, 52*, 596–604.

Rogers, R. W. (1983). Cognitive and psychological processes in fear appeals and attitude change: A revised theory of protection motivation. In J. T. Cacioppo and R. E. Petty (Eds.), *Social psychophysiology* (pp. 153–176). New York, NY: Guilford Press.

Rojek, C. (1999). Deviant leisure: The dark side of free-time activity. In E. L. Jackson and T. L. Burton (Eds.), *Leisure studies: Prospects for the twenty-first century* (pp. 81–95). State College, PA: Venture Publishing, Inc.

Ronis, D. L., Yates, J. F., and Kirscht, J. P. (1989). Attitudes, decisions, and habits as determinants of behavior. In A. R. Pratkanis, S. J. Breckler, and A. G. Greenwald (Eds.), *Attitude structure and function* (pp. 213–239). New York, NY: Erlbaum.

Rosenstock, I. M. (1974). The health belief model and preventive health behavior. *Health Education Monographs, 2*, 354–386.

Samdahl, D. M. and Jejkubovich, N. J. (1997). A critique of leisure constraints: Comparative analyses and understandings. *Journal of Leisure Research, 29*, 430–452.

Scott, D. (1991). The problematic nature of participation in contract bridge: A qualitative study of group-related constraints. *Leisure Sciences, 13*, 321–336.

Shaw, S. M. (1997). Controversies and contradictions in family leisure: An analysis of conflicting paradigm. *Journal of Leisure Research, 29*, 98–112.

Shaw, S. M., Bonen, A., and McCabe, J. F. (1991). Do more constraints mean less leisure? Examining the relationship between constraints and participation. *Journal of Leisure Research, 23*, 286–300.

Shelby, B. and Vaske, J. J. (1991). Resource and activity substitutes for recreational salmon fishing in New Zealand. *Leisure Sciences, 13*, 21–32.

Stebbins, R. A. (2001). *New directions in the theory and research of serious leisure*. New York, NY: The Edwin Mellen Press.

Verhoef, M. J. and Love, E. J. (1994). Women and exercise participation: The mixed blessings of motherhood. *Health Care for Women International, 15*, 297–306.

Wallston, K. A. (1992). Hocus-pocus, the focus isn't strictly on locus: Rotter's social learning theory modified for health. *Cognitive Therapy and Research, 16*, 183–199.

Wallston, K. A., Wallston, B. S., and DeVellis, R. (1978). Development of the Multidimensional Health Locus of Control (MHLC) scales. *Health Education Monographs, 6*, 160–170.

Wheaton, B. (1985). Models for the stress-buffering functions of coping resources. *Journal of Health and Social Behavior, 26*, 352–364.

Chapter 15

The Utility of the Concept of Affordance for Leisure Research

Douglas A. Kleiber (University of Georgia), Michael G. Wade (University of Minnesota), and Angela Loucks-Atkinson (University of Georgia)

If some conditions in the environment constrain leisure behavior, it is also the case that some kinds of behavior and experience are elicited, or "afforded," by those and other conditions. *Affordance* is a concept from ecological psychology (Gibson, 1986; Greeno, 1994) that describes a property of the environment that signals certain opportunities for action. Leisure affordance offers opportunities for leisure experience. This chapter attempts to redress some limitations in the interpretation of affordance theory by leisure researchers, while elaborating on its potential usefulness for further research and for recreation resource management and leisure service delivery.

Applying the Concept of Affordance in Leisure Research

The idea of "affordance" has been suggested as a counterpoint to the concept of constraint (Mannell & Kleiber, 1997). Affordance characterizes what the environment offers a perceiver (Gibson, 1986; Greeno, 1994). If a constraint is that which keeps someone from acting in some way or experiencing some effect, the argument goes, then an affordance provides a "go" message that invites action and experience. A given situation presents limitations to an individual, but it also offers possibilities. One could see the limitations (constraints), or the possibilities (affordances), or both. Leisure, almost by definition, would be a greater source of affordance than constraint. Nevertheless, it is constraint to leisure—interpersonal, intrapersonal, and structural—that has been the focus of so much leisure research (see Jackson & Scott, 1999, for a review, and Wade, 1985, for an early collection), while affordance has been largely ignored.

Mannell and Kleiber (1997) originally advanced the argument that by focusing exclusively on constraint we may be missing the idea of what the environment offers in terms of affordance; that is, the opportunity or the possibilities for leisure that one sees, or could see with a little help, in a given situation. Mannell and Kleiber stated:

> The potential for facilitating leisure participation and enhancing leisure experiences can be understood through the leisure constraints and leisure affordances that are present in the environment or can be created within the environment, as well as the psychological factors within individuals that influence the perception of constraint or affordance. (p. 346)

Nevertheless, by positioning leisure affordance in opposition to constraint, Mannell and Kleiber were not entirely faithful to the idea of affordance as James Gibson originally advanced it. In modifying it they attempted to make it more accessible to an audience unfamiliar with ecological psychology. Simplification can certainly be a virtue if it leads to conceptual clarity or has heuristic value; but in oversimplifying important and useful aspects of the idea were neglected or ignored. Most important among these is affordance is *not* the opposite of constraint on some continuum of appraisal of a situation. Indeed affordance is defined by the constraints as well as the possibilities for action present in a particular situation (Greeno, 1994). For example, the affordances of a public library's reading material include the constraints associated with access and loan regulations and the defining limits of the collection itself. And the boundaries of a field of play circumscribe and thus constrain the action, as do other rules, but in so doing afford the behavioral options assumed for both participating and spectating.[1]

Shogan (2002) pointed out that rules of games have the effect of prescribing, proscribing, and describing action, thereby enabling and facilitating action in addition to constraining it. *Prescriptive rules*, of course, tell what to do (the tennis ball must be served into the opposite front court box on the opponents side). *Proscriptive rules* tell what is disallowed (the ball cannot be hit twice in regulation tennis play, or three times in wheelchair tennis). *Descriptive boundaries* delimit the conditions field of play making the game possible. Games are, of course, a special case of constraint, but the actions proscribed in a given situation (e.g. "please turn off all cell phones") will often raise the level of expectation for other kinds of experience in a given situation.

It is also a mistake, according to the Gibsonian perspective, to see affordance as essentially a subjective matter, as if it were simply a variation of optimistic or pessimistic perspectives on reality. Gibson and others (e.g., Greeno, 1994) view an affordance as a property present (embedded) in the environment, rather than being a matter of subjective interpretation.[2] Gibson (1986) explained affordance referred to properties of the environment offered. These properties are available to be perceived: "The medium, substances, surfaces, objects, places, and other animals have affordances for a given animal. They offer benefit or injury, life or death. That is why they need to be perceived" (Gibson, 1986, p. 143). Affordances, although existing in the environment, must be detected by an individual perceiver (actor) to be meaningful. An affordance is more likely to be perceived if it has importance for an individual's needs and interests. For example, an interest in climbing draws attention to the "climbability" of features of a landscape.

Affordances are only fully perceived through actions that bring the conditions into interaction with the individual. They are the resources both available to and encountered by organisms—resources with which they develop a relationship. Available affordances are not always recognized or acted on. Still they exist, describing species conditions that may not apply to a particular individual member of that species. Behavior affords more behavior, but behavior is regulated with respect to affordances, and perceptual systems must be attuned to an affordance for it to regulate action. The mutuality of the affordances in the environment and the behaviors or actions of an individual is essential to the perception/action sequence. Affordance describes both the agent and the system; it telegraphs to the perceiver/actor what is possible in that environmental context, as in "eat me, I am sweet" or "don't touch me, I will cause pain." A baseball bat has a shape that affords an adequate grip (narrow handle) with some width at the other end to increase the probability of striking the ball when swung. The trail marker is located and presented at the height and angle it is, and with limited verbal information, so as to be clearly instructive to a literate human being with some prospect of getting lost and some interest in avoiding such an outcome. The environment affords an individual such opportunities for action, though detection of the affordances in a setting will depend on needs and interests. Thus, a cliff may be perceived as a place to avoid, presenting primarily danger and injury risk to one who merely wants to descend or ascend safely and comfortably, while for another it affords an opportunity for climbing.

In a provocative challenge to the typical approaches to studying leisure that use goal-directed behavior as the essential paradigm, Pierskalla and Lee (1998) presented an ecological analysis that located the essence of leisure as being discoverable in the environment rather than generated as expectations or received as satisfactions. Leisure for them is rather the result of an encounter with the environment where conditions elicit the experience.[3] In introducing the idea of "leisure affordance" they were rejecting the idea of leisure experience as mental realizations of the satisfaction of leisure needs that existed before the event in question, such as the achievement of victory in a sporting contest. Pierskalla and Lee described recreation as the activity, the "search for information" (p. 68; borrowing terms from Gibson, 1986) that results in the perception of leisure affordances.

In reviewing Gibson's ecological psychology, and in particular his notion of affordance, Pierskalla and Lee demonstrated that separating perception and environment does an injustice to the interaction of perception and action in creating meaning and value in the human environment. Greeno (1994) also pointed out that Gibson's principle of "direct perception" is an interactionist view that rejects the external–physical/internal–mental dichotomy. The environment enables individuals to perceive opportunities. Perception also occurs through action; as the perspective changes, opportunities are redefined. Stepping through the threshold of a museum reveals its affordances far more completely than looking through the museum window.

Leisure Affordance in Outdoor and Social Contexts

Pierskalla and Lee offer a paradigm for understanding leisure experience as the result of exploited opportunity rather than the funneling of behavior by a combination of drives and barriers. However, their analysis is limited in several respects. First, while they introduce the idea of leisure affordance as distinctly characteristic of the environment, they do not fully elaborate on the qualities of that condition or set of conditions. Second, they restrict their attention to the physical environment and leave the social environment for others to explore. Finally, they restrict their critique of the expectancy–valence paradigm to benefits research, while not addressing the same limitations in constraints research. We attempt here to redress each of these limitations.

Leisure Affordance

Pierskalla and Lee's ecological analysis of leisure behavior in the context of outdoor recreation demonstrates the environment possesses information that reveals an individual's opportunities for action and potential for experience. Information is perceived in relation to the mode of activity and the skill level and interests of the perceiver. Further, they argue the environment, mode of activity, and skill level of the actor influence the process of perceiving affordances that offer opportunities for leisure. What constitutes a leisure affordance, however, is not entirely clear in Pierskalla and Lee's analysis. Leisure qualities are not fully described. We submit those qualities include "preferred experience" (Kleiber, 1999), particularly enjoyment, relaxation, and a feeling of comfortable present-centeredness. For example, the juxtaposition of a rock next to a waterfall affords experiences of both sensory stimulation and relaxed tranquility, commonly recognized characteristics of leisure.

A change in the actor's needs or motives does not change an affordance, as affordances are the properties and events present in the environment (Pierskalla & Lee, 1998). However, a change in the actor's needs or motives may change what the actor *perceives* among existing affordances. An affordance can be many things to many people. For example, a lake affords swimming for an individual who possesses this skill but may only afford splashing for a child who cannot swim. For another individual it affords boating and for another, bathing. Therefore, the lake affords certain actions and behaviors depending on the skills, needs, interests, and perceptions of an individual. By manipulating the environment (as Disney World managers, Montessori teachers, adaptive equipment designers, and park engineers do), leisure providers may be able to create an even greater range of opportunities, but they will only be realized if potential actors are sensitized to the possibilities. That is, we cannot create an affordance to be acted on without knowing the actor/perceiver.

Using the example of the individual who cannot swim, we can consider how constraint and affordance perspectives create different orientations. From the perspective of constraints we would be inclined to see individuals as constrained from using the lake to the extent that they lack swimming skills or boating resources. From the affordance perspective, on the other hand, we would examine the environment for what it does offer them in the way of splashing, bathing, and socializing. Or we might manipulate the environment to expand leisure affordances by designing a water slide that does not drop them off into deep water. Helping them to become *attuned* to the possibilities, however, is a critical aspect of the affordance perspective.

Attunement is an important concept for understanding how affordances are perceived. We are all sensitive to opportunities in the environment, but self-tuning, or directed attention, enables the individual to detect the features of the environment that are most relevant and meaningful in relation to his or her abilities and interests. Individuals tune out certain information and attune themselves to other information in the environment. The process of attunement allows individuals to perceive certain environmental properties or events as leisure affordances to the extent they suggest the experiences noted here. Pierskalla and Lee (1998) pointed out "experience is the education of attention" (p. 73), implying that as leisure is experienced the associated affordances are brought into sharper relief.

As Gibson noted, the affordance in an environment may bode well or ill to the perceiver. An affordance that specifies danger will certainly create a different response than an affordance that invites an encounter. Leisure affordances are clearly of the latter kind. And more specifically, we would argue, a leisure affordance is essentially an element of the environment that specifies to the perceiver opportunities for relaxation and/or enjoyment in some measure and variation. Although, to Gibson, affordances are neither pleasant nor unpleasant in general, leisure affordances are clearly of the former kind.

The utility of leisure affordance as a concept is in what it specifies to people about the leisure opportunities available to them. Mannell and Kleiber noted "[r]ecognizing and creating leisure affordance is almost always a partner to managing and negotiating leisure constraints" (1997, p. 346). The notion of creating leisure affordance may be misleading, however; affordances are *not* a consequence of education, persuasion, or even attunement. While these are all important processes that may be addressed in the context of programming and intervention, it is important to reiterate that affordances are present in the perceived environment. Any actual creating of affordance might occur either through environmental design and/or reengineering. We will elaborate on this notion in the final section of this chapter.

Leisure Affordance in Social Environments

As is true of the Pierskalla and Lee (1998) analysis, ecological psychology as a whole has concerned itself mostly with the perception of and interaction with the physical environment and how attunement to its affordances facilitates effective action; but the environment is social as well as physical. Social affordances that individuals perceive come in a variety of forms, including facial expressions, gestures, and kinematic specification, or what is more commonly called "body language" (Runeson & Frykholm, 1983), as well as verbal communication, which are perceived both before and in response to their own actions. The social occasion of a party may be perceived as an enjoyable leisure event for one individual but by another as an uncomfortable social context.

An ecological analysis of a social interaction emphasizes perception rather than cognition (seeing directly what is actually being done by others rather than needing an interpretation of what is seen) in describing an individual's response to the social world (McArthur & Baron, 1983).[4] Individuals (actors) develop understanding directly from information available (Gibson, 1986) in the social environment as they interact with it, rather than requiring internal representation and subsequent interpretation of that environment. This social ecological perspective has been used to describe encounters with the environment that discourage or encourage play in individuals with developmental disabilities (e.g., McArthur & Baron, 1983; Van Acker & Valenti, 1989) or physical disabilities (Goodwin & Watkinson, 2000).

By extension, then, the social ecological perspective should also specify conditions of social affordance conducive to self-expression more generally. As with other kinds of affordance, sensitivity to social affordances changes as a result of a person's characteristics, actions and interactions. As a person enters a novel social situation, the reactions of others (e.g., turning of the eyes, smiling, scowling, or a lack of attention from others) further define the affordances of the context. This makes social affordance more difficult to specify, and yet a recognition of this complexity promises a more complete explanation and understanding of behavior in context. Social psychology of leisure is concerned with understanding and studying leisure behavior and experience of individuals in social situations (Mannell & Kleiber,

1997). Specifying leisure affordance in social situations can provide a more complete description of leisure behavior and experience than has been the case in leisure research to date.

The Perception Problem in Constraints Research

Pierskalla and Lee (1998) noted, "unlike the expectancy–valence theory, this ecological approach does not try to understand the underlying cause of behavior (e.g., motives)" (p. 68). Indeed, they criticize studies using an expectancy–valence approach for separating the "world of mind" from the "world of matter." That is, studies using this framework separate the internal from the external, when perception, meaning, and value are all a function of the interaction (cf. Gibson, 1986). "The key focus of study [from an ecological perspective] is the process rather than the underlying behavioral causes of information seeking" (Pierskalla & Lee, 1998, p. 70). Pierskalla and Lee's critique of the expectancy–valence framework can also be addressed to the leisure constraints framework.

Leisure constraint research also often separates the "world of mind" from the "world of matter." While conceptualizations of constraints have recognized the interplay of internal and external factors in the different categories, as well as the interaction of the categories (e.g., Jackson, 1988, 1997), the prevailing tendency for constraints researchers is to separate constraints into intrapersonal, interpersonal, and structural in a way that is potentially misleading. To do so suggests a separate reality for internal constraints and external constraints, when both are typically involved. For example, it is difficult to categorize the constraint of a woman's chronic pain into "world of mind" (i.e., internal) and "world of matter" (i.e., external). Chronic pain can be associated with structural constraint in that environmental features (e.g., opening heavy doors) may be more challenging to her than others, while interpersonal constraints clearly arise through lack of understanding or social stigma, and certainly the fear associated with aggravating chronic pain would seem to be an intrapersonal constraint. The intervening constraints of chronic pain thus become internalized, resulting in a reduction of interest or desire to participate in certain activities, which then makes them antecedent constraints according to the model. In this example, the utility of separating the reality of the experience into internal and external factors becomes questionable. The experience of chronic pain interacts with the environment, the woman's perceptions, and her actions. This is experienced as a process and not as separate phenomena.

It has been suggested affordance can only be about structural constraint, because it is about the environment (i.e., "out there"). In this case, important intrapersonal constraints, such as shyness, could not be considered vis-à-vis affordance. But that limitation holds true only if one accepts the dichotomy between internal and external. As McArthur and Baron (1983) argued, internal structures must be understood in relation to external ones. Therefore, to understand intrapersonal constraints we must understand structural constraints and external factors. From this perspective, interpersonal constraints may be examined in terms of social affordances, but the intrapersonal impact cannot be separated out in such an approach. Taking the case of a person with a physical disability, one would first see the disability as constraining—"handicapping"—at both a structural level in terms of accessibility and at an intrapersonal level in terms of efficacy expectations. It is obviously also constraining at an interpersonal level in terms of availability of companions, support, and typical attitudes toward disability. But all these things are a matter of perspective. The social stigma faced by people with disabilities, as with other stigmatizing conditions, is structural and societal and even hegemonic, to utilize the perspective of critical social theory. As such it may limit (constrain) behavior in a variety of ways and with some unexpected effects. To illustrate the point further, a study of adolescents with spinal cord injuries revealed a clear preference for engaging in sports with others in wheelchairs versus those who did not require them (Groff, 1998). Furthermore, it was clear participants felt more comfortable with others with similar disabilities and more free to express themselves. Thus a case was made that, while there may be important advantages to recreation participation in integrated settings, the kind of relaxed self-expression that contributes to identity formation probably occurs more effectively in segregated settings (Groff & Kleiber, 2001).[5]

While constraints were not the focus of the Groff and Kleiber study, it is reasonable to assume the participants interviewed would have recognized constraints to their participation in integrated settings at the structural, interpersonal, and intrapersonal levels. The lack of adequate wheelchair accommodations in the sport facility, the lack of awareness of coaches and able-bodied participants, and the anxiety experienced in anticipation of participation would be among the constraining conditions; but separating their influences would not likely reflect the experience of participants. It also may be tempting to suggest that eager participation in the segregated setting was due to the absence of such constraints. Clearly, though, the motivation to participate in the latter setting came about at least as much from the attraction of the situation as from the absence of constraints. Indeed, constraints define any situation according to affordance theory; in this case, even the segregated setting would be daunting to one who had yet to develop the necessary skills, but the signs and signals emitted basically send a "come and learn to play" message, and the other participants in wheelchairs provide exemplars of action that leads to enjoyable self-expression.

The label "physically disabled" is also stigmatizing in ways that may not even be fully understood by a disabled individual, but it is nonetheless determining (constraining) interpersonally and then intrapersonally in an apparently antecedent way. But how useful, then, are such distinctions? Given the importance of perception for all types of constraints, it might be tempting to see everything as socially constructed, as if the perceived world is entirely a personal fiction in its idiosyncratic interpretation (however, the experiences and interpretations may in fact be shared by other subgroups or entire societies), but ecological psychology recognizes the environment as having some tangible conditions that must nevertheless be perceived by the organism. As Greeno (1994) pointed out, the interactionist view is different from the constructionist perspective in saying there is a world out there people attune themselves to more or less successfully through interaction. Social construction of that world, while clearly impactful in itself, must nevertheless be tested in interaction with the environment as it exists. Constraints research could be enhanced by focusing less on the internal–external dichotomy and concentrating on the dynamic interaction of the individual with the environment.

It also bears repeating that leisure affordance is a special kind of affordance. To return to our person with a disability, the environment is often unwelcoming in many ways. In ancient cultures some disabilities were precipitously fatal. As the world has been made more accessible for a wide variety of disabling conditions, affordances have been expanded accordingly, but only where an affordance is appealing and inviting can we conceive of it as a leisure affordance. Specification of affordances for leisure will be an important subject for both future research and practice.

Implications for Research

The majority of the literature on constraints in recreation is arguably provider driven. Earlier constraint research sought to determine the conditions that limit use of a particular service or resource—the resource or service itself being an unquestioned good that may be kept away from a participant for reasons unrelated to its inherent qualities (Crawford & Godbey, 1987; Goodale & Witt, 1989). With respect to a given constraint, the principle was essentially, "if we remove it, they will come." Thus, it has not been uncommon to force a response (as in a ranking of most significant deterrents) from people who haven't felt particularly constrained because they haven't sought the particular activities or experiences. Nevertheless, when study participants are asked to provide an interpretation that fits the experimental demand of the investigator's protocol, they do. This applies especially to supposed "latent" demand (where constraints are argued to be "antecedent"). It is thus largely an attempt to capture the noninvolved market. And even where constraints are clearly felt, turning away from a desired or previously valued activity may be less an indication of defeat and frustration than of changed priorities and interests. In any case, examining the service/resource/activity itself for its intrinsic properties of attraction is rarely included in constraints research. Focusing on the true functional (psychological, emotional) impact of what is lost due to a constraint would seem to be important. And yet it rarely comes up in discussions of constraint, except perhaps more recently where motivation has been considered (e.g., Alexandris & Tsorbatxoudis, 2002; Hubbard & Mannell, 2001).

As a practical research problem, specifying leisure affordance may have heuristic value for those who have been concerned with the issue of negotiating leisure constraints. Rather than having to locate the constraint as internal or external—when it is usually both—it is likely simpler and more direct to assume an interaction and focus instead on the nature of the affordances in a situation and the perception, or absence of perception, of those affordances. Jackson (2000) stated to enhance our understanding of leisure constraints researchers should investigate how individuals turn constraints into opportunities. He suggested we address the following question: "Why are some people particularly successful in their leisure lives, not only negotiating constraints but also viewing constraining factors more positively as opportunities to develop new leisure interests and pursuits?" (Jackson, 2000, p. 66). Perceiving constraining factors as opportunities sounds contradictory, but considerable evidence now suggests constraints are not inevitably deterring to participation and enjoyment. Understanding the way in which constraint in the environment is relativized with respect to the concept of affordance offers a theoretical solution to that conundrum and an explanation for previously ambiguous results. There clearly are leisure affordances in contexts constrained in various ways where individuals find a way to use those conditions to create meaningful leisure experience.

By the usual definition, constraints are not positive factors; however, examining opportunities offered through the perception of leisure affordance might shed light on this process and provide new directions for research. In a similar vein, developmentalists have identified a process of *selective optimization with compensation* (Baltes & Baltes, 1990) that describes how aging forces people to find ways to manage constraints in maintaining high priority activities while disengaging from activities no longer possible or no longer as attractive to do as they once were. This process is consistent with the discrimination/attunement process of assessing affordance and constraint throughout the life course. Indeed, where constraints and limitations are prohibitive, new affordances may be recognized. McGuire and Norman (this volume) use this perspective in identifying the enabling aspects of constraints in their consideration of positive adaptation to the limitations of aging, noting "for some older people constraints...support a disengagement from life that is congruent with physical, emotional, cognitive and financial losses." They use the example of prohibitive activity fees as helping a person with physical limitations adjust to the necessity of giving up some activities, which will in turn allow him or her to perceive other more compelling possibilities within his or her circumstances and to consider how to optimize those.

The process of *constraint negotiation* may also be further clarified from an ecological perspective. Constraint negotiation is largely a matter of persisting in responding to leisure affordance in spite of constraints. Mannell and Kleiber suggested a variety of strategies exist to help individuals overcome leisure constraint and therefore create affordance. However, as noted earlier, that portrayal of affordance misrepresented the concept to some extent; it erroneously suggested affordance is a matter of perspective and interpretation, and a result of optimism (i.e., "the glass is half full"). Affordances are not in this sense "created"; they are more accurately recognized as existing along with and even defined by the constraints that exist. For example, an older person may see an opportunity for leisure in a walk around the block on a 70-degree summer day, weakness in her legs notwithstanding. The winter, on the other hand, does not afford such activity because of the cold and the prospects of slipping. Those constraints accepted, alternatives are sought indoors.

According to Gibson's view of affordance, leisure affordances cannot be viewed as the opposite of leisure constraints. Constraints are conceptualized as being either external to the individual (e.g., lack of a partner to play tennis) or internal to the individual (e.g., lack of skills to play tennis). As previously stated, affordance is not the opposite of constraint on a continuum of invitation to action; affordances are simply the possibilities that exist for action in the situation, and they may or may not be perceived. Leisure affordances do not assist an individual in overcoming or navigating constraint. They are not internal to the individual; rather, they are characteristics of the environment that promise relaxation and/or enjoyment when they are detected. For example, by providing an individual with a tennis partner, a social leisure affordance is not necessarily detected and the constraint of "lack of partner" is not necessarily overcome. Unless the individual perceives the social situation as conducive to leisure experience, the leisure affordance that exists has not yet been recognized.

Recently, Hubbard and Mannell (2001) provided an analysis of negotiation processes we find to be consistent with the idea of affordance. In their assessment of negotiation strategies and resources they isolated "facilitory conditions" (e.g., "having friends with whom to do things or being a person who likes to learn new skills") sometimes seen as the opposite of constraints and used as negative indicator items in measures of constraint. But their research showed these factors operate independently of actual constraints in bringing about behavior, making a case for the separate influence of motivation. However, while this is clearly an advance beyond other leisure constraints research wherein motivation is neglected, the authors still see motivation as internally driven rather than externally elicited. Affordance represents the environmental conditions that elicit motivation (e.g., interest, enthusiasm, approach) in conjunction with felt needs. And for explanatory purposes, it may be a mistake not to distinguish resources in the environment (e.g., "having friends with whom to do things"), which are clearly affordances, from those such as "being a person who likes to learn new skills," which more clearly define the person, even though it is the interaction of these that best describes behavioral reality. The use of negotiation *strategies*, such as "getting up earlier" or "learning to live within my means"[6] also begs for an ecological perspective for understanding the appeal of the environment that makes such strategies important. Finally, Hubbard and Mannell noted the data best supported the constraint/effects/mitigation model, suggesting "a higher level of motivation to participate does not lead to a reduction in perceptions of constraint" (p. 159). From the perspective of affordance theory, this would indicate rather than being the opposite of affordances, constraints simply serve to define them. In other words, in a context that offers the prospect for strongly desired leisure experience, the constraints clearly recognized as part of that context are simply accepted. The weather, the crowds, parking issues, and costs are not negotiated away in at-

tending an outdoor concert; they are considered a full part of the experience (cf. Shogan, 2002).

One of the challenges in using leisure affordance as a construct in research is how to operationalize it. Since affordances must be perceived to result in any kind of meaningful relationship with an individual, or in this case to produce leisure experience, the problem is primarily and essentially a descriptive and qualitative one, at least at first. Techniques that would elicit the perception of affordances—getting the perspective of participants about what is available to them, what they can do and what they can't—might involve the use of interviews about certain situations, either individually or in focus group formats. In their study of gym class participation among individuals with physical disabilities Goodwin and Watkinson (2000) used focus group interviews, visual recordings, and field notes to describe participant perceptions of the affordances in surfaces, objects, spaces, and social circumstances of the physical education environment. They elicited students' perceptions of ramps, water, modified equipment, and peer behaviors in defining the good days and bad days of PE class. For example, they found water afforded movement competence, locker rooms afforded overexposure, changing rooms afforded concealment, high grass restricted movement, and the theater-like setting promoted self-consciousness. Another possible advantage of using focus groups for studying affordances is the action research potential of contributing to attunement. In other words, as individuals participate in focus groups about the affordance of specific leisure environments, they may be attuned or sensitized to their possibilities.

The opportunities for employing quantitative methods in research on leisure affordance may be more limited than those using a qualitative approach. But there is reason to experiment with quantifying some of the judgments that might come in direct assessments and perception of physical and social environments or in their visual representations. For example, Van Acker and Valenti (1989) quantified observed behaviors with Likert scales in their ethological approach to studying social affordance in the environments of children with developmental disabilities. Further, it would be possible to design items on a survey that ask a respondent to record on a numerical scale the strength of a variety of leisure-related experiences if he or she were in a specified setting. Utilizing such quantitative approaches in conjunction with more qualitative interviews would help to sharpen measurement techniques at the same time the complexities of the perceived environment are explored.

Implications for Practice

An ecological perspective on leisure experience, utilizing the concept of affordance, also has much to offer in the realm of professional recreation and the management of leisure services and resources. We will break the discussion into the two sources of influence on behavior: the individual and the environment, focusing on leisure education in the case of the former and leisure resource development in the case of the latter.

Attunement Through Leisure Education

How does one come to detect affordance in the environment? This is essentially a matter of attunement. If a given setting intends to elicit recreation and leisure experience, but a prospective participant detects only the conditions that constrain or inhibit voluntary participation because the experiences anticipated lack the qualities of leisure, then leisure is not being afforded. Ameliorating some of the inhibiting factors might bring about a different view of this situation, but it will be necessary for the perception of the experience to change. In some cases this may be accomplished, not by altering the environment or providing the resources to overcome constraints, but rather through a process of refined projection as to the possibilities. Attunement suggests a merging of action and awareness (cf. flow) that allows a person to interact effectively with the environment in actually experiencing affordance. But there are a wide variety of factors—many of them falling in the various constraints categories—that keep a person from attending adequately and accurately to the possibilities in the environment for desirable experience, whether related to the construction of leisure or other, more instrumental, behaviors.

Leisure education is largely about *facilitation*, a subject that has drawn some attention in the recent constraints literature. Hubbard and Mannell (2001) identified "facilitory" characteristics in the assessment of constraint negotiation resources and strategies, but these facilitating resources, as noted previously, are essentially affordances. Attuning individuals to those resources is a different matter and may in fact be facilitated by educational intervention processes.

In a recent interpretation of Gibsonian ecological psychology, Reed (1996) offered the idea of a "field of promoted action" (p. 131; see also Reed, 1991) as all the affordances made available to or emphasized for the child by others and excluding those that are forbidden. He proceeded to describe parenting/caregiving with the developing infant and young child in these terms, noting, for example, that by three months infants act "prospectively" in interactive frames (i.e., they act to create anticipated action). Their locomotion leads to a sharing of the environment ("triadic interaction") with others. Caregivers are part of the interactive frame that attunes the infant to the environment by both action and coaching. In the area of leisure services, the field of promoted action of leisure educators would include those settings and conditions likely to lead to enjoyable or relaxing interactions and would exclude those expected to elicit self-consciousness and lead to anxiety or boredom.

Creating Leisure Affordance in Environmental Design

Affordances that suggest the likelihood of leisure experience currently exist in a wide variety of settings in both the natural physical environment and in social leisure contexts. Achieving leisure experience in these settings is largely a matter of attunement to the conditions that would interact effectively with individual abilities and interests. Creating additional affordances, on the other hand, involves the manipulation of the environment or the construction or arrangement of new environments. Designing environments that would promote leisure experience, whether in the construction of theme parks, playgrounds, and new trails or in the organization of special events, would benefit from an ecological perspective that recognizes the nature of affordances and the value of creating spaces and opportunities for interaction that have psychological significance (i.e. that have leisure meanings and values for particular individuals).[7]

While the application of affordance principles to the design of environments for adult leisure is largely nonexistent (although suggestions of such in the work of recreation resource planning and design exist), when affordance has been studied in relation to children's environments, the subject of play affordances is prominent. As with adult leisure experience, play is a preferred experience (i.e., intrinsically motivated) and takes advantage of opportunities for enjoyment that revolve around experimentation and diversion. In an interesting analysis using Gibson's affordance principles, Heft (1988) presented a functional approach to describing environmental resources for children and provided a taxonomy based on psychologically meaningful features of the play environment rather than on form-based classifications (e.g., trees, walls, slopes). He noted affordances are psychologically meaningful when adequately detected and are specified relationally in ways such as the following: climb-on-able surfaces, throw-able objects, mold-able materials, walk-on-able surfaces, and hide-behind-able, jump-over-able, and swing-on-able features. **Table 15.1** lists affordances Heft associated with different environmental features. Note that affordances appear in more than one category in some cases. As Heft noted, affordances are determined simultaneously by attributes of the environment (physical and social) and attributes of particular individuals or species. Age also differentiates, as adults and children will overlap only partially. For example, the affordance a child sees in a group of bushes for hiding may not be seen by adults because of both their size and their lack of interest in being concealed. Heft pointed out that functional characteristics of an environment are more important than forms alone since they have "experiential primacy." Indeed, a given form may have multiple functional "significances"—a rock may be perceived as affording grasping, throwing, holding down, propping open, hammering with, but it cannot also be a tree or bush or person. More generally, Heft's analysis suggests, while children are oriented in their play to certain environmental affordances, any environment might be designed, à la Maria Montessori (1964) and others (cf. Moore & Anderson, 1969), to be "autotelic," having features that afford and invite action, create interest which leads to activity, exploration and enjoyment, and/or elicit relaxation.

Conclusions

The concept of leisure affordance not only offers a useful idea for furthering the understanding of leisure behavior, but also should evoke an ecologically sensitive approach to leisure research more generally. While it has been used somewhat inappropriately in the past as the antithesis of leisure constraint, it is more clearly an alternative approach to constraint-related problems. On the one hand, it argues against some of the categories used in leisure constraint research (intrapersonal, interpersonal, and structural) as being artificial in ignoring the interaction of environment and perception, while on the other it treats the environment, physical as well as social, as something real rather than as a social construction.

In keeping with this approach, future research would do well to examine not only what individuals perceive as preventing them from participating in enjoyable leisure experiences, but also what they perceive in the environment that makes leisure experience a distinct possibility. While we recognize the theoretical and practical importance of identifying constraints that limit activity and experience in various ways, we have argued here that considering these from an ecological perspective in relation to leisure affordance offers a more complete picture both for further research and for recreation resource management and the provision of leisure services.

Table 15.1. A preliminary functional taxonomy of children's outdoor environments

1. Flat, relatively smooth surface: affords walking, running; cycling, skating, skateboarding

2. Relatively smooth slope: affords coasting down (e.g., on bike, wagon); rolling, sliding, running down; rolling objects down

3. Graspable/detached object: affords drawing, scratching; throwing; hammering, batting, spearing, skewering, digging, cutting; tearing, crumpling, squashing; building of structures (e.g., raw materials for forts)

4. Attached object: affords sitting on, jumping on/over/down/from

5. Nonrigid, attached object: affords swinging on (e.g., tree branch)

6. Climbing feature: affords exercise/mastery; looking out from; passage from one place to another (e.g., stairs, ladder)

7. Aperture: affords locomoting from one place to another; looking and listening into adjacent place

8. Shelter: affords microclimate; prospect/refuge; privacy

9. Moldable material (e.g., dirt, sand): affords construction of objects (e.g., pottery); pouring; modification of its surface features (e.g., sculpting)

10. Water: affords splashing; floating objects; swimming, diving, boating, fishing; mixing with other materials to modify their consistency

Adapted from Heft (1988)

References

Alexandris, K. and Tsorbatxoudis, C. (2002). Perceived constraints on recreational sport participation: Investigating their relationship with intrinsic motivation, extrinsic motivation and amotivation. *Journal of Leisure Research, 34*, 233–253.

Baltes, P. and Baltes, M. (1990). Psychological perspectives on successful aging: The model of selective optimization with compensation. In P. Baltes and M. Baltes (Eds.), *Successful aging: Perspectives from the behavioral sciences*. Cambridge, England: Cambridge University Press.

Crawford, D. E. and Godbey, G. (1987). Reconceptualizing barriers to family leisure. *Leisure Sciences, 9*, 119–127.

Gibson, J. J. (1986). *The ecological approach to visual perception*. Hillsdale, NJ: Lawrence Erlbaum Associates, Inc.

Goodale, T. L. and Witt, P. A. (1989). Recreation nonparticpation and barriers to leisure. In E. L. Jackson and T. L. Burton (Eds.), *Understanding leisure and recreation: Mapping the past, charting the future*. State College, PA: Venture Publishing, Inc.

Goodwin, D. L. and Watkinson, E. J. (2000). Inclusive physical education for the perspective of students with physical disabilities. *Adapted Physical Education Quarterly, 17*, 144–160.

Greeno, J. G. (1994). Gibson's affordances. *Psychological Review, 101*, 336–342.

Groff, D. (1998). *Exploring identity formation of youth involved in an after school disabled sports program*. Unpublished doctoral dissertation. University of Georgia, Athens.

Groff, D. and Kleiber, D. (2001). Exploring the identity formation of youth involved in an adapted sports program. *Therapeutic Recreation Journal, 35*, 318–332.

Heft, H. (1988). Affordances of children's environments: A functional approach to environmental description. *Children's Environments Quarterly, 5*, 29–37.

Henderson, K. and Bialeschki, D. (1993). Exploring an expanded model of women's leisure constraints. *Journal of Applied Recreation Research, 18*, 229–252.

Henderson, K, Bialeschki, D., Shaw, S., and Freysinger, V. (1996). *Both gains and gaps: Feminist perspectives on women's leisure*. State College, PA: Venture Publishing, Inc.

Hubbard, J. and Mannell, R. C. (2001). Testing competing models of the leisure constraint negotiation process in a corporate employee recreation setting. *Leisure Sciences, 23*, 145–163.

Jackson, E. L. (1988). Leisure constraints: A survey of past research. *Leisure Sciences, 10*, 203–215.

Jackson, E. L. (1997). In the eye of the beholder: A comment on Samdahl and Jekubovich (1997), A critique of leisure constraints: Comparative analyses and understandings. *Journal of Leisure Research, 29*, 458–468.

Jackson, E. L. (2000). Will research on leisure constraints still be relevant in the twenty-first century? *Journal of Leisure Research, 32*, 62–68.

Jackson, E. L. and Scott, D. (1999). Constraints to leisure. In T. L. Burton and E. L. Jackson (Eds.), *Leisure studies: Prospects for the twenty-first century*. State College, PA: Venture Publishing, Inc.

Kleiber, D. A. (1999). *Leisure experience and human development*. New York, NY: Basic Books.

Mannell, R. C. and Kleiber, D. A. (1997). *A social psychology of leisure*. State College, PA: Venture Publishing, Inc.

McArthur, L. Z. and Baron, R. M. (1983). Toward an ecological theory of social perception. *Psychological Review, 90*, 215–238.

Montessorri, M. (1964). *The Montessori method*. New York, NY: Shocken Books.

Moore, O. and Anderson, A. (1969). Some principles for the design of clarifying educational environments. In D. Goslin (Ed.), *Handbook of socialization theory and research*. New York, NY: Rand McNally.

Pieper, J. (1952). *Leisure: The basis of culture*. New York, NY: Pantheon.

Pierskalla, C. D. and Lee, M. E. (1998). An ecological perception model of leisure affordances. *Leisure Sciences, 20*, 67–79.

Raymore, L., Godbey, G., and Crawford, D. (1994). Self-esteem, gender, and socioeconomic status: Their relation to perceptions of constraint on leisure among adolescents. *Journal of Leisure Research, 26*, 99–118.

Reed, E. S. (1991). Cognition as the cooperative appropriation of affordances. *Ecological Psychology, 3*, 135–158.

Reed, E. S. (1996). *Encountering the world: Toward an ecological psychology*. New York, NY: Oxford University Press.

Runeson, S. and Frykholm, G. (1983). Kinematic specification of dynamics as an informational basis for person-and-action perception: Expectation, gender, recognition, and deceptive intention. *Journal of Experimental Psychology: General, 116*, 585–615.

Samdahl, D. M., Hutchinson, S., and Jacobson, S. (1999, May). *Navigating constraints? A critical commentary on negotiation in leisure research*. Wolfville,

Nova Scotia, Canada: Canadian Congress on Leisure Research.

Shogan, D. (2002). Characterizing constraints of leisure: A Foucaultian analysis of leisure constraints. *Leisure Studies*, *21*, 27–38.

Van Acker, R. and Valenti, S. S. (1989). Perception of social affordance with mild handicapping conditions: Implications for social skills training. *Ecological Psychology, 1*, 383–405.

Wade, M. G. (Ed.). (1985). *Constraints on leisure*. Springfield, IL: Charles. C. Thomas.

Endotes

1. That constraint and affordance may not be oppositional in nature is also suggested in recent work on the enabling properties of constraints (Henderson, Bialeschki, Shaw & Freysinger, 1996; McGuire & Norman, this volume; Shogan, 2002).

2. The leisure constraints literature has itself been biased largely to a subjective, interpretivist perspective. Henderson and Bialeschki (1993), for example, noted, "constraints have no intrinsic meaning until they are defined and redefined by individuals within their reality" (p. 223). But Raymore, Godbey, and Crawford (1994), in noting, "interpersonal constraints may be less identifiable because they involve subjective evaluations regarding other individuals" (p. 116), implied other constraints are more objectively identifiable, such as the absence of a playmate or the presence of steady auto traffic across a potential bike path.

3. This might be compared to Josef Pieper's (1952) idea of leisure as an attitude of relaxed openness to whatever presents itself.

4. Standard (traditional) views of perception incorporate it into the cognitive processes that both interpret and generate responses to external (environmental) stimuli. Gibson (1986) removed perception from this process. Direct perception immediately "informs" the perceiver (actor) as to the consequences or opportunities for action. Thus an ecological analysis of a social interaction emphasizes perception rather than cognition.

5. It may be tempting to see this as an example of constraint negotiation, a subject which will be addressed shortly, but rather than being exclusively a barrier to some desired end, the constraint of segregation defines the affordance of unselfconscious participation.

6. "Navigation" has been suggested as a more appropriate word than negotiation (Samdahl, Hutchinson & Jacobson, 1999), given that people more commonly work around constraining conditions than they actually work to change them. We concur and suggest the greatest gains in attunement to affordances come in large part from more clearly specifying constraints rather than trying to change them.

7. Barker and Wright (1955; cited in Heft, 1988) used the phrase "psychological habitat" to describe the niches that provided children with the experience they sought.

Chapter 16

Integrating Benefits to Leisure With Constraints to Leisure

John L. Crompton (Texas A&M University), Edgar L. Jackson (University of Alberta), and Peter Witt (Texas A&M University)

Over the last two decades, leisure studies witnessed the ebb and flow of new substantive topics, emerging theoretical frameworks and concepts, and significant developments in methodological breadth and sophistication. Among the topics that have become increasingly dominant in the field (in North America, at least), signified by the space devoted to them in refereed journals and at scholarly conferences, the issues of constraints to leisure and benefits of leisure stand out.

Much of the leisure research literature directly or indirectly touches on the benefits of leisure, even if it is not couched in that language, and at least one book has been published, *Benefits of Leisure*, edited by Driver and colleagues (Driver, Brown & Peterson, 1991). Driver and Bruns (1999) also provided us with a detailed statement of the "benefits approach to leisure." This framework has been widely advocated across North America from the municipal to the state/provincial levels of government as a philosophical and strategic approach to establishing the importance of leisure and recreation services and resources, as well as for planning, delivering, and managing them. Until the present book, there has been no equivalent of *Benefits of Leisure* for the field of constraints. However, as the book as a whole attests, together with the numerous citations of related research in the individual chapters, there has been a similar amount of interest in constraints as in benefits among leisure researchers.

Given the importance of the benefits and constraints subfields of leisure studies, their influence on theoretical developments and empirical research within the field as a whole, and their potential and actual impact on the delivery of leisure services, what is perhaps most surprising is the two areas of research tended to develop in parallel and distinctly, as opposed to in tandem and in connection with each other. Our purposes in this chapter are to suggest not only there are some important connections between benefits and constraints, but also there is much to be gained from thinking about and examining them simultaneously and in terms of interrelations between them. We suggest there are many ways in which researchers in each field can benefit from awareness and adaptation of the literature in the other. Our goals are

1. to prompt researchers and students to think about constraints and benefits in terms of their linkages rather than as separate, unrelated aspects of leisure.

2. to encourage research that might address benefits and constraints, and their interacting roles in people's lives, simultaneously.

We begin with a brief overview of some key ways in which benefits and constraints, and their associated literature, are—or can be perceived to be—connected. We then turn our attention to one specific example of a research project in which both constraints and benefits were examined for a specific purpose: market segmentation. The results of this research project show the examination of constraints and benefits and their interactions in the same study can be used to develop a segmentation of target markets theoretically more insightful and practically more useful than segmentation based on only one or the other of the two factors. Thus, a more complete understanding of the factors that influence people's choices of tourist and recreation destinations emerges.

An Overview of Connections Between Constraints and Benefits

Despite the current separation of work on constraints and benefits, we propose they also share several important similarities and potential connections. Recognizing the two fields are indeed linked should help to move each of them—and leisure studies as a whole—forward, because of the new insights generated and questions raised, which might profitably be addressed in future research.

If the criteria are defined broadly enough, an imaginative mind can establish a virtually unlimited number of connections between superficially different phenomena and concepts. For the purposes of this chapter, however, we focus more narrowly on what we see as three major linkages between constraints and benefits:

- similar intellectual origins of the two fields, coupled with the new insights each had to offer.

- the idea that the "benefits chain of causality" (Driver & Bruns, 1999), which shows how benefits that accrue to individuals have broader social and economic implications, can also be applied to the understanding of constraints.

- synthesis of concepts related specifically to constraints and to benefits into a single integrated model.

Constraints and Benefits: Origins and Insights

The emerging focus on both benefits of leisure and constraints to leisure arose out of what one might think of as some researchers' "dissatisfaction" with the limitations of previous approaches to understanding these phenomena and leisure in general. These approaches tended to adopt a numerical, "head counting" methodology, in which the implicit model posited leisure behavior as the ultimate dependent variable, usually couched in terms of participation in leisure and recreation activities. The goal of research was essentially to identify and to explain the impact on recreation participation of antecedent and intervening variables (e.g., socioeconomic and demographic factors and motivations) that would assist in the understanding of leisure and recreation choices. Moreover, there was a tendency to focus on the individual, and to view him or her as a "rational decision maker," with little acknowledgment either of limits to rationality (Simon, 1957), or of the context within which leisure decisions are made and their broader subsequent implications.

A crude model of this approach is summarized in **Figure 16.1**. In this simple model, interest in and preferences for an activity are viewed as intermediate or intervening variables that vary in accordance with several variables that describe an individual's socioeconomic and demographic characteristics (exemplified here by age), as well as by motivations. Motivations, too, exhibit socioeconomic variations, including age-based ones, and both of these sets of factors, singly and in combination, are assumed to explain aspects of an individual's leisure choices and recreational activity participation.

Research based on this approach tended to produce findings such as those displayed in the left-hand bar graph in **Figure 16.2**, which is an idealized but typical diagram using cross-sectional survey data to show a sharp age-based decline in participation in an outdoor recreational activity (e.g., downhill skiing). Sometimes findings such as these marked the endpoint of research, particularly in the early days when little was known about who participates in what activities, but more sophisticated studies would go on to ask what it is about age (or some other descriptor variable) that "causes" or explains a decline of this nature. Most frequently the explanation was sought in the realm of the "positive" forces that influence participation, such as motivations, which therefore helped to understand the clearly defined pattern of change in participation over the life cycle implied in the graph.

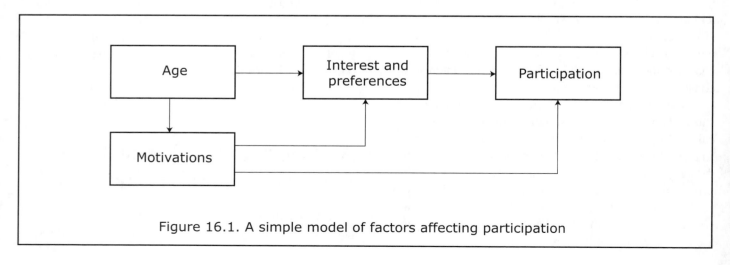

Figure 16.1. A simple model of factors affecting participation

From Participation to Nonparticipation, and From Motivations to Barriers

Work on constraints—or "barriers" as the then-current terminology had it—began when some researchers realized each bar in the histogram identified only a portion of the respective age group, which contained—but hid—nonparticipants as well as the people who actually do participate and who were focused on in most empirical research. Adding these people (as in the center graph in Figure 16.2), and then separating out them out again, inverting the graph, and focusing on nonparticipants (as in the right-hand graph in Figure 16.2) was in retrospect a neat piece of lateral thinking that raised an entirely new central question: "Why does nonparticipation increase with age?" complemented if not replaced the question "Why does participation decline with age?" A host of ancillary questions and new insights followed, summarized in a focus on the more "negative" factors related to participation and nonparticipation—in short, the barriers and constraints that might inhibit, alter, or even block participation.

This new perspective led to research based largely on the simple model shown in **Figure 16.3** (p. 248): the ways in which constraints explain why some people do not develop particular interests and preferences, and which intervene as inhibiting or blocking factors and thus prevent or modify participation even when a person has an interest in and desire for a new activity. This kind of barriers research dominated the field through most of the 1980s (see Goodale & Witt, 1989, and Jackson, 1988, for reviews of the literature toward the end of that decade). Despite the limitations we can detect in hindsight, this stage of barriers research was a necessary step that laid the foundation for the more sophisticated work that came along in the next decade. The key point that cannot be emphasized too strongly, however, is the emerging focus on barriers and constraints was far more than "old wine in new bottles." It fundamentally altered the ways in which many scholars thought about leisure and conducted their research.

From Recreational Activity Preferences to Benefits

Broadly speaking, a similar set of conceptual and theoretical changes characterized the beginnings of the benefits approach to leisure (Driver & Bruns, 1999; Schreyer & Driver, 1989), moving from the previous focus on activities and associated variables, such as recreational activity preferences and satisfaction, to a more sophisticated and inclusive understanding of the ultimate outcomes of leisure. Led by Driver, several researchers realized they should be focusing less on what activities

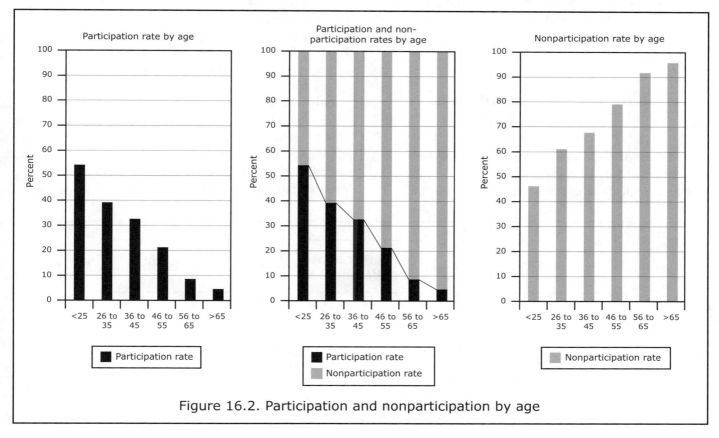

Figure 16.2. Participation and nonparticipation by age

people participate in and more on the benefits people expect to realize (anticipated benefits), hope to realize (desired benefits), and do in fact achieve (realized benefits). In the same way as for constraints, we can draw a crude model of how the benefits approach (**Figure 16.4**) was different from the activity approach (Figure 16.1). The key point is leisure behavior per se was no longer viewed as the ultimate dependent variable to be focused on in research. In other words, inherent in the benefits approach was the recognition participation studies had been investigating means rather than ends.

Two other points should also be made about the new thinking that accompanied the switch to a benefits-based approach. First, the benefits approach more easily allowed for the incorporation of feedbacks than had been possible or had occurred in the activity approach. These feedbacks are of many kinds but are exemplified by those shown in Figure 16.4. The extent to which benefits are realized (or not) is viewed not as the end of the process, but as a key influence on the development of future interests, preferences, and participation. Thus, the benefits approach as summarized in Figure 16.4 was inherently a far more dynamic and interactive one than the rather static, unidirectional model in Figure 16.1 that powered previous, prebenefits research. Second, and equally important, the concept and measurement of benefits encompass not just those that accrue to the individual, but also those that benefit society, the economy, the natural environment and so on (the outcomes of the "benefits chain of causality"; see next section for further discussion).

"Chains" of Benefits and Constraints

One of the most important contributions of the benefits approach to leisure, especially in regards to the practical applications of research, has been to demonstrate the benefits of leisure activity and recreational engagement accrue not simply to individuals—there are "downstream" benefits at a much broader level as well. These may include social, economic, and environmental benefits. As an articulation of this idea, Driver and Bruns (1999) discussed what they referred to as "benefits chains of causality." One example of such a chain is shown in **Figure 16.5**, adapted from the model that Driver and Bruns presented. It suggests a possible process whereby recreational relaxation and enjoyment create economic benefits, first for the individual, then the employer, and ultimately the country's economy.

Of course, it is quite easy to criticize this proposition by arguing such claims for leisure and recreation are mere hyperbole stemming from the enthusiasm of leisure researchers and practitioners promoting their own agendas. It is also easy to overlook the costs inevitably incurred in realizing benefits. Nevertheless, the premise embodied in the idea of a chain of benefits is compelling and deserves recognition and further exploration, not only for its applications to policy and practice, but also for leisure theory and research. Thus, in the same way the benefits approach to leisure helped to shift the focus of study beyond participation (as argued previously and shown in Figure 16.4), the "benefits chain of causality" also extends previous knowledge by demonstrating there are important benefits of leisure and recreation that go far beyond the individual person. While this is a widely held but largely unsubstantiated article of faith among most leisure researchers and practitioners (Driver & Bruns, 1999), the concept of a benefits chain of causality offers a framework for focused empirical investigation.

In reproducing Driver and Bruns's model, we explicitly added a component (the arrow at the foot of the diagram) that demonstrates the "direction" in which benefits are assumed to flow—in this specific case, from the individual to the economy, but more generally and more abstractly from the microscale to the macroscale. It is important to recognize this characteristic of the process

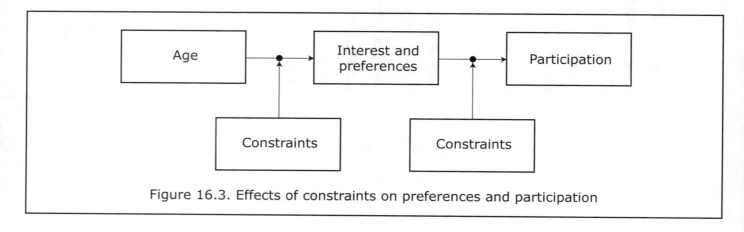

Figure 16.3. Effects of constraints on preferences and participation

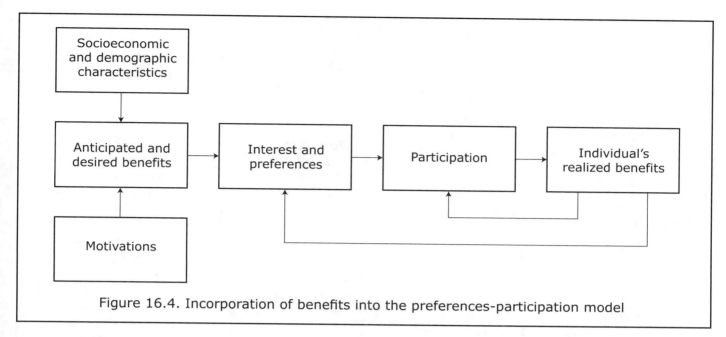

Figure 16.4. Incorporation of benefits into the preferences-participation model

because it helps to make explicit that the process, when adapted and applied to constraints, more than likely operates in the reverse direction: from the macroscale to the microscale.[1] Two hypothetical examples of constraints chains of causality are shown in **Figure 16.6** (p. 250), each of which is self-explanatory. Both examples show how circumstances and trends in society as a whole, generally outside the control of the individual, may produce policies and strategies that translate into more immediate ways in which people's lives may be affected—at which point they become "constraints" that are internalized and much more directly influential on people's immediate lives and leisure choices.

The implications for thinking about constraints in this manner are at least threefold. First, the idea of a constraints chain of causality assists in placing the constraints perceived and/or experienced by an individual in a broader social context that influences, in a variety of

often profound ways, how an individual behaves, even if he or she is not fully aware of such influences (see Shaw & Henderson's discussion of gender and constraints, this volume). Thinking in this way should help to expand questions about constraints in future research. Furthermore, it should also help to alleviate the concern that much of leisure constraints research is not "contextual" or "sociological" enough because it has typically taken "increasing costs of participation" or "time for leisure becomes scarcer" (to choose examples from Figure 16.6) as the starting point for research instead of as an outcome of social, economic, political, and environmental influences.

The second implication is the idea that the experience of constraints is a process (see also Jackson on transitions and constraints, this volume) in that it consists of a series of interlocking and influential—if not causal—components. This in turn suggests the experience of constraints

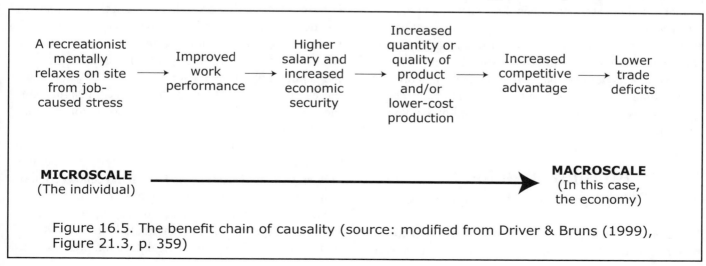

Figure 16.5. The benefit chain of causality (source: modified from Driver & Bruns (1999), Figure 21.3, p. 359)

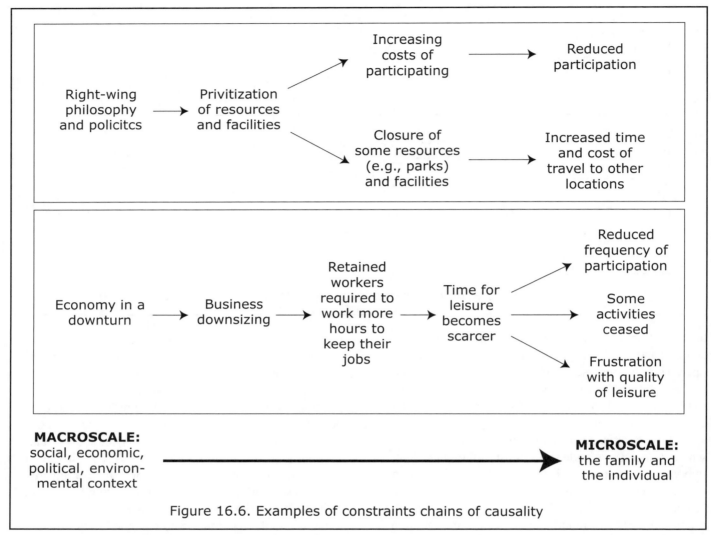

Figure 16.6. Examples of constraints chains of causality

is dynamic and ongoing and not the static response one is virtually forced to assume when conducting survey-based, statistical correlative research on relationships between "snapshots" of constraints and their supposed effects on people's leisure.

The third implication is recognizing the "upstream" influences of constraints on people's leisure, and the "downstream" benefits provide a key to constructing an integrated model of leisure behavior that simultaneously incorporates both constraints and benefits as influences on leisure behavior and places that behavior in a broader social context than has typically occurred to date. This model, shown in **Figure 16.7**, is discussed in the next section.

An Integrated Model of Constraints and Benefits

In the previous paragraphs, we established how incorporating concepts of constraints into research about leisure

helps to understand both participation and nonparticipation (as well as, indirectly, other aspects of leisure, such as preferences, specialization, and enjoyment, as posited in previous work by Crawford, Jackson & Godbey, 1991, and Jackson, Crawford & Godbey, 1993). We have also demonstrated how benefits enter into the equation, both in terms of those that precede preferences (anticipated and desired benefits) and those that occur as a result of leisure engagement (realized benefits)—not to mention "downstream" collective benefits. However, reflecting the parallel but for the most part separate development of these two subfields of leisure studies, new insights and models resulting from the incorporation of constraints and benefits were dealt with separately.

Based on the underlying premise of this chapter—it is desirable to find ways in which to integrate benefits and constraints research—and given the central components in the models shown in Figures 16.3 and 16.4 are identical, the two models are combined in the central portion of Figure 16.7. This integrated model shows that a recreationist's hypothetical decision process of proceeding from anticipated and desired benefits (which themselves are shown to be affected by personal circumstances and motivations, plus attitudes and values), through the establishment of interest and preferences, on to participation, and finally to the realization of benefits, may be constrained at several stages. The primary implication is that a more complete understanding of recreation behavior can be achieved by examining both constraints and benefits in the same study (as we exemplify later in this chapter). To put it another way, studies of benefits without constraints provide an incomplete picture, inherently reflecting an assumption that benefits can automatically be achieved without difficulty. Conversely, adding benefits to the constraints model makes explicit the notion participation is not the key variable to be explained in leisure constraints research, but rather "constraints to benefits realization" is—or should be—the central focus. (Incidentally, this extension should go some way toward satisfying those critics of leisure constraints research who have decried the emphasis on the numerical and easily measurable aspects of leisure, such as activities and participation, to the neglect of more qualitative measures and outcomes of the leisure experience.) Moreover, the integration of constraints and benefits as proposed in Figure 16.7 is consistent with—if not necessarily an identical display of—the hierarchical and negotiation models of leisure constraints (Crawford et al., 1991; Jackson et al., 1993), and in particular the associated "balance proposition," which states, "both the initiation and outcome of the [leisure constraints] negotiation process are dependent on the relative strength of, and interactions between, constraints on participating in an activity and motivations for such participation" (Jackson et al., 1993, p. 9). To alter the language slightly, leisure reflects a balance between benefits and constraints.

Two other key aspects of Figure 16.7 should also be recognized, both of them building on the concepts of chains of benefits and constraints discussed previously. First, the model shows the achievement of benefits at the level of the individual also has implications for broader social, economic, and environmental benefits (and perhaps policy as well). This in turn suggests constraints, and efforts to alleviate them, have implications not only for leisure participation and enjoyment and overall quality of life for individual people, but also for society as a whole. Second, the model shows, from an "antecedent" perspective, an individual's decisions occur within a broader social, economic, political, and environmental context, which itself may be both constraining (as shown in the model) and enabling (see the chapter on affordances by Kleiber, Wade & Loucks-Atkinson, this volume). Moreover, placing the individual within this context provides a model-based reminder there are limitations to the understanding of behavior if it is approached purely from an individual, agency-based, social psychological perspective and may help to move the field toward a more contextual, sociological, and structural understanding of leisure.

Benefits, Constraints, and Market Segmentation

We now turn our attention to an example of one possible set of connections between benefits and constraints: an empirical investigation in which potential visitors to an

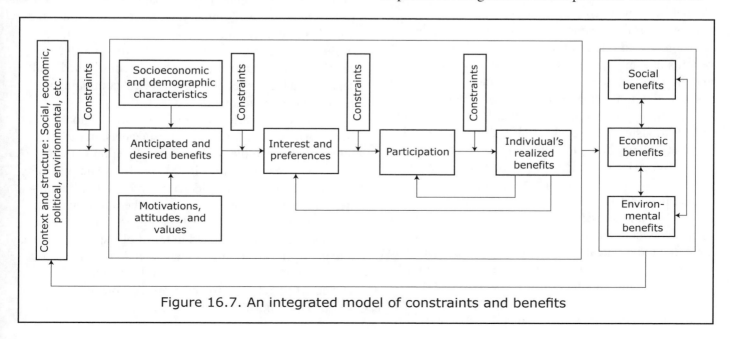

Figure 16.7. An integrated model of constraints and benefits

urban tourism and recreation destination were classified, first on the basis of the benefits visitors were seeking, and then according to clusters of constraints that may interfere with fulfilling anticipated and desired benefits. By combining the two sets of data, the study demonstrates the value of using benefits and constraints data simultaneously to identify market segments and subsequently to propose marketing strategies appropriate for each segment, a goal consistent with one of the core arguments of Scott's chapter (this volume). The key points are

1. both a more sophisticated and conceptually complex classification of actual and potential facility users results from utilizing both components of the data.

2. the ensuing groups aid in the identification of specific strategies that will likely be more successful in achieving agency goals than broader classifications based on either benefits or constraints alone.

We do not mean to imply this example encompasses the entire range of possible connections between constraints and benefits. In addition, the reader should not develop the mistaken impression that market segmentation is the only purpose of identifying such connections and capitalizing on them in research and practice. Nevertheless, the example pertinently illustrates how new insights and practical applications can be derived from the integration of these two superficially disconnected themes in leisure research.

Theoretical Background

There has been general recognition in the tourism literature that if knowledge of an attraction exists, then a decision to visit it is essentially a trade-off between the benefits it is anticipated will occur from the experience and the effort and cost required to surmount constraints associated with the trip (Harris, Driver & Bergerson, 1985; Krumpe & McLaughlin, 1982; Um & Crompton, 1992; Woodside & Lysonski, 1989). Benefits are defined as satisfying psychological outcomes derived from a leisure activity (Driver & Bruns, 1999), while constraints may initially be defined as subsets of reasons for not engaging in an activity (Jackson, 1988).

In the early tourism literature, benefits were almost exclusively defined in terms of visitors' ratings of desired amenities and activities, and this operationalization of benefits remains in use. Illustrative of this approach are the substantial number of image studies that described and evaluated potential visitors' perceptions of destinations' configurations of amenities and activities

(Crompton, 1979; Fakeye & Crompton, 1991; Gartner, 1986; Hunt, 1975; Keown, Jacobs & Worthley, 1984; Mayo, 1973; Um & Crompton, 1992). In the past two decades, a contrasting operationalization of benefits emerged as some tourism researchers conceptualized the tangible attributes of destinations as being merely conduits with the potential to facilitate desired psychological benefit outcomes (Iso-Ahola, 1982; Pearce & Caltabino, 1983). This conceptual shift away from activities and amenities and toward experiential and psychological outcomes or benefits is consistent with the general evolution of definitions across the gamut of leisure subfields (Samdahl, 1991, 1999), including constraints to leisure.

Benefit segmentation was first advocated in the marketing field by Haley (1968). However, it is only in the past decade, with the emergence of more sophisticated statistical tools and computer programs, that its use has become widespread in tourism and leisure research. It has been noted the strength of benefit segmentation is that it "predicts behavior better than personality and lifestyles, volumetric, demographic, or geographical measures, which merely describe behavior without explaining it" (Loker & Perdue, 1992). A number of studies have demonstrated benefit-based segments in the context of tourism are a viable and useful means of segmentation (Davis & Sternquist, 1987; Dybka, 1987; Gitelson & Kerstetter, 1990; Hudson, 2000; Loker & Perdue, 1992; Shoemaker, 1989, 1994). Likewise, some researchers emphasized the usefulness of viewing constraints as a characteristic on which to base segmentation (Hultsman, 1995; Jackson, 1993; Norman, 1995). For example, Jackson (1993) derived constraint domains by a clustering procedure and demonstrated the usefulness of differentiating them by participants' ages and patterns of leisure activities. Similarly, Norman (1995) clustered constraint items relating to a summer vacation trip and differentiated groups on the basis of individuals being relatively unconstrained, being highly constrained, and reporting a high level of constraints but continuing to participate at an unconstrained level.

Some of the early work on image alluded to the importance of constraints in tourists' decision making, although these studies did not formally address their role. For example, Mayo (1975) noted, "the number of alternatives actually considered may, of course, be limited by virtue of financial, time, or other constraints" (p. 14). Similarly, Crompton (1977) suggested destination images were first prioritized in terms of ideal preference, and their prioritization was then amended by the impact of perceived constraints. Based on their review of the choice set literature, Crompton and Ankomah (1993) developed a proposition, which states, the criteria used to evaluate alternatives in the early consideration set will primarily focus on the relative merits of the destinations' attributes, while the criteria used to evaluate alternatives in the late consideration set will primarily focus on the constraints associated with each of the alternative destinations. (p. 469)

However, despite the acknowledged role of constraints in a tourist's decision process, relatively few researchers reported empirical studies in which situational variables or constraints have been incorporated into investigations of a destination's attributes, image, or potential for realizing psychological outcomes. Um and Crompton (1992), in one of the few studies to have done this, noted, "the inclusion of situational variables that were specific to a tourist's decision-making context reduced the unexplained variance in models and increased the management value of research in this area" (p. 18).

Although studies dealing with the tourist's decision process tended to focus on desirable destination attributes, image, and benefits sought, Ellis and Rademacher (1986) pointed out virtually any study in which a tourism phenomenon serves as a dependent variable is related to the topic of constraints. Among those who would select a destination based on the benefits it offers, some proportion of them are likely—because of perceived constraints—to select a substitute destination perceived to offer fewer benefits.

Relatively little empirical work on the nature and effects of constraints has been reported in the tourism literature, but a substantial body of findings emerged in the leisure and recreation literature. There is some agreement with the tourism literature in that constraints can be conceptualized as a mechanism for reducing desired alternatives (Jackson & Searle, 1985). One of the emerging findings from leisure constraints research is that some individuals who report their leisure behavior is impacted by constraints indicate they engage in it anyway, if not exactly in the same way as if they had been constraint free (see the introductory chapter by Jackson, this volume, for an elaboration of concepts and research related to the negotiation of leisure constraints). For example, Kay and Jackson (1991) found

constraints were reported by a number of interviewees who did not reduce their participation at all, despite identifying the constraint as a major influence on their leisure. Through exerting effort to overcome the constraint, these individuals succeeded in maintaining their desired level of participation, despite appearing affected by it. (p. 310)

It appears the benefits accruing from participation were sufficiently substantial; they more than offset the costs associated with the constraints.

Traditionally, it was assumed constraints inhibited visitation. However, the work by Kay and Jackson and others suggested individuals may formulate negotiation strategies to surmount primary perceived constraints. This idea has been explored conceptually (Crawford et al., 1991; Henderson & Bialeschki, 1993; Jackson et al., 1993) and empirically (Henderson, Bedini, Hecht & Schuler, 1995; Jackson & Rucks, 1995; Kay & Jackson, 1991; Scott, 1991). Examples may include adjusting schedules, using time, money, and energy more efficiently to free up opportunities to participate, and becoming better informed of opportunities. It has been reported individuals who exhibit characteristics associated with high involvement with a tourist attraction are most likely to successfully modify or reshape their perceived constraints by decreasing their relative importance to facilitate pursuit of desired activities (Norman, 1995). The adoption of a negotiation strategy stems from a belief that the benefits derived from visitation will compensate for the perceived constraints. The result is they are then surmounted.

A Case Study of Benefits and Constraints in Tourism

Operationalization

Benefits and constraints can be integrated to identify responsive target markets in a tourism context by using a market grid analysis approach (Crompton & Lamb, 1986). This approach analyzes a potential market by using a grid with different characteristics of the market specified on the horizontal and vertical axes. In this case, the axes consist of perceived constraints and perceived benefits.

It seems likely each type of constraint will vary in its applicability to the different benefits sought by participants. That is, a given constraint or set of constraints is more likely to restrict visitation to a particular type of attraction among those seeking particular preferred types of benefits rather than others. In seeking a certain type of benefit from an attraction visit, therefore, individuals, "make themselves more vulnerable to the types of constraints which reflect the characteristics of that [benefit]" (Kay & Jackson, 1991, p. 311). The matrix approach suggested here accommodates this linkage.

To illustrate implementation of the approach and its utility, a study of visitors seeking a cultural tourism experience is briefly described. The location is Galveston,

Texas. The Galveston Historical Foundation (GHF) played a central role in revitalizing the city's interest in restoring its extensive heritage of historic properties and in arousing interest in cultural tourism. As part of its mission, GHF operates six museum attractions in the city, which are the heart of the thrust to develop cultural tourism. However, in recent years all of these properties experienced declines in attendance, some of which have been substantial.

Ongoing research is conducted at the GHF museum properties to monitor visitors' profiles and geographic origin. These data indicated visitors were most frequently individuals with a proclivity to visit museums, rather than visitors who came to Galveston primarily for other purposes and opted to visit a museum while they were there. The data also confirmed a majority of visitors came from the Galveston–Houston area. These findings suggested a central component of an action plan designed to arrest the decline in attendance should be a focus on attracting museum goers in the Galveston–Houston area to the properties. A decision was made to use a constraints–benefits matrix approach to identify characteristics of the potentially most responsive target markets within this interest population. The matrix was developed using a sample of over 1,000 known museum visitors in the Galveston–Houston area. Details of the sampling, instrumentation, and statistical procedures are not included in this chapter because they are incidental to the general description of the procedure; they are discussed in Tian, Crompton, and Witt (1996).

The Benefit Segments

Five benefits sought by museum visitors were identified as socialization/bonding, relaxation, social recognition, self-esteem, and educational entertainment. Respondents were divided into four groups based on the benefits they sought: child-centered adults; extensive benefit seekers; tag-alongs; and non-ego-involved visitors. The characteristics of these groups are briefly described next.

Child-centered adults (34.5% of the sample) contained the largest proportion both of frequent museum goers and visitors to children's museums. Although most of these respondents were in the 26–45 age-cohort, it contained the largest proportion in the 56–65 age group, suggesting that grandparents as well as parents were involved. Scores on all of the benefit domains except social recognition were relatively high. Almost 70% of this cluster were females, and the cluster contained the highest percentage of people who came with children.

Extensive benefit seekers (25.5%) ranked highest on all five benefit domains and contained the highest

proportion of people who said they would come more frequently if constraints were removed. However, they did not visit museums significantly more frequently than other clusters. The cluster included the largest proportion of female respondents, and a larger proportion than other clusters who had visited eight listed Galveston attractions in the past.

Tag-alongs (21.4%) appeared to be rather ambivalent toward benefits from museum visits, since their ratings of each of the domains tended to be around the neutral midpoint of the 7-point scale. Although they contained the highest percentage of respondents whose family income exceeded $80,000, they ranked lowest on the two involvement scales, and contained the lowest proportion of people who said they would come more frequently if constraints were removed. The cluster contained a significantly higher proportion of males and they tended to tag along on visits to museums with their spouse or other adults rather than with children. Hence, they were significantly less likely to visit children's museums than were other clusters.

Non-ego-involved visitors (18.6%) ranked the benefit domains of social recognition and self-esteem low, "strongly disagreeing" that these were benefits they sought from museums. They were relatively infrequent visitors to museums. The cluster contained a relatively large proportion of males. There were no indications of why this cluster visited museums at all, given their relative lack of ego involvement with them. However, their museum visit may fall into the category of meeting the need of "something to do" or "somewhere to go."

The Constraint Segments

Six constraints were identified by this sample: cost, time, difficulty of access, repetition, product failings, and lack of interest. Similar procedures to those used to develop the benefit segments suggested the sample should be divided into five constraint segments: highly constrained visitors, committed localites, unconstrained mature enthusiasts, pac people, and cost-conscious visitors. The characteristics of the five groups are described next.

Highly constrained visitors (27.3%) scored relatively high on all the constraints domains. They had the largest proportion of respondents who were males, and of respondents who were in the highest income group. Even though one quarter of the cluster were members of a museum, it appears that this reflected the interests of others in their family, since a smaller proportion of them indicated they would visit museums more often if constraints were removed than any other cluster. They were particularly uninclined to visit history museums.

Committed localites (23.1%) were relatively high-income, frequent museum-goers, with strong aspirations to visit even more frequently. There was a larger proportion of repeat visitors and museum members in this cluster than in any other. They reported the lowest score on the repetition constraint. Their major constraints were time and difficulty of access, which referred particularly to travel distance, reflecting that most of the sample lived in Houston rather than Galveston.

Unconstrained mature enthusiasts (18.9%) rated low on all six constraints. They were older, medium-income individuals who tended to visit museums relatively frequently with other adults. Although a larger proportion came from outside the Galveston–Houston area than in any other cluster, a relatively large number of these individuals reported having visited other Galveston attractions.

Pac people (15.7%) had more members who visited each of the eight Galveston attractions listed than the members of any other cluster, but they were relatively infrequent museum-goers who engaged in minimal repeat visitation. Their major constraints were time and, to a lesser extent, repetition. The name for this cluster was derived from the Pac-Man game: they appear to "gobble-up" experiences and be characterized by a "been there, done that" mentality. A lower proportion of this group were museum members than any other cluster, and a relatively large proportion were in groups without children.

Cost-conscious visitors (15%) were relatively infrequent visitors, with comparatively high constraint scores on most domains, the highest score of all clusters on the cost constraint, and the lowest average household income. The cluster contained the largest proportion of respondents who were female, and a relatively low proportion were museum members.

Selecting Responsive Target Markets

To determine which target markets may be most desirable for GHF to address, the benefit clusters were cross-tabulated with the constraint clusters. The resulting 20 cell matrix (four benefit clusters by five constraint clusters) is shown in **Table 16.1**. Substantial evidence in both the consumer behavior and the tourism literatures suggests in the initial stages of making a decision the focus is on preference or benefits sought, but as the time to finalize the decision gets closer, situational constraints exercise a modifying influence (Belk, 1975; Hansen,

Table 16.1. Potential target markets derived by cross-tabulation of benefit and constraint clusters

Benefits (%) Constraints (%)	Non-Ego-Involved Visitors (*n* = 189)	Child-Centered Adults (*n* = 356)	Tag-Alongs (*n* = 221)	Extensive Benefit Seekers (*n* = 257)	Percent of the Sample (*N* = 1023)
Cost-Conscious Visitors (*n* = 154)	14% 18	14% 32	12% 17	20% 33	15%
Highly Constrained Visitors (*n* = 278)	24 16	18 24	48 38	24 22	27
Committed Localities (*n* = 238)	23 18	26 39	18 17	24 26	23
Pac People (*n* = 161)	21 24	15 33	13 17	16 26	16
Unconstrained Mature Enthusiasts (*n* = 192)	18 18	27 50	9 10	16 22	19
Percent of the Sample	18	35	22	25	100

Note: Priority target markets are outlined. Markets judged least likely to be responsive to marketing efforts are shaded.

1976; Harris, Driver & Bergerson, 1985; Jackson & Searle, 1985; Park, 1978; Woodside & Lysonski, 1989). Um and Crompton (1992) pointed out this is consistent with the notion that choice is a satisfying behavior (Simon, 1957) that is constraints-driven, rather than an optimizing behavior that is benefits-driven. Given the initial primacy of benefits, the starting point in reviewing the array of potential target markets shown in Table 16.1 was to consider the four benefit clusters.

The *non-ego-involved visitors* and *tag-alongs*, who together accounted for 40% of the potential market, were not considered likely to be responsive to marketing efforts. This large proportion of museum-goers who appeared to be reluctant visitors was a surprising finding to the researchers. Conventional wisdom asserts tourists visit attractions because they have some interest in them or expect to derive some benefits and satisfaction from the experience. However, this was not the case with these visitors. A critical ingredient in the definition of a leisure experience is perceived freedom—visitors should have a strong sense of intrinsic motivation (Iso-Ahola, 1986). These visitors did not exhibit this characteristic. On the contrary, one could describe these groups as "constrained into" visits rather than constraints preventing their visits (Jackson, 1988; Shaw, 1994): their decision was constrained by a sense of obligation to spouse or friends, or by pressure to go somewhere or to do something. These obligations and pressures potentially defined their museum visit as a chore rather than as a freely chosen delight. Hence, the likelihood of these individuals being responsive to efforts to encourage their voluntary visitation is low.

The clusters deemed likely to be most responsive were *child-centered adults* and *extensive benefit seekers*. They constituted 60% of the potential market, but within these two clusters, 18% and 24%, respectively were classified as *highly constrained visitors*. Clearly, these segments did not fit comfortably within the two generally responsive benefit clusters, because they indicated that even if all constraints were removed they were least likely to go to museums, and they were particularly disinclined to visit history museums, which constitute a central segment of GHF's attractions. These 12 cells deemed likely to be least responsive to marketing efforts are shaded in Table 16.1.

The remaining eight potential target markets, identified as being likely to be relatively responsive, made up 48% of the total market of museum goers. It is widely accepted in the marketing literature that to be viable a target market needs to be (a) sufficiently large to be worth serving, (b) measurable, and (c) accessible (Crompton & Lamb, 1986). All other factors being equal,

the best return on marketing investment is likely to come from the largest of these responsive target markets.

The size criterion led to selection of four of the eight groups as priority targets. Together they account for approximately 30% of the total population of interest. They are accessible through direct mail communications using lists purchased from commercial vendors and/or membership lists provided by other museums in the Galveston–Houston area. The four priority target markets whose cells are outlined in bold in Table 16.1 are characterized next.

Child-centered adults who are unconstrained mature enthusiasts. Members of this target market are relatively unconstrained. The attractions' appeals should be to grandparents, inviting them to bring their grandchildren and to use the museums' exhibits as a catalyst for conveying their early life history and experiences to their grandchildren. The appeal may be directed also to parents, suggesting this may be a fun activity for grandparents when they come to visit from out-of-town.

Child-centered adults who are committed localites. The appeal should be to groups of two adults with children who are frequent museum visitors, but are constrained by the travel distance from Houston to Galveston. Child-oriented exhibits and interpretive programs are required. A discounted ticket limited to groups of two adults with children from the Houston area may be effective in surmounting the difficulty and associated costs of access, which is the primary constraint of this group.

Extensive benefit seekers who are committed localites. These are museum enthusiasts whose visitation to the Galveston attractions is inhibited by the need to travel from Houston. Since they seek a wide array of benefits, a discount package permitting unlimited visitation for a two-day period at all GHF attractions may be appealing. Members of this cluster are repeaters, so mailings notifying them of exhibit changes or special events are likely to be good investments.

Extensive benefit seekers who are cost-conscious visitors. These are museum enthusiasts who gain much from the experience, but are infrequent visitors because they are inhibited by both the direct costs and the indirect costs associated with travel distance from Houston. Since cost is a primary concern, they may be responsive to special promotions offering a package of accommodations, meals, and access to the attractions at deep discounts for short time periods at off-peak times, but when children are not in school.

The remaining four groups shown in Table 16.1 identified as likely to be responsive to marketing efforts were substantially smaller, and may not meet the viability criterion of being sufficiently large to be worth a distinctive marketing investment in them. These four groups include the following:

1. child-centered adults who were cost-conscious visitors.

2. child-centered adults who were pac people.

3. extensive benefit seekers who were pac people.

4. extensive benefit seekers who were unconstrained mature enthusiasts.

The groups are not mutually exclusive. They are described by selected core features that best differentiate them from other clusters, but a proportion of respondents are likely to be fringe members who may not be responsive to the suggested marketing strategies. The converse is also likely to be true—that is, there are fringe members of other groups who may be responsive to some of these strategies, so there is likely to be some positive spillover reaction to these marketing efforts.

Conclusions

As academic and applied knowledge, research, and publication grow super-exponentially, it can become difficult for researchers to keep up with intellectual advances and new results in their own area of specialization, let alone other fields that, at first glance, seem to be only superficially connected. One result is the development of increasingly sophisticated yet decreasingly interlinked bodies of knowledge, coupled with an understandable tendency for researchers to associate their academic identity with a given area, or to be so associated by others. Such is the case with benefits research and constraints research. Because the interaction of benefits and constraints directs leisure behavior, it is appropriate that much of the research into leisure behavior is concerned with better understanding these two constructs. Yet relatively little work has addressed the dynamics of their interrelationships.

In this chapter we sketched how the subfields of constraints and benefits evolved essentially in isolation of each other within leisure studies. We also argued, however, the two fields have much in common, and actual and discernible linkages between them are strong enough to propose they be considered together in future research endeavors. We have shown how the two fields arose out of similar circumstances and developments in leisure studies, how a useful concept (the "benefits chain of causality") can be adapted from one field to the other, and how the integration of thinking about both constraints and benefits simultaneously can help to construct a model that has two advantages. First, it incorporates benefits *and* constraints into our understanding of the individual's leisure decision-making process. Second, it places that behavior in context by demonstrating the equal importance of both its antecedents and its outcomes.

Using the example of an applied research project conducted in Texas, we have also demonstrated how investigating constraints and benefits in the same study can itself provide benefits that would likely be missing from a more fragmented approach. We have taken visitors' profiles defined by constraints and benefits, and suggested how they can be used to identify those target markets likely to be most responsive to an organization's marketing efforts. Selecting target markets on the basis of the differing benefits visitors seek has a relatively long pedigree in the leisure field (e.g., Howard & Crompton, 1980), because delivering the benefits visitors seek from using a service is the fundamental reason for the existence of that service. Focusing on one of the two constructs exclusively and disregarding the other is likely to provide an incomplete and potentially misleading view of the characteristics of the different types of visitors, since leisure behavior is a function of the weighting of trade-offs between the two constructs. To the best of our knowledge, this attempt to interface benefits with constraints to derive market segments and select target markets is a new departure.

It is important to repeat the caveat this was a single instance and there are many other opportunities for integrative work on the benefits of and constraints to leisure. Such work could address, for example, the relative strength of the constraints experienced at different stages in the visitation decision process, the threshold levels at which the influence of one prevails over the influence of the other, or the profiling of visitors by the differences in the two constructs which they exhibit. We hope the example presented in this chapter, together with the more general discussion that preceded it, will fulfill the goals of the chapter, namely to prompt researchers and students to think about constraints and benefits in terms of their linkages rather than as separate, unrelated aspects of leisure, and to encourage research that might address benefits and constraints and their interacting roles in people's lives simultaneously.

References

Belk, R. W. (1975). Situational variables and consumer behavior. *Journal of Consumer Research, 2*, 157–164.

Crawford, D. W., Jackson, E. L., and Godbey, G. (1991). A hierarchical model of leisure constraints. *Leisure Sciences, 13*, 309–320.

Crompton, J. L. (1977). *A systems model of the tourist's destination selection decision process with particular reference to the role of image and perceived constraints.* Unpublished doctoral dissertation, Texas A&M University.

Crompton, J. L. (1979, Spring). An assessment of the image of Mexico as a vacation destination and the influence of geographical location upon that image. *Journal of Travel Research, 17*, 18–24.

Crompton, J. L. and Ankomah, P. K. (1993). Choice set propositions in destination decisions. *Annals of Tourism Research, 20*(3), 461–476.

Crompton, J. L. and Lamb C. W. (1986). *Marketing government and social services.* New York, NY: John Wiley.

Davis, D. and Sternquist, B. (1987). Appealing to the elusive tourist: An attribute cluster strategy. *Journal of Travel Research, 25*(4), 25–31.

Driver, B. L., Brown, P. J., and Peterson, G. L. (Eds.). (1991). *Benefits of leisure.* State College, PA: Venture Publishing, Inc.

Driver, B. L. and Bruns, D. H. (1999). Concepts and uses of the benefits approach to leisure. In E. L. Jackson and T. L. Burton (Eds.), *Leisure studies: Prospects for the twenty-first century.* State College, PA: Venture Publishing, Inc.

Dybka, J. (1987). A look at the American traveler: The U.S. pleasure travel market study. *Journal of Travel Research, 25*(3), 2–4.

Ellis, G. and Rademacher, C. (1986). *Barriers to recreation participation.* Unpublished paper submitted to the President's Commission on Americans Outdoors.

Fakeye, P. C. and Crompton, J. L. (1991). Image differences between prospective first-time and repeat visitors to the Lower Rio Grande Valley. *Journal of Travel Research, 30*(2), 10–16.

Gartner, W. C. (1986). Temporal influences on image change. *Annals of Tourism Research, 13*(4), 635–643.

Gitelson, R. J. and Kerstetter, D. L. (1990). The relationship between sociodemographic variables, benefits sought, and subsequent vacation behavior: A case study. *Journal of Travel Research, 28*(3), 24–29.

Goodale, T. L. and Witt, P. A. (1989). Recreation non-participation and barriers to leisure. In E. L. Jackson and T. L. Burton (Eds.), *Understanding leisure and recreation: Mapping the past, charting the future* (pp. 421–449). State College, PA: Venture Publishing, Inc.

Haley, R. (1968, July). Benefit segmentation: A decision oriented research tool. *Journal of Marketing, 23*, 30–35.

Hansen, F. (1976). Psychological theories of consumer choice. *Journal of Consumer Research, 3*, 117–142.

Harris, C. C., Driver, B. L., and Bergersen, E. P. (1985). Do choices of sport fisheries reflect angler preferences for site attractions? In G. H. Stankey and S. F. McCool (Eds.), *Proceedings: Symposium on recreation choice behavior.* Ogden, UT: USDA Forest Service, Intermountain Research Station.

Henderson, K. A., Bedini, L. A., Hecht, L., and Schuler, R. (1995). Women with physical disabilities and the negotiation of leisure constraints. *Leisure Studies, 14*, 17–31.

Henderson, K. A. and Bialeschki, M. D. (1993). Exploring an expanded model of women's leisure constraints. *Journal of Applied Recreation Research, 18*, 229–252.

Howard, D. R. and Crompton, J. L. (1980). *Financing, managing and marketing recreation and park resources.* Dubuque, IA: William C. Brown.

Hudson, S. (2000). The segmentation of potential tourists: Constraint differences between men and women. *Journal of Travel Research, 38*, 363–368.

Hultsman, W. Z. (1995). Recognizing patterns of leisure constraints: An extension of the exploration of dimensionality. *Journal of Leisure Research, 27*, 228–244.

Hunt, J. D. (1975, Winter). Image as a factor in tourism development. *Journal of Travel Research, 13*, 1–7.

Iso-Ahola, S. E. (1982). Towards a social psychology theory of tourism motivation: A rejoinder. *Annals of Tourism Research, 9*(2), 256–262.

Iso-Ahola, S. E. (1986). A theory of substitutability of leisure behavior. *Leisure Sciences, 8*, 367–389.

Jackson, E. L. (1988). Leisure constraints: A survey of past research. *Leisure Sciences, 10*, 203–215.

Jackson, E. L. (1993). Recognizing patterns of leisure constraints: Results from alternative analyses. *Journal of Leisure Research, 25*(2), 129–149.

Jackson, E. L., Crawford, D. W., and Godbey, G. (1993). Negotiation of leisure constraints. *Leisure Sciences, 15*, 1–11.

Jackson, E. L. and Rucks, V. C. (1995). Negotiation of leisure constraints by junior-high and high-school students: An exploratory study. *Journal of Leisure Research, 27*, 85–105.

Jackson, E. L. and Searle, M. S. (1985). Recreation non-participation and barriers to participation: Concepts and models. *Loisir et Sociètè, 8*, 693–707.

Kay, T. and Jackson, G. (1991). Leisure despite constraint: The impact of leisure constraints on leisure participation. *Journal of Leisure Research, 23*(4), 301–313.

Keown, C., Jacobs, L., and Worthley, R. (1984, Winter). American tourists' perceptions of retail stores in 12 selected countries. *Journal of Travel Research, 22*, 26–30.

Krumpe, E. E. and McLaughlin, W. J. (1982). A model of recreationists' decision making process. In *Forest and River Recreation Research Update* (Agricultural Experiment Station Miscellaneous Publication 18; pp. 94–99). St. Paul, MN: University of Minnesota.

Loker, L. E. and Perdue, R. R. (1992). A benefit-based segmentation of a nonresident summer travel market. *Journal of Travel Research, 31*(1), 30–35.

Mayo, E. J. (1973). Regional images and regional travel behavior research for changing travel patterns: Interpretation and utilization. *Proceedings of the Travel Research Association fourth annual conference* (pp. 211–218). Salt Lake City, UT: University of Utah.

Mayo, E. J. (1975). Tourism and the National Parks: A psychographic and attitudinal survey. *Journal of Travel Research, 14*, 14–18.

Norman, W. C. (1995). *Perceived constraints: A new approach to segmenting the vacation travel market.* Abstract from the 1995 symposium on leisure research, Arlington, VA: NRPA.

Park, C. W. (1978). A conflict resolution choice model. *Journal of Consumer Research, 5*, 125–137.

Pearce, P. and Caltabiano, M. (1983). Inferring travel motivation from travelers' experiences. *Journal of Travel Research, 22*(2), 16–19.

Samdahl, D. M. (1991). Issues in the measurement of leisure: A comparison of theoretical and connotative meanings. *Leisure Sciences, 13*, 33–49.

Samdahl, D. M. (1999). Epistemological and methodological issues in leisure research. In E. L. Jackson and T. L. Burton (Eds.), *Leisure studies: Prospects for the twenty-first century* (pp. 119–133). State College, PA: Venture Publishing, Inc.

Schreyer, R. and Driver, B. L. (1989). The benefits of leisure. In E. L. Jackson and T. L. Burton (Eds.), *Understanding leisure and recreation: Mapping the past, charting the future* (pp. 385–419). State College, PA: Venture Publishing, Inc.

Scott, D. (1991). The problematic nature of participation in contract bridge: A qualitative study of group-related constraints. *Leisure Sciences, 13,* 321–336.

Shaw, S. M. (1994). Gender, leisure, and constraint: Towards a framework for the analysis of women's leisure. *Journal of Leisure Research, 26*, 8–22.

Shoemaker, S. (1989). Segmentation of the senior pleasure travel market. *Journal of Travel Research, 27*(3), 14–21.

Shoemaker, S. (1994, Winter). Segmenting the U.S. travel market according to benefits realized. *Journal of Travel Research, 32*, 8–21.

Simon, H. A. (1957). *Models of man: Social and rational mathematical essays on rational human behavior in a social setting.* New York, NY: John Wiley.

Tian, S., Crompton, J. L., and Witt, P. A. (1996). Integrating constraints and benefits to identify responsive target markets for museum attractions. *Journal of Travel Research, 35*(2), 34–45.

Um, S. and Crompton, J. L. (1992). The roles of perceived inhibitors and facilitators on pleasure travel destination decisions. *Journal of Travel Research, 30*(3), 18–25.

Woodside, A. G. and Lysonski, S. (1989, Spring). A general model of traveler destination choice. *Journal of Travel Research, 27*, 8–14.

Endnote

1. The idea that a constraints chain of causality could be developed based on the benefits chain of causality, but with the directions of influence reversed, was first raised during a two-day informal seminar on benefits and constraints held in Denton, Texas, in January 1993. Although participants in the seminar (Bev Driver, Tom Goodale, Karla Henderson, Ed Jackson, Roger Mannell, Sue Shaw, and Peter Witt) agreed the idea had merit, neither the concept nor its possible implications have been articulated prior to the drafting of this chapter.

Chapter 17

Advancing Quantitative Research on Social Cognitive Theories of the Constraint–Negotiation Process

Roger C. Mannell (University of Waterloo) and Yoshi Iwasaki (University of Manitoba)

The evolution of process models of leisure constraint that distinguish types of constraint, the role of social cognitive processes (e.g., motivation, negotiation, self-efficacy), and outcomes other than participation suggests it might be profitable to examine methodological and measurement issues involved in testing models of the constraint–negotiation process. In our own research, we have attempted to explore the social–cognitive dimensions of a variety of leisure experience, stress–coping, and constraint phenomena with quantitative and multivariate methods. The discussion in this chapter will draw on this experience and the efforts of other researchers with a focus on the following issues:

1. methodologies for testing causal, process, and transactional models of constraint–negotiation.

2. accuracy, contextual validity, and meaning of self-reported reasons for nonparticipation.[1]

3. development of standardized and psychometrically sound measures of constraint constructs.

4. measurement of short-term and long-term outcomes other than participation.

Studying Social Cognitive Constraint–Negotiation Processes

Theory and research on leisure constraints suggest ways in which constraints influence participation are complex and dynamic and involve a variety of intervening and process variables. Leisure constraint theory is evolving into a social cognitive theory that goes well beyond suggesting a stimulus–response model of constraints causing nonparticipation. A variety of intervening variables and processes have been identified. Hierarchical constraint theory (Jackson, Crawford & Godbey, 1993) suggests different types of constraint are interconnected in a sequential process driven by motivational and negotiation processes. This perspective is consistent with the social cognitive view (Bandura, 1986) that people are active agents in responding to conditions that impede their goals rather than passive bystanders. A few quantitative studies have been reported in which these constraint processes and intervening variables have been examined and models of them tested (e.g., Alexandris, Tsorbatzoudis & Grouios, 2002; Carroll & Alexandris, 1997; Hubbard & Mannell, 2001; Raymore, Godbey, Crawford & von Eye, 1993). Also, the dynamics of different types of participation decisions (e.g., constraints to being interested in, starting, or continuing participation) on the influence of constraint have been examined (Hultsman, 1993; Jackson & Dunn, 1991; Jackson & Rucks, 1993; Tsai & Coleman, 1999). However, new methods for studying and testing models of these social cognitive processes and other possible intervening processes (Mannell & Loucks-Atkinson, this volume) also need to be adopted and developed.

Analyses of leisure constraints have been almost exclusively based on the collection and use of *cross-sectional data* (i.e., data collected at one point in time). Also, constraints research has been primarily retrospective, regardless of whether survey or qualitative interview methods have been used. Typically, study participants have been asked to look into their pasts and report on the types and levels of constraint they encountered (e.g., Carroll & Alexandris, 1997; Kay & Jackson, 1991; Raymore et al., 1993; Tsai & Coleman, 1999), and more recently, also the negotiation resources they had available and used (e.g., Henderson, Bedini, Hecht & Schuler, 1995; Hubbard & Mannell, 2001; Jackson & Rucks, 1995). As we discuss shortly, this "mining" of the past is open to the vagaries of memory and the "creativity" of participants in their use of cultural explanations and excuses to explain their nonparticipation that may obscure the constraint and negotiation processes operating. In 1991, Jackson expressed his optimism that experimentation with alternative methodologies was on the increase. Some years later, he and Scott (Jackson & Scott, 1999) observed this increase, particularly in the use of alternative quantitative approaches, does not appear to have occurred.

Model Testing With Cross-Sectional Data

Concern with the overreliance on survey methods does not mean survey and cross-sectional data cannot be used to examine social–cognitive processes and variables. While cross-sectional data cannot provide unequivocal support for the existence of the causal links suggested by models, a priori theoretical specification of the causal relationships modeled and the use of multivariate modeling procedures, such as path analysis and structural equation modeling (SEM), do provide a means of determining how well these causal models fit the data collected to test them. With SEM, for example, statistics are available to help in the assessment of whether a model is a good fit to the data and can provide support for the validity of a model and inferences made about the causal relationships proposed (Bollen, 1989). Raymore et al. (1993) and Hubbard and Mannell (2001) demonstrated SEM approaches and cross-sectional survey data can be used for testing models of the relationships among variables specified to operate in the constraint–negotiation process. Raymore et al. (1993) found some support for the hierarchical and sequential operation of intrapersonal, interpersonal, and structural constraints, although in a more recent study Hawkins, Peng, Hsieh, and Eklund (1999) claimed they were unable to replicate this finding. Hubbard and Mannell (2001) tested several models of possible relationships among leisure constraint, negotiation, motivation, and participation and found the best support for a model that suggests higher levels of constraint not only decrease levels of participation but also

trigger greater efforts to negotiate that in turn counteract the negative influences of constraint. Higher levels of motivation appeared to directly increase efforts to negotiate. However, ultimately, research methods other than cross-sectional and retrospective are needed to sort out and to verify the causal relationships suggested by these types of models.

Short-Term Longitudinal, Repeated Assessment, and Prospective Approaches

Despite some success with the use of cross-sectional studies to test constraint–negotiation models, other approaches are better suited to studying the causal links suggested by process models. Short-term longitudinal studies that allow the actual operation of constraint, negotiation, motivation, and other social cognitive processes to be examined as they occur in everyday life are needed. Only a few longitudinal constraint studies of any type have been reported. Jackson and Witt (1994) assessed the change and stability of leisure constraints between two similar groups of people drawn from the same population over a four-year period using the same measures and survey procedures. They found few differences over time. In a panel study with the same group of individuals and using the same measures, Wright, Drogin Rodgers, and Backman (2001) examined leisure constraints and hunting participation in 1989 and 1992. In this type of study, differences in individual levels of constraint and participation and not just group-level differences can be examined. The strength of various constraints for individuals was found to vary over the two time periods and appeared to be associated with participation. The authors argued because researchers are typically interested in the behavior of individuals "it appears more appropriate to employ research designs (e.g., panel, repeated measures) that allow individual-level analyses" (p. 450).

We might add short-term longitudinal and repeated assessment designs that allow the operation of constraints in the context of everyday life are also needed. Phenomena such as constraint–negotiation can be view as *transactional processes*. For example, Lazarus (1993) argued the experience of stress is a transactional process that neither exists solely in the environment nor in the person, but is something that results from the interaction of the person and their environment. Repeated assessments of coping processes involve researchers measuring key variables "in each distinct context repeatedly from moment to moment or encounter to encounter" (Lazarus, 1995, p. 4), and allow data to be collected a number of times from the same individuals across various circumstances. This approach has enabled stress researchers to examine both change and stability in the way a person copes with different stressful encounters over time (Lazarus, 1999; Somerfield & McCrae, 2000; Stone, Shiffman & De Vries, 1999; West & Hepworth, 1991), and it could be applied to the study of constraint and efforts to negotiate.

These short-term longitudinal and repeated assessment studies would also lend themselves to the development of predictive field studies. Data on constraints and leisure participation could be gathered at successive intervals. Such *prospective designs* would allow the monitoring not only of the key causal variables, but also of the intervening and mediating processes as well. In a prospective design, the participant is less influenced by the recall of events than is the case with a retrospective design (Brawley, Martin & Gyurcsik, 1998). If we assume negotiation strategies are process-oriented and situation-specific in nature, and mediate the effects of constraint on participation and other outcomes, we can test a model such as the one suggested by Mannell and Loucks-Atkinson (this volume), in which constraint appraisal, negotiation, negotiation outcomes, and intentions are described as intervening variables between constraint and participation. For example, Iwasaki and his colleagues (e.g., Iwasaki, 2002; Iwasaki & Mannell, 1999–2000; Iwasaki, Mannell, Smale & Butcher, 2002) used a repeated assessment or short-term longitudinal design to examine the effects of leisure coping beliefs and strategies on the impact of major stressful life events and weekly hassles on the health of highly stressed groups of individuals (e.g., police and emergency response service personnel). The purpose of using this type of research design was to comprehensively capture participants' use of stress–coping strategies in their everyday lives, and to examine stress–coping processes across a number of situations. In one study, university undergraduate students participated in a three-phase study over two weeks (Iwasaki & Mannell, 1999–2000). For the first phase of the study, participants were met one at a time and they completed a questionnaire with items measuring the role leisure played in helping them cope with stress, their physical and mental health, and stress. In the second phase of the study, the participants completed a stress and coping log twice a week for two weeks. They recorded daily levels of stress, severity of stressful events encountered, leisure coping strategies used, coping outcomes, and resulting emotional responses. They also provided a written description of each of the stressful

events encountered. The final phase involved each of the participants again meeting individually with a researcher to hand in their logs, and they also completed a post-study questionnaire in which physical and mental health were assessed for a second time.

This design allowed a number of competing models of leisure stress–coping to be tested and various intervening processes were examined. Although the development of the research design, recruitment of participants, and data collection were challenging and demanding, the richness of the information collected was a very positive aspect of this research, and allowed causal links to be more effectively examined. The use of this type of research design appears promising for the study of the constraint–negotiation process, which like the stress–coping process, involves a dynamic transactional process involving active coping or negotiating.

Accuracy, Meaning, and Context of Self-Reported Reasons for Nonparticipation

In addition to the use of research methods that allow the dynamics of the constraint–negotiation process to be better studied, greater attention to the quality of the information being gathered is needed. Indicators of leisure constraints and negotiation strategies have been almost exclusively based on the verbal information people provide in the form of self-reports, usually in the form of numerical ratings on a checklist of written reasons for nonparticipation, or verbal descriptions provided during a qualitative interview. While alternatives to self-report information about type and frequency of various forms of leisure behavior and quality of experience have been utilized (see Mannell & Kleiber, 1997), unobtrusive and behavioral indicators of constraint and constraint-related processes are somewhat more difficult for researchers to identify. Constraints are not necessarily discrete behavioral events or mental acts, but rather complex circumstances. Consequently, it is not an unreasonable assumption that the people who are constrained are in the best position to identify constraints to their own behavior.

In spite of the fact that research using self-report methods has led both to the identification of a wide range of factors that inhibit participation and the subpopulations for whom these factors are particularly problematic (Jackson, 2000; Jackson & Scott, 1999), the detection and measurement of leisure constraint continues to be one of the most significant challenges for constraint researchers. This challenge has been long recognized (e.g., Jackson 1988; Mannell & Zuzanek, 1991) and the capacity of constraint constructs and measures to capture meaningful aspects of people's leisure experience has been questioned (Samdahl & Jekubovich, 1997). The complexity and dynamics of people's leisure intentions, behaviors, resources, and the everyday circumstances in which their behaviors are embedded may limit their ability to recognize constraints. For example, paradoxically, it may be individuals more actively engaged in leisure rather than those less active individuals who are more aware of constraints. Following the analysis of their survey data in which participants sometimes reported being more constrained than nonparticipants, Kay and Jackson (1991) theorized that when individuals report constraints they may include not only factors that inhibit them, but also those they have overcome: "Any act of participation potentially exposes individuals to constraints" and "it is therefore to be expected that high levels of constraint may be reported by those who participate" (Kay & Jackson, 1991, p. 301). It is also likely people lack awareness of some of the constraining factors present in their lives. Shaw, Bonen, and McCabe (1991) pointed out when researchers focus on people's perceptions of constraint, the constraining effects of social structural factors, such as socioeconomic differences, ethnicity, and gender are likely overlooked. These factors may serve as "invisible" constraints because they are part of the pervasive background of values, attitudes, and expectations that play an important role in shaping the social contexts in which people live out their lives.

Though the limitations of self-report data have been the subject of some excellent analyses in the psychological literature during the past few decades, little serious consideration of these problems for constraint research has been forthcoming. Given the possibility that the reasons given for nonparticipation or less than desired levels of participation may under some circumstances not accurately represent constraints on leisure, it is important to give greater attention to the measurement and interpretation of the constraints people report.

Self-Knowledge of Constraints: Cultural Explanations and Stereotypic Reasons

As we noted, survey research methods continue to be used extensively in quantitative studies of leisure nonparticipation and constraints, and it is likely the limitations suggested for measuring leisure participation with surveys (see Chase & Godbey, 1983; Mannell & Kleiber,

1997) also operate when gathering information about reasons for leisure nonparticipation and constraints. The completion of survey items requires respondents report reasons for nonparticipation at a time removed from actual encounters with these factors and the social contexts in which the participation is actually inhibited. Respondents are also expected to recall and summarize the factors contributing to their nonparticipation for substantially lengthy and often unspecified periods of time. Therefore, given that both participation and constraint are typically measured at the same time, it is not surprising that these self-reports may be highly inaccurate and make the constraint process difficult to study with precision.

The limitations of self-report data described by Nisbett and Wilson (1977) in their now classic but largely ignored analysis of the validity of a wide range of psychological self-report measures of needs, beliefs, attitudes, and personality traits would seem to apply to measures of constraints as well. Self-reported constraints are people's beliefs about their reasons for reduced or nonparticipation. Nisbett and Wilson argued, "when people attempt to report on their cognitive processes, that is, on the processes mediating the effects of a stimulus on a response, they do not do so on the basis of any true introspection" (p. 231). Rather, their reports are based on implicit causal theories or judgments about events that are plausible causes of their behavior. Early in the social psychological study of leisure, Iso-Ahola (1980) noted how this process can lead to deficiencies in research on leisure needs and satisfactions.

From time to time, concern has been expressed about respondents' abilities "to recognize and verbalize the reasons why they do not participate" (Jackson, 1988, p. 211). Mannell and Zuzanek (1991) argued Iso-Ahola's concern about self-reports of leisure needs and satisfactions can be applied to self-reports of leisure constraints. For example, if we ask a person why she did not attend all of the skateboarding classes in which she registered, she may answer, "I didn't have enough time." The challenge for the researcher is to determine how the nonparticipant reached this conclusion. This type of *constraint* question may initiate a process whereby the individual starts looking for a reason or cause for her behavior, and she may rely on general culturally furnished rules or theories rather than remember and reconstruct the exact circumstances. One such "theory" quite prevalent in many contemporary societies is *the pace of life is faster today and there is too much to do, therefore I do not have enough time.* In spite of the occasional concerns raised about self-report measures, little attention has been given to this issue. It remains to be determined when reported reasons for reduced or nonparticipation are accurate indicators of leisure constraints and when they are socially or culturally provided explanations.

Constraints and Excuses: The Stories People Tell About Nonparticipation

Inaccuracy may not be the only problem with self-reported constraints. People may consciously or unconsciously misrepresent the real reasons they do not participate in a leisure activity at a level consistent with their stated intentions. In their discussion of barriers to exercise, McAuley, Poag, Gleason, and Wraith (1990) suggested the barriers mentioned by people may be "attributed excuses" rather than real obstacles. The conditions that contribute to inaccurate self-reports may increase the likelihood that the reasons and explanations people provide for their behaviors are excuses. For example, if researchers ask individuals to provide retrospective views of why they do not participate, this open-ended task gives them the opportunity to provide excuses for their leisure nonparticipation. Again consider the lack of time "constraint." On the one hand, this self-reported reason may represent a legitimate lack of time due to caregiving obligations or heavy occupational demands beyond people's control. On the other hand, it may indicate an unwillingness to sacrifice time spent doing something else during free time, such as relaxing, exercising, or volunteering. This self-reported reason may also mask the "true" reason for nonparticipation, such as being too lazy and not wanting to make the effort. We would probably have no difficulty in agreeing the first reason describes a constraint, and the latter reason is a socially acceptable excuse whose main function is to allow the individual to maintain a favorable impression of himself or herself. The second reason, "unwillingness to sacrifice time," is more difficult to classify. Given that participation in the activities that contribute to the lack of time is voluntary, the real reason is the "constrained" activity does not have a high enough priority. The lack of time reason in this case may be a shorthand explanation for this lack of priority or it could be an excuse, particularly if the individual felt that nonparticipation could reflect negatively on the image he or she has of themselves or wishes to project to others.

Meichenbaum and Fong (1993) proposed the use of a constructive narrative perspective to examine the reasons or "stories" people tell to explain their nonparticipation may lead to a better understanding of the factors that really stop them from doing what they say they wish to do. Drawing on the tenets of narrative psychology,

Meichenbaum and Fong argued, "individuals construct and control their own 'minds' by creating narratives [and] persuading themselves" (p. 473) they are good people engaged in appropriate behavior. They also often perceive their excuses to be legitimate, which likely makes them more difficult to overcome.

Meichenbaum (1995) applied this approach to the analysis of the stories people create to help them cope with stressful events, and Meichenbaum and Fong (1993) studied and analyzed the reasons (or stories) people provided for not engaging in healthy behavior (e.g., quitting smoking). Their analysis suggested many of the reasons people gave were self-protective excuses. They also argued these excuses could be distinguished on the basis of the type of psychological process that underlies the excuse, which in turn affects the difficulty involved in changing the person's behavior or enabling them to participate in healthy behaviors. For example, when excuses are based on a lack of knowledge or faulty logic, behavior may be easier to change. However, excuses linked to views people have about themselves or ego-involving beliefs that influence the way situations and information are evaluated likely make it much more difficult to change behavior.

An interesting aspect of applying the constructive narrative perspective to an understanding of leisure constraint is that social cognitions become relevant to the conceptualization and study of perceived constraints. People are psychologically active and generate reasons for not participating influenced by their need to present a positive self-image both to themselves and others, and to develop and protect their personal belief systems. Leisure constraint researchers might benefit from investing more time in studying the social cognitive processes related to the reasons reported for leisure nonparticipation. This knowledge might not only allow the development of research strategies to more effectively measure "true" constraints, but also allow the implementation of more effective interventions to help people participate in leisure activities consistent with their expressed wishes.

Recall, Accuracy, and Veracity of Self-Reports of Constraints

In addition to better understanding the meaning of the reasons people give for nonparticipation, an analysis of the factors that affect the accuracy of recall can lead to the development and use of more effective research methods. The most obvious and chief determinant of accuracy is memory of the events at the time of recall. Inaccuracies in self-reports may be increased by the separation in time between the report and the actual occurrence of the constraining circumstances. When the specifics of an event are forgotten, the "vagaries of memory may allow the invention of factors presumed to be present at the time the process occurred" (Nisbett & Wilson, 1977, p. 253). Stereotypic cultural explanations and excuses contribute to these inventions.

Context also seems to be a factor influencing memory. For example, people likely remember their nonparticipation and not the specifics of the circumstances surrounding it. When the researcher asks a question about constraints, the question may not focus the respondent's attention on the contextual influences. Consequently, study participants may rely on stereotypical reasons or excuses. When people are asked why they did certain things in the past, they are inclined to explain their behavior in terms of what appear to be larger causes rather than the myriad factors a part of the actual contexts of their daily lives "simply because of their smallness and seeming inconsequentiality" (Nisbett & Wilson, 1977, p. 253).

Another aspect of the context of constraint is the variability and stability of various reasons given for nonparticipation. As we have already suggested, the influence of constraints is best seen as an ongoing and dynamic "transaction" between personal characteristics and environmental contexts. Survey methods are limited in their ability to provide information on the nature of constraints as they operate in the context of daily life. The dynamics of this transaction are not likely to be remembered. Constraints that have emerged from many studies, such as time, finances, availability of facilities, and health, tend to be seen as relatively permanent or stable. Survey data collection does not easily allow the contextual variability of the impact of constraints on participation and the use of negotiation resources to be assessed.

Some recognition has been given to the view that reasons and constraints may exhibit different degrees of variability and stability. Boothby, Tungatt, and Townsend (1981) used the terms "relative" and "absolute." In making a distinction between "blocking" and "inhibiting" constraints, Jackson and Searle (1985) suggested the inhibiting influence of a constraint may vary in intensity depending on circumstances, including such factors as time of the week and availability of partners (p. 698). Iso-Ahola and Mannell (1985) proposed a constraint typology of "six major categories or sources of leisure constraints, one-half of which are considered fairly stable and permanent and the other variable and temporary" (p. 115). As noted earlier, Wright et al. (2001) found the intensity of constraints on a particular leisure behavior changed over time.

Mannell and Zuzanek (1991) postulated the salience of the reasons people typically give for nonparticipation varies as a function of the attributes of the social context in which people find themselves. Therefore, the reasons for nonparticipation reported may vary from one situation to another—what might be called constraint switching (Mannell & Zuzanek, 1991, p. 339). One strategy for cutting through cultural explanations and excuses for nonparticipation and assessing the contextual variability of constraint is to monitor the constraints people report during their daily lives as close in time and place as possible to their actual occurrence.

Monitoring Constraints in Daily Life With the Experiential Sampling Method

One of the authors and a colleague (Mannell & Zuzanek, 1991) attempted to monitor the leisure constraints experienced in the context of daily life by adapting the Experiential Sampling Method (ESM). The reasons reported for nonparticipation by older retired adults in physically active leisure during the course of a typical week were examined and compared to those typically identified with surveys. Larson and Csikszentmihalyi (1983) argued the ESM allows a means of collecting quantitative data about an individual's behavior and experience within its situational context and at a time close to their occurrence. Respondents typically carry electronic pagers or watches for a period of several days, usually one week. In response to a random signal or "beep," respondents take out a booklet of brief questionnaires and complete a series of closed and open-ended questions indicating the current activity engaged in, psychological and cognitive states, and the social and physical context of the behavior and experience. The ESM has been used to address a number of leisure-related research questions (see Mannell, 1999). For their study of constraints, Mannell & Zuzanek (1991) incorporated two questions into the ESM questionnaire form, which constituted the Alternative Activity Probe Technique (AAPT). The potentially constrained activity of interest in their study was physically active leisure. The respondents were first asked, "At this moment, would you like to engage in physically active leisure?" The follow-up question was then, "Why or why not?" These two questions were devised to elicit a broad range of reasons used by people to explain why they felt or did not feel like participating in physically active leisure at the moment when signaled. Given that the structured interviews also used in this study indicated the participants were interested in being physically active in their leisure, it was assumed that if a respondent indicated no immediate interest in participating at the moment when signaled (response to the first question), the reason provided (response to the second question) could be a constraint.

The reasons provided by the study participants in response to the AAPT were detailed and context-specific. For example, rather than providing summary statements such as "a lack of time," responses to the AAPT provided evidence the alleged lack of time may have meant other activities had a higher priority at that moment, supporting suggestions by Godbey (1985) and Jackson (1988). Reasons that included "the wrong time," "preference for the present activity," and "plan to participate later" supported the view the participants were busy and their daily lives were filled with other valued, competing activities.

With the AAPT, it was also found the constraints perceived to inhibit participation are variable and temporary in their influence. Clear evidence suggested the respondents "switched" constraints depending on the context. In addition to this type of research alerting researchers to the limitations involved in taking self-reported constraints at face value when collected independent of context, future constraint research could be directed at examining the influence of factors in the social and physical contexts of people's daily lives that influence the constraints experienced. For example, do people feel less constrained at certain times, when engaged in certain types of activities, while experiencing particular mood states, or in the company of certain persons?

There are, however, limitations with methods like the ESM for studying constraints. First, the techniques may not completely enhance the ability of respondents to identify the "true" reasons for their nonparticipation or totally eliminate the use of stereotypic reasons or excuses. However, by having respondents report their reasons for nonparticipation at the moment when faced with a decision, the tendency to provide a stereotypic response or excuse due to forgetting the real reason with the passage of time may be substantially reduced.

Second, the modification of the ESM is more of a methodological departure than the simple addition of another question or two to the ESM form might suggest. The AAPT is an intrusive strategy that requires respondents to switch response mode from simply recording behavior and experience at the occurrence of an electronic signal. The respondents are also asked to consider an alternative to their ongoing activities that presumably activates a sequence of cognitive events involving conscious decision making. The potential for instrument reactivity and the possibility of influencing habitual patterns of thinking and experiencing are increased. However, the potential of research techniques that explore constraints in the contexts of daily life would seem to outweigh these disadvantages.

Qualitative Interviews and Self-Reports of Constraints

Although providing a form of self-report data, qualitative research with the use of in-depth interviews may also allow researchers to circumvent some of the problems of the accurate reporting of constraints. By allowing the researcher and study participant to recreate and explore the context and meaning of self-reported constraints and negotiation strategies, a more accurate assessment of constraining circumstances and responses to them may be obtained. Researchers using qualitative interviews have found when asked people are able to describe in some detail the constraints, negotiation strategies, and contexts in which the dynamics of constraint–negotiation processes occur. For example, the women studied by Henderson, Bedini, Hecht, and Schuler (1995) felt they were successful at becoming involved or staying involved in leisure activities based on the use of negotiation strategies that allowed them to resist gender role expectations, to respond actively rather than passively to constraints, and to balance the benefits and costs of participation. They felt these strategies allowed them to deal with the constraints of energy deficiency, time shrinkage, lack of opportunities and choices, dependency on others, and physical and psychological safety. Similarly, the women in Little's (2002) study of adventure recreation involvement were able to describe a wide variety of constraints and negotiation strategies as well as the specific contexts in which they occurred. Qualitative interview approaches, although still relying on self-reports, may—by focusing on the social context of the experience of constraints—encourage participants to move beyond stereotypical responses. By encouraging study participants to recreate the social context, it may be possible to gain a more accurate picture of the constraining conditions that operate in their lives. However, people's ability to identify and to describe constraints and the ways in which they negotiate to participate is not guaranteed with qualitative interviews. Little (2002) noted sometimes the women she studied appeared to be "unconscious" of what an outside observer might label a constraint as well as the ways in which they negotiated or adapted their circumstances to continue their participation.

Like quantitative methods, qualitative approaches that do not rely solely on one-time interviews may help researchers to more accurately identify the leisure constraints responsible for nonparticipation. For example, in addition to in-depth interviews, Little (2002) had the participants in her study complete an adventure diary for up to six months in which they recorded "actual adventure activities, missed adventures, frequencies, locations, motivations and companions" (p. 162). Participant observation is another qualitative method that can be useful in corroborating interview data. Though a number of studies have utilized participant observation to study various types of leisure behavior (e.g., Fine, 1987; Stebbins, 1992), little research of this nature has been carried out specifically looking at the leisure constraint process. Scott's (1991) year-long study of group-related constraints among contract bridge players continues to be an exception. He used a mixed approach to data collection that combined participant observation with in-depth interviewing. He was able to confirm the group-related constraints the study participants reported were operating to influence their leisure behavior.

Measurement of Constraint Constructs: Psychometric Conundrums

A basic tenet of quantitative research is that the basis of defining concepts or constructs is their measurement. Though researchers may agree on the nominal definition of a concept such as constraint, if they cannot agree on its measurement little progress is likely to be made. The strategy of developing standardized measurement scales of key constructs, and the psychometric development of these scales in establishing dimensionality, reliability, and validity is quite common in social psychological studies of leisure. For example, multi-item scales comprised of one or more theoretically meaningful subdimensions have been developed for the study of leisure motivation (Beard & Ragheb, 1983), leisure boredom (Iso-Ahola & Weissinger, 1990), and the coping functions of leisure (Iwasaki & Mannell, 2000). However, the development of widely used standardized measures of constraint and constraint-related constructs has been limited.

A decade ago Raymore et al. (1993) noted a "lack of previously existing instruments for measuring constraint" (p. 103). If we interpret this statement to mean standardized scales that can be used to study nonparticipation in a wide range of leisure activities, in diverse settings, and with different populations, the situation has not changed greatly. Also, few attempts to develop negotiation scales have been reported (Hubbard & Mannell, 2001). A common strategy in constraint research is to select items on the basis of their relevance to the population, specific leisure activities, and contexts of interest. In developing constraint measures, researchers often construct lists of the constraints on the basis of their own knowledge of the study population, sometimes having in mind various constraint types or dimensions to guide their selection of items. Scales also vary according to whether they focus on a single leisure activity, a narrow range of activities, or all of the activities comprising a person's leisure lifestyle (Jackson & Scott, 1999). A number of items may be selected to represent each of these types. The published literature and discussions with individuals from the population under study may also serve as a source for the constraint items developed and included. Sometimes items are sorted into subscales on basis of their similar appearing meaning, and not infrequently on the basis of exploratory factor analysis carried out after the data have been collected (e.g., McGuire, 1984; Tsai & Coleman, 1999; Wright & Goodale, 1991). The reduction of the large number of constraint items that often comprise constraint scales to a relatively small number of constraint types or dimensions makes it easier for researchers to describe the constraints encountered by a population and to analyze constraint and participation relationships. Typically, scales have been developed and used for single, one-time studies, though a few researchers have used their scales with little or no alteration in several studies with similar populations and types of leisure participation. For example, in several studies of the sport and physical recreation participation of the residents of a Greek city, Alexandris and his colleagues found psychological factors, time, knowledge, facilities, accessibility, partners, and interest emerged as constraints consistently and with good reliability (Alexandris et al., 2002). Also, Wright et al. (2001) found though the strength of various constraint types changed for individuals during their four-year panel study of a group of U.S. hunters and nonhunters, the major attitudinal, cost, opportunity, family, and work constraint dimensions were stable and the items comprising them constituted reliable multi-item scales. Some evidence also shows the same constraint dimensions underlie scales whether they are used to measure constraint to interest in participating, starting to participate, or continuing to participate (Hultsman, 1993; Jackson & Dunn, 1991; Jackson & Rucks, 1993; Tsai & Coleman, 1999). However, these scales were not developed with the intention of being general and widely used measures of leisure constraint.

Raymore et al. (1993) took a different approach, and in the interest of testing the hierarchical constraints model (Jackson et al., 1993) attempted to develop a theoretically driven constraint scale with distinct intrapersonal, interpersonal, and structural constraint subscales that measured "general or global perceptions of constraint on leisure" (p. 103). The results of Raymore et al.'s confirmatory factor analysis appears to provide some support for the existence of the three general subscales, though they were highly correlated. Hubbard and Mannell (2001) were unable to duplicate the three-factor structure with a slightly modified version of this scale tailored to account for constraint to employee recreation and fitness participation. Also, Hawkins, Peng, Hsieh, and Eklund (1999) attempted to replicate the three-dimension structure suggested by the hierarchical constraint model using a forced-choice response format and items they argued paralleled those used by Raymond et al. (1993). In spite of the authors' conclusion the three-factor solution from their exploratory factor analysis was consistent with the three hierarchical constraint types, closer scrutiny of their factor solution suggests the so-called "intrapersonal, interpersonal, and structural" items were substantially intermixed throughout the three factors.

In hindsight, this finding does not seem surprising when dealing with broad constraint types, such as those suggested by the hierarchical model. The items within each dimension (intrapersonal, interpersonal, and structural) are quite heterogeneous and measure a very diverse set of constraints. For example, it would not necessarily follow that a person constrained by shyness would also be constrained by a lack of skill or illness in an activity or any other non-shyness-related intrapersonal constraint.

It seems clear that specific, narrowly defined types of constraint (e.g. shyness, unavailability of coparticipants, limited financial resources) can be measured with multi-item scales, whereas it may be difficult to develop internally consistent measures of broad theoretically driven types (e.g., intrapersonal, intervening) comprised of a heterogeneous collection of constraints. Parenthetically, this heterogeneity does not appear to be a problem for the hierarchical model. The theory is not based on the constraint types being one-dimensional.

It is difficult to see the feasibility of developing standardized constraint scales general enough to be used with a wide variety of populations, activities, or contexts. It is also not practical to develop scales with a high level of internal consistency each time a specific leisure activity, context, and population are studied. Besides developing a pool of constraint items researchers can draw on when tailoring constraint scales to meet their specific research needs, it might prove useful to develop short, multi-item scales for measuring narrow and specific constraints, such as perceptions of lack of skill, lack of com-

panions, or limited accessibility to resources that may be easily and quickly incorporated into scales for specific studies. Based on the stability of the factor structure of several activity-specific scales examined, it also looks feasible to develop activity-specific scales for use in research on specific leisure domains.

As noted earlier, there is growing use of structural equation modeling (SEM) procedures for testing theoretical models in a number of areas of social scientific inquiry into leisure, including constraint research. One of the strengths of structural equation modeling is that measurement models of the key constructs are specified at the same time that the structural relationships are specified and tested. *Structural models* refer to the cause-and-effect links hypothesized to exist among the independent, intervening, and dependent variables in a model. Separate *measurement models* are often created for the structural variables in the model, which include the structural variable and its respective indicators or measures. For example, Hubbard and Mannell (2001) incorporated two indicators of motivation, three of constraint, and five of negotiation into their model to test several competing constraint models. Specification of the measurement models requires that multiple measures or indicators of the key variables be included, preferably measured with several data collection procedures (e.g., self-report, observational, performance; MacCallum & Austin, 2000).

Unfortunately, many constructs studied by social scientists are difficult to measure with other than self-report procedures, which as we have seen is true of constraints. Many social science researchers using SEM opted to use as separate indicators the average scores of the subscales or dimensions of measures of the constructs comprising their models. For example, Hubbard and Mannell (2001) treated average scores for each of the subscales of intrapersonal, interpersonal, and structural constraints as separate indicators of the constraint construct. Therefore, it would be useful to have internally consistent and reliable multidimensional constraint scales for model-testing using SEM procedures, which as we have seen is a challenge. This problem is not unique to constraint measurement. In fact, several statistical approaches and debate about them have emerged relating to ways of developing more effective self-report indicators of the key variables in social science models when reliable and internally consistent subscales are not available (see Finch & West, 1997; Kishton & Widman, 1994).

Another solution to this measurement problem is to use alternatives to self-report measures of constraints. However, these measures are often difficult to identify and collect. In a number of areas of psychological research, in addition to self-report measures, investigators developed rating systems for the third-person (e.g., friend, coparticipant, teacher, program leader, coworker, or family member) assessment of constructs such as people's coping responses (Endler & Parker, 2002), couple conflict (Hahlweg, Kaiser, Christensen, Fehm-Wolfsdorf & Groth, 2000), and depression (Parker et al., 2003). This approach has also been recommended by Brawley et al. (1998) for the study of barriers to exercise and could prove useful in constraint research.

Studying Nonparticipation Outcomes of the Constraint–Negotiation Process

Short-Term and Long-Term Quality of Life Outcomes: Constraint as a Dimension of Lifestyle

Though it has been suggested the leisure constraints people encounter in their lives may influence their satisfaction with their leisure lifestyles, there is little evidence the leisure constraints people report are actually related to their psychological well-being, either directly or indirectly through their influence on leisure participation. It seems reasonable to expect the experience of leisure constraints could cause people to be less satisfied with their leisure lifestyles, and consequently, daily lives and life in general. Of course, it is also possible low levels of well-being and life satisfaction could influence how constrained people feel. It has been suggested experiential outcomes, such as enjoyment and satisfaction, are likely influenced by constraint (Jackson, 1991, 2000; Jackson & Scott, 1999). In spite of research reported by Witt and Goodale (1981) and Francken and van Raaij (1981) that suggested leisure constraint decreases leisure enjoyment and satisfaction, little theorizing or empirical research has been done on constraint to quality of life, well-being, or short-term experiential outcomes. A few exceptions can be found. For example, Cutler Riddick (1985) found transportation barriers were significantly associated with lower leisure participation rates and lower life satisfaction among older adults. Raymore, Godbey, and Crawford (1994) found adolescents who reported higher levels of leisure constraint also had lower self-esteem.

Relationships between the type, frequency, and pattern of constraints reported and other outcomes, such as psychological well-being and life satisfaction, could

be further examined. In fact, people's leisure constraint profile could be seen as a dimension of their lifestyle. Several studies have been reported in which researchers attempted to identify or group people according to their *constraint* profile. For example, Jackson (1993) and Mannell (1994) used cluster analysis to identify six and four groups, respectively, of individuals who shared similar patterns of constraint. Mannell (1994) also examined differences among the resulting groups in leisure participation, life satisfaction, and current levels of psychological well-being. He carried out a series of analyses using data collected with the ESM/AAPT method described earlier. Following factor analysis of the constraints reported by respondents, cluster analysis was carried out based of the frequency with which the six different types of constraint were experienced. Four groups of individuals, each with a distinct constraint profile, were identified. The constraint profiles of the people in three of the four groups were each dominated by different combinations of constraint, and the people in a fourth group encountered all six types of constraint relatively infrequently compared to the other groups.

The short-term happiness and psychological well-being of participants during the study week was found to be associated with their constraint profile rather than just their total level of constraint. Long-term measures of quality of life, such as life satisfaction, were also related to constraint profile. For example, the group of older adults who said they were very busy with other activities and had already done or planned the leisure activity participated in a significantly larger number and diversity of leisure activities during the preceding year. They also had the highest level of leisure satisfaction and affective states during the study week. The unconstrained group had significantly lower levels of leisure participation, life satisfaction, and affect. This finding is consistent with the findings of Kay and Jackson (1991). Constraint appears to be a dimension of lifestyle related to its quality. Further thought needs to be given to the ways in which these short-term and long-term, other-than-participation, outcomes can be studied.

Short-Term Experiential Leisure Outcomes

Future research could be directed at examining the influence of constraint and experience-specific negotiation strategies on the leisure experience itself. It is possible to think of circumstances in which people participate in a leisure activity as frequently as they wish, but feel there are constraints on the psychological experience associated with the activity reducing its desired quality.

Though leisure experiences that do not regularly meet expectations for quality might themselves be perceived as a constraint on participation in the associated leisure activity and eventually lead to discontinuation, people may have a long-time commitment to the activity or feel obligated or compelled to continue to participate for reasons other than the quality of the experience. Consequently, they could experience a constraint on the quality of the experience without discontinuing or reducing participation. Constraint on this leisure experience could include pain due to a disability or injury, low skill level, desire for a more socially compatible partner, or any other factor that might result in the experience not meeting a participant's expectations or needs. Rarely have researchers asked people about constraints on the quality of their experiences, or about the strategies they use to overcome these constraints. It might be profitable for researchers to develop both conceptual frameworks for thinking about experiential constraint and negotiation resource, and measurement and research strategies for examining them.

The small number of studies reported in which actual constraints to enjoyment were examined illustrates the possibilities for future research. Harrington, Dawson, and Bolla (1992) and Harrington and Dawson (1995) asked their respondents specifically about constraint to their leisure enjoyment in general. In the participant observation study discussed earlier, Scott (1991) examined group-related constraints on both participation in contract bridge and the extent to which the participation was enjoyed. He concluded actual enjoyment in the activity was influenced by the extent to which participants' abilities in the activity, their orientation (social vs. serious), and their beliefs and attitudes matched those of their playing partners. Often these same factors served as constraints on participation as well, but not always. In another qualitative study, Whyte and Shaw (1994) found fear of violence often constrained the enjoyment undergraduate women experienced in their leisure activities even when they continued to participate. Not only was enjoyment of travel to and from the activity inhibited by a concern for personal safety, but also, "some women reported that the extra time, energy, and money invested in the planning stage of participation decreased their enjoyment," (p. 16) as did the resulting loss of spontaneity. In a study using both quantitative survey and qualitative interview methods, Frederick and Shaw (1995) found among women who attended aerobics classes, a number of them reported their enjoyment of the classes was constrained by the workout attire they were expected to wear and the competitive nature of the sessions. Given participants' strong motivation to participate to improve their body images, these factors appeared to constrain enjoyment without constraining participation.

It remains to be seen whether nonparticipation models of constraint and negotiation can be applied to an understanding of quality of experience. It would also be interesting to develop constraint–negotiation models that integrate the leisure participation and experience dimensions within a single model. Perhaps, such models might eventually provide a more comprehensive picture of constraints to leisure generally.

It should be possible to develop quantitative measures of experience-specific constraints and negotiation resources. A recent research project completed by Leveille (2003) demonstrated the feasibility of doing so. She developed a quality of experience measure for use with adults playing in a community recreational volleyball league that included not only enjoyment, but also the flow dimensions of time perception, focus of attention, and degree of match between a person's skills and the challenges encountered in the activity. Preliminary evidence supported the idea that people are able to think about constraints and negotiation strategies related to their experiences as distinct from their participation. Leveille also demonstrated it was possible to develop reliable scales of experience-specific constraints and negotiation strategies.

An Optimistic Concluding Note

The evolution of explanations of constraint toward a social–cognitive theoretical perspective demands a variety of theoretical and methodological developments take place that appear to have substantial potential for the further explication of phenomena associated with leisure constraint and nonparticipation. While the possibilities are quite promising, it will require considerably more effort to design and to carry out these types of constraint studies. It no longer seems sufficient only to use surveys with scales measuring participation, constraint, negotiation, and other constraint-related constructs. Though this chapter has focused on quantitative research issues, it is clear qualitative approaches in addition to the in-depth interview are required if our knowledge of the constraint negotiation process is to be advanced. A social–cognitive approach to leisure constraint theory not only requires careful analysis of the meaning of the reasons reported by people when they explain their reduced and nonparticipation and the processes involved, but also examination of their behavior in the contexts of daily life. As we have seen, there are a wide array of research designs and methodological, statistical, and analytical procedures available to examine comprehensive models of leisure constraint that include intervening social cognitive processes and behavioral and experiential outcomes. In conclusion, then, there appears to be good reason to be enthusiastic about the possibility of further study of the constraint–negotiation process.

References

Alexandris, K., Tsorbatzoudis, C., and Grouios, G. (2002). Perceived constraints on recreational sport participation: Investigating their relationship with intrinsic motivation, extrinsic motivation and amotivation. *Journal of Leisure Research, 34*, 233–252.

Bandura, A. (1986). *Social foundations of thought and action: A social cognitive theory*. Englewood Cliffs, NJ: Prentice Hall.

Beard, J. G. and Ragheb, M. G. (1983). Measuring leisure motivation. *Journal of Leisure Research, 15*, 219-228.

Bollen, K. A. (1989). *Structural equations with latent variables*. New York, NY: Wiley.

Boothby, J., Tungatt, M. F., and Townsend, A. R. (1981). Ceasing participation in sports activity: Reported reasons and their implications. *Journal of Leisure Research, 13*, 1–14.

Brawley, L. R., Martin, K. A., and Gyurcsik, N. C. (1998). Problems in assessing perceived barriers to exercise: Confusing obstacles with attributions and excuses. In J. L. Duda (Ed.), *Advances in sport and exercise psychology measurement* (pp. 337–350). Morgantown, WV: Fitness Information Technology, Inc.

Carroll, B. and Alexandris, K. (1997). Perception of constraints and strength of motivation: Their relationship to recreational sport participation in Greece. *Journal of Leisure Research, 29*, 279–299.

Chase, D. R. and Godbey, G. C. (1983). The accuracy of self-reported participation rates. *Leisure Studies, 2*, 231–235.

Cutler Riddick, C. (1985). Life satisfaction determinants of older males and females. *Leisure Sciences, 7*, 47–63.

Endler, N. S. and Parker, J. D. A. (2002). Assessing a patient's ability to cope. In J. N. Butcher (Ed.), *Clinical personality assessment: Practical approaches* (2nd ed.; pp. 335–360). London, England: Oxford University Press.

Finch, J. F. and West, S. G. (1997). The investigation of personality structure: Statistical models. *Journal of Research in Personality, 31*, 439–485.

Fine, G. A. (1987). *With the boys*. Chicago, IL: The University of Chicago Press.

Francken, D. A. and van Raaij, W. F. (1981). Satisfaction with leisure time activities. *Journal of Leisure Research, 13*, 337–352.

Frederick, C. J. and Shaw, S. M. (1995). Body image as a leisure constraint: Examining the experience of aerobic exercise classes for young women. *Leisure Sciences, 17*, 57–73.

Godbey, G. C. (1985). Nonuse of public leisure services: A model. *Journal of Park and Recreation Administration, 3*, 1–12.

Hahlweg, K., Kaiser, A., Christensen, A., Fehm-Wolfsdorf, G., and Groth, T. (2000). Self-report and observational assessment of couples' conflict: The concordance between the Communication Patterns Questionnaire and the KPI observation system. *Journal of Marriage and the Family, 62,* 61–67.

Harrington, M. and Dawson, D. (1995). Who has it best? Women's labor force participation, perceptions of leisure and constraints to enjoyment of leisure. *Journal of Leisure Research, 27*, 4–24.

Harrington, M., Dawson, D., and Bolla, P. (1992). Objective and subjective constraints on women's enjoyment of leisure. *Society and Leisure, 15*, 203–221.

Hawkins, B. A., Peng, J., Hsieh, C., and Eklund, S. J. (1999). Leisure constraints: A replication and extension of construct development. *Leisure Sciences, 21,* 179–192.

Henderson, K. A., Bedini, L. A., Hecht, L., and Schuler, R. (1995). Women with physical disabilities and the negotiation of leisure constraints. *Leisure Studies, 14*, 17–31.

Hubbard, J. and Mannell, R. C. (2001). Testing competing models of the leisure constraint negotiation process in a corporate employee recreation setting. *Leisure Sciences, 23*, 145–163.

Hultsman, W. Z. (1993). Is constrained leisure an internally homogeneous concept? An extension. *Journal of Leisure Research, 25*, 319–334.

Iso-Ahola, S. E. (1980). *The social psychology of leisure and recreation*. Dubuque, IA: Wm. C. Brown.

Iso-Ahola, S. E. and Mannell, R. C. (1985). Social and psychological constraints on leisure. In M. G. Wade (Ed.), *Constraints on leisure* (pp. 111–151). Springfield, IL: Charles C. Thomas.

Iso-Ahola, S. E. and Weissinger, E. (1990). Perceptions of boredom in leisure: Conceptualization, reliability and validity of the Leisure Boredom Scale. *Journal of Leisure Research, 22*, 1–17.

Iwasaki, Y. (2002). Exploring leisure coping processes: Roles of leisure activities and psychosocial functions of leisure coping. *Annals of Leisure Research, 5*, 27–50.

Iwasaki, Y. and Mannell, R. C. (1999–2000). The effects of leisure beliefs and coping strategies on stress–health relationships: A field study. *Leisure/Loisir, 24*, 3–57.

Iwasaki, Y. and Mannell, R. C. (2000). Hierarchical dimensions of leisure stress coping. *Leisure Sciences, 22*, 163–181.

Iwasaki, Y., Mannell. R. C., Smale, B. J. A., and Butcher, J. (2002). A short-term longitudinal analysis of leisure coping used by employees of police and emergency response service workers. *Journal of Leisure Research, 34*, 311–339.

Jackson, E. L. (1988). Leisure constraints: A survey of past research. *Leisure Sciences, 10*, 203–215.

Jackson, E. L. (1991). Leisure constraints/constrained leisure: Special issue introduction. *Journal of Leisure Research, 23*, 279–285.

Jackson, E. L. (1993). Recognizing patterns of leisure constraints. *Journal of Leisure Research, 25*, 129–149.

Jackson, E. L. (2000). Will research on leisure constraints still be relevant in the twenty-first century? *Journal of Leisure Research, 32*, 62–8.

Jackson, E. L., Crawford, D. W., and Godbey, G. (1993). Negotiation of leisure constraints. *Leisure Sciences, 15*, 1–12.

Jackson, E. L. and Dunn, E. (1991). Is constrained leisure an internally homogeneous concept? *Leisure Sciences, 13*, 167–184.

Jackson, E. L. and Rucks, V. C. (1993). Reasons for ceasing participation and barriers to participation: Further examination of constrainted leisure as an internally homogeneous concept. *Leisure Sciences, 15*, 217–230.

Jackson, E. L. and Rucks, V. C. (1995). Negotiation of leisure constraints by junior-high and high-school students: An exploratory study. *Journal of Leisure Research, 27*, 85–105.

Jackson, E. L. and Scott, D. (1999). Constraints to leisure. In E. L. Jackson and T. L. Burton (Eds.), *Leisure studies: Prospects for the twenty-first century* (pp. 299–321). State College, PA: Venture Publishing. Inc.

Jackson, E. L. and Searle, M. S. (1985). Recreation nonparticipation and barriers to participation: Concepts, and models. *Loisir et Sociètè/Society and Leisure, 8*, 693–707.

Jackson, E. L. and Witt, P. A. (1994). Change and stability in leisure constraints: A comparison of two surveys conducted four years apart. *Journal of Leisure Research, 26*, 322–336.

Kay, T. and Jackson, G. (1991). Leisure despite constraint: The impact of leisure constraints on leisure participation. *Journal of Leisure Research, 23*, 301–313.

Kishton, J. M. and Widman, K. F. (1994). Unidimensional versus domain representative parceling of questionnaire items: An empirical example. *Educational and Psychological Measurement, 54*, 757–765.

Larson, R. W. and Csikszentmihalyi, M. (1983). The experience sampling method. In H. T. Reis (Ed.), *Naturalistic approaches to studying social interaction* (pp. 41–56). San Francisco, CA: Jossey-Bass.

Lazarus, R. S. (1993). Coping theory and research: Past, present, and future. *Psychosomatic Medicine, 55,* 234–247.

Lazarus, R. S. (1995). Theoretical perspectives in occupational stress research. In R. Crandall and P. L. Perrewe (Eds.), *Occupational stress: A handbook* (pp. 3–14). Washington, DC: Taylor and Francis.

Lazarus, R. S. (1999). *Stress and emotion: A new synthesis.* New York, NY: Springer.

Leveille, T. (2003). *Empirical examination of the leisure experience: The motivation, constraints and negotiation strategies of competitive–recreational indoor volleyball players.* Master's thesis, University of Waterloo, Ontario, Canada.

Little, D. E. (2002). Women and adventure recreation: Reconstructing leisure constraints and adventure experiences to negotiate continuing participation. *Journal of Leisure Research, 34,* 157–177.

MacCallum, R. C. and Austin, J. T. (2000). Applications of structural equation modeling in psychological research. *Annual Review of Psychology, 51,* 201–226.

Mannell, R. C. (1994). Constraints, leisure participation and well-being among older adults. In D. M. Compton and S. E. Iso-Ahola (Eds.), *Leisure and mental health* (Vol. 1; pp. 79–97). Salt Lake City, UT: Family Development Resources.

Mannell, R. C. (1999). Leisure experience and satisfaction. In E. L. Jackson and T. L. Burton (Eds.), *Leisure studies: Prospects for the twenty-first century* (pp. 235–251). State College: Venture Publishing, Inc.

Mannell, R. C. and Kleiber, D. A. (1997). *A social psychology of leisure.* State College, PA: Venture Publishing, Inc.

Mannell, R. C. and Zuzanek, J. (1991). The nature and variability of leisure constraints in daily life: The case of the physically active leisure of older adults. *Leisure Sciences, 13,* 337–351.

McAuley, E., Poag, K., Gleason, A., and Wraith, S. (1990). Attribution from exercise programs: Attributional and affective perspectives. *Journal of Social Behavior and Personality, 5,* 591–602.

McGuire, F. A. (1984). A factor analytic study of leisure constraints in advanced adulthood. *Leisure Sciences, 6,* 313–326.

Meichenbaum, D. (1995). Disasters, stress and cognition. In S. E. Hobfoll and M. W. deVries (Eds.), *Extreme stress and communities: Impact and intervention* (pp. 33–61). New York, NY: Kluwer Academic/Plenum Publishers.

Meichenbaum, D. and Fong, G. T. (1993). How individuals control their own minds: A constructive narrative perspective. In D. M. Wegner and J. W. Pennabaker (Eds.), *Handbook of mental control* (pp. 473–490). Englewood Cliffs, NJ: Prentice Hall.

Nisbett, R. E. and Wilson, T. D. (1977). Telling more than we can know: Verbal reports on mental processes. *Psychological Review, 8,* 231–259.

Parker, G., Gladstone, G., Mitchell, P., Welham, K., Malhi, G., and Loo, L. (2003). Valid assessment of the clinical features of depression by relatives appears to slip under the RADAR. *Australian and New Zealand Journal of Psychiatry, 37,* 92–96.

Raymore, L. A., Godbey, G. C., and Crawford, D. W. (1994). Self-esteem, gender, and socioeconomic status: Their relation to perceptions of constraint on leisure among adolescents. *Journal of Leisure Research, 26,* 99–118.

Raymore, L., Godbey, G., Crawford, D., and von Eye, A. (1993). Nature and process of leisure constraints: An empirical test. *Leisure Sciences, 15,* 99–113.

Samdahl, D. M. and Jekubovich, N. J. (1997). A critique of leisure constraints: Comparative analyses and understandings. *Journal of Leisure Research, 29,* 430–452.

Scott, D. (1991). The problematic nature of participation in contract bridge: A qualitative study of group-related constraints. *Leisure Sciences, 13,* 321–336.

Shaw, S. M., Bonen, A., and McCabe, J. F. (1991). Do more constraints mean less leisure? Examining the relationship between constraints and participation. *Journal of Leisure Research, 23,* 286–300.

Somerfield, M. P. and McCrae, R. R. (Eds.). (2000). Stress and coping research: Methodological challenges, theoretical advances, and clinical applications. Psychology in the Public Forum. *American Psychologist, 55*(6), 620–673.

Stone, A. A., Shiffman, S. S., and De Vries, M. (1999). Ecological momentary assessment. In D. Kahneman, E. Diener, and N. Schwarz (Eds.), *Well-being: The foundations of hedonic psychology* (pp. 26–39). New York, NY: Russell Sage Foundation.

Stebbins, R. A. (1992). Hobbies as marginal leisure: The case of barbershop singers. *Society and Leisure, 15,* 375–386.

Tsai, E. H. and Coleman, D. J. (1999). Leisure constraints of Chinese immigrants: An exploratory study. *Loisir et Sociètè/Society and Leisure, 22,* 243–264.

West, S. G. and Hepworth, J. T. (1991). Statistical issues in the study of temporal data: Daily experiences. *Journal of Personality*, *59*, 609–662.

Whyte, L. B. and Shaw, S. M. (1994). Women's leisure: An exploratory study of fear of violence as a leisure constraint. *Journal of Applied Recreation Research*, *19*, 5–21.

Witt, P. A. and Goodale, T. L. (1981). The relationships between barriers to leisure enjoyment and family stages. *Leisure Sciences*, *4*, 29–49.

Wright, B. A., Drogin Rodgers, E. B., and Backman, K. F. (2001). Assessing the temporal stability of hunting participation and the structure and intensity of constraints: A panel study. *Journal of Leisure Research*, *33*, 450–469.

Wright, B. A. and Goodale, T. L. (1991). Beyond nonparticipation: Validation of interest and frequency of participation categories in constraints research. *Journal of Leisure Research*, *23*, 314–331.

Endnote

1. The term nonparticipation is used to refer to both a lack of participation and less than desired participation.

Section 4

Constraints Research and Practice

Chapter 18

The Relevance of Constraints Research to Leisure Service Delivery

David Scott (Texas A&M University)

The George Bush Presidential Library and Museum is a big flashy feather in the cap of [Bryan/College Station]....Nearly three-quarters of a million people have visited the museum since it opened in late 1997, which area experts say is impressive. But that number falls short of the goal of 250,000 people a year. (Levey, 2001, p. E1)

Making the parks relevant and welcoming to a broader constituency is a matter of survival and equity for the National Park System in the new millennium. (Wilkinson, 2000, p. 20)

Those of us who are museum professionals have frequently been puzzled by the elusive masses who never enter our museum doors—the non-participants. With all the treasures we offer, why don't we attract a broader spectrum of the public, a larger audience, a substantial clientele that comes regularly rather than just for blockbusters? (Hood, 1983, p. 50)

The three accounts cited here get at the heart of a central question among leisure service practitioners: Why don't people use or make greater use of agency offerings? The very success of many leisure service organizations, particularly commercial or private operations, depends on their being able to attract a steady, if not necessarily loyal, stream of customers. Another issue is at stake among public or quasi-public park and recreation entities: How can programs and services be made attractive to population groups who have historically been underserved or underrepresented with regard to visitation and participation? In democratic societies, issues of equity and fairness are very much at stake in terms of how publicly funded leisure service organizations do (or ought to do) business.

Indeed, findings from a variety of studies show marked disparities among population groups in terms of their frequency of participation in different leisure activities, and their use of local, regional, and national public park and recreation services. Studies show nonusers of local and regional parks are disproportionately female, older, members of a minority group, and have lower levels of education and income (Scott & Munson, 1994). Similar patterns are evident in regard to people's use of locally sponsored recreation programs and facilities (Godbey, Graefe & James, 1992; Howard & Crompton, 1984; Lee, Scott & Floyd, 2001); museums and zoos (Hood, 1993); and national parks, state parks, and historic sites (Dwyer, 1994; Floyd, 1999). Findings like this have led some researchers and policy makers to observe, "leisure has become a source and site of inequality" (Collins & Kennett, 1998, p. 133). Leisure service practitioners may find this indictment harsh. Nevertheless, the consistency of these results should indicate to practitioners they might not fully understand the wants and recreation needs of marginalized groups under their jurisdiction.

Research on leisure constraints can potentially help practitioners to understand why population groups do not make greater use of agency offerings and provide directions about how to allay the conditions that inhibit involvement. Few other areas of leisure research have such an applied focus and roots that stretch back over such a long time. However, as noted by Jackson and Scott (1999), there is little indication that practitioners are applying findings from constraints research to improve service delivery. Both practitioners and students in leisure studies may find constraints research esoteric and lacking in inspiration (Godbey, 1989). If constraints research is to have a positive impact on service delivery, we researchers must do a better job of making our research accessible.

To date, a number of articles and chapters have been written that seek to summarize ideas and findings associated with constraints research (e.g., Goodale & Witt, 1990; Jackson, 1988; Jackson & Scott, 1999). At least two articles have been published whose purpose has been to highlight the practical implications of constraints research. One of these, an article published by Searle and Jackson (1985b), drew attention to four elements of public park and recreation delivery systems that must be examined critically if constraints are to be relaxed. These elements, according to Searle and Jackson, include agency philosophy, policy statements, program planning efforts, and marketing strategies. The other article, written by McGuire and O'Leary (1992), sought to link research to practice by identifying major themes within constraints research. For example, they recognized constraints may shape both preferences and participation, and constraints are more or less important to different groups of people.

Although the pieces by Searle and Jackson (1985b) and McGuire and O'Leary (1992) provided valuable guidance for practitioners, many articles about constraints have been published in the last decade, providing new insights about the relationship between constraints and other facets of leisure behavior. The purpose of this chapter is to provide an up-to-date examination of the practical implications of constraints research. I begin by laying down some general principles gleaned from constraints research. I then summarize findings from studies focusing specifically on constraints to people's use of leisure service amenities. To my knowledge, no published works, including the piece by McGuire and O'Leary, have summarized this body of literature. Finally, I turn to an examination of how organizational practices and beliefs may actually create barriers to involvement.

The primary audience for this chapter is park and recreation practitioners and students who aspire to be practitioners. Although I focus primarily on publicly funded park and recreation agencies, many of the issues discussed are likely to be applicable to commercial providers as well. The success of both public and commercial entities depends, in part, on locating clients/customers and ensuring client/customer satisfaction. Public and commercial entities are equally likely to target services/products to diverse groups of clients/customers. Constraints research can potentially assist both public agencies and commercial providers as they pursue these ends. An obvious difference between public agencies and commercial entities, of course, is that the latter must make profits to survive. A profit orientation necessarily means that commercial providers can be far more selective in terms of the groups they target. Thus, they can ignore a range of constraints and issues necessarily important to public agencies.

General Principles About Constraints

Before I put forth some general principles, I provide the following working definition of leisure constraints:

> factors that limit people's participation in leisure activities, people's use of leisure services (e.g., parks and programs), or people's enjoyment of current activities

As I will show, I do not believe constraints are insurmountable. A similar term—"barriers"—has this connotation. Rather, I regard constraints as factors within the individual's life space that must be successfully negotiated if participation or enjoyment is to occur. The principles in this section are gleaned from an array of studies and articles written about leisure constraints, and to an extent constitute a compilation of important "truths" about what researchers now know about leisure constraints. I believe practitioners and leisure service agencies must understand these ideas if they are to effectively moderate the conditions that make participation or visitation problematic. I also make every effort to highlight the practical implications of the different principles put forward. The principles identified in this section include the following:

- constraints influence both participation and preferences.

- time commitments are the most frequently cited constraints to leisure involvement.

- constraints vary across activities and different dimensions of leisure.

- constraints vary by population groups.

- people may negotiate constraints.

Constraints Influence Both Participation and Preferences

Early studies on constraints focused primarily on factors that inhibited people's participation in desired activities (Jackson & Scott, 1999). Both researchers and practitioners tended to focus on barriers or constraints physical and external to the individual (e.g., lack of facilities). Over time, researchers began to realize constraints could also be internal to the individual and include such things as personality and individual dispositions. In their influential article on barriers to family leisure, Crawford and Godbey (1987) argued persuasively that constraints affect other facets of people's leisure beyond just participation. Indeed, they stated our understanding of constraints is facilitated when we consider how they relate to both leisure participation *and* leisure preferences. They identified three distinct types of constraints—intrapersonal, and interpersonal, structural—that help us to better comprehend these relationships.

Intrapersonal constraints, according to Crawford and Godbey (1987), are those psychological states that inhibit the acquisition of leisure preferences. The notion of antecedent constraints has a similar connotation (Henderson, Stalnaker & Taylor, 1988; Jackson, 1990a, 1990b). Intrapersonal (or antecedent) constraints include personality needs, religiosity, reference group attitudes, prior socialization, and perceived skills and abilities. Intrapersonal constraints lead people to define leisure activities, services, and locales as inappropriate, uninteresting, or unavailable. To date, intrapersonal or antecedent constraints have been documented among women with stereotypic feminine personalities (Henderson et al., 1988), adolescents with low self-esteem (Raymore, Godbey & Crawford, 1994), and individuals who perceive themselves as helpless (Dattilo, 1994). Individuals with these personality traits are more likely than others to state they lack the interests, skills, confidence, and information to participate in a range of leisure activities.

Interpersonal constraints are those barriers that arise out of social interaction with friends, family, and others. In a family context, for example, interpersonal constraints may occur when spouses differ in terms of their respective leisure preferences. As noted by Crawford and Godbey (1987), these differences may impact spouses' participation *and* preferences. Likewise, parenthood often reduces how much time new fathers pursue leisure activities independently and increases the extent to which spouses' leisure activities reflect the preferences of wives (Crawford & Huston, 1993). Interpersonal constraints are probably unimportant in limiting people's involvement in solitary activities, particularly ones pursued close to home. On the other hand, interpersonal constraints appear to be highly important within the context of group activities and may take the form of gatekeeping mechanisms, scheduling problems, and group disbandment (Scott, 1991). Interpersonal constraints may also take the form of fear of crime. Studies have documented that fear of sexual assault keeps many women from visiting parks and other public recreation areas alone (Whyte & Shaw, 1994). Likewise, research indicates some members of ethnic and racial minority groups do not visit public recreation facilities because they are afraid of being harassed or assaulted by Anglo visitors and law enforcement representatives (Harris, 1997; Rideout & Legg, 2000).

Finally, Crawford and Godbey (1987) conceived *structural constraints* as those factors that intervene between leisure preferences and participation. They noted structural constraints are how researchers typically conceive barriers and include a variety of factors outside the control of the individual, including "family life stage, family financial resources, season, climate, the scheduling of work activities, availability of opportunity (and knowledge of such availability), and reference group attitudes concerning the appropriateness of certain activities" (p. 124). While many leisure researchers have used these factors to measure constraints, they are truly structural constraints to the extent they actually inhibit individuals from being able to act on their preference.

In a follow-up article, Crawford, Jackson, and Godbey (1991) theorized the three categories of constraints are hierarchically related. They argued constraints are encountered first at the intrapersonal level. These constraints were believed to be the most powerful because they have a fundamental impact on people's motivation for participation. If preferences are formed, the individual may then encounter interpersonal constraints. Participation may be curtailed if the individual is unable to locate suitable partners. If both intrapersonal and interpersonal constraints are absent or successfully overcome, individuals may then bump into structural constraints. If sufficiently strong, structural constraints may result in individuals not participating in a desired activity or at a level of desired intensity.

The three categories of constraints may also interact with one another in ways that further limit people's ability to use park and recreation facilities (Jackson, Crawford & Godbey, 1993). A few examples highlight how this might work. Fear of being assaulted or harassed at a park (an interpersonal constraint) may inhibit the expression of leisure preferences and result in negative attitudes about outdoor recreation activities in general (an intrapersonal constraint). Similarly, transportation and accessibility problems (typically thought of as structural constraints) may prevent people from acquiring skills and knowledge (intrapersonal constraints) about what kinds of opportunities are available at recreation areas.

These ideas suggest practitioners must recognize constraints may stymie the development of preferences and intervene between preferences and participation. Developing strategies to mitigate constraints will require practitioners to more fully understand how constituents are constrained and incorporate multiple strategies in their attempts to alleviate leisure constraints. For example, providing people easy access to an outdoor recreation area or facility may not result in participation unless there is a simultaneous effort to promote positive attitudes about the outdoors, to facilitate skill development, and to ensure visitor safety.

Time Commitments Are the Most Frequently Cited Constraints to Leisure Involvement

Jackson and Scott (1999) noted a consistent core of leisure constraints that cut across a range of studies and samples, including "time commitments, costs, facilities and opportunities, skills and abilities, and transportation and access" (p. 304). In North America, time commitments stand out as the most frequently cited constraint to leisure across an array of studies. Time constraints are the principal reason why people say they have stopped participating in leisure activities (Jackson & Dunn, 1991), do not participate in fitness activities (Mannell & Zuzanek, 1991; Shaw, Bonen & McCabe, 1991), do not participate in desired activities (McCarville & Smale, 1993), do not participate more often in outdoor recreation activities (Mueller, Gurin & Wood, 1962), do not participate in locally sponsored recreation activities and services (Godbey et al., 1992; Howard & Crompton, 1984), and do not visit local parks (Arnold & Shinew, 1998; Scott & Jackson, 1996; Scott & Munson, 1994).

Time constraints stem from a speeding up of the pace of life (see Godbey, this volume). The pressures of work, economic downsizing, and changing gender roles certainly contribute to this (Hochschild, 1997; Schor, 1991). Two other factors that contribute to a speeding up of the pace of life include a seemingly endless number of goods and experiences people may choose from, and the fact that people are increasingly forced to assimilate an abundance of information. The norm in the United States is to "do it all" and many people tirelessly endeavor to become more "physically fit, better read, more traveled, better dressed, better parents, better tennis players, better homeowners, better lovers, and so on" (Scott, 1993, p. 53). Given the finite amount of free time on their hands, many people feel they simply lack the time to do everything they would like to do. From the point of view of service delivery, practitioners must understand that they are in competition over how people allocate their free time. Leisure service agencies that waste people's time are likely to be shunned by time-conscious constituents, to the point of "committing competitive suicide" (Berry, 1990, p. 31). Leisure service organizations can build into

their marketing and programming efforts specific strategies that mitigate time constraints. Three such tactics include providing expanded opportunities to make reservations for facilities and programs, providing opportunities for shorter, more self-directed leisure experiences, and providing complete information about time requirements in promotional literature (Scott, 1993).

Time commitments also emanate from responsibilities individuals take on as caregivers, a role that typically falls to women. Studies show not only are women far more likely than men to report they are busy because of family responsibilities (Henderson & Allen, 1991; Jackson & Henderson; 1995; Scott & Jackson, 1996; Searle & Jackson, 1985a), but also the caregiving role among women results in their reducing or ceasing involvement in leisure activities (Dunn & Strain, 2001; Kay & Jackson, 1991). Clearly, if park and recreation agencies are to better serve caregivers, a greater effort must be made to help them meet the circumstances of their lives. As noted by Scott and Jackson (1996), constraints related to child care may be assuaged by offering child care, or by providing facilities in which groups of mothers are able to organize their own cooperative child care arrangements. Likewise, Dunn and Strain (2001) indicated women who care for a sick parent might achieve some relief from adult day care programs or other formal services.

Constraints Vary Across Activities and Different Dimensions of Leisure

Although time constraints are pervasive, it is important to note other constraints figure prominently in why some people do not develop preferences for leisure objects (activities, services, or locales) or participate in activities or use leisure services or amenities. With this in mind, research indicates constraints range in importance depending on the kind of activity in which people participate. In a groundbreaking study of leisure constraints, Jackson (1983) found equipment cost was the most frequently mentioned reason by people for not participating in skiing and a variety of other outdoor recreation activities. Equipment costs, in contrast, were generally inconsequential in limiting people's involvement in exercise activities, team sports, and tennis. In the same study, overcrowding was among the most frequently cited reason people said they did not participate in racquetball, tennis, and downhill skiing. Overcrowding was not mentioned often among individuals who wished to participate in creative activities and some types of outdoor recreation activities, including backpacking, canoeing, and cross-country skiing. Jackson (1994) replicated these findings in a more recent study.

Researchers also focused on a variety of criterion variables to measure the influence of constraints against. Some of these variables include nonuse of public park and recreation services, discontinuing/ceasing participation, participation in specific types of activities, inability to increase participation, and insufficient enjoyment of current activities. An important lesson learned from these studies is the intensity of constraints varies across different dimensions of leisure (Hultsman, 1993; Jackson & Dunn, 1991; Jackson & Rucks, 1993; Nadirova & Jackson, 2000). Jackson and Dunn (1991) were the first researchers to systematically examine this issue of "heterogeneity" of leisure constraints in a single study. One interesting finding they reported pertained to impact of equipment costs on initiating and ceasing involvement. Whereas equipment cost was the most important reason why people said they did not *initiate new leisure activities*, people were far more likely to cite other factors as reasons for *stopping participation*. Hultsman (1993), in a study of barriers to leisure among adolescents (10 to 15 years old), found key constraints limiting youths' ability to initiate a new leisure activity included lack of transportation, costs, and parental disapproval. In contrast, program-related factors (e.g., unhappiness with leaders and rules) were the most important factors youths cited for ceasing participation. In a more recent study, Nadirova and Jackson (2000) reported lack of skill was more likely to contribute to people ceasing participation than preventing them from participating in a desired activity. Alternatively, time commitments were more likely to explain why people did not initiate a new activity than it was a cause for ceasing participation.

Collectively, these findings suggest leisure service practitioners

1. will need to be clear about which aspects of constrained leisure they wish to deal with.

2. may have to devise alternative intervention strategies for alleviating constraints to different leisure activities and various facets of leisure behavior.

For example, the results summarized in the previous paragraph suggest program-related factors are likely to play a significant role in why people stop using a leisure service. Thus, practitioners would do well to understand those factors that potentially undermine long-term enjoyment or satisfaction among participants. This is consistent with a model of ceasing involvement developed a decade ago by Searle (1991), who theorized people stop participating in programs "if the rewards do not change

and expand as the duration of participation increases" (p. 284).

Constraints Vary by Population Groups

Findings from surveys show population groups differ in the nature and intensity of constraints experienced. A low income, for example, is associated with a variety of constraints, including lack of access, lack of transportation, fear of crime, and price of equipment (Kay & Jackson, 1991; McCarville & Smale, 1993; Scott & Munson, 1994; Searle & Jackson, 1985a). In contrast, individuals with high income are more likely to cite time commitments as barriers to leisure (Scott & Munson, 1994). Moreover, while time commitments tend to be more problematic among younger and middle-age adults, poor health, lack of companions, and fear of crime are much more likely to keep older adults from participating in leisure activities and visiting local parks (McCarville & Smale, 1993; Scott & Jackson, 1996). Surveys also show the intensity of a constraint increases for individuals who possess two or more "disadvantaged" statuses. For example, people most likely not to use parks because they lack companions are older females with low incomes (Scott & Munson, 1994). Likewise, individuals who do not use parks because they are too busy with family responsibilities are women between the ages of 25 and 45 (Scott & Jackson, 1996).

In-depth and qualitative studies of single population groups have drawn attention to constraints typically ignored in surveys (Jackson & Scott, 1999). These constraints may be particularly problematic for specific segments of the population, as illustrated in the following examples.

- Many women are constrained by an ethic of care (Henderson & Allen, 1991) and a sense of lack of entitlement to leisure (Deem, 1986; Henderson & Bialeschki, 1991). These constraints, which tend to work in tandem, result in many married women putting other people's needs ahead of their own and not spending time practicing and developing their abilities and knowledge in leisure activities. Married women who choose to participate in activities at an advanced level may go to great lengths to ensure time spent in the activity does not interfere with family obligations (Stebbins, 1992).

- Many women are also acutely constrained by a fear of sexual assault, and feel vulnerable when they venture out into public (Franck & Paxson, 1989; Riger & Gordon, 1981; Whyte & Shaw, 1994). Women who participate in outdoor recreation activities will often cope by compromising on location and time of day, participating with companions, and taking a dog along on runs and walks (Bialeschki, 1999).

- Some women are also constrained by a negative body image (Frederick & Shaw, 1995; James, 2000). Girls who feel self-conscious about the way they look may limit their frequency of involvement in certain activities (e.g., swimming) or develop strategies to make themselves less visible, including covering up their bodies.

- Learned helplessness, a trait sometimes found among older adults (McPherson, 1994) and people with disabilities (Dattilo, 1994) greatly constrains leisure. Individuals with this condition believe the environment is not responsive to their actions and see little point in trying to develop strategies that would help them to take control of their lives. Thus, helplessness prevents individuals from developing skills and motivation to participate in a range of leisure activities.

- Studies have shown harassment and discrimination in public places are common incidents experienced by many African Americans (Feagin, 1991; West, 1989). Anticipation of harassment may actually lead many Blacks to avoid using parks and outdoor recreation areas away from home (Harris, 1997; Rideout & Legg, 2000).

- Studies indicate age-related norms are strongly held by older adults (McPherson, 1994; Ostrow & Dzewaltowski, 1986). These norms constrain older adults' involvement in sport and physical activity because participation is felt to be the privilege of younger people.

Results reported in this section strongly point to the need for practitioners to be sensitive to the salience of population-specific barriers and to individualize their planning and marketing strategies for relieving constraints to different population segments. Efforts to assuage constraints to middle-age adults, for example, are potentially very different from efforts to relieve constraints among older adults. Likewise, practitioners will probably need to develop different strategies for reducing constraints among low-income constituents than for upper or middle-income groups. Results reported here also suggest practitioners would benefit by incorporating multiple variables in their planning and marketing

strategies (Jackson & Henderson, 1995). For example, practitioners may develop strategies for reducing barriers among low-income females, middle-age females, low-income older adults, and so on.

People May Negotiate Constraints

It is important to note many people participate in leisure activities despite encountering constraints. In an influential article, Jackson et al. (1993) postulated "participation is dependent not on the absence of constraints (although this may be true for some people) but on *negotiation* [italics added] through them" (p. 4). Negotiation here refers to those strategies that people use, individually or collectively, to overcome the effects of one or more constraints. Jackson and his colleagues proposed a three-category typology of people based on their responses to constraints: Some individuals react by not participating (reactive response), others do not reduce or change their participation (successful proactive response), and others participate but in an altered manner (partly successful proactive response). The typology has been partly supported in a study of constraints negotiation among women with physical disabilities (Henderson, Bendini, Hecht & Shuler, 1995).

A recent study reported by Hubbard and Mannell (2001) indicated the presence of a constraint may actually "trigger negotiation efforts, which appear to...counteract the negative influence of constraints to some extent" (p. 158). Hubbard and Mannell provided evidence individuals who are highly motivated to participate are likely to work hard at negotiating constraints. These findings are consistent with Stebbins's (1999) work on serious leisure, which indicates that highly committed leisure participants persevere despite encountering hardships and disappointments.

Moreover, people's ability to negotiate constraints appears to be related to the types of constraints they encounter. Support for this generalization comes from a study reported by Shaw et al. (1991). In that study, individuals who said they encountered some kinds of constraints (time commitments, costs, quality of available facilities) were actually more likely to participate in physical activities than individuals who did not report them. In contrast, individuals who said they ran into other types of constraints (low energy and poor health) participated less often in physical activities than individuals who did not cite these barriers.

Together, findings reported in this section suggest despite encountering constraints people still participate in leisure activities. On the one hand, these findings could lead practitioners to become complacent and cynical about constraints research in general. Some researchers have publicly articulated this point of view (Samdahl & Jekubovich, 1997). On the other hand, I would hope the findings reported here would actually embolden practitioners. A major implication I draw from all this is that people actively seek to negotiate constraints and practitioners are in an outstanding position to assist them in their efforts.

Constraints to Use of Park and Recreation Services

There now exists a small but growing number of studies devoted specifically to why people do not use public park and recreation services. Either by design or chance, these studies have focused on slightly different aspects of nonparticipation. Some researchers, for example, have examined constraints to greater use of local park and recreation services generally (Godbey, 1985; Godbey et al., 1992; Howard & Crompton, 1984; Schroeder & Wiens, 1986), while others have limited their focus to why people do not use local or regional parks (Arnold & Shinew, 1998; Scott & Jackson, 1996; Scott & Munson, 1994). A few studies sought to determine why people do not use specific facilities, such as public golf courses in Chicago (Gobster, 1998), the Fort Worth Nature Center (Rideout & Legg, 2000), and the Toledo Museum of Art (Hood, 1983). Simultaneously, while most studies focused on nonparticipants, at least one study had participants, in this case park visitors, indicate whether or not different factors limited their use of community or neighborhood parks (Arnold & Shinew, 1998). Findings reported from different studies of nonuse of park and recreation services augment our understanding of constraints in general by providing insight into site-specific constraints to involvement and identifying strategies that may possibly help people to negotiate barriers they encounter.

Site-Specific Constraints

As already noted, time constraints are the most frequently cited reasons why people do not use parks and recreation services (Arnold & Shinew, 1998; Howard & Crompton, 1984; Godbey et al., 1992; Scott & Jackson, 1996). Here we turn our attention to other factors researchers discovered to be relatively important constraints to people's use of park and recreation programs and services. At least two of these—lack of interest and safety concerns—are ones not typically examined by constraints researchers in general.

Lack of Interest

Researchers historically have been uncertain about whether or not to include lack of interest as a leisure constraint. This ambivalence is reflected, for example, in the writings of Ed Jackson. At one point he noted lack of interest is not a "true" barrier to participation (Jackson & Dunn, 1988). Elsewhere he argued, "to exclude from an investigation those people who apparently are not interested in participating will likely underestimate the number of people who experience constraints on their leisure" (Jackson, 1990a, p. 58). Lack of interest can readily be conceived as an intrapersonal constraint because these deal with factors that shape or limit the development of leisure preferences (Crawford et al., 1991; Crawford & Godbey, 1987; Scott, 1991). Furthermore, some public and commercial entities do not have the luxury of ignoring constituents and consumers who eschew their services and products. Stated differently, their livelihood depends on their being seen as relevant.

Howard and Crompton's (1984) study of nonparticipation in Dade County, Florida; Austin, Texas; and Springfield, Oregon, demonstrated lack of interest figured rather prominently as to why people did not use park and recreation services in those communities. In Austin, for example, 27% of residents reported they prefer to stay at home, 21% said they never think about going, and 18% said they were not interested. Corroborating these findings, Schroeder and Wiens (1986) reported lack of interest was the most frequently mentioned reason by residents of Tulsa, Oklahoma, for not using public swimming pools (45%), community centers (53%), and parks and playgrounds (53%). Groups most likely to cite lack of interest, according to Schroeder and Wiens, were older adults and individuals with low levels of income and education. More recently, Gobster (1998) found lack of interest to be an important constraint to people's involvement in golf in Chicago, particularly among Hispanic and African American youth. According to Gobster, they felt golf "was not fun, was boring, uninteresting, lacked excitement, and was not 'up-to-date' compared with the sports most teens currently enjoyed" (p. 55).

Marilyn Hood's (1983, 1989, 1993) research on museum visitors provided valuable insight into lack of interest as a reason for nonparticipation. She pointed out lack of interest stems from the inability of museums to appreciate the benefits that large numbers of people seek during their leisure time. For example, museums tend to ignore the fact that many family groups are looking for places where they can do things together. Hood argued family groups are likely to stay away from museums if this need is not consistently satisfied. A related source of lack of interest stems from mental saturation. Hood opined that "we are still pummeling visitors by overloading them mentally and physically, and then complaining that too few guests read every label, look at every object, or followed the sequence we laid out for them" (Hood, 1993, p. 18). Although it is possible people are not aware museums can provide some of the benefits they desire, Hood's counsel remains valid: Museums must better understand what the public wants and plan accordingly. Park and recreation agencies, in general, would do well to heed this advice.

Lack of Information

Nonparticipation in public park and recreation services can be partly explained by the fact that people lack sufficient information about agency offerings. In a study of nonparticipation of park and recreation services in an eastern city, Godbey (1985) found residents reported varying degrees of awareness of local amenities. While only a handful (9%) of those polled did not know that the city had a zoo, close to 90% indicated they were not aware that the city had community centers. An additional 64% said they did not know that the city had an environmental center, and 40% reported that they did not know about public golf courses or the city's tennis programs. In a nationwide study, Godbey et al. (1992) found lack of information was the second most frequently mentioned barrier, behind lack of time, by Americans for not participating in locally sponsored recreation activities. In this case, one third of Americans said lack of information was why they did not participate in local recreation programs.

A handful of studies indicated specific groups within the population may be more constrained in their use of park and recreation services by lack of information. Young adults and people with lower levels of education were significantly more likely than their respective counterparts to cite lack of information as a reason for not using local parks (Scott & Jackson, 1996; Scott & Munson, 1994). Lack of awareness and knowledge appears to play a role in why ethnic and racial minorities do not use public golf courses in Chicago (Gobster, 1998), do not use outdoor recreation facilities away from home (Scott & Kim, 1998), and do not participate in recreation activities on public lands (Roper Starch, 1998). These results tentatively suggest lack of information is more or less important depending on the amenity in question and may constrain some subgroups more than others.

Safety Concerns

Studies have also documented that safety concerns figure prominently in why some people do not visit parks and outdoor recreation areas. By safety concerns, we refer to fear of crime, harassment, and discrimination, as well as fear of natural elements. Fear of crime was among the most frequently cited reasons why people do not use parks in greater Cleveland (Scott & Jackson, 1996; Scott & Munson, 1994). Nearly one third of nonvisitors said fear of crime was a very important reason for not using local and regional parks. Moreover, among individuals with low incomes, it was the most frequently cited constraint to park use—53% said fear of crime important was very important in limiting their use of parks. Fear of crime was also the most frequently cited reason for not visiting parks among older adults. Women, too, tended to be more constrained by fear of crime than men. Arnold and Shinew (1998), likewise, found fear of crime and gang activity were among the most important factors that limited park visitors' use of community or neighborhood parks in Chicago. Unlike the studies reported by Scott and his colleagues, however, no significant differences were found between males and females or among income groups.

Studies indicate safety concerns figure prominently in why some ethnic and racial minorities may not use public park and recreation areas outside their community. In a study of people's use of regional parks in the Detroit area, West (1989) reported Blacks were twice as likely as Whites to report experiencing racial tensions. Gobster (1998) reported some African Americans feel unwelcome at Chicago golf courses because they are regarded as being used principally by Whites. In their study of why minorities do not visit the Fort Worth Nature Center, Rideout and Legg (2000) found many adult African Americans expressed a fear of discrimination and police harassment in surrounding rural communities. Interestingly, they also found a common barrier among African American youth was fear of natural elements (e.g., fear of snakes). Collectively, these studies indicate park and recreation agencies must be committed to strengthening and sensitizing law enforcement efforts and ensuring park employees are responsive to safety needs among minority visitors.

Opportunities and Access

Leisure researchers have long used opportunity theory to explain nonparticipation in outdoor recreation activities and nonuse of outdoor recreation amenities. The essence of opportunity theory is simple: Involvement in a given activity depends on the availability of facilities and amenities (Hendee, 1969). Support for the perspective is widespread. Using data from the first Outdoor Recreation Survey, Hauser (1962) reported participation in fishing and hunting is higher among people who live in rural areas and outside metropolitan areas. In contrast, participation rates in walking for pleasure and attending outside concerts were higher among urban residents. Likewise, Beaman, Kim, and Smith (1979) found the supply of outdoor recreation amenities contributed significantly to Canadians' participation in skiing, hunting, and fishing above and beyond the effects of sociodemographic factors. A study by Kim and Fesenmaier (1990) demonstrated Texans' use of state parks close to home was positively related to their supply. Moreover, Texans who lived close to many state parks had more options and thereby tended to visit a single park less than those individuals who had had fewer parks close to home.

Hendee (1969) observed one implication of opportunity theory is groups who have historically been denied access to outdoor recreation facilities and amenities will use them if appropriate services are made available. The National Park Service, for example, justified the development of national recreation areas in or near urban areas precisely on these grounds. However, the reality is these and other park and recreation sites continue to be inaccessible to poor individuals. Studies show lack of transportation and fees and charges are major constraints to leisure participation (Kay & Jackson, 1991; Searle & Jackson, 1985a) and use of local and regional parks (Scott & Munson, 1994) among individuals with low levels of income. Scott and Munson, for example, found 28% of individuals with low income (less than $15,000) said lack of public transportation was a very important barrier to their use of parks, compared to less than 1% of individuals with high income (more than $50,000). Moreover, 35% of individuals with low income said parks were too far away, compared to 3% of people with high income. While only 15% of individuals with low income said costs were very important in limiting their use of parks, nobody in the highest income category cited this factor as very important. These results suggest availability of opportunities is indeed related to people's use of parks and outdoor recreation environments, but accessing opportunities is problematic for poor individuals because they are "transportation disadvantaged" and lack the discretionary income to pay for admission fees.

Helping People Negotiate Constraints

While researchers have done a reasonably good job of identifying salient constraints to people's use of park and recreation services, limited information exists about what specific strategies, within practitioners' control,

may potentially ease barriers to involvement. One study that addressed this issue was reported by Scott and others (Scott & Jackson, 1996; Scott & Munson, 1994). They asked nonusers and infrequent users of parks in Northeast Ohio whether or not certain changes in park operations or programming might result in their using public parks more often. More than 70% of those sampled said they might use parks more if they were made safer or more information was provided about existing parks and park programs. Over half said they might use parks more often if more activities were provided or parks were developed closer to home.

The study also revealed striking differences across different population groups. Individuals with low incomes, for example, were far more likely than those with higher incomes to report they might visit parks more often if they were made safer, costs were reduced, parks were developed closer to home, and public transportation to parks was provided. Likewise, women and African Americans reported that if parks were safer they might visit them more often. African Americans were also significantly more likely than Whites to report they might visit parks more often if more activities were provided. These results augment those reported previously: Population groups who report specific constraints to use of parks also report they might use parks more often if these constraints are removed.

Institutional Barriers and Recreation Need

The research we summarized thus far examined constraints from the point of view of the individual. What is missing from constraints research is an examination of how everyday practices within leisure service agencies and practitioners' beliefs about constituents may actually contribute to nonparticipation among segments of the population. These practices and beliefs are deeply embedded in the normal everyday functioning of leisure service agencies and perpetuate inequality in terms of access to park and recreation amenities. Our focus in this section is to show how institutional barriers systematically constrain leisure involvement among disenfranchised groups. The ideas presented here are based, in part, on those published elsewhere (Scott, 2000).

The framework for this discussion borrows from ideas about institutional discrimination and racism developed by Baron (1969), Williams (1985), and Feagin and Feagin (1986). First, the perspective maintains inequalities within major institutional spheres (e.g., economy and labor market, education, housing, and politics) are mutually reinforcing and systematically perpetuate inequality over time. These inequities no doubt impact people's access to leisure opportunities and abilities to acquire leisure skills (see **Figure 18.1**). Second, outwardly neutral organizational practices in the present systematically reflect or perpetuate the effects of preferential treatment in the past. The perspective, thus, encourages us to examine inequality and oppression in terms of longstanding structural arrangements in society. Institutional discrimination is insidious because inequality stems from everyday practices deep-rooted within organizations and perceived by organizational members and nonmembers as being legitimate.

One way leisure service organizations may perpetuate inequality is by adopting an entrepreneurial approach to service delivery. Such an approach gives primacy to revenue production through the use of fees and charges, privatization, and efficiency. In some communities and agencies where these practices are used, social equity appears to be becoming less important in decisions concerning resources and services (Foley & Pirk, 1990). Consequently, many people living in poorer communities find the quantity and quality of available park and recreation services have worsened. These practices have been fairly well-documented and criticized by others (e.g., Goodale, 1991; More, 2002).

A less obvious organizational practice is promoting customer loyalty. Should tax dollars continue to become scarcer, practitioners will probably become increasingly driven to promote customer loyalty. Loyal patrons are desired because they are believed to provide leisure service agencies with long-term sources of income and support for bond measures that potentially expand recreational services (Selin, Howard, Udd & Cable, 1988). To maximize customer loyalty, practitioners are increasingly adopting a service quality perspective. Emphasizing customer loyalty and service quality are laudable, if not necessary goals, but these practices may result in agencies deemphasizing concern over social equity and inclusion. The reason for this is these practices give primacy to the interests and needs of individuals and groups who historically used an agency's facilities and services. For example, the vast majority of interpretive exhibits at national and state parks celebrate European American experiences, conquests, exploration, and heritage (Taylor, 2000). Missing are those stories reflecting the experiences of African Americans, Chinese Americans, Mexican Americans, and so on.

Another factor that keeps many leisure service agencies from better serving marginalized groups is employees do not resemble the population at large. Allison (1999) has done an outstanding job of documenting how park and recreation agencies deal with workplace diversity. Her recent work showed diversity policies and practices tended to be more symbolic than substantive and agencies engage in selective and exclusionary hiring of women and people of color. These policies keep agencies from developing an organizational culture where ideas about diversity and inclusion are fundamental to the organization's mission. Consequently, many practitioners lack the skills to appreciate the needs of disenfranchised groups. Without a multicultural and diverse staff, leisure

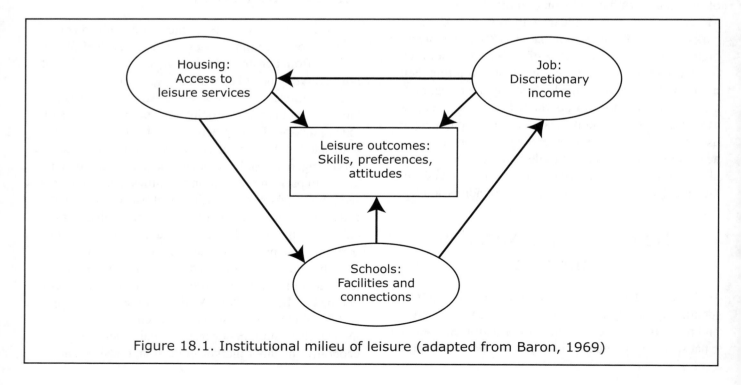

Figure 18.1. Institutional milieu of leisure (adapted from Baron, 1969)

service agencies ultimately fall prey to what Allison (2000b) described as "cultural imperialism." This is the tendency to accept dominant groups' perspectives and experiences as the norm and make invisible the viewpoints of subordinate groups.

Finally, practitioners' definitions of recreation need may create organizational barriers. These definitions may very well be the glue that keeps in place all the other agency practices described here. As noted by Godbey (1994), there are different ways to define recreation need (e.g., expressed need, comparative need, created need, normative need, and felt need) and each carries different value assumptions and beliefs about constituents. According to Godbey, within the context of public and park and recreation delivery, these values and beliefs are necessarily in conflict with one another:

> One believes either that each citizen should have an equal amount of public recreation resources or that some subgroup should be given priority. One believes either that government should seek to be culturally neutral, reacting to what the public says and does during leisure, or that government should promote certain activities and experiences and discourage others. You believe either that experts are in a position to prescribe desirable minimums of certain types of recreation resources, or you do not. (p. 307)

Determining recreation needs is very much a matter of interpretation and definition, and mediated by the interests and beliefs of practitioners, researchers, and other stakeholders (Scott, 1997). How practitioners define recreation needs will ultimately dictate how they interpret nonparticipation and the extent to which they believe leisure constraints are a proper concern of their leisure service organization. From what I have observed, there is a tendency for many agencies to provide services in terms of expressed need. This conception of recreation need, according to Godbey (1994), holds that people's need for leisure is based on what they are currently doing and assumes constituents are fully capable of self-determination, constituents have equal means and access to leisure resources, and there is relatively just distribution of recreation and park resources. Henderson (1997) made a similar point: "Onus is always on individuals.... In North American society, we are socialized to 'pull ourselves up by the bootstraps' and to be personally responsible for our fate" (p. 456). History has seemingly proved practitioners right—many will say their facilities, programs, and campgrounds are already at or near capacity. Organizations and practitioners who provide services using this paradigm need not incorporate a conception of a "constrained constituent" within their planning and

marketing efforts. Nonuse of a given service or amenity can justifiably be explained in terms of strongly held interests in alternative activities, locales, or services.

No doubt most practitioners would be unsettled with the charge they are prejudiced, are insensitive to the needs of disenfranchised populations under their jurisdiction, and engage in discriminatory behaviors. From what I have seen, most practitioners intend to treat all people fairly, but despite their best intentions, in some cases inequality is perpetuated. The practices and beliefs highlighted here are, in the words of Goodale (1999), "externally compelling forces that are systemic." They have a taken-for-granted quality and may well perpetuate inequity in terms of access to leisure services and resources. If leisure service agencies are to better serve marginalized groups and actively reduce leisure barriers from within and from without, they must broaden their conception of recreation need.

Some agencies do just that. In Texas, urban outreach programs, in conjunction with grants provided by the Texas Parks and Wildlife Department, are working to introduce minority youth to a range of outdoor recreation activities. Individuals involved in these programs acknowledge youth will not participate in backpacking, fishing, hunting, and a variety of other outdoor recreation activities unless they are taught to appreciate them first. These organizations have defined, explicitly or implicitly, recreation need in terms of created need. In effect, practitioners involved in these efforts regard youth as being constrained in terms of interests and skills. Commercial leisure service organizations also work within this paradigm as they "seek to create a need through advertising or by teaching people how to participate in or enjoy their services" (Godbey, 1994, p. 307).

Alternatively, some practitioners (and many researchers) embrace the notion of comparative need. The three key value assumptions of this perspective include the following:

1. recreation resources may not be justly distributed.

2. people have varying abilities to access leisure amenities.

3. individuals with low socioeconomic status have a greater need for public park and recreation services (Godbey, 1994).

Individuals working out of this paradigm are far more likely than others to believe park and recreation agencies have a special mandate to meet the recreation needs of marginalized groups in society. They are also far more likely to believe that many people lack the resources to effectively negotiate constraints by themselves

(Henderson, 1997). To more effectively meet the needs of marginalized groups, Allison (2000a) advocated leisure service agencies be antidiscriminatory (as opposed to being nondiscriminatory). To this end, she believes agencies should work toward developing an organizational culture where ideas about diversity and inclusion are fundamental to the organization's mission and strategic plans.

Conclusion

In this chapter I highlighted how constraints research may assist practitioners in their efforts to research population groups who do not make greater use of agency offerings. Findings and principles gleaned from constraints research can be incorporated into policy, planning, and marketing efforts of the leisure service organization (Searle & Jackson, 1985b). As I also noted, barriers or constraints may stem from organizational practices and beliefs about constituents. To more effectively meet the needs of marginalized groups, practitioners must broaden their conception of recreation need.

To conclude this chapter, I put forward two areas of future inquiry I believe are most pressing. First, it is imperative researchers work closely with practitioners to determine how effectively changes in operations alleviate leisure constraints. This is a formidable task. Single-subject methods and field experiments have been used effectively to look at the effects of program design in effecting change among people with disabilities. Similar efforts should be used in assessing the impact of change in park and recreation delivery on changes in use among constituents in general (Jackson & Scott, 1999).

A second area of research is to examine practitioners' attitudes about the utility of constraints research and definitions of recreation need. How practitioners incorporate constraints research into practice will depend on their ability to give prominence to one conception of recreation need over another. Research that reveals how practitioners define recreation need may well provide information that bridges the gap that currently exists between practitioners and researchers.

References

Allison, M. T. (1999). Organizational barriers to diversity in the workplace. *Journal of Leisure Research, 31*, 78–101.

Allison, M. T. (2000a). Diversity in organization perspective. In M. T. Allison and I. E. Schneider (Eds.), *Diversity and the recreation profession: Organizational perspectives* (pp. 4–16). State College, PA: Venture Publishing, Inc.

Allison, M. T. (2000b). Leisure and social justice. *Journal of Leisure Research, 32*, 2–6.

Arnold, M. and Shinew, K. (1998). The role of gender, race, and income on park use constraints. *Journal of Park and Recreation Administration, 16*, 39–56.

Baron, H. M. (1969). The web of urban racism. In L. K. Knowles and K. Prewitt (Eds.), *Institutional racism in America* (pp. 134–176). Englewood Cliffs, NJ: Prentice Hall.

Beaman, J., Kim, Y., and Smith, S. (1979). The effect of recreation supply on participation. *Leisure Sciences, 2*, 71–87.

Berry, L. L. (1990, February). Market to the perception. *American Demographics*, 31.

Bialeschki, M. D. (1999, October). *Negotiation of fear: Women's resistance to social control of outdoor recreation space.* Paper presented at the National Congress for Recreation and Parks, Nashville, TN.

Collins, M. F. and Kennett, C. (1998). Leisure, poverty, and social inclusion: The growing role of leisure cards in public leisure services in Britain. *Local Governance, 24*, 131–142.

Crawford, D. W. and Godbey, G. (1987). Reconceptualizing barriers to family leisure. *Leisure Sciences, 9*, 119–127.

Crawford, D. W. and Huston, T. L. (1993). The impact of the transition to parenthood on marital leisure. *Personality and Social Psychology Bulletin, 19*, 39–46.

Crawford, D. W., Jackson, E. L., and Godbey, G. (1991). A hierarchical model of leisure constraints. *Leisure Sciences, 13*, 309–320.

Dattilo, J. (1994). *Inclusive leisure services: Responding to the rights of people with disabilities.* State College, PA: Venture Publishing, Inc.

Deem, R. (1986). *All work and no play? The sociology of women and leisure.* Milton Keynes, England: Open University Press.

Dunn, N. J. and Strain, L. A. (2001). Caregivers at risk? Changes in leisure participation. *Journal of Leisure Research, 33*, 32–55.

Dwyer, J. (1994). *Customer diversity and the future demand for outdoor recreation* (Gen. Tech. Rep. RM-252). Fort Collins, CO: USDA Forest Service, Rocky Mountain Forest and Range Experiment Station.

Feagin, J. R. (1991). The continuing significance of race: Antiblack discrimination in public places. *American Sociological Review, 56*, 101–116.

Feagin, J. R. and Feagin, C. B. (1986). *Discrimination American style: Institutional racism and sexism* (2nd ed.). Malabar, FL: Robert E. Krieger Publishing Company.

Floyd, M. (1999). Race, ethnicity and use of the national park system. *Social Science Research Review, 1*, 1–23.

Foley, J. and Pirk, H. (1990, Summer). Taking back the parks. *California Parks and Recreation*, 31–33, 35, 37–38.

Franck, K. A. and Paxson, L. (1989). Women and urban public space: Research, design, and policy issues. In I. Altman and E. H. Zube (Eds.), *Human behavior and environment: Advances in theory and research: Vol. 10. Public places and spaces* (pp. 121–146). New York, NY: Plenum Press.

Frederick, C. J. and Shaw, S. M. (1995). Body image as a leisure constraint: Examining the experience of aerobic exercise classes for young women. *Leisure Sciences, 17*, 57–73.

Gobster, P. H. (1998). Explanations for minority "under-participation" in outdoor recreation: A look at golf. *Journal of Park and Recreation Administration, 16*, 46–64.

Godbey, G. (1985). Nonparticipation in public leisure services: A model. *Journal of Park and Recreation Administration, 3*, 1–13.

Godbey, G. (1989). Implications of recreation and leisure research for professionals. In E. L. Jackson and T. L. Burton (Eds.), *Understanding leisure and recreation: Mapping the past, charting the future* (pp. 613–628). State College, PA: Venture Publishing, Inc.

Godbey, G. (1994). *Leisure in your life: An exploration* (4th ed.). State College, PA: Venture Publishing, Inc.

Godbey, G., Graefe, A., and James, S. W. (1992). *The benefits of local recreation and park services: A nationwide study of the perceptions of the American public*. Washington, DC: National Recreation and Park Association.

Goodale, T. (1991). Prevailing winds and bending mandates. In T. L. Goodale and P. A. Witt (Eds.), *Recreation and leisure: Issues in an era of change* (pp. 231–242). State College, PA: Venture Publishing, Inc.

Goodale, T. (1999, October). *The cab driver's horse*. Paper presented at the National Congress for Recreation and Parks, Nashville, TN.

Goodale, T. L. and Witt, P. A. (1990). Recreation non-participation and barriers to leisure. In E. L. Jackson and T. L. Burton (Eds.), *Understanding leisure and recreation: Mapping the past, charting the future* (pp. 421–449). State College, PA: Venture Publishing, Inc.

Harris, E. L. (1997, December). Solo faces. *Outside*, 106–110, 177, 178.

Hauser, P. M. (1962). Demographic and ecological changes as factors in outdoor recreation. *Trends in American living and outdoor recreation: Report to the Outdoor Recreation Resources Review Commission, 22* (pp. 27–59). Washington, DC: U.S. Government Printing Office.

Hendee, J. C. (1969). Rural–urban differences reflected in outdoor recreation participation. *Journal of Leisure Research, 1*, 333–341.

Henderson, K. A. (1997). A critique of constraints theory: A response. *Journal of Leisure Research, 29*, 453–457.

Henderson, K. A. and Allen, K. R. (1991). The ethic of care: Leisure possibilities and constraints for women. *Society and Leisure, 14*, 97–113.

Henderson, K. A., Bendini, L. H., Hecht, L., and Schuler, R. (1995). Women with physical disabilities and the negotiation of leisure constraints. *Leisure Studies, 14*, 17–31.

Henderson, K. A. and Bialeschki, M. D. (1991). A sense of entitlement to leisure as constraint and empowerment for women. *Leisure Sciences, 12*, 51–65.

Henderson, K. A., Stalnaker, D., and Taylor, G. (1988). The relationship between barriers to recreation and gender-role personality traits for women. *Journal of Leisure Research, 20*, 69–80.

Hood, M. (1983, April). Staying away: Why people choose not to visit museums. *Museum News*, 50–57.

Hood, M. G. (1989). Leisure criteria of family participation and nonparticipation in museums. *Marriage & Family Review, 13*(3/4), 151–170.

Hood, M. G. (1993). After 70 years of audience research, what have we learned? In D. Thompson and A. Benefield, S. Bitgood, H. Shettel, and R. Williams (Eds.), *Visitor studies: Theory, research and practice* (Vol. 5). Jacksonville, AL: The Visitor Studies Association.

Hochschild, A. R. (1997). *The time bind: When work becomes home and home becomes work*. New York, NY: Metropolitan Books.

Howard, D. R. and Crompton, J. L. (1984). Who are the consumers of public park and recreation services? An analysis of the users and nonusers of three municipal leisure service organizations. *Journal of Park and Recreation Administration, 2*, 33–48.

Hubbard, J. and Mannell, R. C. (2001). Testing competing models of the leisure constraint negotiation process in a corporate employee recreation setting. *Leisure Sciences, 23*, 145–163.

Hultsman, W. Z. (1993). Is constrained leisure an internally homogeneous concept? An extension. *Journal of Leisure Research, 25*, 319–334.

Jackson, E. L. (1983). Activity-specific barriers to recreation participation. *Leisure Sciences, 6*, 47–60.

Jackson, E. L. (1988). Leisure constraints: A survey of past research. *Leisure Sciences, 10*, 203–215.

Jackson, E. L. (1990a). Variations in the desire to begin a leisure activity: Evidence of antecedent constraints? *Journal of Leisure Research, 22*, 55–70.

Jackson, E. L. (1990b). Trends in leisure preferences: Alternative constraints-related explanations. *Journal of Applied Recreation Research, 15*(3), 129–145.

Jackson, E. L. (1994). Activity-specific constraints on leisure. *Journal of Park and Recreation Administration, 12*, 33–49.

Jackson, E. L., Crawford, D. W., and Godbey, G. (1993). Negotiation of leisure constraints. *Leisure Sciences, 15*, 1–11.

Jackson, E. L. and Dunn, E. (1988). Integrating ceasing participation with other aspects of leisure behavior. *Journal of Leisure Research, 20*, 31–45.

Jackson, E. L. and Dunn, E. (1991). Is constrained leisure an internally homogeneous concept? *Leisure Sciences, 13*, 167–184.

Jackson, E. L. and Henderson, K. A. (1995). Gender-based analysis of leisure constraints. *Leisure Sciences, 17*, 31–51.

Jackson, E. L. and Rucks, V. C. (1993). Reasons for ceasing participation and barriers to participation: Further examiniation of constrained leisure as an internally homogeneous concept. *Leisure Sciences, 15*, 217–230.

Jackson, E. L. and Scott, D. (1999). Constraints on leisure and recreation. In E. L. Jackson and T. L. Burton (Eds.), *Leisure studies: Prospects for the twenty-first century* (pp. 299–321). State College, PA: Venture Publishing, Inc.

James, K. (2000). "You can feel them looking at you": The experiences of adolescent girls at swimming pools. *Journal of Leisure Research, 32*, 262–280.

Kay, T. and Jackson, G. (1991). Leisure despite constraints: The impact of leisure constraints in leisure participation. *Journal of Leisure Research, 23*, 301–313.

Kim, S.-I. and Fesenmaier, D. R. (1990). Evaluating spatial structure effects in recreation travel. *Leisure Sciences, 12*, 367–381.

Lee, J., Scott, D., and Floyd, M. (2001). Structural inequalities in outdoor recreation participation: A multiple hierarchy stratification perspective. *Journal of Leisure Research, 33*, 427–449.

Levey, K. (2001, September 9). Flowering Bush: Center's director sets high attendance goals. *The Bryan/College Station Eagle*, E1–E2.

Mannell, R. and Zuzanek, J. (1991). The nature and variability of leisure constraints in daily life: The case of the physically active leisure in older adults. *Leisure Sciences, 13*, 337–351.

McCarville, R. E. and Smale, B. J. A. (1993). Perceived constraints to leisure participation within five activity domains. *Journal of Park and Recreation Administration, 11*(2), 40–59.

McGuire, F. A. and O'Leary, J. T. (1992). The implications of leisure constraint research for the delivery of leisure services. *Journal of Park and Recreation Administration, 10*(2), 31–40.

McPherson, B. D. (1994). Sociocultural perspectives on aging and physical activity. *Journal of Aging and Physical Activity, 2*, 329–353.

More, T. (2002). "The parks are being loved to death" and other frauds and deceits in recreation management. *Journal of Leisure Research, 34*, 52–78.

Mueller, E., Gurin, G., and Wood, M. (1962). Participation in outdoor recreation: Factors affecting demand among American adults. *Outdoor Recreation Resources Review Commission, Study Report No. 20.* Washington, DC: U.S. Government Printing Office.

Nadirova, A. and Jackson, E. L. (2000). Alternative criterion variables against which to assess the impacts of constraints to leisure. *Journal of Leisure Research, 32*, 396–405.

Ostrow, A. C. and Dzewaltowski, D. A. (1986). Older adults' perceptions of physical activity participation based on age-role and sex-role appropriateness. *Research Quarterly for Exercise and Sport, 57*, 167–169.

Raymore, L. A., Godbey, G. C., and Crawford, D. W. (1994). Self-esteem, gender, and socioeconomic status: Their relation to perceptions of constraint on leisure among adolescents. *Journal of Leisure Research, 26*, 99–118.

Rideout, S. and Legg, M. H. (2000). Factors limiting minority participating in interpretive programming: A case study. *Journal of Interpretation Research, 5*, 53–56.

Riger, S. and Gordon, M. T. (1981). The fear of rape. *Journal of Social Issues, 37*, 71–93.

Roper Starch. (1998, June). Outdoor recreation in America 1998. Retrieved November 7, 2001, from http://www.funoutdoors.com/roper98.html

Samdahl, D. and Jekubovich, N. (1997). A critique of leisure constraints. Comparative analysis and understandings. *Journal of Leisure Research, 29*, 430–452.

Schroeder, T. D. and Wiens, M. (1986). The nonuse of public park and recreation facilities in Tulsa. *Journal of Park and Recreation Administration, 4*(3), 75–87.

Schor, J. (1991). *The overworked American: The unexpected decline of leisure*. New York, NY: Basic Books.

Scott, D. (1991). The problematic nature of participation in contract bridge: A qualitative study of group-related constraints. *Leisure Sciences, 13*, 321–336.

Scott, D. (1993). Time scarcity and its implications for leisure behavior and leisure delivery. *Journal of Park and Recreation Administration, 11*, 51–60.

Scott, D. (1997). The formative nature of conducting research for a metropolitan park district. *Applied Behavioral Science Review, 5*, 25–39.

Scott, D. (2000). Tic, toc, the game is locked and nobody else can play! *Journal of Leisure Research, 32*, 133–137.

Scott, D. and Jackson, E. L. (1996). Factors that limit and strategies that might encourage people's use of public parks. *Journal of Park and Recreation Administration, 14*, 1–17.

Scott, D. and Munson, W. (1994). Perceived constraints to park usage among individuals with low incomes. *Journal of Park and Recreation Administration, 12*, 52–69.

Searle, M. K. (1991). Propositions for testing social exchange theory in the context of ceasing leisure participation. *Leisure Sciences, 13*, 279–294.

Searle, M. S. and Jackson, E. L. (1985a). Socioeconomic variations in perceived barriers to recreation participation among would-be participants. *Leisure Sciences, 7*, 227–249.

Searle, M. S. and Jackson, E. L. (1985b). Recreation nonparticipation and barriers to participation: Considerations for the management of recreation delivery systems. *Journal of Park and Recreation Administration, 3*, 23–36.

Selin, S. W., Howard, D. R., Udd, E., and Cable, T. T. (1988). An analysis of consumer loyalty to municipal recreation programs. *Leisure Sciences, 10*, 217–223.

Shaw, S. M., Bonen, A., and McCabe, J. F. (1991). Do more constraints mean less leisure: Examining the relationship between constraints and participation. *Journal of Leisure Research, 23*, 286–300.

Stebbins, R. A. (1992). Hobbies as marginal leisure: The case of barbershop singers. *Society and Leisure, 15*, 3, 75–386.

Stebbins, R. A. (1999). Serious leisure. In. E. L. Jackson and T. L. Burton (Eds.), *Leisure studies: Prospects for the twenty-first century* (pp. 69–79). State College, PA: Venture Publishing, Inc.

Taylor, D. E. (2000). Meeting the challenge of wild land recreation management: Demographic shifts and social inequality. *Journal of Leisure Research, 32*, 171–179.

West, P. C. (1989). Urban region parks and black minorities: Subculture, marginality, and interracial relations in park use in the Detroit metropolitan area. *Leisure Sciences, 11*, 11–28.

Whyte, L. B. and Shaw, S. M. (1994). Women's leisure: An exploratory study of fear of violence as a leisure constraint. *Journal of Applied Recreation Research, 19*, 5–21.

Wilkinson, T. (2000, January/February). The cultural challenge. *National Parks*, 20–23.

Williams, J. (1985). Redefining institutional racism. *Ethnic and Racial Studies, 9*(3), 323–348.

Chapter 19

A Paradigm Shift in Therapeutic Recreation: From Cure to Care

Stuart J. Schleien, Charlsena F. Stone (University of North Carolina at Greensboro), and Cecilia Y. Rider (Blythedale Children's Hospital)

Diversity is a cornerstone of our society and culture and thus should be celebrated. Including people with disabilities in the fabric of society strengthens the community and its individual members. (Position Statement on Inclusion, National Recreation and Park Association, 2000)

This quote is indicative of what we believe should be the direction of therapeutic recreation (TR) service delivery in the future. Trends suggest no longer should we focus primarily on providing outcome-based TR services in clinical settings. TR providers must possess the willingness and competencies necessary to include consumers with disabilities in the fabric of society. Only then can individuals with disabilities be empowered to participate fully in community recreation and physical activity.

This chapter provides a guide that will serve as a springboard for action that could be taken at the individual and organizational levels to alter the way we think about recreation services. We explore TR from both clinical and community perspectives, and provide an analysis of trends that will impact TR service delivery. Researchers and practitioners in many service professions, including special education, nursing, occupational therapy, rehabilitation medicine, sports medicine, gerontology, public health, mental health, and adaptive sports documented the prevalence of constraints to leisure. As providers of leisure, it is important that TR professionals not only understand what the constraints are, but also have some knowledge of how they might be overcome. Consequently, we next examine TR and constraint-free environments, providing a basis for inclusive community recreation services. Specific constraints to community inclusion for individuals with disabilities are discussed and strategies are offered which could be used to negotiate, to eliminate, or to reduce substantially those constraints. We conclude the chapter with a futuristic perspective of TR to stimulate individual thought and discussion among members of the therapeutic recreation field.

The Changing Nature of Therapeutic Recreation Service Delivery

Therapeutic recreation has been shown to have beneficial consequences for the physical, psychological, and social well-being of people with disabilities (Coyle & Santiago, 1995; Loy & Dattilo, 2000; Mobily, Mobily, Lessard & Berkenpas, 2000). TR practice delivers services through the use of recreation and leisure activities designed to restore, to remediate, or to rehabilitate the functional capabilities necessary for improving independence and reducing or eliminating the effects of illness and disability (Shank, Coyle, Boyd & Kinney, 1996). It has also been defined as the purposive use of recreation/recreative experiences by qualified professionals to promote independent functioning and to enhance the optimal health and well-being of persons with illnesses and/or disabling conditions (Bullock & Mahon, 2000). As is clear from these definitions, TR is concerned with recreation and treatment. Both are important to understanding service goals, and neither should be deemphasized (Stone, Bullock & Brooke, 2004).

Therapeutic recreation can occur in a variety of settings, but is *not* defined by the setting in which it occurs. It is defined by its service, and occurs within agencies/organizations that have clear mandates to provide treatment and therapeutic services. This may include clinical inpatient units or a variety of community options, such as halfway houses, adult day care programs, and independent living facilities. Therapeutic recreation is not any and all recreation services for people with disabilities. Simply having a disability does not qualify one to receive TR services. The individual who has a disability may receive TR services or may receive recreation services (typically referred to as "special recreation," or therapeutic recreation if it occurs in a segregated community-based setting). The distinction between recreation and therapeutic recreation is made on the basis of individual need and a mandate for treatment rather than on disability and setting. Stone, Bullock, and Brooke (manuscript in preparation) suggested to refer to recreation services as "therapeutic" simply because they involve individuals with disabilities or because they occur in clinical settings is not only inaccurate, but also patronizing and stigmatizing to the people who have been so labeled.

While TR services have typically had a more defined role in medical settings, considerable changes have occurred in health and human services that have implications for the provision of TR services. One change in health and human services that impacted and will most likely continue to impact service delivery is increased medical costs. Community-based treatment alternatives are being developed in response to increased medical costs, shorter hospital stays, deinstitutionalization, and other related factors. Coile (2001) presented several trends that will shape health care delivery over the next decade. For example, the average length of stay in hospitals slipped to 5.9 days and outpatient visits to hospitals increased 4.5% during 2000. Additionally, hospitals in the United States have continued to decrease their number of beds from a peak of one million in 1983 to 830,000 in 1999.

Smith (1995) indicated the changing face of health care has forced the restructuring and reorganization of physical rehabilitation units nationwide "as facilities struggle to increase efficiency without jeopardizing the quality of their health care services" (p. 67). In physical rehabilitation, the trend is toward outpatient services and efforts to reintegrate patients into their home communities where they can live as independently as possible. Obviously, a paradigm shift in health care has occurred; that is, a move away from traditional inpatient clinical settings and toward outpatient, community-based options. These alternatives are not only fiscally sound, but also structurally responsive, situating health care and rehabilitation in the community rather than in higher-cost clinical facilities. This paradigm shift suggests we are moving away from the sole-provider model of medical care and treatment to self-care, prevention, and health

promotion teams. According to Shugars, O'Neil, and Bader (1991):

> The health care system, which has been focused largely on the treatment of acute disorders or the acute manifestations of chronic disorders, will move gradually to a system that delays the onset of inevitable chronic disorders through prevention and education. Accompanying this change will be a general shift from *cure* to *care* as the health care needs of the population change. (p. 7)

This shift in emphasis has significant implications for recreation professionals. In our communities, opportunities will be created for TR programs conducive to prevention of illness and disability and health promotion. Collaboration between professionals working in clinical and community settings will become more necessary than ever before. This collaboration between TR specialists in clinical and community settings will help to ensure a continuity of recreation and leisure services for individuals with disabilities, thus reducing the risk of rehospitalization, reinstitutionalization, or reincarceration.

It is clear the therapeutic recreation field must respond to these dramatic and inevitable changes in our health care system. To become more responsive to those we serve, efforts will be made to reintegrate clients into their home communities so they can live as independently or interdependently as possible. The time appears ripe to develop more community-based TR programs in conjunction with existing clinically based treatment and rehabilitation programs. Since most patients leave hospitals now when they are medically stable, therapeutic recreation specialists are beginning to focus on discharge planning during the inpatient therapeutic recreation intervention and are preparing those they serve to transition back to the community.

An increasing number of consumers of TR services are choosing to participate in typical community recreation, physical activity, and social settings. Therapeutic recreation specialists have a legal obligation to accommodate them as they attempt to make the transition back into the mainstream. We must become better prepared to include our patients, clients, and participants in constraint-free environments and to help them succeed within their home communities.

Therapeutic Recreation and Constraint-Free Environments

The three inalienable rights of all citizens of America—life, liberty, and the pursuit of happiness—imply that *all* American citizens have these three rights. Every one of our citizens should have access to all of the services available in one's community, including medical, religious, educational, social, and recreational opportunities.

We have learned a great deal about the impacts of therapeutic recreation service delivery on the people we have served. We are no longer satisfied with merely assisting the allied health team in ameliorating illnesses or with physically integrating individuals with disabilities into various "therapeutic" programs and settings. Our primary goal has become the facilitation of a better quality of life for all of our citizens, particularly those we serve who have been disenfranchised and underrepresented. We attempt to accomplish this by helping people to become socially included within their communities through active, vital, and healthy lifestyles. This lofty service goal was supported by then-President George Bush in 1990 when he eloquently stated, "With today's signing of the landmark Americans With Disabilities Act, every man, woman, and child with a disability can now pass through once-closed doors into a bright new era of equality, independence, and freedom."

Participation in recreation, physical activity, and social settings is an important aspect of life in our society. Active, healthy, and socially connected individuals participate in a wide range of activities within a broad array of environments throughout their lifetimes. This vital lifestyle includes participation in athletic programs in schools and recreational sports on college campuses, as well as in individual, team, and family recreation at home and in the community. Active and ongoing involvement in recreation, sports, and social activities is a positive investment of one's time. Society has begun to recognize the immense value of quality recreation and physical activity programs and facilities. For example, intramural–recreational sport programs are the most regularly attended activities, with the exception of academic classes, by students on today's college campuses. Activities that meet the needs of individuals in community and social settings promote physical health and conditioning and provide them with natural opportunities for developing social relationships and new, and potentially lifelong, skills. It has become essential to find a desirable balance between recreation/socialization and work.

The rationale for designing TR service delivery that seeks to promote healthy and active lifestyles in the community is well-established from both theoretical (e.g., social value) and practical (e.g., deinstitutionalization) perspectives. Services that promote active recreation and social participation in the community offer the individual with a disability opportunities to develop a positive self-concept through successful experiences and satisfying relationships with peers. Channels for choice and self-expression, opportunities to interact with the environment, and establishing a more personally fulfilling way of life are other potential benefits.

Therapeutic recreation preference is shifting from providing specialized and separate services to helping include people with disabilities in more typical community programs. In addition to the substantial changes in health care described earlier, this philosophical change is the result of a series of other international trends propelled by the deinstitutionalization movement of the past three decades and the concepts of normalization and what Wolfensberger (1972, 1983, 1995) labeled "social role valorization."

Normalization is a Scandinavian concept that has served as a guiding principle for all services to people with disabilities since the 1970s. The intent of using normalization as a guiding principle is not to make people with disabilities "normal," but to set a standard by which all services could be measured. Accordingly, these services and the manner in which they are delivered should be as close to the cultural norm as possible. This suggests TR services and activities designed for people with disabilities should not be different or highly contrived, nor should they be separated from those designed for individuals without disabilities, just because the individual has been labeled.

Deinstitutionalization is a social policy change, partially a reflection of adherence to the least restrictive environment; that is, the environment in which the needs of the individual could be met while simultaneously affording the individual the greatest opportunity to interact with peers without disabilities. Deinstitutionalization refers to changing the residential service system so that people with disabilities are less likely to live in institutional settings and more likely to live in community (or more normalized) settings. Consequently, people with disabilities are more likely to be living in the community, and thus, are more likely to be asking for greater access in the community.

As applied to leisure and recreation, a normalization or wellness goal offers people with disabilities opportunities for physical access to settings with nondisabled peers as a means to acquire social, recreational, physical activity, and community skills. Access to socially inclusive programs promotes healthy leisure lifestyles. In short, the concept of normalization implies that recreation providers consider the influence of social inclusion as they design and implement programs.

Wolfensberger (1983) coined the term "social role valorization" to broaden the meaning of normalization: "The most explicit and highest goal of normalization must be the creation, support, and defense of valued social roles for people who are at risk of social devaluation" (p. 234). Social role value, in other words, implies bringing roles and conditions valued by most people to the lives of typically devalued people. Two paths could be followed to reach this goal: (a) further develop the competencies of a culturally devalued individual, and (b) enhance the individual's social image or value in the perceptions of other members of society.

Significant evidence supports the benefits of recreation that target improved quality of life outcomes and valued social roles. For example, increased leisure skills and participation in recreation activity typically result in increases in skill level in a variety of other curriculum areas. As a function of enhanced instruction and participation in recreation and physical activity, collateral skill development has been documented for individuals with disabilities in other areas such as language, problem-solving, cognition, personal–social behavior, gross and fine motor skills, and academics (e.g., reading comprehension and mathematics).

It has been found that increases in recreational competencies relate to decreases in negative and inappropriate excess behaviors. By teaching highly preferred skills and activities referenced against nondisabled peers in the community, individuals are less likely to engage in self-stimulating or excess behavior. Constructive recreation learned through TR services has been shown to be negatively correlated with such excess behavior.

Constructive use of leisure time is related to the success of people with disabilities living in community environments. There is longstanding literature in the disability field that relates success in community living to adaptive behavior and, particularly, to the absence of a need for constant supervision. If a TR program could prepare individuals with disabilities to deal constructively and enjoyably with breaks in routine and free time, and thus reduce the need for supervision and decisions made by others, successful community living could be greatly enhanced.

Finally, having a repertoire of enjoyable and preferred recreation and social activities is essential for quality of life and the development of positive relationships with family and friends. Clearly, any personal relationship—friendships, best friends, family, and intimate relationships with partners and spouses—is nurtured by opportunities to share enjoyable leisure with one another and to explore mutual interests and activities. If an individual has few leisure skills and interests, or is prevented from participating in the kinds of activities enjoyed by his or her peers, one is also effectively being barred from the many opportunities to develop friendships and

other meaningful personal relationships. Surely, few dimensions of an individual's life could be as essential to healthy and quality lifestyles as having good relationships with family and friends.

Therapeutic recreation services that enhance participation in socially inclusive community activities could produce positive, life-changing outcomes for people of varying abilities. And it is not only people with disabilities who benefit from these programs; the community overall benefits from this diversity. As a result of these positive experiences, practitioners in parks and recreation are expanding options that are inclusive for their constituents. Not only do accommodation and inclusion make good sense to consumers and program planners, but also family members of individuals with and without disabilities advocate for these services. For instance, the community benefits as recreation and park professionals grow more accepting and welcoming of individuals with disabilities and accommodating of all people. On attitude assessments, practitioners indicated inclusive services taught them not to be afraid of people who are differently abled, and individuals with disabilities are disabled only to the extent that we perceive them to be. Programming specialists are learning that with careful attention to design and accommodation, inclusion works to everyone's benefit over the long term.

State-of-the-Art Inclusive Community Recreation Services

Since the mid-1970s, the need to provide community services for individuals with disabilities has received increased attention from lawmakers. For example, PL 94-142, the Education for All Handicapped Children Act of 1975, and its recent reauthorization (Marchand, 1997), PL 105-17, the Individuals with Disabilities Education Act (IDEA), address therapeutic recreation as a related service for people with disabilities. Published federal regulations for rehabilitative services, such as Section 504 of the Rehabilitation Act, indicate the importance of recreation programs in the community for individuals with disabilities. Several states' developmental disabilities plans designate recreation/leisure as a priority area for children and adults with developmental disabilities. The Americans with Disabilities Act (ADA) of 1990 comprehensively eliminates discrimination against people with disabilities in the areas of employment, transportation, public accommodations, public services, and telecommunications. Additionally, the ADA states all areas of public accommodation, including recreational areas, must be made accessible, and nondiscriminatory practices must be implemented. ADA guidelines also have implications for other community environments where people play and socialize. For example, playground equipment designers and landscape architects will have to take these guidelines into account in their design of new playgrounds and in modifying old ones. A certain proportion of play components will be required to be accessible, along with accessible surfacing, ramp access, and transfer system access to elevated structures for people with physical disabilities (Burkhour, 2001; Hunter, 2001).

Therapeutic recreation is devoted to using treatment, education, and recreation services to help people of varying abilities to develop and to use their leisure in ways that enhance their health, functional abilities, independence, and quality of life (NTRS, 2001). The National Recreation and Park Association, through its Position Statement on Inclusion (NRPA, 2000) strongly advocated for the encouragement and enhancement of inclusive leisure experiences for people of varying abilities to participate and interact together in activities with dignity. NRPA espoused four concepts:

1. right to leisure for all individuals.

2. quality of life enhancements through leisure experience.

3. support, assistance, and accommodations.

4. barrier removal in all park, recreation, and leisure services.

Unfortunately, programming that includes people who have traditionally challenged our service delivery systems has had relatively low priority in community recreation and sports. Segregated programming was and continues to be the primary service delivery model for people with disabilities. At first, special after-school recreation programs and summer camps were designed for children with developmental disabilities. In 1968, the Special Olympics program began. During the past 30-plus years, there has been a proliferation of segregated recreation and sports services as a number of organizations (e.g., Association for Retarded Citizens of the United States, International Sports Federation for Persons with Intellectual Disability) attempted to meet the needs of their constituents.

Why has there been this proliferation of segregated recreation programs? Several constraining factors that continue to contribute to inaccessible community opportunities for those on the fringes of society and to the continuous growth of homogeneous (i.e., for people with disabilities only) programs include the following:

- In spite of dramatic shifts in health care, the medical model and deficit-oriented approaches to TR services continue to be prevalent ways that services are provided to people who are disabled.

- Voluntary service organizations that provide segregated programs are hesitant to relinquish their participants to agencies that previously had ignored them lest the agency program be inadequate or inferior.

- Many family members and other advocates of individuals who are disabled oppose inclusive programs for reasons including fear of the unknown and limited success with generic agencies previously.

- People with disabilities and their advocates do not voice their desires for greater access loudly enough and to the right people.

- People with disabilities often fail to participate successfully in typical community programs for a variety of reasons, including inability to make good choices, perceived skill deficits, low self-esteem, and minimal programmatic support from the agency.

- Recreation service providers often doubt their own professional abilities to design and implement inclusive programs within the wellness model.

Several studies have attempted to describe and to explain the current state of community recreation and physical activity options for individuals of varying abilities. The findings have been discouraging. In spite of a growing list of laws mandating the inclusion of people with disabilities in all community programs in the least restrictive environment, many constraints remain.

In studies on the social and leisure inclusion of adults with developmental disabilities living in foster homes and small group homes, Hayden and colleagues (Hayden, Lakin, Hill, Bruininks & Copher, 1992; Hayden, Soulen, Schleien & Tabourne, 1996) concluded the movement away from large, institutional settings to small, community-based home environments often involves little more than a change of scenery. Participation in typical community activities by people with disabilities remains low. Most recreation participation takes place in a passive manner. Watching television, listening to the radio, and taking car rides remain prevalent. This lack of participation translates into a lack of opportunity for the development of new skills and positive social relationships. Few residents reported having ongoing social contact with nondisabled peers other than staff and family members. Few residents had more than one friend, and most reported being satisfied without any friends. Most said that their best friend was another resident or a staff member. A majority stated, also, that their best friend was their only friend. These studies indicated that the underparticipation in community activities is, in part, attributable to care providers' low expectations of their dependents' leisure and social potential. It was evident many care providers and service providers offered little opportunity for increased socialization and community participation. It must be understood that the deinstitutionalization movement alone cannot ensure one's active community participation, good health, or improved quality of life.

In an earlier study, Schleien and Werder (1985) surveyed 405 parks and recreation, community/continuing education, and adapted physical education programs in Minnesota to determine the status of recreation services available to individuals with disabilities. Although this study is over 15 years old, we believe it remains relevant today across a broad range of community settings. Results revealed activity selection was based most often on instructor choice. Participant preferences and needs were seldom taken into account. Activities were segregated in nature and provided little variety from the stereotypical norms (e.g., bowling, swimming, arts and crafts). An unwillingness to take ownership and responsibility for providing activities for people with disabilities was glaringly evident. Seventy-eight percent of the parks and recreation agencies stated community/continuing educators should be held responsible for providing services to their constituents with disabilities, while 93% of the community/continuing education respondents said the responsibility belongs to parks and recreation. Less than 20% of the supervisors of adapted physical education reported having collaborated with community agencies, and 33% stated they were not concerned with the recreation or social skill needs of their students because others were already doing so.

More recently, a study was undertaken by the American Park and Recreation Society/National Therapeutic Recreation Society Joint Commission on Inclusion to identify accommodations and barriers encountered in providing inclusive leisure services throughout the United States (Devine & Kotowski, 1999). Although the inclusion of individuals with disabilities into existing recreation programs is becoming more prevalent in our public park and recreation agencies, problems remain. Among the most frequently cited barriers that inhibited inclusive programming were lack of financial resources,

constraints on staff (e.g., accessible community transportation, adaptive equipment, resistance to inclusion by community members), lack of staff training, negative staff attitudes, and too much demand for inclusion. Although a national trend toward more inclusive options was noted, these barriers point to a need to continue to design ways to prepare people and environments so a supply of inclusive opportunities could keep pace with demand for them.

The fact that few inclusive recreation services are available throughout our communities is not confined to any one community, state, or country. Furthermore, few of the existing leisure service delivery systems address the total lifestyle and leisure needs of people with disabilities and their families. Many people with disabilities may now live in the community, but they are not part of the community. Thus, although the delivery of TR services in the least restrictive environment is legally mandated and although many administrators and staff members have at least given lip service to access and accommodation, the necessary personnel, methods, and budgets to implement the mandates and draw people with disabilities into the mainstream of the community have not been developed adequately. A variety of constraints many people encounter on a daily basis as they attempt to become a part of the community mainstream must be identified, studied, and overcome. Only in this way will we be able to design a set of "best professional practices" that will enable even our most challenging citizens to have access and success in their communities.

Prevalence of Constraints

Unfortunately, many individuals with disabilities remain unable to take advantage of the vast recreation and social opportunities in their communities. The challenge to therapeutic recreation specialists is to identify constraints to participation and inclusion and to develop strategies to negotiate or remove them. TR specialists must also provide ample opportunities for participants to develop skills, awareness, and the understanding needed to freely choose leisure experiences. Problems encountered could be a result of any number of circumstances related to organizational or programmatic structures, individual skill deficits, social/cultural issues, and environmental concerns.

Sources of barriers to successful community participation have been categorized in a variety of ways (Crawford & Godbey, 1987; Crawford, Jackson & Godbey, 1991; Henderson, Stalnaker & Taylor, 1987; Malik, 2000; Schleien, Ray & Green, 1997; Smith, Austin & Kennedy, 2001), including intrapersonal, interpersonal, and structural; intrinsic, extrinsic, and political; and antecedent and intervening. While most of the therapeutic recreation literature embraced the intrinsic/extrinsic or internal/external categorization, problems often arise concerning where to place certain constraints. For example, some authors place lack of time and money in the external category while others categorize them as internal. Also, this method of classification fails to account for the relationship between leisure preferences and any environmental factors that inhibit participation. An example would be someone who wishes to play basketball, but who believes facilities are unavailable due to a lack of knowledge on where to look. Would the barrier be with the individual (lack of knowledge) or with the environment (lack of facilities)? Classification in either category fails to show the relationship that exists between the internal and external factors that explain why the individual does not play basketball.

Of the different categorization models, the framework for categorizing barriers first introduced by Crawford and Godbey (1987) best captures this relationship between an individual's leisure preferences and the activities in which he or she actually participates. Therefore, we have chosen to use the categories of intrapersonal (psychological), interpersonal (social), and structural (environmental). *Intrapersonal barriers* stem from the person's psychological state and include feelings of inadequacy or incompetence, fear of failure, and individual behavioral issues that might affect the individual's leisure preferences. *Interpersonal barriers* generally stem from an individual's social interactions and include the attitudes of family/significant others and participants without disabilities, lack of family support, and social/cultural issues that intervene between an individual's leisure preferences and participation. *Structural barriers* are those that interfere between an individual's leisure preferences, capabilities, and actual participation, and include architectural, geographic, or physical obstacles in the environment and economic or financial restrictions (Jackson, Crawford & Godbey, 1993).

Intrapersonal Barriers

Intrapersonal barriers stem from the person's particular psychological state and pertain to concerns such as limitations in social, leisure, physical, or functional skills and abilities and knowledge of recreational opportunities (Crawford, Jackson & Godbey, 1991; McAvoy & Lais, 1999; Schleien, Ray & Green 1997).

Skill Limitations

People need various skills and abilities to participate actively in recreation, physical, and social activities. Many people with disabilities do not possess the appropriate skills to enjoy a number of leisure pursuits. These limitations may be attributed to a lack of or limited leisure competencies and skills, lack of opportunities for leisure, and lack of functional skill development as a result of a particular disability. The inability to participate physically in various recreation activities secondary to loss or lack of physical endurance, balance, strength, and flexibility has also been found to be a constraint to community participation (Dattilo, Caldwell, Lee & Kleiber, 1998). The physical skill requirements of many recreation and sports activities discourage many people from participating.

Additionally, individuals with disabilities have traditionally been excluded from opportunities to interact socially with their peers. Because of this, many lack the social skills necessary to engage in positive and appropriate behaviors within community settings. Often times, recreation activities require partners, making it necessary for participants to display appropriate social skills. We believe TR in the community recreation setting is an ideal place for an individual with a disability to gain social skills, and perhaps to develop genuine friendships.

Sometimes the very nature of a person's disability may limit further skill development. However, more often than not, individuals are not provided opportunities to develop the skills necessary to enhance their participation. Consequently, they have low self-esteem, resulting in a belief they are incapable of participation. This often means noninvolvement and minimal community participation.

Modifications could be made to accommodate the current skill levels of participants with disabilities. For example, functional skill limitations are a result of the unique disability characteristics of the individual. TR specialists should be encouraged to conduct functional, strength-based assessments and to discuss the individual's current skills and abilities with him or her, family members, teachers, and advocates. They could discuss past leisure participation patterns and identify any limitations and barriers related to functional skills. At that point, task and activity analyses could be conducted and appropriate modifications made to enable the individual to successfully participate at his or her optimal skill level. If deemed appropriate, programs could then be developed that encourage socialization among participants with and without disabilities. Appropriate social skills could be modeled by staff as well as peers as socially inclusive programs provide opportunities to observe and imitate peers' appropriate behaviors in natural social contexts.

Lack of Knowledge

An additional barrier to an appropriate leisure lifestyle is the lack of knowledge about leisure and recreation. Consumers are placed at a major disadvantage when they lack information concerning available community recreation programs and support systems needed to access those programs. An adequate knowledge of programs, facilities, transportation options, legislative rights, and other resources is needed to make informed choices.

Some people, such as those with learning disabilities or mental retardation, possess cognitive limitations that interfere with learning about recreation or social opportunities. Knowledge deficits usually result from inadequate information and lack of opportunity. Several possible solutions to these problems are addressed next.

Leisure education programs, sponsored by recreation agencies or initiated in collaboration with TR specialists who work in clinical facilities from which many individuals with disabilities are being discharged or transitioned, could be instituted. A primary goal of such programs is to develop an awareness of accessible programs in the community, their importance, and how to access them. TR specialists may also wish to consider implementing leisure education programs that incorporate systematic procedures for transitioning people into inclusive community programs.

Another suggestion is to develop written or web-based materials that describe accessible recreation and social programs available within the community, such as a resource booklet or resource file. Recreational and social opportunities could be described that include specific details about accessibility, program dates/times, activity fees, and skill requirements. These materials must be developed in a user-friendly manner, and should be made available on the Internet for broader access. Agency staff and volunteer advocates could be trained as liaisons between community recreation and other agencies to ensure program and resource information is continuously updated and disseminated.

Interpersonal Barriers

Interpersonal barriers stem from an individual's social interactions. This type of barrier includes attitudes of family/significant others and participants without disabilities, the extent of dependence on others for assistance to participate, and poor communication that may

all interfere with an individual's leisure preferences and participation.

Negative Attitudes

One of the most difficult barriers to overcome is the existence of negative attitudes of people without disabilities, professional service providers, and care providers. Attitudinal barriers experienced by consumers in recreational settings could manifest themselves in the form of stigmas, stereotypes, unequal treatment, lack of social acceptance, and lower expectations of abilities (Bedini & Henderson, 1994; Devine & Broach, 1998; Hayden et al., 1996).

Despite legislative mandates and the good intentions of advocates of people with disabilities, recreational programs and services are developed and conducted in ways that keep people with disabilities socially isolated. Schleien, Germ, and McAvoy (1996) surveyed 484 community leisure service agencies to identify barriers encountered and inclusive practices employed. Twenty-nine percent of the agencies cited the program in and of itself as being resistive to inclusion (e.g., too dangerous, highly competitive, unadaptable equipment, highly technical material). Thirteen percent of the respondents cited poor public attitudes as a barrier, and reported unaccepting beliefs in the community at large to be more of a barrier to inclusion than the attitudes of participants with disabilities (12%) or program staff (6%). Negative attitudes of the participants with disabilities included the strong desire to be with like (disabled) peers, perceived skill deficiencies, fear of a novel situation/failure, and negative reaction of others in the program.

Positive attitudes toward people with disabilities could be nurtured through opportunities for personal contact and education, organized small group work, the use of team and cooperative experiences, and improving the social skills of people with and without disabilities. Additionally, community agencies and schools could host educational workshops or other educational forums to help people with and without disabilities learn how to facilitate socially inclusive programs. TR providers could also solicit the perspectives of consumers regarding misconceptions about disabilities and develop recreation and physical activities free of assumptions about their capabilities.

Dependence on Others

Closely related to skill deficits discussed in the intrapersonal barriers section is the physical and/or psychological dependency people with disabilities develop on others (Henderson, Bedini, Hecht & Schuler, 1995;

Smith, Austin & Kennedy, 2001). People with disabilities often depend on others to meet their recreational, physical, and social needs. This dependency may lead to losing, or never gaining in the first place, the ability to function independently. This dependency may be physical in nature, such as when the presence of an aide may be necessary to transport the participant to an activity. Psychological dependency, on the other hand, could be imposed by family members and care providers who foster an atmosphere of dependency. When this occurs, the individual typically makes few choices and does not develop an appropriate repertoire of independent living skills. For example, Henderson et al. (1995) conducted in-depth qualitative interviews with 30 women with physical disabilities concerning the influences of disability on leisure. Their results suggested solitary and more passive activities were performed at home, while going into the public to participate in more active recreation generally required some type of assistance or companionship. The authors stated the women with physical disabilities who had not developed support systems, such as family, friends, disability support groups, or community groups, were more constrained by dependency on others.

Similarly, Dattilo, Caldwell, Lee, and Kleiber (1998) interviewed 14 individuals with spinal cord injuries after being discharged from a rehabilitation center. These researchers identified lack of support and companionship as the primary constraints to leisure participation within their communities. Social supports appear to be an important factor in the community inclusion of people with disabilities. When a disability leads a person to feel physically or psychologically dependent on others, the result often is noninvolvement. It is not a simple task to request assistance from others, particularly in the physical domain, as people become embarrassed, feel inferior, or do not have the skills to request assistance in the first place. Following are a few guidelines for decreasing physical and psychological dependency barriers.

People with disabilities should be provided opportunities to make decisions and to advocate effectively for themselves. It may be necessary for the TR specialist to conduct self-advocacy training sessions that may include family members, as well. The family may be one of the more important sources of support to the individual. It is crucial that family members and other advocates allow individuals with disabilities to participate in community recreation activities with only minimal support and assistance. They should be encouraged to assist only when necessary. An additional suggestion is to determine when personal assistance is absolutely necessary, and then modify programs to encourage and to support appropriate levels of independence.

Poor Communication

For individuals whose speech and language abilities are affected by developmental or congenital disorders (e.g., cerebral palsy, hearing impairments), acquired neurologic disorders (e.g., stroke, head injury), or progressive degenerative disorders (e.g., Parkinson's disease), communication may be compromised or limited. Problems associated with communication present barriers that may inhibit leisure participation and satisfaction. Communication difficulties may occur during the interactions with nondisabled peers because some people with disabilities do not function as an active and equal member in the communication exchange. Dattilo and Light (1993) stated engaging in reciprocal communication "enhances a person's ability to communicate preferences, make meaningful choices, and subsequently, experience leisure" (p. 167). Recreation professionals could compound communication problems if they lack the necessary skills, such as sign language and telecommunication systems (e.g., TDD) to communicate effectively. Schleien, Ray, and Green (1997) suggested lacking such skills and systems within an agency is predominantly an external barrier issue, even though having such impairments is an individual barrier encountered by the potential consumer. Following are possible strategies that TR providers could use to overcome communication constraints.

A major component to successful communication is being comfortable with the person with whom one is interacting. For many people, there is some awkwardness in attempting to communicate with people with disabilities. They are unsure of how to act and what to say. Learning more about people's disabilities, including their strengths and interests, will increase the comfort level in interactions with them. When interacting with people with disabilities, it is important to extend them the same respect shown to others. One of the major accomplishments in communicating with and about people with disabilities is "people-first" language. People-first language emphasizes the person and not the disability. By placing the person first, the disability is no longer the primary, defining characteristic of the individual, but one of several aspects of the entire person (McCormick, 1999). Accommodations could be provided in community recreation programs to reduce communication concerns, including the use of adaptive equipment (e.g., assistive listening devices), personal assistants (e.g., readers), and alternative means of communication (e.g., large print materials, sign language interpreters). Another strategy is to invite a communication disorders specialist to conduct in-service training on communication disorders and alternative communication systems (e.g., electronic devices, word boards) to TR specialists and community recreation personnel. Additionally, TR specialists and other leisure service personnel should consider enrolling in sign language courses.

Structural Barriers

Although an individual's disability may inhibit access to a full range of community activities, structural barriers place additional restrictions on the individual. Organizations and other environmental factors may further reduce the likelihood people with disabilities will successfully engage in community experiences. Architectural or physical obstacles, economic or financial restrictions, and lack of transportation could all potentially interfere with successful participation.

Architectural or Physical Obstacles

People with disabilities cannot participate in community activities when they are unable to maneuver through doorways or throughout facilities. Lack of adequate and accessible facilities is frequently reported as the primary obstacle to participation. Devine and Broach (1998) identified physical barriers in an agency, such as lockers mounted too high and the unavailability of raised lettering or Braille signage, that prevent many people from participating successfully. Dattilo et al. (1998) reported numerous instances of accessible recreation facilities and activities, but indicated there were also occasions where participation was constrained due to lack of physical access or difficult terrain. Getting to the setting where an activity is taking place is crucial, particularly for individuals with limited mobility.

Eliminating architectural constraints is not as difficult or expensive as many believe. In the event facilities and areas cannot be made completely accessible, agencies could make reasonable accommodations or program modifications that may not necessarily require physical changes to the environment. For example, a program could be moved to the ground floor or to a more accessible facility rather than requiring expensive architectural changes. Community mapping could be used to develop a comprehensive inventory of potential resources in the community, including people and facility resources. This implies identifying resources available in organizations throughout the community before the fact and developing plans that integrate each organization into the community as a whole. If necessary, arrangements could then be made with other organizations, such as community centers, schools, YMCAs, or churches/synagogues to use

their facilities and/or other resources for support. A TR specialist could also implement a "buddy system" where a person with a disability is paired with a nondisabled companion to assist one another to overcome physical barriers in the environment. For example, a person with one arm paired with another individual could work together to perform gardening tasks, such as planting seeds and transplanting small plants.

Architectural accessibility surveys of indoor and outdoor environments, using the Americans with Disabilities Act Accessibility Guidelines (ADAAG), should be conducted under the direction of recreation service agency staff. Accessibility specialists, including TR specialists, could serve as agency consultants to conduct these surveys, to make recommendations, and to prepare reports of their findings to park and recreation personnel and board members. It is beneficial to include individuals with disabilities, as self-advocates, on park and recreation boards and commissions, as they could make significant contributions in planning to remove constraints.

Financial Restrictions

People with disabilities typically have less discretionary funds available to spend on recreation and physical activities. This could be attributed to the fact that employment rates of people with disabilities are lower than those of their nondisabled peers. One purpose of the ADA was to increase the employment rates of people with disabilities by making it illegal to discriminate against people who happen to have a disability. However, October 1994 through January 1995 survey data confirmed that employment rates, while gradually increasing, continue to be a problem for people with disabilities. For example, 82% of people without a disability had a job or business, compared with 77% of those with a nonsevere disability, and 26% of those with a severe disability (McNeil, 2000). Also, low wages, limited assistance from social service agencies such as Medicare, and greater expenses associated with the need to purchase specialized equipment, such as vans with wheelchair lifts and/or custom-made clothing, come into play.

Financial constraints may also affect staffing patterns, facilities, equipment, and supplies. Municipal park and recreation departments often work with limited budgets, restricting their ability to develop new programs and services, to make their buildings more architecturally accessible, to hire qualified staff, and to acquire necessary specialized equipment and materials. Possible solutions to these barriers are discussed next.

We must challenge assumptions that financial resources are limited. Sliding-scale user fees for participants with personal financial constraints based on one's ability to afford to pay for the activity could be used. People with disabilities could donate their services in other areas of an agency to offset the cost of activity participation. For example, an individual with a disability could volunteer her time in a recreation agency by staffing the front desk in exchange for activity fees in a desired cooking class. Perhaps recreation staff and volunteers could sponsor funding drives and use the money raised to establish scholarships for individuals with financial need. Collaborative efforts between leisure service and civic or corporate agencies could also be useful in developing innovative strategies for supplementing funding needed by people who are unable to pay for services.

Financial constraints of agencies and program priorities also interfere with the ability to hire staff with the appropriate skills to implement inclusive programs. TR consultants could be hired to train various park and recreation agency staff in areas such as conducting needs assessments and modifying programs, as necessary. Well-trained volunteers with and without disabilities are also valuable assets to agencies that lack funds to hire additional staff. Providing in-service training to existing agency staff, as an investment, could reduce the need for specialized staff to design and implement inclusive programs.

There are times when specialized equipment is required to ensure program accessibility. Agencies could pursue funding from outside sources, such as private foundations and corporate agencies, to purchase expensive equipment. This may be accomplished through grant applications written by skilled agency staff in collaboration with advocacy organizations, universities, and so on. Homemade equipment and materials could be developed that are more cost-effective than commercially marketed adapted equipment.

Lack of Transportation

One of the most prevalent constraints individuals with disabilities face relates to transportation. Securing accessible transportation often proves to be extremely difficult for people with mobility problems. And, when accessible transportation is available, its quality and reliability are sometimes called into question. Public transportation systems, such as city buses and private taxis, may not be physically accessible, or may be too expensive. If adapted vehicles are used, they are typically available on a limited, reservation-only basis. Consumers often report available transportation is distanced too far from home, transportation services to their neighborhoods are generally unreliable, and vehicles are inaccessible. Individuals with disabilities are often faced with the choice of either staying home or asking family members or friends to transport them to recreational activities.

Accessible transportation is essential if individuals with disabilities are to lead more independent lifestyles and become more involved in community experiences. Following are possible solutions to consider.

According to the ADA, communities are obligated to provide transportation to people with disabilities as they do for people without disabilities. Door-to-door transportation for people with disabilities who cannot travel to a recreation or park facility could be provided. TR specialists could provide individualized services and support, such as home visits when appropriate, to teach functional skills in preparation for future community recreation participation. The costs associated with providing door-to-door transportation or home visits may be prohibitive, and therefore more immediate and practical considerations may become necessary. For example, recreation agency personnel could consider offering rate reductions for users of accessible transportation with limited incomes, or establishing car or van pools using volunteers, parents, and advocates. Individuals with disabilities or their advocates could contact public or private transportation agencies to determine the availability, costs, and scheduling information of accessible vehicles. Examples of these transportation agencies include city or county transit systems, private taxicab companies, or churches/synagogues. It is imperative that TR specialists, family members, advocates, and educators teach participants how to independently access and utilize available transportation systems within their communities.

What Next? Future Perspectives

It was our intent to shed some light on those issues that best exemplify the types of constraints people with disabilities address each day to become active, healthy, and socially connected members within their communities. If people are to become valued socially, TR services must facilitate opportunities for people who have traditionally been excluded to participate actively. To return to the recently adopted position of the National Recreation and Park Association (2000), opportunities, programs, and environments will have to foster the physical, social, and psychological inclusion of people with diverse experiences and skill levels. In this manner, therapeutic services, community supports, and attitudinal changes that reflect functional abilities, independence and interdependence, self-respect, dignity of the human being, and self-determination will be facilitated.

Current national health initiatives that support the overall health and well-being of our citizens have recently been promoted by the Centers for Disease Control's "Healthy People 2010" (U.S. Department of Health and Human Services, 2000). To promote a healthy citizenship, this report supports helping all people—including people with disabilities—to become more active to prevent depression, and to spend more time in social and community activities. Special attention was given to the reduction of environmental constraints that inhibit participation across all of life's domains (Sable, Craig & Lee, 2000).

If consumers, advocates, and professionals are to support the new mandates of the National Recreation and Park Association, the Centers for Disease Control, and the Americans with Disabilities Act, we will have to be creative in the ways we design, market, and implement our services. Recreation and physical activity programs will need to be designed so their participants become valued socially. Leisure service organizations and the other institutions that deliver "therapeutic" recreation services will have to eliminate the constraints that lead to dependence and a lack of social value and social inclusion (Devine, 1997). Structural, as well as intrapersonal and interpersonal, solutions must become the focus of our agencies and services. Smith, Austin, and Kennedy (2001) and Schleien, Ray, and Green (1997) suggested our efforts at eliminating barriers go well beyond the obvious intrinsic (internal) barriers we have addressed in years past through therapeutic recreation services.

Hahn (1987) and Devine and Dattilo (2000) argued we have traditionally attempted to improve the physical, cognitive, and emotional skills of people with disabilities to address their well-being. We are discovering that traditional medical model cures, remediation, and amelioration of illness do not often lead to social acceptance and health-promoting lifestyles. We must become aware of the many forms that constraints take, including the roadblocks we confront in our services, environments, and society. Rather than continue to require people of varying abilities to conform to society's ways and stereotypes by improving peoples' functional abilities only, it may be time to radically alter our "therapeutic" approaches to help society conform to individual differences. Possibly, the more effective approaches to supporting social acceptance, healthy lifestyles, and community inclusion will include the reduction of stereotyping and stigmatizing people who have been underrepresented and disenfranchised.

Although mandates for independence/interdependence, self-determination, social inclusion, and accessibility seem clear, a wide range of constraints that impede progress toward achieving these goals continues to exist. Society's negative role perceptions of people with disabilities, as well as its low tolerance for individual differences, increase the likelihood obstacles such as community and organizational stigmas and other pervasive negative attitudes will continue to support the medical versus wellness model, decrease leisure service delivery, and diminish rates of participation by people with disabilities. A more positive view suggesting the individual with a disability is a person first may help to change societal perceptions. A change toward more open and inclusive service systems could be a reflection of these perception and attitude changes. Passing the ADA, including its comprehensive discussions of rules regulating play, recreation, and physical activity environments, is reflective of these attitudinal changes and provides helpful guidelines for ensuring that citizens of all abilities are reasonably serviced, accommodated, and ultimately, included in programs.

We have attempted to identify and categorize persistent constraints to successful leisure lifestyles of people with disabilities. It is our firm belief many constraints could be avoided or eliminated if recreation professionals incorporated the perspectives and strategies that have been presented to change and improve existing therapeutic recreation and leisure service delivery systems. Taken as a whole, this chapter presented a direction for service delivery that welcomes people with disabilities who want to participate in our communities and enhances their feelings of self-worth and sense of belonging to the communities and neighborhoods in which they live, learn, work, and play. In an interview by Mobily (2000), Iso-Ahola noted therapeutic recreation will make a huge difference in our society if it can make people believe in themselves (e.g., self-efficacy) on the one hand and make them motivated about life and various activities on the other: "Believing in your skills and capacities (however limited), and finding enthusiasm for life's activities, set the stage for subsequent improvement in psychological and physical well-being" (p. 302).

Ongoing cooperation among key players, including therapeutic recreation specialists in both clinical and community settings, recreation programmers, advocates, consumers with disabilities, and their family members should ensure the recreation and social needs of people with disabilities are met in the community. Socialization and the development of relationships with nondisabled peers will be stressed, and the spirit and intent of the ADA will be realized. Both TR and other recreation professionals are reminded to take a proactive, rather than a reactive, approach to systems and personnel change and to avoid making the erroneous assumption that constraints to inclusion and accessibility are created solely by the individual characteristics of people with disabilities.

If therapeutic recreation professionals begin to engineer environments to remove constraints to social inclusion—in addition to improving the functional abilities and health of the people they serve—they will have progressed in developing and manifesting positive, accepting attitudes toward citizens with disabilities. To serve as a role model, the people of Sweden have adopted a social sense of collective responsibility, whereby all members of the community are valued for who they are. A central premise in the Nordic countries is that all people have a right to a decent standard of living. Efforts are made to discover the value and talents of each individual so every person could make his or her unique contribution for the good of all. As a result, all members of Swedish society are viewed as valuable, and it is understood and accepted that all people with disabilities will receive whatever support is necessary to become active and contributing citizens of society (Pedlar, 1990).

The inclusion of people with disabilities in programs and communities is an essential element in recognizing the inherent dignity of every member of our society. Successful social inclusion requires that major stakeholders of our service delivery systems espouse philosophies and value systems that reflect the right of every individual to participate to one's fullest potential. Of central importance in this philosophy is the recognition that all individuals have valuable contributions to make. Agencies must articulate and practice a policy of making existing programs inclusive. The creation and provision of service delivery based solely on the correction of disability is exclusionary and results in the further alienation of people with disabilities from the remainder of society.

In conclusion, the following four principles should guide the development of exemplary recreation service delivery:

1. Programs designed for all people must be age-appropriate and based on personal interest, not diagnosis and stereotypes, or the preferences of agency staff only.

2. To the maximum extent possible, programs must occur within home communities, and not in restrictive, contrived, or irrelevant environments.

3. Continual communication and coordination among participants, family members, advocates, therapists, recreation practitioners, and program administrators must occur to ensure program longevity in the community.

4. Participants with and without disabilities, family members, and programmers must share the responsibility to ensure that every community member's needs and interests are met, including the recreation, health, social, physical, and lifestyle needs of entire families.

As potential contributors to overall health and wellness, family members, peers, and recreation practitioners continue to advance inclusive community services for people of all abilities; they help to enhance the development of community life itself. No longer shunted off to constricted, contrived, and segregated environments, people of varying abilities who live in, learn in, and use the community also teach their peers without disabilities new lessons in diversity, personal growth, empowerment, and self-fulfillment. Until we are able to empathize with others who are disenfranchised and on the fringes of community life, we will be unable to mature into the fine professionals and citizens we aspire to be. We must work to broaden the community's definition of diversity by bringing those who have been excluded into the discussion. By building a creative vision of wellness, inclusion, and self-efficacy, rather than continuing to adopt and nurture solely deficit-oriented and clinical perspectives, a common vision of truly welcoming and inclusive communities could appear and take hold. We must build organizations committed to community and disperse our services throughout communities.

A mandate for welcoming and accommodating communities makes us all responsible as advocates, educators, role models, catalysts, and spokespersons. The Brazilian story of the hummingbird's work during a destructive forest fire exemplifies this point. The hummingbird was observed flying back and forth carrying water in its minuscule beak, and dispersing droplets over the overwhelming fire, while other, much larger and stronger animals were running briskly in the opposite direction. An observant "king of the forest," the mighty lion, asked the tiny bird if she understood it was impossible to extinguish the ferocious forest fire with such tiny droplets of water, and in fact, would probably get killed in the process. Without missing a wing flap or beat, the exhausted hummingbird simply replied, "I'm just doing my part!" It is time that we all begin to do our small parts in making our communities more welcoming, inclusive, and stronger. It is our responsibility and it is our area of expertise.

References

Bedini, L. A. and Henderson, K. A. (1994). Women with disabilities and the challenges to leisure service providers. *Journal of Park and Recreation Administration, 12*(1), 17–34.

Bullock, C. C. and Mahon, M. (2000). *Recreation services for people with disabilities: A person-centered approach*. Champaign, IL: Sagamore Publishing.

Burkhour, C. (2001). ADA accessibility design guidelines play areas update. *NTRS Report, 26*(1), 23.

Bush, G. (1990). Remarks of President George Bush at the signing of the Americans With Disabilities Act. Retrieved from http://www.eeoc.gov/ada/bushspeech.html

Coile, R. C. (2001). A millennium mindset: The long boom. *Journal of Health Care Management, 46*(2), 86–90.

Coyle, C. and Santiago, M. (1995). Exercise and depression in adults with physical disabilities. *Archives of Physical Medicine and Rehabilitation, 76*, 647–652.

Crawford, D. W. and Godbey, G. (1987). Reconceptualizing barriers to family leisure. *Leisure Sciences, 9*, 119–127.

Crawford, D. W., Jackson, E. L., and Godbey, G. (1991). A hierarchical model of leisure constraints. *Leisure Sciences, 13*, 309–320.

Dattilo, J., Caldwell, L., Lee, Y., and Kleiber, D. A. (1998). Returning to the community with a spinal cord injury: Implications for therapeutic recreation specialists. *Therapeutic Recreation Journal, 32*(4), 13–27.

Dattilo, J. and Light, J. (1993). Setting the stage for leisure: Encouraging reciprocal communication for people using augmentative and alternative communication systems through facilitator instruction. *Therapeutic Recreation Journal, 27*(3), 156–171.

Devine, M. A. (1997). Inclusive leisure services and research: A consideration of the use of social construction theory. *Journal of Leisurability, 24*(2), 3–11.

Devine, M. A., Broach, E. (1998). Inclusion in the aquatic environment. *Parks and Recreation, 33*(2), 60–67.

Devine, M. A. and Dattilo, J. (2000). Social acceptance and leisure lifestyles of people with disabilities. *Therapeutic Recreation Journal, 34*, 306–322.

Devine, M. A. and Kotowski, L. (1999). Inclusive leisure services: Results of a national survey of park and recreation departments. *Journal of Park and Recreation Administration, 17*(1), 56–72.

Hahn, H. (1987). Civil rights for disabled Americans: The foundation of a political agenda. In A. Gartner and T. Joe (Eds.), *Images of the disabled, disabling images* (pp. 181–202). New York, NY: Praeger.

Hayden, M., Lakin, K. C., Hill, B., Bruininks, R., and Copher, J. (1992). Social and leisure integration of people with mental retardation in foster homes and small group homes. *Education and Training in Mental Retardation, 27*, 187–199.

Hayden, M., Soulen, T., Schleien, S., and Tabourne, C. (1996). A matched, comparative study of adults with mental retardation who moved into the community and those who remained at the institution. *Therapeutic Recreation Journal, 30*(1), 41–63.

Henderson, K. A., Bedini, L. A., Hecht, L., and Schuler, R. (1995). Women with physical disabilities and the negotiation of leisure constraints. *Leisure Studies, 14*, 17–31.

Henderson, K. A., Stalnaker, D., and Taylor, G. (1987, May). *Personality traits and leisure barriers among women*. Paper presented at the meeting of the Fifth Canadian Congress on Leisure Research, Dalhousie University, Nova Scotia, Canada.

Hunter, J. (2001). The final word on playground accessibility. *Today's Playground, 1*(1), 22–31.

Jackson, E. L., Crawford, D. W., and Godbey, G. (1993). Negotiation of leisure constraints. *Leisure Sciences, 15*, 1–11.

Loy, D. P. and Dattilo, J. (2000). Effects of different play structures on social interaction between a boy with Asperger's syndrome and his peers. *Therapeutic Recreation Journal, 34*(3), 190–210.

Malik, P. B. (2000). *Utilizing resources: Supporting consumers transitioning from clinical to community settings*. Paper presented at the National Institute on Recreation Inclusion, Deerfield, IL.

Marchand, P. (1997). The Individuals with Disabilities Education Act (IDEA) amendments of 1997. Retrieved from http://www.thearc.org/ga/qa.html

McAvoy, L. and Lais, G. (1999). Programs that include persons with disabilities. In J. D. Miles and S. Priest (Eds.), *Adventure programming* (pp. 403–414). State College, PA: Venture Publishing, Inc.

McCormick, S. (1999). *Removing barriers: Tips and strategies to promote accessible communication*. Raleigh, NC: The North Carolina Office on Disability and Health and Woodward Communications.

McNeil, J. M. (2000). *Employment, earnings, and disability*: Survey of income and program participation. Washington, DC: U.S. Bureau of the Census. Retrieved from http://www.census.gov/hhes/www/disable/emperndis.pdf

Mobily, K. (2000). An interview with professor Seppo Iso-Ahola. *Therapeutic Recreation Journal, 34*, 300–305.

Mobily, K. E., Mobily, P. R., Lessard, K. A., and Berkenpas, M. S. (2000). Case comparison of response to aquatic exercise: Acute versus chronic conditions. *Therapeutic Recreation Journal, 34*(2), 103–119.

National Recreation and Park Association. (2000). Position statement on inclusion. *NTRS Report, 25*(1), 18.

National Therapeutic Recreation Society. (2001). Definition statement. Alexandria, VA: Author.

Pedlar, A. (1990). Normalization and integration: A look at the Swedish experience. *Mental Retardation, 28*, 275–282.

Sable, J., Craig, P., and Lee, D. (2000). Promoting health and wellness: A research-based case report. *Therapeutic Recreation Journal, 34*, 348–361.

Schleien, S., Germ, P., and McAvoy, L. (1996). Inclusive community leisure services: Recommended professional practices and barriers encountered. *Therapeutic Recreation Journal, 30*(4), 260–273.

Schleien, S., Ray, M. T., and Green, F. (1997). *Community recreation and people with disabilities: Strategies for inclusion* (2nd ed.). Baltimore, MD: Paul H. Brookes.

Schleien, S. J. and Werder, K. J. (1985). Perceived responsibilities of special recreation services in Minnesota. *Therapeutic Recreation Journal, 19*(3), 51–62.

Shank, J. W., Coyle, C. P., Boyd, R., and Kinney, W. B. (1996). A classification scheme for therapeutic recreation research grounded in the rehabilitative sciences. *Therapeutic Recreation Journal, 30*(3), 179–196.

Shugars, D. A., O'Neil, E., and Bader, J. D. (1991). *Healthy America: Practicioners for 2005, an agenda for U.S. health professional schools.* Durham, NC: The Pew Foundation Health Professions Commission.

Smith, R. W. (1995). Trends in therapeutic recreation. *Parks and Recreation, 30*(5), 66–71.

Smith, R. W., Austin, D. R., and Kennedy, D. W. (2001). *Inclusive and special recreation: Opportunities for persons with disabilities* (4th ed.). New York, NY: McGraw-Hill.

Stone, C. F., Bullock, C. C., and Brooke, P. (2004). Community versus clinical: A false dichotomy in therapeutic recreation. Unpublished manuscript.

U.S. Department of Health and Human Services, Office of Disease Prevention and Health Promotion. (2000). Healthy people 2010. Atlanta, GA: Centers for Disease Control.

Wolfensberger, W. (1972). *The principle of normalization in human services.* Toronto, Ontario, Canada: National Institute on Mental Retardation.

Wolfensberger, W. (1983). Social role valorization: A proposed new term for the principle of normalization. *Mental Retardation, 21*, 234–239.

Wolfensberger, W. (1995). An "if this, then that" formulation of decisions related to social role valorization as a better way of interpreting it to people. *Mental Retardation, 33*, 163–169.

Chapter 20

Spatial and Temporal Constraints to Natural Resource Recreation and Tourism: A GIS Perspective

M. A. Tarrant (University of Georgia) and R. P. Porter (Ithaca College)

In this chapter we demonstrate the application of geographic information systems (GIS) to explore spatial and temporal access constraints to natural resource based recreation and tourism opportunities. In response to Jackson and Scott's conclusion "the most pressing need is for diversification of research approaches" (1999, p. 314) in future leisure constraints work, GIS represents a unique and novel method for examining geographic access constraints. Critical questions explored in this chapter include the following:

1. Is there a conceptual framework for examining geographic access constraints to leisure?

2. How can GIS improve our understanding of leisure constraints?

3. What is the role of GIS in improving the leisure practitioner–researcher relationship?

We argue GIS can help to identify potential inequities in the distribution and allocation of leisure opportunities and resources, as a critical step in alleviating spatial and temporal geographic constraints and improving access.

Conceptual Framework

Executive Order 12898 (Federal Actions to Address Environmental Justice in Minority Populations and Low-Income Populations; Federal Register, February 1994) requires all federal land management agencies to assess the environmental justice implications of their policies, practices, and programs. Although only federal programs (including areas within National Forests, National Parks, National Wildlife Refuges, and Wilderness Areas) fall within the mandate, Order 12898 also raises a broader concern of constrained allocation in the supply of, and access to, public leisure resources, including Greenways, urban open spaces, recreation centers, and safe transportation networks.[1]

Environmental justice concerns potential inequities in the distribution and effects of environmental resources and encourages nondiscriminatory activities in government regulations and actions. Traditionally, the emphasis has been on hazardous land uses (e.g., landfills, chemical plants, factories), but recently the focus was expanded to include all types of land uses, both desirable and undesirable (e.g., Faber, 1998; Salazar, 1998; Tarrant & Cordell, 1999; Tarrant & Porter, 1999). The environmental justice movement is now predicated on the concept that the environment consists of not only the places in which we work and live, but also the places where we play (Di Chiro, 1998). An injustice occurs when certain groups receive an unfair portion of the costs or benefits of management actions, which, in the case of natural resources, involve strategies that potentially favor some people and constrain others (Salazar, 1998).

The environmental justice issue reportedly began in the early 1970s with the discovery of toxic waste in a schoolyard near Niagara Falls, New York, in the now infamous Love Canal community. The increased rate of birth defects and presence of serious childhood illnesses prompted local citizens to fight to get reimbursement for their homes. In response to Love Canal, the government passed the Superfund Law, providing tax money for the cleanup of toxic areas. The next issue that received national attention was the decision to locate a landfill for PCB (polychlorinated biphenyl) contaminated soil in predominantly African American Warren County, North Carolina, in 1982. The PCB proposal passed (albeit in another majority non-White county in North Carolina), but the issue provoked subsequent research showing ethnicity to be one of two primary factors (along with income) in the location and/or clean-up of commercial hazardous waste sites (Bullard, 1983, 1994; Bullard & Wright, 1992; Commission for Racial Justice, United Church of Christ, 1987; Mohai & Bryant, 1992; U.S. General Accounting Office, 1983). The U.S. General Accounting Office, for example, found communities surrounding three of four hazardous sites in the Southeast United States to be predominantly non-White. The Commission for Racial Justice of the United Church of Christ (1987) reported zip code areas with one commercial hazardous waste facility had twice the non-White population (24%) than those without a facility, while communities with multiple facilities had an average of 38% non-White population. According to Mohai and Bryant (1992), White residents in Detroit were four times less likely to live close to a hazardous waste site than non-White populations.

Other studies support income as either the primary factor (e.g., Hamilton, 1995; Kriesel, Centner & Keeler, 1996) or a related influence along with ethnicity (e.g., Costner & Thorton, 1990; Foreman, 1996; Glickman, 1994; Lavelle & Coyle, 1992; U.S. Environmental Protection Agency [EPA], 1992) in the siting of undesirable land uses. Kriesel et al. (1996), for example, reported significant differences in exposure to toxic releases (as measured using the EPA's Toxic Release Inventory) were associated with income, but not ethnicity. Similarly, Hamilton (1995) found ethnicity was not a significant factor in explaining the capacity expansion of hazardous waste facilities when income was included. Costner and Thorton (1990), however, found communities in which hazardous waste incinerators were located to be made up of 89% more non-Whites, and 15% lower-income residents than national averages. Lavelle and Coyle (1992) indicated the cleanup of waste sites takes considerably longer in poor and non-White communities than in more affluent white neighborhoods. A U.S. EPA (1992) report concluded exposures to air pollutants, hazardous waste facilities, and other environmental costs are higher than average in non-White and low-income communities.

If one supports the view that studies of minority groups are studies of constraints (Goodale, 1992, cited in Jackson & Scott, 1999), it is a logical extension to apply the environmental justice framework within constraints research, generally. However, recreation resources (and access to them) are rarely undesirable land uses (as is the case with hazardous waste facilities).[2] Implicit in the constraints work is that leisure is a desirable good for which barriers should be negotiated and/or alleviated. Only recently has the environmental justice debate addressed desirable, as well as undesirable, land resources. In response to Executive Order 12898, the U.S. EPA (1998) recognized agencies should address minority interests in terms of the communities' "reliance on natural resources for [their] economic base" (p. 17). Salazar (1998) called for "a comprehensive conception of environmental justice [to] take into account environmental goods as well as bads" (p. 52). The political context of natural resource planning, including recreation and tourism, renders a concern over whether certain management actions have constrained access to (desirable) resources for some groups of people and not others.

Faber (1998) based his concerns for environmental justice on the "neoliberal efforts to contain and roll back policies establishing...protections for wilderness, forest, wild rivers, wetlands, and endangered species" (p. 40). These efforts include the exploitation of old growth forest in the Pacific Northwest, the unearthing of coal deposits in homelands of the Hopi and Navajo Indians, and the grazing of sheep on environmentally sensitive lands. Often the economic revenues of these multiple use practices provide no benefit to the local community and may devalue the local resource, especially in terms of recreation, aesthetics, and the tourism they attract.

The charges of Salazar and Faber imply a need to examine possible inequities in the distribution of, and access constraints to, all types of land uses (including recreation and tourism), both desirable and undesirable. For example, West, Fly, Marans, Larkin, and Rosenblatt (1995) found lower income and minority anglers consumed more contaminated fish (up to 23.9 grams/person/day) on average than White anglers (17.9 grams/person/day). Tarrant and Porter (1999) found race to be a primary factor in national forest fish advisory areas; poor fisheries habitat was more likely to be located in predominantly non-White than White communities. In urban environments, low income and non-White communities were shown to have fewer local open park spaces than predominantly White, affluent residents (Wemett & Henderson, 1998). Together, these studies indicate that non-White populations may have the closest access to impaired recreational resources, but constrained access to desirable land uses. Clearly, the environmental justice model provides one approach for exploring access constraints to leisure services, particularly for certain segments of society.

GIS Applications to Leisure Constraints

The use of GIS in leisure studies is rare (Bertazzon, Crouch, Draper & Waters, 1997); indeed, only a handful of studies have applied GIS techniques to examine environmental justice issues (e.g., Glickman, 1994; Mohai & Bryant, 1992; Stockwell, Sorenson, Eckert & Carreras, 1993; U.S. General Accounting Office, 1995). In the leisure field, Tarrant and his colleagues advocated a one-mile buffer/radius around national forest recreation sites (wilderness areas, fisheries, and campgrounds) to compare the demography of census block groups within and outside the buffer (Tarrant & Cordell, 1999), as well as a straight-line distance method to calculate the spatial distance of minority populations from fish advisory areas (Tarrant & Porter, 1999). Wemett and Henderson (1998) used GIS to combine census data, aerial photos, and digitized maps of land cover and park use patterns to examine the distribution of urban parks.

GIS represents a sophisticated computerized mapping tool for analyzing, querying, displaying, and organizing spatial information (e.g., points, lines, shapes), with nongeographic features (Harris, Gimblett & Shaw, 1995; Johnson, 1990). GIS, for example, can be used to merge coverage areas (e.g., wilderness areas, lakes, county boundaries), spatial points (e.g., campgrounds, leisure centers) and lines (e.g., rivers, transportation networks, trails) for analyzing spatial interactions. The power of GIS lies in an ability to incorporate raw data from a number of databases (e.g., leisure supply and demand statistics, patterns of visitor flow) and to convert it to digital form, permitting data to be manipulated and reclassified into a common system. More generally, GIS is a data input, storage, retrieval, analysis, and reporting approach for processing spatial data into information typically used in land management decisions. It is used to collect spatial data from various sources; to store, retrieve, and edit data; to manipulate data by estimating new parameters and performing modeling functions; and to report and produce results of data in tabular, graphic, and/or map formats (DeMers, 1997). Because of the versatile nature of GIS, the processes can be performed quickly, providing results that would otherwise be time-consuming, if not impossible, using analog maps.

Recently, the EPA (1998) recognized "GIS provide a much more powerful tool for identifying and locating populations of concern" and advocated using GIS to address issues of environmental justice. The various functions of GIS (e.g., spatial analysis, spatial modeling, network analysis, and mapping) permit researchers and managers to sculpt them into an appropriate tool for a specific job (DeMyers, 1997). Queen (1992), for example, stated GIS "provides a vehicle for integrating diverse resource perspectives to aid in resource management decisions" (p. 1). In the next section of this chapter, we briefly discuss the issue of geographic scale in GIS applications to leisure constraints research and describe two analytical GIS methods (straight-line distance and network analysis) and their applicability to understanding geographic (spatial and temporal) access constraints in leisure studies.

Geographic Scale

In any GIS analysis the issue of geographic scale is of critical importance. For example, environmental justice has been examined at different scales of analysis, including county (Hird, 1993), city (Mohai & Bryant, 1992), zip code (Hamilton, 1995), and census block group (Kriesel, Centner & Keeler, 1996), at times with conflicting results. (One argument is that much information is lost in larger versus smaller units of analysis.) Census block groups represent an amalgamation of census blocks, containing about 250 to 550 housing units. (The U.S. Bureau of the Census does not collect information on income, occupation, etc., at the block level, thus limiting the utility of census blocks for social research studies.) County, city, and zip code levels are probably less appropriate scales for examining issues in leisure constraints because the populations of interest (e.g., non-White, low-income, elderly, single-parent households) are typically concentrated in small geographic units. For example, people with low-incomes tend to live in close proximity to one another (i.e., in neighborhoods) because of how affordable housing has been planned and developed.

Straight-Line Distance and Network Analysis

Straight-line (i.e., "as the crow flies") methods in GIS measure spatial access to resources. Living in close physical proximity to a wilderness area, for example, may provide scenic vistas and cleaner air and water that might be less available (or unavailable) for people living further away from natural resources. Ribeiro da Costa (1996) used a straight-line approach to calculate distances between towns and tourist attractions in the Mediterranean; Tarrant and Porter (1999) used a similar method to measure the spatial distance of minority populations from fish advisory areas.

Network analysis, a vector-based approach,[3] calculates the actual distance traveled, taking into account the shape of a road or stream and other factors, such as speed limit or rate of water flow. Network analysis has the capability of converting spatial distance into a temporal measure (e.g., average time to commute from point A to B, controlling for road types, speed limits, stop signs). Lewandowski and McLaughlin (1995) used network analysis to manage hiker movement through a trail system to minimize use at ecologically sensitive areas. The method enabled the researchers to evaluate the success of alternative strategies in redistributing use. Spear and Contrill (1993) used a prototype network approach to create a viable road system for visitor use in Yellowstone National Park. Potential visitor demand for tourism sites in England has also been identified using predicted travel times from origin to destination (Bateman, Lovett & Brainard, 1999).

Network analysis has proven to be more accurate than a straight-line method, at least for determining actual distances (Bhat, Bergstrom & Bowker, 1997), and probably has greater applicability for leisure studies because it measures both spatial and temporal access constraints. For undesirable land uses, the facility's proximity, in a straight-line, is the factor that determines exposure to hazardous environmental conditions (e.g., windborne air pollutants, soil and water contamination, and toxic exposure). However, direct use of desirable land uses, such as wilderness areas, recreation facilities, and tourism sites, is most always a function of road access. Given travel time is one of the most important influences on decisions to visit a recreation site[4] (Bateman et al., 1999; Brainard, Bateman & Lovett, 1995), road access can be a critical constraint (or benefit) for those wishing to take advantage of recreational opportunities. Queen (1992) stated, "roads are an integral part of the recreational opportunities that exist in any given area... areas with roads provide access to recreational facilities" (p. 4). Time constraints increase exponentially as distance from the site increases, because people often do not have sufficiently large blocks of time (e.g., a single five-hour period) to access and use a resource. The closer one lives to a desirable recreation site, the greater the opportunities because large time blocks are not required (i.e., the resource can be accessed in multiple and shorter times of 1–2 hours, for example). To this end, Salazar (1996) called for resource managers to "promote equal access to natural resources and ensure that the least powerful receive a fair share of the benefits" (p. 35). Correspondingly, a complete examination of leisure constraints should include both spatial and temporal access to opportunities.

Structural and Intrapersonal Constraints

GIS (especially network analysis) has the potential to be a viable method for identifying the influence of both intrapersonal and structural constraints. First, it has been shown that preferences for leisure opportunities can be a function of physical proximity and past exposure, an intrapersonal constraint (Jackson, 1994; Jackson & Scott, 1999). People who do not live near alpine ski areas, for example, are much less likely to develop preferences for snow skiing. Furthermore, such people are less likely to be socialized into the activity and therefore unlikely to develop the skills and knowledge for effective engagement. Such an assertion is supported by Jackson (1994) who reported "the absence of recreational and leisure opportunities close to home and the cost of transportation, do in fact act as deterrents to people's leisure and recreational participation" (p. 119).

The second category that involves geographical constraints to leisure is structural. For example, an individual may not be able to afford the time or money to travel to a recreation site. Such constraints may be of intermediate importance, suggesting they should be examined in terms of not only spatial and/or temporal distance, but also sociodemographic characteristics, such as income, occupation, and race (Jackson & Scott, 1999). By overlaying spatial shapes (e.g., census block group boundaries containing demographic information) with points and lines (e.g., recreation centers, hiking trails), the geographic (temporal and spatial) relationships among the phenomena can be displayed, analyzed and queried. Once distances are computed, data can be exported to a statistical package for further analysis. Within a network analysis, the least cost (i.e., optimal) road system between a community or census block group (comprised of about 250–550 housing units) and a recreation destination can be calculated. Constraints to travel, such as speed limits and highway interchanges, can be included in the network to produce an estimated travel time. The sociodemographic makeup of communities can be analyzed as a function of their spatial and/or temporal distance to destinations. If, for example, populations surrounding a wilderness area are predominantly White and low-income, while actual users of the area are White and upper-income, we may conclude income is a possible constraint in using the resource.

GIS has several general limitations, including an inability to perform statistical analysis directly within the software (without exporting to an external software package), time-consuming database development and preparation (especially for network analysis), and a reliance on (predominantly) secondary data sources. In terms of leisure constraints research, one of the primary concerns is that it does not take into account the psychological aspects of travel access (Bateman et al., 1995). People do not always choose the fastest or shortest route to access an area, especially recreation and tourism resources. Some will prefer a lengthier scenic drive, while others will choose the most direct route. Therefore, GIS are limited in their ability to assess only quantitative aspects of access.

The Leisure Practitioner–Researcher Relationship

Geographic access is one of many antecedent constraints to leisure, and alleviating temporal and/or spatial access may do little to promote equitable opportunity and redress environmental injustices associated with recreation and tourism opportunities. The existence of other structural and intrapersonal as well as interpersonal constraints (i.e., opportunities dependent on social interactions and situations) suggests relocating or providing additional resources and services to improve access will not alone ameliorate leisure constraints. However, perhaps one of the greatest contributions of a GIS-driven, environmental justice perspective to leisure constraints is pragmatic application, especially in improving the planning and marketing of leisure services. Jackson and Scott (1999) proposed, "leisure constraints research cannot impact professional practice until academics develop more potent partnerships with practitioners and leisure service agencies" (p. 310). As a marketing and planning tool, GIS may be an effective avenue for promoting such relationships.

GIS is widely used in many fields, ranging from biomedical sciences (mapping the physiology of the human body) to city transportation planning and airport control. Researchers often provide the databases, critical for GIS analysis, while planners can shape the analytical tools, available in GIS, to examine a specific problem or issue. By identifying both who is served and who is not served in a community, GIS lends itself very well to market segmentation and the target marketing of underserved populations. Scott (this volume), for example, describes the ways in which "research on leisure constraints can potentially help practitioners understand why population groups do not make greater use of agency offerings and provide directions about how to allay the conditions that inhibit involvement." Clearly, GIS has direct application to alleviating such constraints. Traditionally, however, many leisure agencies have delivered services based on

an "expressed need" (or product orientation), making the assumption that resources are equitably distributed and demand is determined by user tastes, preferences, and needs (Jackson & Scott, 1999). The utility of GIS is it can provide planners with information on those who (a) have easy access yet do not use the resources, (b) have poor access yet often use the resource, and (c) have poor access and do not use the resource. By focusing only on direct users of the resource, leisure agencies have typically evaluated the success of their programs, facilities, and services through profits and/or attendance figures, often ignoring the constraints of an underserved population.

Conclusion

Access is clearly a more complex and broader issue than simply defining it in terms of spatial and/or temporal geography involving a person's social structure (e.g., family, peer group) and sociodemography (e.g., education, race, class). Addressing geographic access constraints to leisure within an environmental justice framework permits assessment of sociodemographic influences in natural resource based recreation and tourism management decisions and practices. While such land use practices were probably rarely intentionally discriminatory (in terms of site location), they are fundamentally political decisions that warrant investigation under Executive Order 12898 (Salazar, 1998). To the extent particular segments of society may receive an inequitable share of the costs or benefits of public recreation resources, indirect discrimination (i.e., with no intent to harm minorities) may have occurred. Either way, Bullard (1994) suggested environmental injustice includes "any policy, practice, or directive that differentially affects or disadvantages (whether intended or unintended) individuals, groups, or communities" (p. 98). As part of a much broader civil rights issue, the environmental framework, examined using GIS techniques, provides a novel and recent approach to understanding spatial and temporal access constraints to leisure opportunities, especially (though not exclusively) for certain groups in society. Clearly, as the push for an outcomes-based approach to leisure management and service provision continues, managers and planners must become increasingly aware of who is receiving the benefits of such services (and where) and who is constrained. Within the context of environmental justice, the issue becomes one of balancing benefits (and costs) of leisure services while considering economic growth, environmental protection, and social equity. In this way, efforts can be made to ensure decisions regarding the use and allocation of public resources do not unfairly benefit one group over another. When inequities do arise, either the cost should be borne proportionately by all those who benefit, or individuals who bear the costs can be fairly compensated and/or receive additional support to overcome constraints that may impede their share of the benefits.

References

Bateman, I. J., Garrod, G., Brainard, J. S., and Lovett, A. A. (1995). *Using geographical information systems to apply the travel cost method: A sensitivity analysis of woodland recreation value*. Centre for Rural Economy (CRE) Working Paper. Newcastle-upon-Tyne, UK: Department of Agricultural Economics, University of Newcastle-upon-Tyne.

Bateman, I. J., Lovett, A. A., and Brainard, J. S. (1999). Developing a methodology for benefits transfer using geographical information systems: Modeling demand for woodland recreation. *Regional Studies, 33*(3), 191–205.

Bertazzon, S., Crouch, G., Draper, D., and Waters, N. (1997). GIS applications in tourism marketing: Current issues, an experimental application, and future prospects. *Journal of Travel and Tourism Marketing, 6*(3/4), 35–59.

Bhat, G., Bergstrom, J., and Bowker, J. M. (1997). *Integration of geographical information systems based spatial analysis in recreation demand analysis* (Faculty Series Working Paper FS 96-26). Athens, GA: Department of Agricultural and Applied Economics, The University of Georgia.

Brainard, J. S., Bateman, I. J., and Lovett, A. A. (1995). Modelling recreation demand using geographic information systems. In M. M. Fischer, T. T. Sikos, and L. Bassa (Eds.), *Recent developments in spatial information* (pp. 163–174). Hungary: Geomarket Co.

Bullard, R. D. (1983, Spring). Solid waste sites and the black Houston community. *Sociological Inquiry, 53*, 273–288.

Bullard, R. D. (1994). *Dumping in Dixie: Race, class, and environmental quality*. Boulder, CO: Westview Press.

Bullard, R. D. and Wright, B. H. (1992). The quest for environmental equity: Mobilizing the African-American community for social change. In R. E. Dunlap and A. G. Mertig (Eds.), *American environmentalism: The U.S. environmental movement, 1970–1990*. Philadelphia, PA: Taylor and Francis.

Commission for Racial Justice, United Church of Christ (1987). *Toxic wastes and race in the United States: A national report on the racial and socio-economic characteristics of communities with hazardous waste sites*. New York, NY: United Church of Christ.

Costner, P. and Thornton, J. (1990). *Playing with fire*. Washington, DC: Greenpeace.

DeMers, M. N. (1997). *Fundamentals of geographic information systems*. New York, NY: Wiley.

Di Chiro, G. (1998). Environmental justice from the grassroots. In D. Faber (Ed.), *The struggle for ecological democracy* (pp. 104–136). New York, NY: Guilford Press.

Faber, D. (1998). The political ecology of American capitalism. In D. Faber (Ed.), *The struggle for ecological democracy* (pp. 27–59). New York, NY: Guilford Press.

Federal Register (1994, February 11). Executive Order 12898 (59, 7629). Washington, DC: U.S. Government Printing Office.

Foreman, C. H. (1996). A winning hand?: The uncertain future of environmental justice. *Brookings Review, 14*(2), 22–25.

Glickman, T. S. (1994). Measuring environmental equity with geographical information systems. *Resources, 116*, 2–6.

Hamilton, J. T. (1995). Testing for environmental racism: Prejudice, profits, political power? *Journal of Policy Analysis and Management, 14*, 107–132.

Harris, L. K., Gimblett, R. H., and Shaw, W. W. (1995). Multiple-use management: Using a GIS model to understand conflicts between recreationists and sensitive wildlife. *Society and Natural Resources, 8*, 559–572.

Hird, J. A. (1993). Environmental policy and equity: The case of Superfund. *Journal of Policy Analysis and Management, 12*, 323–343.

Jackson, E. L. (1994). Geographical aspects of constraints on leisure and recreation. *The Canadian Geographer, 38*(2), 110–121.

Jackson, E. L. and Scott, D. S. (1999). Constraints to leisure. In E. L. Jackson and T. L. Burton (Eds.), *Leisure studies: Prospects for the twenty-first century* (pp. 299–321). State College, PA: Venture Publishing, Inc.

Johnson, L. B. (1990). Analyzing spatial and temporal phenomena using geographical information systems: A review of ecological applications. *Landscape Ecology, 4*(1), 31–43.

Kriesel, W., Centner, T. J., and Keeler, A. G. (1996, Fall). Neighborhood exposure to toxic releases: Are there racial inequities? *Growth and Change, 27*, 479–499.

Lavelle, M. and Coyle, M. (1992). Unequal protection: The racial divide in environmental law. *National Law Journal, 15*(3).

Lewandowski, J. P. and McLaughlin, S. P. (1995). Managing visitor's environmental impact in a system of sites: A network approach. *The Pennsylvania Geographer, 33*(2), 43–58.

Mendelsohn, R. and Markstrom, D. (1988). The use of travel cost and hedonic methods in assessing environmental benefits. In G. L. Peterson, B. L. Driver, and R. Gregory (Eds.), *Amenity resource valuation: Integrating economics with other disciplines* (pp. 159–166). State College, PA: Venture Publishing, Inc.

Mohai, P. and Bryant, B. (1992). Environmental racism: Reviewing the evidence. In B. Bryant and P. Mohai (Eds.), *Race and the incidence of environmental hazards: A time for discourse.* Boulder, CO: Westview Press.

Queen, L. P. (1992). *Integrating spatial models of recreation, wildlife, and timber resources.* Proceedings, GIS Symposium, Vancouver, British Columbia, Canada: Forestry Canada.

Ribeiro da Costa, J. (1996). Assessing tourism potential: From words to numbers. In S. Morain and S. L. Baros (Eds.), *Raster imagery in geographic information systems* (pp. 149–155). Sante Fe, NM: OnWord Press.

Salazar, D. (1996). Environmental justice and a people's forestry. *Journal of Forestry, 94*(11), 32–38.

Salazar, D. (1998). Environmental justice and natural resource management in the Pacific Northwest. *Northwest Science Forum, 72*(1), 52–57.

Spear, B. D. and Cottrill, B. (1993). GIS manages Grand Teton, Yellowstone Park roads. *GeoInfoSystems, 3*(10), 52–55.

Stockwell, J. R., Sorenson, J. W., Eckert, J. W., and Carreras, E. M. (1993). The U.S. EPA geographical information system for mapping environmental releases of toxic waste chemical release inventory (TRI) chemicals. *Risk Analysis, 13*(2), 155–164.

Tarrant, M. A. and Cordell, H. K. (1999). Environmental justice and the spatial distribution of outdoor recreation sites: An application of geographic information systems. *Journal of Leisure Research, 31*(1), 18–34.

Tarrant, M. A. and Porter, R. (1999). Environmental justice and the spatial distribution of fish advisory areas in the Southern Appalachians: A geographic information systems approach. *Human Dimensions of Wildlife, 4*(3), 1–17.

U.S. Environmental Protection Agency. (1992). *Environmental equity: Reducing risks for all communities* (EPA-230-R92-008). Washington, DC: U.S. Government Printing Office.

U.S. Environmental Protection Agency. (1998). *Final guidance for incorporating environmental justice concerns in EPA's NEPA compliance analysis.* Washington DC: U.S. Government Printing Office. Retrieved from http://es.epa.gov/oeca/ofa/ejepa.html

U.S. General Accounting Office. (1983, June 1). *Siting of hazardous waste landfills and their correlation with racial and economic status of surrounding communities* (GAO/RCED 83-168). Washington, DC: U.S. Government Printing Office.

U.S. General Accounting Office. (1995). *Hazardous and non-hazardous waste: Demographics of people living near waste facilities.* Washington, DC: U.S. Government Printing Office.

Wemett, J. and Henderson, J. (1998). Parks for the people: Whittier College's environmental project. *GeoInfoSystems, 8*(3), 27–32.

West, P., Fly, M., Marans, R., Larkin, F., and Rosenblatt, D. (1995). Minorities and toxic fish consumption: Implications for point discharge policy in Michigan. In B. Bryant (Ed.), *Environmental justice: Issues, policies, and solutions*. Washington, DC: Island Press.

Endnotes

1. While there have been attempts by President George W. Bush to rollback several environmental actions of the former administration, Executive Order 12898 remains active on the political agenda (e.g., http://www.honolulu-pacific.feb.gov/newsbite/newsbiteaug02.doc).

2. Although hazardous waste sites do provide local employment opportunities and contribute to local economies, the social, personal, and environmental costs of such facilities are generally considered to outweigh the benefits. Similarly, while recreation resources can have a detrimental effect on local communities (e.g., through generating traffic and noise pollution), the benefits of such uses generally outweigh the costs.

3. Vector-based approaches permit the representation of geographic data using strings of (x, y) coordinate pairs. As such, much of the space between the graphical representations is implied rather than explicitly defined. To overcome this limitation, a series of either regularly or irregularly placed points act as vertices that are connected to form a vector. (For more information see DeMers, 1997).

4. Travel time is a factor in several travel cost methods used in recreation and tourism demand modeling (e.g., Mendelsohn & Markstrom, 1988).

Section 5

Critique

Chapter 21

The Ontology of Exclusion: A European Perspective on Leisure Constraints Research

Neil Ravenscroft, Andrew Church, and Paul Gilchrist
(University of Brighton, England)

The departure point for this chapter is an observation (Ravenscroft & Curry, 2004; Uzzell et al., 2000) there is an apparent absence of a strong tradition of leisure constraints research outside North America (and North American journals). Indeed, it is hard to identify any constraints literature in the leading European leisure journals, such as *Leisure Studies* and *Managing Leisure*. With the exception of Kay and Jackson's (1991) seminal British work on negotiating constraints (published in a North American journal) and a paper by Ravenscroft and Curry (2004) (in an Australian journal), most development in the field would appear to have taken place outside Europe. Indeed, in his recent paper on discourses of constraint, Ravenscroft (2004) argued North American work is sufficiently ubiquitous, in the absence of a strong European tradition; it has influenced policy in the UK (and other European countries), although often in inappropriate and untested ways (Curry & Ravenscroft, 2001).

Yet, paradoxically, there are vibrant bodies of European research on constraints, although often not related solely to leisure and often not published in leisure-related journals and books. Three areas that have received particular attention are sustainable transport (Botma, 1992; Department of the Environment, Transport and the Regions, 1999; Dijkstra et al., 1998; Downward & Lumsdon, 2001; Green Party, 2000; Ravenscroft, 2004; Ravenscroft & Rogers, 2003; Ravenscroft, Uzzell & Leach, 2002), the impacts of people's fear of crime (Bairner & Shirlow, 2003; Montgomery, 1995; Oc & Tiesdell, 1997; Ravenscroft et al., 2002; Scraton & Watson, 1998; Thomas & Bromley, 1996), and the long-standing tradition in geography of research into time–space constraints on human activity (Hagerstrand, 1978) recently critiqued and extended from a feminist perspective (Hanson & Pratt, 1995; Kwan, 2000). Although often bearing comparison with North American constructs of constraint, what tends to distinguish this European work is the sociopolitical ontology of relative exclusion from specific spaces or aspects of the public realm (Centre for Leisure and Sport Research, 2002; Curry, Joseph & Slee, 2002). This is consistent with Shogan's (2002) epistemological critique of constraints research, as well as wider understandings of the people–environment relationships that formed the basis of this research (Pierskalla & Lee, 1998).

Therefore, in this chapter we wish to argue, far from being absent, European constraints research is both present as a field of study and active as a prism through which to challenge orthodox ontologies of conflict and constraint. This argument is informed by the comparative analysis of leisure studies and leisure sciences undertaken by Fred Coalter (1999), particularly in contrasting European constructs of society in leisure (and other social fields) with the North American tradition of studying leisure without society. This inevitably leads us to Coalter's (1999) comparison of the underlying normative and applied theory of much European research (social outcomes) with the more cognitive approach in North America (what is leisure?). This we illustrate through reference to the development of research in a number of European countries into exclusion from social practices, including leisure. We conclude the chapter with a recent case study of recreational conflict in England that illustrates both the similarities and the differences between research in Europe and North America.

Theoretical Framework: Power and Social Practice

Coalter (1998, 1999) suggested normative theorizing about strategic social policy dominate British leisure studies, with scant regard for robust evidence to support policy development. While there have been attempts by the government in the UK to shift strategy toward "evidence-based policy" (Department of Transport, Local Government and the Regions, 2001; Office of the Deputy Prime Minister, 2003), there is as yet little evidence of this becoming a dominant paradigm for academic writing. Equally, a commitment to evidence-based policy may not always be reflected in the process of policy evolution. Rather, much of Coalter's (1999) rhetoric remains valid, with the key themes of European research remaining avowedly sociological in perspective (Coalter's construct of "leisure as not leisure"), with an often implicit focus on the interplay of power relations within social practices, as recognized by Sugden and Tomlinson (2002, p. 3) in the introduction to *Power Games*:

> The centrality of power in sociological analysis hardly comes as a surprise to those grounded in the classical debates of modern Western social science. What has always been at issue is the source of power, and the nature of the context within which power relations are lived out: the mode of production for Marx; new forms of the division of labour for Durkheim; particular forms of authority for Weber; and the individual drive or will to acquire and use power for theorists such as Habermas, Freud and Nietzsche.

As Giddens (1994) argued, it is not so much a question of who does or does not have power, but rather that power relations are an inherent part of social interaction. This implies the use of power in any situation does not denote particular types of conduct (as much North American constraints research has hypothesized), but rather, action. Thus, power is not a finite commodity traded between people (as is often portrayed in conflict situations), but a relative factor present in all relationships, such that even though one party may dominate, subordinate people still have some power to resist or counter the dominant force (Layder, 1995). Alternatively, individuals may draw on the resources of power to self-regulate in a manner supportive of dominant forces and hegemonic structures (Allen, 2003). From this perspective, power is seen as spatially varied and diffuse, and the "roundaboutness of power" (Allen, 2004) means it may be unused or wasted. In contrast to the ideas of freedom and choice (and thus constraint) that informed the analysis of person–person interactions in North America, therefore, much European work has focused on constructs of social and cultural reproduction, such that cognition of the broader context of any interaction is privileged over the dynamic of the interaction itself (see Coalter, 1999).

This constitutes, in Goffman's (1974) terms, a particularized frame or paradigm for social conduct, imparting both a sense of what is going on (meaning), as well as a normative expectation of how fully individuals are "carried into the activity organized by the frame" (involvement; Burns, 1992, p. 345). Negotiating interactions, in the context of this frame, thus becomes a generative social practice, undertaken as a form of "apprenticeship" (Haworth, 1997) in embodying the habitual actions consistent with the occupation of a particular social field (Bourdieu, 1984). Equally, the power to shape social interactions can be vested into key institutions, but their "reach" into particular situations and individual negotiations will be mediated by time and space (Allen, 2003).

In the UK and much of Europe, these forms of social practice and habitual actions that constrain individuals' actions have traditionally been seen as being generated by class, gender, race, sexuality, disability, work, and to a lesser extent religious affiliations (Aitchison, 2003; Jarvie & Maguire, 1994; Roberts, 1997; Warde, 1995). These types of divisions have been highly influential in informing all elements of social and bodily practice, including patterns of food consumption (Mennell, 1985; Savage, Barlow, Dickens & Fielding, 1992), leisure participation (Aitchison, 2003; Clarke & Critcher, 1985; Roberts, 1999), and tourism (Ryan, 1997; Wagner, 1998). As a result we argue—in contrast to North America—"choice" has been a highly constrained and constructed term, especially when related to particular activities (Jarvie & Maguire, 1994). Rather than any significant element of freedom, our argument is choice has been—and continues to be—socially structured, reflecting clear class and social dispositions in the form of a strongly identifiable body habitus (Bourdieu, 1984). By this we mean individual people's "choices" have been circumscribed by their internalization of existing social structures, reflecting Bourdieu's (1977, p. 95) understanding of habitus as "an acquired system of generative schemes objectively adjusted to the particular conditions in which it is constituted."

Rather than understanding these habitual dispositions as subject, however, the domain construction (certainly in much conflicts research) has been oppositional—what the others are not. Individual people's habitual dispositions (their internalized responses to given stimuli) with respect to certain leisure practices have thus tended to concentrate on distancing, for example, "environmentally acceptable" activities from those perceived to be environmentally damaging (Adelman, Heberlein & Bonnicksen, 1982; Gramann & Burdge, 1981; Jackson & Wong, 1982; Knopp & Tyger, 1973; Watson, Williams & Daigle, 1991). For Schor (1999) this type of logic is inherently comparative and competitive—there are no absolutes, merely comparisons with the other. This leads to what Schor sees as defensive behavior, based on the dualism of the dismissal or appropriation of the other.

While taste and preference have been strongly associated with established class dispositions, it is equally recognized they are capable of appropriation in attempts to signify new or changing dispositions, as subject subsumes other (Elias, 1978; Elias & Dunning, 1986). This is very much the case as existing dispositions are subjected to challenge. Rather than being absolute, therefore, Elias argued such dispositions should be viewed as both relative and hierarchical, to the extent social prestige can be gained by acquiring the taste signifiers deployed by those whom an individual seeks to emulate (see Wagner, 1998).

Rather than being concretized binary opposites, therefore, Elias shows us subject and other are relative and hierarchical descriptors. For while sociation A (subject) may be trying to emulate the taste dispositions of sociation B (other), sociation B (subject) will be, simultaneously, trying not only to distance itself from sociation A (other), but will also be trying to emulate the taste dispositions of sociation C (other). As a consequence Wagner (1998), elaborating on the work of Elias and Bourdieu, suggested the relationship between subject and other should be read not as isolated or binary opposites, but as a surface on which there is a continual interplay between agentive humans, in all directions, each simultaneously being both subject and other. As such "choice," in this context, is viewed as inherently socially informed and constructed:

> choice is socially structured, reflecting the possession and deployment of varying degrees and combinations of economic, cultural and symbolic capital. Taste reflects and embodies class disposition, a body habitus. The body is the most indisputable materialisation of class taste.
> (Jarvie & Maguire, 1994, p. 205)

It is this relativist construction of the body and embodied action at the core of our argument: the recognition of the bodily performance (embodiment) of ontology—the undoubted linkage of subject and other. Rather than the unidirectional nature of Urry's (2002) gaze, we posit a more fluid version, in which there is a "meeting" of narratives and knowledges. Following Horne (1992), our understandings of our own dispositions are thus contingent on our understandings of the dispositions of others—which are, of course, contingent on their own internal cognitive processes and their consequent understandings of the dispositions of others, and so on. Furthermore, as geographical writings confirm (Crouch, 1999), embodiment and ontological construction are not just mediated by space but involve the use and coconstruction of leisure spaces.

Case Study: Conflict and Constraint in the Use of Nonmotorized Routes

In illustrating the theoretical framework set out here, we will consider the Europe-wide interest in promoting walking and cycling as sustainable leisure and local transport practices. The volume of car-related accidents involving pedestrians and cyclists in Britain is among the highest in Europe (Walters, 2001), and is the principal reason why many parents will not allow their children to walk or cycle to school (Policy Studies Institute, 1991). In recent cycling studies, pollution from cars and fear of accidents with cars have been identified as two of the main barriers to cycling (Department of the Environment, Transport and the Regions, 1999; Green Party, 2000). In addition, there is a wider fear of accidents in unregulated spaces. Research in Paris, for example, found among cultural factors constraining the use of inline skating as a mode of recreational transport (e.g., concerns over fashion and the compulsory wearing of protective gear), other intervening factors also contributed to its constraint (e.g., risk of accidents both with cars and pedestrians, problems caused by physical obstacles, prohibited use and access in certain zones; Carré, 2003, p. 24).

The potential of nonmotorized shared-use routes has been recognized widely as a potential solution to people's fears, with the European Commission funding a major project to examine the ways in which short car trips can be replaced by walking or cycling (Danish Council of Road Safety Research, 1998). Walkers and cyclists have to negotiate several forms of discomfort, including the following:

- noise and air pollution.

- degraded urban environment and landscape.

- narrowness of the special areas available to them (footpaths, tracks, lanes).

- lack of maintenance (subways, footpaths, cycling facilities).

- unlawful parking.

- cluttering up of footpaths by urban furniture (e.g., permanent seating, litter bins, picnic tables).

These discomforts form part of a wider set of physical and psychological vulnerabilities cyclists and walkers face in urban and rural environments (Carré, 2003). This has led to best practice guidance for promoting cycling and walking, based on the premise such a shift will only occur if the appropriate level, range, and quality of facilities are available (Dijkstra et al., 1998).

In addition to the environmental sustainability associated with promoting walking and cycling in place of cars, there is also a strong emphasis on the potential safety gains from shared-use routes. While recognizing some pedestrians may feel threatened by the presence of bicycles, Sustrans (1999) makes the point forcibly both pedestrians and cyclists are in much greater danger from accidents with cars. This is supported by work in Denmark (Jensen, 1998), which identifies the improved safety of both pedestrians and cyclists, particularly after dark.

Despite the numerous benefits, much anxiety remains about the growth of shared-use routes. This is exemplified by a recent publication from the Ramblers' Association (1997). While endorsing the potential public benefits of shared-use routes, members of the Ramblers' Association are concerned about the hazards presented by cyclists, particularly when they approach at speed from behind. While there are as yet few reported accidents between walkers and cyclists (British Waterways, 1997), and while many people may be both walkers and cyclists at different times (Watson, Asp, Walsh & Kulla, 1997), the anxiety is clearly evident: "We know that there are genuine concerns about shared use voiced by different users, notably pedestrians and in particular elderly and visually impaired people" (Sustrans, 1999, p. 1).

A recent report in the UK by the Commission for Integrated Transport (2001) highlighted the lack of investment in nonmotorized routes for walkers and cyclists in the UK compared to other European countries. Where they are provided, however, nonmotorized shared-use routes are generally well-regarded by users (Uzzell et al., 2000). Although some claims suggest such routes generate interpersonal conflict between users (e.g., Cyclists' Touring Club, 1999), a recent study for the Countryside Agency concluded few people experience either actual or perceptual conflict when using the routes (Uzzell et al., 2000).

While the level of concern may be greater than the current risk of accidents, such anxiety and perceptions of

risk can undermine people's confidence, leading them to avoid using such routes (Sustrans, 1999). This accords with the earlier work by Burgess (1995) with respect to recreational visits to the urban fringe. Given the relatively low incidence of accidents on shared-use routes, there has been a tendency to blame the few inconsiderate or poorly behaved users (Ramblers' Association, 1997), with the majority of pedestrians feeling "cohabitation" between walkers and cyclists takes place without incident (Morel, 1999).

In all of these cases there is an emphasis on design and maintenance to ensure shared-use routes are, and remain, fit for their purpose (Carré, 2003). However, there is a depth of opinion, regardless of design and maintenance, that such routes have a limited utility and capacity, particularly to accommodate pedestrians and cyclists. For example, the current Local Transport Note relating to shared-use routes (LTN 2/86) makes clear Highways Authorities should attempt to cater for cycling on the road (Department of Transport and Welsh Office, 1986). This is broadly endorsed in the National Cycling Strategy (Department of Transport, 1996) and the work on cycle friendly infrastructure (Institution of Highways Transportation, Cyclists Touring Club, Department of Transport Bicycle Association, 1996), where it is recommended shared use should only be developed following careful consideration of the alternatives.

It is thus apparent the development of shared-use routes takes place within a complex policy arena. On one side, the promotion of multiple uses, particularly those not involving the car, is seen to be part of a wider initiative to promote sustainable and efficient transport networks. This is allied to a wider recognition of the dangers posed to pedestrians and cyclists by cars. Against this, however, is a concern about the erosion of both pedestrian rights (Ramblers' Association, 1997) and safety—rather than solving safety issues, shared use merely shifts the problem from carriageways to other routes. Consequently, shared use does no more than redefine the existing hierarchy of use, by taking pressure away from roads and onto new, often nondefinitive routes.

What this means is users continue to experience constraint, but within a narrower, more tightly defined boundary (Ravenscroft, 2004). This very much reflects Coalter's (1999) argument about the normative and collective sociological focus of much European leisure research. It also underscores Kay and Jackson's (1991) arguments about people's ability to negotiate constraints, suggesting constraints should be understood in relative rather than absolute terms. As such, leisure activity is but one example of a social practice through which people negotiate their entry to, and use of, social and often public spaces. In this way leisure is, as Coalter (1999) argued, "not leisure" per se, but rather a practice through which people deploy their relative power to achieve particular sociopolitical distinctiveness.

Social Exclusion and the European Project

This understanding of the different ways in which constraints act on individual people is increasingly at the core of the European political project, in which a central tenet of the European Union (EU) is the collectivization and equalization of power to participate in social (including leisure) practices:

> The objective in the coming period must be to preserve and develop the European Social Model as we move towards the 21st century, in order to give the people of Europe the unique blend of economic well-being, social cohesiveness and high overall quality of life which was achieved in the postwar period. (European Commission, 1994, p. 7)

The use of the term European Social Model (ESM) denotes the social conditions of Europe's citizens are a prime matter of public concern. Over the last decade, Member States have made a series of policy commitments and recommendations that formed the framework of a common social policy (the ESM) that institutionally and prescriptively recognizes the social conditions of well-being in determining an individual's quality of life (Blanc, 1998; European Commission, 1993; Ferrera, Matsaganis & Sacchi, 2002; Greenspace Consortium, 2003; Mayes, 2002; Paugam, 1996). Indeed, social policy can now readily be identified as an intrinsic element in the road to integration, or Europeanization. Risse, Green Cowles, and Carporosa (2001, p. 3) defined this as

> the emergence and development at the European level of distinct structures of governance, that is, of political, legal and social institutions associated with political problem solving that formalises interaction among actors, and of policy networks specialising in the creation of authoritative European rules.

Foremost among the core aspects of the ESM has been a discursive construction of social exclusion as a common area of concern facing members of the union. By this we mean the emphasis on addressing social exclusion reflects a reasoned (rather than intuitive) approach to improving the welfare of Europe's citizens.

This commitment to addressing exclusion was extended in the Lisbon European Council of March 2000, which agreed to take the necessary steps toward the eradication of exclusion by 2010. Perhaps the most important initiative, however, is the *Joint Report on Social Inclusion* (Council of Europe, 2001). This is the first single policy document to assess common challenges to be met by member states in the prevention and elimination of social exclusion and the promotion of social inclusion from an EU perspective. The report argues the challenge facing public policy is to ensure a host of social, political, and economic institutions, which distribute opportunities and resources (including the labor market, the tax system, and the systems providing social protection, education, housing, health, and other services, including leisure) become "sufficiently universal to address the needs of those who are at risk of poverty and social exclusion and to enable them to access their fundamental rights" (Council of Europe, 2001, p. 8). Hence, this should enable citizens to enjoy a standard of living and quality of life regarded as acceptable by the society in which they reside.

Yet, within European constructions of social exclusion employment is emphasized as a panacea to this particular ill and its associated symptoms (e.g., deprivation and disadvantage). Employment is seen to have both a productive element (as a way of maximizing national product and as a means to the provision of goods and services) and a social element (as a key instrument to reduce inequalities and promote social cohesion through participation in the labor market; Council of Europe, 2001, p. 6; European Commission, 1994, p. 9). This naturally has consequences for the present and future capacities of citizens to sustain independent living, family formation, and access to social practices, such as leisure and recreation.

As such, we argue the ESM institutionalized a normative and welfarist ideological position that recognizes real freedom from constraints (formal political equality and a minimum level of resources), rather than solely recognizing individuals as self-sufficient, self-determining, and rights-bearing. In official policy discourse, therefore, the construction of social exclusion—and thus constraint—is centered on intervening social conditions beyond the individual that dislocate him or her from society, rather than one based around internal or volitional constraints to participation (e.g., natural capacities and culturally governed preconditions). To borrow from Van Parijs, by coordinating policy and political actors at a supranational level, Europe has encouraged the creation of a society where "may," not "can," is the arbitrator in freedom (Van Parijs, 1995, p. 23), and so replicates a collectivist welfare perspective toward social problems.

The problem of exclusion is clearly located at a structural level—a property of social relationships and groups—rather than resting with the individual. Atkinson (1998, p. 7) wrote, "social exclusion often manifests itself in terms of communities rather than individuals, an illustration being the use by financial institutions of street postcodes for purposes of credit rating." This moves away from an individualized reading of the conflict that leads to exclusion (Murray, 1984). In contrast to many North American constructs of conflict, the exclusion that can arise from relative powerlessness is seen not as a "state," but as an active social process.

There are, however, some fundamental differences among European states in the approaches they make toward welfare, and concomitantly to social exclusion, which has resulted in different regimes of social policy despite broadly similar objectives (Bulpett, 2002; Esping-Andersen, 1990). Yet states have faced similar problems in the midst of globalization, which has led to economic pressures on the ability of the state to provide and guarantee social citizenship and hence the full participation of individuals and groups within society. Gvozdeva's (1999) work on post–Soviet Russia reveals how macroeconomic pressures, as part of a wider political and social transformation, led to a division of leisure opportunities between urban–rural and the genders, as the state prioritized the funding of cultural and leisure provision in areas of densely concentrated populations. Thus, while women may benefit from an expansion of civic and political rights, this means little at the microlevel if it leads to a reentrenchment of traditional ideologies of gender and domesticity which constrain their leisure and cultural participation (Kay, 1996, 2000; Shaw, 1994).

A further aspect of the political and social construction of space as a form of exclusion has been policies relating to spatial planning and the microarchitecture of streetscapes. At one level, central and local authorities have intervened to create "safe" public spaces in which diverse leisure and cultural experiences can be found. This has been achieved, for example, through renovation, regeneration, and challenging urban design (Oc & Tiesdell, 1999; Tiesdell & Oc, 1998), at the expense, some might argue, of traditional working-class and masculine (night-time) cultures, rooted around the alehouse and social club (see Chatterton & Hollands, 2001). Through measures such as the removal of undesirables and the provision of safety and surveillance equipment (e.g., extensive street lighting and the closed-circuit television monitoring of the use of public spaces), urban space has been reformed in a socially inclusive manner, to lessen intervening and external constraints, such as the fear for safety and fear of crime, in the interests of the public good (Ravenscroft, 2000). In some cases perceptions of fear tend to overrule questions of justice (e.g., discrimination) in removing unwanted elements. As Young (1998, p. 79) commented, "the policing of core areas…aimed at removing uncertainties, of sweeping the streets clean of alcoholics, beggars, the mentally ill and those who congregate in groups…is an actuarial police…moving on the inappropriate rather than arresting the criminal."

According to Oc and Tiesdell, in both British and continental European cities part of the problem has been a lack of suitable provision: "for urban spaces to become peopled and animated, the public realm has to offer what people want and desire" (Oc & Tiesdell, 1999, p. 278). This has necessitated increasing the range of activities available and encouraging more minority and excluded groups to use the city center.

In policy terms, this has been enacted in countries like the Netherlands, which hopes to create vibrancy and vitality in its towns and cities through carefully planned and designed urban spaces that take account of social, leisure, and recreational needs (Schwanen, Dijst & Dieleman, 2004). The idea of the compact or short-distance city should be noted here. This idea is based on various means of action to stimulate the development of compact centers and neighborhoods and to restrict retail sprawl, which aim to limit the spatial range of journeys, from residential, commercial and industrial areas, to increase the density of the urban area, reclaiming it as an active and public space (Carré, 2003, p. 55). Graz (Austria) and Groningen (Netherlands) are among the towns that apply this principle. The Fourth Physical Planning Memorandum, as set out by the Dutch Ministry of Housing, Physical Planning and the Environment, introduced a policy whereby firms were asked to locate to central and accessible urban locations to reduce motorized transport use and encourage cycling and walking (see Schwanen et al., 2004, p. 582). While questions remain as to whether this policy was successful, it serves to highlight the types of nonmotorized transport used for a host of activities (e.g., shopping, commuting, leisure, and recreation) and to create high-quality environments for the welfare of all in which leisure activities are of central concern.

Undoubtedly these contextual political agendas have influenced the nature of some academic research on leisure and constraint (Gratton & Henry, 2001). The ontologies of leisure research in Europe, however, are not just constructed by the political discourse on social exclusion or the theoretical developments in sociology and geography discussed earlier. The material nature of the spaces, activities, and social practices that make up leisure experiences in Europe will also coconstruct the nature of constraints research. In densely populated nations and regions, such as the Netherlands or England, the spaces of outdoor leisure are often subject to many other demands and land-use pressures. Any constraints and conflicts cannot simply be understood as arising from interpersonal relations, but must also be examined in relation to the broader economic, social, political, environmental, and legal processes that are the context for leisure activities in Europe. To exemplify the interplay between the material world of leisure and the nature of research on constraints, the next section outlines the findings of recent research on the use of inland water for leisure activities in Britain. The examples presented are drawn from two research projects recently completed by the authors (Church, Curry, Ravenscroft & Burnside, 2001; Ravenscroft, Church, Gilchrist, Hickey & Hammond, 2004) commissioned by the national government in the UK.

Case Study: Leisure on Inland Water in Britain and the Politicization of Constraint

In Britain, constraints on leisure activities and the resulting social conflicts have shaped political discourse at the national level, leading to major pieces of national legislation that significantly influenced the nature of outdoor leisure. In the 1930s, for example, the lack of access for walkers to moorland in northern England resulted in mass trespasses by organized groups of walkers on to the upland estates of wealthy landowners. The legislative outcome of these actions and other political campaigns was the 1949 National Parks and Access to the Countryside Act, which served to establish access to the countryside for leisure activities as a clear component of the political discourse in the United Kingdom (see Shoard, 1999). More recently, the election of the Labour party to national government in 1997 resulted in the passing in 2000 of new legislation, the Countryside Rights of Way Act, designed to improve access to open countryside, especially in upland areas. In most circumstances, the Act does not extend to inland water partly because the legislative context was distinctive and in some cases problematic. The omission of inland water served to highlight the longstanding constraints and conflicts affecting certain forms of water-based leisure. In particular, there have been long-running disputes between canoeists and anglers over the use of certain rivers. This

has culminated in violent actions by some individuals and organized mass rallies by canoeists on rivers where canoeing has been prevented, such as on the River Dee in 2004 (British Canoe Union, 2004). These high-profile events, however, are symbols of the wider problem of access to inland water that constrains some water-based leisure activities.

The Lake District in northwest England is one of the best-known international symbols of the English countryside. The name of this national park alone indicates the popularity of water as an element in countryside recreation in the UK. In 1998 12% of the adult population visited inland water for recreational purposes (Church et al., 2001).

Regular participation in sports that make use of inland water involves a smaller proportion of the population. The limited data available suggest 3% of adults regularly participate in outdoor water-related sports, including angling[1], and 4% take part occasionally (Mintel, 1998). Participation is dominated by males, who make up around three quarters of participants (Sport England, 1999; Sports Council for Wales, 2003). Participation data for individual sports highlight some contrasting trends. Canoeing, with approximately 100,000 regular and perhaps one million occasional participants, is experiencing a growth in participation, as is rowing, especially among young people. Windsurfing, after initial growth in the 1980s, has seen participation decline slightly (Mintel, 1998). In terms of participation rates, angling is by far the most popular outdoor sport making use of inland water, with over one million people being members of angling clubs and approximately three million individuals regularly participating. These levels of participation have been relatively static, but certain types of angling, especially coarse fishing on inland rivers, have seen a decline in participant numbers (Church et al., 2001).

Despite the overall situation of static participation, there has been considerable debate among water users and a variety of government bodies about the degree to which constraints create unmet demand or deter potential new participants. The evidence concerning how antecedent constraints affect potential participants presents a complex picture. In general, the rising incomes of many working British adults have been accompanied by increased time constraints (Kay, 1998),[2] such that a number of studies have argued new facilities for outdoor countryside recreation will not necessarily stimulate an increase in participation (e.g., Curry & Ravenscroft, 2001). In water-based sports many activities require significant blocks of time, especially if travel is involved to access suitable inland waters. Some bodies representing water sports suggest time constraints lie behind a shift in the nature of involvement, with participants increasingly choosing to use pay-and-play facilities rather than undertake the commitments involved with joining clubs (Church et al., 2001). The growth of pay-and-play facilities may also influence the nature of antecedent economic constraints. There are significant startup costs for some water-based sports, such as sailing, which can be avoided by using pay-and-play facilities. For many water sports, such as angling and canoeing, startup costs are quite modest and compare favorably with those for other popular land-based activities, such as golf or horse riding (Church et al., 2001).

It is true the effect of these time and economic constraints will be partly determined by personal choices. However, currently complex social processes and environmental factors also shape the nature of antecedent constraints, and it is attention to these that, in part, distinguishes work on constraints in the UK from its North American counterpart. Certain water-related sports in the UK, especially sailing, game fishing, and rowing, have a long history of providing individuals with a source of social distinction linked to the consumption habits of the middle classes. By contrast, many coarse angling clubs have their origins in working class urban society of the 19th century (Franklin, 2002). A recent analysis of nonparticipants' attitudes to water-related sports suggests while certain activities are still associated with people from particular backgrounds, this does not act as a direct constraint on participation. Instead these social associations are part of a more complex set of social anxieties deterring involvement based on environmental worries about pollution in inland waters in Britain and the fear of doing the "wrong thing" or making a "fool of yourself" in public (Church et al., 2001). These pollution concerns are rarely based on any actual evidence and are influenced by everyday narratives, which conflate pollution with the appearance of green sediment-filled water in UK lakes and rivers. Fear of acting in an inappropriate way confirms how constraints are in part a response to personal dispositions and the dispositions of others and overcoming constraints involves individuals negotiating certain perceived social barriers. For particular social groups, however, constraints are more easily identifiable. A major survey of young disabled people and sport in Britain found 37% felt limited in their participation by their health or disability, 20% were inhibited by the discriminatory attitudes of the general public, and 20% identified a lack of facilities as a constraint (Sport England, 2001).

When considering the constraints on particular social groups, Slee, Joseph, and Curry (2001) argued (in relation to outdoor countryside recreation) care must be taken not to confuse exclusion with a more general

preference not to participate. Thus, constraints, which may appear circumstantial, may in part be self-imposed. Nevertheless, the UK government's policy agenda for sport and leisure outlined in the *Game Plan* document reflects the wider European discourse on social exclusion and places a strong emphasis on increasing participation among marginalized groups (Cabinet Office Strategy Unit, 2002). Some of the organizations involved with water-related sports in the UK argue this policy discourse encourages the development of new leisure facilities and initiatives to support participation in sport among groups experiencing social exclusion even when unmet demand or constraints are not immediately apparent (Church et al., 2001).

While the evidence about the effects of antecedent constraints on nonparticipants presents a complex picture, certain constraints on usage facing regular users of inland waters are much more apparent and clearly linked to a wider social context. A number of national bodies representing water-based sports claim certain activities are limited by a complex range of economic and regulatory constraints that affect both water and riparian land. For example, rowing requires quite extensive land-based facilities, but a number of rowing clubs in England are currently concerned about their ability to maintain existing facilities. A number of clubs were established in urban areas during the early 20th century and developed clubhouses on riparian sites acquired through 99-year land leases. Today these clubs find themselves located on valuable waterfront urban sites with their leases coming to an end and landlords who may prefer to redevelop the sites for other uses (Church et al., 2001).

Current constraints on canoeing also arise from the system of property rights, but additionally they are shaped by the wider social construction of constraints and conflicts. The British Canoe Union, the national governing body for the sport, recently joined with other partners to launch a rivers access campaign, which is pushing for more rivers in the England and Wales to be available for navigation (British Canoe Union, 2002). In England and Wales all the tidal sections of rivers can be used for canoeing and other boating activities, but currently only a quarter of the nontidal major river and canal network is available for navigation by canoes (Ravenscroft et al., 2004). On these rivers the public acquired rights to passage usually through legal enactments or prescriptive rights. Also, angling is permitted on most of these rivers by the government bodies now responsible for the rivers, such as British Waterways and the Environment Agency. This situation differs markedly from other European countries, such as Germany and Hungary, where all rivers are available for navigation with limits on usage being determined by the characteristics of the craft (Peter Scott Planning Services, 1991, 1998; University of Surrey Consortium, 1999; Westerlund, 1996).

In England and Wales the system of property rights means the underlying bed of a river is owned by the riparian landowner. This allows the owner to sell off certain lesser rights to third parties. These might include the right to take fish or the right to access riparian areas. Over the last century many fishing clubs or individuals have acquired, either through purchase or leasing of land, the necessary rights to guarantee them access in return for payments for exclusive use of many rivers and banks. Recent estimates suggest angling promoted in guidebooks occurs on nearly half of the major rivers and canals in England and Wales, but many anglers claim it is possible to fish on many other rivers providing one knows whom to ask and is willing to pay (Church et al., 2001). Consequently, where anglers have acquired exclusive rights they are able, if they so choose, to deny access to other leisure activities whose participants wish to use the water. The national bodies that represent angling see this as a perfectly acceptable situation based on legal property rights and payments. Indeed, anglers stress in addition to making payments to landowners they have to buy a license from the government's Environment Agency each year, which permits them to own a fishing rod.

Many river-based activities, such as rowing or canal boating, can function perfectly satisfactorily under this situation since they are well served by the rivers where navigation is permitted. For canoeing, however, a number of complex constraints arise reinforced by a politicized discourse of conflict involving national representative bodies. The restrictions on access to rivers do not result in canoeing being affected by a simple demand-and-supply imbalance. The rivers where navigation is permitted, along with many lakes and other enclosed waters, provide canoeists with plenty of "flat water" suitable for training and certain canoe disciplines, such as racing. There is, however, a lack of supply of specific resources, especially fast-moving water for whitewater canoeing and slalom and also long stretches of river for canoe touring (Ravenscroft et al., 2004). The national and local bodies that represent canoeing have sought to access additional rivers through negotiating voluntary access agreements with landowners. While landowners have been willing over the years to develop such agreements with angling, which is a static activity, the need for passage for canoeing makes access agreements more complex, often involving a number of landowners. Consequently, voluntary access agreements in England and Wales only provide canoeing on an additional 800 kilometers, and most agreements only permit

canoeing in the angling closed season, which is between three and five months. As a result many canoeists and individuals develop personal and group solutions to problems of access. Some canoe clubs develop unwritten informal access arrangements with local landowners that permit canoeing mainly by known locals. Many canoeists, however, finding themselves constrained by a lack of access to rivers have to resort to what has become known as "bandit" or "stealth" canoeing, which involves using rivers without formal or informal permission from landowners. Indeed, published and web-based guidebooks promote canoeing on nearly half the major rivers where there is no right of navigation or formal access agreement (Church et al., 2001).

In such a situation it is no surprise significant conflicts occur between canoeists and both landowners and anglers. Some of the most significant conflicts involve fast-moving rivers attractive for whitewater canoeing that also provide high-quality game fishing. Clearly, the leisure conflicts on Britain's rivers will involve many individual incidents that might be understood from a goal interference perspective on conflict (Jacob & Schreyer, 1980). The wider social and political discourses associated with this conflict suggest, however, even a social values or visitor response approach to conflict (Schneider, 2000) may not fully encapsulate the complex way conflict and constraint have evolved on Britain's rivers.

The national bodies that represent angling and canoeing have sought to influence a politicized discourse about the use of inland waters. Usually this involves constructing one position as reasonable while emphasizing the unreasonable attitudes of others. The governing bodies for angling have opposed a "right to roam" along all major rivers for canoeing on the grounds it would conflict with established property rights built up by the voluntary efforts of angling clubs (Knight, 2003). Furthermore, anglers argue the unreasonable attitudes of canoeists are typified by a general unwillingness to pay for access. The current position of the British Canoe Union (2002) in its campaign for more access to rivers is canoeists are willing to pay for land-based facilities, but should not have to pay to move along rivers, since passage differs in its nature to static angling. For canoeists the anglers' position is portrayed as unreasonable, because it seeks to maintain exclusive use of water space and to deny others the opportunity to pursue a low-impact leisure activity in the countryside (British Canoe Union, 2002).

Not surprisingly, this discourse around access and constraint is imbued with differences of opinion concerning environmental conservation. The evidence regarding the impact of canoeing on fish stocks in England and Wales remains inconclusive (Environment Agency,

1999), although Wolter (2000) argued evidence from Germany indicated nonpowered craft can negatively affect stocks of rarer fish species. Nevertheless, the bodies that represent angling seek to portray anglers as the leading recreational contributors to aquatic habitat and species conservation, partly because the income generated by the sales of rod licenses is used to fund the government's activities to maintain inland fisheries. At the same time canoeists are presented in a negative light environmentally. For example, Paul Knight (2003), the director of the Salmon and Trout Association for the UK, claimed recently:

> Of those in competition with anglers for water, canoeists frighten us most. Canoeing is an Olympic sport, and so has the ear of politicians. Canoes have the ability to wreck a day's fishing over many miles if their crews so chose, yet canoeists do little to help protect the environment or contribute to the maintenance of the resource.

Not surprisingly, bodies representing canoeing counter this view, claiming their sport operates in harmony with the environment. A former president of the British Canoe Union claimed:

> Canoes are quiet, and do not pollute the environment, nor do they have any adverse effect on the ecology of the river. They pass down and away and leave no evidence of their passing. Let us cling to this reputation for sportsmanship in competition, courage in the face of danger, oneness with all other creatures living in, on, or by our waterways. Through courtesy we may even win the tolerance of angling bodies, for we already have many friends amongst individual anglers. (Stott, 1999)

Recently, the national government has sought to intervene in this conflict, commissioning research to advise on the potential for extending voluntary agreements to increase the water space available to canoeing (Ravenscroft et al., 2004). In the case of Britain's rivers, conflict and constraint cannot be understood, for example, by analyzing users of joint trails. Instead, constraints on inland rivers have become part of political discourse where different user groups jostle for power to influence the nature of outdoor recreation.

Concluding Remarks

We commenced this chapter by suggesting, in comparison to North America, there is no strong European tradition of constraints research. At the level of the individual—commonly the subject of North American research—this is largely the case. However, as we have argued, this lack of focus on the individual disguises a rich vein of research on the social and collective nature of constraints and exclusion, very often driven by an overtly political agenda (the European Social Model). Thus, rather than the broadly social psychological grounding of much North American constraints research, its European counterpart is more commonly grounded in sociology and politics, thus substituting the concentration on interpersonal interactions with a more overt focus on the sociopolitical structures that inform and govern these interactions in public spaces.

At the core of the European Social Model there is an acute understanding that power relations are an inherent part of social interaction—all actors have power, although not necessarily sufficient in any given context to be able to secure their goals at the expense of others. As a result, European research—such as reported in the case studies—tends to privilege "frames" of organization (Goffman, 1974) associated with normative expectations of how individuals will interact within the frame. This is consistent with Bourdieu's (1977, 1984) construct of habitus, in which people's dispositions and relative power are a function of the extent to which they have internalized existing social structures. Rather than starting with questions about the nature and identity of leisure, therefore, European researchers tend to view leisure as "not leisure" per se (Coalter, 1999) but rather as one of myriad processes and interactions through which individual people experience—and confirm their membership of—society.

While making this distinction—and with it the separation of two research traditions—it is important to recognize despite their differences these traditions share many common attributes. For example, while the legal governance of inland water-related recreation may differ between the UK and North America, the types of issue raised in the case study are familiar to North American researchers (in addition to North American anglers and canoeists). Thus, it is not so much that social interactions are experienced differently—there is no evidence to suggest this is the case—but they are understood from a different perspective, in which individual rights and choices are framed (constrained) by a broader social policy context. The negative angler/boater interaction thus ceases to be significant for its interplay of personal power and rights, but becomes increasingly emblematic of a broader issue about how land policy is framed in a way can recognize and address multiple uses and claims. Similarly, the walker/cyclist interactions gain social and political significance through what they tell researchers and the broader policy community about the issues informing the nonmotorized shared use of confined public spaces.

As such, the European approach to constraints research does not fully reflect the dichotomous other proposed by Coalter (1999), nor does it really offer an alternative to the more conventional North American approach. Rather, what it does do is offer a different frame of reference for understanding how conflict arises and can be understood as an example of the multiple ways in which power is inherent in all social interactions. As the angler/boater case study illustrates, the European model neither starts from the position of oppositional conflict nor expects an absolute (win/lose) solution to be achieved. Rather, what it offers is a way of comprehending how conflict arises, what significance such conflict has for the achievement of the European Social Model, and as a consequence, what political action—if any—is required to rectify any power imbalances that may compromise broad policy goals.

References

Adelman, B. J. E., Heberlein, T. A., and Bonnicksen, T. M. (1982). Social psychological explanations for the persistence of a conflict between paddling canoeists and motorcraft users in the Boundary Waters Canoe Area. *Leisure Sciences, 5*(1), 45–61.

Aitchison, C. C. (2003). *Gender and leisure: Social and cultural perspectives*. London, England: Routledge.

Allen, J. (2003). *Lost geographies of power*. Oxford, England: Blackwell.

Allen, J. (2004). The whereabouts of power: Politics, government and space. *Geografiska Annaler, 86B*, 19–32.

Atkinson, T. (1998). Social exclusion, poverty and unemployment. In *CASE Paper, CASE/4* (pp. 9–24). London, England: Centre for Analysis of Social Exclusion, London School of Economics.

Bairner, A. and Shirlow, P. (2003). When leisure turns to fear: Fear, mobility and ethno-sectarianism in Belfast. *Leisure Studies, 22*(3), 203–222.

Blanc, M. (1998). Social integration and exclusion in France: Some introductory remarks from a social transaction perspective. *Housing Studies, 13*(6), 781–792.

Botma, H. (1992). Method to determine level of service for bicycle paths. *Transportation Research Record, 1502*, 38–44.

Bourdieu, P. (1977). *Outline of a theory of practice*. Cambridge, England: Cambridge University Press.

Bourdieu, P. (1984). *Distinction: A social critique of the judgement of taste*. London, England: Routledge.

British Canoe Union. (2002). *Access strategy: England*. Nottingham, England: Author.

British Canoe Union. (2004). Welcome to the BCU. Retrieved May 25, 2004, from http://www.bcu.org.uk

British Waterways. (1997). *Accidents to towpath visitors*. Watford, England: Author.

Bulpett, C. (2002). Regimes of exclusion. *European Urban and Regional Studies, 9*(2), 137–149.

Burgess, J. (1995). *Growing in confidence* (CCP 457). Cheltenham, England: Countryside Commission.

Burns, T. (1992). *Erving Goffman*. London, England: Routledge.

Cabinet Office Strategy Unit. (2002). *Game plan: A strategy for delivering the government's sport and physical activity objectives* (A Joint DCMS/Strategy Unit Report). London, England: Author.

Carré, J -R. (with Mignot, C.). (2003). *Eco-mobility: Non-motorised transport—Walking, cycling, rollerblading, key elements for an alternative in urban mobility*. Paris, France: PREDIT.

Centre for Leisure and Sport Research (2002). *Count me in*. Report to the Department for Culture, Media and Sport. Centre for Leisure and Sport Research, Leeds Metropolitan University.

Chatterton, P. and Hollands, R. (2001). *Changing our 'toon': Youth, nightlife and urban change in Newcastle*. Newcastle, England: University of Newcastle-Upon-Tyne.

Church, A., Curry, N., Ravenscroft, N., and Burnside, N. (2001). *Water-based sport and recreation: The facts*. Report to Department for Environment, Food and Rural Affairs. Brighton, England: School of the Environment, University of Brighton. Retrieved from http://www.defra.gov.uk/wildlife-countryside/resprog/findings/watersport.pdf

Clarke, J. and Critcher, C. (1985). *The devil makes work*. Basingstoke, England: Macmillan.

Coalter, F. (1998). Leisure studies, leisure policy and social citizenship: The failure of welfare or the limits of welfare? *Leisure Studies, 17*, 21–36.

Coalter, F. (1999). Leisure sciences and leisure studies: The challenge of meaning. In E. L. Jackson and T. L. Burton (Eds.), *Leisure studies: Prospects for the twenty-first century* (pp. 507–519). State College, PA: Venture Publishing, Inc.

Commission for Integrated Transport (2001). *Study of European best practice in the delivery of integrated transport* (Summary Report). Retrieved from http://www.cfit.gov.uk/research/ebp/exec/index.htm

Council of Europe (2001). *Joint report on social inclusion* (Council Document No. 15223/01). Strasbourg, France: Author.

Crouch, D. (1999). *Leisure/tourism geographies*. London, England: Routledge.

Curry, N. R., Joseph, D. H., and Slee, W. (2002). To climb a mountain? Social inclusion and outdoor recreation in Britain. *World Leisure Journal, 43*(3), 3–15.

Curry, N. and Ravenscroft, N. (2001). Countryside recreation provision in England: Exploring a demand-led approach. *Land Use Policy, 18*(3), 281–291.

Cyclists' Touring Club. (1999). *Cyclists and pedestrians: Behaviour in shared facilities*. Godalming, England: Author.

Danish Council of Road Safety Research. (1998). *Transport research—Fourth framework programme. Adonis—Analysis and development of new insight into substitution of short car trips by cycling and walking*. Luxembourg City, Luxembourg: Office for Official Publications of the European Communities.

Department of the Environment, Transport and the Regions. (1999). *Cycling for better health* (Traffic Advisory Leaflet 12/99). London, England: Author.

Department of Transport. (1996). *The national cycling strategy*. London, England: Department of Transport.

Department of Transport and Welsh Office (1986). *Shared use by cyclists and pedestrians* (Local Transport Note 2/86). London, England: HMSO.

Department of Transport, Local Government and the Regions (2001). *Strong local leadership—Quality public services*. Cm 5327. London, England: TSO.

Dijkstra, A., Levelt, P., Thomsen, J., Thorsen, O., Van Severen, J., Vansevenant, P., et al. (1998). *Best practice to promote cycling and walking*. Copenhagen, Denmark: Danish Road Directorate.

Downward, P. and Lumsdon, L. (2001). The development of recreational cycle routes: An evaluation of user needs. *Managing Leisure, 6*, 50–60.

Elias, N. (1978). *The civilising process: The history of manners*. New York, NY: Urizen.

Elias, N. and Dunning, E. (1986). *Quest for excitement: Sport and leisure in the civilising process*. Oxford, England: Blackwell.

Environment Agency. (1999). *Effects of canoeing on fish stocks* (Research and Technical Report W266). Bristol, England: Author.

Esping-Andersen, G. (1990). *The three worlds of welfare capitalism*. Cambridge, England: Polity Press.

European Commission. (1993, June). *Growth, competitiveness, employment—The challenges and ways forward into the 21st century* (White Paper). Brussels, Belgium: Author.

European Commission. (1994, July). *European social policy—A way forward for the union* (White Paper). Brussels, Belgium: Author.

Ferrera, M., Matsaganis, M., and Sacchi, S. (2002). Open coordination against poverty: The New EU 'Social Inclusion Process.' *Journal of European Social Policy, 12*(3), 227–239.

Franklin, A. (2002). *Nature and social theory*. London, England: Sage.

Giddens, A. (1994). *Beyond left and right*. Cambridge, England: Polity Press.

Goffman, E. (1974). *Frame analysis*. New York, NY: Harper Row.

Gramann, J. H. and Burdge, R. (1981). The effect of recreation goals on conflict perception: The case of water skiers and fishermen. *Journal of Leisure Research, 13*, 15–27.

Gratton, C. and Henry I. P. (2001). *Sport in the city: The role of sport in economic and social regeneration*. London, England: Routledge.

Green Party (2000). *Greater London authority elections 2000—Green Party cycling strategy for London: Action, freedoms and responsibilities*. London, England: Author.

Greenspace Consortium. (2003). *Annual report*. Dublin: Environment Centre, University College Dublin.

Gvozdeva, G. (1999). Time balance changes and women's use of their right to rest. *Loisir et Sociètè/Society and Leisure, 22*(1), 131–143.

Hagerstrand, T. (1978). Time geography. In T. Carlstein, D. Parkes, and N. Thrift (Eds.), *Timing space and spacing time*. (Vol. 2; pp. 122–145). London, England: Arnold.

Hanson, S. and Pratt, G. (1995). *Gender, work and space*. London, England: Routledge.

Haworth, J. T. (1997). *Work, leisure and well-being*. London, England: Routledge.

Horne, D. (1992). *The intelligent tourist*. McMahon Point, Australia: Margaret Gee Publishing.

Institution of Highways Transportation, Cyclists Touring Club, Department of Transport and Bicycle Association (1996). *Cycle friendly infrastructure: Guidelines for planning and development*. Godalming, England: Cyclists Touring Club.

Jackson, E. L. and Wong, R. (1982). Perceived conflict between urban cross-country skiers and snowmobilers in Alberta. *Journal of Leisure Research, 14*, 47–62.

Jacob, G. R. and Schreyer, R. (1980). Conflict in outdoor recreation: A theoretical perspective. *Journal of Leisure Science, 12*(4), 368–380.

Jarvie, G. and Maguire, J. (1994). *Sport and leisure in social thought*. London, England: Routledge.

Jensen, S. U. (1998). *Pedestrian safety—Analyses and safety measures* (Report 148). Copenhagen, Denmark: Danish Road Directorate Division of Traffic Safety and Environment.

Kay, T. (1996). Women's work and women's worth. *Leisure Studies, 15*(1), 49–64.

Kay, T. (1998). Having it all or doing it all? The construction of women's lifestyles in time-crunched households. *Leisure and Society, 21*(2), 435–454.

Kay, T. (2000). Leisure, gender and family: The influence of social policy. *Leisure Studies, 19*, 247–265.

Kay, T. and Jackson, G. (1991). Leisure despite constraint: the impact of leisure constraints on leisure participation. *Journal of Leisure Research, 23*, 301–313.

Knight, P. (2003, February). A question of access. *Salmon and Trout*, 12.

Knopp, T. B. and Tyger, J. D. (1973). A study of conflict in recreational land use: Snowmobiling versus ski-touring. *Journal of Leisure Research, 5*, 6–17.

Kwan, M. (2000). Gender differences in time space constraints. *Area, 32*(2), 145–156.

Layder, D. (1995). *New strategies in social research*. London, England: Blackwell.

Mayes, D. G. (2002). Social exclusion and macro-economic policy in Europe: A problem of dynamic and spatial change. *Journal of European Social Policy, 12*(3), 195–209.

Mennell, S. (1985). *All manners of food: Eating and taste in England and France from the middle ages to the present*. Oxford, England: Basil Blackwell.

Mintel International Group. (1998). *Activity holidays, Mintel marketing intelligence*. London, England: Mintel International Group.

Montgomery, J. (1995). Urban vitality and the culture of cities. *Planning Practice and Research, 10*, 101–109.

Morel, C. (1999). *Cyclists and pedestrians: Enemies or brotherhood?* Paper presented at *Velocity* conference, Geneva, Switzerland.

Murray, C. (1984). *Losing ground*. New York, NY: Basic Books.

Oc, T. and Tiesdell, S. (1997). The death and life of city centres. In T. Oc and S. Tiesdell (Eds.), *Safer city centres: Reviving the public realm* (pp 1-20). London, England: Paul Chapman Publishing.

Oc, T. and Tiesdell, S. (1999). The fortress, the panoptic, the regulatory and the animated: planning and urban design approaches to safer city centres. *Landscape Research, 24*(3), 265–286

Office of the Deputy Prime Minister (2003). *Local Government Act 1999. Part 1: Best Value and Performance Improvement* (Circular 03/2003). London, England: Author.

Paugam, S. (1996). *L'Exclusion, L'État des Savoirs*. Paris, France: le Découverte.

Peter Scott Planning Services (1991). *Countryside access in Europe* (SNH Review No 23). Edinburgh, Scotland: Scottish Natural Heritage.

Peter Scott Planning Services. (1998). *Access to the countryside in selected European countries: A review of access rights, legislation and associated arrangements in Denmark, Germany, Norway and Sweden* (SNH Review No 110). Edinburgh, Scotland: Scottish Natural Heritage.

Pierskalla, C. D. and Lee, M. E. (1998). An ecological perception model of leisure affordances. *Leisure Sciences, 20*, 67–79.

Policy Studies Institute (1991). *One false move*. London, England: Author.

Ramblers' Association (1997). *Shared-use cycle routes* (circular 97/25). London, England: Author.

Ravenscroft, N. (2000). The vitality and viability of town centres. *Urban Studies, 37*(13), 2533–2549.

Ravenscroft, N. (2004). Tales from the tracks: Discourses of constraint in the use of mixed cycle and walking routes. *International Review for the Sociology of Sport, 39*(1), 27–44.

Ravenscroft, N., Church, A., Gilchrist, P., Hickey, R., and Hammond, B. (2004). *Improving Access for Canoeing to Inland Waterways in England.* (Countryside Research Note 79). Cheltenham, England: Countryside Agency.

Ravenscroft, N. and Curry, N. (2004). Constraints to participation in countryside recreation in England. *Annals of Leisure Research,* 7(4).

Ravenscroft, N. and Rogers, G. (2003). A critical incident study of barriers to participation on the Cuckoo Trail, East Sussex. *Managing Leisure,* 8(4), 184–197.

Ravenscroft, N., Uzzell, D., and Leach, R. (2002). Danger ahead? The impact of fear of crime on people's recreational use of non-motorised shared use routes. *Environment and Planning C: Government and Policy,* 20(5), 741–756.

Risse, T., Green Cowles, M., and Carporosa, J. (2001). *Europeanisation and domestic change: Transforming Europe.* Ithaca, NY: Cornell University Press.

Roberts, K. (1997). Same activities, different meanings: British youth cultures in the 1990s. *Leisure Studies,* 14(3), 202–216.

Roberts, K. (1999). *Leisure in contemporary society.* Wallingford, Oxon, England: CABI Publishing.

Ryan, C. (Ed). (1997). *The tourist experience: A new introduction.* London, England: Cassell.

Savage, M., Barlow, J., Dickens, P., and Fielding, T. (1992). *Property, bureaucracy and culture.* London, England: Routledge.

Schneider, E. I. (2000). Revisiting and revising recreation conflict research. *Journal of Leisure Research,* 32(1), 129–132.

Schor, J. (1999). The new politics of consumption. *Boston Review, 24*(3), 1–11. Retrieved November 19, 1999, from http://bostonreview.net/BR24.3/schor.html

Schwanen, T., Dijst, M., and Dieleman, F. M. (2004). Policies for urban form and their impact on travel: The Netherlands experience. *Urban Studies, 41*(3), 579–603.

Scraton, S. and Watson, B. (1998). Gendered cities: Women and public leisure space in the 'postmodern city.' *Leisure Studies, 17,* 123–137.

Shaw, S. M. (1994). Gender, leisure, and constraint: Towards a framework for the analysis of women's leisure. *Journal of Leisure Research,* 26(1), 8–22.

Shoard M (1999). *A right to roam.* Oxford, England: Oxford University Press.

Shogan, D. (2002). Characterizing constraints of leisure: A Foucaultian analysis of leisure constraints. *Leisure Studies,* 21, 27–38.

Slee R. W., Joseph, D., and Curry N. R. (2001). *Social exclusion in countryside leisure in the United Kingdom: The role of countryside recreation in addressing social inclusion.* A Report to the Countryside Recreation Network, March. Cheltenham, England: Countryside Agency.

Sport England. (1999). *General household survey: Trends in adult participation in sport in Great Britain, 1987–1996.* London, England: Author.

Sport England. (2001). *Disability survey 2000: Young people with a disability and sport.* London, England: Author.

Sports Council for Wales. (2003). *Sports update: Sport and rural Wales.* Cardiff, Wales: Author.

Stott, T. (1999). *The river and waterway environment for small boat users. An environmental guide for recreational users of rivers and inland waterways.* Nottingham, England: British Canoe Union.

Sugden, J. and Tomlinson, A. (2002). Theory and method for a critical sociology of sport. In J. Sugden and A. Tomlinson (Eds.), *Power games: A critical sociology of sport* (pp. 3–21). London, England: Routledge.

Sustrans (1999). *Shared use routes* (Information Sheet FF04). Bristol, England: Sustrans.

Thomas, C. J. and Bromley, R. D. F. (1996). Safety and shopping: peripherality and shopper anxiety in the city centre. *Environment and Planning C: Government and Policy, 14,* 469–488.

Tiesdell, S. and Oc, T. (1998). Beyond 'fortress' and 'panoptic' cities—Towards a safer urban realm. *Environment and Planning B: Planning Design, 25*(4), 639–655.

University of Surrey Consortium (1999). *Access to 'other' open countryside: Advice to the Countryside Agency.* Guildford: School of Management Studies for the Service Sector, University of Surrey.

Urry, J. (2002). *The tourist gaze* (2nd ed.). London, England: Sage.

Uzzell, D. L., Groeger, J., Leach, R., Parker, G., Ravenscroft, N., and Wright, A. (2000). *User interactions on unsegregated non-motorised shared use routes* (Report to the Countryside Agency). Guildford, England: Department of Psychology, University of Surrey.

Van Parijs, P. (1995). *Real freedom for all: What (if anything) can justify capitalism?* Oxford, England: Oxford University Press.

Wagner, W. (1998). Modernisation and prestige: Tourism as a motor of social change. In W. Nahrstedt and T. Pancic Kombol (Eds.), *Leisure, culture and tourism in Europe. The challenge for reconstruction and modernization in communities* (pp. 27–34). Bielefeld,

Germany: Institut fur Freizeitwissenschaft und Kulturarbeit.

Walters, J. (2001, November 25). Gridlocked UK: Now it's official. *The Observer*, p. 16.

Warde, A. (1995). Cultural change and class differentiation: Distinction and taste in the British middle classes, 1968–88. In K. Roberts (Ed.), *Leisure and social stratification* (Publication No 53; pp. 27–47). Eastbourne, England: Leisure Studies Association.

Watson, A. E., Asp, C., Walsh, J., and Kulla, A. (1997). The contribution of research to managing conflict among national forest users. *Trends, 34*(3), 29–35.

Watson, A. E., Williams, D. R., and Daigle, J. J. (1991). Sources of conflict between hikers and mountain bike riders in the Rattlesnake NRA. *Journal of Park and Recreation Administration, 9*, 59–71.

Westerlund, S. (1996). *The right of free access to nature and the countryside in Europe: Issues and overview*. Stockholm: IMIR Institute for Environmental Law.

Wolter, C. (2000). Conservation of fish species diversity in navigable waterways. *Landscape and Urban Planning, 53*, 135–144.

Young, J. (1998). From inclusive to exclusive society: Nightmares in the European dream. In V. Ruggerio, N. South, and I. Taylor (Eds.), *The new European criminology: Crime and social order in Europe* (pp. 64–91). London, England: Routledge.

Endnotes

1. We use the term "angling" (and "angler") to denote all forms of fishing with hooks, lines and (usually) rods. In contrast, we use the term "fishing" to cover all forms fishing (thus including netting).

2. This finding is consistent with North American research; see the chapter by Jackson on transitions and constraints, this volume.

Chapter 22

Making Room for "Silly" Debate: Critical Reflections on Leisure Constraints Research[1]

Diane M. Samdahl (University of Georgia)

To chronically debate the relative merits of any theoretical system amounts to little more than theoretical silliness, needlessly postponing the necessary and admittedly more difficult and less entertaining task of rolling up our sleeves and getting to work collecting the evidence required to support, refute, or revise the theory at hand. (Crawford & Jackson, this volume)

It is hard to talk about leisure without making reference to freedom. We see this in definitions that refer to leisure as *freedom from* and *freedom to*. In a similar vein, it's hard to talk about freedom without implying some dimension of constraint. After all, freedom is inherently defined in relation to those (absent) constraints that have the power to restrict our freedom. It would make sense, then, for leisure scholars to be particularly intrigued with the study of constraints that impinge on leisure.

In spite of the commonsense importance of leisure constraints, I find myself feeling dissatisfied and unfulfilled by this large and growing body of research. This is somewhat surprising, since my own early work focused on this very topic—the relationships between freedom and constraint as characterized in leisure. Leisure constraints research represents the largest and most cohesive body of research in the field of leisure studies, and it has been a foundation for some very good scholarship, as the chapters in this book attest. Yet I find myself asking: What have we learned by this extended collective endeavor? The culminating effect of two decades of research on leisure constraints has not, in my mind, significantly enhanced our understanding of the dialectic of freedom and constraint at the heart of leisure. Nor does it engage in what I find to be the more significant issues facing our field.

My goal in this chapter is to explore those concerns and to examine this body of research in ways that reveal and highlight the assumptions and presumptions on which leisure constraints research has been built. These reflections capture *my* concerns; they are not intended as an authoritative final statement or malicious critique. However, I contend they are much more than "silly debate." Some of these issues have been acknowledged, and to some extent addressed in more recent discussions of leisure constraints; other issues have been and continue to be contested and reflect a difference of opinion that might never be resolved. My goal in laying out this review is to engage others in an ongoing reflection of the constructed nature of leisure constraints research. Even adherents of leisure constraints should find this process useful for sharpening and strengthening the foundational premises of their work.

The Early Critique

In an earlier critique (Samdahl & Jekubovich, 1997a) I raised several concerns about the fundamental conceptualization of leisure constraints. One concern was most of this research focused on explaining leisure activity participation. This, I pointed out, was in stark contrast to contemporary theoretical developments that had shifted away from activity toward the examination of leisure as a context or state of mind. I questioned the utility of a concerted effort to explain participation. This concern has been voiced by others as well (cf. Jackson & Scott, 1999; Nadirova & Jackson, 2000). Indeed, Jackson (1997) claimed the original models (i.e., Crawford & Godbey, 1987; Crawford, Jackson & Godbey, 1991) did not posit nonparticipation as the exclusive outcome of leisure constraints; rather, those models implied constraints could be evidenced in other ways, such as in the formation of leisure preferences. Goodale and Witt (1989; see also Nadirova & Jackson, 2000) suggested the behavioral consequences of constraints be replaced by a broader interest in how constraints affect the enjoyment or subsequent benefits that stem from leisure engagement.

In spite of this ongoing concern, a significant portion of contemporary research still focuses on constraints to activity participation.

More significant was my assertion that leisure constraints should be viewed as a conceptual tool designed to assist in our understanding of leisure, not as an entity to be documented and confirmed. In support of this I referred to philosopher Karl Popper, who spoke about the hidden danger of treating a conceptual tool (essentially, a paradigmatic way of looking at things) as if it were truth rather than a subjective explanation and interpretation of events. Offering an example of Freudian "theory" (which he discredited as not really theory), Popper said, "Once your eyes were thus opened you saw confirming instances everywhere; the world was full of verifications of the theory...[but] what did it confirm? No more than that a case could be interpreted in light of the theory" (1962, p. 35). This characteristic, Popper argued, was evidence Freudian psychology was not a theory.

Popper's admonition was against mistaking a theory (which makes predictions that could possibly be proven wrong) for a paradigm (which is comprised of accepted beliefs not subject to validation). The key, he said, is that theories must be falsifiable. In that early paper I argued leisure constraints, like Freudian psychology, are not inherently falsifiable because they represent a label, a lens, a way of interpreting factors that influence people's leisure.

For me, the abundance of research that documented leisure constraints has done little more than confirm that events could be interpreted in light of this "theory."[2] As Popper predicted, once our eyes were opened we could see verification of leisure constraints everywhere. I found myself asking, so what? How did using the lens of leisure constraints (rather than other paradigmatic lenses, such as symbolic interaction or life stage development) enhance our understanding of what people do or experience in their leisure? The research on leisure constraints seemed descriptive and stopped short of asking deeper, more interesting questions.

As discussed in Samdahl and Jekubovich (1997a), the design of constraints research contributes to this problem. Much of the data stem from questionnaire items such as, "Think of a leisure activity which you would like to do but don't participate in as often as you wish." Ignoring the fact that this question produces abstract and hypothetical data, it also shapes respondents' answers toward the very thing researchers are trying to uncover (see Auster, 2001, for a discussion of other methodological limitations in leisure constraints research). This style of question seems intent on studying the constraints model rather than using that model as a tool to enhance our understanding of some other aspect of leisure. This research could not, for example, reveal the possibility that constraints might not be the most effective or insightful way to study leisure. It is not inherently falsifiable.

That was the central point in the earlier critique by Samdahl and Jekubovich (1997a). In that paper we analyzed one set of interviews in two ways: first using the leisure constraints model and then using a more inductive qualitative data analysis. When we entered the data looking for leisure constraints, we found wonderful examples that corresponded with aspects of Crawford et. al's (1991) model. Originally that had been the sole purpose of our analysis. However, although we found the evidence we were looking for, we felt this analysis did not effectively capture the rich and complex factors people spoke about as they described what shaped their leisure. That dissatisfaction led us back into the data for a qualitative analysis grounded more closely in the interviews.

That qualitative analysis, reported in detail in that paper, highlighted the interactional processes through which people structured their lives to create space for leisure. It was clear people were not just responding to constraints; these people purposefully worked to create leisure opportunities they could share with special friends and family. Though constraints were visible (if we chose to call them that), leisure patterns and motivations were much more dynamic and complex than what had been captured as leisure constraints. We were left with serious concerns about the utility of constraints as a broad framework for understanding leisure.

A central feature of our paper was that our data could be interpreted as evidence in support of leisure constraints or as evidence the constraints model is too limited. The decisive question, then, came from asking which approach produced the better insights, and in that study the framework of leisure constraints did not significantly enhance our understanding of leisure. Our point was to show the constraints model is simply a conceptual tool that should be abandoned when something else more effectively serves its purpose. Surprisingly, we were critiqued for not using our data as a "vehicle for enhancing [the constraints] framework" which "in the long run [would] have been [a] far more productive contribution to knowledge" (Jackson, 1997, pp. 462, 465; see also Henderson, 1997). In our view (Samdahl & Jekubovich, 1997b) this response missed the central purpose of our paper. Whereas our intent had been to question the utility of the constraints framework, these comments tried to pull us back inside that model. The very nature of that critique, including its tenacious allegiance to the constraints framework, seemed to illustrate the pervasive and commanding nature of a paradigm as it "forc[es] nature into the preformed and relatively inflexible box that the paradigm supplies" (Kuhn, 1970, p. 24).

The Ubiquitous Nature of Constraint Negotiation

The aforementioned study initiated my examination of leisure constraint negotiation. Early on, researchers discovered constraints do not necessarily impede participation, but are often negotiated through actions and strategies that help people to overcome those constraints. Samdahl and Jekubovich (1997a) asked why, when it was obvious leisure occurred in spite of constraints, the field didn't simply discard the constraints model as an ineffective tool for explaining leisure behavior. For those who viewed leisure constraints as a theory, evidence of participation in spite of constraints should have become the falsifying evidence that proved the theory wrong.

However, from a paradigmatic point of view, constraint negotiation provided an interesting perspective on broader factors that shape leisure engagement. Examining the ways people encounter and negotiate constraints opened a potentially powerful bridge that linked leisure to other social theories (as evidenced in many of the chapters in this book). But constraint negotiation also posed a pitfall for the field through its wide and indiscriminate application. This wide-ranging application is evident, for example, in Jackson and Rucks's (1995) claim that all modifications of leisure are examples of leisure constraint negotiation. Similarly, in a study of sports participation, Alexandris and Carroll (1997) claimed participants either encountered no constraints or had successfully negotiated through their constraints. And Nadirova and Jackson (2000) proposed successful negotiation of one constraint could increase the salience of other constraints and thus not result in participation at all. The all-pervading nature of these statements is overwhelming: all modifications of leisure reflect the negotiation of constraints; all forms of participation are explained in terms of the absence, presence, or negotiation of constraints; and while the presence of constraints does not preclude participation, neither does the successful negotiation of constraints assure participation. Constraint negotiation seems relevant to everything—and therefore to nothing.

Jackson (1997; see also Jackson & Scott, 1999) spoke of this as the Pac-Man problem and cautioned the field to be wary of overextending leisure constraints through application beyond its intended purpose. The problem, in his view, was most characteristic of constraints research in the early years and has been less evident in more contemporary research that integrates constraints with other theoretical perspectives. (Note, however, the previous examples reflect Jackson's own work in the latter half of the 1990s.) Crawford and Jackson (this volume) suggest this problem occurs most often when leisure constraints are extended to macroscopic levels of analysis beyond the "appropriate boundaries" that delimit its purpose; unfortunately, "appropriate" was left undefined.

Moreover, Crawford and Jackson denounce the "detractors" who dwell on this point, saying constraints research is being criticized "for not doing what we never said we were going to do in the first place." As one of those detractors, I feel they have laid blame in the wrong place. To point out weaknesses or flaws in the application of a model is much more than a silly distraction; it represents an integral part of the checks and balances central to the scientific process Crawford and Jackson embrace.

Deconstructing Leisure Constraints Research

In subsequent papers (Samdahl, Hutchinson & Jacobson, 1999; Samdahl, Jacobson & Hutchinson, 2001) I engaged in a more critical examination of leisure constraints research. This was spurred by several concerns, most notably my own desire to better understand and articulate those factors at the heart of my unwillingness to embrace this growing body of work. In those papers my colleagues and I attempted to deconstruct the literature on leisure constraints. Deconstruction entails a critical reading of the text to uncover underlying values and assertions that shape a particular line of work. It proceeds by examining not only what *is* in the literature, but also what *is not* said or represented, thereby highlighting conditions or characteristics implicitly valued over their alternatives. In this manner, deconstruction makes visible the taken-for-granted parameters that direct and shape a line of work, often representing those parameters through binary relationships that expose hidden assumptions and beliefs. Deconstructing the leisure constraints literature disclosed several key factors that initially appeared unremarkable, but on further reflection were seen to exert a defining influence on the study of leisure constraints.

Decontextualizing Participation

Our[3] analysis initially led to a fuller understanding of the implications that stem from focusing on activity participation in isolation from other social factors. This activity focus, as mentioned previously, has been criticized for not mirroring current theoretical definitions of leisure and represents a limited interpretation of the original constraints model, yet participation persists as a significant dependent variable in much of the research on leisure constraint negotiation. Successful negotiation, after all, is typically defined as participation in an activity that had been somehow constrained. Giving participation such a central role often strips that activity from the broader contexts of an individual's life and hides ramifications that might stem from successfully negotiating that constraint. For example, negotiating a constraint might require resources, such as time or money, that could have been used elsewhere, with implications not only to that individual, but also to family and others.

Whether or not this is a concern depends on the intent of the researcher. This narrow focus is most appropriate in research on constraints to consumer behavior (cf. Petrick, Backman, Bixler & Norman, 2001; Stemerding, Oppewal & Timmermans, 1999), particularly when studied from the perspective of marketing aimed at influencing a specific behavioral choice. That is perhaps the best practical application of leisure constraints and constraint negotiation, for marketing researchers are very clear about their desire to influence participation in a specified activity. However, most of the research on leisure constraints attempts to understand leisure in a broader social context, which makes that narrow focus on activity much too limiting. For example, researchers concluded time is a constraint that significantly distinguishes between those who do or do not participate in recreational sports (Alexandris & Carroll, 1997). If our intent is simply to increase participation in recreational sports, understanding time as a constraint might be important. But if our intent is more broadly defined in terms of understanding what motivates some people to engage in recreational sports more often than others, time constraints must be understood within the complex and often competing demands of work, family, and modern lifestyles. When time is discussed only as a constraint to sports we miss the cascading ramifications that would occur if individuals were to alter the rest of their lives to make more time for that activity. This approach barely captures the complexity within which individuals make choices about their leisure.

Perhaps a better example is research that examines fear of violence as a constraint to women's leisure (see Bialeschki, this volume). Fear clearly shapes and constrains women's leisure choices and activities, and can affect leisure experience even when participation is achieved. Overcoming that fear (i.e., negotiating that constraint) can take enormous emotional resources plus strategies and equipment for self-protection. However, because this fear stems from broad cultural patterns that shape the gendered nature of leisure, women who successfully negotiate their fear are going against cultural norms that define "proper" women's behavior. Although they may attain participation, these women still risk being labeled deviant or lesbian for their involvement in such activities. (See, for example, Auster's [2001] claim about the importance of supportive social networks for women who decide to ride motorcycles. It often takes two or more years of riding before these women can comfortably discard the gender stereotypes that define motorcycling as inappropriate for women.)

Decontextualizing participation from other facets of people's lives allows leisure constraints to be represented as a simplistic but unrealistic binary—people either face constraints or they are free to engage in that activity. But when participation is placed within the multidimensional nature of people's lived experience we see the relationship between constraints and freedom isn't nearly so clean. Constraints and negotiation cannot be understood simply in relation to participation; they are interwoven with other factors and have meaning that extends well beyond participation. The leisure constraints model has created a way of thinking that inevitably and regrettably isolates leisure from other elements of our lives.

Portraying Constraints as Negative Barriers

A closely related tenet in the leisure constraints research is a discourse that presents constraints as negative and restrictive. This perspective is inherent in the use of the word "constraint" and follows directly from the original model, which established a binary between constraints (bad) and participation (good). Most of the ensuing constraints research proceeded within this framework by selecting and studying negative factors that keep people from engaging in presumably desirable leisure activities.

At times this is an obvious and acknowledged position. Marketing research, as noted previously, proceeds from the premise that increased participation in the specified activity is desirable. We also see this in some research with broader social foundations. For example, in a study of constraints to active recreation for mothers of young children, Brown, Brown, Miller, and Hansen (2001) take a clearly visible stance that increased active recreation would be beneficial for these women. They do this by embedding their study in a discussion of the health benefits of exercise and evidence mothers of young children engage in less exercise than other women. In contemporary society, it would be hard to argue against the value of increased exercise (we must be cautious, though, about accepting this stance without uncritical reflection).

While perhaps justified in the aforementioned study, the portrayal of constraints as negative can be problematic in other situations. For example, using leisure constraints as a framework for understanding employee participation in corporate recreation (Hubbard & Mannell, 2001) carries an implicit but unacknowledged assumption these constraints are blocking access to a desired activity—that assumption is inherent in the binary that defines constraint in relation to participation. Questionnaire items are framed within this perspective (e.g., *I am too shy; I don't have the right clothes*), effectively ensuring the data provide explanations for why that "desired" behavior does not happen. But do these constraints actually impede an activity that would otherwise occur? Perhaps the employee who didn't have the right clothes intentionally left those clothes at home to have an excuse for not participating. Until we know whether or not participation was desired by the employees it is premature to call these factors constraints.

Some researchers address this concern by asking participants to select their own example of a leisure constraint, often by asking them to "think of a leisure activity which you would like to do but don't participate in as often as you wish." However, that wording still imposes a binary between constraint and participation and casts constraints in a negative light. The view that constraints are negatively restrictive is so central to the leisure constraints framework it is difficult to escape.

One way to reveal that framework is to envision a situation in which the binary is reversed; for example, where acquiescing to a constraint is more desirable than negotiating around it to achieve participation. Such an example is provided by McGuire and Norman (this volume) who discuss constraints in relation to successful aging. McGuire and Norman point out constraints can serve a valuable role by helping people focus attention and energy in later life. Using the metaphor of a stoplight that controls the flow of traffic, they suggest constraints can ultimately enhance the quality of life for seniors by imposing restrictions that contribute to their overall well-being. In fact, constraints might actually sanction the right to remain "blissfully inactive" by providing an excuse for not engaging in a more active lifestyle. When viewed in this manner, we are forced to acknowledge constraints are not always bad. And in that acknowledgment lies a revelation about the narrow way leisure constraints have been envisioned.

Another reversal of this binary comes from examples where constraints prevent activities that are proscribed, so negotiating those constraints is actively discouraged. We see this throughout society in the multitude of constraints that keep uncivil or objectionable behaviors in check. For example, curfews are a definite constraint on teenagers' leisure; likewise, rules of etiquette constrain talking and movement during a theatrical performance. Like stoplights, these constraints are imposed to regulate people's actions to presumably enhance our collective well-being. In a similar fashion, alcoholics impose constraints on themselves by limiting where they will go and with whom, with a belief that these constraints will enhance their personal well-being. Like time, money, and friendship, these forms of social and personal constraints are significant factors that shape and restrict leisure engagement; however, they have not been studied as leisure constraints.[4]

Perhaps the best critique of the negative portrayal of constraints comes from those who see constraints as simultaneously good and bad. Shogan (2002, p. 29) addressed this dialectical nature of constraints by saying, "Constraints act by prescribing certain actions, proscribing other actions, and describing the boundaries or contexts within which these actions make sense." She noted constraints make possible many actions and experiences that would not otherwise occur. Hutchinson and Kleiber (this volume) carry this a step further in their examination of positive consequences that emerge in the aftermath of negative life events. The constraints they discuss stem from traumatic disruptions such as a protracted illness or disabling injury, yet coping with those events often fosters forms of personal growth that under other circumstances would not have been achieved.

The tenet that constraints are negative barriers is indeed much too simplistic to facilitate a full understanding of the influence of constraints on leisure engagement. Likewise, revising the model to incorporate the positive benefits of constraints resurrects the Pac-Man problem. Why, when circumstances have a multitude of diverse consequences on our leisure, do we persist in calling those circumstances constraints? To do so will limit rather than advance our understandings of leisure.

Valuing Negotiation

Complementing the belief that constraints are bad is an equally prevalent belief that negotiating constraints must therefore be worthwhile. The implication is it is better to negotiate a constraint than to passively acquiesce to its controlling influence, with a related assumption that negotiation necessarily leads to positive outcomes. Though not openly acknowledged or examined, this positive connotation is clearly visible in the literature.

We see this first in the language used when negotiation is discussed. Crawford et al. (1991, p. 314) made an early reference to negotiation by proposing that constraints must be "overcome" to achieve participation.

Jackson, Crawford, and Godbey (1993, p. 2) claimed people who negotiated through constraints would "succeed" in leisure participation. Hubbard and Mannell (2001, p. 147) claimed negotiation provides "enhanced opportunities" to participate in leisure. In these and other examples, negotiation is championed for its liberating effects as it resolves problems and facilitates positive outcomes.

Even though negotiation has been portrayed in a positive light, it has been granted a fairly narrow goal. Successful negotiation means coming as close as possible to participating as "normally" as possible in the specified activity. This is illustrated in Henderson, Bedini, Hecht, and Schuler's (1995) study of leisure constraints for women with disabilities. In their analysis the authors distinguished between the "attempters" (those forced to significantly modify their involvement in a leisure activity as a result of the disability) and the "achievers" (those successfully able to participate in spite of the disability). Clearly, these labels frame successful negotiation in relation to achieving near-normal participation in a traditional sense. The attempters, though getting some credit for trying, are not granted the same status as the achievers. James (2000) used comparable labels by classifying people as "compromisers" or "achievers," though she offered a rationale for why the activity in her study (swimming) should be promoted, which at least gives contextualized meaning to the label "achiever." By defining negotiation in relation to normative participation, most researchers give little attention or credence to the multitude of other ways people respond to leisure constraints (cf. Goodale & Witt, 1989; Jackson & Scott, 1999; Nadirova & Jackson, 2000).

As we did before, we can reverse this binary to illustrate its restrictive nature. One example comes from McGuire and Norman's discussion of beneficial constraints (this volume). For seniors who want to remain "blissfully inactive," the presence of constraints might be a welcomed excuse to slow down and disengage. In this situation, negotiating constraints is less attractive than accepting and living within them. Removing the constraint might bring about unwanted ramifications.

Undoubtedly this is true in other situations as well, though researchers rarely examine their assumption that negotiating constraints will be beneficial. Why do we want employees to engage in corporate recreation? Why should retirees overcome constraints that prevent them from traveling more often? Why should African Americans negotiate constraints that limit their presence in the national parks? We seem to blindly assume negotiating these constraints will facilitate increasingly positive outcomes (and those outcomes will accrue to the participant rather than the employer, the travel industry, or an agency under criticism for prejudicial practices).

It is important to understand there are many alternative responses to constraints and engaging in the constrained activity might not be the most attractive or rewarding alternative for all participants.

Another way to reverse this binary is to look for examples where constraint negotiation is perceived as bad or undesirable. The clearest examples of this are in situations where people exhibit deviant behavior. For example, stealing a car is one way to negotiate a constraint brought about by the lack of transportation but it is not a desired alternative we would want to promote. Robertson (1993) studied adolescent boys who planned for and carried out criminal acts, such as burglary and drive-by shootings, showing these acts were exceedingly similar to "legitimate" recreation activities (e.g., Boy Scout camping trips) in terms of planning, engagement, enjoyment, and reminiscence. If anything, the deviant boys faced more constraints because of the illicit nature of their activities. Stebbins (1997) and Rojek (1989) also discussed deviant forms of leisure whereby people overcame significant barriers to engage in crime, witchcraft, drugs, or other illicit acts. It spite of this work that links leisure and deviance, leisure researchers have not applied the constraints framework to the sorts of barriers that keep people from engaging in deviant leisure. The relative absence of that discussion highlights the fairly narrow way constraint negotiation has been embraced by our field.

Individualized Responsibility

Leisure constraints are typically portrayed as obstacles or conditions that can sometimes be overcome "through some combination of privilege and human will" (Crawford et al., 1991, p. 313). Jackson et al. (1993) outlined several ways people confront and adapt to leisure constraints, including modifications to leisure or to the nonleisure aspects of one's life. Constraint negotiation was described to include behavioral strategies, such as gathering information or developing skills, and cognitive strategies, such as changing the way one perceives an activity so it becomes less important. This work laid an important foundation that has been carried forward as researchers examine the modifications people make as they confront and negotiate leisure constraints.

This approach is clearly delineated by an emphasis on the individual and a belief that individuals are often capable of finding solutions to their own constraints. This focus on individualized response is evident in the array of negotiation strategies outlined here as well as in the wording of questions used for data collection. For example, Jackson and Rucks (1995) asked participants to think about free-time activities "in which you manage to take part even though you have problems doing so....What have you done to overcome those problems?" In this question the researchers clearly seek individual responses to the constraint; the ensuing data (and the research question which elicited them) are driven by this emphasis on the individual.

Not so obvious, however, is an equally prevalent implication that individuals therefore carry responsibility for finding solutions to their own constrained status. The pervasiveness of this belief is made evident by contrasting responses to the previous question with answers that would have been obtained had they asked, "What could be done to make this activity possible for you?" While the original question was oriented to elicit actions and responses of an individualized nature, this alternative question is framed to encompass social or environmental modifications as well. This choice of words is not unimportant, nor is it always conscious. The way we ask questions is driven by the types of answers we seek, and both are the product of the models and paradigms that shape the way we think.

There is a practical utility to focusing on ways individuals encounter and negotiate obstacles to their leisure, especially in the context of leisure counseling or interventions aimed at increasing self-efficacy. Personal action is often the most immediate recourse available for redressing a problem. However, individualized response is only one way to alleviate a constraint; collective action designed to change the structures that generate constraints is another (overlooked) solution. The effectiveness of collective action is best illustrated through the political lobbying that resulted in passage of the Americans With Disabilities Act. While individuals had to negotiate barriers, such as curbs and stairs, by devising creative strategies to get around them, collective action brought about removal of those barriers altogether. The conceptual foundation of leisure constraint negotiation kept us focused on the limited realm of individual action, and in doing so effectively held individuals responsible for finding their own solutions to the constraints that impact their leisure.

I argue this approach stems from the broader social psychological paradigm that shapes and drives most North American leisure research (see Coalter, 1997, for further discussion). Within that paradigm, attention is focused on individuals, and behavior is explained in terms of personal characteristics (e.g., attitudes, demographics) or responses to environmental stimuli. The pervasiveness of social psychology can be seen in research on leisure attitudes, motives, and behaviors, as well as in concepts such as leisure lifestyles and leisure constraints. Indeed,

definitions that highlight perceived freedom or a subjective state of mind reify this social psychological view by placing the individual at the center of our understanding of leisure. In contrast, leisure research that comes from Europe is often embedded in critical theory or Marxist theory and engages in analysis of concepts like culture, class, and institutionalized power rather than individual experience.

To focus on constraints and negotiation from a social psychological perspective ignores the powerful cultural influences that shape leisure behavior and puts undue responsibility on individuals for things they cannot control. Factors like time scarcity, discrimination, and lack of money are much more than constraints to leisure—they are the consequences of a structural order in our society by which some people benefit at the expense of others. When these factors are studied only as obstacles to leisure, the hegemonic systems that create and perpetuate those constraints remain invisible and unscathed. As Henderson (1997) so aptly stated, "To consider constraints negotiation as only an individual's problem is to miss an important aspect of social responsibility" (p. 457).

When we frame leisure constraints from the social psychological perspective we are unable to see and ultimately to change the social and cultural systems that prevent equitable access to leisure for all. Feminist leisure researchers were among the first to move away from this social psychological framework in their examination of constraints that stem from gender roles and expectations (see Shaw & Henderson, this volume). Not coincidentally, feminist researchers aspire to use their research to create change that will enhance women's lives. In a similar fashion, the rest of leisure research would become more relevant if it addressed how societal norms and institutions create "constraints" that impinge on people's lives.

The purpose of deconstruction is to reveal hidden values and judgments that have shaped the way a topic is portrayed. It is clear from this discussion leisure researchers have engaged in a fairly narrow definition of constraints, driven (and limited) by the central binary that poses a dialectical relationship between constraint and participation. In doing so it has blocked from its vision a broad array of factors that constrain people's leisure, overlooked alternative effects constraints might have on leisure, and engaged in analysis removed from the complex realities that shape people's leisure choices. Responding to these concerns will require a reconceptualized framework less committed to activity participation and more responsive to social context. Though many alternative frameworks are possible, I describe one approach next that provides new meaning for the terms "constraint" and "constraint negotiation."

A New Understanding of Negotiation

As noted previously, the leisure constraints model has been used to understand why people don't participate in presumably desirable leisure activities. Constraint negotiation in that framework refers to the actions individuals take to engage in activities in spite of constraints. According to Samdahl, Hutchinson, and Jacobson (1999), this model portrays constraints as if they were obstacles or conditions around which individuals must successfully steer, similar to the way a canoeist maneuvers around rocks and boulders in a stream. Since negotiation of this type depends entirely on individual action, we suggested the terms *navigation* or *accommodation* would be more appropriate than negotiation. Navigation implies individuals have control and responsibility for avoiding obstacles as they travel toward their desired destinations. Accommodation, as used in the social sciences, has a similar meaning and refers to ways that individuals adapt to existing conditions by making relevant modifications. We argued the terms navigation and accommodation better capture the way our literature discusses the process of encountering and overcoming constraints than the more common word negotiation.

An example of this can be seen in the behavior of lesbians and gays who often pass as heterosexual in public leisure spaces. For these individuals, passing as heterosexual may be preferable, because it avoids problems that might arise if they were to openly identify as lesbian or gay. Passing, therefore, is an effective way to negotiate the constraint of homophobia. However, passing does little to challenge or to change people's homophobic attitudes. It allows lesbians and gays to avoid confrontation, but it does not change the homophobic world in which they live. Using the term accommodation in this situation serves to remind us this solution is individualistic and asymmetrical; it does not entail a mutual compromise through which the world is made more tolerant. Leisure researchers, we argued, focused almost entirely on this type of negotiation, whereby individuals successfully navigate around factors that constrain their leisure using individualistic strategies of adaptation and accommodation.

That is different than the way negotiation is typically used in the broader social sciences. *Merriam-Webster's Collegiate Dictionary* (10th edition) offers this alternative definition of negotiation: *to confer with another so as to arrive at the settlement of some matter*. This definition places negotiation within a broad context of social interaction and requires at least two parties, each of whom hopes to accomplish something through the

assistance or compliance of the other. This meaning is illustrated through the negotiation of a treaty where two countries engage in a process of give and take. The negotiation results in a new arrangement shaped by the demands of each side, with each country required to alter its behaviors to comply with the newly negotiated order. Within this definition, activities undertaken alone or unilateral decisions that do not entail compromise are not seen as negotiation. Thus, negotiation as it has been addressed in leisure constraints research does not fit this definition.

Surprisingly, this view of negotiation is not unknown in leisure studies; it just has not been strongly integrated into the framework of leisure constraints. Interactive negotiation is at the heart of symbolic interaction, a paradigm that had great influence on leisure research in the 1980s and early 1990s (cf. Kelly, 1983; Samdahl, 1988), the same period when the leisure constraints models were being proposed. Those early models focused primarily on understanding the constraints (it wasn't until much later that constraint negotiation became the focus), which might explain the lack of cross-breeding between these two contemporaneous lines of research.

Negotiated Meaning

In the literature outside leisure studies, this type of negotiation is commonly examined in conjunction with ideology and symbolic meanings. Even when there are tangible ramifications from negotiation, the real mediation is seen to occur within the sphere of negotiated meaning. (See Strauss, 1978, for further discussion of the negotiation of social order.) Samdahl, Hutchinson, and Jacobson (1999) argued this focus on negotiated meaning is an essential missing component in leisure constraints research. For example, a woman who negotiates the demands of motherhood to create leisure opportunities for herself might have simply achieved a guilt-laden escape from the house for a few hours, or she might have reached a mutually accepted understanding with her partner that honors and facilitates her independent leisure needs. Without examining the negotiation of meaning, leisure researchers miss the important symbolic contexts that surround and define leisure activity.

This portrayal of negotiation applies not only to interaction between two individuals but also to interaction between an individual and internalized cultural systems of meaning (see Mead, 1934/1962). Negotiation with internalized systems of meaning was illustrated in Auster's (2001) study of women motorcycle riders; those women clearly were torn between their desire to ride a motorcycle and their internalized stereotypes that told them riding was not appropriate for women. This struggle with internalized beliefs is also evident in James's (2000) study of adolescent girls at a swimming pool. These girls were concerned about the ways their bodies would be seen "as refracted through male eyes" (p. 275). Their reactions were based on an imagined audience, even though the people at the pool responded quite differently than what these girls imagined. One set of girls (whom James labeled "rationalizers") adapted to this situation by learning to care less about what others thought about their bodies. When confronting cultural constraints in this fashion, negotiation takes the form of changed beliefs or expectations that (hopefully) become accepted and reciprocated by those with whom one interacts.

In women's studies, researchers study the negotiation of gender in this fashion. Gender roles are proscriptive and constraining similar to leisure constraints. Researchers who study gender negotiation examine what it means to be a woman, wife, mother, or any other gendered label, with emphasis on how people negotiate a meaning that allows them to fulfill those roles in personally satisfying ways. Gender negotiation thus becomes a process by which gender ideologies are enacted, resisted, and/or changed. Research on women's leisure, particularly work on leisure as a site of resistance (cf. Green, 1998; Shaw, 2001), has shown this alternative definition of negotiation to be a valuable framework for studying leisure.

Competing Discourses

One immediate outcome of this framework is insight into the nature of constraints and the associated need for negotiation. The leisure constraints model offers no basis for understanding the formation of constraints other than to explain they are factors that interfere with participation. Working from this alternative definition of negotiation, we see that conflict (constraint) that requires negotiation occurs when two individuals or organizations have competing agendas. Applying this concept to leisure, we might argue constraints arise when two competing discourses offer alternative options for action.

Discourses are sets of ideas and meanings that structure some facet of life; they affect the ways people act and are perceived/received in the social world. For example, cultural discourses about gender refer to the diffuse and often internalized messages that shape people's beliefs about the behaviors, attitudes, and "proper" life course agendas for a man or a woman. The concept of discourse is often associated with Foucault, who believed modern society is governed by invisible and internalized systems of power (discourses) rather than

external coercive power. As people are socialized into those pervading discourses they become complicit (willing victims) in the power relations that constrain them.

Foucault used the concept of discourse to explain how hegemonic power relations are reaffirmed and maintained through everyday language and action. Contradictory discourses, however, pose a challenge because they require an individual to choose between competing messages. This occurs when there is a disjuncture between cultural expectations and personal desires, or between two conflicting cultural ideologies that produce incompatible expectations or understandings. For example, the ideology of motherhood and the demands it made on women became problematic in the late 20th century when a competing ideology arose that promoted autonomy and self-fulfillment. Today, new first-time mothers feel the pull from each set of beliefs and are forced to negotiate some resolution to these incompatible discourses (Wearing, 1990). Negotiating that disjuncture requires compromise in one realm or the other, which comes in the form of weakened commitment to the proscriptions and meanings inherent in one of those discourses.

Conflict between competing discourses inevitably makes visible a dominant (constraining) discourse that otherwise was not seen as problematic. Once alternatives become visible, the original discourse is open to negotiation. Thus, the negotiation of cultural discourse brings with it the very real possibility of resistance and an opportunity to create new social order. Green (1998) explained, "At the intersection of contradictory discourses, resistance to imposed…constraints can occur, in which case people can be perceived as active agents rather than as passive recipients of constraining structures" (p. 172). It is through this process the cumulative effect of individual negotiations can facilitate social change.

The Power to Negotiate

As one last point, this interactive view of negotiation offers insight into the resources necessary to negotiate leisure constraints. The existing literature addressed some of those resources, including resourcefulness in finding extra time or money, social skills for effective interpersonal interaction, and enhanced self-esteem to overcome intrapersonal factors that constrain leisure. Crawford et al. (1991) spoke about a "hierarchy of social privilege" by which social class relates to constraints; this has been born out in research showing people with higher income/education mention fewer leisure constraints (Brown et al., 2001).

I would add people also need an understanding of the constructed nature of social order, or at least the ability to see alternatives to the existing nature of things. (Auster's [2001] discussion of the "enrichment hypothesis" is relevant to this.) Without that vision it is difficult even to see the constraint, much less to be motivated to negotiate it. For example, in a study of women with brain injuries, Hutchinson (reported in Samdahl, Jacobson & Hutchinson, 2001) noted some were incapable of envisioning their lives in any form other than what it was like prior to their injuries; these women were doomed to frustration since they no longer had the cognitive capabilities necessary for living that earlier lifestyle. Not being able to envision a satisfying alternative, these women were unsuccessful in negotiating many of the constraints brought about by their disabilities. Likewise, unless they had partners and family members who were willing to adapt as well, these women were powerless to negotiate new roles and expectations that better fit their current capabilities.

It is clear people need a certain amount of social power to effectively engage others in negotiation toward their own goals. Until we study that element of power, we will miss an important resource central to leisure constraint negotiation.

Discussion

My goal in this chapter was to examine the assumptions and presumptions on which leisure constraints research has been built in an effort to better understand my lingering discomfort with this growing body of research. I now see two general sources of that dissatisfaction. First, the focus on participation at the heart of the leisure constraints framework is much more insidious than simply using the wrong dependent variable, as my earlier critique implied. Defining constraints in relation to participation established a binary that decontextualizes leisure, employs a narrow framework for understanding constraints and negotiation, and frames negotiation from a perspective that reifies individual action. Second, this work derives from a definition of negotiation incapable of capturing the complex and dynamic interactions through which people enter in to leisure engagements.

As shown throughout my discussion, many of these concerns about leisure constraints research have been raised by others as well. There is a growing body of research that attempts to step beyond these limitations by examining positive constraints, understanding contextual influences on constraint negotiation, and analyzing the negotiation of meaning. In addition, researchers are positing concepts that complement and extend the leisure constraints model, such as affordance (Kleiber, Wade & Loucks-Atkinson, this volume), facilitation (Raymore, 2002), and enhancement (Auster, 2001). Nonetheless, I remain skeptical about the collective utility of leisure constraints research as a mechanism for enhancing our understanding of leisure.

That skepticism, in part, reflects a concern that much of this newer work is attaching itself to leisure constraints only in a nominal fashion. That is, this work applies the term constraints as it talks about factors like health or body image, but constraints are not an integral conceptual premise for those discussions. We see examples of this in Hutchinson and Kleiber's discussion of coping (this volume), James's (2000) study of adolescent girls at the swimming pool, Auster's (2001) discussion of women motorcyclists, and many other studies. References to constraints could be removed from those papers without significantly altering the meaning of the remaining discussion. To the extent the theoretical contributions of these studies exist outside of the constraints framework, I find myself questioning the utility of describing those situations as constraints and constraint negotiation.

I am aware some might say the constraints framework could be modified in response to many of the concerns I've raised. We could examine constraints to experience as well as to participation, and we could address beneficial as well as restrictive constraints. We can apply the constraints model to the negotiation of meaning as well as to more visible forms of constraints, and we can use it to understand broad forms of control such as cultural discourse. Undoubtedly we can. However, that course of action seems more loyal to the constraints framework than to the larger goal of understanding leisure. I'm reminded of Popper's admonition against Freudian psychology: Though the world was full of verifications, they simply confirmed that a case could be interpreted in light of that model. And I want something more than that.

Leisure constraints are a conceptual tool we employ in attempt to make sense out of what we see. That is true of any scientific label, model, or paradigm; these things do not inherently exist and have meaning other than through their utility in helping us to understand the world around us. The points outlined in this chapter raise serious doubts about the ability of the leisure constraints framework to provide rich understandings of people's leisure behaviors or experiences. As I've argued, the framework of leisure constraints does not capture the complexity of people's lives and cannot address some of the more interesting questions we could be pursuing.

I've challenged leisure researchers to step back from the social psychological paradigm that pervades our field and to acknowledge individuals shape and create their lives in a dynamic world of symbolic meaning. Broad cultural ideologies and hegemonic structures define what is expected and what is socially valued. These beliefs are enacted and reinforced, as well as negotiated and changed, in the daily interactions that occur between individuals. Constraints are not objective barriers; they are the consequence of imposed social order and result from competing desires and expectations. Negotiation of and within this broader world of constructed meaning is a rich topic for exploration that remains hidden through our commitment to the leisure constraints framework.

Concluding Thoughts

The quote from Crawford and Jackson that opened this chapter challenges us to undertake the "difficult…task of rolling up our sleeves and getting to work collecting the evidence required to support, refute, or revise the theory at hand." More specifically, Crawford and Jackson dismiss the relative merits of introspective debate and call instead for activities that lead to solid empirical "evidence" in support of that critique. They stated:

> Leisure scholars do not comprise a debating society, but rather a scientific community wherein research is the rule of law. Theory without research is philosophy and, while we clearly recognize the importance and value of philosophy, we would note that such contributions rightfully occur in departments of philosophy, not science. (Crawford & Jackson, this volume)

I am afraid this chapter will win little favor from those who hold to that belief. I have tried my best to engage in a thoughtful examination of my concerns about leisure constraints research, but I have provided no objectively verifiable "evidence" Crawford and Jackson would find convincing. I have not, in their terms, put the rubber to the road. But I am reminded of Kuhn's comment: A paradigm cannot be dismantled from within for it is incapable of producing evidence that would refute it. Standing outside of the leisure constraints framework—indeed, outside the positivist epistemology from which it is derived—I know I am incapable of providing the evidence Crawford and Jackson seek; likewise, they are unlikely to accept the evidence that I have just provided. Hopefully, however, there remains some value in holding this discussion. I don't care if they want to label this philosophy, but perhaps we could compromise and call it a philosophy of science.

References

Alexandris, K. and Carroll, B. (1997). Demographic differences in the perception of constraints on recreational sports participation: Results from a study in Greece. *Leisure Studies, 16,* 107–125.

Auster, C. J. (2001). Transcending potential antecedent leisure constraints: The case of women motorcycle operators. *Journal of Leisure Research, 33,* 272–298.

Brown, P. R., Brown, W. J., Miller, Y. D., and Hansen, V. (2001). Perceived constraints and social support for active leisure among mothers with young children. *Leisure Sciences, 23,* 131–144.

Coalter, F. (1997). Leisure sciences and leisure studies: Different concept, same crisis? *Leisure Studies, 19,* 255–268.

Crawford, D. W. and Godbey, G. (1987). Reconceptualizing barriers to family leisure. *Leisure Sciences, 9,* 119–127.

Crawford, D. W., Jackson, E. L., and Godbey, G. (1991). A hierarchical model of leisure constraints. *Leisure Sciences, 13,* 309–320.

Goodale, T. L. and Witt, P. A. (1989). Recreation nonparticipation and barriers to leisure. In E. L. Jackson and T. L. Burton (Eds.), *Understanding leisure and recreation: Mapping the past, charting the future* (pp. 421–449). State College, PA: Venture Publishing, Inc.

Green E. (1998). Women doing friendship: An analysis of women's leisure as a site of identity construction, empowerment and resistance. *Leisure Studies, 17,* 171–185.

Henderson, K. A. (1997). A critique of constraints theory: A response. *Journal of Leisure Research, 29,* 453–457.

Henderson, K., Bedini, L., Hecht, L., and Schuler, R. (1995). Women with physical disabilities and the negotiation of leisure constraints. *Leisure Studies, 14,* 17–31.

Hubbard, J. and Mannell, R. C. (2001). Testing competing models of the leisure constraint negotiation process in a corporate employee recreation setting. *Leisure Sciences, 23,* 145–163.

Jackson, E. L. (1997). In the eye of the beholder: A comment on Samdahl & Jekubovich (1997), "A critique of leisure constraints: Comparative an analyses and understandings." *Journal of Leisure Research, 29,* 458–468.

Jackson, E., Crawford, D., and Godbey, G. (1993). The negotiation of leisure constraints. *Leisure Sciences, 15,* 1–11.

Jackson, E. L. and Rucks, V. C. (1995). Negotiation of leisure constraints by junior-high and high-school students: An exploratory study. *Journal of Leisure Research, 27*, 85–105.

Jackson, E. L. and Scott, D. (1999). Constraints to leisure. In E. L. Jackson and T. L. Burton (Eds.), *Leisure studies: Prospects for the twenty-first century,* (pp. 299–321). State College, PA: Venture Publishing, Inc.

James, K. (2000). "You can feel them looking at you": The experiences of adolescent girls at swimming pools. *Journal of Leisure Research, 32,* 262–280.

Kelly, J. R. 1983. *Leisure identities and interactions.* London, England: Allen & Unwin.

Kuhn, T. S. (1970). *The structure of scientific revolutions* (2nd ed.). Chicago, IL: University of Chicago Press.

Mead, G. H. (1934/1962). *Mind, self, and society.* Chicago, IL: University of Chicago Press.

Nadirova, A. and Jackson, E. L. (2000). Alternative criterion variables against which to measure the impacts of constraints to leisure. *Journal of Leisure Research, 32*, 396–405.

Petrick, J. F., Backman, S. J., Bixler, R., and Norman, W. C. (2001). Analysis of golfer motivations and constraints by experience use history. *Journal of Leisure Research, 33*, 56–71.

Popper, K. R. (1962). *Conjectures and refutations: The growth of scientific knowledge.* New York, NY: Basic Books.

Raymore, L. A. (2002). Facilitators to leisure. *Journal of Leisure Research, 34*, 37–51.

Robertson, B. J. (1993). *An investigation of leisure in the lives of adolescents who engage in delinquent activities for fun, thrills, and excitement.* Unpublished doctoral dissertation, University of Oregon, Eugene.

Rojek, C. (1989). Deviant leisure: The dark side of free time activity. In E. L. Jackson and T. L. Burton (Eds.), *Understanding leisure and recreation: Mapping the past, charting the future* (pp. 81–95). State College, PA: Venture Publishing, Inc.

Samdahl, D. M. (1988). A symbolic interactionist model of leisure: Theory and empirical support. *Leisure Sciences, 10*, 27–39.

Samdahl, D. M., Hutchinson, S., and Jacobson, S. (1999). *Navigating constraints? A critical commentary on negotiation in leisure research.* Paper presented at the Canadian Congress on Leisure Research, Wolfville, Nova Scotia, Canada.

Samdahl, D. M., Jacobson, S., and Hutchinson, S. (2001). When gender is problematic: Leisure and gender negotiation for marginalized women. In J. White and S. Clough-Todd (Eds.), *Women's leisure experiences: Ages, stages and roles* (pp. 139–146). Eastbourne, England: Leisure Studies Association.

Samdahl, D. M. and Jekubovich, N. J. (1997a). A critique of leisure constraints: Comparative analyses and understandings. *Journal of Leisure Research, 29*, 430–452.

Samdahl, D. M. and Jekubovich, N. J. (1997b). A rejoinder to Henderson's and Jackson's critique of "A critique of leisure constraints." *Journal of Leisure Research, 29*, 469–471.

Shaw, S. M. (2001). Conceptualizing resistance: Women's leisure as political practice. *Journal of Leisure Research, 33*, 186–201.

Shogan, D. (2002). Characterizing constraints of leisure: A Foucaultian analysis of leisure constraints. *Leisure Studies, 21*, 27–38.

Stebbins, R. A. (1997). Causal leisure: A conceptual statement. *Leisure Studies, 16*, 17–25.

Stemerding, M., Oppewal, H., and Timmermans, H. (1999). A constraints-induced model of park choice. *Leisure Sciences, 21*, 145–158.

Strauss, A. (1978). *Negotiations: Varieties, contexts, processes, and social order.* San Francisco, CA: Jossey-Bass.

Wearing, B. (1990). Beyond the ideology of motherhood: Leisure as resistance. *Australian New Zealand Journal of Sociology, 26,* 36–58.

Endnotes

1. Debate and disagreement are essential components of the scientific process. I am deeply indebted to Ed Jackson who, in spite of claims (in this book and elsewhere) that my critiques have been misguided, was adamant this book include my critical reflections. He and I have agreed to disagree in a friendly and hopefully productive academic debate about leisure constraints.

2. In their early work Crawford, Jackson, and Godbey posited leisure constraints as a model. However, subsequent researchers have used it as if it were a theory in terms of documenting, measuring, and making predictions based on the model of leisure constraints. Crawford and Jackson's chapter in this book offers a more extensive discussion of this point, and contrary to the position I take here, they argue leisure constraints indeed has become a theoretical body of research.

3. An initial draft of these ideas was developed in D. M. Samdahl and S. L. Hutchinson's, *The 'negotiation' of leisure constraints: Implicit assumptions and conceptual alternatives*, an unpublished manuscript available from the author.

4. I say this with some trepidation, not wanting to encourage leisure constraints to become any more pervasive than it already is. However, the absence of this discussion in the constraints literature is significant.

Other books by Venture Publishing, Inc.

21st Century Leisure: Current Issues, Second Edition
by Valeria J. Freysinger and John R. Kelly

The A•B•Cs of Behavior Change: Skills for Working With Behavior Problems in Nursing Homes
by Margaret D. Cohn, Michael A. Smyer, and Ann L. Horgas

Activity Experiences and Programming within Long-Term Care
by Ted Tedrick and Elaine R. Green

The Activity Gourmet
by Peggy Powers

Advanced Concepts for Geriatric Nursing Assistants
by Carolyn A. McDonald

Adventure Programming
edited by John C. Miles and Simon Priest

Assessment: The Cornerstone of Activity Programs
by Ruth Perschbacher

Behavior Modification in Therapeutic Recreation: An Introductory Manual
by John Datillo and William D. Murphy

Benefits of Leisure
edited by B. L. Driver, Perry J. Brown, and George L. Peterson

Benefits of Recreation Research Update
by Judy M. Sefton and W. Kerry Mummery

Beyond Baskets and Beads: Activities for Older Adults With Functional Impairments
by Mary Hart, Karen Primm, and Kathy Cranisky

Beyond Bingo: Innovative Programs for the New Senior
by Sal Arrigo, Jr., Ann Lewis, and Hank Mattimore

Beyond Bingo 2: More Innovative Programs for the New Senior
by Sal Arrigo, Jr.

Both Gains and Gaps: Feminist Perspectives on Women's Leisure
by Karla Henderson, M. Deborah Bialeschki, Susan M. Shaw, and Valeria J. Freysinger

Boredom Busters: Themed Special Events to Dazzle and Delight Your Group
by Annette C. Moore

Client Assessment in Therapeutic Recreation Services
by Norma J. Stumbo

Client Outcomes in Therapeutic Recreation Services
by Norma J. Stumbo

Conceptual Foundations for Therapeutic Recreation
edited by David R. Austin, John Dattilo, and Bryan P. McCormick

Dementia Care Programming: An Identity-Focused Approach
by Rosemary Dunne

Dimensions of Choice: A Qualitative Approach to Recreation, Parks, and Leisure Research
by Karla A. Henderson

Diversity and the Recreation Profession: Organizational Perspectives
edited by Maria T. Allison and Ingrid E. Schneider

Effective Management in Therapeutic Recreation Service
by Gerald S. O'Morrow and Marcia Jean Carter

Evaluating Leisure Services: Making Enlightened Decisions, Second Edition
by Karla A. Henderson and M. Deborah Bialeschki

Everything From A to Y: The Zest Is up to You! Older Adult Activities for Every Day of the Year
by Nancy R. Cheshire and Martha L. Kenney

The Evolution of Leisure: Historical and Philosophical Perspectives
by Thomas Goodale and Geoffrey Godbey

Experience Marketing: Strategies for the New Millennium
by Ellen L. O'Sullivan and Kathy J. Spangler

Facilitation Techniques in Therapeutic Recreation
by John Dattilo

File o' Fun: A Recreation Planner for Games & Activities, Third Edition
by Jane Harris Ericson and Diane Ruth Albright

Functional Interdisciplinary-Transdisciplinary Therapy (FITT) Manual
by Deborah M. Schott, Judy D. Burdett, Beverly J. Cook, Karren S. Ford, and Kathleen M. Orban

The Game and Play Leader's Handbook: Facilitating Fun and Positive Interaction, Revised Edition
by Bill Michaelis and John M. O'Connell

The Game Finder—A Leader's Guide to Great Activities
by Annette C. Moore

Getting People Involved in Life and Activities: Effective Motivating Techniques
by Jeanne Adams

Glossary of Recreation Therapy and Occupational Therapy
by David R. Austin

Great Special Events and Activities
by Annie Morton, Angie Prosser, and Sue Spangler

Group Games & Activity Leadership
by Kenneth J. Bulik

Growing With Care: Using Greenery, Gardens, and Nature With Aging and Special Populations
by Betsy Kreidler

Hands On! Children's Activities for Fairs, Festivals, and Special Events
by Karen L. Ramey

In Search of the Starfish: Creating a Caring Environment
by Mary Hart, Karen Primm, and Kathy Cranisky

Inclusion: Including People With Disabilities in Parks and Recreation Opportunities
by Lynn Anderson and Carla Brown Kress

Inclusive Leisure Services: Responding to the Rights of People with Disabilities, Second Edition
by John Dattilo

Innovations: A Recreation Therapy Approach to Restorative Programs
by Dawn R. De Vries and Julie M. Lake

Internships in Recreation and Leisure Services: A Practical Guide for Students, Third Edition
by Edward E. Seagle, Jr. and Ralph W. Smith

Interpretation of Cultural and Natural Resources, Second Edition
by Douglas M. Knudson, Ted T. Cable, and Larry Beck

Intervention Activities for At-Risk Youth
by Norma J. Stumbo

Introduction to Outdoor Recreation: Providing and Managing Natural Resource Based Opportunities
By Roger L. Moore and B. L. Driver

Introduction to Recreation and Leisure Services, Eighth Edition
by Karla A. Henderson, M. Deborah Bialeschki, John L. Hemingway, Jan S. Hodges, Beth D. Kivel, and H. Douglas Sessoms

Introduction to Therapeutic Recreation: U.S. and Canadian Perspectives
by Kenneth Mobily and Lisa Ostiguy

Introduction to Writing Goals and Objectives: A Manual for Recreation Therapy Students and Entry-Level Professionals
by Suzanne Melcher

Leadership and Administration of Outdoor Pursuits, Second Edition
by Phyllis Ford and James Blanchard

Leadership in Leisure Services: Making a Difference, Second Edition
by Debra J. Jordan

Leisure and Leisure Services in the 21st Century
by Geoffrey Godbey

Venture Publishing, Inc.
1999 Cato Avenue
State College, PA 16801
Phone: (814) 234-4561
Fax: (814) 234-1651